Women in a Globalizing World
Transforming Equality, Development, Diversity and Peace

Women in a Globalizing World
Transforming Equality, Development, Diversity and Peace

edited by

Angela Miles

INANNA Publications and Education Inc.
Toronto, Canada

Published in Canada by
Inanna Publications and Education Inc.
210 Founders College, York University
4700 Keele Street, Toronto, Ontario M3J 1P3
Telephone: (416) 736-5356 Fax (416) 736-5765
Email: inanna.publications@inanna.ca Website: www.inanna.ca

The publisher gratefully acknowledges the support of the Canada Council for the Arts and the Ontario Arts Council for its publishing program.

The publisher is also grateful for the kind support received from an Anonymous Fund at The Calgary Foundation.

Note from the publisher: Care has been taken to trace the ownership of copyright material used in this book. The author and the publisher welcome any information enabling them to rectify any references or credits in subsequent editions.

Printed and Bound in Canada.

Cover Design: Val Fullard
Interior Design: Luciana Ricciutelli

Library and Archives Canada Cataloguing in Publication

     Women in a globalizing world : equality, development, diversity and peace / edited by Angela Miles.

Includes bibliographical references.
ISBN 978-1-926708-19-5

     1. Sex role and globalization. 2. Women—Social conditions. 3. Women—Economic conditions. 4. Globalization—Social aspects. 5. Feminism. I. Miles, Angela Rose.

HQ1233.W6569 2013   305.42   C2012-907267-2

For Rosalie Bertell (1929-2012)
and Roxana Ng (1951-2013)

Contents

I. UN DECADE FOR WOMEN AND BEYOND

II. RIGHTS AND REFORMS

III. ALTERNATIVES AND RESISTANCE

Acknowledgements

Editing this large book has been a long labour of love. Our grand aim has been to produce a major Canadian-focused feminist resource for understanding the profound globalizing processes of our time. This ambitious undertaking has been shared throughout by my friends Luciana Ricciutelli publisher extraordinaire and Sheila Molloy index impresario. Their contributions to the book are inestimable. Ajamu Nangwayu, Yukyung Kim Cho, Soma Chatterjee, Kate Bojin, Andrea Weerdenberg and Ebru Bag provided much appreciated graduate assistance at various stages of this long march. Thanks also, to my sisters of the Antigonish Women's Resource Centre who provided crucial material and logistical support and political inspiration while I worked on this book during my nourishing sabbatical time with them.

The strength of this collection rests on the fine work of contributors grounded in, drawing on and contributing to the theory and practice of Canadian and global women's movement. We are deeply indebted to the authors' generous co-operation in swiftly updating earlier articles and rushing to complete new ones. And we are more grateful than we can say for their graciousness in the face of an unexpectedly drawn out publishing process. We hope that they and our readers find the volume worth the wait.

ANGELA MILES

Introduction

> *If ... survival ... is now the most pressing problem in the world, and if women are the crucial human links in that survival, then the empowerment of women is essential if new, creative and cooperative solutions to the crisis are to emerge.... This is why we ... affirm that feminism allows for the broadest and deepest development of society and human beings free of all systems of domination.... Equality, peace and development by and for the poor and oppressed are inextricably interlinked with equality, peace and development by and for women.*
>
> —Development Alternatives with Women for a New Era (DAWN)

FEMINISM IS NECESSARILY an internationalist politics, for the systems of exploitation and control we resist are global. Many in North America have long understood that to win our full freedom and not merely ameliorate *some* women's conditions we will have to transform global as well as national and local structures of power. The ascendance of neo-liberalism since the 1980s and growing relationships with feminists from the economic south have deepened this awareness in the economic north and increased both the necessity and possibility of global resistance and transformation. The exciting rise of Indigenous women's activism we are seeing today offers new hope for this struggle.

The articles in this volume have been selected because all their varying critical and/or visionary approaches are informed by and open the way to feminist politics deep enough to sustain global solidarity. They are presented in the context of the developing global women's movement that their analyses are shaped by and contribute to.

Women have worked together across boundaries of nation, class, race, and culture for a century and a half—against slavery and war and for women's rights. Early international organizing was predominantly among European, Scandinavian, North American, Anzac, and Latin American women. International conferences and networks supported women's struggles in significant ways in each of their home nations while providing a powerful international voice and presence for women (Steinstra).

1

By the mid-1980s, international links among a new wave of feminists had grown into a more truly "global" movement than in the earlier period (Antrobus; Miles 1996). Feminists, today, are cooperating internationally to develop analyses and strategies, and to support local and international action through newsletters, conferences, workshops, courses, and joint lobbying efforts at the United Nations (UN) and other international venues. They are creating new forms of ongoing dialogue and are organizing in loose, decentralized networks very different from women's earlier international associations which tended to bring together official national representatives. Now, feminists from any region, nation or locality/ies may initiate international actions when a need is felt. Current initiatives are more numerous and flexible with generally closer ties to local activism and more opportunity for direct mutual learning among women in very different situations and struggles. Unlike the earlier period, leadership tends to come from the economic South where women have been more intensely and longer aware of international systems of power and the need for global understanding.

All over the world women have for decades been engaged in environmental, economic, health, shelter, food security, social-justice, human rights, land rights, peace, anti-debt, anti-globalization, pro-democracy, anti-violence, and anti-fundamentalist struggles of major proportions (Basu; Davies 1983, 1986; Marx-Feree and Tripp; Morgan; Naples and Desai; Ricciutelli, Miles and McFadden; Rowbotham and Linkogles).

Vibrant international identity-defined, issue-based and regional feminist networks and gatherings have grown from this local activism. From these networks a myriad of international non-governmental organizations (INGOs), funding networks, member organizations, campaigns and projects have developed. All these forms of cooperation foster dialogue, research, theory building and activism across regions and across issues and are making major contributions to the development of broad and inclusive feminist politics.[1]

Feminists' ability to act together at the global level is extremely important. However, it is only one facet of global feminist movement which is at heart a multitude of globally aware local feminisms. The "World March of Women" (WMW), with 5,000 member groups in 164 countries, inspired originally by Quebec feminists, is a vibrant example of direct grassroots to grassroots international links.[2]

All these forms of organized cooperation are accompanied by institutional and individual web sites, chat rooms, open and closed e-mail and Skype consultations, Twitter and Facebook communication. In fostering mutual learning and organizing among feminist individuals and groups all over the world, these newer forms of communication build on and supplement regional and international gatherings and campaigns and other actions.

Women, as individuals and as members of diverse groups, are located very differently, often in antagonistic relation to each other within their local communities and the world system and often with very different immediate needs, interests, and strategic priorities and very distorted views of each other. Global feminist interactions that link the many centres of multi-centred feminist practice offer challenging and vitally important spaces for educating each other and discovering women's shared interests in change.

Four UN World Women's Congresses held in 1975, 1980, 1985, and 1995 (with growing numbers and diversity of women and ever increasing leadership from the "two thirds world') have been central in this process. UN conferences on Environment and Development (1992, 2002, 2012), Human Rights (1993), Population (1994), Social Development (1995), Food Security (1996), Racial Discrimination (2001), next year's first World Congress of Indigenous Peoples and annual meetings of the UN Commission on the Status of Women and the UN Committee to Eliminate all Forms of Discrimination Against Women (CEDAW) have also been and continue to be crucial sites for the collective achievement of feminisms critical and visionary enough to sustain global solidarity.

In this volume, Canadian feminist analyses of neo-liberal globalization and possible alternatives are presented in the context of this exciting history of global feminist dialogue and activism. Together, the articles present a comprehensive critical feminist overview of the agenda and processes of neo-liberal globalization, women's activist responses to the consequent environmental and social destruction, and visionary alternative feminist worldviews and values.

Decades of accessible cutting-edge articles in *Canadian Woman Studies/les cahiers de la femme* (*CWS/cf*), many of them revised and updated, have been an inestimable resource in this project and have been supplemented by invited contributions on the most recent developments. We have drawn, for instance, on important journal issues focused on Environment, Development, Migration and Trafficking, Women's Labour Rights and Women's Human Rights. In addition, journal issues published in conjunction with the United Nations World Congresses of Women in Nairobi (1985) and Beijing (1995), and the Canadian women's movement's millennium celebration (2000) have enabled us to present this material in historical context. And, thus, to capture something of the dynamic of political challenge and discovery among women from all regions of the country and the world that has nurtured the transformative feminist perspectives that are traced and reflected in this volume.

INTRODUCTION: FEMINIST ANALYSIS AND VISION

Seven articles by First Nations, Canadian, Costa Rican, German, Indian and U.S. authors open this volume. All call for a deeply different world which sustains and honours life; not simply for a fair share of wealth and work in this divided and unequal world organized around production for profit for a few. Their varied visions of a world and worldviews honouring individual, community and ecological survival in a world of dignity, respect, and security for all, are core challenges to neo-liberal globalization.

Two political statements bookend this section: "Women's Action Agenda 21

Preamble" reflects the political understandings and commitments reached by 1,500 women from 84 countries at the World Women's Congress for a Healthy Planet, and the closing "Position Paper for a Peaceful World" was circulated at the World Social Forum in hopes that other social movements would engage with transformative feminist perspectives. Between these two statements, Eva Johnson, Bear Clan Kahnawake Mohawk Nation, invokes just such an alternative worldview and set of values in her article on "Native culture and the environment"; Vandana Shiva calls for an "Earth Democracy," rather than a share-holding democracy; Sylvia Federici speaks of "re-enchanting the world"; Alda Facio calls for "feminist spirituality as a strategy for action"; and Maria Mies writes of the new "moral economy" offered by a subsistence perspective.

All these writers bring holistic economic, social, cultural, spiritual, and environmental approaches to the whole world, not only to "women's issues." In varying ways and with differing emphases, they insist passionately on the central importance of the reproduction and sustenance of all of life—a concern marginalized, trivialized, and left largely women's under-resourced responsibility in colonial capitalist patriarchy. They recognize the leading role Indigenous women and marginalized women play in all women's struggle for another world.

PART ONE: NEO-LIBERAL RESTRUCTURING: SOCIAL AND ENVIRONMENTAL COSTS

Key to these transformative perspectives is an understanding that the unequal, competitive, individualistic, market relations that define this system were established historically through the conquest and control of nature, women, workers, and traditional cultures and communities in both "first" and "two-thirds world" (Mies). Dominant forms of "globalization" today continue to be shaped by these destructive processes (Miles 2001).

In the industrial nations of the economic north, we are taught on the contrary, that "modernization," "development," and "globalization" represent unambiguous and benign (if "complex") progress for everyone. Since the Second World War, keeping national income accounts has been a requirement of UN membership even for nations in which very little of people's livelihood is supplied through the market. These national accounts measure a country's Gross Domestic Product (GDP), that is, the value of goods and services that pass through the market. GDP measures leave all non-market value invisible (i.e., unpaid products and services, nature, personal safety, and health) and register all costly disasters and behaviours as positive growth. Nevertheless, GDP is used as the prime indicator of a nations' wealth and well-being and GDP growth is read as an increase in general wealth and well-being. This sleight of hand legitimizes neo-liberal policies which maximize GDP growth and the opportunity for profit for a few over all other social and environmental priorities. Yet, as articles in Part One of this volume show, agendas to maximize economic growth, including privatization, deregulation, devaluation, cuts to social welfare, downsizing, wage reductions, enclosure and intensified commodification actually have huge costs for people everywhere and for the planet.

Two framing articles (Green; Armstrong and Armstrong) are followed by articles organized in three sections to critically examine, the logic, agenda and policies of neo-liberal globalization and its impact on women and their communities. The articles include reports of original survey, interview and case study research, political statements, policy analysis and personal accounts from across the country and abroad. They are written by rural and farm women, migrant women, women workers, trade unionists, lawyers, social service providers and clients as well as academics—most authors being more than one of these.

Restructuring/"Liberalization" critically explores the meaning and consequences of neo-liberal "restructuring" (often called "liberalization") with attention to its constitutive policies under the headings: Free Trade, Privatization, Cutbacks. Following an overview of the current global crisis (Federici), articles deal with the implications of globalization for women (Cohen et al.); the impact of neo-liberal trade policies on garment workers (Ng); why privatization is a women's issue (Stinson); the consequences of re-structuring for women workers in British Columbia health care (Cohen, Ritchie, Swenarchuk and Vosko); the impact of government cut-backs on women workers' safety (Mosher and Evans); on occupational health (Baines); and for women in prison (Pate).

Enclosure, Commodification and Theft examines the processes of enclosure and commodification of common wealth for the benefit of a few that lie at the heart of capitalist economic growth and globalization. Measures of wealth that count only what passes through the market register private appropriation for profit as economic growth a presumed increase in general wealth. "Sustainable development" as generally understood is dedicated to sustaining this economic growth, not to sustaining communities and environment. Thus, its policies offer false "solutions" to the problems of poverty and ecological destruction caused by growth focused maldevelopment.

Articles critically analyze the politics of sustainable development at the UN (Isla) and the centrality of land and the food question to globalization and resistance (Dalla Costa). They explore the commodification of women (Hartsock) and the significance of women's unpaid work (Waring); the commodification of life itself through intellectual property rights (Shiva; Forsey); the brutal consequences of Canadian mining's intensifying resource exploitation for women in Latin America (Isla) and of unchecked climate change for rural women, especially in the economic south (Milne).

Displacement, Migration and Violence examines the connection between this form of neo-liberal global development and the oppressive security and lucrative militarism required to enforce policies of impoverishment, to police increasing inter-communal tensions from resulting scarcity, and to manage and control migrating individuals and populations displaced by such violence and/or economic and environmental collapse.

Articles present the essential violence of neo-liberal globalization (Shiva);

the oppressive legal regulation of cross-border movements globally (Kapur); migrant women's vulnerability in Canadian and international law (Macklin); and migrant workers experience in Canada as live in care providers (Velasco) and farm workers (Preibisch); the growing trafficking in women for the sex industry as a central aspect of neo-liberal globalization (Poulin); and the connection between growing poverty and violence against women in Canada (Lakeman).

PART TWO: ORGANIZING FOR ANOTHER WORLD

Following two introductory articles (Grant-Cummings; Green) three sections provide snap shots of feminist responses to globalization across a broad spectrum of issues in local as well as global contexts over the full period of neo-liberal emergence and continuing dominance.

UN Decade for Women and Beyond collects personal accounts and political statements written by participants at the United Nations World Women's Congresses in Nairobi and Beijing and the World Women's Congress for a Healthy Planet. These articles offer a rare window into the vibrant feminist global engagement of the 1980s and 1990s which forged the deep critiques and transformative perspectives that continue to ground transformative feminist action today.

Political statements are by the Third World feminist network DAWN (Development Alternatives with Women for a New Era) and the Indigenous Women's Caucus at Nairobi, and by the International Indigenous Women's Caucus, Women of the South Caucus, and the North American Regional Caucus at the World Women's Congress for a Healthy Planet. Personal accounts are written by women active at these conferences around the status of women (Wetzel), peace (Fulton), health (Tudiver), environment (Kettle), women's human rights (Bunch, Dutt and Fried), alternative development (Christiansen-Ruffman), Indigenous rights (Sillett), sexual rights (Day), and food security and land rights (Pedersen).

In the second and third sections, articles exemplify the diversity and energy of more recent feminist practice in response to neo-liberal policy and its impacts on the ground. *Rights and Reform* focuses on feminist organizing for change in government policy, practice and perspectives that will move us closer to another world. Articles report on women's global peace activism (Bunch); Canadian women's constitutional activism (McPhedron); the failure of Gender Based Analysis (GBA) as currently understood to provide a "culturally-affirming gender re-balancing framework" that honours First Nation worldviews (Stirbys); the ways a human rights approach can bring feminist environmental and reproductive rights struggles together (Cooper and Kelly); the realities of Black women's experiences of HIV/AIDS (Tharao and Massaquoi); Canadian child care politics and activism (Friendly); and virtual activism in the pro-choice movement (McTavish).

Alternatives and Resistance gathers accounts of community and movement focused activity aimed at building new relations, economies and cultures while speaking truth to power. The section opens with an account of Aboriginal women's peaceful and healing water walk and ceremony that was called in downtown Toronto to "bring attention to Idle No More and the fight against the changes to the Navigational Waters Protection Act Bill C45" (Nanibush).

The articles that follow present the challenges and possibilities of women working together for peace in ethnically divided societies (Abseykara); the promise a guaranteed livable annual income offers for women's equality and security and social development (Lakeman, Miles and Christiansen-Ruffman); the many "blossoming initiatives to create local, community ... [that are] helping people survive the vicissitudes of world market fluctuation and ... [are laying] the seeds for more fundamental economic transformation" (Perkins); the radical cultural and economic potential of an agriculture where ecologically grown food is a relationship rather than a commodity (McMahon); the ways organizing an LGBTQ Community Safety Initiative in small town Nova Scotia revealed that "the rural sphere can be radical and ... can even surprise those who call these communities home" (Marple and Latchmore); the central importance and challenges of Aboriginal women organizing against the racist and sexist violence they face (Harper); the experiences and reflections of women farm leaders working in the National Farmers Union and globally to defend rural communities and food sovereignty (Desmarais); the perspectives and practice that women of the economic North and South bring to struggles around energy, sustainability and climate change (Milne); the power and importance of diverse anti-patriarchal women's voices for peace (Starhawk); a personal experience of vulnerability and courage in anti-globalization activism (Foster); and the influence and promise of feminist presence and principles in Occupy activism (Rebick; Boler).

Angela Miles is a Professor in the Adult Education and Community Development Program and co-founder of the International Women's Human Rights Education Institute at the Ontario Institute for Studies in Education at the University of Toronto; editorial board member of Canadian Woman Studies/les cahiers de la femme; *founding member of Toronto Women for a Just and Healthy Planet, The Feminist Party of Canada, and The Antigonish Women's Association. Her publications include the book* Integrative Feminisms: Building Global Visions *(1996) and the co-edited collection* Feminist Politics, Activism and Vision: Local and Global Challenges *(2004).*

[1]Formative issue-based networks include the Coalition Against Trafficking in women (CAT-W); Development Alternatives with Women for a New Era (DAWN); Global Coalition on Women and AIDS; International Women and Health Network; Women's Environment and Development Organization (WEDO); Women Against Fundamentalism; Women's Global Network for Reproductive Rights (WGNRR); Women Human Rights Defenders International Coalition; Women's International League for Peace and Freedom (WILPF).

Regional networks include the Association of African Women on Research and Development (AAWORD); the Asian Pacific Forum on Women, Law and Development (APWLD); the Caribbean Association for Feminist Research and Action (CAFRA); and the Latin American Feminist Encuentros. Examples of non-governmental organizations include African Women's Development Fund; Association for Women's Rights in Development (AWID); Feminist International Radio Endeavour (FIRE); Global Fund for Women (GFW); International Feminist Network for a Gift Economy; International Women's Rights Action Watch (IWRAW); Peace Women Across the Globe; Women's International News Gathering Service (WINGS).

[2]In 1995, at the Fourth World Women's Congress in Beijing, Quebec feminists, inspired by the success of their march "*Du pain et des roses*" earlier that year, called on women's groups around the world to organize coordinated local events related to these themes in their own countries beginning on March 8, 2000 (International Women's Day), and ending on October 17, 2000, the final day to be marked with national marches in all the participating countries and an international march on the United Nations and the International Monetary Fund in New York City. This massive global initiative drew on women's political strengths in 157 countries (August 2000 count), highlighting both the uniqueness and connections of each group, nation and region. Local groups organizing events as part of the 2000 and subsequent 2010 World Marches and other WMW campaigns experience themselves and are revealed to each other as unique centres of diverse practice in a multi-centred global movement in which any one of its many centres can invoke the power of global solidarity.

REFERENCES

Antrobus, Peggy. *The Global Women's Movement: Origins, Issues and Strategies.* London: Zed Books, 2004.

Basu, Amrita, ed. *Women's Movements in the Global Era: The Power of Local Feminisms.* Boulder, CO: Westview Press, 2010.

Davies, Miranda, ed. *Third World, Second Sex: Women's Struggles and National Liberation.* Vol 1. London: Zed Books, 1983.

Davies, Miranda, ed. *Third World, Second Sex: Women's Struggles and National Liberation.* Vol 2. London: Zed Books, 1986.

Development Alternatives for Women With a New Era (DAWN). "Development Crisis and Alternative Views: Third World Women's Perspectives." *Canadian Woman Studies/les cahiers de la femme* 7.1,2 (1986): 31-33.

Marx-Ferree, Myra and Ali Mari Tripp, eds. *Global Feminism: Transnational Women's Activism, Organizing, and Human Rights.* New York: New York University Press, 2006.

Mies, Maria. *Patriarchy and Accumulation on a World Scale: Women in the International Division of Labour.* London: Zed Books, 1986

Miles, Angela. *Integrative Feminisms: Building Global Visions, 1960s-1990s.*

Routledge, 1996.

Miles, Angela. "Women's Work, Nature and Colonial Exploitation: Feminist Struggles for Alternatives to Corporate Globalization." *Canadian Journal of Development Studies* 22 (2001): 855-878

Morgan, Robin, ed. *Sisterhood is Global: The International Women's Movement Anthology.* Garden City, NY: Anchor Press/Doubleday, 1984.

Naples, Nancy A. and Manisha Desai, eds. *Women's Activism and Globalization: Linking Local Struggles and Transnational Politics.* New York: Routledge, 2002.

Ricciutelli, Luciana, Angela Miles and Margaret McFadden, eds. *Feminist Politics, Activism and Vision: Local and Global Challenges.* Toronto/London: Inanna Publications and Education and Zed Books, 2004.

Rowbotham, Sheila and Stephanie Linkogle, eds. *Women Resist Globalization: Mobilizing for Livelihoods and Rights.* London: Zed Books, 2001.

Stienstra, Deborah. *Women's Movements and International Organizations.* Basingstoke, UK: Macmillan, 1994.

World March of Women (WMW). *A Score for Women's Voices: A March to Change the World.* Prod. Les Productions Virage Inc., in coproduction with The National Film Board of Canada, Montréal, Québec, 2002.

Feminist Analysis and Vision

Preamble

Toward a Healthy Planet

P EOPLE EVERYWHERE ARE FRIGHTENED by mounting evidence of the deterioration of Earth's lifegiving systems. Human beings are part of the web of life, not above its laws. We have a special responsibility to respect all of the Earth community, including our air, water, soil and natural resources, our fauna and flora, and the atmosphere that shelters us.

We, women of many nations, cultures and creeds, of different colours and classes, have come together to voice our concern for the health of our living planet and all its interdependent life forms.

We have listened to each other speak of the ills of our societies, our families and children, our sacred Nature. We have been inspired by the courage and commitment of our sisters throughout the world who protect and repair our natural heritage.

As caring women, we speak on behalf of those who could not be with us, the millions of women who experience daily the violence of environmental degradation, poverty, and exploitation of their work and bodies. As long as Nature and women are abused by a so-called "free market" ideology and wrong concepts of "economic growth," there can be no environmental security. Rainforest dwellers, island peoples, and inhabitants of fragile arid zones are threatened with displacement and dispossession due to human disruption and pollution of vulnerable ecosystems. In a world that condones such practices, there lies little hope for long-term survival or peace among peoples.

We are deeply troubled by the increasing quality of life disparities between inhabitants of industrialized nations and those in so-called "developing" nations and by the growing numbers of poor within the rich countries. In all instances, women, children, minorities, and Indigenous peoples are the chief victims.

We are outraged by the inequities among children the world over, with millions denied food, shelter, health care, education and opportunities for a full and productive life. We condemn the racism and disrespect of diversity on which this inequity feeds.

We equate lack of political and individual will among world leaders with a lack of basic morality and spiritual values and an absence of responsibility towards future generations.

We will no longer tolerate the enormous role played by military establishments and industries in making the twentieth-century the bloodiest and most violent in all of human history. Militarism is impoverishing and maiming both the Earth and humanity. It is urgent that resources currently consumed by the military be redirected to meet the needs of people and our planet.

We believe that a healthy and sustainable environment is contingent upon world peace, respect for human rights, participatory democracy, the self-determination of peoples, respect for Indigenous peoples and their lands, cultures, and traditions, and the protection of all species.

We believe that basic human rights include access to clean air and water, food, shelter, health, education, personal liberty, and freedom of information.

We come together to pledge our commitment to the empowerment of women, the central and powerful force in the search for equity between and among the peoples of the Earth and for a balance between them and the life-support systems that sustain us all.

Women are a powerful force for change. In the past two decades, thousands of new women's groups have been organized in every region of the world, ranging from community-based groups to international networks. Everywhere, women are catalysts and initiators of environmental activism. Yet policy-makers continue to ignore the centrality of women's roles and needs as they make Fate of the Earth decisions.

We demand our right, as half the world's population, to bring our perspectives, values, skills and experiences into policy-making, on an equal basis with men, not only at the United Nations Conference on Environment and Development (UNCED) in June 1992 but on into the twenty-first century.

We pledge to undertake our Action Agenda 21 on behalf of ourselves, our families, and future generations. We appeal to all women and men to join in this call for profound and immediate transformation in human values and activities.

Excerpted from Women's Action Agenda 21, developed for the UN Conference on Environment and Development (UNCED) held in Rio de Janeiro, Brazil, in 1992. Full text available at: <http://www.iisd.org/women/action21.htm>.

VANDANA SHIVA

Economic Globalization, Ecological Feminism and Earth Democracy

G LOBALIZATION HAS A VERY POSITIVE RING TO IT. However, economic globalization as we are seeing it unfold is not a process of ever widening circles of inclusion. It is a process of ascending hierarchies that concentrate power and exclude people from participating in the political and economic life of their societies.

The "global" in the dominant discourse is the political space in which the dominant local seeks global control, and frees itself of local, national, and global control. The global in this sense does not represent the universal human interest; it represents a particular local and parochial interest which has been globalized through its reach and control. A group of the (seven [G7], and later eight [G8]) most powerful countries dictates global affairs, but remains narrow, local, and parochial in terms of the interests of all the world's communities. The World Bank is not really a bank that serves in the interest of all the world's communities. It is a bank where decisions are based on voting weighted by the economic and political power of donors, and in this decision-making the communities who pay the real price and are the real donors (such as the tribals of Narmada Valley) have no say. The "global" of today reflects a modern-day version of the global reach of the handful of British merchant adventurers who raided and looted large parts of the globe as the East India Company, and which then became the British Empire.

The "global" as construct does not symbolize planetary consciousness. In fact, it excludes the planet and peoples from the mind, and puts global institutions in their place. The concept of the planet is invoked by the most rapacious and greedy institutions to destroy and kill the cultures which use a planetary consciousness to guide their daily actions in the concrete. The ordinary Indian woman who worships the tulsi plant worships the cosmic as symbolized in the plant. The peasants who treat seeds as sacred see in them a connection to the universe. Reflexive categories harmonize balance from planets to plants to people. In most sustainable traditional cultures, the large and the small have been linked so that limits, restraints, and responsibilities are always transparent and cannot be externalized. The large exists in the small, and hence every act has not just global but cosmic implications. Treading gently on the Earth becomes

15

the natural way to be. Demands in a planetary consciousness are made on the self, not on others.

The moral and political framework of economic globalization is the opposite. There are no reflexive relationships, only coercively imposed structures such as General Agreement on Tariffs and Trade (GATT) and Structural Adjustment Programs (SAPs).

Economic globalization is exemplified by the trade liberalization imposed by SAPs, and by "free-trade" treaties and the establishment of the World Trade Organization (WTO). However, globalization is deeper and wider than SAPs or Free Trade—it is the ruling ideology that centres on the replacement of governmental and state planning by corporate strategic planning and the establishment of global corporate rule. Even though globalization is made to appear as natural, spontaneous, and inevitable, it is in fact a political process shaped by the dominant interests of society, especially the transnational corporations.

There are two shifts entailed by globalization. The first is the movement of political and economic control from the local and national space to the global space. The core of the "free-trade" or trade liberalization measures is a change in the location of decision-making power from the local and the national space to the global space. This political shift is aimed at expanding the scope of trade, both geographically in space as well as in content

Thus, trade is moving rapidly from taking place predominantly at the local and national level to taking place at the global level. Further, new areas are being brought into global trade such as intellectual property rights, services, investment. In effect, all aspects of everyday life are being transformed into globally-traded commodities. Food, land, seeds, plants, and animals are now all commodities on international markets. The impact of globalization is, therefore, to take resources and knowledge that have hitherto been under women's control, and the control of Third World communities to generate sustenance and survival, and put them at the service of corporations engaged in global trade and commerce to generate profits.

The imperialistic category of global is a disempowering one at the local level. Its coercive power comes from removing limits for the forces of domination and destruction and imposing restrictions on the forces of conservation.

The ecological category of global is an empowering one at the local level because it charges every act, every entity, with the largeness of the cosmic and planetary and adds meaning to it. It is also empowering because precisely by embodying the planetary in the local, it creates conditions for local autonomy and local control.

FROM AN EARTH DEMOCRACY TO A SHARE-HOLDING DEMOCRACY?

There is a story that elders tell to their children in central India to illustrate that the life of the tribe is deeply and intimately linked to the life of the soil and the forest.

The forest was ablaze. Pushed by the wind, the flames began to close in on a beautiful tree on which sat a bird. An old man escaping the fire, himself, saw the bird and said to it, "Little bird, why don't you fly away? Have you forgotten you have wings?" And the bird answered, "Old man, do you see this empty nest above? This is where I was born. And this small nest from which you hear the chirping is where I am bringing up my small child. I feed him with nectar from the flowers of this tree and I live by eating its ripe fruit. And do you see the dropping below on the forest floor? Many seedlings will emerge from them and thus do I help to spread greenery, as my parents before me did, as my children after me will. My life is linked to this tree. If it dies I will surely die with it. No, I have not forgotten my wings." (Rane 15)

In total contrast to this story I recently read another one in the *Guardian* with the heading, "Children to Learn Finance." The most powerful financiers in London's financial centre had concluded that the world of work is precarious and that secondary school children should be taught to take responsibility for their own financial affairs. As traditional full-time staff jobs disappear and state care is eroded, youngsters should turn to "financial security" in a share-owning democracy. The problem is that there is no security for most in a world led by the global financial system. And the share-owning democracy is not a democracy, it is a casino.

Long before the far reaching and continuing financial crisis that we are facing today, it was becoming increasingly evident that the financial system is not a source of security but risk. The global casino is hardly the place for our children to be looking for security when the dominant economic system is not able to provide job security, social security, or ecological security. As David Korten states in his recent book, *When Corporations Rule the World*:

> Financial institutions that were once dedicated to mobilizing funds for productive investment have transmogrified into a predatory, risk-creating, speculation-driven global financial system engaged in the unproductive extraction of wealth from tax payers and the productive economy.

This extractive economy takes away the wealth from nature and society. Even the shareholders are not in charge. It is a myth that shareholders control the corporation and have full power over it. Only a small portion of funds used by corporations comes directly from stockholder investment. As John Kenneth Galbraith has said plainly, "the stock holder … has no power and hence no role in the running of the firm."

The corporation is controlled by its management, who reward themselves at excessive levels, and through economic globalization control our lives. As Ralph Estes has stated,

Thus we have a small group, not elected by the populace but chosen by themselves, from among themselves, a managerial elite whose members hold great power, and whose personal morality is kept on hold while acting in their corporate roles (which for some is practically twenty-four hours a day). To a substantial extent they collectively decide where and how we will work, how safe our job will be, when we will lose our jobs (possibly for the rest of our lives), what we will eat, what we will wear, how we will clean it, how we will get around, how we will communicate, how much we will make in wages and as a return on our investments, what we will do for entertainment, and yes, through control of the media with its influence over our culture, even what we will think.

This sounds rather like pre-perestroika Russia. There the government controlled the quality, price, purity, safety, and choice of food, and of all other consumer products. It ordained the quality, safety, and wage rate of the job. The government was not one of checks and balances, not seriously constrained by a constitution, and not elected by or accountable to the mass of citizens. It was chosen and perpetuated largely by itself.

Strangely, in capitalist societies that opposed the Russian communist system throughout its existence, we appear to have come to accept a very similar arrangement. Our system is marked by a relatively small number of individuals, with no accountability, controlling great power for the benefit of narrow interests, while the broad public interest is carried along as a captive passenger, a hostage.

We would not long tolerate a government without accountability, a dictatorship answerable to no one. But we allow unaccountable corporations to control more of our lives than government has ever attempted. (76-77)]

THE REINVENTION OF "NATION"

Globalization has rendered the relationship between the community, the state, and the corporation totally fluid or, to use Marc Nerfin's more colourful categories, the relationship between the citizen, the prince, and the merchant. The appeal of globalization is usually based on the idea that it implies less red tape, less centralization, and less bureaucratic control. It is celebrated because it implies the erosion of the power of the state.

Globalization does mean "less government" for regulation of business and commerce. But less government for commerce and corporations can go hand-in-hand with more government in the lives of people. As globalization allows increasing transfer of the resources from the public domain—either under the control of communities, or that of the state—discontent and dissent necessarily increase, leading to law and order problems. In such a situation, even a minimalist state restricted only to policing and law and order will become enormously large and all-pervasive, devouring much of the wealth of society and intruding into every aspect of citizens' lives.

Most of the ideological projection of globalization has focused on the new relationship of the prince and the merchant, the state and the corporation, the government and the market. The state has been stepping back more and more from the regulation of commerce and capital. India's Finance Minister Manmohan Singh was reflecting this ideology of deregulation when he stated that, "power should move to the Board room" i.e., from the state to the corporations ("The Hindu"). However, the shift from the rule of the nation-state to that of the corporations does not imply more power to the people. If anything, it implies less power in the hands of people both because corporations, especially transnational corporations, are more powerful than governments and also because they are less accountable than governments to democratic control.

The erosion of the power of the nation-state from outside and above leads to a concentration of power in the hands of corporations. It does not devolve power to the people. It does not move power downwards into the hands of communities. In fact, it takes power away from the local level, and transforms institutions of the state from being protectors of the health and rights of people to protectors of the property and profits of corporations. This creates an inverted state, a state more committed to the protection of foreign investment and less to the protection of the citizens of the country. The inversion of the state is well exemplified in a recently announced proposal that foreign security experts would train Indian police to protect the "life and property of foreign investors" ("The Hindu").

Narrow nationalism in fact feeds on economic globalization which robs people of all security and positive identity and leaves them with negatively defined identities.

The homogenization processes of globalization do not fully wipe out differences. Differences persist not in an integrating context of plurality, but in the fragmenting context of homogenization. Positive pluralities give way to negative dualities, each in competition with every other, contesting for the scarce resources that define economic and political power. Diversity is mutated into duality, into the experience of exclusion.

The intolerance of diversity becomes a new social disease, leaving communities vulnerable to breakdown and violence, decay and destruction. The intolerance of diversity and the persistence of cultural differences sets up one community against another in a context created by a corporate rule creating monocultures. Difference, instead of leading to richness of diversity, becomes the base for diversion and an ideology of separatism and terrorism. Thus narrow nationalism and economic globalization go hand in hand.

A political response to both requires creating an inclusive nationhood. The reinvention of the state has to be based on the reinvention of sovereignty. Sovereignty cannot reside only in centralized state structures nor does it disappear when the protective functions of the state with respect to its people start to wither away. The new partnership for national sovereignty needs empowered communities which assign functions to the state for their protection. Communities defending themselves demand such duties and obligations from state structures. On the other hand, transnational corporations (TNCs) and international agencies promote the separation of community interests from state interests and the fragmentation and divisiveness of communities.

As TNC totalitarianism destroys the ecological and economic security of citizens throughout the world, how should feminist movements respond? While feminism has always been pluralistic, there are currently two major trends with respect to economic globalization.

Ecological feminism sees in the current trend the ultimate concentration of capitalist patriarchy and its violence against nature and women. While feminism based on reductionist constructivism is unwittingly becoming a partner of TNC totalitarianism by supporting the political and technological paradigm of economic globalization. Reductionist constructivism is the philosophy that nature or the nation are nothing but a social construction of patriarchy. Some feminists have thus supported the erosion of national sovereignty and any form of people's protection instead of reclaiming the nation as an extension of feminist ideology's inclusion of all members of a society.

THE REINVENTION OF "NATURE"

The rise of industrialism led to a patriarchal construction of nature as passive, inert, and valueless and gendered these constructed qualities. Reductionist constructivism perceives nature as mere construction. In the absence of an ecological framework, feminist theorizing, especially the stream characterized by reductionist constructivism (the view that nature and its diversity is nothing but a social construction) has an unintended convergence with the dominant reductionist philosophy of genetic engineering. Ironically, while beginning as a critique of dominant science, it ends up speaking the same language. Thus both genetic engineering and feminist theories of biotechnology contribute to the invisibility of the organism, and to the disappearance of ordered biodiversity which is the basis of ecological stability (Braidotti). In a reductionist approach to biotechnology, issues of social justice also vanish along with concern for ecology.

If the post-modernist tradition of feminism is to avoid supporting the uncritical acceptance of the new biotechnologies, it must open a fresh dialogue with those working on equity, ethics, and ecological aspects of genetic engineering. It must become more ecological and this implies rethinking some of the categories whose origins lay in challenging the status quo, but which now support it. Two of these categories are "essentialism" and "crossing boundaries."

The machine metaphor for organisms is one arising from patriarchal rationality, which, when applied to organisms, denies their self-organizing, self-healing properties. Technologies based on the perception of living organisms as living systems and not machines are ecological, not engineering technologies.

Unfortunately, post-modern feminists have adopted this limited view of technology as mechanization. They therefore see an increased degree of freedom not as the freedom of an organism to adapt, to grow, to shape itself from within but as the mechanistic addition of "metal" to "flesh" and the "machine" to the "body." The inevitable consequence is to see the one without the other as incomplete. Haraway's cyborg imaginary was supposed to suggest a way out of the maze of the dualisms in which we have explained our bodies and our tools to ourselves.

The post-modern discourse was supposed to question the privilege of the white male individual and to enable recognition of other forms of historical experience. Much western academic feminist thinking, however, is converging closely with the perspectives of the global patriarchal elite. It is reinstituting the world view of powerful white males as a norm in an era where concern for preserving diverse forms of life, both biological and cultural, is emerging as a major challenge.

Reductionist constructivism in feminist theorizing and genetic reductionism underlying the genetic engineering industry converge in a move to genetic essentialism, which treats genes as more basic and essential than organisms as self-organizing systems, and species as separate and identifiable entities. However, a shift to genetic essentialism does not make essentialism disappear, but merely relocates it.

All paradigms treat something as basic and essential. Reductionism shifts the basis of life from organisms and their interactions to the gene. As Fox Keller has pointed out, genetic reductionism leads to the:

> relocation of the essence (or basis) of life. The locus of vital activity was now to be sought neither in the physical-chemical interactions and structures of the organism-niche complex, of the organism itself, nor even of the cell, but rather, in the physical-chemical structure of one particular component of the cell; namely, in the genetic material, or more exactly, in the gene. (Keller 96)

It is not that molecular reductionism eliminates essentialism; it merely relocates it in the gene. Post-reductionist biology needs to relocate the basic unit in the internal and external relationships of organisms.

RETHINKING BOUNDARIES

Boundaries have been an important construct for ecological restraint. "Removing boundaries" has been an important metaphor for removing restraints on human actions, and allowing limitless exploitation of natural resources. Boyle referred to the "removal of boundaries" that Native Americans had constructed to respect and conserve nature:

> that the veneration, wherewith men are imbued for what they call nature, has been a discouraging impediment to the empire of man over the inferior creatures of God: for many have not only looked upon it as an impossible thing to compass, but as something impious to attempt, the removing of those boundaries, which nature seems to have put and settled among her productions; and whilst they look upon her as such a venerable thing, some make a kind of scruple of conscience to endeavour so to emulate any of her works, as to excel them. (qtd. in Keller 96)

Two centuries later, Muller, the father of molecular biology, said:

> We cannot leave forever inviolate in their recondite recesses those invisibly small yet fundamental particles, the genes, for from these genes ... there radiate continually those forces, far-reaching, orderly, but elusive, that make and unmake our living worlds. (Muller qtd. in Keller 96)

In the reductionist paradigm, it is species boundaries that are crossed, and the boundaries created are those that separate the gene from the whole organism, and the patent holder from the rest of society. Crucial to the creation of transgenic organisms is the breaking down of species barriers, and the construction of the fictitious Weismann barrier that made the gene the casual determinant of the organism's evolution.

"Nature," "limits and boundaries," "organisms," and "species" have emerged as central to the discourse and politics of ecology. Biodiversity conservation in particular includes the recognition of the intrinsic worth of species and of ecological barriers that make diversity and distinctiveness flourish. Post-modern feminists and the genetic engineering establishment have, however, treated nature and boundaries as mere constructions, which can and should be dispensed with.

Mad Cow Disease and the equally mad sacrifice of millions of cattle to restore consumer confidence is an example of the risks of crossing ecological boundaries. When cattle were fed carcasses of infected cows and sheep, converted from being herbivores to cannibals, new risks were created for the transfer of infections across species. The links of new cases of Creutzfeldt-Jakob disease (CJD) on humans with bovine spongiform encephalopathy (BSE), the Mad Cow Disease, should create a humility in us that species boundaries are not mere fictions— they are an ecological reality and they need to be respected.

This species integrity is in fact the ethics of an earth democracy, the democracy of all life. To treat a species merely as a momentary organization of a chunk of information opens the flood gates of unlimited manipulation and unlimited hazards. Whether it is in the context of new technologies or in the context of political and economic restructuring, the reintroduction of limits in human affairs is becoming an ecological and political imperative to tame the excesses and ravages and predation of economic globalization.

Excerpted from a speech presented at the Sixth International Interdisciplinary Congress on Women, held in Adelaide, Australia, from April 21-26, 1996.

Vandana Shiva is an internationally renowned activist for biodiversity and against corporate globalization, and author of Stolen Harvest: The Hijacking of the Global Food Supply; Earth Democracy: Justice, Sustainability, and Peace; Soil Not Oil; *and* Staying Alive.

References

Braidotti, Rosi. "Organs Without Bodies." *Differences* 1 (1989): 3-16.

Estes, Ralph. *Tyranny of the Bottom Line: Why Corporations Make Good People Do Bad Things.* San Francisco: Berrett-Koehler Publisher, 1996. 76-77.

Haraway, Donna. *Simians, Cyborgs, and Women: The Reinvention of Nature.* New York: Routledge, 1991.

"The Hindu." *Indian Express* 1 October 1995.

Keller, Evelyn Fox. *Secrets of Life, Secrets of Death.* New York: Routledge, 1992.

Korten, David C. *When Corporations Rule the World.* San Francisco: Kumaran Press and Berrett-Koehler, 1995.

Rane, Ulhas. "The Zudpi Factor." *Sanctuary* 7.4 (1987).

Shiva, Vandana, and Radha Holla Bhar. "IPRS, Community Rights, and Biodiversity: A New Partnership for National Sovereignty." Conceptual Approach Paper prepared for the Seminar on the subject. New Delhi, 20 Feb. 1996.

EVA JOHNSON

An Open Letter

Native Culture and Environment

GREETINGS. I would like to submit a brief observation from the perspective of a Native North American Woman and a Mohawk National. Should we attempt to go back 500 years to chronicle events which have systematically undermined the "matriarchal society" established by the Five Nations Confederacy, now commonly known as the Six Nations Confederacy? As I am not a professional historian, I can only provide general observations beginning with the disease which was brought from across the seas along with many bad habits. The rights of Indian women were taken away from them almost as soon as the non-Native observed that women had such a high place in Native culture.

Respect for women was part of "Indian" culture long before the feminist movement had breath. The way the Iroquois Confederacy government operated was the first true "democratic" form of government in North American history. Although we are very rarely credited with this, it is still how true traditional governments operate. The women, in particular the clan mothers, have a very big role to play to ensure the peaceful existence of our people and yours.

We did not have a dominant male society, and it wasn't necessary to have a "class" system within our culture. Women had their duties and the men had their duties; it was understood that in order for balance to exist within our communal society, everyone had to tend to their particular tasks. This was the only way our people were guaranteed survival; there was no room for chauvinism of any sort. Children were also given specific duties in their training to become responsible adults.

We are a people who have a disciplined "religious" belief. It is not the same sort of discipline as non-Natives in which people worship on a scheduled weekly basis. Our "worship" was and still is structured by the seasons; we have ceremonies and feasts to commemorate each aspect of the different seasons. Our ceremonies are scheduled according to the cycle of the moon, and our feasts are "thanksgiving" feasts for all that our Creator has given us. Our feasts give thanks for what we have today, what was given to us yesterday, and what we must work for tomorrow.

Mother Earth is automatically thanked for what is provided to us. We dance in thanksgiving to our Creator and all other elements of the bird life, fish, animal, and plant life. Everything has to be put into perspective; no one organism is more important or has more place in our society than another.

Traditional "worship" does not call for idols, religious symbolism, once-a-week repentance and forgiveness of transgressions. This is where we differ: no human is given the power to "absolve" us if we stray from our 'original instructions' to care for the earth and each other. We have to look inward to find an answer and forgiveness. Only in very extreme cases would clan mothers or other persons who hold titles intervene; but, if help is asked of us, we do not have the power to say no. It is one of our "original instructions" that we have to extend help where it is needed. This holds true for domestic disputes, child care needs or any other element in today's society.

Violence against Mother Earth and violence against women in North America were unheard of before the migration of non Natives to our homelands. We are now called various names such as non-productive and unambitious because we do not have the same "goals" and aspirations as the majority of non-Native society. Mind you, some of our people (especially those who were adopted and educated by outsiders or who were torn away from their families and children) think a lot like big business people. They have been indoctrinated into the industrialized society and put more effort into making more money than they need and less effort into caring for their environment and people.

It was unheard of in our ancient ways to do anything which would endanger and jeopardize our well-being. Our Clan system ensured that we maintained a well-balanced lifestyle. Our Clan Mothers, Chiefs, Men's and Women's Societies all had their duties. Our system was foolproof; our Constitution (the Great Law) guided us in every aspect of our lives. Those who have been made to stray from this Constitution have done so unknowingly; it was so systematic that people did not know what hit them.

In fact, it has taken some 500 years to almost destroy North America and Native North Americans, but, somehow, we survived. But, our language and culture is barely surviving—this too was a long, strategic endeavour to prohibit us from speaking our languages and practising our beliefs . Even today, the well planned genocide is being carried out; it is very low key in some areas but very apparent in others. In fact, some of our own people chastise those of us who still believe in our traditional ways. These oppressors are called "apples" (red on the outside, white on the inside). They believe themselves to be the most holy and righteous people; this is what they have been taught by the Jesuits and other foreign religious fanatics. Those of us who are fighting desperately to hold onto the very small portion of land which hasn't been totally desecrated by industry are called militants and other fashionable names. Besides having to work very hard against outside aggression, we also have to overcome internalized oppression. This is an enormous task and it is what keeps violence in our communities. Both Native and non-Native populations can see the aggression of governments— governments have become big business and overpower the average, every day person. They keep hard feelings alive and perpetuate hatred by dividing us into classes; we have the oppressed (poor people) and the oppressors (well-to-do people), although this analogy is not totally true any more as some people are beginning to realize that this system is what almost destroyed our nations in the first place.

As men became dominant in North America and began the process of putting women "in their place," they also brainwashed our men and women into believing that this arrangement is natural. Some of our women still believe the *Indian Act*'s rhetoric which gave Indian men the power of marrying a non-Indian and turning her into an instant Indian, giving her the rights to own our land. This same destructive legislation stripped the Indian women of their ancestry if they happened to marry a non-Native. This process managed to replace Indian women with non-Indian women and was the beginning of the end for our languages and cultures.

The governments knew exactly what they were doing when they began to legislate over the Indian peoples; their plan was so intricate that we never knew what hit us. All of a sudden there was a big shift in our society. The esteem which our men had held for women for centuries began to diminish. We suddenly became second-class citizens in our own homes, and the process of extinguishing us was set in motion. Every element of our existence was modified to fit the model of the more dominant, westernized society. It is no wonder that we are living a lifestyle which is detrimental to our environment, your environment, our people and your people.

Eva Johnson, Bear Clean, Kahnawake Mohawk Nation, has been the Coordinator of the Kahnawake Environment Protection Office for 20 years.

SILVIA FEDERICI

Re-Enchanting the World

Technology, the Body and the Construction of the Commons

A PRECONDITION in the production of alternatives to the patriarchal capitalist conception of our relation to the earth is demystifying industrial technology and capitalist development as creators of abundance and higher forms of social cooperation. "Re-enchanting the world" re-imagines the knowledges and human powers that have been repressed in the capitalist rationalization of the world, not in view of an impossible return to the past, but as a step towards a better understanding of what constitutes the commons and what contemporary struggles best bring them into existence. The concept of the "commons" here defines a society built upon the sharing of a common wealth, the commitment to cooperative relations, and the organization of economic activity to satisfy our most basic needs.

INTRODUCTION

Almost a century has passed since Max Weber, in "Science as a Vocation" (1918-1919), argued that "the fate of our times is characterized, above all, by the disenchantment of the world," a phenomenon he attributed to the intellectualization and rationalization produced by the modern forms of social organization (155). By "disenchantment" Weber referred to the vanishing of the religious and the sacred from the world. But we can interpret his warning in a more political sense, as the emergence of a world in which our capacity to recognize the existence of a logic other than that of capitalist development appears everyday more problematic. This "blockage" has many sources combining to prevent the misery we experience in everyday life from turning into transformative action. The restructuring of production, which the globalization of the world economy has activated, has dismantled working class communities and forms of organization, products of a century of struggle, and deepened the divisions that capitalism has planted in the body of the world proletariat. There is, however, something else at work that we must acknowledge and demystify.

I propose that what prevents our suffering from becoming productive of alternatives to capitalism is also the seduction that the products of capitalist "technology" exert on us, as they appear to give us powers without which it would seem impossible to live. It is the main purpose of my article to challenge this myth. This is not to engage in a sterile attack against technology, yearning for an impossible return to a primitivist paradise, but to acknowledge the cost of the technological innovations by which we are mesmerized and, above all, to remind us of the knowledges, powers, and reasons that we have lost in the process of their production and acquisition. It is the discovery of other logics than that of capitalist development and the reconstitution of these powers and reasons that I refer to when I speak of "re-enchanting" the world, a practice, I believe, that is central to today's most anti-systemic movements and a precondition for resistance to domination. For if all we know and crave is what capitalism has produced, then any hope of truly revolutionary change is doomed. For *any* society not prepared to scale down the use of industrial technology must face ecological catastrophes (see Sarkar), competition for diminishing resources, and a growing sense of despair about the future of the earth and the meaning of our presence in it. In this context, struggles aiming to re-ruralize the world—e.g. through land reclamations, resistance to deforestation, the liberation of rivers from dams and, central to all, the *revalorization of the work of reproduction*—are crucial to our survival. These are the paths not only to the possibility of our physical survival, but to a "re-enchantment" of the earth, for they reconnect what capitalism has divided: our relation with nature, with others, with our bodies, enabling us not only to escape the gravitational pull of capitalist technology, but to regain a sense of wholeness in our lives.

TECHNOLOGY, THE BODY, AND AUTONOMY

With these questions in mind, I argue that the seduction that technology exerts on us is the effect of the impoverishment—economic, ecological, cultural—that five centuries of capitalist development have produced in our lives, even (or above all) in the countries in which it has climaxed. This impoverishment has many sides. Far from creating the material conditions for the transition to communism [as Marx imagined], capitalism has *produced scarcity* on a global scale,[1] devalued the activities by which our bodies and minds are reconstituted after being consumed in the work-process, and overworked the earth to the point that it is now less capable of sustaining our life. As Marx put it with reference to the development of agriculture:

> All progress in capitalist agriculture is a progress in the art not only of robbing the worker, but of robbing the soil; all progress in increasing the fertility of the soil for a given time is a progress towards ruining the more long term sources of that fertility. The more a country proceeds from large-scale industry as a background of its development, as in the case of the United States, the more rapid is this process of destruction. Capitalist production, therefore, only develops the techniques and

the degree of combination of the social process of production by simultaneously undermining the original source of all wealth—the soil and the workers. (Marx 638)

This destruction is not more obvious because the global reach of capitalist development has placed many of its social and material consequences out of sight, so that it becomes difficult for us to assess the full cost of any new forms of production. As the German sociologist Otto Ullrich has written, only our inability to see the cost, the suffering caused by our daily usage of technological devices, and the separation of our personal advantage from our collective danger, allows the myth that technology generates prosperity to persist. In reality, capital's application of science and technology to production has proven so costly, in terms of its effects on human lives and our ecological systems that, if it were generalized, it would destroy the earth. As it has often been argued, its generalization would only be possible if another planet existed also available for plunder and pollution (Wackernagel and Rees).

There is, however, another form of impoverishment that is less visible and yet equally devastating, one that the Marxist tradition has largely ignored. This is the loss produced by the long history of capitalist attacks on our autonomous powers, both through the regimentation of production and through our separation from nature, our separation from our own bodies, and the de-collectivization of our reproduction. By "autonomous powers" I refer to that complex of needs, desires and capacities that millions of years of evolutionary development in close relation with nature have sedimented in us, which constitute one of the main sources of resistance to exploitation. I refer to the need for the sun, the winds, the sky, the need for touching, smelling, sleeping, making love, being in the open air, instead of being surrounded by closed walls (keeping children enclosed within four walls is still one of the main challenges that teachers encounter in many parts of the world). Insistence on the discursive construction and nature of the body has made us lose sight of this reality. Yet, this accumulated structure of needs and desires, that has been the precondition of our social reproduction, has been a powerful limit to the exploitation of labour which is why, from its earliest phase of its development, capitalism had to wage a war against our body, making it a signifier for all that is limited, material, opposed to reason.[2] Foucault's intuition on the ontological primacy of resistance,[3] and our capacity to produce liberatory practices, can only be explained on this ground. That is, it can only be explained on the basis of our bodies' constitutive interaction with an "outside"—which I call the cosmos, the "world of nature"—that has been immensely productive of capacities and collective visions and imaginations, though obviously mediated through social/cultural interaction. All the cultures of the South Asian region— Vandana Shiva has reminded us—have originated from societies living in close contact with the forests. Also the most important scientific discoveries have originated in pre-capitalist societies in which people's lives were, at all levels, profoundly shaped by a daily interaction with nature. Four thousand years ago Babylonians and Mayan sky-watchers discovered and mapped the main constellations and the cyclical motions of heavenly bodies (Connor 63-4). Polynesian sailors could navigate the high seas in darkest nights, finding their way to the shore by reading the ocean swells—so attuned were their bodies to changes in the undulations and surges of the waves (Connor 55).[4] Pre-conquest Native American populations produced the crops that now feed the world, with a mastery unsurpassed by any agricultural innovations introduced over the last five hundred years, generating an abundance and diversity that no agricultural revolution has matched (Weatherford). I have turned to this history, so little known or reflected upon, to underline the great impoverishment that we have undergone, in the course of capitalist development, which no technological device has compensated for. Indeed, parallel to the history of capitalist technological innovation we could write a history of the dis-accumulation of our pre-capitalist knowledges and capacities, which is the premise on which capitalism has developed our capacity to work. Not surprisingly. The capacity to read the elements, to discover the medical properties of plants and flowers, to gain sustenance from the earth, live in woods, forests, mountainous regions, be guided by the stars and winds on the roads and the seas was and still remains a source of "autonomy" that had to be destroyed. The development of capitalist industrial technology has been built on that loss and has amplified it.

Not only has capitalism appropriated the workers' knowledges and capacities in the process of production, so that (in Marx's words) " the instrument of labour appears as a means of enslaving, exploiting and impoverishing the worker..." (638). As I argued in *Caliban and the Witch* (Federici 2003), the mechanization of the world was premised on and preceded by the mechanization of the human body, which in Europe was realized through the "enclosures," the persecution of vagabonds and the sixteenth- and seventeenth-century witch-hunts—all manifestations of what Michel Foucault has defined as "bio-power."

It is important here to remember that technologies are not reducible to any particular devices, but involve specific systems of relations, "particular social and physical infrastructures" (Ullrich), as well as disciplinary and cognitive regimes, capturing and incorporating the most creative aspects of the living labour used in the production process. This remains true in the case of digital technologies. Nevertheless, it is difficult to disabuse ourselves from the assumption that the introduction of the computer has been a benefit to humanity, that it has reduced the amount of socially necessary labour and increased our social wealth and capacity for communication and co-operation. Yet, an account of what computerization has required casts a long shadow on this optimistic view of the information revolution and knowledge-based society. As Saral Sarkar has reminded us, just to produce one computer requires on average 15 to 19 tons of materials and 33 thousands of liters of pure water, obviously taken away from our commonwealth, plausibly the common land and waters of communities in Africa or Central and Latin America (126-7; see also Shapiro). Indeed, to computerization we can still apply what Raphael Samuel has written about industrialization: "if one looks at [industrial] technology from the point of view of labour rather than that of capital, it is a cruel caricature to present machinery as dispensing with toil ... quite apart from the demands which machinery itself imposed there was a huge army of labour engaged in supplying it with raw material" (26-40).

Computerization has also immensely increased the military capacity of the capitalist class and its surveillance of our work and lives—all developments compared to which the benefits we can draw from our personal computers pale (Mander).[5] Most important, computerization has not reduced our work-week, the promise of all techno-topias since the 1950s, nor the burden of physical labour. We now work more than ever. Japan, the motherland of the computer, has led the world in the new phenomenon of "death by work." Meanwhile in the United States a small army of workers—numbering in the thousands—dies every year of work accidents, while many more contract diseases that will shorten their lives (Wypijewski).[6]

Not last, with computerization, the abstraction and regimentation of labour is reaching its completion and so is our sense of alienation and de-socialization. What levels of stress digital labour is producing can be measured by the epidemic of mental illnesses—depression, panic, anxiety, attention deficit, dyslexia—now typical in the most technologically advanced countries like the U.S.—epidemics which (not alone) I read as forms of passive resistance, refusals to comply, to become machine-like and to make capital's plans our own (Berardi).

In brief, computerization has added to the general state of misery, bringing to fulfillment La Mettrie's idea of the "man-machine." Behind the illusion of interconnectivity, it has produced a new type of isolation and new forms of distancing, and separation. Thanks to the computer millions of us work now in situations where every move we make is monitored, registered, possibly punished; social relations have broken down, as we spend weeks in front of our screens forfeiting the pleasure of physical contact, eye-to-eye conversation; communication has become more superficial as the attraction of immediate response replaces pondered letters with superficial exchanges. It has also been noted that the fast rhythms to which computers habituate us generate a growing impatience in our daily interactions with other people, as these cannot match the velocity of the machine.

In this context, we must reject the axiom, common in analyses of the occupy movement, that digital technologies (Twitter, Facebook) are conveyor belts of global revolution, the triggers of the "Arab Spring" and the movement of the squares. Undoubtedly, Twitter can bring thousands to the streets, but only if they are already mobilized. And it cannot dictate how we come together, whether in the serial manner or the communal, creative way we have experienced in the squares, fruit of a desire for the other, for body-to-body communication, and for a shared process of reproduction. As the experience of the Occupy Movement in the United States has demonstrated, the internet can be a facilitator, but transformative activity is not triggered by the information passed online; it is by camping in the same space, solving problems together, cooking together, organizing a cleaning team, confronting the police, all revelatory/experiences for thousands of young people raised in front of their computer screens. Not accidentally, one of the most cherished experiences in the Occupy Movement has been the "mic check"—a device invented because of the police ban on the use of loudspeakers in Zuccotti Park, now symbolic of freedom from dependence on the state and the machine, and a signifier of a collective expression of desire, a collective voice, will, and practice. "Mic check!" people now say on many occasions, even when not needed, rejoicing in this affirmation of collective power, the power to make our voices heard regardless of permissions by capital and the state. "Mic check is more powerful than a sword," stated a graphic designed on the pavement of New York's Union Square this Mayday.

All these considerations fly in the face of arguments attributing to the new digital technologies an expansion of our autonomy, and the parallel assumption that it is those who work at the highest levels of technological development who are in the best position to promote revolutionary change. In reality, the regions less technologically advanced from a capitalist viewpoint are today those in which political struggle is the highest and most confident in the possibility of changing the world. The main examples of "autonomy" come from the everyday struggles and autonomous spaces constructed by peasant, indigenous communities of the Americas, which Gustavo Esteva and Michael Hardt and Alvaro Reyes have described. I argue that this is the case because, despite centuries of colonization, the communities involved have never completely lost their connection with that "other" logic that is inscribed in our bodies by a life in close contact with the world of nature.

Today the material foundations of this world are under attack as never before, being the target of an incessant process of enclosures conducted by mining, agribusiness, bio-fuel companies. That even reputedly "progressive" Latin American states seem unable to overcome the logic of extractivism is a sign of the depth of the problem. The present assault on lands and waters is compounded by an equally pernicious attempt by the World Bank and a plethora of NGOs to bring all subsistence activities under the control of monetary relations, through the politics of rural credit and micro-finance, which has already turned multitudes of self-subsistent traders, farmers, food and care providers, mostly women, into debtors (see, among others, Ibanez). But despite this attack, this world which some have called "rurban" to stress its simultaneous reliance on town and country, refuses to wither away. Witness the multiplication of land squatting movements, water wars, and the persistence of solidarity practices like the *tequio*[7] even among immigrants abroad. Contrary to what the World Bank would tell us, the "farmer"—rural or urban— is a social category not yet destined for the dustbins of history. Some, like for example, the Zimbabwean sociologist Sam Moyo, speak of a process of "re-peasantization," arguing that the drive against land privatization and for land re-appropriation, sweeping from Asia to Africa, is possibly the most decisive, certainly the most fierce, struggle on earth (Moyo and Yeros).

From the mountains of Chiapas to the plains of Bangladesh many of these struggles have been led by women, a key presence in all land squatters' land reclamation movements. Faced with a renewed drive toward land privatization and the rise in food prices, women have also expanded their subsistence farming, appropriating for this purpose any available public land, in the process transforming the urban landscape of many towns. As I have written elsewhere, regaining or expanding land for subsistence farming has been one of the main battles for women in Bangladesh, leading to the formation of the Landless Women's Association that has been carrying on land occupations since 1992 (Federici 2004). In India as well, women have been in the forefront of land reclamations, as they have in the movement opposing the construction of dams. They have also formed the National Alliance for Women's Food Rights, a national movement made of thirty-five women's groups that has campaigned in defense of the mustard seed economy that is crucial for many rural and urban communities, but has been under threat since the attempt by a U.S. corporation to patent it. Similar struggles have taken place in Africa and Latin America, and increasingly in industrialized countries as well, with the growth of urban farming and various forms of solidarity economies in which women have had a prominent part.

What we are witnessing, then, is a "transvaluation" of political and cultural values. Whereas a Marxian road to revolution would have the factory workers lead the revolution, we are beginning to recognize that the new paradigms may come from those who from the fields, kitchens, fishing villages across the planet struggle to disentangle their reproduction from the hold of corporate power and preserve for all of us access to the "commonwealth." In the industrialized countries as well (as Chris Carlsson has documented in his *Nowtopia*), more people are seeking alternatives to a life regulated by work and the market, both because in a regime of precarity work can no longer be a source of identity formation, and because of their need to be more creative. Along the same lines, workers' struggles today follow a different pattern than the traditional strike, reflecting a search for new models of humanity and new relations between human beings and nature. We see the same phenomenon in the growing discourse and practice of the "commons," which is already spawning many new initiatives, like time-banks, urban gardens and accountability structures. We see it also in the preference for *androgynous* models of gender identity, the rise of the Transexual and Intersex movements and the queer rejection of gender with its implied rejection of the sexual division of labour. We must also mention the global diffusion of the passion for tattoos and the art of body-decoration, that is creating new and imagined communities across sex, race and class boundaries. All these phenomena point not only to a breakdown of disciplinary mechanisms, but to a profound desire for a remolding of our humanity in ways very different from, in fact the opposite of, those that centuries of capitalist industrial discipline have tried to impose. How profound is the desire for a humanity not shaped by capitalist relations and the industrial organization of our reproduction can be gauged by the popularity of a movie like *Avatar*, canonic in its anti-Cartesian celebration of "savage life," with its complete interpenetration of body and mind, the human, the natural and the animal and its pervasive communalism.

As this volume well documents, women's struggles over reproductive work play a crucial role in the construction of the "alternative." As I have written in "Feminism and the Politics of the Commons" (Federici 2010), because of their limited access to monetary income and engagement in reproductive work, women have engaged in strenuous struggle to maintain autonomous forms of sustenance, as traders, subsistence farmers, care providers. More importantly, there is something unique about reproductive work—whether in the form of subsistence farming, or education, or child-raising and domestic labour—that makes it particularly apt to regenerate our conception of work and social and ecological relations. Producing crops or human beings is in fact a qualitatively different experience and practice than producing cars, as it requires a constant interaction with natural process whose modalities and timing we do not control. As such, reproductive work potentially generates a deeper understanding of the natural constraints within which we operate on this planet, which is essential to the re-enchantment of the world that I propose. Not accidentally, the attempt to force reproductive work within the parameters of an industrialized organization of work has had especially pernicious effects. Witness the consequences of the industrialization of childbirth that has turned this potentially magical event into an alienating and frightening experience (Kahn).

In different ways, through these movements, we glimpse the emergence of another rationality not only opposing social and economic injustice but reconnecting with nature, reinventing life as a process of experimentation and redefining what it means to be a human being. This new culture is only on the horizon, for the hold of the capitalist logic on our subjectivity remains very strong. The violence that in every country men of all classes display against women is a measure of how far we must travel before we can speak of "commons." I am also concerned that some feminists cooperate with the capitalist devaluation of re-production. Witness their fear to admit that women can play a special role in the reorganization of reproductive work, evidence in my view of an inability to conceive reproductive activities other than as forms of drudgery. This, I believe, is a profound mistake. For reproductive work, insofar as it is the material basis of our life and the first terrain on which we can practice our capacity for self-government, is the "ground zero of revolution."

This paper was originally presented at the conference "The Anomie of the Earth" held at the Institute of the Arts and Humanities of The University of North Carolina at Chapel Hill, May 3-5, 2012.

Silvia Federici is a feminist writer, activist, teacher. She is Emerita Professor at Hofstra University in Hempstead, New York.

[1]It is necessary to clarify, however, that this is not a call for a policy of "de-growth" that in the present political context can only become a support to further austerity programs. The argument that capitalism produces scarcity should also not be confused with the theory that there are "limits" to capitalist expansion, presumably placed on it by the finite character of "natural resources"—a theory which is empirically and politically problematic, as it encourages a "wait and see attitude" and the expectation of a "naturally" developing capitalist crisis. By "production of scarcity" I refer both to the ongoing, eternally recurrent assault on the most basic means of subsistence on which we rely for our reproduction, be these lands, forests, fisheries or wages, pensions, and other common entitlements, and to the very logic of capitalist relations which demands the creation of a population of property-less workers as a preconditon for the extraction of surplus labour.

[2]On this matter, see Federici 2003, especially Chapter 3.

[3]Referred to in Negri and Hardt (31).

[4]Conner also reports that it was from native sailors that European navigators gained the knowledge about winds and currents that enabled them to cross the Atlantic Ocean.

[5]According to Wypijewski, more than 5,000 workers died on the job in 2007, with an average of 15 corpses a day, and more than 10,000 maimed or hurting. She calculates that "[b]ecause of under-reporting the number of injured workers every year is likely closer to 12 million than the official 4 million" (2).

[6]See especially Chapter 4, "Seven Negative Points About Computers."

[7]*Tequio* is described by Wikipedia as a form of collective work, dating back from pre-colonial Mesoamerica, in which members of a community join their forces and resources for a community project, like a school, a well, or a road.

REFERENCES

Berardi, Franco "Bifo." *Precarious Rhapsody.* London: Minor Compositions, 2009.

Carlsson, Chris. *Nowtopia*, Baltimore: AK Press, 2008.

Conner, Clifford D. *A People's History of Science. Miners, Midwives and Low Mechanics.* New York: Nation Books, 2005.

Esteva, Gustavo. "Enclosing the Encloser: Autonomous Experiences from the Grassroots Beyond Development, Globalization and Postmodernity." Paper presented in the conference "The Anomie of the Earth," University of North Carolina at Chapel Hill, May 3-5, 2012.

Federici, Silvia. *Caliban and the Witch: Women the Body and Primitive Accumulation.* London: Autonomedia, 2003.

Federici, Silvia. "Feminism and the Politics of the Commons." *Uses of a*

Whirlwind: Movements, Movement and Contemporary Radical Currents in the United States. Ed. Craig Hughes, Stevie Peace and Kevin Van Meter for the Team Colors Collective. Edinburgh: AK Press, 2010

Federici, Sylvia. "Women, Land Struggles and Globalization: An International Perspective." *Journal of Asian and African Studies* 39.1/2 (2004): 48-62.

Hardt, Michael and Alvaro Reyes. "'New Ways of Doing': The Construction of Another World in Latin America: an Interview with Raúl Zibechi." *South Atlantic Quarterly* 111.1 (Spring 2012): 165-191.

Ibanez, Graciela Toro. *La Pobreza: Uun gran negocio*. La Paz (Bolivia): Mujeres Creando, 2006.

La Mettrie, Julien Offray de. *Machine Man and Other Writings*. Cambridge: Cambridge University Press, 1996.

Kahn, Robbie Pfeufer. "Women and Time in Childbirth and Lactation." *Taking Our Time: Feminist Perspectives on Temporality*. Ed. Frieda Johles Forman with Caoran Sowton. New York: Pergamon Press, 1989. 20-36.

Marx, Karl. *Capital*. Vol. 1, Chapter 15: "Machinery and Large Scale Industry." London: Penguin 1976.

Mander, Jerry. *In the Absence of the Sacred: The Failure of Technology and the Survival of the Indian Nations*. San Francisco, Sierra Club Books, 1991.

Moyo, Sam and Paris Yeros, eds. *Reclaiming the Land: The Resurgence of Rural Movements in Africa, Asia and Latin America*. London: Zed Books, 2005.

Negri, Antonio and Michael Hardt. *Commonwealth*. Cambridge, MA: Harvard University Press, 2009.

Samuel, Raphael. "Mechanization and Hand Labour in Industrializing Britain." *The Industrial Revolution and Work in Nineteenth Century Europe*. Ed. Lenard Berlanstein. London: Routledge, 1992. 26-40.

Sarkar, Saral. *Eco-Socialism or Eco-Capitalism? A Critical Analysis of Humanity's Fundamental Choices*. London: Zed Books, 1999.

Shapiro, Tricia. *Mountain Justice. Homegrown Resistance to Mountain Top Removal For the Future of Us All*. Baltimore: AK Press, 2010.

Shiva, Vandana. *Staying Alive. Women, Ecology and Development*. London: Zed Books, 1989.

Ullrich, Otto. "Technology." *The Development Dictionary*. Ed. Wolfgang Sachs. London: Zed Books, 1992. 275-287.

Wackernagel, Mathis and William Rees. *Our Ecological Footprint: Reducing Human Impact on the Earth*. Gabriola Island, BC: New Society Press, 1996.

Weatherford, Jack. *Indian Givers. How the Indians of the Americas Transformed the World*. New York: Fawcett Columbine, 1988.

Weber, Max. "Science as a Vocation." (1918-1919). *For Max Weber: Essays in Sociology*. Eds. H. H. Gerth and C. Wright Mills. New York: Oxford University Press, 1946. 129-158.

Wypijewski, Joann. "Death at Work in America." *Counterpunch*. April 29, 2009. Web.

ALDA FACIO

Confronting Globalization

Feminist Spirituality as Political Strategy

G LOBALIZATION IS NOT A NEW PHENOMENON. More than five thousand years ago the process of globalizing patriarchy was begun, and has continued with such success that today there is no question that patriarchy has been completely globalized on planet Earth. Economic globalization is not a new process either. In the last five centuries, the economically strongest countries have imposed their way of viewing the world through trade and "production activities" in the "discovered and/or colonized" territories. What is more, the strategy of globalizing policies, economies, systems, and beliefs, which we see so prominently today, is not new and it has not only been used for imposition and domination. The socialist, pacifist, anti-colonial, pro-human rights, feminist and other emancipatory movements of the past centuries have also aspired to the globalization of their visions, but they have not called these dreams "globalization."

The neoliberal strategy of giving the name "globalization" to the process by which the most powerful men have managed to demolish national economic barriers, empowering financial institutions and transnational companies as never before, is very effective. Neoliberal ideologists have made us believe that "financial globalization" is about the free "exchange" of people, goods and services and more progress for the benefit of humanity. They have made us believe that globalization is the technology that has made it possible and that we cannot have the best of it if at the same time we have protections against the flow of capital into or out of a poor country. Furthermore, their strategy is even more successful because they have declared globalization synonymous with more freedom, progress, leisure and goods. The globalization that we are experiencing, however, which was developed at the end of the twentieth century and the beginning of the twenty-first, needs an adjective: *neoliberal globalization*. What has really been globalized is the market. In fact, the only thing that circulates freely around the world is capital. That is to say, only imperialistic financial globalization is total, while the globalization of merchandise, products or services is partial and that of people almost non-existent.

For example, every month we hear of "wetbacks" who were left to die or were otherwise abused by "coyotes" trying to get them into the U.S. or Europe. The mere existence of these coyotes is proof that there is no freedom of migration for the majority of poor people. In our region, hundreds of Colombians and Mexicans are denied entrance into the United States, Canada or any other country that has become a haven for migration from war, poverty or violence. And yet the Free Trade treaties that the U.S. and others have forced Latin American countries to sign do not deal with the problem of migration from poverty to the the U.S., while insisting on the free flow of capital. In fact, financial liberalization has been the hallmark of neoliberal globalization, due mainly to the "advice" of the international financial institutions and to the idea put forward by neoliberal economists, that there would be great benefits derived from opening up to inflows of international capital for "developing" nations. And even though the financial crisis we are experiencing worldwide[1] has more than demonstrated the perils of the free flow of capital, the trade negotiators are still insisting on it. This neoliberal financial globalization is what I am referring to when I speak of the nightmare of globalization for women today. And although women are the poorest, the most violated and the most alienated thanks to globalization, many feminists feel that we have to "look on the bright side" of it because we have been sold the idea that to be against globalization is to be against progress. It is time that we clearly identify this process of globalization so we understand that it does not have a bright side and it has not produced any benefits for the majority of people in the world. We must be clear that the globalization that dominates today is capitalist globalization in a neoliberal incarnation, so that if we decide to oppose or resist it, we are clear about what we are up against.

While some people identify a myriad of factors and processes implicated in globalization, we should be clear that the Internet, scientific advances, social movements, environmental struggles, pacifism, and feminism are not international thanks to globalization. They are internationally opposed to globalization and they are international in spite of globalization and/or before it. If there be any doubt, consider HIV/AIDS. It is because of feminist research and Internet communications that today we know that this pandemic is primarily affecting women. Furthermore, it is because of technological and scientific advances that today we could end the AIDS crisis. It is thanks to globalization, however, that a few transnational companies have the power to put their avarice and greed before the possibility of ending the AIDS pandemic with impunity. *Why?* Because thanks to the globalization of the neoliberal ideology, it is not considered a crime against humanity to make a lot of money at the expense of the lives of the majority by denying needed medications to those who cannot afford to pay for them.

Moreover, globalization has permitted the country with the strongest market in intangible goods and the military force to support its dominance, to be seen by too many people in many parts of the planet as a world leader in questions unrelated to its economic-military power. In Latin America, for example, the political, medical, legal and educational systems of the United States of America are viewed as models to be emulated in spite of the fact that the U.S. is full of corrupt politicians, there is no public health system to speak of, prisons are full of ethnic minorities and women lack pre- and post-natal leave. Moreover, women's greater access to higher education in the U.S. undermines their awareness of their own oppression and the fact that the privileges offered by this system come at the expense of millions in both north and south who cannot even aspire to basic education. And even though the world is increasingly critical of the power that emanates from this center of arrogance, pride and despotism, which has set itself up as the global policeman, few question U.S. technology, science, medicine or U.S. interventions such as the Plan Colombia or Plan Merida.[2] Few seem to realize that these products of the United States reduce, rather than increase our leisure, liberty, health and peace.

Neoliberal globalization has not meant progress, interdependence, equality, peace or happiness for the majority of the world's population, and even less so for women who are worse off than ever, as has been shown and re-proven in too many studies by academic, development, human rights and women's institutions. So why is it that the feminist movement does not have a plan and consolidated strategies to combat this process called globalization, whose greatest impact has been the imposition of a necrophilic and misogynist culture on the whole world?

I believe our objective has been obscured because in our desire to eliminate the discrimination that we suffer as women of different ages, races, classes and abilities, we have been thinking only of the "possible" within the state. We have stopped dreaming of new worlds. In this effort to work within the parameters of the possible, we embrace all women, independent of whether they identify with feminist thinking or not. We are so accepting of women today that you can be considered a feminist and also be on the executive board of the International Monetary Fund, the president of a neoliberal party or commander of a platoon. This is a crucial problem. I am not saying that women in those positions cannot be feminist or that they shouldn't be feminist. I am only saying that if feminism is something so diffuse and abstract that it can include an ideology such as neoliberalism which is responsible for impoverishing millions of women, maiming and killing many and making life more difficult for most, then we have a problem. And if we have a problem, we must begin to face it instead of pretending it does not exist.

Furthermore, while I recognize that we have achieved quite a lot, many of us act as if our successes within the existing structure are what is presently needed to end patriarchy. It is undeniable that in the 1980s and 1990s, this movement made incredible achievements in the public sphere. Consider, for example, the formal recognition of gender-based violence as a social problem and a violation of human rights; the repeal of almost all openly sexist laws; more women at most levels of decision-making and the creation of ministries or offices of women's affairs; the promulgation of laws and policies with a gender perspective; and the international and regional conferences that adopted platforms for action, which if implemented would end the discrimination and exploitation of women on the basis of our gender. Moreover, in the private sphere we also made some gains for some women, including more freedom of expression, greater freedom of movement, and more paths open for more women.

However, it is also undeniable that gender-based violence has not only increased, but has become more sophisticated; that justice continues to be androcentric in spite of the repeal of most sexist laws and in spite of hundreds of training sessions, innovations and conventions with a gender perspective; that power continues to be masculine although it now may paint its nails; and that poverty continues to be a Chicana, Mulatto, Black or Indigenous woman, even though our enemies now use the language of diversity. So while for some women there are more freedoms today, it is also true that almost all women are prisoners of fashion, publicity, fundamentalisms, legal or illegal drugs or even of that self-same "sexual freedom," technological "advances," and the innumerable messages telling us we are always ill, foul smelling, too fat, and of the wrong age, color, hair-type and personality.

We cannot simply rely on those strategies vis-à-vis the state that were successful in the past. Instead, I think that we have to (re)construct a movement capable of confronting both the old and the new challenges of neoliberal globalization. This kind of movement requires us to ask questions and respond to them from a loving heart and from an emotional space that is free of judgement or blame. This is not easy because as women, we have been indoctrinated in distrust of each other and in the idea that women are always "guilty" of something.

THE SPIRITUAL IS POLITICAL

I believe that our most urgent task in creating a movement capable of confronting the onslaughts of capitalist globalization in its neoliberal incarnation is to recreate, redefine and reaffirm ourselves as feeling, thinking beings, autonomously interdependent and eternally finite. We need to reaffirm ourselves as beings capable of thinking lovingly, living in the present without denying the past or forgetting the future, and perceiving ourselves as both unique and at the same time as part of a larger whole. This, I believe, is spirituality.

But instead of our understanding of ourselves proceeding in this spiritual direction, advertising by huge transnational corporations has created a globalized culture of people who need to consume and accumulate in order to fill the emptiness of our lives. We have become so alienated, fragmented and isolated from our interior selves that we look to the accumulation of objects and power to fill the emptiness that we feel. Because of this overwhelming tendency, I believe that the spiritual is very political at this particular historical moment. The spiritual is a transgressor of the demands of the market because it is about interior wholeness and the dialogue that we establish within ourselves. The spiritual is about a state of ultra-consciousness that lets us see and understand who we really are. My suggestion for global women's movements, therefore, would be to actively pursue feminist spirituality and develop a "feminist ultra-consciousness."

This feminist ultra-consciousness goes beyond a feminist consciousness, which is understood as a mindset that allows us to "see" sexism. A feminist ultra-consciousness would allow us not only to see sexism in societal structures but also how sexism operates within us and how it is linked to all other forms of oppression. It would also allow us to see the energy flowing in and out of these oppressions so that we do not reproduce this energy in our solutions. For example, the energy that flows out of gender violence towards women is misogynist and the energy that flows out of misogyny is hatred of the opposite sex. If the solution we propose for gender violence is only or mainly punishment of perpetrators, without regard or compassion for their construction as males, would this not be equivalent to "hating men'? Are these not similar energies? Should we not try to find a solution that flows with a different energy? How about love or compassion or forgiveness? Not easy, definitely, but it is probably necessary.

When I speak of needing a feminist spirituality, I am *not* speaking about a religion as such. I am definitely *not* proposing that the creation of female religious authorities or praying to the goddess in place of a god is a political act *per se*. Of course, if someone wishes to do either of these things, that is their prerogative. It is not, however, the spirituality of which I am speaking when I say that the spiritual is political. Political spirituality is what allows us to re/create ourselves as interdependent and infinite beings, capable of confronting impositions from outside with a creative bravery. We need to be brave and creative because in the quest to discriminate between our conditioning and our true feelings, we will need to step into lonely and unknown lands. As I said earlier, spirituality has to do with a state of feminist ultra-consciousness that allows us to see ourselves as the women we are. But to be in touch with the women we are, we need to strip ourselves of thousands of years of indoctrination in patriarchal values and ways of understanding reality. We need to be able to identify which are our genuine feelings and which are those we have been taught to feel.

As women, we need to find this state of "ultra-consciousness" that allows us to love intelligently as we think with our hearts, so we can undo the false dichotomies into which we have been divided by patriarchal ideology. With this new consciousness, we will be able to feel and think about the world in new ways that will lead us to imagine, dream and create alternative attitudes towards everything around us. In time, it will allow us to build lifestyles that are less consumerist, more cooperative and especially more respectful of the other beings that inhabit this planet. It will permit us to find ways of "being our bodies" instead of treating them as objects that we inhabit.

One thing that is abundantly clear in this era of neoliberal globalization is that we need different attitudes and different values in order to resist it. We cannot continue in the disjunction of assuming "the masculine" as our own, or presuming "the feminine" to be superior. We have to end the masculine/feminine dichotomy and replace it with values of real inclusiveness. We need lifestyles that are less violent and misogynist; we definitely need more love, more forgiveness, more tolerance in our lives.

I believe that the fight against globalization can help us find these values that we need so badly to recover, and these new attitudes and ways of life that we need to adopt if we want to continue to exist on this planet. But we also need to remember that we are not only people within the globalized world, but also women for whom globalization is impoverishing, violating and fragmenting. We therefore cannot simply join in the fight against neoliberal globalization. We need to create a strong feminist movement that has something unique to contribute to the anti-globalization movement. The power and strength of our movement will rest in this contribution.

In order to recover and recreate the feminine on which we can base our contribution to the fight against neoliberal globalization, we should turn our eyes to the beginnings of patriarchy. We know that in prehistory, that is, before patriarchy, god was female. Understanding how the first patriarchs displaced the goddess can give us a clue to how to recover and re/create her for our contemporary purposes. Our goal is not to adore her like a god, but to recover our love for the feminine and everything associated with it, such as caring, nurturing and giving. We know that one strategy of the patriarchs was to rend from female bodies their transcendent and spiritual meaning. As a result, the body came to be understood as devoid of all sacredness, while the soul was viewed as the repository of everything divine, spiritual and superior. The pre-patriarchal religions, however, did not make this distinction. For them the body was sacred because it was one with the spirit or soul. Female bodies, capable of giving life to other human beings, were therefore considered not only sacred, but divine. And as the body was sacred, so too was pleasure. The patriarchal religions not only took away our capacity for transcendence but also our capacity to feel pleasure without guilt.

Once again we need the spiritual to create a feminist movement that offers pleasure to women: sexual pleasure, bodily pleasure, mental pleasure, pleasure of the soul, and also pleasure in work and in activism. We do not need a feminist movement that kills us with work but a movement that dances, laughs and delights in the creation of choreographies against globalization. This is where feminist spirituality comes in. In contrast to that created by patriarchs, feminist spirituality does not deny pleasure; rather it illuminates for us the thousands of ways of enjoying each moment of consciousness, of work, of activism, of our power and especially of our bodies.

Feminist spirituality also teaches us that pleasure cannot be accumulated, reproduced, sold, or possessed. Perhaps it is because pleasure is not merchandise that neoliberal globalization is not interested in it. For this reason, then, feeling pleasure and being happy can be our biggest rebellion against the dominant economic order. Why? Because a culture based on a market economy such as the one globalization has imposed on us, needs people to buy and buy and buy. And, if one is happy and content with what one has and with what one is, one buys less. Thus, it is only logical to assume that a market economy needs people who are unhappy with who they are and with what they have. The strategy is to make us feel unhappy, unworthy, dirty, sick, foul smelling and dependent so we can buy things that will make us clean, healthy, free and independent. You only need to see any television commercial to understand this.

Furthermore, the spiritual is political because how one sees oneself and understands reality is how one behaves. If we see ourselves as the victims of men, we will behave with vengeance. If we see ourselves as superior, we will behave towards men as they have towards us. If we believe that we are only flesh without spirit, or if we believe that there is a god only outside of us, surely we will not fully feel the happiness and pain of others. But if we see ourselves as distinct expressions of the same energy and the divine, we will behave with the love and respect that this consciousness gives us. And that is political!

TOWARDS A SPIRITUAL FEMINIST MOVEMENT AGAINST GLOBALIZATION

It is true that in the face of patriarchy we need public policies with a gender perspective in order to alleviate poverty and violence against women, but the current incarnation of patriarchy that is bringing us militarized and neoliberal globalization requires something more than just different strategies. In reality, the majority of our states and their governments do not have the desire or the capability to solve problems on their own. Moreover, globalization is not a process that has been decided on by us as citizens but rather by a few rich men disguised as the free market. National policies, therefore, are of ever less importance in the free market because it is outside the reach of politics. What should our strategies be then?

I am convinced that the feminist movement should not simply seek the same power that men have exercised. In the 1960s and 1970s, we met in consciousness-raising groups to discuss our position as women in the patriarchy and to seek the feminine that the patriarchy had made invisible and trivialized. We still need this type of mutual support and consciousness-raising. Today, we need a movement made up of thousands of women's groups ready to dream and to build the possibility of a new world, because, as the most revolutionary movement of this new millennium says, "another world is possible." It is around this realization, I would suggest, that we need to formulate our anti-globalization strategies.

In (re)constructing a feminist movement in the face of neoliberal globalization, a fundamental step will be to stop speaking in the abstract and to use the new feminist consciousness that I have been speaking about to give "love," "sisterhood," and "friendship" substance. This implies feeling them and giving them space, not only in our everyday interpersonal relationships, but also in our public actions.

For example, in our public actions we need to continue to denounce the discrimination and violence that we as women face on a daily basis, but we also need to celebrate our life, our friendships, our history with art festivals, with posters, concerts, poems and theater. We need to envision a life with no discrimination and no violence. We need to create feminist utopias that describe in detail how societies without sexisms would look. And we definitely need to laugh at our own mistakes and learn from them.

Globalization poses several distinct challenges to women, human rights and our planet in general. First, globalization is imposing one single culture throughout the world: the American Way of Life, which is spoon fed to the world through cable television and through what we eat in the shopping malls, what we wear in the streets and what we study in our schools. In response, with our new consciousness we need to create a feminist counter-culture. This requires losing the fear that others will brand us as self-referential, ineffective or antiquated idealists, *mujeristas*, *hembristas* or lesbians. We have to permit ourselves to be transgressors, without becoming malcontents who are useful to the system. We can only do this if we become a feminist movement dedicated to building and creating outside of the limits that are imposed on us by mainstreaming gender into state laws and policies.

Creating a feminist counter-culture does not mean imitating the misogynist culture that has been imposed by globalized patriarchy on us. It implies the creation of arts, technologies, sciences, languages, symbols and myths from our true internal selves in connection with all other beings. This requires raising the veils that obstruct our clear vision of ourselves: veils of romanticism, Greek tragedy, patriarchal myths and ancestral guilt; veils that prohibit pleasure and that do not allow us to feel, smell, touch, see, hear or even dream about another world without patriarchal biases. Again, in order to achieve this, we need a spirituality that permits us to see ourselves as we are, without fear, without excuses, and above all, without judgments.

Creating this counter-culture will not be easy and that is why we need to work in consciousness raising groups so we can collectively see the patriarchy's underbelly. But we must also work individually, with strategies that permit us to know ourselves and grow as human beings, such as meditation and yoga. Creating a counter-culture is difficult because it implies not believing or accepting ideas that have been held by humanity as universal truths for centuries: the nuclear family as the basic unit of society, obedience and discipline as values that make people better, guilt as god-given, good and evil as always recognizable and the body as separate from the soul or mind. We would also need to see how we have internalized the notion that erotic pleasure and violent and degrading treatment go together, that beauty is thin and young or skin deep, and that security is more important than freedom. And all these things we would not only have to understand as half-truths or outright falsehoods, we would have to *feel* them as such in our bodies.

Decoding our feelings or even feeling them to begin with requires a sense of entitlement and bravery. But the challenge is not only to get in touch with our bodies by becoming our bodies, but also to create a context that makes this awareness possible and that validates our response. Individual feelings of anger or outrage for what has been considered "natural" or "god-ordered" for centuries requires a cultural legitimacy and that can only happen if we create this culture which will validate our feelings.

Of course, feminist counter-culture would not be linear or a mono-culture, but a diversity of different options. Just as there are many feminisms, so too are there many utopias and many feminist cultures. These different utopias, and maybe even conflicting utopias, may be a source of discontent in the future. But if we work on ourselves, if we create a space in and out of ourselves for friendly debate, the discontent may be minimized. Maybe in learning to create from the heart and not only from the mind we will be able to stop competing for the truth.

A second key challenge of the neoliberal incarnation of globalization is that it is substituting for an economy based on production of goods, an economcy based on speculation. To achieve an alternative vision in the face of a globalization whose success is based on contempt for human reproduction, of a globalization that so easily moves from overvaluing tangible goods to super-valuing intangible goods, we need a feminist movement that truly values reproduction and bases its economy both on this reproduction and the production of material goods needed for our welfare without destroying the planet. Our movement must make the other groups resisting neoliberal globalization see that it is essential that every one of us incorporate the entire gamut of issues of human reproduction, including eroticism and pleasure, but also valuing maternal thinking and nurturing as part of their vision.

As feminists aware that structural adjustment policies have impoverished even more those women who were already poor, we can not pretend that the neoliberal state can really benefit us because it supports the criminalization of some forms of gender-based violence or institutes quotas for political representation. The type of economy which the neoliberal state is creating demands that the feminist movement itself be leftist, socialist and in favor of the elimination of all privileges in order for it to be effective. We need a movement that is based on the belief that patriarchy is hateful, not only because it is based on masculine domination, but also because it promotes domination and control as ends in and of themselves. We must be a movement that opposes all forms of domination and strives to create economies and political structures based on principles of substantive equality.

When I speak of a leftist and socialist movement, I am *not* speaking of The Left or of patriarchal socialism. I am speaking of a left that is against domination of any kind. I am speaking of a socialism that has still not been realized anywhere on this planet. If feminists have had the patience to train those who govern on "gender" and "gender-mainstreaming," why would we not have the same patience to convince the leftists and socialists that domination based on gender is as shameful as that based on class, race or any other category? Oppression based on sex and gender is, after all, the oldest form of domination and perhaps the most difficult to eradicate. I believe it is worth our effort to undertake this challenge because I am convinced that we can achieve much more by incorporating a gender perspective in socialism then in neoliberal policies or traditional parties. We were so successful in reconceptualizing human rights, democracy, and public policies to include our needs and interests, I do not see why we would not be able to reconceptualize socialism so that it includes our desires for a society without domination or discrimination against women. But more importantly, it should include the construction of a society that values the caring and nurturing of human beings more than the production of goods and far more than the accumulation of power.

Speaking of desires, I am convinced that a very powerful strategy against neoliberal globalization would be to know how to fill this internal emptiness that so many of us feel. We should ask ourselves why evangelical churches, as well as conservative and religious parties are attracting so many women. I am not proposing that we imitate them in order to sell women more lies, as they do, or in order to create another religion imposed from outside, but in order to understand what it is that they offer to women which we do not. It could be that their success is due to the fabrication of the illusion of filling the internal emptiness that the stock exchange has left us. For this reason we need a movement that proselytizes, a movement that is willing to promote feminist ideas and practices in multiple new ways. Furthermore, we need a feminist movement that is relevant to the large majority of women.

The third element of neoliberal globalization that I would like to highlight is its tendency to fragment us even more by promoting the divisions between us and by capitalizing on our diversity. To counteract this, we need a feminist movement that does not fall into the patriarchal trap of diversity as political identity. As women we are not a homogenous group, and neither are we as black women, lesbians, indigenous women, or young women. Within the category of black women for example, there are rich and poor women, and there are lesbians, bisexuals and heterosexuals. Similarly, in the category of lesbians there are Chinese and indigenous lesbians, there are young and old lesbians, there are lesbians from the North and from the South, lesbians who are disenfranchised and lesbians that are over-privileged. Identities are infinite and if we give them primacy we cannot defeat the patriarchy that is the root of our particular oppressions. Rather than fight over our multiple identities, we have to fight against domination, privilege and control as values that dehumanize us all.

We should celebrate our diversity and we need to recognize that among us there exist racism, homophobia, and ageism, among other blindnesses. However, we should do this within the connecting framework of feminist struggle, always keeping in mind that what unites us is the fight against patriarchy in its capitalistic incarnation. If the most constant values during patriarchy's different incarnations have been misogyny, domination and control of women, then we must fight against these values both inside and outside of ourselves. It is important that we also recognize that racism, homophobia and intolerance do not have a gender, sex, race, ethnicity, class or age; they live in all of us no matter how discriminated against we are. For this reason, I believe that instead of accusing each other of being racist, homophobic, ageist or classist, we should struggle constantly against all these forms of oppression and make a daily effort to eliminate privileges, whatever and wherever they are.

THE FIRST STEP

In all of my suggestions I am not speaking of abstract concepts. I am speaking of our feminist movement being made up of women who are not only of distinct physical or social conditions, but distinct in the ways in which we have internalized patriarchy and also in the ways that we have survived in it. I am speaking of a feminist movement made up of women who must change attitudes and behaviors not only in the intimacy of our internal selves but also in the public and private spheres. We must remember that our movement is about the transformation of a system that does not exist only in the public sphere, but also, where perhaps it is strongest, in our relations with ourselves. In order to obtain our objective successfully, we need to feel love and respect for others, *but we need to begin with ourselves.* We need the ability to put ourselves in each other's shoes and understand each other, to agree or disagree healthily, without treating each other cruelly. And we can only do this if our relationship with ourselves and with our interior self is loving, respectful and honest. Again, for that we need the path of spirituality.

As I have emphasized throughout this essay, we need a movement willing to bravely confront its errors, prejudices and foolishness. We do not need a movement made up of women who will judge, accuse and bring each other down. For that reason, we need to exile the misogyny that lives in each one of us, and we will not be able to do it without the ability to see it, understand it and remove it from our lives with love and understanding. The path of feminist spirituality can help us with this since it teaches us to love or at least understand ourselves, even our "evil side," because it allows us to see that we can learn from it. What is more, when we understand how internalized misogyny works, we have the most important keys to eradicating it.

The poorly named "anti-globalization movement" is against the existing globalization, not against a globalization of the best that humanity has invented and imagined. For this reason, they repeat the slogan, "another world is possible" over and over. I believe that this movement needs feminism and feminists so that this other world that really is possible also includes our dreams of a world without discrimination against women, a world that values the caring and nurturing of others. Moreover, it is only with the inclusion of our desires that this other world will really be possible. But for that, we need a feminist movement strong in the recognition of its weaknesses, united in respect for its diversity, happy with the consciousness of pain and loving because we know there is a reason for it. *Is this so impossible?*

An earlier version of this article was published in The Future of Women's Rights: Global Visions and Strategies, *edited by Joanna Kerr, Ellen Sprenger, and Alison Symington (2004). ©Aldio Facio. Reprinted with permission of the author.*

Alda Facio is a feminist human rights defender, jurist and writer who has published hundreds of articles on feminist issues for different international and national magazines. She was a correspondent for FEMPRESS, a feminist Latin American news agency based in Chile, for fourteen years. She has lectured extensively and been a visiting professor in several universities around the world, as well as in human rights and women's organizations and law centers. In 2003, she was the 7th Dame Nita Barrow Distinguished Visitor at the CWSE at the University of Toronto. Since then, she has continued to teach the Women's Human Rights in an Era of Globalization Education Institute at this same Center. For three years she was a professor at the United Nations University for Peace where she taught a course on women's human rights. Since 1996, she has also been teching a course on CEDAW during the CEDAW sessions at the UN.

[1]Consider violence against women in the domestic sphere, for example. In Latin America, the emphasis has been on criminalizing domestic violence and for many years the women's movement has dedicated most of its energy towards this. To me, this is an ineffective strategy in the long run because it stems from the desire to punish those who harm us, which in the end is a desire for vengeance. Punishment and vengeance for domestic abusers, as with punishment and vengeance for terrorists, will only bring about more violence. We need to find strategies that come from a spiritual space that flows with compassion and understanding, even for our abusers, in order to end this violence.

[2]The term Plan Colombia refers to a piece of U.S. legislation which under the guise of procuring peace in Colombia and curbing drug smuggling is really aimed at combating a left-wing insurgency in this country. More than 78 percent of the funds, contributed not only by the U.S. even though it is a U.S. law, went to the Colombian military and police for counternarcotics and military operations. This law is criticized because it mandates aerial fumigation to eradicate coca and marijuana plantations which not only damages legal crops but has adverse health effects upon those exposed to the herbicides.

The Mérida Initiative, called Plan Mexico or Plan Merida by its critics because of its similarity with Plan Colombia, is a security cooperation "agreement" between the U.S. and the governments of Mexico and Central America, with the declared aim of combating the threats of drug trafficking, transnational organized crime, and money laundering. Both plans are criticized for combating the supply of drugs rather than focusing on prevention and treatment and education programs to curb U.S. demand. This suggests they have nothing to do with combating drugs and all to do with militarizing the region to make it safe for big corporations to exploit the region's incredible natural richness.

MARIA MIES

Do We Need a New "Moral Economy"?

I T IS WELL KNOWN by now that the biggest problems the world is facing today—ecological destruction, hunger and poverty in the "Third World," and the danger of war—are an outcome of the prevailing development model of unlimited growth of goods and services, of money revenue, of technological progress, and of a concept of wellbeing, identified as an abundance of industrially produced commodities. It should also be known that this model, which prevails in the affluent countries of the North, cannot be generalized to the rest of the world.

MORALITY—A BAD WORD IN ECONOMICS

The moral problem of the modern, capitalist market economy consists above all in the fact that ethics, morality, have been excluded and externalized from the so-called economic sphere proper. When the fathers of the new political economy of capitalism developed their theories they were keen to establish that economic laws were functioning like natural laws, like the law of gravity of Newton, for instance. Economics was a science, like other sciences, and as such was set apart from the sphere of moral values. It was supposed to be "value-free" and to follow only universal objective laws of supply and demand.

This externalization of morality from the political economy of capitalism is not only similar to the exclusion of values from modern science, but is also directly linked to the externalization of ecological, social, and other costs, which the capitalists are not ready to pay. These costs have been apparently pushed outside the economic sphere of the core nations of world capitalism and onto colonies. We have identified women, nature, and foreign countries in the South as the main colonies of "white man," i.e. the modern capitalist world system (Mies, Bennholdt-Thomsen, and Werlhof). Because, if we include those colonies into the analysis of the functioning of the market economy we realize, that the growth of wealth in the core countries in this world-system (Wallerstein) is based on increasing pauperization in the colonies, that the laws of supply and demand, functioning apparently automatically, are based on coercion and violence. Polanyi has convincingly shown that the markets for money, land, and labour had to be created by direct and coercive state intervention in England; they did not grow out of the new economics by themselves. And if we include the external colonies, nature, and women into our analysis of the political economy of the new world market system we see clearly that coercion, robbery, and direct and structural violence are still the main forces behind the apparently, "value-free," "objective" law of supply and demand.

We can conclude, therefore, that the basic philosophy on which the capitalist market system is based, has not been able to solve the ethical dilemma, it has only pushed the moral questions outside the sphere which it has defined as "economy." This system can, therefore, not be called a "moral economy" in the sense this term has been used so far.

THE LIMITS OF GROWTH AND THE IMPOSSIBILITY OF "CATCHING-UP DEVELOPMENT"

It is a well-known fact that the resource base within our limited globe is limited and that the economic philosophy of unlimited growth will necessarily reach the ecological limits of this planet. And yet, practically all conceptions and strategies of development, both national and international ones, are explicitly or implicitly based on the assumption that the poor nations will eventually reach the standard of living of the U.S. or Europe.

However, if we keep in mind that the six percent of the world's population who live in the U.S. annually use up 30 percent of the fossil energy produced, then it should be dear, that the rest of the world's population, of which about 75-80 percent live in the poor countries of the South, cannot also consume as much energy per person (Global 2000: 59). But even if the world's resource base were not limited, it would take about 500 years for the poor countries to reach the standard of living prevailing in the rich countries of the North. And this would be possible only if these rich countries would not continue with this growth model. To catch up with this model of development is impossible for the poor countries of the South. It is not only impossible because of the limits of the resource base and the uneven distribution of their consumption. Above all it is impossible because the growth model in the rich industrialized countries is based on a colonial world order in which the gap between the two poles is getting wider and wider, at least as far as economic development is concerned.

The living standard in the rich countries of the North could not be so high if the colonized South had not been exploited and continue to be exploited. If all labour, incorporated in the commodities sold in the rich countries was paid at the rate of a skilled (male) worker of Germany then most of these commodities would be so expensive that only a small minority could buy them. So-called development is not an evolutionary process from a lower to a higher stage but a polarizing process in which some are getting richer and richer because they make others poorer and poorer. Two hundred years ago the western world was only five times as rich as the poor countries of today. In 1960, this relationship was already twenty to one, and in 1983 it was forty-six to one, the rich countries being 46 times richer than the poor countries (Trainer). The wealth in the rich countries grows ever faster, and within a limited world this means it grows at the expense of others, of what I continue to call colonies: nature, women, the so-called Third World.

If one aims at sustainability, then one has to transcend the industrial world market and profit-oriented growth model. This transcendence is, as Vandana Shiva has convincingly shown, for the poor, for women and children in the poor countries and regions, a matter of survival. They fight explicitly against "development" and modernization because they know that this development will destroy their survival base—their access to the commons: land, water, air, forests, their communities, their culture. They are the ones who have to pay the price for urban and male industrial development.

The prevailing world market system, oriented towards unending growth and profit, cannot be maintained unless it can exploit external and internal colonies: nature, women, and other countries. The only alternative is a deliberate and drastic change of lifestyle, a change of consumption quantities, and consumer patterns in the affluent societies of the North. Such a change of lifestyle would, however, imply something like a "new moral economy."

HISTORICAL ROOTS OF THE "OLD MORAL ECONOMY"

The concept "moral economy" has been used by economic historians like E. P. Thompson to describe the undivided complex of social, economic, cultural, religious, and ethical norms which were the base of the pre-capitalist society and which was broken up by the new capitalist political economy.

The protest movements of the European peasants, craftsmen, and petty traders in the eighteenth and nineteenth century, the corn and bread riots, the Jacobin revolts, drew their legitimacy from the values of the "old moral economy." And this economy was based on what Scott calls "subsistence ethics," which means that each person, living in a community has a right to subsistence. And all economic transactions, for example the price of bread, are not based on the laws of supply and demand because they can be manipulated by force—but on the right to subsistence, even of the poor. In the "old moral economy" the bread price was always a moral, or political price. The poor had a right to subsistence and a right to prevent food from leaving the country and to set up prices which they could afford to pay (Thompson 1979; Scott).

THE "MORAL ECONOMY" OF PEASANTS AND WOMEN

The "old moral economy," based on a subsistence ethics, was thus rooted in the reality of peasants. In this reality the economic, social, cultural, political, and moral spheres and activities were not segregated, but formed one whole. Otto Brunner called this whole the "whole house." The well-being of this "whole house" depended not on money income and external markets but on the work of all who lived in this unit. This work was not motivated by the objective of profit maximization but by the need for subsistence security and self-provisioning. In this unit the relationship between the human being and the soil necessarily had to be a caring and ecological one. The peasant who exploited his land and his animals too much in one year would possibly have starved the next year. The three-field-system rotation which the German peasants invented in the Middle Ages is an example of this ecological relation to the land.

The relationship between people also had to be such that everyone had a guarantee of subsistence security. These relationships were, no doubt, patriarchal and unequal, but the head of this household, the householder, was quite different from a modern manager. He had to be a teacher, a caretaker, a doctor, an economist, an agriculturist etc., all in one person (Brunner). "Economy" as commerce and profit-seeking was not his main concern but the well-being and the security of all. Brunner shows that the word "economy," which stems from the Greek word *oikos*, originally meant exactly this type of subsistence relationships to the land and the people which ensured that the survival of everyone, including the land, was not jeopardized. The central value in this "moral economy" of the peasants was not wealth but subsistence security. This involves a long-term perspective (Scott).

To guarantee this subsistence security on a given plot of land and within a given village community and a given region, with a given geography and climate it was necessary to maintain certain norms and institutions, in short a subsistence ethics. As Scott puts it: "Although the desire for subsistence security grew out of the needs of cultivators—out of peasant economics—it was socially experienced as a pattern of moral rights and obligations" (6). This system of rights and obligations made sure that nobody within the community was threatened by individual starvation (Polanyi). Everybody had a right to subsistence. This subsistence ethics was based on mutual help, village reciprocity, generosity (even sometimes forced generosity), patron-client relations and, above all on the village commons, on which the poor had a claim and a right.

THE "MORAL ECONOMY" IS NOT MORALISTIC

It is important to stress that these norms, obligations, and institutions do not fit into a moralistic, or ethical framework which only differentiates between "good" or "bad." These norms, obligations, and institutions were neither good nor bad. They were necessary, they oriented human behaviour in such a way that survival of all was possible, even in times of scarcity. The "morality" of the "moral economy," therefore, is based on a realistic recognition of the ecological, social, and economic limits of a given area and the people living there. According to Scott the subsistence peasant does not ask "how much is taken"—by the landlord or the state—but rather "how much is left" and whether his basic subsistence needs are respected.

Everybody had a right to subsistence. When this right was violated by landlords and the state the peasants and the poor in general had a right to rebellion and their seizure of land, grain, flour, etc. was considered legitimate: "At the core of popular protest movements of urban and rural poor in eighteenth- and nineteenth-century Europe was not so much a belief in equality of wealth and landholding but of the more modest claim of a right to subsistence"(Scott 33).

If we look closer at the popular protest movements of the eighteenth and nineteenth century, we see that the bread and corn riots in England and France were to a large extent led by women. E. P. Thompson writes that such bread or food riots could be found in England "in almost every town and country until the 1840s" (1979: 67), and that not wages "but the cost of bread was the most sensitive indicator of popular discontent" (1979: 68). The poor women were the ones who marched to the market and who saw to it that the food prices were such that poor families would not starve. When, for example, all the corn had been bought up by one of the new merchant capitalists in Ireland who wanted to bring it out of the country, a mob entered the Dutch ship, brought the corn to the market, and sold it for the owners at the common price.

Even today we find that women everywhere in the world protest first when the prices of basic food are rising too high. In 1973-75, the women of Bombay started a massive agitation, called the Anti-Price-Rise Movement against inflation of food prices. But the resistance of women against the introduction of the money and market economy and its "rational logic" is not restricted to the past and to the sphere of consumption. Women, particularly rural women, are also found in the forefront of movements which try to defend the ecological base of their survival or subsistence. Women are in the forefront of the Chipko Movement in India (Shiva; Hegde), they are the initiators of the Green Belt Movement. Women like Medha Pathakare also leaders of movements against big dams, like the Narmada Dam project in India, sponsored by the World Bank.

And, as the women of the Chipko movement make explicit, these women do not want to sacrifice their subsistence security, their subsistence base for all the promised wealth which modernization, development, and the capitalist market are supposed to bring them. They, too, like their sisters in the eighteenth and nineteenth centuries in Europe, know pretty well that this wealth is not meant for them but for the urban elites. And even if it was, they do not want it. They have a different concept of freedom, equality, and good life than the one which the capitalist market economy promises. Their ethics is still a subsistence ethics, based on the recognition that their survival is better guaranteed when they cooperate in the same careful manner with "mother nature" as they did before than when they gave up this "moral economy" for short-term monetary income.

The "moral" or subsistence economy of the women of the forest-agriculture has never destroyed the forest, has never exploited nature to an extent that she could not regenerate herself. This "moral economy" is not only based on a respectful and careful relationship to nature, but also on a system of social relations which makes sure that all can survive in dignity and without the threat of individual starvation. When in one of the women's agitations against a chalk mine in the Himalayas the mine owners tried to bribe the young men of the community by offering them money and jobs, one of these men, the son of one of the women leaders, said: "Money I can get anywhere, but my mother's dignity comes from the village community, and we can never sacrifice that" (Mies and Shiva 243). It is this sense of honour, of dignity, which goes much deeper than the short-term egotistic interest in money and material gains which gives the "moral economy" the strength to resist the fascination and the glamour of the capitalist supermarket. But, as was already said earlier, this "stubborn" insistence on a subsistence ethics, on values like honour, dignity, self-reliance, reciprocity towards humans and nature, freedom based on one's own food production, community-based solidarity, and mutual respect, are not moralistic in the sense that they are better or worse than other values. They are not part of an ethics that is segregated from everyday life. They are based on a realistic assessment of the ecological and social conditions which are necessary to guarantee survival. They are based on a worldview, a cosmology which does not consider these necessary conditions of survival, the limits of nature and of human life as a handicap to our freedom and wellbeing but rather as preconditions for these goals.

These values stand in sharp contrast to the philosophy and ethics of the European Enlightenment which considers man's dominance over nature by virtue of his rationality the precondition for his freedom. Feminist scholars have criticized this concept of rationality and ethics not only because of its androcentric bias (Merchant; Harding; Fox-Keller) but also, because it is an ethics that considers values like caring or nurturing, responsibility for the maintenance of everyday life, and humaneness as only private values, for which women have been made responsible. Such an ethics cannot help women or nature. Lieselotte Steinbrügge has shown that the Enlightenment philosophers tried to solve the contradiction between the market values (egotism and competition) and the claim to build a more humane society by making women the "moral gender," that is by making them responsible for maintaining human values like mercy, solidarity, love, caring within an aggressive, competitive economy based on individual self-interest. Because of this heritage mere demands for social justice will not do for women writes Veronika Bennholdt-Thomsen. Instead women should demand more reciprocity and mutuality, the values of a "moral economy."

THE NEED FOR A "NEW MORAL ECONOMY"

A solution for the fundamental questions of our time: the problem of poverty in the South, the women's question, or the problem of patriarchy and, above all, the ecological question, cannot be found within the paradigm of the existing growth-oriented, industrialist market system. What is needed is a "new vision" based on new values, on a new ethics, which respects the limits of nature, of human beings, the diversity and dignity of all life forms and is not based primarily on Hobbes' anthropology of individual self-interest, egotism, and competition but on solidarity, mutuality, love, cooperation, caring, and responsibility as basic human characteristics.

Many analysts of the present crises agree there is a need of a new vision, of new ethics. But they would hesitate to go all the way from their analysis to spelling out the basic premises and principles of a "new moral economy." But this is exactly what is needed today. We will not be able to solve the global crises we are experiencing today unless we have the courage to think at least about this "new moral economy."

One of the problems one faces is the recurring argument that the "old moral economy" was nothing to be nostalgic about, that, on the contrary poverty, disease, exploitation, and feudal and patriarchal dominance could only be overcome by the new market economy of the modern era, by the combination of modern science, progress, and the development of a "rational" economic system, called market economy. Without this modernization process we would all still live in abject poverty and misery. A "moral economy," therefore, will not be easily accepted as something that could help overcome our crises. But I think we have no other choice today but to look for radical alternatives to the present economic and social system. And I am not afraid to call this search a search for a "new moral economy."

Of course, it should be obvious, that the "new moral economy" cannot just be a replica of the "old moral economy," described above. It certainly cannot have the same feudal and patriarchal structures and institutions. But certain characteristics and principles of the "old moral economy" will have to be preserved or reactivated if we want to develop a truly sustainable, non-exploitative, nondestructive relationship between human and non-human nature, between women and men, between different people and countries. Most of the characteristics of such a moral economy are identical with those which I have spelled out for an eco-feminist perspective of a new society (Mies).

The first insight is the recognition that our planet earth, that nature, is limited and that we as human beings are limited. Within a limited universe there cannot be unlimited economic growth lest people and nature are being progressively exploited and destroyed. This means, a "new moral economy" will have to be developed from a new cosmology and anthropology in which the *de facto* limits of our universe will be respected. It will therefore be a kind of global *oikos* or household, an *oikos* embracing the whole world.

The second principle to be reactivated from the "old moral economy" would be the reinclusion of subsistence ethics into economic activity. The externalization of morality from the economic sphere—and the division of labour between economics and science on one side and ethics and politics on the other—has led to the present irresponsible behaviour both of consumers and producers. Only if ethical considerations are again present in all everyday economic, social, and cultural activities can we hope to overcome the vicious circles of destructive growth mania.

But, as was said before, such everyday survival ethics would not be moralistic. It would not be based on a Protestant work ethic, on asceticism, and this-worldly or other-worldly deferred gratification. It would be based on the realistic recognition of the necessary conditions of survival for all and on the right to subsistence for all because it is this right which is violated everywhere by modern development. Glaring examples are the big dams or the destruction of the survival base of people and of nature for the sake of luxury production for 20 percent of the worlds' population. This destruction has been made invisible by the world market and its global division of labour.

This, of course, implies, that the concept of what constitutes "a good life" changes, both in the affluent countries and in the hitherto poor countries. Only when the notion that "good life" is identical with the production, possession, and consumption of ever more material and non-material commodities is given up—first in the rich countries and the rich classes of the North but also in the poor countries of the South can we hope that people will be able to overcome the suicidal myth of "catching-up development."

The concept of "good life" within the framework of a "moral economy" will not mean that people are not able to satisfy their fundamental human needs, on the contrary, it will mean that these needs will rather be satisfied by direct human interaction and mutuality instead of only by the purchase of goods in a supermarket. This non-commoditized satisfaction of human needs will be a greater source of happiness.

SOME FEATURES OF A "NEW MORAL ECONOMY"

A "new moral economy" will be based on a different concept of labour. This concept of labour will again combine work as a burden and work as enjoyment. This will necessarily also lead to a different concept of time, a concept of time which does not split up a human lifetime in periods of burdensome and alienated work only and of pleasure and alienated leisure time. Further consequences of a different concept of labour in the framework of a "new moral economy" would be the restoration of meaningfulness, of a sense of purpose to human work, of a direct interaction with non-human nature as a precondition for our happiness, and a closer link between production and consumption (Mies).

It is obvious that such a concept of work transcends the framework of an economy based on ever-expanding growth of monetary revenue and of ever-expanding forces of production in terms of high technology development. As this paradigm has led to "overdevelopment" of some nations at the expense of "underdevelopment" of women, nature, and colonies, a concept of work oriented towards the production of life requires a reversal and a transcendence of this framework.

The first basic requirement of an alternative economy is a change, both in the overdeveloped and in the underdeveloped societies, from dependency for basic subsistence needs—food, clothing, shelter—from economies outside their national boundaries and a movement towards greater self-sufficiency. Only societies which are to a large extent self-provisioning in the production of these basic necessities can maintain themselves free from political blackmail and hunger. In this, self-sufficiency in food is the first requirement.

Malcolm Caldwell has shown that such self-sufficiency in food, as well as in energy, would be quite possible in Britain, with the available cultivable land and its present population. It would equally be possible in any other of the overdeveloped countries of Europe or North America. But what is more, if the governments of these overdeveloped countries had not bribed their working people by importing cheap food, cheap clothes, cheap raw materials, etc. from so-called "cheap labour" countries, these countries in Asia, Africa, and Latin America could all be self-sufficient in food, clothing, shelter, etc. If the protein food imported to Europe from Third World countries in the form of animal feed to produce milk seas, butter mountains etc. was used to feed the local people there, there would be no hunger in any of these regions (Collins and Moore-Lappé). A largely self-provisioning economy would necessarily lead towards a change of the existing exploitative and non-reciprocal international world order, a contraction of world trade and of export-oriented production both in the industrialized countries, whose economy is dependent on export of industrial products and of underdeveloped countries who have to pay back their credits by exports of mainly primary goods, cheap labour, or raw material.

A further consequence of a more or less self-provisioning economy would be a drastic reduction of all non-productive work, in the sense I use the term, particularly in the tertiary sector, a change in the composition of the workforce with a movement away from employment in industries towards employment in agriculture. If people of a given region want to live mainly by the natural and labour resources available in that region then it follows that many more people will have to do necessary manual labour in food production. Within such a finite region people would also be careful not to destroy the very ecology on whose balance the survival of all depend on. It would lead to the narrowing down of the gap between production and consumption and to more autonomy of producers-consumers over what they produce and consume. As Caldwell points out, this radical restructuring of the economy is not only a beautiful dream or a case of exhortatory politics, but will increasingly become a necessity particularly for workers who have been made redundant for good by the rapid development of high technology and automation. He reminds us that already in 1976 massive unemployment in Italy had led to a big movement of workers back to the land. About 100,000 workers returned to farming. A similar movement back to the land happened in India during the strike of the textile workers in Bombay in 1982-83, which lasted for almost a year. These workers started a movement for alternative agriculture and water management, inspired by a subsistence perspective (Patankar; Mies and Shiva).

The brief description of an alternative economy, spelled out by Caldwell, however, is silent about the non-reciprocal, exploitative division of labour between the genders. The perspective of a self-provisioning "moral economy" based on non-exploitative relations to the ecology, other peoples, people within a region, and on small, de-centralized units of production and consumption, is for feminists not broad enough if it does not start with a radical change in the sexual division of labour. In most ecological writings, however, the "woman question" is either not mentioned at all, or is simply added on to a long list of other more urgent, more "general" issues. This "adding on" will no longer do if we want to change the existing inhuman men-women relation. The concept of a "moral economy" is therefore not only incomplete without the goal of transcending the patriarchal sexual division of labour, it will rather be based on the illusion of change and therefore not be able to truly transcend the status quo.

A feminist conception of a "new moral economy" will include all that was said before about self-provisioning and decentralization. But it will place the transformation of the existing sexual division of labour (based on the breadwinner-housewife model) at the centre of the whole restructuring process. This is not mere narcistic self-indulgence of women but the result of our historical research as well as our analysis of the functioning of international capitalist patriarchy. Feminists do not start with the external ecology, economy, and politics, but with the social ecology, the centre of which is the relation between men and women. Autonomy over our bodies and lives has been the first and most fundamental demand of the international feminist movement. Any search for a "new moral economy" must start with the respect of the autonomy of women's bodies, their productive capacity to maintain life through work, their sexuality, and procreation. A change in the existing sexual division of labour would imply first and foremost that the violence that characterizes capitalist patriarchal man-woman relations worldwide will be abolished not by women but by men. Men have to refuse to define themselves any longer as Man-the-Hunter or Warrior. Men have to start movements against violence against women if they want to preserve the essence of their own humanity.

This demand of autonomy over women's bodies also implies that any state control over women's fertility has to be rejected. Women have to be freed of their status of being a natural resource for individual men as well as for the state as the Total Patriarch. True women's liberation will be also the cheapest and most efficient method to restore the balance between population growth and food production.

Secondly, in a "new moral economy" men have to share, as far as possible, the responsibility for the immediate production of life, for child care, housework, the care of the sick and the old, the relationship work, all the work so far subsumed under the term "housework." This means men would have to share in the ethics of care. In a community keen to preserve its autonomy and keen to follow a non-exploitative ecological path of human development this "housework" could not be paid. It would have to be free work for the community. But each man, each woman, and also children would have to share this most important work. This would then immediately have the effect that men would have less time for their destructive production in industry, less time for their destructive research, less time for their destructive leisure activities, less time for their wars. Positively put, they would regain the wholeness of their own bodies and minds, they would re-experience work as both a burden and enjoyment, and finally also develop a different scale of values altogether with regard to work. It would also mean the end of the breadwinner-housewife-model.

These processes of liberation are interrelated. It is not possible for women in our societies to break out of the cages of patriarchal relations unless the men begin a movement in the same direction. A men's movement against patriarchy would not be motivated by benevolent paternalism but by the desire to restore to themselves a sense of human dignity and respect.

As the path of "catching-up development" is neither possible for all, nor is it desirable, the only solution of this dilemma can be a voluntary reduction of the living standard and a change of consumer patterns in the rich countries and classes. Such a change of consumption patterns and of lifestyles will only occur when people begin to realize that less is more, when they begin to define what constitutes a good life differently from what the managers of the corporations think. This new definition of "good life" will emphasize different values which in our consumer societies are underdeveloped or even destroyed: for example, self-sufficiency, cooperation, respect for all creatures on earth and their diversity, belief in the subjectivity not only of human beings but also of non-human beings, communality instead of "catching up with the Joneses," joy of life that springs from cooperation with others, and an understanding of the meaningfulness of what one does.

A different definition of the "good life" and an improvement of the quality of life implies different forms of satisfaction of fundamental human needs. Max-Neef and his colleagues, who developed this concept of fundamental human needs, stress that fundamental human needs are universal, but the means and ways these needs are satisfied may vary according to culture, region, and historical conditions. They have identified nine of these fundamental human needs, namely: subsistence (health, food, shelter, clothing etc.); protection (care, solidarity, work etc.); affection (self-esteem, love, care, solidarity etc.); understanding (study, learning, analysis etc.); participation (responsibilities, sharing of rights and duties); idleness (curiosity, imagination, games, relaxation, fun); creation (intuition, imagination, work, curiosity etc.); identity (sense of belonging, differentiation, self-esteem); and freedom (autonomy, self-esteem, self-determination, equality).

As these fundamental human needs are universal they are the same in rich and poor, "overdeveloped" and "underdeveloped" countries. In overdeveloped industrial societies these needs are satisfied almost exclusively by satisfiers which have to be bought in the market, which are produced industrially, and which not only very often are pseudo-satisfiers, because they do not in the end satisfy the need—like cars which are bought for status purposes—or cosmetics, which are bought to satisfy the need for love—they are sometimes simply destructive. The arms race, for example, is legitimized by the need for protection, the need for subsistence, the need for freedom.

If we try to break out of the mental framework which industrial society has created and which it has exported to all poor countries we discover that there would be many different ways, many of them not dependent on the market, to satisfy those fundamental needs. This could mean for children, for example, that one would spend more time with them or play with them instead of buying them ever more toys. Many of the non-commoditized satisfiers have the advantage of being synergetic. This means they satisfy not only one need but several at a time. If one takes time to play with children a number of needs are satisfied: the need for affection, for protection, for understanding, for idleness, freedom, identity. And this applies both to the children and to the adults. If fundamental human needs are satisfied in non-commercial ways—I call them subsistence ways— then these processes of satisfaction are often reciprocal ones. The one who gives something also receives something.

If such a change of lifestyle were to happen in the rich countries on a big scale this would not only halt the destruction of the ecology and stop the exploitation of the "Third World," it would also change the model for imitative and compensatory consumption which middleclass people in the North provide both for the lower classes in their own country and for people of the South. Because patterns of consumption of the North are imported into countries of the South and are imitated there by political and economic power groups, these consumption patterns then lead to more dependency, indebtedness, internal imbalances, and a loss of cultural identity.

Max-Neef and his colleagues stress the need to break away from these imitative consumption patterns in the "Third Worlds" in order to free these countries from economic and cultural dependence and to make a more efficient use of their own resources for their own wellbeing. It would be a necessary step for "Third World" countries towards self-reliance. In my view, however, a breaking away from the imposed consumption patterns would also be a necessary step towards self-reliance of hitherto overdeveloped, affluent societies. Most of these depend, as we saw, to a very large extent on the exploitation of the "Third World" countries and their resources. If sustainability and self-reliance are considered the correct path for countries of the South, then they must necessarily also be the correct path for the countries of the North.

This article was excerpted from Challenges: Science and Peace in a Rapidly Changing Environment, *proceedings from the International Congress of Scientists and Engineers, Berlin, November 29-December 1, 1991.*

Even after retirement Maria Mies has remained active in a number of international feminist and other socio-political movements. She was co-founder of the International

Feminist Network of Resistence to Reproductive and Genetic Engineering (FINRRAGE). *and continues to part in the worldwide struggles against the neoliberal restructuring of the global economy. At 82, she is still active in the ecological movement and in the peace movement, particularly against the new war mongering of the superpowers. Her articles and books on these issues have been published widely. Her main concern is to end the capitalist-patriarchal system and to bring about a new vision of society, which she calls the Subsistence Perspective. She is the co-author, with Veronika Bennholdt-Thomsen, of* The Subsistence Perspective: Beyond the Globalized Economy *(1999). Her most recent publicatation is her autobiography,* The Village and The World *(2010).*

REFERENCES

Bennholdt-Thomsen, Veronika. "Gegenseitigkeit statt sozialer Gerechtigkeit. Zur Kritik der kulturellen Ahnungslosigkeit im modernen Patriarchat." *Ethnologische FrauenforJrhung.* Ed. Brigitta Hauser-Schaublin. Berlin: Dietrich Reimer Verlag, 1991.

Brunner, Otto. "Vom 'Ganzen Haus' zur Familie." *Familie und Gesellschaftsstruktur.* Ed. Heidi Rosenbaum. Frankfurt: Fischer Verlag, 1974.

Caldwell, Malcolm. *The Wealth of Some Nations.* London: Zed Books, 1977.

Collins, J. and F. Moore-Lappé. *Food First: Beyond the Myth of Scarcity.* San Francisco: Institute for Food and Development Policy, 1977.

Danziger, Sheldon, and Jonathan Stern. "Ursachen und Folgen der Armut von Kindern in den USA." *Frankfurter Rundschau* 9 July 1990.

Fox-Keller, Evelyn. *Reflections on Gender and Science.* New Haven: Yale University Press, 1985.

Global 2000. *The Global 2000 Report to the President.* Eds. Council of Environmental Quality. Washington: U.S. Government Printing Office, 1980.

Harding, Sandra. *The Science Question in Feminism.* Ithaca, NY: Cornell University Press, 1986.

Hegde, Pandurang. *Chipko and Appiko: How the People Save the Trees.* Nonviolence in Action Series Quaker Peace and Service. Jan. 1988.

Max-Neef, Manfred. *Human Scale Development: Conception, Application, and Further Reflection.* London: Zed Books, 1991.

Merchant, Carolyn. *The Death of Nature: Women, Ecology, and the Scientific Revolution.* San Francisco: Harper and Row, 1983.

Michelsen, Gerd, ed. *Der Fischer Öko-Almanach.* Freiburg Öko-Institut, 1984.

Mies, Maria. *Patriarchy and Accumulation: Women in the International Division of Labour.* London: Zed Books, 1994.

Mies, Maria, and Vandana Shiva. *Ecofeminism.* London: Zed Books, 1993.

Mies, Maria, Veronika Bennholdt-Thomsen, and Claudia V. Werlhof. *Women: The Last Colony.* London: Zed Books, 1987.

Müller, Michael. "SPD—Experten orten Krise des Kapitalismus in naher Zukunfi." *Frankfurter Rundschau* 25 Mar. 1991: 3.

Patankar, Bharat. "Alternative Water Management: The Case of Balinaja Dari." *Our Indivisable Envrionment: A Report of Perspectives.* Bangalore. 1-7 Oct. 1990. Unpublished. 51-52.

Pietilä, Hilkka. "Environment and Sustainable Development." IFDA-*Dossier 77* (May-June 1990): 61E.

Polanyi, Karl. *The Great Transformation.* Frankfurt: Suhrkamp, 1978.

Sarkar, Saral. "Die Bewegung und ihre Strategie—Ein Beitrag zum notwendigen Klärungsprozess." *Kommune* (Frankfurt) 5 (1987): 39-45.

Shiva, Vandana. *Staying Alive, Women Ecology, and Survival in India.* Delhi: Kali for Women, 1988.

Scott, James C. *The Moral Economy of the Peasant: Rebellion, and Subsistence in Southeast Asia.* New Haven: Yale University Press, 1977.

Steinbrügge, Lieselotte. *Das moralische Geschlecht. Theorie und literarische Entwürfe über die Natur der Frau in der französischen Aufklärung.* Weinheim: Beltz-Verlag, 1987.

Thompson, E. P. "The 'Moral Economy' of the English Crowd in the 18th Century." *Past and Present* 50 (1971).

Thompson, E. P. *The Making of the English Working Class.* Hammondsworth: Pelican, 1979.

Trainer, Ted F. *Developed to Death: Rethinking Third World Development.* London: Green Print, 1989.

Wallerstein, Immanuel. *The Modern World-System: Capitalist Agriculture and the Origins of the European World Economy in the Sixteenth Century.* New York: Academic Press, 1974.

Zenwas, Hans-Jörg. *Arbeit ah Besitz—Das ehrbare Handwerk zwischen Bruderliebe und Klassenkampf.* Reinbek: Sororo, 1988.

Position Statement for a Peaceful World

International Feminists for a Gift Economy is a group of feminist activists and academics from many countries, who meet irregularly, share ideas, and speak about the gift economy on panels at local and international gatherings. This Statement was written in October 2001 and presented at the World Social Forum in 2002. It has been circulated widely since that time and is available at: <www.gift-economy.com>.

FROM THE DAWN OF TIME women's gifts have been creating and sustaining community, and we have struggled to make the world a better place. In recent years women have been articulating new forms of protest, refusing war and all forms of violence, protecting the environment and all life, creating new multi-centred and diverse political spaces and defining new politics of care, community, compassion, and connectedness.

Women, from both North and South especially from the margins of privilege and power, are creating alternative visions. Over the last decades the growing feminist movement has developed analyses, changed paradigms, built solidarity through listening to each other. We are rethinking democracy, creating new imaginaries, even reconceptualizing the foundations of political society.

The anti-globalization movement is grounded in the new political space women have created. The global dialogue and networking among men, so celebrated today as a new achievement, post-dates the growing global women's movement by many years. Yet this is rarely acknowledged and feminist leadership is seldom invited. Feminist perspectives remain largely invisible in the struggle against globalization, impoverishing not only women but the struggle as a whole.

We, women of many countries, believe that the death dealing elements of patriarchal capitalist colonial globalization are rooted, not in unequal exchange alone but in the mechanism of exchange itself. The creation of scarcity, the globalization of spiritual and material poverty, and the destruction of cultures and species are not failures of a wealth creating system. They are essential expressions of a parasitical centralizing system which denies the gift giving logic of mothering.

Traditional gift-giving societies integrated the logic of mothering into the wider community in many ways. Now socio-economic systems based on the logic of exchange degrade and deny gift giving while co-opting the gifts of most women and many men, dominating the gift givers and destroying the remnants of traditional gift giving societies.

Nevertheless, mothering is a necessity for all societies. Because children are born vulnerable, adults must practice unilateral gift giving towards them. Women are socialized toward this practice which has a transitive logic of its own. Men are socialized away from mothering behavior and towards a self-reflecting logic of competition and domination. The gift logic, functional and complete in itself is altered and distorted by the practice of exchange which requires quantification and measurement, is adversarial, and instills the values of self interest and competition for domination. Exchange, especially monetized exchange, the market, and the capitalist and colonial economies that derive from them are formed in the image of masculinist values and rewards. For this reason we can characterise capitalism as patriarchal.

In the present stage of capitalist patriarchy, corporations have developed as disembodied non-human entities made according to values of dominance, accumulation and control and without the mitigating rationality and emotional capacity a real human being would presumeably have.

Corporations have an internal mandate to grow or die. However, even simple market exchange superimposes itself on gift giving at all levels, cancelling and concealing its value and appropriating its gifts, renaming them as its deserved profits.

Women's free labour is gift labour and it has been estimated as adding some forty percent or more to the GNP in even the most industrialized economies. The goods and services provided by women to their families are qualitative gifts that create the material and psychological basis of community. These gifts pass through the family to the market, which could not survive without them.

Profit is a disguised and forced gift given by the worker to the capitalist. Indeed the market itself functions as a parasite upon the gifts of the many. As capitalism "evolves" and spreads, its market becomes needy for new gifts, commodifying free goods which were previously held in common by the community or by humanity as a whole. The destructive methods of appropriation which feed the market also create the scarcity necessary for the exchange-based parasite to maintain its control. Since gift giving requires abundance, the parasite can only keep the gift giving host from gaining power by creating artificial scarcity through the monopolization of wealth.

Northern patriarchal capitalism has grown exponentially by invading the economies of the South and extracting their gifts. In the past whole continents have been appropriated, their territories and peoples divided into private property of the colonizers, their gifts commodified. Today, in a new form of colonization, traditional indigenous knowledge and plant species, as well as human, animal, and plant genes are being patented and privatized so that the gifts of the planet and humanity are passing again, at a new level into the hands and profits of the few.

The mechanisms of exploitation are often validated by the very institutions that are established to protect the people. Laws are made in the service of the patriarchal parasite and justice itself is formed in the image of exchange, the payment for crime. Apologists for patriarchal capitalism exist at every level of society from academia to advertising. The very language they use has been stolen, the common ground of its meanings distorted and co-opted in the service of the perpetrators of economic violence. Thus "free trade" apes the language of the gift and liberation while it is only short hand for more exploitation and dominance.

While fair trade seems to be better than unfair trade, it is not the liberating alternative we seek. Exchange itself and not just unequal exchange must give way to the gift. The answer to the injustice of the appropriation of the abundant gifts of the many is not a fair return in cash for the theft but the creation of gift based economies and cultures where life is not commodified.

While such a radical change may appear extremely difficult, it is more 'realistic' than simply continuing in our attempts to survive and care for one another in the frighteningly destructive and increasingly toxic world we know today, for these attempts are doomed to failure in the long term.

Women have worked to transform political spaces and have made important, though fragile and highly contested gains in the last decades in affirming women's legal, sexual and reproductive rights, challenging fundamentalisms, opposing violence, and war, improving women's education, health and economic conditions. These struggles have broken new ground while remaining within the exchange paradigm. Our successes and failures challenge and inspire us to seek new terrain, recognizing that "the masters tools can never be used to dismantle the masters house" (Audre Lord).

WE WANT A MARKET-FREE SOCIETY, NOT A FREE-MARKET SOCIETY

We want:
•A world of abundance where bodies, hearts and minds are not dependent on the market.
•A world where gift-giving values of care are accepted as the most important, the leading values of society at all levels.
•A world where women and men enjoy taking care of children and each other.
•A world where everyone is able to express their sexuality in life-loving ways, where their spirituality is treasured and their materiality is honored.
•A world where trust and love are the amniotic fluid in which all our children learn to live.
•A world where boys and girls are socialized without gender limits as gift-giving humans from the very beginning. ·
•A world where mother nature can be seen as the great gift giver, her ways understood and her infinitely diverse gifts celebrated by all.
•A world where humans and all species can reach their highest potential in relationship rather than their lowest potential in parasitism and competetion.

We want:
•A world where money does not define value nor legislate survival.
•A world where all the categories and processes of parasitism and hate - racism, classism, ageism, ablism, xenophobia, homophobia are regarded as belonging to a shameful past.
•A world where war is recognized as expressing unnecessary patriarchal syndromes of dominance and submission in a ridiculously sexualized death ritual using phallic technological instruments, guns and missiles of ever greater proportions.
•A world where the psychosis of patriarchy is recognized, healed, and no longer validated as the norm.
We will create the world we want while keeping intact our full humanity, humor and hope.

(NB: This document is not patented, commodified or copyrighted. Anyone can use it. Please respect its integrity.)

If you would like to join this dialogue, learn more about the gift economy, and help formulate and express the ideas, especially in relation to your own tradition and reality, see <http://www.gift-economy.com> and contact Genevieve Vaughan <genvau@aol.com>

Part One
Neo-Liberal Globalization:
Social and Environmental Costs

JOYCE A. GREEN

Resistance is Possible

WHEN I WROTE this article in 1996 (reprinted below), Canada had emerged from over a decade of political struggle over the wisdom of adopting neoliberalism and neoconservatism. It was a struggle won by the proponents of those changes, and most actively prosecuted by the Mulroney governments federally, but supported also by their Liberal successors and by virtually all their provincial counterparts. Neoliberalism was consolidated through the 1990s and into the present; it is generally framed as an ineluctable and non-ideological (that is, non-political) set of structural and policy frameworks. Opposition to neoliberalism (and to a lesser extent, to neoconservatism) is still framed by those with power as both futile and as misguided. "Resistance is Possible" was written in the context I have just described, in an attempt to encourage citizens to engage in critical conversations and actions with each other, in search of a compassionate and just civil society characterized by a more thoroughgoing democracy than mere electoral engagement. Were I writing today, I would entitle my work "Resistance is Necessary" as I did my article that appears later in this volume.

*

The Non-Governmental Organizations' Beijing Declaration following the Fourth World Women's Congress in 1995, warns that:

> The globalization of the world's so-called "market economies" is a root cause of the increasing feminization of poverty everywhere. This violates human rights and dignity, the integrity of our ecosystems and the environment, and poses serious threats to our health. The global economy, governed by international financial institutions, the World Trade Organization and transnational corporations, impose Structural Adjustment Programs on countries in the South and economic restructuring on countries in the North in the name of fiscal health. The result is increasing poverty, debt, and unemployment. The resulting reductions in social programs and services in the areas of health, education, and housing harm the very people they purport

to assist. The media, controlled by transnational corporations, acts as an instrument of social control, denying women's right to free communication.

How was and is this still relevant to Canadian women? Let's look at the evidence as Canada's provincial and federal governments eagerly embraced policies dictated by this process of neo-liberal globalization. In Canada, in February 1996, the Toronto Stock Exchange broke 5,000 for the first time, and set its tenth record level in less than a year. Then in April it beat its February high. In the last quarter of 1995, the Big Five Banks posted their highest profits ever, over $5 billion, while cutting 2,800 jobs. World-class corporations, household names to all of you, are making record profits ... and cutting jobs. In 1995, General Motors made $1.4 billion, and cut 2,500 jobs. Bell Canada cut 3,200 jobs. Inco cut 2,000 jobs; its labour and environmental practices have been questionable; its CEO got an honourary doctorate and it has just bought most of Voisey's Bay, the largest nickel deposit in the world, situated squarely on unceded Aboriginal lands in Labrador. The Alberta government raked in an unearned windfall in petrodollar royalties, much of which is extracted from unceded Lubicon Cree lands, sold off the profitable and unionized liquor stores, privatized whole chunks of government, slashed millions from welfare, education, and health and thousands of tax-paying jobs from the public sector. The Harris government in Ontario adopted the same strategy. The Chretien government has eliminated the federal Canada Assistance Plan (CAP) (federal-provincial partnership) funding for post secondary education, social programs, and such, which further eroded the financial base of the programs that define us as a nation and provide the basics for citizens.

What's happening here? We are experiencing life at the nexus of economic, social, and political forces in the phenomenon known as globalization, and interpreted through the dominant economic ideology known as neoliberalism.

Here I want to offer you some definitions. "Neoliberalism" is an ideology that advocates an economic arena free of government regulation or restriction, including labour and environmental legislation, and certainly, free of government action via public ownership. It advocates a retreat from the welfare state's publicly funded commitments to equality and social justice. It views citizenship as consumption and economic production. This, not coincidentally, is compatible with, and advances in tandem with "neoconservatism," an ideology advancing a more hierarchical, patriarchal, authoritarian, and inequitable society. "Civil society" is comprised of citizens located in communities, associations, and movements, in relation and subject to state and economic structures and relations of dominance, but with the capacity to name them, agree to them, or resist them up to and including revolution. Finally, "globalization" refers to the emerging world economic order, characterized by multilateral "free trade" blocs designed for capital mobility; globalization of world capital markets; financial deregulation; disaggregated production; and instantaneous communications (Grinspun and Kreklewich; Gill; Teeple). The trade blocs essentially erode political sovereignty while creating zones of market sovereignty, which has the effect of constraining state domestic policy.

Neoliberalism and neoconservatism come together to form a powerful alliance that detrimentally affects women in the paid workforce, in the family, and in society, through the under-valuation or nonvaluation of our work and the appropriation of our labour in the family and through "volunteerism" (see Dacks, Green and Trimble).

The profitability of neoliberalism rests in large measure on the foundation of women's un-and underpaid labour; on the commodification of the land and of society; and on the state's retreat from regulatory policy, and yes, from spending, that supports the family, the community, and women as women in a gendered and discriminatory world.

The consequence is the erosion of the foundation of relationship: the priority of family, of community, is lost to the priority of individual responsiveness to the imperatives of the labour market. These imperatives are phrased as the need for a "re-educated" workforce, or for a "more flexible" workforce, or for sequential career changes as a norm, or for reduced expectations on the part of citizens … and always, for the least possible government intervention in the market, except to discipline society and ensure profitability. This means the preference for no or little regulation of labour standards, environmental consequences, and so on. It also means limitations on dissent, for the success of neoliberalism depends on citizens buying the Big Lie that there is no alternative.

I want to sketch the connections between economic globalization, governments' political responses to that phenomenon, and erosion of both political democracy and civil society. But I do not mean to argue that there is no alternative. Rather, I argue that the Canadian provincial and federal governments have sold us out and have defined themselves as tools for the interests of transnational capital rather than the instruments for democracy. When I am done I hope you will be convinced of two things: first, this agenda is only logical within its internally consistent universe of neoliberalism and neoconservatism. It is not the only possible response to the challenges of contemporary global capitalism. Second, citizens must act to reclaim and redefine the political and economic agenda, in order to save democracy and civil society.

Let me make five main points to you:

1. We are in the era of a global phenomenon, the globalization of markets and of the conditions for profitability of an elite composed of certain transnational corporations and agents for investment capital. This capital moves around the world with the flick of a computer key, occasionally destabilizing national currencies in its wake, as, for example, in the 1994 Mexican currency crisis. Most recently, the 2009 global economic crisis has established the fragility of the global economic system.

Global capitalism is the contemporary expression of the evolution of capitalism, and is part of the historical strand that arguably emerged in the fifteenth century as part of the age of imperialism. The meaning that we attach to its practice, to its consequences, depends on our moral, theological, and ideological stances, but there is no doubt about the reality or the dynamics of its existence.

2. The interests of transnational capital are served by policy decisions at the state level, and it is in the ability of transnational capital and its smaller state-based counterparts to assist or disrupt national economies (through "capital ebb and flow") that this elite finds its power over state governments.

3. Domestic economies and the global economy, then, are being reconfigured by governments to conform to the interests of transnational capital, the former through neoliberalism and the latter through multinational not-so-free trading blocs. This means that where interests collide, governments work to meet the criteria of capital—profitability—not that of society, which is well-being.

4. There is a congruence between many of the interests of transnational capital, and domestic corporate elites. These domestic elites are influential. Their approval of policy and politics is desired by governments, who anticipate it in policy matters. For example, the Business Council on National Issues (now renamed the Canadian Council of Chief Executives [CCCE]) and others funded advertising in support of the Canada-United States Free Trade Agreement (CUFTA) and the North American Free Trade Agreement (NAFTA). In Alberta, many corporate players eagerly anticipate passage of so-called "right to work" legislation, which amounts to legislated union-busting. Consider the implications, also, that the day of Paul Martin's 1995 budget, the Edmonton Journal budget story was on one side of the front page; the other side read "Wall Street Pleased." The consequences of all this include the dominance of monetarist policy, the ascendance of neoliberalism, and consolidation of hemispheric and multinational trading blocks, which have the effect of entrenching global economic inequities. At the same time, national sovereignty and constitutional rights and responsibilities are subordinated to undemocratic and unaccountable international trade panels and corporate boardrooms.

The weight of popular support behind the government policies of cuts to social programs, and public sector restructuring through privatization and wage and benefit rollbacks, demonstrates the power of populism, and of the effective use of language and images, primarily through the media. Resistance seems futile. The government and its corporate cheerleaders have expertly used language and culture to convince the public (1) that there is no option to the neoliberal, neoconservative agenda; (2) to focus public pain and anger on governments; and (3) to provide the illusion of democratic consultation for its policies while it selectively marginalizes opposition to these, and co-opts "opinion leaders." Even the most marginal dissent is suppressed, while the majority of citizens accept what government and opinion leaders serve up as analysis: the mantra of debt and deficit elimination through the imperative of public sector cuts and privatization.

We must see populism for what it is—often reactive, often un- or misinformed, and always majoritarian. This means that common prejudices, tested by political polling or by mail-in questionnaires on public expenditure,[1] can substitute for political responsibility and accountability. The informed citizen, like the accountable government, takes this responsibility seriously. This means getting and weighing information and engaging in political debate and considering all interests, not just having an opinion.

Politics as debate about the nature and purpose of government is silenced. This constraint on debate and opposition undermines citizenship. Consider the disciplinary impulse behind the rhetoric of "special interest groups"; that is, those who dissent from the government/ business agenda. Those who support this agenda are called "all Albertans," "ordinary folks" and "families."

The government invokes the deficit as the reason why society must drink from the cup of debt reduction and government restructuring. But we are told there is a bright side: we are restructuring to become competitive in a global economy.

The legitimacy of this global economy, or our role in it, remains unexamined while society is restructured to make incorporation in it inevitable. This has significant negative implications for our social and political agenda. In the words of the late, great political economist Ralph Miliband, "Democracy has no access to corporate boardrooms" (Miliband). Nor, we might add, does it have access to multi-lateral trade negotiation and arbitration panels.

Both citizenship potential and constitutionalism are eroded, as the legal and permanent effects of regional bloc trading agreements such as NAFTA and CUFTA effectively circumscribe the policy options available to government, while removing decision-making power about a host of matters from public accountability and parliamentary review and vesting it in multinational review bodies. Multinational trade agreements function to coerce governments to privatize and deregulate even central strands of the social safety net. Economist Marjorie Cohen warned:

> while the United States may not directly say "change your tax system, your health care system, your unemployment insurance system, and your regional development schemes," these programs may be forced to change if Canada is to continue to trade with the United States. The pressure to conform will be indirect ... through the mechanism of American trade remedy legislation.

What are "trade barriers" to NAFTA are Canada's domestic policy options, potentially illegal if challenged under NAFTA. Now, the decision of Alberta, for example, to privatize all or a portion of health care, may well result in a permanent change: under the conditions of the NAFTA we may not be able to reverse this or similar decisions without "compensating" our trading partners for our internal policy choices.

A combination of the some 300 transnational corporations which currently dominate the global economy, together with fluid and mobile investment capital, disciplines governments to impose policy measures on their societies to enhance profitability, regardless of national populations' material well-being and political development. Corporate agents can move investment and production around the globe, in search of cheap labour, compliant governments, and maximum profits.

In response to the chaotic social conditions resulting from globalization, states have moved to monetarist policy and restrictive social policy, characterized by "deregulation, free trade, and technological change" (Lipietz) intended to maximize "competitiveness"; that is, to appeal to the robber barons of capital.

There are also domestic advocates of restructuring for globalization. Through the political and economic power of domestic corporate elites pressure is brought to bear on democratic processes of the state to adopt policy measures that further the neoliberal and neoconservative agenda; and through corporate and political influence over the media, the public is taught the wisdom of restructuring in terms which make it inevitable and desirable.

Consider the relentless torrent of *Globe and Mail* editorials and columns on this subject, together with the frequent appearance of these same writers on television and radio programs to propound the gospel of neoliberalism.

We, the people, the taxpayers, equality seekers, service users, panhandlers, voters, are asked to vest a simplistic trust in the largely unanalyzed marketplace. There is virtually no policy discussion of the economy as a tool of society. Rather, society is cast in the service of The Economy. This unquestioned economic imperative is increasingly shaping our politics, our relationships, our career prospects, our education, health care, and other policy options in fundamental ways. And, the restructuring of the state also reduces the ability of citizens to challenge or monitor government choices. Even information is commodified.

Additionally, the notion of "citizen" is reconstructed as "consumer" or "worker," rather than as the one who holds the right and obligation to engage in public discourse and political activism. We are being commodified: our significance now lies in our utility to the economy as wage-earners, investors, and consumers but not as citizens or as human beings. Commodities have no rights and don't talk back. Alternatives to the undisputed crises of the welfare state, such as a reduced work week and a move from a consumption-driven perpetual growth economy to a stable-state economy, are ignored, despite the existence of sound analysis and theory-building in these areas.

In the environment of globally active corporate monopolies, public policy is increasingly defined as the conditions most attractive to corporate non-citizen interests. These interests are invariably contrary to the interests of the majority of state citizens. Governments have allowed national and provincial economies to become so dependent on the presence of increasingly mobile and transnational capital(ists) that the interests of the latter have become conflated with national interests in national economic and civic decision-making.

But the logic of transnational capital, and of neoliberal state policy, and of international competitiveness as the leading indicator of success, is no logic for civil society. It coerces workers of the world to compete, to scrabble after any job, regardless of conditions, of fulfillment, of social or environmental cost. It privileges consumption over social production, so that child labour in some jurisdictions and prison slavery in others makes cheap goods possible for consumers in relatively privileged states. It leads to economic "recovery" without jobs. It creates a large and growing "marginal" class here and elsewhere, people who may never know full employment, stable employment, meaningful work, or work at all. And as governments comply with neoliberal dictates, eroding and eliminating the social safety net and the social component of public policy, a cruel Malthusianism[2] kicks in: blaming the poor and the marginal for choosing to be poor and marginal.

Human beings find greatest meaning as individuals in the context of community—in families, in communities, in society. What it means to be fully human is being eroded by the emerging economic order. Resistance is a moral imperative. So where are our sites of resistance to this overwhelming consensus? Politics at the level of communities and within and among national and international social and political movements will foster awareness, commitment, and solidarities. In these arenas, we can create space for the practice of citizenship: create the power to rein in the state; and to capture The Economy as a tool created by and for human well-being. In partisan matters, beware neoliberal governments ... and neoliberal opposition parties.

And always, we have the touchstones of feminist experience. Sisterhood is powerful: we are called to solidarity with one another. The personal is political: the power relations that affect our lives most intimately are an expression of politics writ large, and must be named and contested. And, none of us has made it till all of us have made it. Together, in all of our diversity, we can forge a better alternative than the neoliberal neocons suggest.

This paper was presented to the conference "Alberta Through the Eyes of Women," May 3-4, 1996; organized by the Adhoc Committee on Alberta-Beijing and Women's Program, Faculty of Extension, University of Alberta, to follow up on the impetus of Beijing. The title "Resistance is Possible" is a play on the creed of the Borg in the TV series "Star Trek." The Borg, a semi-mechanized fascist life form, went around the universe assimilating others, repeating "resistance is futile."

In 1996, Joyce Green was a Ph.D. Candidate and occasional sessional lecturer in the Department of Political Science, University of Alberta. She is now a Professor of Political Science at the University of Regina, where she teaches Canadian politics, critical race and post colonial theory, and the politics of decolonization in Canada. Her recent publications include an edited book, Making Space for Aboriginal Feminism *(Joyce Green, ed.) (2007); and the articles: "Canada the Bully: Indigenous Human Rights in Canada and the United Nations Declaration on the Rights of Indigenous Peoples,"* Prairie Forum *36 (Fall 2011): 9-31; "Parsing Identity and Identity Politics,"* International Journal of Critical Indigenous Studies *2 (2) (December 2009): 36-46; and "From Stonechild to Social Cohesion:*

Anti-Racist Challenges for Saskatchewan," Canadian Journal of Political Science *39 (3) (2006): 507-527.*

[1]As, for example, the Klein government recently did to ask households how it should spend the Alberta budget surplus.

[2]Malthusianism refers to inheritors of the views of Thomas Malthus, who argued in 1798 that society owed the poor nothing, as they were responsible for their own misfortune because of their prolific breeding and indigence or incapacity.

REFERENCES

Cohen, Marjorie Griffin. *Free Trade and the Future of Women's Work: Manufacturing and Service Industries.* Toronto: Garamond Press and the Canadian Centre for Policy Alternatives, 1987.

Dacks, Gurston, Joyce Green, and Linda Trimble. "Road Kill: Women in Alberta's Drive Toward Deficit Elimination." *The Trojan Horse: Alberta and the Future of Canada.* Eds. Gordon Laxer and Trevor Harrison. Montreal: Black Rose Press, 1995.

Gill, Stephen. "Globalization, Market Civilization, and Disciplinary Neoliberalism." *Millennium* 24.3 (1995).

Grinspun, Ricardo and Robert Kreklewich. "Consolidating Neoliberal Reforms: 'Free Trade' As a Conditioning Framework." *Studies in Political Economy* 43 (Spring 1994): 46.

Lipietz, Alain. *Towards a New Economic Order.* New York: Oxford University Press, 1992.

Miliband, Ralph. *Socialism for a Skeptical Age.* Cambridge: Polity Press, 1994.

Non-Governmental Organizations Beijing Declaration, February 11, 1996, Interim Version.

Teeple, Gary. *Globalization and the Decline of Social Reform.* Toronto: Garamond Press, 1995.

PAT ARMSTRONG AND HUGH ARMSTRONG

Thinking Globally

Women, Work and Caring

T HE AMERICAN FEMINIST DEBORAH STONE, an eloquent analyst of women's caring, talks about being a "'lumper' rather than a 'splitter'"(91). For "lumpers," the emphasis is on what is common about women's work, on what women share. At the same time, there remains in her publications a clear recognition of tensions and differences. Miriam Glucksmann's revealing analyses of British women's work speaks of "slicing" data, theory and concepts to create multiple and complex pictures of particular peoples in particular places (16). Her purpose is to look at the various ways work is divided up within what she calls the "total social organization of labour."

This article is about both lumping and slicing. It attempts to explore what is common, not only among women but also across time and space. At the same time, it seeks to examine different slices of the same questions. Such slices are meant to help expose the complex and contradictory nature of the concepts we use in considering women's work and of the current state of women's work. It assumes that contexts and locations matter, and that while women face considerable pressures from forces outside their immediate control, they also are active participants in shaping their own lives.

WHY LUMP?

Everywhere throughout recorded time, there has been a division of labour by gender. Every society we know about has defined some work as men's and some as women's. And every society we know about has made distinctions between what women can and should do. Women have primary daily responsibilities for children and for the sick or disabled, as well as for much of the other work in domestic domains. They do most of the cooking, washing, cleaning, toileting, bathing, feeding, comforting, training for daily living, shopping and planning for domestic consumption and care. And it is women who bear the children.

This division of labour is combined with a gap between average male and female wages. Jobs mainly done by men pay more than those mainly done by women. Women are much more likely than men to work part-time or part-year and to have interrupted career patterns or casual, temporary jobs. When self-employed, they are much less likely than men to employ others. And much of the work women do pays no wage at all.

Feminists have long been struggling to make the full range of women's work both visible and valued. Lumping has allowed them to do this. They began in the early 1960s by focussing on domestic labour, understood as the unpaid work women do in households, and by revealing the institutional and social arrangements that combine to produce systemic discrimination in the paid workforce. Initially, the emphasis was on what was termed the reproduction of labour power on a daily and generational basis. This meant having babies and providing for their needs, along with those of their breadwinning fathers. As the research on women's work expanded, the picture of this work became both more refined and more complex. More categories of work, such as care for the elderly, the sick and the disabled, appeared in the literature. Then this care category, too, was further refined to include care management, assistance with daily living and personal as well as medical care, and it came to be seen as a relationship rather than simply as a work category. Similarly, the picture of women's work in the labour force was further developed to encompass the detailed division of labour found within occupations and industries and the nature of workplace relationships. Within the formal economy outside the home, working in the public sector was distinguished from the private sector, and then this private sector itself divided between the for-profit and the not-for-profit, or what came to be called the third sector. Within this not-for-profit sector, women's work as volunteers was distinguished from their paid employment. Locations in the underground economy, where women worked for pay as cleaners, prostitutes, babysitters and secretaries, and in formal economy jobs that they did in their own homes, also have been exposed.

Lumping also allows us to explore the social, economic and institutional arrangements as well as the policies and practices that contribute to these patterns in women's work. But lumping is not only about processes remote from the individual lives of most women, about abstract concepts or far-away decision-makers. It is also about how women's work is shaped at the level of the hospital, day-care, community centre, clinic, home and office; about the fine divisions of labour; the ways policies are played out in daily lives and the ways women act to create spaces in their own lives or to limit those spaces. So, for example, lumping allows us to ask what kinds of caring work women and men do, and what kinds of government funding support or undermine this work.

Lumping, then, is appropriate because there are so many common patterns in women's work. Lumping allows us to see what women, as women, share, in terms of the nature of both the work and the work relationships. It also helps us to expose the forces that keep these patterns in place and change them.

WHY SLICE?

Although there is a division of labour by sex everywhere, there is also no common division of labour across time and space and often not even within countries during a particular period. What is defined and practised as men's work or women's work varies enormously, and most cultures have at least some women who do men's work. Moreover, the actual division of labour can contradict the prescriptions or accepted practices. Equally important, there are significant differences among women related to class, race, culture, age, marital status, sexual orientation and spatial locations, as well as for the same women over time.

Once, those paid to do secretarial and teaching work were mainly men; now, most are women. Those paid as chefs are mainly men, while women do most of the unpaid cooking. However, in Canada at least, if the unpaid cooking is done outside on the barbeque, it is men who do the work, but the unpaid kitchen jobs are still primarily left to women. In the USSR, most doctors were women at the same time as North American medicine was dominated by men. The care provided by women in a Bosnian refugee camp differs fundamentally from that provided in a household in Ottawa's exclusive Rockcliffe neighbourhood. While care work is women's work, there are multiple forms of women's paid and unpaid caring. There are also considerable variations in what is defined as women's caring work. Our grandmothers, for example, did not clean catheters, insert needles or adjust oxygen masks as part of the care work they did at home.

There may also be large gaps in both places between what women and men think they should do and what they are able to do. There is, in other words, often a gap between practices and ideas about appropriate practices. For example, while most Canadian and British men think they should equally share the domestic labour, there is little evidence that such sharing actually happens in practice. Yet many men who think care is women's work find themselves providing care for ill and aging partners. Many women who provide care do not necessarily think that it is their job, nor do they necessarily have the skills to do the work. At the same time, many women who think they should provide care cannot do so because they have too many other demands on their time, because they do not have the skills, because they do not have the other necessary resources or because they do not have the physical capacity. Many who do provide care, providing services such as meal preparation, comforting and cleaning, may not even see this as care because it is so much a part of their daily lives.

Not only within countries at particular times, but also within workplaces, there may be significant differences among women. A hospital, for example, may have women working as managers and women working as housekeepers. The managers are more likely to be white, Canadian-born, with English or French as a first language and relatively young, while the housekeepers are more likely to have migrated to this country, to have neither English or French as their mother tongue and to be older than the female managers. And, of course, there are significant differences between these groups in terms of power, pay and ideas about work, and in their political, material and symbolic resources related not only to their positions in the paid work force, but also to their positions in their households and neighbourhoods.

But slicing is not only necessary to draw out the differences related to women's various spatial, physical, social, psychological, economic, work and age locations, it is also necessary in order to see the different ways of understanding the evidence, different ways of developing evidence and different views on the same processes. It is, for example, possible to look at care from the perspective of the care provider or from that of those with care needs, or to examine care as a relationship. Furthermore, the family as a group may see care issues one way, and the government, the agencies and the paid providers in other ways. Indeed, each household member may have a specific way of slicing the situation. Equally important, the tensions among these may not be possible to resolve but possible only to recognize and handle. By beginning with a recognition of contradiction, by taking this slice, it is possible to base and develop policies and practices that seek to accommodate such tensions rather than setting out single solutions based on notions of harmony.

Analysis can begin from a number of different questions: asking, for example, what does this mean in the short term and what does it mean in the long term? What does it mean for those immediately involved, and what does it mean for the country or the world? It can also begin by acknowledging that some practices, conditions and situations are contradictory. Women, for example, may at one and the same time want to provide care and find it impossible to do so. They may love the person for whom they provide care but, precisely because of this love, hate to provide care.

Slicing can expose the different kinds of care work involved in providing for children with and without disabilities: for teenagers who join gangs and for those unable to attend university because there is no money, for adult neighbours with chronic illness and for those with marital problems, for healthy elderly and severely ill old people. It can also reveal what it means to provide this care at home or in an institution and what different kinds of institutions and homes there are.

It is also possible to begin with quite different purposes. For example, most policies are about helping households and families adapt to the demands of paid work and services. It is also possible, as some Norwegian policy analysts make clear, to start by figuring out how paid work can adapt to family lives (Brandth and Kvande). Instead of asking what resources the growing number of elderly require, the questions could be about the resources they bring and the services they provide. Rather than asking how care can be made an individual responsibility, we can ask what conditions make it possible to care without conscripting women into caregiving. Rather than assuming, as we do in Canada, that public care is what supplements family care done mainly by women, we could assume that families supplement public care.

Slicing adds both a recognition of difference and the possibility of developing different views of the same issues, circumstances and evidence.

WHY WOMEN?

On the one hand, we have a universal pattern in terms of a division of labour by sex and women embracing caring work. On the other hand, we have an incredible range of labour done by women and defined as women's work. We also have women resisting caring work. Indeed, American historian Emily Abel argues that some nineteenth century women "complained bitterly that caregiving confined them to the home, caused serious physical and emotional health problems, and added to domestic labour, which was gruelling even in the best of times" (Abel 5). What factors, ideas, structures and processes contribute to this universality and difference, this embracing and resistance? More specifically, why do women provide the care but in so many different ways? There are no simple answers to these questions. Rather there are a number of answers that help contribute to a better understanding of care as women's responsibility.

We do know that only women have babies. But we also know that the meaning, experience and consequences of having babies varies enormously, not only across time and with location and culture, but also for individual women from one baby to another. Having a baby is fundamentally different for Celine Dion than it is for an Aboriginal woman who must leave her northern Quebec community if she is to receive medical assistance. Moreover, there is no necessary connection between having babies and rearing them; that is, to providing care. Bodies, then, are a factor in all of women's lives, but these bodies themselves are embedded in social, economic and political structures that are continually influencing how bodies work, as well as how they are defined and valued. They cannot provide much of the explanation for why women provide most of the care, not only for the babies they bear, but for other people as well.

Although there is plenty of evidence to suggest that women are more likely than men to identify with the emotional aspects of caring, there is very little evidence to suggest that this is connected to the way women's bodies or minds are physiologically constructed or that men are physiologically incapable of such caring emotions. There is also evidence to suggest that girls are taught and expected to exhibit such caring, and they are also more likely than their brothers to be assigned the caring jobs in the home. What sociologists call early socialization obviously contributes to women's skills in and attitudes about care, as well as to their brothers' notions of who is responsible for care and knows how to care. However, the pressures on women to provide care do not end and perhaps are not primarily created by early learning. Just as children are born and formed within a social context, so too are women carers daily created and shaped within social relationships, processes and structures. At the same time, women are active in creating these same relationships, processes and structures, albeit often from a weaker position than that of men.

These relationships, processes and structures are about power, not only in the sense that governments, employers, community organizations and husbands have specific powers and protect specific rights, but also in the more general sense of whose preferences, ways of acting and ideas prevail in daily practices. And they are about resources and the principles, as well as the mechanisms for their distribution. Power and resources in the formal and underground economies, in community organizations and households are often mutually reinforcing and are definitely linked. They are also unequally distributed, not only between women and men, but also among women. Women do have resources and are active participants in creating caring work. However, most women have fewer resources than most men, and the resources, as well as the means of participating they have, are frequently different from those of men.

There is, then, very little that is "natural" about women's work in general or their caring work in particular. Contexts matter much more than bodies in creating and maintaining women's caring work. Caring can be understood only as women's work within unequal relationships, structures and processes that help create women as carers and undervalue this caring work.

THINKING GLOBALLY: THE LARGEST CONTEXT

Globalization has become a familiar term in recent years. While familiar, though, teasing out its meanings and its implications for women in different locations is a complicated task. Globalization implies a process that is drawing the world and its occupants closer together on what is often seen as an inevitable and undirected path. At the core of this process are giant corporations centered in one, usually Northern, country but operating throughout the globe. These transnational corporations (TNCs) helped create the technologies that have themselves contributed both to the corporation's multinational form and their power. Such technologies make it possible to move money rapidly around the globe, thus allowing these corporations to avoid or at least threaten to avoid any particular government's taxes and regulations by moving their investments. The technologies also make it possible to move work around the world, thus allowing the corporations to avoid or threaten to avoid demands from workers or restrictions on the use of labour imposed by governments. In order to facilitate this movement of goods, money and work, the giant corporations have been central in promoting what is often called free trade. Free trade is far from new, and traders have always enjoyed considerable freedoms as well as considerable power. It may well be, however, that the speed of transactions has altered along with the size of the corporations directing them. As a result, their power may be greater than ever before.

Instead of combining to resist this pressure, many governments have come together to support the process of achieving greater and easier movement of goods, services and money. At the international level, the First World countries (also called northern, developed or industrial countries) in particular, have worked through the International Monetary Fund, the World Bank and the World Trade Organization to promote the removal of restrictions on trade, a process which entails both de-regulation and re-regulation. Countries owing enormous debts have been required to introduce structural adjustment programs that involve the removal of many restrictions on foreign investment and labour practices, as well as the sale of public corporations to private ones, cutbacks in public services and the adoption of market strategies within the public sector that remains. The impact on women has been mixed and contradictory, both within and across nations.

Some women have been able to get new jobs on the "global assembly line," producing goods and even services previously produced mainly by women in the highly industrialized countries. Precisely because firms have relocated in these countries in order to avoid high wages and restrictions on working conditions, these jobs for women have rarely been good jobs. But they have offered some new possibilities for work, income, shared locations and minimal protections. More common has been the expansion of paid work for women outside the factory walls within the underground or informal economy where few, if any, rules apply. Women have been drawn into small-scale retail and service work, into domestic and homework, or simply into semiclandestine enterprises (see Ward). Here the boundaries between household and formal economy, between public and private space, and between employment time and non-employment time are blurred and protection along with visibility absent. At the same time, the withdrawal of public services has meant that women have had to do more of this work without pay or support within the confines of their private worlds, where the work is less visible and less available. For many women within these countries, there is no paid work at all. The poverty and unemployment that follow in the wake of structural adjustment policies push many to search for jobs in those First World countries that have created these policies. Women, in particular, have sought work as what Grace Chang calls "disposable domestics." Separated in time and space from their children, these women often do the domestic and caring work for First World women under conditions supported in the First World by the combination of government regulations, women's working conditions, and the failure to provide care services. Like free trade, the movement of women to do such work is not new, but the scale has altered. The result is a growing gap among women within and between countries, a gap that is frequently linked to racialized categories, as well.

In addition to imposing structural adjustment programs on Third World countries (or what are often called southern or developing countries), First World countries have entered into trade agreements that promise to support the movement of goods, services, money and, to a lesser extent, people across borders. This has not necessarily meant less government, but it has meant more measures to allow corporations to operate with less regard to national practices and preferences and fewer taxes or other contributions to national economies. It has also meant less local and democratic control as more decisions are being made by these international trading groups. Facing debt pressures themselves, these countries have adopted strategies similar to those imposed on the Third

World. First World countries have acted more like entrepreneurs at the same time as they have handed over more of the services previously provided by governments to private, for-profit firms.

These shifts have had critical consequences for women. The expansion of the public sector had provided many, and often quite good, jobs for women. Indeed, "in 1981, between 65 and 75 percent of college-educated women in Germany, Sweden and the U.S. were employed in the 'social welfare industries'" (Pierson 130). Many of these jobs disappeared or their character changed in the wake of the global reforms. Trade agreements did allow some women to move to other countries in search of work. Registered nurses, for example, left Canada in large numbers when hospitals closed, acquiring jobs in the United States. But those women from Third World countries seeking work in Canada found it more difficult to gain full citizenship status, providing just one example of how free trade has not worked in the same way for everyone. As public services have declined, more of the services have been provided for sale in the market.

This process, often described as commodification, determines access primarily on the ability to pay rather than on need. More of the women in First World countries, as compared to those in the Third World, have had the means to pay for commodified services. However, women in both Worlds have continued to earn less than men, and women have continued to bear primary responsibility for care and domestic work. Faced with fewer public services and relatively low pay, but still in need of income to purchase these services, women in the First World have sought the cheapest means of paying for care or other supports. These means have often involved the even poorer women from the Third World. This is not to suggest that most First World women have completely escaped unpaid work or that the majority of women could afford to pay for services. Indeed, the reduction in public services has meant that a considerable amount of this work, formerly done by women for pay in the market, is now done by women without pay in the home. In other words, it has been de-commodified but not eliminated. Rather, it is to stress the linkages among women created by globalization and the growing gaps among women that these linkages often entailed.

Globalization does not simply refer to economics, however. It also refers to the ways people, ideas and cultures are brought closer together around the world. This has, in many ways, meant the spread of First World, and especially U.S., practices. Along with music, movies, fashions and food have come ideas about all aspects of social life, including women's work. This dissemination of ideas is also linked in many ways to the corporations, both through their ownership of companies that produce these goods and through their influence over the media. In these global sources, the emphasis is increasingly on the individual as a consumer with choices being based on the capacity to purchase. Like the relocation of jobs, the spread of ideas is a mixed blessing. On the one hand, feminist ideas have spread rapidly around the world. On the other hand, the

First World version of feminism was what has spread most rapidly, and this version too often fails to take context and difference into account.

This notion of shared international perspectives is not particularly new. Indeed, after the Second World War there was much talk of a postwar consensus. This consensus was based on a commitment to expanded government-provided services to a mixed economy that combined public and private enterprise, and to policies of full-employment along with sustained economic growth (Pierson 125). Redistribution of goods and services was part of the package, as were collective responsibility and shared risk. Now, this consensus seems to have fallen apart, only to be replaced by a new, and quite different, one. Public rights are replaced by private ones, with markets rather than states as the preferred means of allocating jobs, goods and services. But markets are unable to respond to many human needs and are especially ill-equipped to promote equity and full employment or to avoid long-term problems like pollution or other health consequences. Instead, they result in greater inequality, especially for women. As British theorist Ian Gough puts it, "Markets paradoxically require altruistic, collective behaviour on the part of women in the household in order to enable men to act individualistically in the market" (16).

Globalization has allowed much more than money, people, goods, and services to move quickly around the world. Diseases, too, face more permeable borders. New epidemics, such as HIV/AIDS, are transported along with old ones, like tuberculosis and hepatitis, around the globe with relative ease, transported in and by airplanes, as well as by service workers. Increasing inequality, not only in the Third World but also in the First, encourages their development and prevents their treatment. Diabetes has become much more common, especially among marginalized groups in large urban centres and on reservations. At the same time, protections under free trade rules for pharmaceutical patents frequently leave treatments beyond the reach of many.

One way, then, to slice globalization is to reveal the increasing dominance of transnational corporations, the converging of governments around market strategies, the declining democratic controls and the growing gap for and among women. Another way to slice it is to expose the counter tendencies. The same technologies that support corporate power allow various kinds of social and labour movements to organize around their interests. We see evidence of this not only in the "battle of Seattle" and in the streets of Quebec, but also in the Beijing Conference on Women that reached a consensus around means of promoting women's equality and in the attempts to protect sweat shop workers encouraged by the success of Naomi Klein's book *No Logo*. The movement of people around the globe has meant that many of us are more familiar with other cultures and practices.

We also see counter tendencies in the escalation and power of terrorism. Although many governments have adopted strategies taken from the for-profit sector, there is still an incredible variety in the ways these governments operate. Important public programs that reflect a continuing commitment to social rights and collective responsibility remain in many countries. Others have taken a route that emphasizes family values while still others have turned to religion and ethnicity. Moreover, the trade alliance among members of the European Union has served to improve working conditions for many women and help improve services for others. Instead of de-regulation, we see on occasion the extension of regulation. Britain, for example, has been required to provide protections for part-time workers and to introduce both minimum wage and equal pay legislation, all of which improve women's market jobs. Several countries are resisting the high drug prices that prevent them from treating mothers with HIV/AIDS, a sign that not all countries are willing to put property rights above people's right to life. And perhaps most importantly, there is ample evidence to demonstrate that spending on social programs can enhance rather than prevent trade, and that gender-based analysis linked to effective programs is essential to economic development.

Contradictions within global developments, as well as those among particular kinds of developments, are important in understanding where and how change may occur or is occurring. It is equally important to examine the details of how global agreements and patterns are played out within specific locations, because practices may well defy or transform intentions.

In short, globalization is about processes that result from actual decisions and practices rather than about forces beyond human control. While there is strong evidence to demonstrate that corporations are powerful players that are often supported by governments, there is also evidence to suggest that there are both limits on this power and contradictory patterns. There are choices to be made. These choices can have important consequences for women and their work and have to be considered in developing strategies for care.

Excerpted from "Thinking it Through: Women, Work and Caring in the New Millennium" published by "A Healthy Balance," a research program located in the Atlantic (formerly Maritime) Centre of Excellence for Women's Health. Reprinted with permission of the authors. The original version of this article was funded by the Healthy Balance Research Program, through the Canadian Institutes of Health Research, Maritime Centre of Excellence for Women's Health (MCEWH) and the Nova Scotia Advisory Council on the Status of Women (NSACSW). It expresses the views and opinions of the authors and does not necessarily reflect the official policy of the MCEWH or NSACSW, or any of its sponsors.

Pat Armstrong is a Distinguished Research Professor in Sociology and in Women's Studies at York University, Toronto. Hugh Armstrong is a Distinguished Research Professor in Social Work and in Political Economy at Carleton University, Ottawa. Together, and separately, they have written widely on women and work and on health care. Recent publications include Critical to Care: The Invisible Women in Health Services *(2008) with Krista Scott-Dixon;* About Canada: Health Care *(2008); and* They Deserve Better: The Long-Term Care Experience in Canada and Scandinavia *(2009) with Albert Banerjee, Marta Szebehely, Tamara Daly and Stirling Lafrance. Part Armstrong is the Principle Investigator and Hugh Armstrong one of the Co-investigators for their current SSHRC-funded project, "Re-imagining Long-Term Residential Care: An International Study of Promising Practices."*

REFERENCES

Abel, Emily K. "A Historical Perspective on Care." *Care Work: Gender, Labour and the Welfare State.* Ed. Madonna Harrington Meyer. London: Routledge, 2000.

Brandth, Berit, and Elin Kvande. "Flexible Work and Flexible Fathers." Paper presented to the conference on "Rethinking Gender, Work and Organization." Keele University, England, June 2001.

Chang, Grace. *Disposable Domestics: Immigrant Women Workers in the Global Economy.* Cambridge, MA: South End Press, 2000.

Glucksmann, Miriam. *Cottons and Casuals: The Gendered Organization of Labour in Time and Space.* London: British Sociological Association, 2000.

Gough, Ian. *Global Capital, Human Needs and Social Policy.* New York: Palgrave, 2000.

Klein, Naomi. *No Logo: Taking Aim at the Brand Bullies.* Toronto: Knopf Canada, 2000.

Pierson, Christopher. *Beyond the Welfare State: The New Political Economy of Welfare.* Second Edition. Oxford, Blackwell, 1999.

Stone, Deborah. "Caring by the Book." *Care Work: Gender, Labour and the Welfare State.* Ed. Madonna Harrington Meyer. London: Routledge, 2000.

Ward, Kathryn. Ed. *Women Workers and Global Restructuring.* Ithaca, NY: Cornell University Press, 1990.

I. Restructuring/"Liberalization"

SILVIA FEDERICI

The Global Crisis

FOR MORE THAN THREE DECADES one part or another of the world has been in crisis. We had the "debt crisis" of the 1980s and 1990s that swept much of the former colonial world into a neo-colonial status. Then came the "Asian crisis" of 1997 and the "financial crisis" of 2008, followed by the threatened default of several countries until recently considered fairly prosperous like Greece, Italy and Spain. At the same time, "Crisis" of one sort or another, has become a constant component of social economic discourse, as in "water crisis," "climate crisis," "peak oil crisis," or "healthcare crisis." In fact "crisis" has become the main socio-analytic category of the age and the prism through which most social realities are now being interpreted and evaluated.

What does "crisis" mean in this over-determined context? One quick answer is that the concept is losing its power to designate the specificity of the moment and the situation in which we are living. But a more useful response is to see how we can demystify the use that is being made of it. The first question then is *whose crisis* are we speaking about? Like every other social-economic concept, "crisis" has a class dimension and we should not assume that *their* crisis is *our* crisis and *vice versa*. Unless we make this distinction many of today's world-historical events cannot be deciphered.

Second, we should recognize that since at least the 1940s, capitalism has been able to plan economic crises (periods of high unemployment and declining wages for workers and increasing numbers of bankruptcies for marginal capitalists) as much as it has planned development. The times of the "anarchy of production" are long gone. Rather than an unexpected, uncontrollable event, economic crisis has been a tool in the arsenal of class war, to impose a new balance of power and dismantle social economic structures no longer profitable. This is not to suggest that capitalist relations cannot be undermined, but it is to alert us to the fact that crises are not only real effects of people's resistance to being exploited, but can be tools used to restore discipline and dis-accumulate this resistance.

Third, under the concept of "global crisis" we should include not only economic but environmental and cultural trends, as the loss of clean waters and airs, and the loss of solidarity ties and hope in the future are as disastrous, if not more, as the loss of income and employment.

A GLOBAL CAPITALIST CRISIS?

Given these premises, then, what is the character of the "global crisis" today seen from the capitalist viewpoint? Can we say, for instance, that capitalism is in crisis? The answer is yes and no. No, if by crisis we refer to a lack of available funds for investment. The global crisis is not a "liquidity" crisis, nor it is a crisis produced by excessive regulation of capital markets. On the contrary. In the U.S. at least, big corporations are flush with cash and the interest rates on loans for such corporations is nearly at zero percent. In addition, despite the outcry that "sub-prime mortgage lending" and the "financial crisis" raised also in financial circles, Wall Street has not changed its *modus operandi*. Wall Street firms are now even more deregulated than in the past. Hedge funds are as conspicuous as they were in 2008, and so are all the other speculative maneuvers that were faulted as the cause of the financial meltdown. In other words, in the aftermath of the Wall Street financial meltdown, less regulation and bolder speculation are more than ever the order of the day. It is also well-known that the U.S. banks are stuffed with money, being the beneficiaries of one of the biggest transfers of public wealth into private hands in U.S. history. Companies too are enjoying record profits, having decimated their work-forces while increasing the workload of those still employed. Yet, both in Europe and the U.S., capital is on strike, freezing investment (except in the energy sector), degrading assets, bringing countries to the edge of default. As a result, not only are unemployment rates reaching record highs and consumption rates collapsing with effects felt across the world, but in three of the main economies of Western Europe (Britain, Italy and Spain), measured by the size of the GDP, conditions are worse now than during the Great Depression.

What conclusions can we draw from this description? First the "crisis" is not economic but political. It is not due to lack of capital, but to the lack of conditions favourable to profitable investment, and it is not meant to be resolved but perpetuated until, at least, its objectives are achieved. These objectives can be deduced from the concessions the high unemployment regime is extracting from workers: (a) deregulation of labour relations and reduction of the cost of labour-production, both at the higher and lower end of the wage scale, through the freezing of wages, the removal of entitlements, the imposition of restrictions on the right to organize; (b) consolidation of corporate control over the world's economies and natural resources, especially those on which people rely for their survival, with the consequent dispossession of large parts of the world population from their farms, their markets, and even their homelands; (c) creation of a political framework guaranteeing the unimpeded flow of goods and capital across the world, which involves a remolding of governments and other institutions to fit this goal, and a further centralization of economic planning, of the type now proposed in Europe, completing the task begun with the creation of the Euro-zone.

In sum, what we are witnessing is a redefinition of the relation between capital and workers in *an attempt to create a work force without rights, completely malleable and subordinate to the needs of the world labour market.* And there is no doubt that to some extent this plan is succeeding. Already in the U.S.—in the aftermath of industrial relocation and the sub-prime lending crisis—a new population of jobless and homeless workers has emerged, constantly moving to the areas where jobs are opening up, travelling on buses, trailers, trucks. And this trend is likely to accelerate, as it is agreed that a return to employment levels of the '50s and '60s will never occur. On a broader scale, too, a large part of the world proletariat is today made up of immigrants and refugees.

Through these maneuvers—which unify the capitalist class from Detroit to Bombay—capitalism may gain another quarter of a century of rule and perhaps more. But if the events of the last year are any indication, we are now entering a phase of major turmoil in which only the utmost level of repression will keep the lid over a world population every day more determined to even risk its life to bring the system down, because it truly has "nothing to lose but its chains."

Stuffed with money, the capitalist class is in crisis, because after 500 years of rule, it can only maintain its power with torture chambers and the threat of bombing those who do not comply, and it has no deal to offer to the multitudes who are increasingly demanding a share of the wealth they have produced. Indeed, though neo-liberalism has been declared dead many times over, no other system is on the horizon to replace it. And even those governments, in Latin America, that have implemented more populist regimes, like Venezuela and Bolivia, have done so on the basis of extractivist economies fully in line with the historical trends of capital accumulation, especially in the "colonies."

Certainly the epicenter of the capitalist system is shifting and it is quite possible, as some predict, that the "BRICs," emerging economic powers Brazil, Russia, India, China, may become the new industrial world powers. But it is now clear that the promise capitalism once made of bettering the conditions of living of people across the globe—which prompted many decolonized countries to imitate the so-called "Western" model—is not to be realized. Far from it, capitalism is only spreading the very scourges it once claimed to have come into the world to eliminate: famines, poverty, diseases, war and death.

That from a capitalist viewpoint the crisis is hardly soluble, is also evidenced by both the state of permanent warfare to which the leading capitalist countries are committed, and the reckless race to appropriate what is left of minerals and fuels in the entrails of the earth, and the complete disregard for the consequences of "global warming" or the continuous ecological disasters.

The prevailing ideology is that we live in "risk society" and nothing should stop the "machine," no matter how deadly the catastrophes it produces, for after all it all serves to "create jobs." Thus, less than two years after the British Petroleum contamination of the Gulf of Mexico, even more dangerous drilling techniques are now being used, increasing the depth and danger of oil extraction. In the effort to squeeze the last drop of gas out of the North American soil, "fracking" has also been introduced, a sort of geological torture by which water is injected into the earth in thousands of different places to pump the gas out, a method that not only poisons the earth but has been known to cause earthquakes. Meanwhile, the Appalachian mountains are being chewed up by the strip mining of coal. In Alberta, Canada, Tar Sand production, which requires 349 million cubic meters of waters a year, is destroying 140,000 square km. of forest a year. Even the Fukushima nuclear disaster—the worst in a century—has been completely normalized, though radiation from it is now circulating through the planet's air and water currents and no method has been found to stop the continuous discharge of nuclear material into the skies and seas of Japan. Meanwhile the long corporate encirclement of the strategic zones of the planet, those where the oil, diamond, coltan and lithium (among other riches) are concentrated, continues unabated, with the institution of a regime of permanent warfare.

Given this situation, it is not surprising that even George Soros, the internationally renowned investor—whose capital movements in the '90s destabilized entire countries—is today pessimistic about capital's future and, in preparation for the Davos Summit of February 2012, declared that the world faces one of the most dangerous periods of modern history—a period of "evil," in which not only Europe will descend into chaos and conflict, and in America there will be riots on the streets, but the global economic system could collapse.

CRISIS FOR AND IN WORLD STRUGGLE: OPPORTUNITY OR ENCLOSURE?

While the capitalist crisis is to some extent manufactured, no uncertainty can exist about the reality of the crisis for the world proletariat. The "neo-liberal deal" promised that in exchange for the removal of job security and other "guarantees," workers would be compensated by a boom in new opportunities for better employment. This "deal" had many different institutional expressions in Western Europe and the U.S., in the former socialist countries and in the former "Third World," and was represented by political figures as varied as Clinton, Yeltsin and Mubarak. But this "deal" never materialized for a large portion of the world working class. From whatever viewpoint we may look at it—wage or employment levels, access to benefits, entitlements, reproductive services (like education, employment training), length of the work-day and working-life, political rights—the economic situation for the bulk of the world population in the last five years, especially, is not only almost uniformly negative, but it reveals a steady deterioration across the last decades with no hope of betterment in the future except through a fierce struggle. Global statistics and trends in the last few years speak clearly in this respect.

The precarization of labour is now a general condition. A further trend is the dismantling of any "welfare system," that is, any state investment in our reproduction. Almost everywhere education has been fully commercialized and subjected to fees, nowhere as high as in the U.S. where student debt is now surpassing any other form of debt in the country, totaling more than a trillion dollars. Similarly publicly-supported healthcare is everywhere under attack and so are pensions, even in Europe where until now these entitlements were more guaranteed. Conditions are even worse in the rest of the world. In China. workers at a Microsoft supplier are threatening mass suicide in protest against low wages and long hours of work. Even in the United States, considered one of the richest countries in the world, 50 percent of workers are now classified as "low income," and the number of those in dire poverty—that is unable even to feed themselves—now has reached more than 30 million (about ten percent of the population) while the number of the homeless is now officially 3.5 million.

It is also clear that the new austerity does not affect all workers uniformly. As often in crises, it is women who suffer most, as they bear most of the cost of reproduction, and are expected to compensate for all the services that no longer exist. As the crisis has escalated, there has also been an increase in the violence against women.

In this case, too, the crisis is not only economic, but it is also political. Worse perhaps than the collapsing standard of living are the divisions among workers that the economic collapse has produced. Anti-immigrant movements, mystified as culture/religion wars are now a key aspect of working-class politics throughout the "developed" world, legitimizing repressive immigration measures that make immigrants a population without rights. Divisions have emerged also with regard to investment choices. Many Canadian workers, for instance, support the exploitation of the Alberta Tar Sands, although it will destroy the livelihood of the First Nations inhabitants of the region, in the same way as many workers in the Gulf refused to fight for the termination of deep sea oil drilling in the Gulf and signed contracts that bound them to keeping their knowledge of the crimes of British Petroleum a secret.

WHAT IS BEING DONE? FROM CRISIS TO STRUGGLE

All these divisions will undoubtedly intensify as there are also powerful corporate forces fanning the flames. Yet counter-tendencies are also emerging, which (as Soros well predicts) ensure that we are entering a period of permanent conflict, if not permanent revolution.

Wherever we turn we see populations in revolt and it is not only the Middle East and North Africa that are on fire. Garment workers are rebelling against low wages in Bangladesh's Free Zones; Nigerians have brought the North of the country to a paralysis to protest against the increased price of fuel. Romanians are up in arms against an austerity budget imposed to pay back an IMF loan; Greece has witnessed months of protests and, in Athens, during the summer of 2012, repeated episodes of urban warfare. Italy is presently paralyzed as truckers, taxis, trains are on strike; and in February 2013, 100,000,000 Indian workers are planning a strike for better work conditions, it will be the largest strike in history recorded.

Most important is the new quality of the struggles. Fewer and fewer protests take the form of the classic union negotiation or remain confined to the classic workplace. More commonly workers use forms of direct action like blocking a highway, even if it is to demand a minimum wage (as workers have successfully done in Jakarta), or blocking the gate to a city (as workers have done in Jordan). In Chile, in July 2012, high school students occupied a television network to protest the lack of coverage for their mobilization, while in the (U.S.) state of Wisconsin, during the winter of 2011, the Governor's decision to strip public workers of their union rights was fought by thousands of people, both public workers and others, who occupied the state house for weeks at a time.

As shown by the phenomenon of the "squares" and the "occupy" movements, now spreading worldwide (from Tunisia to Egypt and recently Nigeria and South Africa, as well as to the U.S., among other places), people are not just fighting for better wages or union demands, but to shake off decades of subordination, and for the freedom to decide their future.

Along these lines, witness also the growing attempts—also worldwide—to create alternative economies. For as secure employment becomes a chimera and government-financed services are slashed, the re-appropriation of the means of reproduction and creation of solidarity economies (local currencies, time banks, various form of free exchange and barter) become a realistic goal. These are still limited initiatives, but nevertheless important, for they represent the first steps towards the new forms of reproduction we need in order to construct an alternative to capitalism. They teach us to think of ourselves as capable of self-government, and prepare the creation of institutions by which we can control the land we walk on, the food we eat, and the water we drink. Most important, they win us away from placing our hopes and energies in electoral politics and the path of political representation that, today, can only be an opium of the masses.

Silvia Federici is a feminist writer, activist, teacher. She is Emerita Professor at Hofstra University in Hempstead, New York.

MARJORIE GRIFFIN COHEN, LAURELL RITCHIE,
MICHELLE SWENARCHUCK AND LEAH VOSKO

Globalization

Some Implications and Strategies for Women

THE NATIONAL ACTION COMMITTEE on the Status of Women (NAC) was one of the first organizations in Canada to understand the significance of globalization for women and the first feminist organization in the North to actively confront its implications. Beginning with the initial campaign against the Free Trade Agreement (FTA) in the mid-1980s, NAC argued that women's work would be negatively affected by the trade agreement. But as the actual terms of the agreement became known, it became clear that much more was at stake and that the agreement itself would be vanguard for further far-reaching international agreements. The ways in which public policy would be undermined, and the effect this would have on all kinds of initiatives women had worked to achieve, became the focus for our actions.

The women's movement understood that the whole point of public policy was to counter the market's failures and to bring about social goals that could not be fulfilled through the normal workings of the market. During the past 150 years, feminists in western industrialized nations have challenged the idea of an unregulated market as the best and most efficient way to meet human needs. Women did not need lengthy analyses of economic theory to realize that the acts of buying and selling on the market were not sufficient to meet their needs: the market could not recognize the value of their work (paid and unpaid), eliminate discrimination and oppression, or overcome chronic unemployment and poverty. Women had experienced first-hand the power of the market to keep them in their place and knew that only attempts to control the market could begin to rectify their circumstances of oppression. In fact, the great social projects of the twentieth-century occurred when people confronted the structures of power in society in order to make those societies more humane. While feminists have been dissatisfied with many of the results, the gains we have made are in great jeopardy with the form of globalization that is now taking shape.

The effects of the free-trade initiatives on labour, social programs, the environment, and the quality of our lives have been examined in NAC publications.

Specifically we have discussed the way in which globalization destabilizes existing social institutions and replaces them with impersonal market relationships and the ways in which it reduces the power of nations to regulate business, tax corporations, and provide for the needs of people. In doing this, we have been mindful that the effects of globalization are not homogeneous and that some groups of people are disproportionately affected as compared to others.

The focus in this article[1] is on two specific areas which feminists have not yet devoted significant attention to but are indicative of the direction in which globalization is taking us. The first section looks at the ways in which the new legal processes that are emerging as a result of globalization threaten our democratic institutions as they currently exist. The main point is that, at both the international and national levels, the legal processes that epitomize our notions of democracy are being shifted from those that are accessible, open, and public processes, to secret proceedings that exclude public scrutiny. The new institutions that are being established are not democratic, do not replace the market-controlling functions of nations, and shift power decidedly in the favour of international corporations.

The second section deepens this theme by specifically discussing changes in the International Labour Organization (ILO) and how its focus is shifting to accommodate the market-creating needs of international capital. While this section treats the attempts to restructure the ILO as a case study, it demonstrates how existing international institutions that have a specific function to support non-corporate groups, could, through the institutions of globalization, become part of the de-regulation framework. This analysis rests on examples of the changes in the ILO's position in two industries that are particularly significant for women's paid work.

Both of the sections show how the new so-called "standards" which are being created could be easily mistaken for international regulation designed to replace the regulations now imposed by nations. In fact, this is the impression perpetuated by proponents of the new "standards." However, in reality, the institutions are incorporating a de-regulation process that will lead to a serious weakening of national and international standards and regulations.

The final section gives a brief overview of the directions that could guide feminist activity in the future.

THE LEGAL FRAMEWORK OF GLOBALIZATION

The legal framework used to facilitate globalization is found in the international trade agreements, particularly the World Trade Organization. For Canada, the Canada-U.S. FTA and the North American Free Trade Agreement (NAFTA) are equally important.

Investment treaties have also been signed to prevent government "interference" in the daily movement of over one trillion dollars ($US) around the world. These include the NAFTA investment chapter and over 1600 bilateral agreements around the world. Canada has signed or is currently negotiating 60 investment agreements with developing countries and Eastern European countries. The Multilateral Agreement on Investment (MAI), was designed to remove government investment regulations in the world's 29 richest countries.[1]

The legal system in Canada has always been problematic. It is male-dominated, too expensive and time-consuming for most citizens to use, and much more accessible to rich individuals and business than to average people. However, NAC and other social and environmental activists have continually fought for positive changes in laws and legal processes. Examples of these positive changes include measures to ensure equal pay, more protection for battered women, bans against cancer-causing chemicals and drugs like thalidomide, and laws against pollution of our air and water. The pillars of our democratic system are elected Members of Parliament who are accountable to the people for the enactment of laws, and an open, visible justice system that is charged with enforcement of those laws.

In the past ten years, Canadians have experienced fundamental changes in the laws that govern us, as well as our access to those laws and to lawmakers. These changes have led to a deterioration in democratic processes and democratic rights.

SECRECY OF TRADE NEGOTIATIONS

A key feature of trade agreement negotiations has been the way they have been pursued behind "closed doors," in entirely secret "diplomatic" processes. To justify this secrecy, the agreements have been described to the public as simple tariff agreements. In actuality, they are comprehensive international agreements that have far-reaching consequences. They bind governmental powers in all countries and are designed to prevent governments from using powers within their national constitutions to uphold the interests of citizens. They are said to concern only cross-border trade, but actually affect all areas of policy, including policy on health, education, employment, resource use, pollution control, and culture.

The trade and investment negotiations occur in cities all around the world away from the scrutiny of peoples affected.

Leaks of preliminary documents related to the FTA, NAFTA and MAI were invaluable to groups active in opposing them. While the negotiations in all three cases were already well advanced, the public scrutiny allowed people to understand what was happening and led to a debate over the social issues affected by these new agreements. Critics of these agreements, including NAC, were ridiculed when they demanded openness in trade negotiations, but they were proven right: the impact of public scrutiny and the resulting openness can be seen in the defeat of the MAI. This does not mean, however, that openness is an established principle. It is one that will need to be continuously placed at the forefront of demands by women, green, labour, and health activists in the future.

One difficulty confronting groups that want to challenge the current globalization process is the proliferation of simultaneous negotiations on critical issues. For example, negotiations continued on agriculture and intellectual property at the World Trade Organization (WTO), comprehensive trade agreements being negotiated through the Asia Pacific Economic Cooperation (APEC) and the Free Trade Area of the Americas (FTAA), significant changes to the rules/regulations governing the operations of the International Monetary Fund (IMF) and the United Nations (UN).

There are other practical difficulties for poorly-funded groups trying to monitor these processes, much less to actually participate in discussions and negotiations. All these negotiations continue to occur behind closed doors in cities around the world.

The conduct of these negotiations provides clear evidence of the need for strong national and local governments close to those affected. Without such governments to represent the interests of people, there is no genuine possibility of democratic participation nor is there any way to ensure the accountability of the politicians and bureaucrats who negotiate the agreements.

International treaty negotiations could, of course, be conducted differently. The UN approach, for example, as seen in the Beijing women's conference, the Kyoto climate change conference, and the Copenhagen social summit, requires sessions that are open to public scrutiny and that are attended by NGOs including women's groups. The precedent for more open trade negotiations already exists; under the UN system, negotiations for a trade and environment treaty covering international sales of genetically modified plants and animals are being conducted in public.

It is possible to work with our international contacts to ensure that all future negotiations are made public. This is critical. People must not be confronted with completed, signed deals that cannot be significantly changed. Activist groups need to work together to require that all trade negotiations be conducted in public, especially as they affect so much more than trade and tariffs.

SECRECY OF CANADIAN GOVERNMENT

The growing dominance of corporate thinking and goals in government has led to an increased culture of secrecy within Canada. In particular, secrecy has accompanied the de-regulation process.

In 1996, the federal government tried to enact the *Regulatory Efficiency Act*, a sweeping law that would have allowed corporations to avoid compliance with existing regulations by signing private deals with government officials. In other words, they would write their own regulations and avoid, without limit, all public requirements. The sectors targeted for rapid de-regulation included health and therapeutic products, and various environmental laws. The bill would have also allowed the Canadian government to sign private agreements with foreign governments regarding the administration of Canadian laws. A vocal national campaign killed the bill. Had it been enacted, Canadians would have been stripped of any right to stop the decimation of public protections.

This failed Act was followed by a *Regulations Act*. It was passed by the House of Commons in 1997 but died because it had not passed the Senate prior to the federal election. The new bill would have given the government unlimited powers to refuse the publication of regulations—denying citizens their fundamental right to know the laws that govern them. Department of Justice lawyers actually stated in testimony before a House of Commons committee that there was no need to publish regulations because affected companies usually knew of them in advance. No consideration was given to the rest of us, citizens and organizations, or our need to know the ways in which we are or are not protected. Their comments reveal what government officials now think of law making: it is a process that is planned secretly in concert with industry lobbyists, without citizens' rights of participation or any right to information.

The *Regulations Act* would have also authorized the replacement of binding Canadian environmental laws with the non-binding, voluntary approaches of certain international bodies, frequently corporate-dominated and inaccessible to citizens.[2]

SECRECY OF TRADE AND INVESTMENT DISPUTE PANELS

The sweeping limitations on governmental powers that are found in the trade agreements are enforced by dispute panels whose procedures are entirely confidential. No citizens or organizations have access to the process, although what is at stake is nothing less than the capacity of our national governments to maintain laws, often for the public's protection. These trade panels have now authorized the removal of:

- •Canadian law that required salmon and herring caught off the BC coast to be landed in Canada for biological sampling prior to export;
- •American law that required tuna fishing that does not kill hundreds of thousands of dolphins;
- •Canadian law that prevented "split run" American magazines in Canada; and
- •American laws to reduce air pollutants in gasoline.

Canada has also used international trade laws to eliminate citizen protections in other countries. In 1997, the Canadian government, acting for the beef industry, won a case against the European Union (EU), which required the EU to drop its ban on hormone-treated beef. This decision was modified on appeal, and the EU has tried to maintain the ban using a new assessment of risks. The fact remains that the hormone ban exists in Europe because citizens who were motivated by concerns about the health impacts of hormone residues spent ten years organizing for the ban. The Canadian government's instigation of this case is particularly offensive since it negates the wishes of European citizens and creates a precedent that can be used against Canadian food standards in the future.

This insidious and damaging use of secret mechanisms in international agreements can also work against Canada in direct ways. For example, a large US. company, Ethyl Corporation, has cited the secret investment panels of NAFTA in its claim for $350 million from the Canadian government as compensation for a Canadian ban on the nerve-poison MMT, an additive in gasoline. This hidden process resulted in a government climb down—to a corporate polluter—at a time when our public institutions were crumbling under the weight of government funding cuts. Canadians had no opportunity to watch or participate in the process, a situation that would not be permitted under Canada's domestic laws. Other companies attacked two Mexican bans on polluting waste dumps, using these same NAFTA provisions.

In contrast, lawsuits (in a legal system which is public) would permit citizens to see the documents, to know what position the government is arguing, and possibly, to intervene. The press can cover trials, and MPs and ministers can be held to account. The secret dispute panels used in international trade organizations were obviously designed to evade these democratic rights and processes. Their considerable power now seriously undermines our democratic parliamentary system.

PUBLIC INTEREST STANDARD-SETTING BY REMOTE INTERNATIONAL INSTITUTIONS

The Canadian government is an enthusiastic supporter of the attacks on so-called "non-tariff barriers to trade." These "barriers" are actually the laws and regulations countries have in place to control products and include health, safety, and environmental laws. With the *Beef Hormone* case, Canada and the WTO gave a boost to standard-setting by the Codex Alimentarius Commission, a Europe-based body whose standards, up to now, have been only advisory. With the trade agreements, its standards became mandatory. The dominant players in the Codex include the major agri-business corporations, and their government allies. Very few citizens or ngos are able to participate.

Both NAFTA and the WTO promote the authority of international bodies to set standards, although some of these bodies have little experience and are not subject to any public accountability. Applying the same logic, trade agreements are being cited by the federal government (and some provincial governments) to evade their responsibility to enact protective standards at home. Meanwhile, funding cuts to our health system and government regulatory agencies are eroding the enforcement of existing standards.

The following section describes one example of a standard-setting institution—the International Labour Organization (ILO). The ILO has been increasingly influenced by international capital, despite its explicit design as an institution that would take its direction from workers, employers and national governments—and be held accountable to all three parties.

LABOUR STANDARDS: DE-REGULATION AND RE-REGULATION

The ILO was formed in 1919, in part as a post-World War peacekeeping measure—with the express goal of protecting workers' interests. With it came the adoption of "workers' clauses," the closest thing we have to a universal charter of labour rights. Over the years these clauses have enshrined the right of association, the eight-hour workday and weekly rest period, the abolition of child labour, equal remuneration for work of equal value, and the general principle that "labour is not a commodity." From its inception, the ILO was named the guardian of these principles.

Starting in the 1920s, the ILO became a forum where states gathered to discuss, debate and agree upon the content of labour legislation. Consequently, its Constitution provides for an annual conference to which each country sends a voting delegation composed of two government representatives, one employers' representative and one workers' representative.

The ILO has two formal functions: the setting of international labour standards through conventions and recommendations, and the provision of technical assistance to member states who request help with the design and implementation of labour legislation. After World War II, participating countries ("Member States") expanded the ILO's mandate to embrace wider objectives related to economic security and social justice. Full employment, social security measures, comprehensive medical care, the provision of adequate nutrition and housing, the assurance of equality of educational and vocational opportunities, and provisions for child welfare and maternity protection—all have been central objectives.

The ILO's 1919 Constitution and the expanded mandate that it adopted in 1944 also established the ILO as a forum where organized labour could address labour issues at the international level. The ILO itself is formally organized on a tripartite basis, a feature that makes it unique among the organizations that come under the auspices of the United Nations. This tripartite structure is intended to promote mutual understanding between workers, employers, and governments. The ILO likewise encourages tripartism within each member state and a 'social dialogue' that involves trade unions and employers in the formulation and, where appropriate, implementation of national policy on social and economic affairs affecting labour. From its inception until quite recently, the ILO has operated fairly effectively with this tripartite model, while fulfilling its constitutional mandate.

Up until the 1980s, the function and role of the ILO was relatively straightforward: it provided its member states with models for new labour legislation and technical assistance in implementing international labour standards. In recent years, however, there has been a marked shift in the role of the ILO. This shift has been influenced by the adoption of international trade agreements including the GATT, NAFTA and the now stalled MAI, as well as the growing power of international institutions such as the Organisation for Economic Co-operation and Development (OECD), the World Bank and the WTO.

Since the late 1980s, there has been an observable deregulation agenda at the ILO. The ILO has backed off from its historic role in setting new international labour standards that protect workers' interests, and improving existing standards. Even more recently, employer representatives have moved into a re-regulation mode. If fully implemented, their aggressive agenda would recast the existing enforceable standards that advance workers' rights and shape, instead, a set of new standards that promote corporate competitiveness and self-regulation. These patterns are emerging alongside the rapidly expanding business lobby inside the ILO itself and the growing ties with the World Bank and the WTO. Standards that have for many years provided for basic workers' rights are now being replaced by business-friendly standards. The message seems clear: "it's our rules or no rules." As anticipated, employers wanted to defeat the labour standard-setting role of the ILO (reflecting the deregulation agenda) and, in particular, to ensure that no further countries ratified the 1991 Convention 172, *Working Conditions In Hotels, Restaurants & Similar Establishments*. Worker representatives were caught off guard however when employers presented their own resolutions on ILO standards—setting the terms for debate and paving the way for their re-regulation agenda.

This development threaten workers' rights on an international scale. In the case of the new convention on *Private Employment Agencies*, they have undermined labour rights that have been in place since the inception of the ILO in 1919.

Given the growing power of international organizations such as the WTO and the OECD, the shift at the ILO has far-reaching implications. Surely, the need for strong, effective, and enforceable labour standards is vitally important in an era of proliferating free trade agreements, globalization, and a shift towards undemocratic, supra-national governance. Most labour unions and social justice organizations like NAC would share this view.

Unfamiliar with the shifting terrain at the ILO, some of these same groups assume a labour-friendly or at least neutral ILO as a policing body for workers' rights if and when such rights are codified. Clearly, new developments and an uncertain balance of power at the ILO suggest we need to rethink our interventions and strategies. There is a need for international, market-controlling institutions but they need to be democratic, representative, and accountable to the people on whose behalf they are supposed to function. This will not be the case if international business is successful in its bid to hijack these institutions.[4]

WHAT TO DO?

Feminists are in the ideas business. It was not because of an internal logic in our social or economic systems, but by pursuing the ideas of women's rights that feminists have been able to reach some of their goals. These ideas about eliminating women's subordination have been advanced over long periods of time, in the face of extraordinary odds and against the self-interests of the most powerful in society. For this reason, that is, the ability to succeed despite overwhelming odds, feminists are well-placed to advance the ideas for egalitarian projects internationally in the twenty-first century.

The major issue to be understood and reversed is the ability of international institutions to insist on uniform economic policies regardless of the historical, cultural, or geographical problems of any country. While differences in economic and political institutions were tolerated internationally in the past, now uniformity through the discipline of the market is required as a condition of international trade regulations. Uniform economic policies greatly aid the mobility of capital, but they also greatly undermine the power of people to shape societies in their own interests.

Women have struggled with the necessity of recognizing distinct conditions among different groups of women: we know that women's experiences are not uniform and a single analysis reflecting women's conditions is inadequate. We know too that the notion of "one policy fits all" simply does not work, mainly because different cultural and political realities are at the heart of our experiences in the world.

This idea of tolerance for unique needs is one that we, as feminists, need to advance at the international level. Women's interests cannot be met as long as we cannot be part of the governing structures of our individual societies and we have everything to lose when power shifts away from people who are accountable to us. The shift in power in favour of corporations and capital mobility distorts ideas—our ideas—like freedom and equality, which tend to get defined in limited ways to reflect narrow notions of self-interest, efficiency, and productivity.

The following suggestions for the future recognize our need to be active in both the local and the international arenas as we confront globalization. Some of these ideas clearly are not short-term measures but will take long, concerted political action to achieve. The long-term nature of establishing international control of corporate behaviour does not mean that our only course of action need focus on the distant future.

AT THE INTERNATIONAL LEVEL

At the international level five main inter-related initiatives should be the focus for action of progressive groups. First, we need to continue to be strategic in order to push back the trade regime that is now in place. To do this we need to identify the sectors in which negotiations will take place, and concentrate on them with our international allies. For the next few years, the focus will be on "non-tariff barriers" (such as environmental, public health, the public sector itself, and food regulations), trade in services, agriculture, and patent laws (including those covering human genes, plants, and animals).

Second, there is a need to initiate actions and demands that lead to the creation of international institutions that can exercise some control over hypermobile capital. The current unwillingness or inability of nation states to assert the kind of control over capital that is necessary to minimize unemployment, protect the environment, and defend citizens' quality of life, reflects the unprecedented power that corporations now have to intimidate or otherwise gain the cooperation of national governments.

We must find ways to deal with international corporations at both the international and national level. It is simply not enough to focus on disciplining the nation state alone. The very rationale for capital mobility is to take advantage of the economic climate in countries that are either politically corrupt or too weak to protect their people or their environments. International institutions that disciplined corporations, rather than countries, would begin to replicate some of the work of national institutions that were effective when nations exerted more power over corporate behaviour. Virtually all of our regulatory regimes work through the nation state; they assume states are responsible for the discipline of corporations. Increasingly, however, corporations are able to escape these controls. While not an exclusive response, there is a need for an additional focus on international instruments to discipline corporate behaviour.

Third, in addition to designing international institutions to control capital, there is also a need to imitate the redistributive functions of the nation-state at the international level so that we can move towards a more equitable sharing of the world's wealth.

As long as the enormous disparities which exist world-wide continue, the corporate sector will be able to blackmail nations into submitting to their demands for a "favourable" climate for business. The interest in developing a tax on international financial speculation (the "Tobin Tax") in order to both discourage excessive speculation and to raise money could be one starting point for the new international vehicles we need for the control and redistribution of capital.[5]

Fourth, there is an urgent need to begin what will be a long-term project to counter the very politically successful propaganda of the right with regard to the efficiency of the self-regulating market. This could begin with analyses that show the economic inefficiencies and real human misery that follows from imposing a uniform economic system around the world.

The call would be for recognition of economic, social, and environmental pluralism in international trade agreements. A tolerance for economic pluralism requires the recognition that different goals, conditions and cultures throughout the world require very different solutions to problems. One system, the western model based on a U.S.-style economic and social system, will not serve the needs of all people in all circumstances.

The attempt to use international trade agreements to impose uniform economic and social policy worldwide creates impossible positions for people in countries that have vastly different problems and resources, in addition to different values and goals. We in Canada have devised an economic and social system that is different from the U.S. because, in part, we have needed to accommodate the conditions of relatively few people living in a huge and often hostile geographical area. Canada is being forced to change many of these systems as a result of trade liberalization and, however difficult it will be for many groups in this country, the problems arising from conformity are infinitely more serious for poor countries with very different types of social and economic organizations.

In the process of demanding economic uniformity, corporate capital has taken away from poor countries any innovative ways in which they might be able to find unique solutions to their problems. Poor countries will never be able to escape poverty if they are required to abide by the employment and environmental standards of wealthy countries while, at the same time, they are required to maintain a competitive, market-based economic system.

The case for economic pluralism is a natural political position for feminists. The political activism of minority and disadvantaged groups has made more visible the different circumstances of groups of people in our society. This has led to the demand for distinct social policy to recognize these different needs. This pluralistic approach to public policy is an important starting point for an analysis that recognizes the need for pluralism in social and economic systems.

Any attempt to change the international rules seems an Amazonian task, particularly because the power of the corporate sector has been so enhanced by the changes in the trading rules. However, the very real likelihood that these policies will fail to meet the needs of peoples around the world and the more recent economic crisis gives new approaches a chance to flourish. A project which begins to analyze the ways in which international institutions could be organized to allow for economic, social, and environmental pluralism will find a welcoming audience when the promises of the existing trade regimes are not fulfilled.

Fifth, it is essential for people in Canada to work with people in other countries that are negatively affected by the rule of international corporations. In this, feminists, trade unionists, environmentalists, and peace activists throughout the world are well-positioned to lead discussions for a future that would make a global economy socially viable. All of these groups have strong international connections that can be strengthened through attempts to control corporate power together.

As the trajectory of trade liberalization continues to unfold, the experiences of all of us in different parts of the world will be distinct, but the ability to learn from each other and to explore ideas for collective action could lead to significant political initiatives for change. In particular, we could unite in the demand for open trade negotiations, on the UN model, so that secret, far-reaching regimes, with secret dispute processes, can no longer be concluded without public intervention.

The political work involved in bringing about international institutions to control capital and to permit economic pluralism may appear overwhelming: this work not only requires long-term planning and concerted organizational efforts, but it will also need a strategy to confront the full might of corporate power. As with any long-term political strategy, there must also be ways for people to work toward similar goals at the local level. If there is nothing concrete that can be suggested for action in the normal course of our daily lives, people will become discouraged and apathetic. Changing the world, or at least the current trajectory, is an important goal, but most people will be unable to respond to this long-term initiative if there is not some relationship between it and their immediate political concerns.

AT THE NATIONAL LEVEL

It is critical that all progressive groups—feminists, trade unionists, and environmentalists—maintain actions that focus on supporting social welfare, equitable distribution systems, and making the state more democratic.

The overwhelming nature of the globalization process has forced us into a reactive posture, rather than a pro-active one. As such, our actions have often been the target of criticism, both by our supporters and our detractors. But, as is frequently noted, there is no consensus in Canada about the vision of the future and public support for some of the central institutions of the social system continues to be strong; so, although resisting the dismantling of social programs is "reactive," it nonetheless can be successful.

While the international structures supporting trade liberalization give the corporate sector a great deal of leverage over public policy within nations, there are sufficiently different possible courses of action so that the uniform "race to the bottom" can be resisted with credibility.

It is very important to point out that the social systems of all countries in the west are not uniform. The substantial national differences in social policies in countries within the European Community, despite free trade and the free movement of capital, indicates that the convergence of social welfare policy is not inevitable (despite what many of us argued during the anti-free trade campaign). Not all nations have such raw approaches to the well-being of their citizens as the U.S. There are differences in social programs that can be tolerated, even within what appears to be a rapid process of economic homogenization. The main point is that we need not allow the existence of international trade agreements to prevent the defense of a decent social system.

Canada is a country that has never been wealthier. The argument must be made, continually, that we can afford to maintain and enhance our social programs. The decisions taken, for example, to reduce the number of people receiving unemployment insurance benefits; to slash federal funding for health and education; and to abandon promises to provide a national childcare scheme are political decisions based on ideological and cultural values. These are decisions that can be contested on moral and democratic bases—they have not been made "inevitable" because of globalization.

Some critics of trade liberalization tend to overstate the powerlessness of nations in the face of corporate power. The ability of nation states to stand up to the corporate sector's demands, although constrained, is still strong—if there is a political will. Because government remains the primary avenue for people within a nation for addressing their interests, it is critical that political action focus on ensuring that government does act in people's interests. By maintaining the "watchdog" roles that are so familiar to feminists, we can focus on fighting increased secrecy and falling health and green standards.

At the international level, national governments are all that exist to represent the collective point of view of people of a nation. While it is important to recognize Quebec's right to self-determination, it is equally important that all of us work to resist the political fragmentation that is occurring in English Canada. This fragmentation accelerates as each region demands more and more autonomy over social and economic programs. While the Canadian government continues to be a champion of trade liberalization and, in some circumstances, is far more ardent than even the U.S. in pursuing new free trade deals, this does not mean that some time in the future Canada could not take a different lead in shaping international institutions. To encourage this shift, we not only need a strong federal government, but one that is truly democratic and represents the will of this nation at the international level. Democratic representation has not occurred with trade liberalization issues: people within Canada repeatedly have voiced their opposition to free trade, yet the government continues to support the interests of the corporate sector.

We are all aware that our world, as troubled as it is, can become even worse. We feel that the actions of people should be able to make a difference. They can, but only if we can devise ways to replicate, at the international level, those initiatives established in an earlier period.

A longer version article was written in 1998 for the National Action Committee on the Status of Women and is reprinted with permission from the authors.

Marjorie Griffin Cohen is an economist who is professor of Political Science and Gender, Sexuality and Women's Studies at Simon Fraser University. Her most recent book is Public Policy for Women: The State, Income Security, and Labour Market Issues *(2009). Laurell Ritchie is a labour representative and works for the Canadian Auto Workers. Michelle Swenarchuk was a lawyer with the Canadian Environmental Law Association. She died in 2008. Leah Vosko holds a Canadian Research Chair in Women's Studies at York University. All were active in NAC, served on its Employment and Economy Committee, and have written extensively on women and trade.*

[1]Since this article was written a massive popular sector action prevented the MAI from being instituted.
[2]The struggle continues. In 2010, Canadian environmentalists were dismayed

to discover the Canadian Nuclear Safety Commission had secretly set a new Clearance Standard allowing recycled steel with potentially low level radioactive contamination to be used in everyday consumer products. Activists have called for the regulation to be withdrawn until public hearings are conducted.

[3] By April 2011, only 15 out of 181 member countries had ratified the 1991 ILO Convention on working conditions in the tourism sector. Canada was still not among them.

[4] In 2009, the ILO developed a Global Jobs Pact to address the social and employment impact of the global economic crisis. It promoted the idea of a recovery centered on public investments, jobs and social protections. After a hopeful start with the endorsement of G-20 leaders meeting in Pittsburgh later that year, it was moved off stage at later G-20 meetings and then undermined by austerity measures and further deregulation in these same countries.

[5] The "Tobin Tax," named after the man who proposed it James Tobin, is now frequently referred to as the "Robin Hood Tax."

ROXANA NG

Freedom for Whom?

Globalization and Trade from the Standpoint of Garment Workers

"GLOBALIZATION" AND "RESTRUCTURING" are buzz words of the new millennium. They are seen in positive and negative lights. On the one hand, governments and corporations see globalization as a positive process enabling businesses to move around the globe in search of markets and "flexible" labour, thereby augmenting profits. Predicting the world in 2001, Dudley Fishburn, editor of this special issue of *The Economist*, states:

> 2001 will be a year in which the world becomes a richer and sharply more decent place. Europe {will have] expanded its wealth at the fastest rate for a decade.... the 2.3 billion people of China and India will organise their societies so as to double their prosperity every ten years.... Globalisation will raise the standards of human rights, law, ethics and corporate governance around the world, even in dismal Africa. The revolution in communications lies behind this imperative.... No pollution, no barriers, no dogmas, no sweatshops exist in the freer exchange of information. (9)

On the other hand, organized labour in Canada, as well as elsewhere, argue that globalization has led to work restructuring, job loss, and depression of wages, thereby impoverishing the livelihood of working people. Who is right? How do we see and understand the manifestation of these abstract, macro processes as concrete and actual relations that shape people's everyday lives?

This article will examine aspects of globalization in relation to the changing working conditions of garment workers in Canada. I will first explain what I mean by globalization and restructuring. I will then describe briefly the changing reality of the garment industry within a Canadian context. Trade agreements will be explored as a component in the conglomerate of processes that shape the working conditions of garment workers against the backdrop of globalization and work restructuring.

Globalization, which should be called more appropriately "economic globalization," refers to the integration of national economies around the world into an international, global economy and market. It signals a stage of capitalist development where capital, embodied in multi- and transnational corporations, has developed the capacity to move across national boundaries. This capacity is partly facilitated by the electronic revolution (*vis-à-vis* the industrial revolution, which was an earlier stage of capitalist development that began in the nineteenth century), by computers and telecommunication systems that have the ability to "capture" and direct the market (the exchange of commodities and services virtually) simultaneously through cyberspace.[1] The movement of capital globally has also led to a corresponding movement of people around the world, either in search of employment, a better livelihood, or through the displacement of their homes by the lack of secure economic and social opportunities, or by warfare. This latter phenomenon often is not considered part of globalization. However, it *is* economic globalization and colonization that have led to the displacement of people from their indigenous livelihood (Sassen 1998).

In some ways, globalization is not new. Some argue that colonization, especially European colonization of the rest of the world, has been with us for several hundred years. What is new in this era of globalization is the ability of capital to move sites of production across national borders with relative ease, and the virtual and instantaneous character of exchange (e.g., through stock market activities). Thus, it is worth investigating how the current processes of globalization affect us because the forms of profit augmentation and labour exploitation are changing.

Closely related to globalization is a process called "work restructuring." However, I don't want to posit a direct, causal relationship between restructuring and globalization, because things are more complicated than that. Restructuring is quite specific, and dependent on local conditions. and how those involved in particular sectors respond to and innovate around local, regional, national, and international changes. The restructuring of the Canadian garment industry in the last two and a half decades, for example, presents an interesting and complex case of Canadian manufacturers' responses to pressures imposed by the various processes related to globalization. Indeed, some analysts suggest that one of the effects of globalization is intense localization (Murphy). The varied responses within the garment sector in Canada seem to bear out this hypothesis.

WHAT IS HAPPENING TO THE CANADIAN GARMENT INDUSTRY?

The garment industry is predominantly Canadian-owned; it was the eighth largest provider of manufacturing jobs in the country. However, since the 1980s, it has experienced rapid decline, and by 2007, it has had become one of the smallest industries. According to Industry Canada calculations, the size of the garment labour force dropped by 28 percent between 1989 and 1994; it dropped by a further 28.5 percent between 1998 and 2004. By 2008, the total number of workers were reduced to 44,400. These figures are not definitive, as precise statistics are hard to get. They nevertheless illustrate the scale of the decline of this sector, which largely made use of and continues to comply female immigrant workers. Historically and presently, the industry has relied on low wages for competitive advantage, and makes use of immigrants as a pool of inexpensive labour. The industry is internally differentiated by gender and ethnicity. In the period immediately after the war, many garment workers were immigrant men from Europe. As they acquire skills and seniority and move up the production hierarchy (e.g., by becoming cutters, who are seen to be more skilled than sewing machine operators), women replace them as sewing machine operators at the bottom of the garment production hierarchy. It is noteworthy, although not surprising, that in employing immigrant women as sewing machine operators, the skills they have acquired in domestic settings (such as mending and sewing) can be readily transferrable to the industrial context; thus these workers are seen by employers as unskilled or semi-skilled (*vis-à-vis* cutters who are seen to be skilled).

Historically, homeworking and sweatshop operation were an integral part of the garment trade. With the formation of the International Ladies Garment Workers' Union (ILGWU), first in the U.S. and later in Canada, garment workers became the few unionized female work force that enjoyed decent wages and employee benefits. Unlike some other sectors with heavy concentration of female immigrant workers, garment workers were protected by labour standard legislation and rights to collective bargaining since the 1930s.[2]

Since the 1980s, control within the industry has shifted from manufacturers to large transnational retail chains, such as Walmart. Manufacturers have responded to their slip in control in different ways. Some retired and got out of the business altogether. Some become importers or contractors to retailers and sub-contract out work to plants in low-waged countries through a vast and expanding global production network, taking advantage of trade agreements between/among governments, and of the establishment of free trade zones in third world countries (Yanz, Jeffcott, Ladd and Atlin). Some reorganize production locally by sub-contracting to smaller shops and jobbers to lower cost and increase productivity, for example by scaling back on their plants and by using home-based workers for the bulk of their production (Ng 1999b). The effects of this restructuring are job loss and the re-emergence of home-based work and sweatshop operations in the Canadian context.

To illustrate this, my 1999 study on homeworkers and their working conditions (Ng 1999a) found that the wages of sewing machine operators had not risen since the 1980s. In her classic study in *The Seams Allowance: Industrial Home Sewing in Canada*, Laura Johnson reported that the piece rate for skirts was two dollars (Johnson and Johnson). In the 1990s, workers also make two dollars for a skirt. A shirt is around three dollars, and a dress pays four to five dollars. These are clothes retailed for up to 200 dollars. For section work (that is, sewing on pockets or collars), workers make between 20 to 50 cents per piece. Based on the piece rate and number of items completed per hour, the average hourly rate can be estimated at between six to eight dollars.

The highest hourly rate reported is $17.00 per hour for evening gowns. The lowest is two dollars per hour.

What is more critical to note is that as home-based workers become skilled at what they are sewing and begin to make more than minimum wage (about seven dollars per hour), the employers drop the piece rate so their earning is effectively reduced. For example, one woman reported that depending on the complexity of the design, she used to get three to four dollars per skirt; now she is paid from $2.80 to $3:00. This finding concurs with a larger study on the garment trade, which reported a decline in the piece rate (Yantz et al.). Some of the other problems mentioned by the women in the study include: the employer will not give information on piece rate until the garments are completed; late payment or being paid less than the agreed upon amount; no vacation pay but employers include vacation pay on the T4A issued at year end to give the appearance of conforming to employment standards. In these situations the women feel that their only recourse, after pursuing the employer repeatedly, is to discontinue work with a particular employer. The story of this worker illustrates non- or late payment:

> I don't have very serious problem with getting paid. What may happen sometimes is getting late payment. One time there was this employer who owed me about $500-600. He admitted to it and kept saying sorry. But I still haven't got any pay from him. It was six to seven years ago. He later referred me to another sub-contractor, who sent the fabric from Montreal to his place. So I would go to his place to pick up the fabric and my pay. Another time, he asked me to lend him money. I did. And he has never paid me back. I still see him from time to time, but I do not work for him any more.

In addition to the low pay rates and non-payment of benefits, liberalization of provincial employment standards and government cut-backs across the country also mean that health and safety regulations may not be adhered to in the smaller shops. The overall picture, from the standpoint of garment workers, is one of decreasing protection and lower wages, deepening exploitation.

THE NEW REGIME OF RULING IN THE ERA OF GLOBALIZATION

Elsewhere, I have argued that the changes we witness in terms of increasing competition among employers and workers, and decreasing security for jobbers and workers alike, are not inevitable. They are the result of what I call a "globalized regime of ruling" that produce, in part, the local conditions we find in centres of garment production in Canada and around the world (Ng 1998, 2001). I use the term, "regime" after George Smith, to indicate that these are not accidental processes. They are planned and effected by actual people in their everyday activities, working toward the integration of markets, including labour markets, on a global scale. With regard to garment production, I have identified four sets of processes that work in concert to produce the phenomenon we see around the world. I will mention them briefly, but will focus on trade agreements in this article.

First, the increasing concentration of capital through corporate mergers and takeovers has had a tremendous impact on the present-day configuration of the garment industry. The shift of control away from manufacturers to large retail chains such as the Hudson's Bay Company (which also owned Zellers) and increasingly to transnational retail chains such as Walmart, has centralized control of the industry while production is progressively fragmented. By fragmentation I am referring to the sub-contractual nature of most garment production, especially in sub-sectors such as ladies and childrens wear. In response to their slip of control, manufacturers scale down production by reducing plant size, retaining a couple of cutters, thereby becoming *contractors* to retailers. The making of garments is contracted out to a network of *sub-contractors*, called jobbers, who may use home-based workers or sweatshop operations to minimize operating costs and maximize profit margins. In Canada, we also witness the increasing penetration of large U.S. chains into the retail sector, pushing local retailers and manufacturers out of business. Apart from deepening class exploitation and creating new classes of workers, these kinds of shifts produce further inequalities between men and women because of women's location at the bottom of the production hierarchy.

Second, under the ideology of neo-liberalism (that is, the mentality of "letting the market decide"), many governments at all levels have cut back on or privatized social provisions, deregulated industries and services, and "liberalized" employment standards. For example, in spite of the increasing phenomenon of home-based work, the Ontario government has consistently resisted reforming labour legislation to enable home-based workers such as domestic and garment workers to unionize across work sites (Mirchandani). Furthermore, in Ontario the legal working hours for the work week have been extended to 60, effectively lengthening the work week of all workers without giving them protection against possible employer exploitation. This development works in concert with coercive regulation of worker mobility, for example by tightening immigration and refugee policies, especially since the September 11, 2001, terrorist attacks on the U.S. Accompanying this move, in Canada, is the increasing use of workers on work permits, effectively restricting the mobility and citizenship rights of groups of workers, frequently from third world countries (Sharma). What we see here is not only the international division of labour between the economic North and South, but also the creation of third world enclaves within the North and the maintenance of racial hierarchy worldwide.

Closely related to the deepening exploitation of citizens as workers is the increasingly coordinated international networks of human trafficking across national borders. Indeed, analysts monitoring this situation assert that human trafficking is the number one illegal activity across the globe, surpassing illegal trafficking of drugs and firearms (Kwong; Murphy). Illegal migrants are used to supply industrialized countries such as Canada and the U.S. with a cheap labour force, thus creating a new category of workers called "undocumented workers." These undocumented workers and illegal migrants are seen frequently as a third world phenomenon arising out of the appalling economic, social and political conditions of southern countries.[3] It is imperative that we interrogate the way in which demand for cheap and docile labour in the developed and industrialized countries creates the impetus and incentive of illegal migration. Illegal migration is often perceived as an accidental phenomenon. In fact, it is an activity that requires a great deal of planning, coordination, and cooperation among groups of people (the intermediaries, those working in transportation companies and border control, to name a few). It is therefore through and through an integral part of the present condition we call globalization.

Finally, the forging of trade agreements between Canada and the U.S., not to mention internationally, has had a profound impact on the garment industry in Canada. It is to this that I will now turn.

TRADE AGREEMENTS AND THEIR IMPACT ON GARMENT WORKERS

I mentioned in the beginning of this article that what distinguishes this period of globalization from previous colonizing efforts by western powers is the increasing capacity for capital to move across national borders. This capacity is facilitated by trade negotiations between and among nations and international trade organizations such as the World Trade Organization (WTO). These negotiations, leading to the signing of trade agreements, govern trade and investment between and among countries. The Canadian government has taken a progressively active role in these trade agreements, especially since the 1980s, beginning notably with the negotiation and implementation of the Canada-U.S. Free Trade Agreement (the CUSFTA or simply the FTA) in 1989. It is not possible to outline all the trade agreements negotiated between Canada and other countries. I will only highlight the major agreements that concern the garment industry directly. I will then look at the implications of these agreements for the industry and for workers' security and conditions.

Until the 1980s, Canada's garment industry was relatively protected by tariffs and quotas.[4] Trade liberalization in the garment sector began with the signing of the FTA in 1989. The FTA is a bilateral agreement between Canada and the U.S. Before the FTA, Canada's major apparel suppliers were China, Hong Kong, and Korea. With the signing of the FTA, there was a significant increase in the value of U.S. garments imported to Canada. According to Industry Canada statistics, between 1988 and 1995 apparel imports from the U.S. increased at an average rate of over 25 percent (cited in Yanz *et al.* 79). Although as a bilateral agreement, the scope of the FTA was limited, it is an important legal document because it set precedents for future trade negotiations, such as negotiations around the North American Free Trade Agreement (NAFTA).

Trade liberalization was accelerated with NAFTA, released on September 6,

1992 and implemented in January 10, 1993. It played a major role in the re-configuration of the garment sector because this agreement enables the movement of production and goods more freely between/among Canada, the U.S. and Mexico. Specifically, it enabled manufacturers to invest in, set up, or out-source to garment plants in Mexico where labour costs are much lower relative to U.S. and Canadian wages. Indeed major Canadian manufacturers such as Nygard International, which manufactures women's wear, and Gildan, the largest T-shirt manufacturer in Quebec, established plants in Mexico, Latin America, and the Caribbean Basin. This resulted in significant job loss, depression of Canadian wages, and the restructuring of garment manufacturing in the Canadian context (MSN). One strategy used by U.S. manufacturers, for example, is to ship U.S.-produced textile to Mexico, where garments can be made much more cheaply, and then import the finished products back to the U.S. market taking advantage of the free tariff and quota agreement of NAFTA (Vosko).

With the signing of NAFTA, Canada's apparel export to the U.S. has also increased. However, the advantage of NAFTA to Canadian manufacturers is contradictory. According to Vosko, the "rules of origin" in NAFTA limit Canadian manufacturers in two ways.[5] First, these rules stipulate that duty is only exempted for products containing textile made in North America. The high-end clothing produced in Canada, however, is made mainly with textile imported from Europe. Since much Canadian-made clothing would be considered non-originating, the work of Canada's apparel manufacturers and their employees are effectively devalued. Thus, NAFTA sets unfair export limits and duties on Canada's most competitive garments. Second, the same rules also force Canada and Mexico to import yarn from the U.S., thus giving U.S. textile and apparel manufacturing an unfair advantage.

In terms of international agreements, Canada first participated in the World Trade Organization's (WTO) Multi-Fibre Agreement (MFA) in 1974. The MFA involved negotiation, country by country, bilateral quotas concerning the quantity of garments that exporting countries from the South could send into Canada and other northern countries. This protected the Canadian industry from southern countries that have a competitive edge in terms of lower labour costs, lower labour standards, and fewer work place health and safety requirements. In 1995, a new agreement, the Agreement on Textiles and Clothing (ATC) came into effect, which replaced the MFA. Under the ATC, worldwide apparel and textile quotas were phased out in 2005. This has enabled countries such as China to dramatically increase apparel and textile exports to western markets. The complete lifting of important quotas in 2005 saw the practical annihilation of garment production in Canada.

It is clear that where production persists, globalization of the negotiation of trade agreements, has led to increasing competition among workers across national borders, and ultimately in this case and others, the decline of the industry in Canada. For example, Canadian workers, who historically received protection through unionization and strict tariffs and quotas, now face intense competition from workers in countries such as Mexico and China, who are paid much less. This has led and will lead to further depression of wages and erosion of labour protection for Canadian workers. To keep existing manufacturers and investors and attract new ones, provincial governments have responded by further de-regulating labour standards. This was the strategy of the Conservative Ontario (Harris) and the Alberta (Klein) governments. This strategy is being valiantly pursued by the Liberal government in British Columbia. Sweatshops and home-based work has increased, as manufacturers and jobbers compete in the international market for garment production. Another logical and empirical extension of this trend is to use even more undocumented workers, thereby augmenting the demand for illegal migration and human trafficking. Canadian garment workers face increasingly similar working and living conditions as their third-world counterparts. I have argued elsewhere that immigrant garment workers from third world countries are undergoing re-colonization in the first world (Canadian) context (Ng 1998). This trend is exacerbated with the trade agreements we examined above. Workers everywhere face more adverse working conditions as manufacturers compete for price advantage *vis-à-vis* their buyers—the transnational retail chains.

WHAT CAN BE/IS BEING DONE?

Given the tremendous odds faced by garment workers in Canada and globally, it is clear that drastic measures are needed to ameliorate increasing labour rights violations. In addition to the efforts of unions and labour rights groups, there are at least three areas in which concerned citizens can be involved, and these are: *research, public education, and activism*. While I have separated them for the purpose of identifying areas of action, in fact they work in concert with each other.

First of all, we need more and better research done on tracking the global production and organization of apparel and textile. Due to the private nature of ownership and the secretive character of garment production, it is very difficult to trace the extensive network and chain of garment production in Canada and globally. Tracking the global inter-connections between/among garment plants therefore requires researchers with different knowledge and skills. For example, statistical analysis of export and import figures of garment manufacturing coupled with interviews with garment workers illuminate the multi-faceted and contradictory nature of garment production. Tracking investment patterns of manufacturers indicates the movement and places of garment production across national borders. It is only through collaboration and partnership among researchers in different locations (e.g., in the academy, in unions, in the community) that we will begin to unravel the complex nature and organization of garment production in Canada and elsewhere.

Second, we need to bring to public awareness the complex system of exploitation of workers and the strategies used by retailers and large manufacturers to augment profit. Instead of de-regulation, governments need to put in better protective and monitoring legislation and regulation. But governments will only become more accountable with tax-payers' forceful insistence. Thus, research and public education need to be bolstered by activism on the part of citizens. For example, as a result of lobbying by students and other concerned citizens, the University of Toronto developed, in 1999, a Code of Conduct for Trademark Licensees to ensure that suppliers of the university's trademarked merchandise (such as T-shirt, sweatshirts, and souvenirs), meet minimum employment standards regarding such issues as wages and benefits, working hours, and overtime compensation. When the University learned about the allegations directed at Gildan Activewear, mentioned above, regarding their unethical treatment of workers in the third world through the CBC-TV program called "Disclosure," aired on January 22, 2002, the administration asked Gildan to account for allegations about poor working conditions in its factories. Increasingly, these kinds of campaigns and advocacy are taking place globally (Garwood). They put some pressure on manufacturers and retailers to be more accountable to workers and consumers.

Finally, we need to develop alliances and multi-pronged strategies, not only to work with workers in Canada, but to make linkages with workers and groups in the South. Given the intimate connection of garment production between northern and southern countries, gains by one group of workers will have a ripple effect on other groups. An example of an organization that combines these three areas of action I identified above to show the feasibility of this approach is the Maquila Solidarity Network (MSN). This Toronto-based non-profit network of 400 plus organizations concerned with labour issues worldwide has been at the forefront of research and advocacy on garment production. It traces Canadian manufacturers' involvement in garment production in Mexico, Central America, the Caribbean Basin, and Asia. In addition to research, MSN is also collaborating with women's and labour rights organizations in the economic South, for example by advocating the development and implementation of codes of conduct governing garment production. Working in coalition with labour and other social action organizations, the network has initiated and organized campaigns in Canada to bring to light the situation of garment workers worldwide, and what Canadians can do to ameliorate the plight of these workers. Their latest disclosure and no sweat campaigns are an innovative, multi-pronged strategy that integrates research, public education, and worker education. These multi-pronged efforts enable researchers and activists to trace the global network of garment production by Canadian manufacturers.[6] It is also a way of educating Canadians about the nature of garment production.

Eliminating inequity is the responsibility of us all. It is by working together in solidarity and cooperation that we can push back or push away the detrimental effects of globalization, and work toward a global system that would benefit the majority of the world population.

The research, on which this article is based, is funded by the Social Sciences and Humanities Research Council of Canada. Thanks are due to Patty Simpson and Ann O'Connell for research assistance, and to Jonathan Eaton for feedback.

Roxana Ng researched immigrant women for over 30 years. She taught in the adult education and community development program at the Ontario Institute for Studies in Education of the University of Toronto, Canada.

[1]Some analysts and lay people use the term "globalization" to refer exclusively to the electronic and communication revolution. While this is not inaccurate, I insist that this development must be understood in the context of the transnational movement of capital. Technological innovations in communication should be seen as an integral part of economic globalization.

[2]The International Ladies Garment Workers Union (ILGWU) was formed in 1900, and the Amalgamated Clothing Workers of America (ACWA) was founded in 1914 to organize the men's clothing industry in the U.S. While both unions quickly moved into Canada, workers did not win labour laws such as the *Industrial Standards Act* in Ontario and the Decree Law in Quebec until the 1930s. Thus, there was a time lag between unionization and when workers gained legislative protection. I thank Jonathan Eaton for providing this detail. Unfortunately, with the weakening of garment manufacturing in Canada, union activities are correspondingly diminished. There is no longer a union that represents garment workers exclusively in Canada.

[3]I am using the terms "third world" and "the economic South" or southern countries here interchangeably to refer to the common sense understanding between the developed and developing world. I recognize that these terms are problematic, because they reinforce, rather than name, power differential between and among nations. Indeed, elsewhere I have argued for a re-thinking of these categories with the advent of globalization (see Ng 1998).

[4]The Multi-Fibre Agreement (MFA), an international agreement negotiated through the World Trade Organization (WTO), is an example that offers Canadian clothing manufacturing some protection against cheaper imports. How the MFA worked is explained later on in the article.

[5]For an outline of the trade agreements being negotiated up to 1998, consult *Review – The North-South Institute Newsletter*. The G20 summit that took place in Toronto, Ontario in the summer of 2010 is a recent example of the escalating trade and other negotiations by nation-states worldwide.

[6]For the work of the MSN, which is also the secretariat of the Ethical Trading Action Group, see their website <www.maquilasolidarity.org>.

REFERENCES

Ethical Trading Action Group. MaquilaSolidarity.org. Web.

Fishburn, Dudley. "Editorial." *The Economist – The World in 2001.* 9 (2001).

Garwood, Shae. "Politics at Work: Transnational Advocacy Networks and the Global Garment Industry." *Gender and Development* 13 (3) (2005): 21-33.

Johnson, Laura and Robert Johnson. *The Seam Allowance: Industrial Home Sewing in Canada.* Toronto: The Women's Educational Press, 1982.

Industry Canada. *Clothing Industry Statistical Data.* 1996

Kwong, Peter. *Forbidden Workers: Illegal Chinese Immigrants and American Labor.* New York: The New Press, 1997.

Maquila Solidarity Network (MSN). *A Needle in a Haystack: Tracing Canadian Garment Connections to Mexico and Central America.* Toronto: MSN, October 2000.

Mirchandani, Kiran. "Shifting Definitions of the Public-Private Dichotomy: Legislative Inertia on Garment Homework in Ontario." *Advances in Gender Research* 3 (1998): 47-71.

Murphy, Brian. "International NGOs and the Challenge of Modernity." *Development in Practice.* 10 (3&4) (2000): 330-347.

Ng, Roxana. "Homeworking: Home Office or Home Sweatship? Report on Current Conditions of Homeworkers in Toronto's Garment Industry." Toronto: The Ontario Institute for Studies in Education, 1999a.

Ng, Roxana. "Homeworking: Dream Realized or Freedom Constrained? The Globalized Reality of Immigrant Garment Workers." *Canadian Woman Studies/les cahiers de la femme* 19 (3) (Fall 1999b): 110-114.

Ng, Roxana. "Work Restructuring and Recolonizing Third World Women: An Example from the Garment Industry in Toronto." *Canadian Woman Studies/les cahiers de la femme* 18 (1) (Spring 1998): 21-25.

Ng, Roxana. "Exploring The Globalized Regime of Ruling from the Standpoint of Immigrant Women." Public Lecture delivered at the University of Victoria, February 13, 2001.

Review – The North-South Institute Newsletter 2 (1) 1998.

Sassen, Saskia. *Globalization and Its Discontents: Essays on The New Mobility of People and Money.* New York: The New Press, 1998.

Sharma, Nandita. "The Social Organization of 'Difference' and Capitalist Restructuring in Canada: The Making of 'Non-Immigrants' and 'Migrant Workers' Through the Formation of the 1973 Non-Employment Authorization Program." Unpublished Ph.D. dissertation, Department of Sociology and Equity Studies, OISE/University of Toronto, 1999.

Sharma, Nandita. "The True North Strong and Unfree: Capitalist Restructuring and Non-Immigrant Employment in Canada, 1973-1993." Unpublished MA thesis, Department of Sociology and Anthropology, Simond Fraser University, Burnaby BC, August 1995.

Smith, George. "Accessing Treatments: Managing the AIDS Epidemic in Ontario" *Knowledge, Experience, and Ruling Relations.* Eds. M. Campbell and A. Manicom. Toronto: University of Toronto Press, 1995. 18-34.

Vosko, Leah F. *The Last Thread: Analysis of the Apparel Goods Provisions in the North American Free Trade Agreement and the Impact on Women.* Ottawa:

Canadian Centre for Policy Alternatives, February 1993.

Yanz, Lynda, Bob Jeffcott, Deena Ladd and Joan Atlin. *Policy Options to Improve Standards for Garment Workers in Canada in Internationally.* Ottawa: Status of Women Canada, January 1999.

JANE STINSON

Why Privatization is a Women's Issue

THE PRIVATIZATION OF PUBLIC SERVICES has tremendous implications for women who account for the majority of public sector employees whose jobs are being privatized, especially in the health and social service sectors. Governments are keen to privatize almost any public service, claiming greater efficiency will be achieved through the private market. Rarely, however, do governments consider the gender implications of this policy direction. Yet there is alarming evidence that privatization is eliminating and eroding good jobs for women in the public sector as well as a range of public services designed to support women's participation in the labour market (Armstrong et al.; Bakker; Broad; Gaffney et al.; Hall and de la Motte; Leys; Martin; Prokosch). Nowhere is this more evident these days, than in the case of sub-contracting health services in British Columbia (see Cohen and Cohen in this volume).

Privatization not only undermines good paid employment for women, it can also make women's life at home more difficult by intensifying, if not increasing, domestic labour and household relations, for which women are primarily responsible. We need more gendered analyses of the implications of privatization to identify the consequences of this privatization on gender equality. This is particularly important with the privatization of health and social services since the nature of work in these sectors is most similar to the unpaid, domestic reproductive labour by women in the home.

We also need analysis that explores the racial implications of privatizing public services. We need to know how women of colour are being affected by this process. Are there differences based on race, and, if so, what are they? What are the patterns of subordination, exploitation and exclusion that can be revealed through a gendered and racialized analysis of the process of privatization? But first, what do we mean by privatization? And how is it affecting women workers? Below, we look primarily at the gender implications of different forms of privatization.

FROM KEYNESIAN WELFARE STATE TO NEO-LIBERAL STATE

Privatization represents a major shift in public policy that started in the 1970s in the United Kingdom with Margaret Thatcher's steps to strengthen the market and to sell off public enterprises in transportation, telecommunications, and utilities to private, for-profit companies. Since then privatization has spread like a global virus to Canada and throughout the world and has multiplied in the forms it takes.

The term privatization is used here to refer to a range of practices that transfer state assets and activities to private actors. Typically this involves transferring the operation and sometimes the ownership of public enterprises, assets or services to a private, for-profit company or consortium of companies. In this article, privatization also includes the transfer of paid work, mainly by women providing public services, to the private, domestic sphere of unpaid, care-giving work in the home.

Below we examine these dominant forms of privatization and their gender implications. It is argued that privatization of work through sub-contracting or outsourcing as well as the transfer of work from the public, paid sphere to the private, unpaid domestic sphere are both forms of lowering labour costs. The case of privatization through sub-contracting or outsourcing is a means to lower labour costs by downloading or transferring work to a cheaper, labour force within the formal labour market. Privatization, by downloading or transferring paid work into the home or to community volunteers, lowers labour costs even more, through women's unpaid domestic labour. Both forms of privatization have serious consequences for women's equality at work and at home.

PRIVATIZATION IS FUNDAMENTALLY CHANGING THE NATURE OF THE STATE

At the level of the state, privatization represents the shift from a Keynesian welfare state to a lean, mean, neo-liberal state where public services are reduced and the private sector plays a much stronger role in their delivery. Privatization is a key element in the transition from a Keynesian welfare state to a neo-liberal state, as the notion of collective, social or public responsibility is weakened and as a market system based on labour flexibility and individual, self-reliance is strengthened (Cossman and Fudge 4).

The transition from the Keynesian welfare state to neo-liberal state involves a process of renegotiating what we think of as public and private at another level—in the relationship between private households and the state, particularly around the provision of public services. As the state withdraws or weakens public services in favour of greater individual responsibility, another form of privatization is encouraged—the transfer of formerly paid work in the public sector, often performed by women, into unpaid work in the home.

The process of renegotiating the relationship between the state and the private household is complicated and mediated by the growth of the community or voluntary sector, sometimes also called the "social economy." The community sector has grown as new services have been developed and as the state devolves the operation of some services to non-profit, community and volunteer organizations. A full analysis of the transfer of public services from the state should involve monitoring changes at the level of the community as well as the household. Given the limits of this article, it is not done here.

DOES PRIVATIZATION TRANSLATE INTO MORE DOMESTIC LABOUR FOR WOMEN?

To what extent are we seeing a transfer of women's work, first from the home into the state, primarily through the growth of public services that characterized the Keynesian welfare state and now from the state into the home through the processes of privatization?

Previous studies have shown that women, particularly of child-bearing age, have a heavy burden from combining paid and unpaid work and, as a result, were the most stressed out in the population (Fast and Frederick; Zukewich 1998). A more recent Statistics Canada analysis of trends in paid and unpaid work from 1986 to 2005 shows that women continue to perform more unpaid, care-giving work in the home than do men and women generally tend to feel more stressed for time than men do, regardless of how long the workday is, or whether they have children (Statistics Canada 2006). Part of the explanation for this lies in the amount of time women spend on domestic labour. Women do more unpaid domestic work than men even though most women are working outside the home as well (Statistics Canada). This is true even when both parents hold full-time jobs, particularly during the early years of childrearing (Jackson; Statistics Canada 2010).

Slowly men are taking on more housework. The proportion of men aged 25-54 doing some houswork daily increased slightly from 1986-2005, as did the number of hours, due mainly to an increase in daily housework (not including childcare) from 1.0 to 1.4 hours a week such as making lunch, vacuuming or taking out the garbage. The amount of women's average hours of unpaid housework, not including childcare, fell slightly from 2.8 hours to 2.4 hours a week as their hours of paid work rose by 1.1 hours a week over this period. (Statistics Canada 2006).

Despite these recent developments, women still normally do most of the daily housework of cooking, cleaning and laundry as well as most of all forms of childcare, personal care to household adults, transportation, assistance, housework and cooking and other unpaid help to adults in other households. Not only are women more likely to perform unpaid care giving, but they also spend more time than men doing so (Zukewich 1998; Statistics Canada 2010). Men normally do the occasional chores like household maintenance, car repairs and yard work. While men are spending more time with children, it is often gendered, with fathers spending more time in play or leisure-type activities while mothers do more custodial and routine work related to caring for children

(Zukewich 1998; Statistics Canada 2010).

The estimated value of unpaid, domestic work primarily by women is staggering. Statistics Canada has calculated that unpaid work is worth between 30.6 percent and 41.4 percent of the GDP or Gross Domestic Product. The spread of almost 12 percent is due to the fact that two valuation methods were used: the first is *replacement method* (the cost of replacing unpaid workers with paid workers) and the second is *opportunity method (calculated on the amount those women would be earning if they were in the paid labour force)*. According to Statistics Canada, the replacement value of unpaid work in Canada in 1992 was $284.9 billion dollars, while that of opportunity value was $318.8 billion (Dresher).

Using the replacement method, the value of unpaid informal care giving was estimated at $50.9 billion in 1998 if parallel services were purchased on the market. That is more than the labour income generated by the health care and social assistance industry ($42.1 billion), education services ($40.1 billion) or the finance, insurance and real estate industry ($43.4 billion). A small portion of the unpaid informal caregiving by women in the home is help and care to adult households. That was worth $5.3 billion, close to the value of labour income of the arts, entertainment and recreation industry ($5.8 billion) (Zukewich 2003).

If even a small portion of these hours of informal care were shifted from the home to the paid labour market—for example, the 156 million annual hours women spend in the home providing medical care for example, to those discharged quicker and sicker from hospitals—this would be equivalent to approximately 77,000 full-time jobs (Zukewich 2003: 18). Imagine what moving that small part of what women do in the private household sphere to the paid labour market could do to improve women's economic status and free up time for women outside of paid work.

A closer examination of the amount, nature and shifts in unpaid work in the home by women and men is needed as the privatization process deepens to see whether domestic labour increases and/or intensifies for women and men and in what ways.

HOW IS PRIVATIZATION AFFECTING WOMEN'S PAID WORK?

From the post-World War Two period up to the early 1970s there was tremendous growth in public services such as health care, education, social services and childcare. Partly because these new jobs resembled women's unpaid work in the home, many women were hired to provide these public services. In this way, the Keynesian welfare state assumed responsibility for some work that had previously been unpaid work done primarily by women in the home and over time public services grew.

Direct government employees are highly unionized, as are employees providing public services such as health care, education and some social service. Over time, given collective efforts, these public sector jobs became a source of good jobs for Canadian women workers. Public sector jobs are by far, the main source of unionized jobs for women. Three out of four women in the public sector are unionized. In contrast, only one in seven women in the private sector are unionized (Jackson) (This is particularly due to the growth of the private, non-unionized service sector including private services like banks, insurance companies, McDonalds, Walmart, and many other fast food and retail outlets).

Women's involvement in their unions resulted in higher wages in the public sector than for women on average, better benefit and pension plan coverage, paid sick leave and vacations and other rights in the workplace for these women. For example, unionized women make on average, $5.44 per hour more than their non-union sisters. And over two-thirds of women in the public sector have a pension, compared to less than one-third of women in non-union jobs (Jackson 25-27). Privatization undermines these union advantages for women working in public services by rolling back these gains women workers made over the past 20 to 50 years, largely as a result of collective action through their union.

SUB-CONTRACTING USED TO ROLL BACK WORKING WOMEN'S GAINS

Privatization often refers in Canada to the practice of sub-contracting the delivery of part of a public service to a private firm: for example, to have the cleaning of a hospital, school or university building performed by employees of a private contractor, who periodically bids for the contract to do the work. "Outsourcing" is another term for sub-contracting or contracting out, most often used when referring to the practice in the private sector, when a large company decides to move part of its production process to another company who supplies the needed product or service.

What are the implications of sub-contracting or outsourcing for women?

Plenty. Public and private sector employers are using sub-contracting and outsourcing to drastically lower women's wages and benefits and turn back the clock on pay equity gains. Two glaring examples arise: 1) the impact of sub-contracting health care support services (cleaning, laundry, food services) on women workers' wages and benefits in British Columbia; and 2) the outsourcing of Bell Canada operator jobs to another private company over the past decade to avoid having to pay female employees higher wages because of federal pay equity legislation that applies to Bell.

In the British Columbia case, the provincial government paved the way for regional health authorities to decide to contract out support services in hospitals and long-term care centres by passing legislation that gutted key job security provisions from the provincial collective agreement of the Hospital Employees Union (part of the Canadian Union of Public Employees). The government's legislation eliminated previously negotiated protection against contracting out and other job security measures.

The effect of sub-contracting health care support services has been to roll back the clock about 30 years on the gains made to women's wages through their union's collective bargaining and pay equity efforts. British Columbia hospital workers had high wages partly due to a multi-million dollar pay equity settlement their union won through an arbitration award in the fall of 2000. The union received $100 million in retroactive pay equity adjustments that brought their members' wages in health care facilities into line with those of comparable workers employed directly by the province of British Columbia (Stinson).

The move to sub-contract cleaning, laundry and food services in certain health regions caused the wages to drop drastically from the highest in Canada to the bottom for comparable unionized jobs. This affects mainly women workers. Many of whom are immigrant women of colour.

The change in service delivery meant thousands of mainly women workers lost their jobs as the services they provided now had a new intermediary—a private company. The multinational companies that won the large cleaning contracts, cut hourly wages for hospital cleaners in half, from over $18.00 to $9.00. Coverage for extended health care benefits and pension plan coverage was lost with the old collective agreement. And many jobs were cut from full-time to part-time with less defined hours of work—a key feature of "flexible labour," such an important element in reducing labour costs through privatization (Cohen and Cohen).

Bell Canada used out-sourcing as effectively as British Columbia hospitals used contracting out, to lower women's wages and avoid pay equity gains. Bell has been battling a multi-million dollar pay equity case for over ten years. It is being pursued under the *Canadian Human Rights Act* by the telephone operators' union (now CEP) and Action Femmes. It has taken over ten years from the date of filing the pay equity complaint to get Bell Canada's lawyers in front of a tribunal that will hear the merits and decide the outcome.

The Bell pay equity case is clearly one of "justice delayed is justice denied." Over the years of resisting the case, Bell has slashed the workforce through sub-contracting to an American-based company that paid about half the wages, technological change and attrition. When the union filed the pay equity complaint initially, it covered over 5,000 telephone operators. Now there are only a few hundred telephone operators left working with Bell Canada, many getting into their 50s and 60s. Some have retired and others have passed away without ever getting the money they were entitled to under the law (Stinson).

In both cases of B.C. health services and Bell telephone operators, contracting out or out-sourcing was used to drastically lower women's wages by terminating established employment relationships where workers had made significant gains over time, in favour of using a private contractor who could provide those services with a new, cheaper workforce.

CONCLUSION

Privatization is an attack on the high rate of unionization in the public sector and the wages and working conditions that have been won there through trade union struggles and pay equity legislation. Privatization not only threatens women's economic equality, it also threatens greater equality in gender roles by shrinking welfare state social programs. Privatization is eliminating and eroding public services that women in particular rely on to aid with social reproduction—like childcare, health care, education, and a broad range of social services (Berhardt and Dresser).

These social support services were designed to encourage and support women's entry into the paid labour market, especially during childbearing years. Now, while women are participating in the labour market in unprecedented numbers, these social supports are being withdrawn and weakened. How can women be expected to continue to "do it all" without these supports?

It is essential that the restructuring of the state and the privatization of public services does not occur on the backs of women, with women bearing the greatest costs in term of worsened labour market position—less unionization, lower wages, fewer benefits, weaker workplace rights, more precarious employment, uncertain work hours—more onerous unpaid, domestic labour and more intense responsibilities for family and household work and relations because of the elimination and deterioration of public services.

Jane Stinson worked for many years from the national office of the Canadian Union of Public Employees (CUPE) as a research and education officer, Research Director as well as Managing Director of National Services and Union Development. She developed campaigns, workshops and articles about raising women's wage, ending discrimination, promoting equality for all disadvantaged groups and fighting privatization. She is currently involved in CRIAW (the Canadian Research Institute for the Advancement of Women) as a volunteer and project director of FemNorthNet.

REFERENCES

Armstrong, Patricia et al., eds. *Exposing Privatization: Women and Health Care Reform.* Toronto: Garamond. 2001.

Bakker, Isabella. Ed. *Rethinking Restructuring: Gender and Change in Canada.* Toronto: University of Toronto Press, 1996.

Bernhardt, A. and L. Dresser. *Why Privatizing Government Services Would Hurt Women Workers.* Washington: Institute for Women and Policy Research, 2002.

Broad, Dave and Antony W. *Citizens or Consumers? Social Policy in a Market Society.* Halifax: Fernwood Publishing, 1999.

Canadian Union of Public Employees (CUPE). *Annual Report on Privatization.* Ottawa: CUPE, 2003, 2002, 2001. Web.

Cohen, Marjorie Griffin and Marcy Cohen. *A Return to Wage Discrimination: Pay Equity Losses Through the Privatization of Health Care.* Vancouver: Canadian Centre for Policy Alternatives – BC, April 2004.

Cossman, Brenda and Judy Fudge, eds. *Privatization and the Law, and the Challenge to Feminism.* Toronto: University of Toronto Press, 2002.

Dresher, Evelyn. "Valuing Unpaid Work." Keynote address at UNPAC's "Counting Women's Work Symposium." Brandon, Manitoba, May 1999. Web.

Fast, Janet and Judith Frederick. *The Time of Our Lives: Juggling Work and Leisure Over the Life Cycle*. Ottawa: Statistics Canada, 1998.

Gaffney, D., A. M. Pollock, D. Price and J. Shaol. "Series on PFIs in the NHS." *British Medical Journal* 319 (1999): 48-51, 116-119, 179-184, 249-253.

Hall, David and Robin de la Motte. *Dogmatic Development: Privatization and Conditionalities in Six Countries. A PSIRU Report for War on Want*. Greenwich, UK: Public Services Research Unit, Feb. 2004. Web.

Jackson, Andrew. "Is Work Working for Women?" Research Paper No. 22. Canadian Labour Congress. Ottawa, May, 2003. Web.

Leys, Colin. *Market-Driven Politics: Neoliberal Democracy and the Public Interest*. London: Verso. 2001.

Martin, Brendan. *In the Public Interest? Privatization and Public Sector Reform*. London: Zed Books/Public Services International, 1993.

Prokosch, Mike and Daren Dolan, eds. *Our Communities Are Not For Sale! Local-Global Links in the Fight Against Privatization*. Boston: United for a Fair Economy/Institute for Policy Studies, 2001. Web.

Samson, Melanie. *Dumping on Women: Gender and privatisation of waste management*. Published by the Municipal Services Project (MSP) and the South African Municipal Workers' Union (Samwu), 2003. Web.

Statistics Canada. General Social Survey – 2010. "Overview of the Time Use of Canadians. Table 1.1 Average time spent per day on various activities, for the population and participants aged 15 and over, by sex." Canada, 2010. Web.

Statistics Canada. "General Social Survey: Paid and Unpaid Work." *The Daily* July 19, 2006. Web.

Stinson, Jane. "Show Us Our Money: A Pay Equity Cross-Country Check-Up." *Our Times* (February/March 2004): 37-44.

Zukewich, Nancy. "Work, Parenthood and the Experience of Time Scarcity. Days of Our Lives: Time Use and Transitions Over the Life Course." Statistics Canada Research Paper. No. 1, 1998.

Zukewich, Nancy. "Unpaid Informal Caregiving." *Canadian Social Trends* (Autumn 2003). Statistics Canada Cat. No. 11-008.

MARCY COHEN AND MARJORIE GRIFFIN COHEN

The Politics of Pay Equity
in B.C.'s Health Care System

The Role of Government,
Multinational Corporations and Unions

LEGISLATION INTRODUCED by the B.C. Liberal government in 2002 and 2003 (Bill 29 and 94) eliminated job security and prohibitions against contracting out in the health sector in B.C. This legislation opened up the door for the wholesale privatization of health support work (i.e., housekeeping, food services, security, and laundry in hospital and long-term care facilities). The impact of privatization on wages and conditions has been immediate and stunning: wages for privatized support services have been cut almost in half, benefits have been either eliminated or drastically reduced and guaranteed hours of work abolished. Eighty-five percent of the workers in this sector are women—many of whom are the primary wage earners for their families. A high proportion of these women are older, visible minority and/or from immigrant backgrounds.[1]

The impetus to lower wages through privatization was facilitated by multinational service corporations who were more than willing to provide health support services utilizing a low-paid contingent workforce. These efforts were further realized when one local of the Industrial, Wood and Allied Workers of Canada (IWA), Local 1-3567, with no previous history in representing health support workers, signed a unprecedented six-year agreement with the multinational service corporations, without negotiations and prior to the hiring of the new workforce (i.e., while the unionized, in-house workers were still in place). The actions of local 1-3467 have created deep divisions within the labour movement, and undermined the role of the Hospital Employees' Union (HEU), the union that has represented the vast majority of health support workers for more than 50 years.

TURNING THE CLOCK BACK ON PAY EQUITY

In the absence of pay equity legislation, as exists in most other Canadian provinces and territories, pay equity in B.C. has been achieved primarily through the efforts of unions and the requirement, through the NDP government of the 1990s, that pay equity in the public sector be addressed in collective bargaining.

131

Historically, women working in the health support sector in B.C. were paid significantly less than men doing similar work or work of equivalent value. The struggle of health support workers to redress the wage gap has spanned several decades and in the last 30 years has proved remarkably successful. During the 1970s the union pursued several different strategies to achieve pay equity including bargaining, human rights complaints, lobbying and arbitrations. Despite these efforts, in 1991 there was still a wage gap between men and women of between 10 and 29 percent.

In 1992, shortly after the NDP was elected, the HEU undertook a major strike to make pay equity a reality. As a result of that strike, 90 percent of the union's membership received pay equity increases on top of general wage increases. As part of this agreement a Job Value Comparison Plan was established with the provision that up to one percent of payroll per year would to be allocated for pay equity implementation until pay equity was achieved in each classification. As a result, by 2001, the wage gap had been reduced from .2 to 11 percent.

These pay equity gains, however, are being reversed through privatization. In May 2001, a new Liberal government was elected in B.C. In January of 2002 they passed legislation (Bill 29), *The Health and Social Services Delivery Improvement Act*) that unilaterally altered signed collective agreements between health care employers and unions and removed essential provisions related to job-security protection and contracting out. Bill 94 (*The Health Sector Partnerships Agreement Act*), passed in 2003, strengthened the privatization process by prohibiting unions from negotiating any language that would limit the ability of the contractor to sub-contract work in response to union efforts to improve the wages and working conditions.

The legislations' goals were very explicit: to provide new investment and business opportunities for private corporations in the health care sector and to reduce compensation for health care support workers. These changes cleared the way for government and its health authorities to privatize health care support work in hospitals and long-term care facilities and to lay off thousands of health care support workers across the province.

With strong legislation in effect, health authorities, primarily in British Columbia's Lower Mainland and on Vancouver Island, have initiated plans to privatize most or all of their housekeeping, security, laundry, and food services work in hospitals and in many long-term care facilities. More than 10,000 union health care workers have lost their jobs. Most of them are women and many are from immigrant and visible minority backgrounds.

The largest out-sourcing contracts, for housekeeping and food services, are with the three largest multi-national service corporations in the world— Compass, Sedexho, and Aramark. None of these corporations are Canadian; all operate internationally with head offices in the United States, Britain and France and have various reputations for poor labour relations and/or union bashing.

THE MULTI-NATIONALS AND THE IWA

Because of government legislation, multinational companies bidding for health support service contracts were not required to hire the existing workers or recognize the union's successorship rights. To even further limit the possibility that the Hospital Employees' Union would organize these workers, the multinational companies took the unprecedented step of approaching a number of other trade unions to offer them "voluntary recognition agreements." In "voluntary recognition agreements" the terms and conditions of employment are established by mutual agreement between the union and company *prior to hiring the workforce*. The overwhelming majority of the B.C. Federation of Labour affiliates recognized HEU's right to organize this work, and refused to co-operate with the outside contractors. There was, however, one notable exception, Local 1-3567 of the Industrial, Wood and Allied Workers of Canada (IWA).

Local 1-3567 of the of the Industrial, Wood and Allied Workers of Canada (IWA) has signed "voluntary recognition agreements" with each of the three largest private service providers—Sedexho, Compass, and Aramark. Until this point, the IWA had no experience in the health care sector. Its main role had been to represent workers in forest industries who are overwhelmingly male.

The "voluntary recognition partnership agreements" between Local 1-3567 of the IWA and the multi-national companies are all very similar. To give one example, the six-year agreement between Local 1-3567 of the IWA and Aramark was signed on July 17, 2003.[2] Thirteen days later, on July 30, 2003, Aramark was awarded the housekeeping contract for the Vancouver Coastal Health Authority (all sites from Powell River to Vancouver, including Vancouver Hospital, UBC Hospital, Lion's Gate Hospital, St. Paul's Hospital and many long-term care and smaller acute care hospitals). Throughout the fall, Aramark advertised job recruitment fairs to hire housekeepers to work at the various facilities in the Vancouver Coastal Health Authority. Representatives of Local 1-3567 were at the job fairs and people interested in working for Aramark were required to sign a union card with the IWA prior to the completion of the hiring process.

Under the Aramark/IWA partnership agreement a housekeeper earns $10.25 an hour, with no guarantee of how many hours she will work from one week to the next. After six years her hourly rate increases to $11.38 an hour. These severe wage reductions are clearly unorthodox and exploitative, particularly for workers in a province with such high costs of living.

If a worker manages to work 30 hours a week, her yearly earnings would be $15,980. If she works 40 hours a week, she would earn about $21,315. Wages for housekeepers (cleaners) have decreased by 44 percent from what had been bargained under the Health Facilities Collective Agreement contract. This is 26 percent less than the national average for this same work.

Under these new rates, B.C. dropped to the lowest pay scale in the country— and not by a few percentage points, but by substantial amounts (i.e., between

14 and 39 percent less than anywhere else in Canada). Even relatively low wage provinces like Newfoundland, Prince Edward Iland, and New Brunswick pay considerably more an hour than the wages negotiated under the Aramark/IWA contract. These wages are so low that they place the purchasing power of housekeepers, for example, at about what it was some 35 years ago.

This represents a tremendous loss for women's work by any standards. It is even more disturbing when one compares the wages negotiated by the IWA under the Aramark contract to current wages for the same occupations under a standard IWA contract for male cleaners. Under the IWA Master Agreement (2000-2003) janitors are paid $21.92 an hour, which is 2.1 times greater than the wage rate negotiated for hospital cleaners. In this context, the Aramark/IWA agreement is not only a setback for pay equity, it is also a complete rejection of the concept that women and men should be paid equally for the same work—an understanding that has been in place in Canada since the 1950s. Even as far back as the IWA Master Agreement of 1983-1986, wage rates for cleaners were not as low as what has been negotiated for the women working at Vancouver Hospital. In the mid-1980s, almost 20 years ago, the IWA negotiated $13.48 an hour for its janitors (male)—$3.23 an hour more than it is willing to negotiate for its cleaners (female) today.

While the reduction in wages and the loss of guaranteed hours of work are the most dramatic and obvious changes under the IWA/Aramark contract, additional concessions to the employer radically change other aspects of compensation for health care support work. For example, pensions, long-term disability plans, and maternity leave provisions have been eliminated and vacations are reduced to the two weeks mandated by the *Employment Standards Act*.

THE IWA AND THE UNION MOVEMENT

The relationship between Aramark and Local 1-3567 of the IWA, as established through this "voluntary recognition agreement," sets an alarming precedent for employer/union collusion in the organizing of B.C.'s health care workers. Because the agreement was in place before the employees had worked a single day, they had no opportunity to have a say in their union representation or in negotiating their collective agreement. Union/management collusion is also evident in the "statement of partnership" at the beginning of the agreement. In this commitment, the IWA accepts "joint responsibility for the profitability and competitiveness of Aramark."

Traditionally, trade unions in Canada are independent of employer or government influence. In stark contrast to those countries where "company unions" or employer-dominated unions are typical (such as Mexico), Canadian workers have had the right to choose their own union. They have also had a say in setting the terms and conditions of their collective agreements. Exceptions to this exist in the building trades and in forestry work, where work is short-term and specific trade unions have long established records in protecting workers rights in these industries. In these limited cases setting up a "voluntary recognition agreement" between the employer and the trade union before the work actually begins protects workers from having to build a union from the beginning each time a new short-term job begins. In fact, it guarantees them the wages and benefits already standard in the sector. But this is a very different circumstance from the work in hospitals, where voluntary recognition agreements are undercutting wages in an established sector and where an ongoing work relationship with a different union already exists.

What is clear, however, is that as more time passed, multi-national service corporations became firmly entrenched within the health support sector, and lower wages and benefits for contracted-out support workers are becoming the norm. This has put tremendous pressure on the HEU and other established health care unions to negotiate significant concessions as employers use the threat of contracting out or decertification of the union to pressure workers to accept contract concessions.

A DOMINO EFFECT

The B.C. government's actions—to set aside pay equity gains for women in traditionally low-wage categories—is a precedent that will likely have repercussions that will go well beyond health care workers. Typically when public sector wages and conditions of work deteriorate significantly, as they are doing in this case, it sets the example for the private sector. If the government reduces women's wages, it is a signal to the private sector that they too can set aside arguments about the necessity for decent wages for women's work.

In fact, the actions by the B.C. government have influenced legislation in other parts of the country. In both Quebec and Ontario new Liberal governments passed legislation modeled on Bill 29. In Ontario, Bill 8, the so-called *Commitment to the Future of Medicare Act* was introduced in November 2003. The third section of this bill gives the health minister broad, binding and unprecedented powers to intervene in health facility administration including the ability to issue directives that override collective agreement language and force facilities to contract-out health support services.[3] In Quebec, Bill 31, passed by the National Assembly in December of 2003, has an even broader mandate. It covers all unionized workers, overrides job security provisions, removes successorship rights, and eliminates provisions requiring new employers to retain the terms of the existing agreements for a minimum of one year.

While government intervention in labour relations has a long history, legislation aimed at altering collective agreement provisions is rare and where it does occur, it is usually limited to changes in compensation rates.[4] In an analysis of Bill 29, Joseph Rose, a professor in the Faculty of Business at McMaster University, noted only three other occasions in Canadian history where governments infringed on statutory or collectively bargained job security provisions. In all of these cases government interventions were intended "to limit or foreclose" future bargaining on job security; they did not "void collective agreement provisions during their term."[5] In this respect the provisions of Bill 29 are highly unusual, and yet quite clearly they established a new precedent that is taking hold across the country.[6]

CONCLUSION

British Columbia has since been condemned by a United Nations committee report looking at discrimination against women. It specifically noted the large poverty rates for single mothers, Aboriginal women and women of colour and the negative impact government cuts were having on women and girls. The privatization initiatives such as the ones in health care appear to deepen an already disturbing trend. Not only will women's wages in some sectors deteriorate relative to men's, but they are also likely to exacerbate an already large and growing gap between different of classes of women workers.

A full explaination of this issue is available through the Canadian Centre of Policy Alternatives–BC. The title of the study by Marjorie Griffin Cohen and Marcy Cohen is A Return to Wage Discrimination: Pay Equity Losses Through the Privatization of Health Care.

Marcy Cohen is retired from working as senior researcher at the Hospital Employees Union. She continues to published articles on working conditions and work restructuring in long-term care in BC.

Marjorie Griffin Cohen is an economist who is professor of Political Science and Gender, Sexuality and Women's Studies at Simon Fraser University. Her most recent book is Public Policy for Women: The State, Income Security, and Labour Market Issues *(2009).*

[1]Information for this section comes from McIntyre and Mustel Research Ltd.
[2]Aramark and IWA Local 1-3567, Partnership Agreement, July 17, 2003
[3]Sack Goldbaltt Mitchell, Memorandum re: Bill 8, the *Commitment to the Future of Medicare Act*, December 15, 2003, page pages 6-7.
[4]Affidavits of Joseph B. Rose in The Supreme Court of British Columbia in reference to Plaintiffs: The Health Services and Support-Facilities Subsector Bargaining Association, The Health Serices and Suport-Community Health Bargaining Association, The Nurses' Bargaining Association, The Hospital Employees' Union, The British Columbia Government and Service Employees' Union, The British Columbia Nurses' Union, Josephine Chauhan, Janine Brooker, Amaljeet Jhand, Leona Fraser, Marguerite Amy McCrea, Sally Lorrain Stevenson and Sharleen G.V. Decilla; and Defendant: Her Majesty the Queen in Right of the Province of British Columbia, page 15.
[5]Ibid., page 17.

[6]HEU and other unions affected by Bill 29, have launched a Charter of Rights court challenge under three provisions of the Charter: equality rights (Section 15), freedom of association (Section 2) and security of persons (Section 7). This challenge was turned down at the B.C. Supreme Court in September of 2003, but the unions will be taking the case as far as the Supreme Court of Canada. A positive ruling by the Supreme Court would be very significant in that it would establish a legal precedent for the recognition of gender based wage discrimination as a violation of equality rights under the Charter.

REFERENCES

Marjorie Griffin Cohen, *Destroying Pay Equity: The Effects of Privatizing Health Care in British Columbia.* Vancouver: HEU, March 2003.

Marjorie Griffin Cohen, *Do Comparisons Between Hospital Support Workers and Hospitality Workers Make Sense?* Vancouver: HEU, 2001.

Marjorie Griffin Cohen and Marcy Cohen. "Privatization: A Strategy for Eliminating Pay Equity in Health Care." *Social Reproduction: Feminist Political Economy Challenges Neo-liberalism.* Eds. Kate Bezanson and Meg Luxton. Montreal: McGill-Queen, 2006.

David Fairey, *An Inter-Provincial Comparison of Pay Equity Strategies and Results Involving Hospital Service and Support Workers.* Revised ed. Vancouver: Trade Union Research Bureau, Jan. 2003.

Sylvia Fuller, *The Case for Pay Equity.* Vancouver: Canadian Centre for Policy Alternatives–B.C., 2001.

Nitya Iyer, *Working Through the Wage Gap: Report of the Task Force on Pay Equity.* Victoria: B.C. Government, Feb. 28, 2002.

McIntyre and Mustel Research Ltd. *HEU Member Profile Survey.* Vancouver: McIntyre and Mustel, March 2002.

JANET MOSHER AND PAT EVANS

Welfare Policy

A Critical Site of Struggle for Women's Safety

ACCESS TO ADEQUATE FINANCIAL RESOURCES that is dependent neither upon the batterer's co-operation nor labour market participation is critical to the safety of women abused in their intimate relationships. Without such access many abused women and their children remain locked in abusive relationships with no hope of escape, or are forced to trade subjugation to abuse for abject poverty, homelessness, and profound social exclusion. Yet often our strategies to aid women in abusive relationships have been premised upon too narrow a conception of safety, focusing on ending the physical assaults, rather than on ensuring that women have access to the means to meet their basic human needs of shelter, food, transportation, and belonging (Davies; Schechter). Adequate, non-punitive and respectfully bestowed welfare benefits must be understood as a crucial component of Canadian anti-violence policy and strategies.

Disturbingly however, the direction of welfare reforms of the past decade, propelled by concerns about welfare dependency and reducing social spending, has been to restrict access, reduce benefits, impose workfare, and dramatically increase the scrutiny under which recipients must live. Concerned by these major changes to social assistance policy, and aware of the emerging American research documenting the harmful impact upon abused women of similar welfare reforms in the United States, we undertook a research project to learn from women of their experiences with Ontario's new welfare regime. The research included qualitative interviews with 64 women who had been in an abusive relationship with intimate partner/s and received social assistance (either Ontario Works [OW] or Ontario Disability Support Program [ODSP]) at some point since 1995, when major reforms were initiated through changes to existing regulations and subsequently through new legislation, the *Ontario Works Act, 1997* and the *Ontario Disability Support Program Act, 1997* (Mosher, Evans, Little, Ontario Association of Interval and Transition Houses & Ontario Social Safety Network). We discovered very quickly as they shared their experiences how powerfully social assistance can operate to make women less, rather than more, safe. When social assistance intersects with policies and practices in other arenas (such as immigration, criminal justice, child welfare) it constrains and complicates even further the limited options women are able to exercise as they attempt to end the violence in their lives. Our findings not only confirm the central importance of access to adequate state income support for women's safety, but detail the myriad ways in which Ontario's present welfare system is failing abused women and shoring up the power of abusive men.

As women contemplated the complex question of whether to stay or leave, many were acutely aware that they could not support themselves and their children through labour market participation. A number of women had no family or friends they could turn to for support and assistance, and for many, this was wholly or in part attributable to the social isolation their batterers had enforced. Perhaps not surprisingly then, several of the women expressed gratitude for the welfare benefits they were receiving, observing that they had absolutely nowhere else to turn and no other possible avenue of financial support. While on the one hand this makes clear that welfare can and does provide a crucial avenue of escape for abused women, it is equally clear that inadequate rates and a punitive and demeaning environment compel some women to return to abusive relationships while compelling others to never leave.

The rates are profoundly inadequate having been slashed by 21.6 percent in 1995, resulting in a maximum monthly benefit for a single person of $520. No increases occurred again until 2004, and since that time, very modest increases have been implemented, leading by 2010 to a maximum of $592/month for a single person. Women reported regularly going without adequate food, shelter, transportation or clothing, and several women were without phones. They were hugely concerned about the impact of poverty and the stigma of welfare for their children. Similar to our findings, several American studies have also found that leaving an abusive relationship greatly increases the risk of food insufficiency and homelessness (Tolman and Rosen).

Nine of the women we interviewed remained in abusive relationships because they knew how much they would receive on welfare and felt that they could not provide adequately for themselves and their children; seven women reported returning to an abusive relationship in situations where their struggle to survive on welfare was *the* reason, or one of the one main reasons, for returning; and six women were contemplating returning at the time of the interview or had considered returning to the abusive relationship because of the difficulties of surviving on welfare. Women also commonly referred to their friends and other women who they had come to know in shelters or elsewhere and offered their observation that many women were remaining in or returning to abusive relationships because of the welfare rates. Earlier research undertaken by the Ontario Association of Interval and Transition Houses (OAITH) shortly after a 21.6 percent rate cut was introduced in the mid-90s came to the same conclusion; all of the shelters surveyed reported that women were remaining within, or returning to, abusive relationships as a direct result of the decrease in financial assistance. It is clear that the horrendous "choice" confronting many women is that of continuing to endure abuse or face the inadequate provision of the means essential to bare human sustenance, let alone necessary for human flourishing or full citizenship.

It is also important to pay attention to the even starker choice facing women without legal status in Canada. In Ontario, women without legal status are categorically ineligible for social assistance benefits, unless an application for permanent residence or refugee status has been initiated. The denial of welfare benefits leaves some women with virtually no choice but to remain in the abusive relationship (Mosher). As was painfully clear from our interviews, inadequate rates diminish, even extinguish hope. We collectively give abusive men more power—we enable their taunts of "you can't live without me"—because we have failed to make adequate financial support available to abused women.

Our research also makes clear that not only the adequacy of rates, but other features of the social assistance delivery system play a critical role in relation to women's safety. Two centrally important features, both integral to the reforms of the mid-1990s, are workfare and the policy of zero tolerance for welfare fraud. In 1997 the *Ontario Works Act* came into effect, tying eligibility for social assistance to participation in a range of activities geared to provide not the best, but the shortest, route to employment. Workfare applies to those considered "employable" with temporary deferrals for those caring for children too young to be in school part-time or other family members requiring care, or to anyone who "has declared himself or herself to be a victim of family violence."

Contrary to the assumptions of mandatory workfare, women in our study viewed paid work as critical to improving their economic security. What we learned from women, however, was that workfare failed women ready for employment as surely as it failed women who were not job-ready. While paid work may be particularly important in order to lessen or remove the power of violent partners (Brush), seeking employment may be impossible because of the impacts of abuse, and/or because women's efforts risk intensifying the abuse (Moe and Bell). The findings from our study document with chilling clarity the kind of interference and harm that women experience when they are employed or try to find employment. Equally clear from our findings are the many ways in which the practices of workfare operate to ignore these harms.

Partners used a number of tactics to sabotage women's efforts to get and maintain a job or to improve their employment prospects. These included burning books, harassing women by repeated telephone calls or visits at work, and leaving them without transportation home when women worked night shifts. Women were forbidden to take a job, go to school, and made to feel guilty about the care of children and household. Talking about employment was risky and could provoke an escalation of abuse, and many women were subjected to continual put-downs about their ability to hold a job. The control exercised over women who were newcomers to Canada, especially those who were sponsored, was particularly powerful as partners were usually well positioned to isolate them, at times completely, from members of their own communities. Women were very clear about the nature and purpose of the control the men exercised. Capturing a common refrain, one woman explained: "He never permits me to master any skills. I guess he might be thinking that if I live a life of a simpleton, it would be easier for him to dominate me and put me down."

Our research also documented the physical and psychological harm women suffered. Roughly half reported serious and continuing impacts that included; chronic and severe back pain and headaches, depression, anxiety, suicidal thoughts, sleep problems, ulcers and eating disorders. In addition to their own health issues, they were also concerned about the effects of violence and poverty on their children.

How did women fare in relation to workfare requirements? Some women reported that they were pleased that workfare was in place, and hopeful of the help it might provide. With few exceptions, women spoke of their considerable frustration and great disappointment. They found little support beyond resumé workshops and were rarely given any help to locate the unpaid community service that was required of them. Also, their own efforts to access education and training were often thwarted. In recounting her unsuccessful attempts to get her worker to refer her to a training program, a woman explains that it made her feel: "Like you're a lost cause and there's no programs. Just keep you on welfare, keep you down, keep you low ... you end up living in that rut...." A woman who works thirty hours a week and has her low wages topped up by welfare wants to access computer training in her spare time but is told she is not eligible: "If I want to take some training, I have to save money. And with two kids some times that is hard...."

Other women experienced the workfare requirement as an almost unbearable additional pressure on lives that were already replete with stress from the impacts of abuse on their own health, the health of their children, and safety concerns. Despite recent hospitalizations for nervous breakdowns one woman struggles to meet the requirement of 120 hours a month of unpaid community service. Suffering from severe back problems and depression, another explains that she had no help from her worker to access a medical deferral. Yet another woman sees no option other than to apply for ODSP because she cannot manage the workfare requirements: unable to bear physical proximity to people, she had to flee an interview when told that the employees were like "one big happy family." Proof of a full-time job search was required, despite the fact that one woman attended university full-time; falling ill, she was terrified that benefits would be cut off because she could not produce the necessary list of job contacts.

Workfare can endanger the security of women and children. A worker insisted that one young mother leave her infant in the care of an abusive boyfriend and then contacted him directly to inquire whether it was true that he had abused her. In apparent contravention of the legislation, several women were expected to meet their workfare requirements outside their children's school hours: "But as soon as she went to school ... I had to look for a job—even weekends, or anything I could get." A woman looks back on her struggle to meet the obligations of workfare, and at the same time, the needs of her children:

> *I find that if you have children … they push you out the door to go to work. I understand that the government is trying to cut back, but the people that do have children need to be with their children…. I was working and I had no problem with working but it was also a very difficult thing to do with three children especially with what my children had been through in the past. And that's when my problems began with my kids because … I wasn't home for my children and the only type of employment I could find was a job where I was working in the evenings. It's not easy to just go out the door and find a 9:00 to 4:00 job where your kids are at school. It's really hard.*

Given this discussion, it was particularly troubling to find that less than one quarter of the women we interviewed were aware that they could be deferred from workfare because of the violence they experienced. In fact, only nine of 55 women knew about this possibility. Twenty-two reported that workfare requirements were applied, although their worker knew of the abuse. Seven women were deferred, but most frequently for reasons unrelated to the abuse, such as the age of their children or other medical conditions. Two women were told about the deferral but did not want one. The findings from our study show, so very clearly, that the deferral does not meet its presumed intention of providing some necessary time free from participation requirements for women who have experienced violence.

While it is evident that the possibility of a deferral on the grounds of family violence is not working for women, it is also not easily repaired (Mosher et al.; Lyon). Even if appropriate information is made available, many women do not feel safe in disclosing the abuse they have experienced to welfare workers. The reasons given for not disclosing the abuse include the prospect of being judged negatively, being suspected of lying, and having to answer intrusive questions and provide documentation (police/medical/shelter reports) that they do not have. But there are other compelling reasons. Women have legitimate fears of potential reports to child welfare authorities, retaliation by the abuser who may learn of the disclosure, the launch of an investigation into whether she is living with a spouse and risking not only an assessment of an over-payment but a possible fraud charge. Additionally, for newcomers, there is grave concern that such a disclosure may further jeopardize their status in Canada. Rather than attempting to set up deferrals to apply to abused women as a separate category of those who receive social assistance, regulations and practices need to be in place that resonate with, rather than operate against, the realities of women's lives which include the prevalence of violence in their lives, their needs and the needs of their children, employment barriers, and their own aspirations. In order for Ontario Works to work for and to be fair to women, a shift must be made to high quality programs in the context of voluntary participation and decent levels of income support.

As noted above, an additional feature of the reformed social assistance regime in Ontario that has had a profoundly negative effect on all recipients, with particularly pernicious effects on abused women, is the policy of zero tolerance for fraud. Having constructed a problem of rampant welfare fraud—a problem not borne out by even its own data—the government proceeded to introduce a series of additional measures to detect and punish fraud (Mosher and Hermer). Included among these measures were expanded powers for eligibility review officers, information sharing agreements, consolidated verification procedures, a toll -free welfare fraud snitch line and increased penalties upon conviction (a lifetime ban on receipt of benefits was introduced by the Conservative government but later revoked by the Liberal government, but in conjunction with the introduction of a new get tough on fraud policy directive).

The system's focus on fraud, and the more general denigration of those dependent upon the system, led many women to draw both explicit and implicit parallels between life in an abusive relationship and life on welfare. Women described being mistrusted, being constantly under surveillance and treated as criminals, as prisoners and as garbage. As with their husbands who did not trust them and constantly monitored them to ensure compliance, women in receipt of welfare assistance are not trusted by the deliverers of the program and are constantly monitored to ensure their compliance with an impossibly complex and impenetrable set of rules governing welfare receipt. Many women felt routinely demeaned, dehumanized and disrespected in their interactions with the system. The message that they were stupid, incompetent, lazy, not fully human, and unworthy was disturbingly reminiscent of the negative messages delivered by their batterers. As one woman explained,

> Okay, you've left. You've made this great decision, but we're [welfare] gonna' keep you this big because you're never gonna' get anywhere else.... I've left an abusive man to deal with an abusive worker.... Like you don't have to make me feel bad. I already feel bad … and you're groveling all the time. Well, that's the situation I just left. And I'm sure that there are lots of women who feel that way. All I did was grovel. Now I have to beg you?

Just as in their abusive relationships, the welfare system also exercises a form of power through its control over access to information. Many women drew parallels between the lack of control over their lives experienced on welfare with the lack of control felt in their abusive relationships. Distressingly, some women returned to abusive relationships because they had greater control over their lives in the abusive relationship; the welfare system, especially as it interacted with other systems (child welfare, immigration, criminal justice, family law) was wildly unpredictable and uncontrollable.

Furthermore, the welfare fraud regime operates in a very direct way to shore up the power of abusive men. Current or past partners threaten to report, and in some cases actually do report allegations of fraud to welfare offices; they can do so anonymously and with absolutely no repercussions for false reports. The potential or actual suspension or cancellation of benefits, the possibility of an overpayment being assessed and the looming threat of a criminal fraud charge, operate to keep women entrapped and silent about the abuse. Women described how accepting small amounts of money, or even a few groceries, could lead to their literal entrapment. So too, could the formation of a relationship itself. One woman on welfare met a man and they began to spend more and more time together. She was very hopeful that a permanent relationship would develop and that he would be her "ticket off welfare." But when she suggested he move in and share expenses, he flatly refused. He became more and more abusive, constantly threatening that he would call welfare and report that he was living with her, although in fact he refused to commit to the relationship and rather than providing for her, sponged off of her. However, because they did spend a lot of time together, he may well have been found to be a "spouse" for welfare purposes, creating the possibility not only of her being cut off and assessed with an over-payment, but charged criminally with fraud. In her words:

> I mean you can't even get a guy outta' your house because now he has all the power in the world. Welfare fraud, welfare, that's what it's all about. They just gained the biggest stronghold they could ever gain and there'll be so many women that will be affected by that…. I just got into an abusive relationship that I could no longer get out of because now someone could accuse me of fraud…. Now I was bound because… that just gave him the control…. See that's the whole problem with how it's set-up now 'cause now women can't get out. Now they are definitely trapped. They are trapped … they're going to basically life sentence you when you need some help.

Our study, consistent with both historical and contemporary research in the United States, makes clear that access to adequate financial support is crucial to women's ability to leave and remain separated from their abusive partners (Davies; Lyon; Raphael). Our research also demonstrates that attention to adequacy of benefits alone is insufficient in formulating sound public policy that takes anti-violence objectives seriously. The conditioning of benefits upon mandated employment or employment readiness activities flagrantly ignores what is known about both the dangers employment can pose for abused women, and about the tremendous importance of access to meaningful employment in the long-term for women's safety and ability to live violence-free lives. Building a system upon a presumption of fraud emboldens abusive men while entrapping abused women.

Disturbingly, Ontario's 2005 *Domestic Violence Action Plan*—its blueprint for protecting women and children—is silent on the links between poverty and violence and on the harms of current welfare policies. While modest initiatives in relation to housing and employment are included, the plan fails to take seriously the evidence that violence makes women poor and keeps them poor, and that the realities of social assistance can be harsher than the abuse. As such, the plan fails to create for women one of the crucial pathways to safety: access to a system of income support grounded in fundamental human rights.

The support of the Social Sciences and Humanities Research Council in funding this research is gratefully acknowledged.

Janet Mosher is an Associate Professor at Osgoode Hall Law School, York University. Violence against women, the welfare state and access to justice are her primary research interests.

Pat Evans is an Professor Emerita at the School of Social Work, Carleton University. Her research and writing highlights women's issues related to welfare and paid and unpaid work.

REFERENCES

Brush, Lisa. "Battering, Traumatic Stress, and Welfare-to-Work Transition." *Violence Against Women* 6 (10): (2000): 1039-1065.

Davies, Jill. "Policy Blueprint on Domestic Violence and Poverty." *Building Comprehensive Solutions to Domestic Violence.* 2002. Publication #15. Accessed June 30, 2006. Web.

Lyon, E. "Welfare and Domestic Violence Against Women: Lessons from Research." *National Electronic Network on Violence Against Women.* 2002. Accessed June 30, 2006. Web.

Moe, Angela and Myrtle Bell. "Abject Economics: The Effects of Battering and Violence on Women's Work and Employability." *Violence Against Women* 10.1 (2004): 29-55.

Mosher, Janet, Pat Evans, Margaret Little, Ontario Association of Interval and Transition Houses and Ontario Social Safety Network. *Walking on Eggshells: Abused Women's Experiences of Ontario's Welfare System.* 2004. Accessed June 30, 2006. Web.

Mosher, Janet. "The Complicity of the State in the Intimate Abuse of Immigrant Women." *Racialized Migrant Women in Canada Essays on Health, Violence, and Equity.* Ed. Vijay Agnew. Toronto: University of Toronto Press, 2009: 41-69.

Mosher, Janet and Joe Hermer. *Welfare Fraud: The Constitution of Social Assistance as Crime* (Law Reform Commission of Canada) 2005. Accessed June 30, 2006. Web.

National Council of Welfare. *Welfare Incomes 2004.* Ottawa: National Council of Welfare, 2005.

Ontario Association of Interval and Transition Houses (OAITH). *Locked In, Left*

Out: The Impacts of the Budget Cuts on Abused Women and Their Children. Toronto: Ontario Association of Interval and Transition Houses, 1996.

Raphael, Jody. *Saving Bernice: Battered Women, Welfare, and Poverty,* Boston: Northeastern University Press, 2000.

Schechter, Susan. "Expanding Solutions for Domestic Violence and Poverty: What Battered Women with Abused Children Need from Their Advocates." *Building Comprehensive Solutions to Domestic Violence.* Publication #13 September 2000. Accessed June 30, 2006. Web.

Tolman, Richard M. and Daniel Rosen. "Domestic Violence in the Lives of Women Receiving Welfare." *Violence Against Women* 7 (2) (2001): 141-158.

DONNA BAINES

Women's Occupational Health in Social Services

Stress, Violence and Workload

IN LARGE PART, downsizing and restructuring of public sectors around the world has removed barriers to corporate infiltration and domination of markets and regions (Stanford; Panitch and Gindin; Esping-Andersen). In Canada and elsewhere, this has occurred alongside the introduction of private sector management schemes such as New Public Management, lean production, and flexible work organization (Baines 2004b; Lewchuk; Foster and Hogget). These changes have had highly gendered and disproportionately negative impacts on women.

The gendered impact on the occupational health of women workers is one area of restructuring and downsizing that has been under explored. Occupational health's preoccupation with hazards common to sites in which men work means that far less is known about the kinds of hazards encountered in "women's" work sites and during the continuity of tasks that occur as part of women's paid and unpaid work days (Feldberg, Northrup, Scott and Shannon; Hall; Messing 1999, 1998, 1995; Mergler, Brabant, Vezina and Messing; Sprout and Yassi). Indeed, little is known about the kinds of occupational health risks women encounter in traditional female job ghettos, such as care work. A few studies show that occupational health hazards typical of women's work, such as heavy workloads, violence, and stress, have increased in the public and non-profit service sector in general (Mayhew; Newhill; Wigmore; Pizzino) and that particularly high levels of workplace violence, injury, and stress exist in Canadian social services, where the work force is predominantly female, poorly paid, and a work ethic of "caring" predominates (Baines, Evans and Neysmith; Canadian Union of Public Employees; Wigmore). Possibly the most debilitating characteristic of care work is the extent to which it is saturated with the ideology of women's care as self sacrificing, elastic, and dependable regardless of working conditions or safety. Indeed, the assumption that care work is something that any woman can and should do rather than a distinct and sophisticated set of skills and knowledge (Baines et al.) is one of the reasons why wages in the sector remain low, the workforce remains insecure and easily replaced, and employers are able to extract large quantities of unpaid overtime and volunteer work from a labour force that has strong loyalties to the clients it serves.

This article summarizes the findings of a three-site study of restructuring and occupational health in a small, subsector of the social services known as development services. I will argue that health risks experienced by the predominantly female labour force have multiplied as workers struggle to maintain heavy workloads of paid and unpaid caring labour in the context of strained resources and new forms of work organization that increase health risks. The context and methods of the study will be very briefly summarized followed by a short discussion of new private sector-like forms of work organization and flexible staffing, and their impacts on women workers including stress, workload, and violence. Well documented in Europe, but under researched in Canada, the emerging issue of workplace bullying will be analyzed in relation to decreased funding, increased demands on workers and managers, and the gender-specific form it took in this study. The article ends with recommended changes in policy.

THE STUDY

The data used in this article come from a three-site study of restructured work in the developmental services, a subsector of the social services which provides community services to people with intellectual disabilities. While complete integration into all aspects of social life was the goal of de-institution in the 1970s, inadequate funding has led to new community-based forms of warehousing and stigmatization of people with intellectual disabilities, rather than their full integration into a caring community (Braddock and Hemp; Taylor and Bogdan; Traustadottir). The three agencies studied were fairly typical for the sector in that they were non-profit,[1] unionized (with the Canadian Union of Public Employees), and provided a range of services for people with intellectual disabilities.[2] Data collection involved 41 interviews,[3] eleven participant observations, and a review of agency documentation. The interview sample was predominantly female, with an average age of 37.1 years and an average of 9.9 years employment in the agency. Interview transcripts, participant observation and field notes were read multiple times for similarities and differences until themes could be developed and patterns emerged.

PRIVATE SECTOR-LIKE FORMS OF WORK ORGANIZATION

Like much of the industrialized world, since the mid-1980s, Canadian social services have been impacted by cuts in funding, privatisation, and a reshaping of the mandates, types and breadth of services (Baines 2004a; Clarke and Newman; Fabricant and Burghardt). As Lena Dominelli and Ankie Hoogvelt note, social service workers have been transformed from professionals with a fair degree of discretion and control over their work to deskilled workers who meet managerial agendas and complete repetitive, standardized tasks in set times frames. Rather than full-time, permanent, unionized jobs, new forms of private sector work organization have been introduced to public sector and non-profit social services which emphasize flexible staffing arrangements such as: "thin" staffing as in solo shifts; lean shifts (one or two workers per site, sometimes with cell phone access to workers or supervisors at other sites); split-shifts (wherein staff work an hour or two in the morning and return in the evening for a few more hours of work); part-time, contract, casual, and other forms of temporary work; and expanded reliance on volunteer work (Baines 2004b; Aronson and Sammon; Lewchuk). Economically, employees experience increased job insecurity, decreased income, and few or no benefits, while agencies save costs in these same areas. In most cases, employers have resisted the inclusion of new job categories in collective agreements, meaning that the majority of these workers do not receive the wage levels, benefits packages, and protection of a union contract. As noted earlier, the workforce in social services is predominantly female; thus one of the impacts of restructuring has been the loss of a significant number of good, public sector jobs for women and their replacement with insecure, non-standard, deskilled types of employment.

WORKLOAD: INCREASED PACE, INTENSITY AND STRESS

The level of care required by many clients increased concomitant with cuts in levels of funding and numbers of staff. Many of the clients who were the first wave of de-institutionalization are now geriatric or near-geriatric, while many of the new clients entering service programs have been living with parents who are too elderly to continue to provide care. New clients are not necessarily elderly, although most require a high level of support as they adjust to a new way of life.

Workers involved in this study reported high levels of stress connected to increased volume and intensity of workload, as well as frustration that a general lack of programming funds mean there were no resources for programming and no time to plan activities. Commenting on workload, one veteran day-program worker noted, "When I started here I had a case load of 18, and now it's 30 with no increase in resources." Another worker added, "very little of the day is spent preparing or planning because there is no time for it. Most of the day is spent flying by the seat of your pants." These situations are particularly distressing for workers who have strong emotional connections to their clients and their frustration at being unable to properly support and care for clients was palpable in many of the interviews conducted for this study. Stress is the by-product of this hectic pace and frustration. Stress-related symptoms such as headaches, fatigue, stomach disruptions, insomnia, and other sleep disruptions, depression, high blood pressure, chronic fatigue syndrome, and various body pains were reported by workers during interviews and participant observations.

Worker compensation plans developed in the early 1900s reflect the compromises that the predominantly male workforce could wrest from employers during an era of intense industrialization. Indisputable, instantaneous, workplace occurrences such as severed limbs were accepted as compensable injuries while longitudinal illnesses such as black lung and cancers were hotly contested by employers who rejected the notion that workplaces contributed to illnesses that may take years of repeated exposure before they develop. Women in care work sites experience longitudinal and cumulative stress, which may develop into health problems only after years of exposure. Like the employers and compensation boards during the early days of worker compensation plans, those currently in power continue to resist compensation for stress-related health problems claiming that there is no proof that these illnesses result directly from the conditions of work, and that compensation systems will collapse from the sheer volume of claims should stress-related and longitudinal illnesses be included in compensation plans. Currently many of the health problems women workers face in the new economy are not compensable under government plans. This reflects a further aspect of the gendering of occupational health. A direct impact of this gendering is that social service workers who are ill as a result of workplace stress are not eligible for insured time off. An indirect impact is that women must use their sick time or unpaid leaves to recover from work induced illnesses and injuries. This creates dilemmas for part-time and casual staff who usually do not have sick time benefits and cannot afford to take unpaid sick time. As a result, many women continue to work while ill, burned-out, injured or all three.

STRESS AND NON-STANDARD JOBS

Although women often gravitate towards part-time and shift work as a way to balance the gendered demands of home and employment, the workers in this study reported that they rarely received enough part-time hours to support themselves, hence stress and stress related health symptoms were particularly acute for the part-time and split shift employees involved in this study. The women employed in non-standard positions needed all the paid work they could get and reported that it was very anxiety-provoking to keep themselves free to accept extra shifts in the event that they were called in at the last minute. Processes for filling extra shifts also generated significant stress. Downloading managerial responsibilities with no increase in pay or control, one agency had staff, not supervisors, make calls to find replacements when workers called in sick. This increase in workload often occurred just before shift change, a time when clients generally require additional supports. Workers found themselves making multiple calls under pressured conditions, leaving shifts knowing that clients were upset and unsettled rather than comfortable and ready for the next part of their days and sometimes, even filling the shift themselves when replacements could not be found. In the context of a workforce that derives considerable satisfaction from caring for, not just about, clients (Baines et al.), this source of stress was particularly acute.

In one of the agencies, if a staff member turned down a shift (for example, a ten hour shift), the shift hours were counted against the maximum 70 hours part-timers were allowed to work in a two-week period. The staffer was considered to have only 60 left to work, constituting a ten-hour loss in wages. Commenting on these dilemmas, one part-timer, a sole support parent, noted that,

> *It's almost impossible to pay my bills on part-time, but that's all they'll give us. I had to take another part-time job just to support myself and my son. But, that means I am less available for my first job and they got peeved and cut back my hours. I'm scared they're going to fire me now.*

An inability to plan life outside of work and the challenges of juggling family life with irregular work commitments was another major source of stress for split-shift workers, part- timers, and multiple job holders. Finding and paying for childcare at odd hours of the day proved to be very difficult for the women involved in this study, as were long absences from children. One multiple job-holder reported that "I barely see my kids," while a part-timer wondered how her "family is going to survive." Women also reported feeling "stretched to the breaking point," "like I've got nothing left inside," and completely "burnt out." Employers like to blame stress on home life as if it somehow exists separately from the organization of paid work life. However, data from this study suggest that the feelings of intense stress reported above occur because of the way that new forms of work organization interrupt and disorganize home life, as well as how this new work organization interacts with enduring social assumptions that domestic work, and child and elder care are the private responsibilities of women.

UNPAID WORK IN THE WORKPLACE

Unpaid work takes many forms in the social services sector and in the lives of the female social service workers. Indeed, it is a messy and highly permeable concept. For female social service workers there is often a continuity of tasks, intensity and emotional content in the work performed for pay in the workplace, and for free as unpaid overtime, formal or informal volunteering, and caring for children and elderly people in the home (Baines 2004c). Downsizing of the welfare state and cutbacks in human services have intensified the paid and unpaid care workload for many women, and for social service workers in ways that are specific to the sector in which they are employed. While volunteers have long been a feature of work in the social services sector, cutbacks and restructuring have inspired employers to expand their use of the unwaged workforce. An unexpected feature of this expansion is the use of predominantly female workforce as the main source of unpaid volunteers. Workers reported expectations from management that they would take on major, even week-long, full-time unpaid volunteer assignments on top of their regular duties (in one case a week-long, out of town camping expedition). Consistent with findings across the social services sector (Baines 2004b), managers confirmed that they prefer to use their own employees as volunteers because they are more dependable, knowledgeable, and most of all, workers can be disciplined or threatened with discipline if they fail to show up, try to leave early, or perform in a substandard manner. Thus, the women involved in this study not only juggled paid caring work at their place of employment and unpaid caring work in their homes and communities, they were also pressured to perform increasing amounts of unpaid "volunteer" work in their places of employment. For workers, unpaid hours in the workplace are, in many ways, a wage cut, extending their hours of work with no increase in pay. For employers in any context, this is a bonanza. The only thing better than a work force who works for free, is a trained, highly skilled, entirely dependable workforce that works for free. For employers in the context of under-resourcing and pressures to integrate private-market efficiency, dependable paid employees working in unpaid "volunteer" capacities provide the ultimate flexible workforce—shift length, start and end time, and job content can all be determined at the last possible moment and best of all, the work force is highly skilled, familiar with local routines and clients, and works for free. Given the impetus for employers to expand their reliance on the volunteer labour of paid workers, it is likely that increasing numbers of female social service workers will experience serious the health impacts associated with high levels of overwork and stress. It is questionable whether new forms of work organization could survive without it (Baines 2004b).

VIOLENCE

Workplace violence is an expanding problem for developmental workers and the data from this study show that women absorb a disproportionate amount of it. Evidence from British Columbia shows a tenfold increase in claims from care workers (Boyd).[4] The majority of these claims are the result of injuries caused by client violence against staff.[5] The responsibility for much of this increase can be laid at the feet of flexible staffing and other forms of lean work organization which disrupt vulnerable clients and make it difficult for workers to learn site-specific violence prevention skills, daily routines, and the particular personalities of the clients with whom they work. New workers often have little contact with more experienced workers, thus reducing opportunities to learn safety and conflict reduction skills from more experienced workers, while flexible shifts mean that workers move from site to site within an agency as well as between jobs, never getting the opportunity to develop the kinds of in situ knowledge that keeps workers and clients safer. This leaves many workers and their clients at greater risk of violent assault and ill prepared to handle outbursts when they occur.

Most workers reported that they were reluctant to report violence, due, in significant part, to fear of management or co-worker retaliation and blame (Duncan, Hyndman, Estabrooks, Hesken, Humphrey, Wong, Acorn and Giovanetti; Macdonald and Sirotech; Morrison; Lanza and Carifio; Lion, Synder and Merrill). However, workers primarily feared negative repercussions for clients, many of whom they care about deeply despite the violence (Koss, Goodman, Browne, Fitzgerald, Keita and Russo; Taylor). Noting the similarities between worker tolerance of violence and partner assault in the home, a day program worker commented that she and her colleagues were as "bad as a bunch of battered women for staying with people who slap us around." Other parallels to wife assault exist. Participants in this study, like women who are battered in the home, often blame themselves for the violence (Lanza and Carifio 1991) and rightfully question whether laying charges will solve anything (see Danis; Harrell and Smith, regarding difficulties associated with laying criminal charges against male partners). Currently, in the underfunded developmental services, employers can depend on workers' capacity to translate an ethic of care and sense of vulnerability in the labour market into tolerance for unsafe working conditions including violent assault, thus relieving the employer of responsibility to enact possibly costly changes in work organization and job design. The association between under reporting, caring and violence also masks and normalizes workplace violence against women, relieving wider society of any knowledge of this growing reality and any responsibility to act.

WORKPLACE BULLYING

In one study site, efforts to discipline and motivate employees had moved into the realm of ongoing intimidation and harassment, known in the literature as bullying. Research participants reported that certain individuals and groups, such as union and environmental activists, received repetitive humiliating, taunting and insulting behaviour at the hands of management, and sometimes at the hands of a small group of workers overtly aligned with management.[6] Most of this bullying was highly gendered as female workers were repeatedly taunted for their body weight, miscarriages, emotionality, sentimentality, unattractive appearance, or a combination of these factors. The men interviewed for this study confirmed that bullying existed but that they had not been victims. One of the men knew that bullying was a problem for his some of his closest female colleagues but sensed that his gender insulated him from becoming a direct target. Indeed, workplace bullying operates in the same larger social context as other gendered forms of aggression in which women's more marginal position within the economy, political apparatus, and criminal justice systems mean that they more likely to be victims, in part because they have little access to deterrence, protection and redress.

A work environment that is bullying can foster widespread harassment by managers and co-workers (Tehrani; Einarson 1999) producing a climate that is traumatic to all who are present including workers who are not even remotely involved in the interactions and clients who may happen to be near by. Research in Europe shows that overall, bullying environments produce more work related stress than all other work-related stressors put together (Einarsen 1999; Zapf, Knorz and Mulla; Niedl). In tandem with these findings, workers involved in this study were concerned about violence and heavy workloads; however, bullying dominated their workplace priorities and they reported alarmingly high levels of stress and mental health impacts.

Bullying is a growing phenomenon in the restructured public sector, particularly where managers are over-stretched and under-skilled, and/or imported from the private sector with little knowledge of the logics and caring relationships that characterize the public and non-profit service sector (Tehrani; Zapf et al 1996; Niedl; UNISON). Research in the UK shows that bullying has taken over from pay as the top concern among workers (Anaova). One of the most debilitating aspects of bullying is that it is difficult to address, particularly in situations where management is participating in the persecution of a group or individual. Victims, and workers not even directly involved in the situation, fear retaliation if they raise concerns and feel powerless to resist. Coupled with increasingly heavy workloads and pro-business managers who may not have the skill or time to address the challenge of today's public and non-profit environments, there is ample reason to believe that bullying will become a more frequent workplace health hazard.

CONCLUSIONS AND POLICY RECOMMENDATIONS

The workplace is rarely thought of as the source of women's health concerns (Messing 1998) and yet the findings discussed in this article suggests that women's occupational health concerns have increased with the introduction of funding cuts and new private-sector models of work organization. Poor working conditions and poor occupational health in the social services sector contribute to low workplace morale and an overall lowering of expectations among the predominantly female workforce. This aids in the creation of a low demand, compliant workforce and undercuts women's capacity to improve their working conditions and labour's capacity to mobilize their increasingly female membership. Leo Panitch and Sam Gindin argue that labour's capacity to assert improvements for workers is antagonistic to neoliberal agendas of unregulated labour markets, hence curtailing women's expanding participation in public sector unions is likely an intended, although not explicit, goal of new forms of social service work organization. Finally, consistent with the creation of a residual welfare state, the expansion of a low-wage, low demand workforce willing even to perform unpaid labour is essential to the profitability of this sector as portions of it are spun off to for-profit enterprises.

The predominantly female social service unions active in this sector have advocated for the inclusion of stress, workload, and violence as compensable health concerns and the findings of this study suggest that these changes are long overdue. Unions and the participants in this study also favour solutions such as increased levels of funding arrangements and full staffing—full complements of full-time, permanent, well waged, fully trained, fully resourced, well supported staff. Referring to the demand for increased staff and funding levels, one young activist asserted, "what we really want is the right to supply people with enough supports." This comment underscores the way that, in this sector, improved occupational health dovetails with themes of caring and that improved occupational health is likely to have reciprocal benefits for clients and communities. However, improved levels of funding and staffing are not sufficient solutions, as women's occupational health concerns in this sector predate restructuring and downsizing.

In order to address the roots of stress, overwork, and violence issues in social service workplaces, the consensus that caring equals endless tolerance for poor working conditions must be broken. Unions, workers and employers of goodwill must challenge the notion that putting up with work organization that impairs the health of workers is a good way to demonstrate caring for clients. Just as feminist campaigns against wife assault assert that women do not deserve to be hit, workplace campaigns must assert that no one should have to work under conditions that include violence, bullying, and high levels of negative stress. Neither in the long- nor the short-term are these kinds of conditions in the best interests of workers, clients, or communities. As an adjunct to fair funding, grounded in a strong sense of entitlement to healthy workplaces, occupational health regulatory bodies must be renewed and revived to aggressively monitor workplaces, enact preventive strategies, and hold management (and funders) responsible for ensuring safe and healthy workplaces. Building on the proactive approaches of some of the more comprehensive workplace harassment policies, themselves borne of the activism of generations of women, workplace models should be developed that are proactive and promote the prevention of women's occupational health hazards through the nurturing of healthy work cultures and work designs that reflect the lived realities of women's work lives, their sources of stress, and health concerns (Baines forthcoming). Regulatory bodies must hold agencies liable and enact strict penalties in situations where employers permit environments in which high levels of stress, violence and heavy workloads are part of the everyday work lives of women (and some men).

It may appear that employers have little incentive to participate in these strategies. After all, they currently have a relatively compliant and caring workforce that absorbs workplace stress, violence and funding cuts. Moreover the link between gender and caring means that employers can rely on female workers to extend their working hours infinitely and absorb workplace stress and violence in the name of caring for clients. However, liability rates are soaring in this sector, sick time is at near-crisis levels, and staff turn over rates are high and rising. Thus, employers have ample incentive to accept measures that improve employee health at the same time as they provide much needed improvements in the quality of life of clients and their communities. Ironically, it is not likely that a commitment to fair treatment of women will compel public sector and non-profit employers to address women's growing occupational health issues. Rather, it may be the crippling cost of compensation insurance that may cause employers to adopt measures that reduce injury and illness in the predominantly female care work labour force.

The author would like to thank the entire research team and dedicate this article to Karen Hadley whose passion for social justice continues to inspire.

Donna Baines teaches in Labour Studies and Social Work at McMaster University. Her research is in the area of women's paid and unpaid care work, restructuring social services, and anti-oppressive and social justice social work.

[1]The non-profit services sector in Canada receives approximately 85 percent of its funding from government, but has been loosely unregulated in terms of quality and accountability until recently. These agencies can opt out of portions of provincial health and safety standards such as paying into government worker compensation plans (although they must then purchase private compensation insurance) and enacting the mandated joint worker-management health and safety committees.
[2]Study sites were sought that could provide the greatest difference and similarity.
[3]Workers of colour and youth have been identified in the literature as more vulnerable to stress and injury, therefore a small sample of each of these groups was interviewed. This data has been analyzed and will be written about separately.
[4]Boyd notes that during the period he studied (1982 to 1991) an increase in the number of workers covered by the provincial workers' compensation program may account for about 20 percent of this increase.
[5]Workplace violence is perpetrated by a range of individuals including management, clients, workers and current or past domestic partners of workers (Santana and Fisher). In this study, client violence against workers was explored.
[6]Research identifies the following risk factors as predictors of a bullying or traumatic environment: low morale, job insecurity, conflicting goals and priorities, and negative leadership behaviour in managers (Brown 2002: 161). All were present in the bullying site discussed in this article.

REFERENCES

Ananova. "Bullying is the worst problem in workplace." *Ananova News Service* (September 2002): 2.

Aronson, J. and S. Sammon. "Practice Amid Social Service Cuts and Restructuring: Working With the Contradictions of Small Victories." *Canadian Social Work Review* 18 (2) (2001): 9-24.

Baines, C., P. M. Evans and S. M. Neysmith. "Caring: Its Impact on the Lives of Women." *Women's Caring. Feminist Perspectives on Social Welfare.* Ed. C. Baines, P. M. Evans and S. M. Neysmith. Toronto: Oxford Press, 1998. 3-22.

Baines, D. "Pro-Market, Non-Market: The Dual Nature of Organizational Change in Social Services Delivery." *Critical Social Policy* 24 (1) (2004a): 5-29.

Baines, D. "Caring for Nothing: Work Organisation and Unwaged Labour in Social Services." *Work, Employment and Society* 18(2) (2004b): 267-295.

Baines, D. "Seven Kinds of Work—Only One Paid: Raced, Gendered and Restructured Care Work in the Social Services Sector." *Atlantis. A Women's Studies Journal* 28 (2) (2004c): 19-28.

Baines, D. "Criminalizing the Care Work Zone? The Gendered Dynamics of Using Legal and Administrative Strategies to Confront Workplace Violence." *Social Justice: A Journal of Crime, Conflict and World Order* 32 (2) (2005): 132-150.

Baines, D., K. Hadley, S. Pollack, B. Slade, A. S. Brooker, K. Fay, W. Lewchuk, S. Preston, and D. Dimatrova. *Improving Work Organization to Reduce Injury and Illness: Social Services, Stress, Violence and Workload—Final Report.* Hamilton: McMaster University Institute for Work in a Global Society, 2002.

Boyd, N. "Violence in the Workplace in British Columbia: A Preliminary Investigation. *Canadian Journal of Criminology* (October 1995): 491-519.

Braddock, D. and Hemp, R. "Towards Family and Community: Mental Retardation Services in Massachusetts, New England and the United States." *Mental Retardation* 34 (4) (1997): 241-56.

Brown, O. "Why Workplace Bullying and Violence Are Different: Protecting Employees from Both." *Violence at Work. Causes, Patterns and Prevention.* Ed. Gil, M., B. Fisher and V. Bowie. London: Willan Publishing, 2002. 151-160.

Canadian Policy Research Networks (CPRN). *The Non-Profit Sector: Struggling to Make Work Pay.* Ottawa: Canadian Policy Research Networks, Inc., 2003.

Canadian Union of Public Employees (CUPE). *Overloaded and Undergird. Report of Ontario Social Services Work Environment Survey.* Ottawa: CUPEHealth and Safety Branch, 1999.

Clarke, J. and J. Newman. *The Managerial State.* London: Sage, 1997.

Danis, Fran S. "The Criminalization of Domestic Violence: What Social Workers Need to Know." *Social Work* 48 (2) (2003): 237-245.

Dominelli, L. and A. Hoogvelt. "Globalization and the Technocratization of Social Work." *Critical Social Policy* 16 (1996): 45-62.

Duncan, S. M., K. Hyndman, C. A. Estabrooks, K. Hesketh, C. K. Humphrey, J. S. Wong, S. Acorn, and P. Giovannetti. "Nurse's Experience of Violence in Alberta and British Columbia Hospitals." *Canadian Journal of Nursing Research* 32 (4) (2001): 57-78.

Einarsen, S. "The Nature and Cause of Bullying at Work." *Journal of Manpower* 20 (1/2) (1999): 379-401.

Esping-Andersen, G. *Social Foundations of Postindustrial Economies.* Oxford: Oxford University Press, 1999.

Fabricant, M. B. and S. Burghardt. *The Welfare State Crisis and the Transformation of Social Service Work.* New York: M. E. Sharpe, 1992.

Feldberg, G., D. Northrup, M. Scott and T. Shannon. *Ontario Women's Work Related Health Survey Descriptive Summary.* Toronto: York University Centre for Health Studies and the Institute for Social Research, 1996.

Foster, D. and P. Hogget. "Change in the Benefits Agency: Empowering the Exhausted Worker?" *Work, Employment and Society* 13 (1) (1999): 19-39.

Hall, E. M. "Double Exposure: The Combined Impact of the Home and Work Environments on Psychosomatic Strain in Swedish Women and Men." *International Journal of Health Services* 22 (2) (1992): 239-60.

Harrell, A. and B. E. Smith. "Effects of Restraining Orders on Domestic Violence Victims." *Do Arrests and Restraining Orders Work?* Ed. E.S. Buzawa and C. G. Buzawa. Thousand Oaks, CA: Sage, 1996. 214-242.

Koss, M. P., L. A. Goodman, A. Browne, L. F. Fitzgerald, G. P. Keita, and N.F. Russo. *No Safe Haven: Male Violence Against Women at Home, at Work and in the Community.* Washington, DC: American Psychological Association, 1994.

Lanza, M. L. and J. Carifio. "Blaming the Victim: Complex (Nonlinear) Patterns of Casual Attribution by Nurses in Response to Vignettes of a Patient Assaulting a Nurse." *Journal of Emergency Nursing* 17 (5) (October 1991): 299-309.

Lewchuk, W. *Workload, Work Organization and Health Outcomes: The Ontario Disability Support Program.* Hamilton: Institute for Work in a Global Society, 2002.

Lion, J. R., W. Snyder and G. L. Merrill. "Underreporting of Assaults on Staff in a State Hospital." *Hospital and Community Psychiatry* 32 (7) (July 1981): 497-498.

Mayhew, C. "Occupational Violence in Industrialized Countries: Types, Incidence Patterns and 'At Risk' Groups of Workers." *Violence at Work: Causes, Patterns and Prevention.* Ed. Martin Gil, Bonnie Fisher, and Vaughan Bowie. Portland, OR: Willan Publishing, 2002. 21-40.

Macdonald, Grant and Frank Sirotech. "Reporting Client Violence." *Social Work* 46 (2) (April 2001): 107-114.

Mergler, D., Brabant, C., Vezina, N. and Messing, K. "The Weaker Sex? Men in Women's Working Conditions Report Similar Health Symptoms." *Journal of Occupational Medicine* 29 (5) (1987): 417-21.

Messing, K. *Integrating Gender in Ergonomic Analysis. Strategies for Transforming Women's Work.* Brussels: Trade Union Technical Bureau, 1999.

Messing, K. *One-Eyed Science. Occupational Health and Women Workers.* Philadelphia: Temple University Press, 1998.

Messing, K. "Introduction." *Invisible: Issues in Women's Occupational Health.* Ed. K. Messing, B. Neis, and L. Dumais. Charlottetown, PEI: Gynergy Books, 1995. ix-xv.

Morrison, E. F. "What Therapeutic and Protective Measures, as well as Legal Actions Can Staff Take When They Are Attacked by Patients?" *Journal of Psychosocial Nursing* 30 (7) (1992): 41-42.

Niedl, K. "Mobbing and Well Being: Economic and Personnel Development Implications." *European Journal of Work and Organizational Psychology* 5(2) (1996): 239-249.

Newhill, C. E. "Prevalence and Risk Factors for Client Violence Toward Social

Workers." *Families in Society: The Journal of Contemporary Human Services* (October 1996): 488-495.

Panitch, L. and S. Gindin. "American Imperialism and EuroCapitalism: The Making of Neoliberal Globalization." *Studies in Political Economy* 71/72 (Autumn 2004): 7-38.

Pizzino, A. *Report on CUPE's National Health and Safety Survey of Aggression Against Staff.* Ottawa: CUPE Health and Safety Branch, 1994.

Richmond, T. and J. Shields. "NGO Restructuring: Constraints and Consequences." Paper presented at the 11th Biennial Social Welfare Conference, Ottawa, Ontario, June, 2003.

Santana, S. A. and B. S. Fisher. "Workplace Violence in the USA: Are There Gender Differences?" *Violence at Work: Causes, Patterns and Prevention.* Eds. Martin Gil, Bonnie Fisher and Vaughan Bowie. Portland, OR: Willan Publishing 2002. 39-52.

Sprout, J. and A. Yassi. "Occupational Health Concerns of Women who Work with the Public." *Invisible: Issues in Women's Occupational Health.* Ed. K. Messing, B. Neis and L. Dumais. Charlottetown, PEI: Gynergy Books, 1995. 104-124.

Stanford, J. "The North American Free Trade Agreement. Context, Structure, and Performance." *The Handbook of Globalization.* Ed. J. Michie. Oxford: Oxford University Press, 2004. 261-282.

Taylor, I. "For Better, for Worse: Caring and the Abused Wife." *Women's Caring: Feminist Perspectives on Social Welfare.* Ed. C. Baines, P. Evans and S. Neysmith. Toronto: McClelland and Stewart, Inc, 1991. 204-233

Taylor, S. J., and R. Bogdan. "On Accepting Relationship Between People with Mental Retardation and Nondisabled People: Towards an Understanding of Acceptance. *Disability, Handicap and Society* 4 (1989): 21-36.

Tehrani, N. "Violence at Work: Supporting the Employee." *Violence at Work: Causes, Patterns and Prevention.* Ed. M. Gil, B. Fisher, and V. Bowie. Portland, OR: Willan Publishing, 2002. 192-209.

Traustadottir, R. "Disability Reform and Women's Caring Work." *Care Work. Gender, Labour and the Welfare State.* Ed. Madonna Harrington Meyer. London: Routledge, 2000. 249-269.

UNISON. *Bullied: UNISON Members' Experience of Bullying at Work.* London: UNISON, 1994.

Wigmore, D. "'Taking Back' the Workplace." *Invisible: Issues in Women's Occupational Health.* Ed. K. Messing, B. Neis and L. Dumais. Charlottetown, PEI: Gynergy Books, 1995. 321-352.

Zapf, D., C. Knorz and M. Kulla. "On the Relations Between Mobbing Factors, and Content, Social Work Environment and Health Outcomes." *European Journal of Work and Organizational Psychology* 5(2) (1996): 215-237.

KIM PATE

Advocacy, Activism and Social Change for Women in Prison

I WANT TO START THIS ARTICLE by honouring those women who have the lived experience about which we, your allies and co-activists, presume to speak. I urge you to continue to unite and together to challenge and hold us accountable for all we say and do, not just here, but in our daily work and lives, especially when we try to describe or represent your realities.

Given the urgency we all feel, or should feel, about the increased criminalization of women and girls worldwide, my hope is that we will truly engage and work to correct what is fundamentally flawed and wrong about current attempts to reform and correct or change individual and/or groups of women, when it is the laws and policies within which we all work that are increasingly coming in to conflict with people's lives. This is especially true for women and all the moreso for women who are poor, racialized, and/or have disabilities. We have no choice but to challenge our pre-conceptions and therefore our approaches, responsibilities, language—in short, everything, about how we are working and envisioning the future.

Women are the fastest growing prison population worldwide and this is not accidental (Correctional Investigator). In Canada, we recognize that our links to the United States has meant that we were amongst the first countries to be impacted by the now globalized capitalist lunges for cash and products, which are occasioning the destruction of social safety nets—from social and health services to economic and education standards and availability (CAEFS; Davis 2005). The result, as we have recognized very concretely by the change of the Canadian Association of Elizabeth Fry Society's mission to recognize the reality that it is the conflicts with peoples' lives that are created by more restrictive and invasive laws and policies that are increasingly resulting in the virtual inevitability of criminalization for growing numbers of the most vulnerable and marginalized, nationally and globally.

Although crime and incarceration rates are on the decline, the rates at which women are criminalized and imprisoned are on the increase (CAEFS; Balfour and Comack). Statistics Canada reports that although crime rates have been dropping since 1996, the fear of crime and the criminalization of women and girls have both increased (see CAEFS). In fact, worldwide, women are the fastest growing prison population. In Canada, this is especially true for Indigenous and other racialized women, poor women, and women with disabling mental health issues (Arbour; Correctional Investigator). This phenomenon coincides with the government budget cuts of the mid-1990s.

The decline in basic support systems for Canadian women, combined with our amplified reliance on the use of imprisonment, has resulted in the increased criminalization of women, especially those who are racialized and those with mental health and intellectual disabilities (Mauer; Human Rights Watch; Martin). In fact, women are the fastest growing prison population worldwide and this is not accidental. In Canada, we recognize that the now globalized destruction of social safety nets—from social and health services to economic and education standards—is resulting in the increased abandonment of the most vulnerable, marginalized, and oppressed. For example, it is incontrovertible at this stage, that since the 1996 elimination of the Canada Assistance Plan, we have witnessed in Canada the shredding of our social safety net.

In 2003, Canada was criticized by the United Nations Committee examining Canada's record regarding the Convention on the Elimination of All Forms of Discrimination Against Women. Criticisms included: neglect of women, particularly with regard to social welfare, poverty, immigration policy; the treatment of Aboriginal women and trafficked women; lack of funding for equality test cases; and lack of funding for crisis services and shelters for victims of violence against women. Current and proposed criminal justice laws and policies are increasingly coming into conflict with peoples' lives, resulting in the virtual inevitability of criminalization, pathologizing, homelessness, and even death of those who are most marginalized and disadvantaged by virtue of their sex, race, class, and/or disability.

Women are also often the victims of physical and sexual assault at the hands of family members, partners and even sometimes the police. Most incidents of violence against women are not reported to police, and those that are sometimes are not even recorded, often do not lead to a conviction, and rarely result in incapacitation. There are not only problems in recording and investigation, but also in court proceedings and sentencing practices, that have prevented the effective criminalization of the victimization of women (CAEFS).

There are no provinces where social assistance rates are actually adequate to support the poor. In order to survive, most people, especially poor mothers who are the sole supports of their families, are required to obtain income by means that would be considered fraudulent if social assistance authorities become aware of it. Accordingly, by creating criminally low welfare or social assistance rates, renaming it as workfare, and even placing bans on receipt of state resources, many poor people are immediately relegated to an economic underclass that is infinitely criminalizable (Boulding et al.; Carlen 1998). Rather than resulting in the criminalization of poor women for welfare fraud, prostitution, drug trafficking or whatever other survival strategies are employed and the like, if we were truly interested in addressing fraudulent transactions that harm others, then criminally low welfare rates should result in the criminalization of those who craft, those who pass, and those who enforce the laws and policies, *not* those subjected to them. Query the value of enabling the creation of laws and policies that effectively criminalize poverty, disabilities, and the resisters of colonization.

They are not the cause of the greatest real or perceived risks to others yet we continue to perpetuate the myth by focusing on risk assessments and correctional programs, when it is those responsible for and/or complicit in the destruction of our social safety net who are in the greatest need of correction. Just as the people had to examine their own actions and inaction following the genocidal results of German policies and practices in the 1920s and 1930s, those who fail to address these matters will be faced with the reality that they too could be directly impacted implicitly and possibly explicitly, depending upon their personal, economical, and professional circumstances. It is simply not acceptable to merely hide our heads in the sand and wallow in despair, nor is it acceptable to set up new and improved versions of the same old flawed system. Really, whom do we think we are fooling as we re-arrange the proverbial deck chairs on the Titanic as the system becomes more overwhelmed and sinks?

In the United Kingdom, noted policy leaders such as Pat Carlen and the Howard League are amongst those calling for decarceration and social (re) investment (Carlen 1994, 1998, 2002; The Howard League). For those of you interested in this analysis, I commend Angela Davis' book entitled, *Are Prisons Obsolete?* (2003). Indeed, Davis and others characterize the push to criminalize the most dispossessed as the present manifestation of race, ability, class, and gender bias, and argue that this demands we examine our fundamental beliefs and notions of whose interests and biases are privileged by and for our social and criminal justice approaches (Balfour and Comack; Christie; Reiman).

It seems ludicrous that we continue to pretend that telling women and girls not to take drugs to dull the pain of abuse, hunger or other devastation, or tell them that they must stop the behaviour that allowed them to survive poverty, abuse, disabilities, et cetera, in the face of no current or prospect of any income, housing, medical, educational or other supports. Surely releasing women and girls to the street with little more than psycho-social, cognitive skills or drug abstinence programming, along with the implicit judgment that they are in control of, and therefore responsible for, their situations, including their own criminalization. Many of us doing this work, myself included, reject and resist such notions.

In Canada, in 1996, we decided to follow the U.S. lead when the federal government eliminated the Canada Assistance Plan and therefore the essential nature of Canadian standards of social, medical, and educational resourcing. We have now experienced the same sorts of cuts and knee-jerk band-aid responses—all of which presume criminality and perpetuate the problems of the past, be they crime prevention, homelessness, restorative justice, or other responses.

Imagine the results if we instead decided to ensure that every prisoner learned about the history of the use of criminal law to colonize Indigenous peoples and separate them from their land and culture, the criminalization of the indigent and homeless through laws prohibiting vagrancy and night walking, while simultaneously failing to condemn the abuse of power and force by police and prison personnel, the neglect of institutionalized persons. Imagine if we chose to reject current theories of crime and criminality and instead chose to focus on trying to prevent—and when unsuccessful punish—those who perpetrate the most harmful behaviours; those who wage war for sure, but also those who hoard essential goods, make excess profits, irresponsibly and negligently handle toxic cargo, crimes against social harmony, economic, and/or even governmental order. What would the system look like if we prosecuted and sentenced people for lying while running for office, wrongful use of access to government power and public resources?

Too many of us spend our time vibrating between rage and despair as we strive to act in ways that will directly benefit and change the status quo for those most oppressed. Let's use that anger to fuel our action, but let's not stop there; let's also decide to remember to celebrate our resisters and revolutionary thinkers and doers.

For each of us, this picture might look a little different. In Canada, we would focus on the Indigenous women who have taken our federal government to the United Nations and forced them to look past the rhetoric and crap from the official reports, causing Canada to drop from no. 1 to something like no. 7 in the world ratings of the standard of living for citizens (*Corbiere v. Canada*; *International Covenant on Economic, Social and Cultural Rights*). We would focus on the workers who led the Winnipeg general strike and other labour leaders who helped bring us our work weeks—and, perhaps more importantly, our weekends. We would toast the working-class feminist organizers who insisted that women and children no longer be considered the property of the men who sired or married them, who insisted that violence against women and children must no longer be tolerated, while hiding those same women from the men who tried to kill them and their children. We would follow the young people who demand that we fight globalization and capitalism; the students in Quebec who went on strike to fight the increased privatization of prisons, health care and education and corresponding cuts to public funding of these essential services as well as rising student tuitions (Jones); the First Nations who blockade highways and logging roads to draw attention to the rape of the land; Canada's pledge to Aboriginal women of women's and Indigenous groups who for 20 years refused to accept "never" as an answer as they demanded that 500 missing and murdered Aboriginal women in Canada did not continue to be abandoned by the criminal injustice system and the penal industrial machine. The lawyers, Anne Derrick and Rocky Jones, who were sued, censured even by some of their professional colleagues, and nearly lost their livelihood when they labeled the racism of the police when they strip-searched three 12-year-old girls in a Halifax-area school (CBC News) and Corinne Sparks, the African Nova Scotian judge who took judicial notice of the racism of police (*R.D.S. v. The Queen*).

And, the many youth, men, and especially the women prisoners who refuse to succumb, who will not stand-down or over, but instead walk with, their sisters inside; who courageously authorized the release to the media of what has now come to be known as the April 1994 incident, when women were illegally stripped, shackled, transferred to a men's prison, then were held for nine months in isolation until the videotape of the degrading, humiliating, and illegal treatment they suffered was broadcast around the world (Arbour)!

It is the responsibility of each and every one of us to refuse to collude. It is always in our collective interest when the oppressed rise up to challenge their oppressors and oppression. Increasing prisoner access to the justice and equality occasioned by social inclusion will benefit all of us, and all of our communities of interest. If the State thinks shutting us out will shut us up, they have not been paying attention! Telling us we can be part of the work on their terms and as long as we mind her Ps and Qs is asinine and insulting. It is also a show of who and what they stand for, and how uninterested they truly are in assisting women. It shows that they are all about power, control, and oppression and that they will try to smash anyone who challenges them. We cannot allow this to happen. Everyone should act now to express our outrage at simple-minded bully tactics and demonstrate that although they may keep trying to keep jailing the resisters, they won't succeed in stopping the resistance.

To use a perhaps over-used cliché—if you are not outraged, you are not paying attention. If we become complacent, if we accept the status quo, if we do not daily challenge our paycheques—those of us who have them—and all of our other privilege, then we should do something else. We must all act and question how future generations will judge all of us if we fail to challenge the lawlessness of government officials and corporate interests, and join the growing worldwide political, economic, and social coalition to de-institutionalize and counter the prison industrial complex.

As Lilla Watson, an Aboriginal woman in Australia has stressed, we need to work together to correct current injustice. She said,

> *If you have come here to help me,*
> *you are wasting our time.*
> *If you have come here because your liberation is bound up with mine,*
> *then let us work together.*

If our government does not think we deserve justice and equality, then we must be ungovernable.

Kim Pate, a teacher and lawyer by training, has also completed post-graduate Masters work in Forensic Mental Health, teaching at the University of Ottawa, Faculty of Law, and recipient of numerous awards, including three honorary doctorates. Kim is in her 22nd year as the National Director of the Canadian Association of Elizabeth Fry Societies, and has worked for approximately 30 years with marginalized, victimized, criminalized, and institutionalized women, men and youth. Most importantly, she is the proud mother of Michael and Madison, her hopes for the future.

REFERENCES

Arbour, L. *Commission of Inquiry into Certain Events at the Prison for Women in Kingston*. Ottawa: Public Works and Government Services Canada, 1996.

Balfour, G. and E. Comack. *The Power to Criminalize: Violence, Inequality and the Law*. Halifax: Fernwood Publishing, 2004.

Boulding, J. A., P. Evans, M. Little, E. Morrow, J. Mosher and N. Vanderplaats. *Walking on Eggshells: Abused Women's Experiences of Ontario's Welfare System*: Social Sciences and Humanities Research Council of Canada, 2004.

Canadian Association of Elizabeth Fry Societies (CAEFS). *Fact Sheets*. 2013. Web.

Carlen, P. "Why Study Women's Imprisonment? Or Anyone Else's?" *Prisons in Context*. Eds. R. D. King and M. Maguire. New York: Oxford University Press Inc., 1994. 131-140.

Carlen, P. *Sledgehammer: Women's Imprisonment at the Millenium*. Chippenham: Antony Rowe Ltd., 1998.

Carlen, P. *Women and Punishment: The Struggle for Justice*. London: Willan Publishing, 2002.

CBC News. *Rocky Jones and Anne Derrick Lose Defamation Case*. 2001. Retrieved May 10, 2001. Web.

Christie, N. *Crime Control as Industry: Towards Gulags Western Style* 3rd ed. London: Routledge, 2004.

Corbiere v. Canada (Minister of Indian and Northern Affairs) [1999] 2 S.C.R. 203.

Correctional Investigator. *Annual Report of the Office of the Correctional Investigator 2005-2006*. Ottawa: Government of Canada, 2006.

Davis, A. Y. *Abolition Democracy: Beyond Empire, Prisons and Torture*. New York: Seven Stories Press, 2005.

Davis, A. Y. *Are Prisons Obsolete?* New York: Seven Stories Press, 2003.

Human Rights Watch. *Ill-Equipped: U.S. Prisons and Offenders with Mental Health Illness*. Washington, DC, 2003. Retrieved May 4, 2004. Web.

Howard League, The. *The Howard League for Penal Reform*. 2006. Retrieved January 10, 2007. Web.

International Covenant on Economic, Social and Cultural Rights, 993 U.N.T.S. 3, Art.11(1).

Jones, K. *Quebec: Student Strikes Exemplify Mounting Social Discontent*. 2005. Retrieved August 10, 2006. Web.

Martin, M. "Critics say new state prison defies logic." *San Francisco Chronicle* January 5th, 2004.

Mauer, M. *Comparative International Rates of Incarceration: An Examination of Causes and Trends*. Washington, D.C.: The Sentencing Project, 2003.

R.D.S. v. The Queen, [1997] 3 S.C.R. 484,

Reiman, J. *The Rich Get Richer and the Poor Get Prison*. 3rd ed. New York: Macmillan Publishing Company, 1990.

II. Enclosure, Commodification and Theft

ANA ISLA

The Politics of Sustainable Development

From Rio 1992 to Rio+20 in 2012 – A Subsistence View

OVER THE PAST TWENTY YEARS sustainable development has been proposed as a means to confront the environmental and social crises that we are currently experiencing around the world. The environmental crisis is evidenced by, among other things, the effects of green house gas emissions, acid rain, and global warming; oceans rising and hurricanes; higher temperatures; toxic chemicals, soil erosion and depletion; desertification, acidification, and the depletion of ground water among other things. The social crisis is reflected in growing poverty and destitution; rising sexism; ethnicism, and racism; increased numbers of environmental, economic and political refugees; the spread of terrorism, trafficking, militarism and violence.

This article examines the limitations of "sustainable development" as a solution for these crises as presented at the three linked United Nations Conferences on Environment and Development (UNCED)—the first, or the Earth Summit, held Rio de Janeiro in 1992, the second, or Rio+10, held in Johannesburg in 2002, and the third, Rio+20, held in Rio de Janeiro 2012.

In Rio (1992), development and environment were first linked together in *Agenda 21*, a plan of action negotiated by governments during the Summit. In it sustainable development was defined as "development that meets the needs of the present without compromising the ability of future generations to meet their own needs" (WCED). Sustainable development was thus equated with economic growth which was to be ensured by a globalization of the economy that would rescue poor countries from their poverty, even in the most remote areas of the world (Pearce and Warford).

The Earth Summit held in Johannesburg in 2002 marked the ten-year anniversary of the original Earth Summit in Rio. While at the Rio 1992 conference, government/states were seen as responsible for organizing sustainable development in Johannesburg, responsibility for sustainable development was transferred to corporations and their shareholders. According to the United Nations, the Summit in Johannesburg:

[W]ill be remembered not for the treaties, the commitments, or the declarations it produced, but for the first stirring of a new way of governing the global commons[1]... [by] oriented partnerships that may include non-government organizations, willing governments and other stakeholders. (United Nations)

The environmental impact of industrial production by transnational corporations (TNCs) was disregarded throughout the (UNCED) process, although a voluntary code of conduct was adopted (see t "A Struggle for Clean Water and Livelihood: Canadian Mining in Costa Rica in the Era of Globalization" in this volume). Instead, proponents of economic growth portrayed the poor of the world, *campesinos*/peasants and Indigenous populations as the prime enemies of the rainforest in ways which legitimize the expropriation of their commons and their exclusion from those commons (Hecht 1990). Michael Goldman states:

As long as the commons is perceived as only existing within a particular mode of knowing, called development, with its unacknowledged structures of dominance, this community [TNCs] will continue to serve the institution of development, whose *raison d'être* is restructuring Third World capacities and social-natural relations to accommodate transnational capital expansion. (47)

Martin Khor, from the Third World Network, argued the ten years between Rio and Johannesburg had thus been a triumph of corporate-driven globalization (Khor 2002) that resulted in the imposition of global control on the civil commons—education, health-care, welfare, unemployment insurance, etc. (McMurtry), and the natural commons (Martinez-Alier)—land, water, biodiversity, rivers, lakes, oceans, atmosphere, forest, and mountains—at the national, regional, and municipal levels. For women and men who depend on the local commons, the assault on their surroundings means loss of dignity and independence, security, livelihood, health, and, sometimes, loss of life. Nevertheless, as governments and corporations seek to expand the economic growth of globalized capitalist accumulation by appropriating the everyday commons of women, households, Indigenous peoples and peasants, a new ecological-gendered-class-ethnic-based movement has been emerging over the use of ecological resources for livelihood.

Moreover, Rio+20, held over three days in June 2012 saw full corporate capture of the Summit. At the Rio-Centre conference, "greenbusiness" proposed to save capitalism from its economic crisis by pricing on the stock exchange the services that nature offers such as the capacity of the forest to absorb CO_2 Thus a fictitious market for speculation has been organized to issue permits (commercial papers) to the industrial world to continue contamination. "Conservation" within sustainable development has expanded economic growth and capital accumulation by creating "natural capital" through expanding the price system. This is actually transforming to merchandize or paper money the water we drink, the biodiversity we eat, and the air we breathe. This facilitates land expropriation, exploitation and marketing of the common goods, and more oppression of unpaid and/or to poorly paid workers, while climate change and the social crises continue without interruption.

This article applies an ecofeminist perspective to a review of the social practice of sustainable development and the social responses to it during the twenty years from Rio in 1992, through Rio+10 to Rio+20 in 2012. Ecofeminists, in coming to terms with the causes and consequences of the social and environmental crises have contested the dominant concepts of sustainable development. Ecofeminists value nature and the knowledge and experience of women as sources of the reproduction and sustenance of individual and community life. For Ecofeminists neo-liberal economic globalization is an assault on the livelihood and resources of the world's population.

Ecofeminists note the intimate connection between the ways women, peasants, Indigenous people, and nature are treated, and argue that it has been possible to sustain the illusion that economic growth is a positive and benign process only because the costs have been borne by the Third World, women, peasants, Indigenous people. They have searched for a perspective on the liberation of women, nature, and the maldeveloped world that does not rest on the continuation of exploitation, colonization, and catch-up development. Veronika Bennholdt-Thomsen and Maria Mies propose the subsistence perspective (see also Mies in this volume). "Subsistence production or production of life includes all work that is expended in the creation, re-creation and maintenance of immediate life and which has no other purpose. Subsistence production therefore stands in contrast to commodity and surplus value production for profit" (20). They have proposed a form of economy that resists the effects of global capitalism and acknowledges that "life comes from women and food comes from the land" (Bennholdt-Thomsen and Mies 80). Ecofeminists see Indigenous subsistence economies as model to inspire the entire world if we want to have social, economic, gender, and environmental justice (Mies and Shiva; Salleh). Thus all over the world there are experts who can help us recover autonomous ways of living, starting from territorial autonomy, food security in small farms, and energy efficiency. These changes will transmute the international division of labour.

Vandana Shiva uncovers an important Western cultural bias in the myth of subsistence provision as poverty. Shiva points out that "subsistence economies which satisfy basic needs through self-provisioning are not poor in the sense of being deprived" (10). These economies could only be universally labeled as 'poor' when, after the Second World War, Gross National Product (GNP), which counts only goods and services that pass through the market, was introduced as the international standard to measure a nation's wealth. Gauging value and wealth by money alone leaves the wealth of nature and the everyday skills and production of women, peasants and Indigenous peoples invisible. It allows the very maldevelopment that destroys this wealth and brings misery and deprivation to these communities to be legitimized as poverty reduction. Recognition of the wealth and support of the work and knowledge required to ensure subsistence and survival will transform the nature of our society and economy, including the existing sexual division of labour and give women autonomy over their bodies and lives.

The three following sections of this article illustrate the ways sustainable development revives colonization and subordinates the environment to economic growth by presenting three specific cases, each an example of the particular sustainable development orthodoxy of a different period. The first illustrates the politics of state-based sustainable development advocated at UNCED in Rio de Janeiro in 1992 through a critical examination of Plan Puebla Panama (PPP) project around Central America. The second exposes the logic and consequences of the private-side of sustainable development advocated at Rio+10 in Johannesburg in 2002 through an examination of the struggles that have emerged around the South American Regional Infrastructure Integration Initiative (IIRSA). The third explores the concept of "green capitalism" as propounded at Rio+20 in Rio de Janeiro in 2012.

THE POLITICS OF SUSTAINABLE DEVELOPMENT AFTER UNCED IN 1992

At the first Earth Summit economists proposed that ecology must be embedded in the economic system through the price system, that is, the economy requires a fully monetized world in order to be protected. This meant that atmosphere, oceans and seas, land, forest, mountains, biological diversity, ecosystems, fresh water etc. needed to be priced. Following this logic, the World Bank (WB) developed "genuine" saving measures that "broaden the usual national accounts definitions of assets to include human capital, minerals, energy, forest resources and the stock of atmospheric CO_2," (Hamilton), thus legitimizing the privatization of the commons. Robert Smith and Claude Simmard subsequently expanded the concept of natural capital into three categories: *natural resource stocks*, the sources of raw materials (priced or unpriced) used in the production of manufactured goods; *land*, essential for the provision of space for economic activity to take place; and *environment systems* (or ecosystems), necessary for the services that they provide directly and indirectly to the economy, including purifying the air and water, providing biodiversity, stabilizing climate, providing protection from solar radiation, and providing stable flows of renewable natural resources. This framework was articulated in the Kyoto Protocol. However, using an ecological economics perspective, Juan Martinez-Alier questions translating such environmental values as water and air into monetary values. He believes that most environmental resources and services are not and cannot be in the market. Their value is so vast that the economy cannot measure them to assign prices. Further money is, in any case, not the relevant standard of comparison for people who are not yet wholly immersed in the generalized market system. Money prices require the endowment of property rights in common wealth. More than anything else, they reflect the global distribution of income. For instance, it is cheaper to produce carbon credits using the forest of Third World Countries than to produce them in the Industrial world.

At the NGO Global Forum that was taking place parallel to the official conference in Rio, women's organizations and many other groups, were proposing to work for cancellation of Third World countries' foreign debt and reparation for the damage caused by 500 years of colonization as a necessary part of environmental activism. The foreign debt of Third World Countries (TWCs) is the sum of the principal and resulting interest on loans received by governments, businesses and individual residents of these countries from other governments, commercial banks, private agencies, and multilateral institutions, such as the IMF and the World Bank. These loans/debts are the result of unequal terms of trade and high interest rates controlled by the lender nations of the economic North. These have ensured that, despite the fact that over the post-war period and for centuries before, there has been a net transfer of wealth from the South to the industrial centres of the North, and the debtor countries have repaid the principal of their loans many times over, their debt not only persists, but is larger than ever. Merely servicing this debt requires continued borrowing which further increases their debt and keeps these nations dependent. It means they cannot refuse the socially and environmentally dammaging Structural Adjustment Programs (SAPs) that are imposed by the IMF as a condition of receiving World Bank loans. Also, today "repayment" of the never diminishing "debt" is made, not only with money, but through the transfer of ownership of national industries, banks, natural resources, nature, and other assets from South to North.

The suffering of subsistence producers, women, peasants, and Indigenous peoples in the indebted world at the hands of commercial banks, the International Monetary Fund (IMF) and the World Bank (WB), and the stabilization and Structural Adjustment Programs (SAPs) inspired solidarity among women and others from all corners. The Debt Treaty signed by the NGOs at the Global Forum, exposed the ecological debt of the industrial world. Its introduction commits the signers to struggle to achieve:

> the international recognition of ecological debt and… the recognition of the ecological creditors (ethnic groups, communities, countries and regions affected by the exhaustion of resources), the ecological debtors (responsible for environmental and social deterioration) and the necessity of applying measures of ecological adjustment (modifications and changes in the present patterns of production and consumption) so that actions of devastation and contamination do not continue to be taken. (Debt Treaty signed by the NGOs at the Global Forum, 1992)

However, despite the Debt Treaty signed in 1992, and the subsequent Debt Treaty Movement (DTM), which raised the profile of the debt and the problems arising from development (by the end of the 1990s by sustainable development in particular), indebtedness had expanded and led to ecological destruction that legitimates ecological appropriation of indebted countries' nature, particularly in Latin America. Since the late 1980s, the expropriation—initiated by the commercial banks, which previously made loans to Third World countries, multilateral institutions such as the International Monetary Fund (IMF) and the World Bank (WB)—continue by an inflow of private portfolio funds and debt-for-nature investments or "debt swaps." Debt swaps are financial mechanisms that offer repayment of loans held by creditors (commercial banks, governments) in return for handing over ownership of national industries, public enterprises, bank assets, and natural resources. Particularly since 1988, capital accumulation relies on debt-for-nature investments. Debt-for-nature investments, one of the major outcomes of the first UNCED in 1992, are the core sustainable development mechanisms of choice for the WB, the IMF, UNESCO, and large environmental corporations. Since then, the Global Environmental Facility (GEF) under World Bank management has established funding for numerous NGOs involved in debt-for-nature swaps to "protect" the global environment (Isla 2003). The sustainable development framework is thus simply economic development, understood as economic growth. As the price mechanism becomes over-extended with respect to the natural environment, and economic growth captures the local commons, locality has become a site of confrontations, where the new forms of domination, exploitation, and oppression encounter responses (Escobar). However, resistance is no longer only at the local level, it has brought international political mobilization and solidarity.

Rio's State-Based Development: Plan Puebla Panama (PPP) in Central America

The Plan Puebla Panama (PPP), also called the Mesoamerican Biological Corridor, has been regarded as the principal initiative of sustainable development of the Central American region arising from Agenda 21 (WB). Proposed and accepted by the eight countries in Central America (Mexico, Guatemala, Belize, El Salvador, Honduras, Nicaragua, Costa Rica, and Panama), PPP, involving an area of 1,026,117 square km and 62,830,000 inhabitants, is supposedly aimed at poverty reduction and environmental reparation. As a development project, PPP comprises eight initiatives: a) road and highway integration; b) human development; c) hydro-electric production; d) promotion of eco-tourism; e) partnership for sustainable development; f) prevention and mitigation of disasters; g) building of functional customs houses; and, h) development of a telecommunications network. As it was presented, PPP complemented the neo-liberal programs of privatization of public resources such as water, energy, and public services with the expansion of commercial markets, highways and transport infrastructures, dams, direct investments in *maquiladoras* (sweat shops) and transnational businesses (Ornelas). As an environment project, the World Bank presents the PPP as a project aimed at identifying and quantifying the biodiversity of the area. WB Director of Environment, Kristalina Georgieva, declared that the PPP was necessary as "there are over 45 million people in the region, of which 60 percent live on less than $2 a day" (World Bank). Poverty defined as the absence of western consumption patterns, cash incomes and industrialization (Mies and Shiva), is thus the excuse for the new assault on Central American commoners.

Despite capital's global reach, corporations still depend on nation states and ruling elites, who expect to benefit by co-operating in the extension of the boundaries of economic activity by bringing more land into development. None of the inhabitants beyond the elites of the eight countries involved were consulted about PPP (Ornelas, 2003). Eucebio Figueroa belongs to an organization called "*Por la Vida y por la Gente*" (For Life Itself and People's Livelihood) that represents a large network opposing PPP. In Figueroa's words, the main goal of PPP is to use what is left of Indigenous peoples' land and cultural domains as the new frontiers for global capital's colonization project. In this way, Indigenous communities are targeted for disintegration. To the resisters, which include Indigenous people, local poor and rural women, PPP is a war against "our culture and ways of life, because we live from subsistence agriculture" (Figueroa). To defend the threatened commons, in 2001 more than 300 organizations of local communities and thousands of Indigenous people met in Xelaju Forum, Quetzaltenango, Guatemala and wrote a document in which participants,

> [R]eject this "forced globalization" ... and denounced the fact that PPP's main goal is to create an infrastructure to facilitate the export of goods, the exploitation of our natural resources, biodiversity and labour of our people; but which does not answer in any way [our] social problems ... [further] we were not consulted ... as a result it violates the autonomy of our countries. (Saldivar 80)

In Mexico, roads and highways have been built as part of the PPP project in order to increase industrial transportation and mobilize commodities produced in the area. PPP makes Oaxaca and Chiapas central areas of development by building the Trans-Isthmus Megaproject and superhighways along the Pacific and Gulf coasts of the country, through the lands of the Indigenous peoples, the Choles, Zoques, Tojolabales, Tzotziles, Mames and Tzeltales. The human development component of sustainable development is reduced to people's value as cheap labour. Peasants and Indigenous peoples' "integration" into the global system underlies the break-up of rural families and the forced mobility of women. Sustainable development claims to increase the equality of women through their insertion into the new sexual division of labour by providing the cheap sex-labour and labour-intensive *maquiladora* (sweatshop) production.

In Guatemala, to produce hydro-electricity for *maquiladoras* and for U.S. consumption, PPP proposed to build 72 dams along the Rio Usumacinta, between Chiapas in Mexico and Peten in Guatemala. The building of dams has been displacing more than 100 communities and cooperatives that belong to these Indigenous communities by flooding (approximately 400 square km. in southern Mexico and 300 square km. in Peten (in northern Guatemala). Indigenous communities of Chole, Chontales and Lacandones have shared this river for millennia. In 1985, Chixoy dam in Baja Veracruz displaced around 5,000 people, killing 900 Indigenous women and children in the surrounding area of Caño Negro, and inundating sacred Mayan land (*Usumacinta, lugar del mono sagrado-video*). The communities affected by the dams are *Piedras Negras* (Mayan sacred temple, *El Cayo and Macabillero* (land of the Lacandon people), *La Pasadita* (Mayan ceremonial centre) and others (Figueroa).

In Costa Rica, debt-for-nature swaps have expanded the market economy. One area of expansion is eco-tourism. It is promoted as an activity that contributes toward economic growth and generates income for local communities—all while protecting the environment. But eco-tourism has had a significant impact on vulnerable species and their habitats as increased deforestation to build cabins and resorts has resulted in an irreparable loss of diversity in species, and endangered wildlife habitat by provoking mudslides, biotic impoverishment, and species-forced migration. Ecotourism can also radically alter ownership claims. Around the Arenal Volcano in La Fortuna de San Carlos, entire communities have been forcibly evicted. While the majority of the land around the volcano is not arable or adequate for cattle ranching, small farms had existed in the area. In 1994, this land was expropriated by the government's Ministry of Environment and Energy (MINAE) to expand the National Park. Peasants who had organized their lives by clearing land for agricultural production and pasture around the Arenal Basin were thrown off the land. Former property owners have become hut renters (*ranchos*) or slum inhabitants (*tugurios*). The personal effects of the *campesinas/os*, such as cars and small electrical appliances, were taken by the commercial banks when they could not afford to repay their loans acquired for economic development. When in desperation some of them returned to their land to plant yucca, beans, corn, and other subsistence foods, they were declared to have broken the law and some were thrown in jail. Their lands, pastures, homes and roads have been converted into expensive resorts, more environmentally destructive than the original uses, with access limited to tourists who can afford recreational activities (Isla 2003). The redesigning of the rainforest as a primary eco-tourism destination has made Costa Rica a sex tourism "paradise" (Schiefter).

As the commons are "enclosed" and commoners' access to nature is curtailed, it becomes a "national security" issue. Land enclosure legitimizes a military presence and assaults on any groups who want to reclaim their right to use nature for their livelihood or differently than capital circumscribes.

Resistance to PPP

In Mexico, for example, an intensive militarization of Southern Mexico started with the Zapatista uprising. On January 1, 1994, the *Ejercito Zapatista de Liberacion Nacional* (EZLN), declared war on the Mexican federal government by occupying seven municipalities/cities in Chiapas. On that day, *Zapatistas* demanded:

•A new pact between Indigenous Peoples and the national society in search for a new state project and a new constitution that includes ethnic diversity and recognition of Indigenous Peoples as part of the nation;
•Land restitution, because lands were commons rather than state property; and
•Expulsion of the municipal officers that have been deepening poverty by enforcing neo-liberal social and economic policies expressed in the Free Trade Agreement (FTA). (Muñoz)

Indigenous peoples know that they have no other recourse to resist state and international development except through direct action. For the Zapatistas, therefore, "This [declaration of war] was a last resort against misery, exploitation and racism, basically, it was a last resort from oblivion" (Muñoz). To break their courage, Indigenous communities that resist are confronted with paramilitary organizations in alliance with the regular army, rich landowners, and *narcotrafico* (Salazar Perez). Further, Salazar Perez argues that the Central America PPP is connected to Plan Colombia, and Plan Dignity in Chapare, Bolivia.[2] The three Plans declare the same objectives: strengthening of democracy, poverty reduction, anti-drug efforts, elimination of drug trafficking, sustainable development, and support of the U.S. anti-terrorism struggle. In support of each of these plans, some politicians and corporations have engaged in counter-insurgency practices, stirring up paramilitaries to attack civilians. The impact on the lives of rural women is significant. Women in the South of Mexico, for example, because of the threat of rape by soldiers, are unable to work and forced to remain in their homes (AWID 2002b). In the northern part of Mexico, women's transition from farmwoman to "independent *maquila*" workers continues to exact a high-price. In Ciudad Juarez, on the Mexico-U.S. border, over 800 women working in *maquiladoras* have been kidnapped, raped and murdered with seeming impunity (AWID 2002a).

Indigenous people, peasants, and all women in these communities want to continue with the time-tested ways of life that depend on them keeping their land. As a consequence, in association with environmentalists, they are fighting each of these projects embedded in PPP and are building international solidarities. They are forging an international campaign of *hermanamiento* (in Spanish this means accompaniment by sisterhood and brotherhood) of individuals, organizations and universities to establish a permanent physical presence in the areas threatened by sustainable development. They believe that an international presence will force the democratization of their societies, and will support their collective rights to land integrity, where currently women's rape and the assassination of community leaders is increasing and social and environmental collapse caused by development as enclosure is threatening.

TEN YEARS LATER RIO+10 IN JOHANNESBURG: THE PRIVATE SIDE OF SUSTAINABLE DEVELOPMENT

The Earth Summit in Johannesburg resulted in the launch of 60 voluntary partnerships to support efforts to implement sustainable development, reflecting the success of neo-liberal corporate campaigns for a voluntary approach instead of government regulation. These voluntary, non-negotiated partnership, were an outcome of this Summit. They actually meant the privatization of the implementation of jobs that are under the category of sustainable development. The justification for this approach was that state/government actions during the last ten years have been so inadequate that encouraging voluntary partnership initiatives might bring new impetus to the implementation of the various commitments. The logic behind the multi-stakeholder model is that by bringing together the "Major Groups" identified by the UN, consensus can be reached on certain outcomes, which are in turn easier to implement and more legitimate. Behind this approach were: The International Chamber of Commerce (ICC), the World Business Council for Sustainable Development (WBCSD), and Business Action for Sustainable Development (BASD). BASD submitted for formal consideration as sustainable development various initiatives, among which were the Energy and Biodiversity Initiative, the Marine Stewardship Council, the Chemical Industry Responsible Care Program, and the Global Mining Initiative. It was during the Johannesburg Earth Summit (Rio+10), in 2002, that mining qualified as sustainable development despite its fossil-fuel centered industrial model, which greatly contributes to climate change.

The Triumph of Corporate Driven Globalization: The South American Regional Infrastructure Integration Initiative

It was in Johannesburg that responsibility for 'sustainable development' (understood as economic growth) was transferred to corporations and their shareholders. Quite naturally as a result, infrastructures for sustainable development were established before and shortly thereafter in South America. The South American Regional Infrastructure Integration Initiative (in Spanish, (Iniciativa para la Integracion de la Infraestructura Regional Sudamericana or IIRSA) is the "sustainable" development program for South America. The IIRSA project trapped Amazonia in the middle of multiple capitalist appetites. It is an area of 8,187,965 square kilometers of natural resources, distributed among eight countries: Bolivia, Brazil, Colombia, Ecuador, Guyana, Peru, Suriname, and Venezuela.

With the help of the Inter-American Development Bank (IDB) and the International Bank for Reconstruction and Development (IBRD), IIRSA was created. It started in 2000, in Brasilia, when twelve South American presidents met under the auspices of Brazil and the protection of the IDB, the Cooperacion

Andina de Fomento (CAF), European Investment Bank (EIB), Banco Nacional de Desarrollo Economico y Social de Brazil (BNDES), Financial Fund for the Development of the Plate Basin (FONPLATA), and other international financial institutions to discuss credits for governments interested in the construction of large sustainable development projects, such as infrastructure for ports, airports, highways, hydro-electrical systems, railways, gas pipelines, and others.

For Brazil, IIRSA has two objectives: Internally, to penetrate or remove existing natural barriers (the Amazon jungle, the Orinoco basin and the Andean mountains to have access to the natural resources), legal barriers (modify, reconcile, and deregulate national laws with international law), and social barriers (eliminate peasant and indigenous resistance of those affected by mega projects) (Antentas).

Externally, to contribute to globalization and its free trade frameworks by creating the infrastructure needed to expand cheaper transportation for commerce liberalization with North America, Europe, and Asia; increase the export of raw material, natural resources, environmental services, and products from the Atlantic to the Pacific; and control of Amazonian natural resources and biodiversity.

IIRSA harbors 506 infrastructure projects, involving 59.53 percent of highways, 44.44 percent of energy and 0.03 percent of communication, representing around USD$68 billion. As Brazil is a G20 member, it plays a role of sub-imperialist power, and is the major beneficiary of IIRSA projects. Brazil's plan for development requires providing electricity to its cities, moving its products from the Atlantic to the Pacific Ocean, and strengthening its geo-politic presence in South America. According to Raul Zibechi:

> The type of integration arising from this model is "exogenous" integration that goes "outwards" from the continent—i.e., the aim is not to integrate the continent itself internally, but rather to integrate it into international markets. (qtd. in Antentas 13)

Antentas, referring to IIRSA-Bolivia said that it is a project that involves the forging of a multi-modal system of connections that would put in place new export-oriented manufacturing installations in key areas, while building links that would open well identified parts of the Amazon Basin to less costly access and more systematic resource exploitation through the integration of a hemispheric system of interconnected river systems (Antentas). It will interconnect river systems, creating global shipping channels linked to a motor and rail transport system.

Here I will concentrate my attention on IIRSA in the Peruvian Amazonia (second only to the Brazilian Amazonia), which represents 13.05 percent of continental Amazonia. IIRSA plans see Peru as a peripheral state which will play a role similar to that of Bolivia, as a transit country and a distribution centre for oil, bio-fuel monoculture, biopiracy and ecotourism for multinational corporations. But reshaping the country this way will threaten the subsistence economies, societies, and environment of Peru and the rest of South America to serve the demands of the world market.[3] Peru has 78 projects in the package of infrastructure investments, which have increased its external debt by USD$6 billion. This plan and its projects are unknown to Peruvians nationally and locally. Nevertheless, the Peruvian government and elites are interested in developing monoculture and cattle ranching projects along the railway lines and Brazil is being connected with the Peruvian Amazonia by:

IIRSA-North on the Peruvian Amazonia side has built a highway between Tarapoto-Yurimaguas to connect with Callao in Lima and Paita in Piura. The main beneficiary in Yurimaguas is the Romero Group (RG), the largest Peruvian corporation which produces oil palm and other exports. In Loreto, IIRSA also plans a hydro project involving the dredging of the Napo River from Peru to Ecuador to link large ships with Manaos and Belem in Northeastern Brazil.

IIRSA-Centro, the Inter-Oceanic Centre, will link Cruzeiro do Sul (Brazil), with Pucallpa, Tingo Maria Huanuco, Cerro de Pasco and Lima, in Peru. The objective of that highway is to be a secondary route to the Pacific Ocean. In addition, the installation of large electric power lines is anticipated between Cruzeiro do Sul and Pucallpa as part of the connection and energy integration accords. Once installed, the line will cross the same Inter-Oceanic Centre region, rich in biodiversity and the traditional territories of indigenous peoples. To add to the problem, in 2008, the governments of Brazil and Peru approved, without any consultation, projects to construct a rail line between Cruzeiro do Sul and Pucallpa, which will also affect the territories of the Serra do Divisor National Park (PNSD) and the Isconahua Territorial Reserve. The rail line will transport soy products from the west-central region of Brazil to the coastal ports of Peru (Paita), and from there, to Asian markets. Brazil has invested USD$100 million to stimulate economic growth (land tenancy, agriculture in deforested areas, health care and public education) while Peru invested USD$20 million (Alvarado).

IIRSA-South will connect the state of Acre, Brazil. It will construct the Inter-Oceanic Centre, which connects Cruzeiro do Sul (Acre in Brasil), and the city of Pucallpa in Ucayali, and Madre de Dios (Inapari, Iberia, Puerto Maldonado), Cuzco (Urcos), Azangaro, Puno (Juliaca), Arequipa (Camana and Mollendo) in Peru[4] will build the Inter-Oceanic South Highway, which connects Rio Branco and Peru, passing through the municipality of Assis. Construction has been completed on the Brazilian side and continues on the Peruvian side. Developers on the Peruvian side are Odebrecht, Graña and Montero, J. J. Camet and IICSA and on the Brazilian side Andrade Gutierrez, Camargo Correa, and Quiroz Galvao Groups (Luna).

Brazil and Peru have also developed joint plans for hydroelectric generation. In April 2009, in the state of Acre, their presidents signed a memorandum of understanding to cooperate in the construction of six hydroelectric generating stations in the Peruvian Amazon, where indigenous peoples live. Five of them will reach a potency of 6.673 MW. The consortium Amazonas Sur Electric Generation Company (EGASUR), which includes the Brazilian firms of OAS,

Electrobrás, and Furnas, is conducting early engineering and economic viability studies. The cost will be USD$16 billion from the (Brazilian) National Bank of Economic and Social Development (BNDES). Corporations that will own the project are: Electrobras in association with private enterprise financed by BNDES (in Brazil) and Electroperu (in Peru). The concession will be for 30 years.

The promoters of IIRSA are large corporations. Ricardo Verdum has shown that the principal Brazilian and international business groups involved in the construction of these highways (which begin at the Brazilian border and cross Bolivia and Peru) have a close relationship with mineral, petroleum, lumber, and agribusiness extraction. Major Brazilian conglomerates present in building infrastructure include: Gerdau, Votorantim, Odebrecht, OAS, Queiróz Galvão, Camargo Korea, Petrobrás, Vale, and others. These firms are the same in Peruvian territory (Verdum), and have been linked with the sectors of the Peruvian economy that are active in international markets.

Resistance to IIRSA

The sustainable development framework argues that corporate globalization is a natural law, and the reproductive sector, especially the subsistence economy, is seen as an obstacle that must disappear in order to expand the market. Consequently, IIRSA-North, ignores the Amazon's Indigenous people as a different society. The President of *Organizacion Secoya del Peru,* Guido Sandoval, denounced Petro-Peru and Petrobras for assaulting his community—Nueva Augusilla, and announced that 100 *Apus* (chiefs), from 100 communities, have rejected IIRSA, particularly oil production. He said "we do not want to live like our brothers of Rio Corrientes. We look at the suffering of their children with lead in their blood. That is why we reject oil production in our territory"(Sandoval). In the words of the AIDESEP president, Alberto Pizango, "Indigenous people want to exercise their free-determination, reclaim their ancestral land as the only guarantee of survival and development of future generations, recover their rights to indigenous jurisdiction and legalization of their ancestral rights, guarantee the protection of collective knowledge, ensure the right to consultation, construct a multicultural, multiethnic, and multilingual National State, assure that the new Constitution includes Indigenous peoples' rights, and build, at the highest level, a special instance to address Indigenous people's problems." In sum, Amazonian Indigenous people have precise borders and identities and demand recognition of their identity, autonomy of their territories, and have their own representation. Their agenda looks like this: Indigenous peoples want to be recognized and included as a different society in a new Peruvian state. At the same time, they want to assure that their children will continue living in freedom, using traditional lands from the forest. Thus, they reject development that entails deforestation, contaminates rivers, destroys their livelihood, and converts their children into cheap labour.

In IIRSA-Centre, one electric plant, Paquitzapango, has provoked uprising from the indigenous Central Ashaninka del Rio Ene (CARE) organization because its construction threatens to flood the lands of seven Ashaninka communities living along the river, in contravention of the country's constitution. In IIRSA-South, Inambari Hydroelectric Station has been the source of the most organized and active resistance from Indigenous people, peasants, and environmentalists, from the departments of Cuzco, Puno, and Madre de Dios. It represents an investment of USD$4 billion that in five years should produce 2,000 megawatts, of which 75 percent will be transferred to Brazil. The builder and the operator are the Brazilian *Empresa OAS* and *Electrobras* respectively. It is considered the largest hydroelectric project to be constructed in Peru, forecast to flood 41,000 hectares of forest, including agricultural land; peasant land that includes 3,400 homes in 42 towns, and extensive areas of flora and fauna of native jungle (including Bahuaja Sonene National Park). In addition, it will flood 61 km of Inter-Oceanic Highway (Prado). According to Brazilian experts "an engineering work of such dimensions will impact the river, because it will destroy the process that organizes biodiversity. It won't destroy a group or species, instead it will destroy the process that generates and maintains biodiversity" ("Central de Inambari"). The opposition insists on forcing EGASUR out from the area ("Dicen no al proyecto"). EGASUR assures that it will create 19,000 job openings and an electric system that might create industry in Peru's south, and connection with Acre and Rondonia in Brazil. EGASUR has proposed to pay compensation for forest destruction and reduce the level of operation from 540 meters to 525; reduce flood from 240,000 to 221,000 ha; and increase the megawatts from 2000 to 2200.

As land-forest is seized, unknown impacts are experienced and social conflicts increased. In Peru's Defensoria del Pueblo (Ombudspeople's office), the office of *Prevention of Conflicts and Governability*, argued that economic growth linked to resource exploitation near or within community common land has been producing struggles. He indicated that the absolute majority of conflicts (128 cases in 2009) were socio-environmentally related, such as mining, hydro-electric, gas pipeline, oil production, and forest concessions ("Defensoria detecta"). The office maintains that 86 percent of the dialogue processes in the country occur after violence has taken place, "because the State has no conflict prevention policy, when conflict happens, it tries in a hurry to find solutions by generating accords that are difficult to comply with, [thus they return]." In 2009, each month had seen between 10 and 15 new conflicts. In June 2009, there were 273 registered social conflicts, 226 active, 14 new cases and only two were resolved (Mendoza). In Bagua, 2009, Indigenous people have risen in defense of their territories as common land and their society as sufficient. Their subsistence perspective has produced "the good life," which is based on simple and practical knowledge that for millennia conserved a healthy forest, wildlife, biodiversity, and society in general. This Indigenous subsistence perspective holds the secret of abundance, sufficiency, security, a good life, preservation of the economic and ecological base, and cultural and biological diversity. For defending their land, Garcia's administration shot them from helicopters, and persecuted their leaders (Isla).

TWENTY YEARS LATER IN RIO (RIO+20): GREEN CAPITALISM

Between June 20 and 23, 2012, the United Nations Conference on Sustainable Development–(Rio+20) met in Rio Centre to redefine international environmental policies. Between June 15 and 23, 2012, the People's Summit, which is the global civil society, met parallel to the official conference in Flamingo Park, Rio de Janeiro. According to Martin Khor, Director of South Centre, "[Rio+20] was meant to celebrate the Earth Summit of 1992, to reaffirm the political commitments made then, and to come up with up-to-date action plans to counter the crises which have become much more serious than 20 years ago" (Khor 2012). Instead the disagreements widened, as Rio Centre government negotiators promoted "green business," while People's Summit supported the defense of the commons and called the "green economy" a false solution. Through replacing nature's commons with the privatization of nature and thus creating "natural capital," "green capitalism" provides support for continued economic growth. Proponents of sustainable development argue that growth in real income per capita can be achieved without major environmental degradation, by getting the price of nature right. That price calculations to allocate use of "scarce" resource (e.g. water, air etc.) should be based on the laws of supply and demand operating in the market place. Prices in the market place would then reflect the private costs of production and the rise or fall in price deter or induce purchase and ensure the efficient allocation of scarce resources. Hence the emergence of new markets in the green economy, for instance, in carbon credits, bio-fuels, biopiracy, will increase in size.

Under the term "green capitalism" is included all the present intensification of capitalism. "Green capitalism" prioritizes a model of huge corporations with enormous projects, which are beneficiaries of governments' cheap credit, but with high costs for the environment and society. The negative externalities (impacts) on the environment and the local population are invisibilized and/or hidden. Consequently, I will examine mega-projects fostered in the context of the Peoples' Summit in Rio+20. The Summit focused on "green capitalism" or mega-projects, financed by mega-banks. Government negotiators disregarded land fragility and conceded huge areas for the oil, mining, soja agro-industry, bio-fuels (such as cana brava, sugarcane, and peanuts), hydroelectric projects, and forest industries with strong impact on ecosystems and resources. BNDES, a Brazilian bank that financed many Rio+20 events, is four times bigger than the World Bank (Kato) and reproduces and expands economic development in Brazil and South America through the IIRSA project.

To reveal this hypocrisy Instituto Mais Democracia de Brasil,[4] a citizens organization to control governments and corporations, organized three visits in Rio de Janeiro to areas impacted by BNDES mega-projects exposing corporate social irresponsibility in all. One visit was to Compania Siderurgica do Atlantic-TKCSA's installations in Rio de Janeiro, a joint venture between the German Thyssenkrupp Steel and the Brazilian Vale, located in Santa Cruz, Baía de

Sepetiba. The people in the area are divided in relation to the project some associations accept the promises of jobs and other forms of cooptation, others do not and are not intimidated by the threats they experience. These associations, such as fishermen, promote protest and create consciousness about the crimes of the corporations. Thanks to these groups a number of participants at the People's Summit witnessed how the high levels of steel particles spread by the steel industry produced environmental and social conflicts, destroying people's economy in the area based on artisanal and industrial fishing and tourism. At the same time, the industry is killing the ecosystem of rivers, green areas, manglares and other sea biomass, as well as the refuges of coastal birds. At the fishermen's centre, around 25 women and men informed the visitors, with pictures and x-rays, how heavy metals have been impacting their health and their livelihood. This project violates the ecological rights of animals and plants by disappearing thousands of forest hectares, threatening biodiversity; and violates the economic rights of local communities.

During the People's Summit, June 18, 2012, thousands of Indigenous people and their supporters reached the doors of Banco de Desarrollo de Brazil (BNDES) with big investments in Amazonia, calling for an immediate halt to land-grabbing, particularly to stop the hydroelectric project of Belo Monte in Amazonia, and the financialization of the "green economy." This project is expected to produce 11,000 megawatts of electricity-the third biggest hydro-electric generating capacity in the world after China's Three Gorges and Brazil's Itaipu dams. Belo Monte will flood an area of 500 square kilometres. The Coordinator of Indigenous Organizations of the Amazon Basin (COICA), representing the interest of 390 Indigenous Communities (around two and a half million people) stated "We cannot be separated from our land and our territories, they are spaces of conservation and living totalities in a permanent and vital relation between human beings and nature" (Preamble, COICA Rio+20). Despite the fact that their territorial rights have been recognized and guaranteed by International instruments, such as the ILO Convention 169, and the UN Declaration on the Rights of Indigenous Peoples, they continue to be displaced by force.

On the same day, the Articulacion de Mujeres Brasileras, World March of Women, and Via Campesina marched in outrage as government negotiators avoided reaffirming the original Rio equity principle, and failed to recognize Women's Reproductive Rights. They also marched against the commodification of life promoted by the "green economy," to affirm food sovereignty as a peoples' right, and in support to Indigenous peoples' claims of respect.

On June 20, on the first day that the heads of state met, the streets of Rio de Janeiro were transformed with different manifestations during the morning, close to Rio Centre. In the afternoon, People's Summit organized a Global March outraged by the failure of governments to tackle climate change and the social crisis. Thousands of people—from Indigenous groups, women, NGOs, Friends of Earth, Green Peace, solidarity groups, students, Brazilean citizens, Via Campesina etc.—marched together raising diverse demands.

CONCLUSION

Plan Puebla Panama in Central America, and IRSA in South America revealed the neo-colonial relations of sustainable development. In both cases, there is a clear connection between global capital and nation/states. Sustainable development of the neo-liberal regime cannot be expanded without the direct intervention of the nation/state against local inhabitants and their commons.

What distinguishes these stories is that local struggles have reached across borders, involving activists around the world in a truly "globalized" campaign against the worst aspects of sustainable development and corporate globalization. In the ecological, gendered, ethnic, class struggle, local communities are building resistance. Democratic forces from Europe, Canada, and the U.S., made up of individuals, grassroots groups and NGOs, internationalize their struggle. This new feature of massive resistance in this period is a reponse to the internationalization of productive and financial capital, which is clearly revealing its tendency for dispossession of the very means of survival of people who follow the rhythm of nature. The awareness of this new context is developing an international class struggle, drawing massive solidarity and support to local struggles led by women, Indigenous peoples, and the local poor.

In each Earth Summit, rural women, Indigenous people and peasants have shown that the politics of sustainable development are not separate from their everyday life. As the capitalist priority of economic growth is emphasized, women's livelihoods are jeopardized and the natural world is externalized and annihilated. Maria Mies and Veronika Bennholt-Thomsen (1996, 1999) proposed subsistence economies for women's equality and local sustainability, in order to stop the rapacious dependence of developed societies on the resources and labour of the underdeveloped other. This perspective championed by many eco-feminists is a necessary basis to defeat neo-liberal development pursued globally by state and corporate "partnerships" in the name of sustainable development.

Ana Isla is an Associate Professor at the Department of Sociology and the Centre for Women's and Gender Studies, Brock University. She is an active member of Women for a Just and Healthy Planet.

[1]The commons are natural resources (water, air, atmosphere, genes, biodiversity, etc) and social wealth (education, health care, security etc.) owned in common by society. The Global Commons are being privatized to expand capital accumulation.

[2]Plan Colombia is publicly justified under the "War on Drugs." Established in July 2000, it is the largest foreign aid package ever sent to a Latin American government, making Colombia the third largest recipient of U.S. aid in the world (only Israel and Egypt surpass this amount) and the number one recipient of military aid (two million dollars per day). As a result of the military presence,

Plan Colombia has displaced more than 500,000 rural people, mostly Afro-Colombians and Indigenous populations. According to Colombians, however, it is a response to more than 50 years of struggle between large landowners and small peasants, between cattle ranching and subsistence agriculture. Plan Dignity, initiated in 1998 to eradicate coca production in Chapare, Bolivia, involves the building three new military bases in the region. To be built with six million dollars in U.S. assistance, the bases will permanently deploy 1,500 troops in the area, a move bitterly opposed by local residents and many human rights groups.

[3]For detailed description see the special issue of Integración y Comercio, Vol. 12, No. 28, 2008, published by the Inter-American Development Bank.

[4]See their documentation at Instituto Mais Democratico <www.maisdemocracia.org.br/arquivos/DOCpoliticoFinalMaio2011.pdf>.

REFERENCES

Alvarado, G. "Explotacion desenfrenada puede devastar la Amazonia Peruana en el ano 2041." *La Republica* February 16, 2010: 10.

Antentas, J. M. "The Madeira River Complex: Socio-Environmental Impact in Bolivian Amazonia and Social Resistance." *Capitalism Nature Socialism* (2009): 12-20.

Association of Women in Development (AWID). *Globalizing Actions Against Impunity of Feminicides in Ciudad Juarez*. Paper presented at the Reinventing Globalization conference, Guadalajara, Mexico, 2002a.

Association of Women in Development (AWID). *In Solidarity with the Independent Movement of Women in Chiapas: Resistance to Neoliberal Globalization*. Paper presented at the Reinventing Globalization conference, Guadalajara, Mexico, 2002b.

Bennholdt-Thomsen, V. and M. Mies. *The Subsistence Perspective, Beyond the Globalized Economy*. London, New York: Zed Books, 1999.

"Central de Inambari destruira la biodiversidad." *La Republica* 16 March 2010: 14.

"Defensoria detecta 18 nuevos casos de conflicto." *La Republica* 8 September 2009: 6-7.

"Dicen no al proyecto Inambari." *La Republica* 3 March 2010: 11.

Escobar, A. "Culture Sits in Places: Reflexions on Globalism and Subaltern Strategies of Localization." *Political Geography* 20 (2001): 139-174.

Figueroa, E. "Plan Puebla Panama." Paper presented at the Guatemalan-Maya Speaker event at Brock University, St. Catharines, Ontario, 2003.

Goldman, M., ed. *Inventing the Commons: Theories and Practices of the Commons' Professional*. New Brunswick, NJ: Rutgers University Press, 1998.

Hamilton, K. "Genuine Savings, Population Growth and Sustaining Economic Welfare." Paper presented at the Natural Capital, Poverty and Development Conference, Toronto, Ontario, September 5-8, 2001.

Hecht, S. a. A. C. (1990). *The Fate of the Forest. Developers, destroyers and defenders of the Amazon*. England: Penguin Books.

Instituto Mais Democratico. "Transparência e controle cidadão de governos e empresas." Documento Politico. Rio de Janeiro,Brasil, maio de 2011. Accessed on August 10, 2012. Web.

Isla, A. "Land Management and Ecotourism: A Flawed Approach to Conservation in Costa Rica. *Natural Capital, Poverty and Development*. Ed. Adam Fenech. Amsterdam: Kluwer Publishing, 2003.

Isla, A. "The Eco-Class-Race Struggles in the Peruvian Amazon Basin: An Ecofeminist Perspective." *Capitalism Nature Socialism* 20 (3) (2009): 21-48. 187.

Isla, Ana and Shirley Thompson. "Environmental Economics Reality Check: A Case Study of the Abanico Medicinal Plant and Organic Agriculture Project." *Natural Capital in Ecology and Economics: An Overview*. Eds. Adam Fenech, Jay Foster, Kirk Hamilton and Roger Hansell. New York Springer Science + Business Media, 2003.

Kato, K. *Companhia Siderurgica Do Atlantico—TKCSA. Impactos e Irregularidades para o Cono Sul*. 3rd Edition. Rio de Janeiro: Instituto Politicas Alternativas para o Cono Sul – PACS, 2012.

Khor, M. "TWN Briefings for WSSD No.1. WSSD Jo'burg 2002: Where We Are and What's Needed Now." Third World Network, 2002. Web.

Khor, M. "Rio+20 Summit: The Key Issues." June 15, 2012. Policy Innovations. Web.

Luna, A. N. "La Integracion sobre el tapete." *El Comercio* 25 April 2010: A8.

Martinez-Alier, J. Ecological Economics and Ecosocialism. *Is Capitalism Sustainable? Political Economy and the Politics of Ecology*. Ed. M. O'Connor. New York: The Guilford Press, 1994.

McMurtry, J. "The Life-Ground, the Civil Commons and the Corporate Male Gang." *Canadian Journal of Development Studies* 22 (2001): 819-854.

Mendoza, R. "Cazador de conflictos." *La Republica* 12 July 2009. Web

Mies, M. and V. Shiva. *Ecofeminism*. London: Zed Books, 1993.

Muñoz, G. "Diez años de lucha y resistencia zapatista." *Rebeldia* (2005): 3-16.

Ornelas, J. "El Plan Puebla Panama y la Globalizacion Neoliberal." *Lectura Critica del Plan Puebla Panama*. Ed. R. S. Perez. Mexico: Libros en Red – Insumisos Latinoamericanos, 2003. 19-54

Pearce, W. D. and J. J. Warford. *World Without End: Economics, Environment and Sustainable Development*. New York: Oxford University Press, 1993.

Prado, E. "Hidroelectrica Inambari genera discordia." *La Republica* 8 March 2009: 9.

Salazar Perez, R. "El Vinculo Militar del Plan Colombia y el Plan Puebla Panama." *Lectura Critica del Plan Puebla Panama*. Ed. R. S. Perez. Mexico: Libros en Red – Insumisos Latinoamericanos, 2003. 135-165.

Saldivar, A. "El Plan Puebla Panama: Una Locomotora sin Vagones de Segunda." *Lectura Critica del Plan Puebla Panama*. Ed. R. S. Perez. Mexico: Libros en

Red – Insumisos Latinoamericanos, 2003. 75-110.

Salleh, A. *Ecofeminism as Politics. Nature, Marx and the Postmodern.* London: Zed Books, 1997.

Sandoval, G. "Iniciativa para la Integracion de la Infraestructura Regional Sudamericana (IIRSA)." Iquitos, Peru, 2010.

Schiefter, J. *Viejos Verdes en el Paraiso. Turismo Sexual en Costa Rica.* San Jose: Editorial Universidad Estatal a Distancia, 2007.

Shiva, V. *Staying Alive, Women, Ecology and Development.* London: Zed Books, 1989.

Smith, Robert and Claude Simmard. "A Proposed Approach to Environment and Sustainable Development Indicators Based on Capital." Paper presented at the Natural Capital, Poverty and Development Conference, Toronto, 5-8 September 2001.

United Nations. "The Johannesburg Summit Test: What Will Change" United Nations, 2002. Web.

Verdum, R. "The New Developmental Extractivism in South America." Americas Program Report, Center for International Policy, Washington, DC, 2010. Accessed: January 25, 2010. Web.

World Bank (WB). "Briefing. Shareholders and Donors of Mesoamerican Biological Corridor Conference from 12-13 December 2002." Conference Center of the World Bank in Paris, 2003.

World Commission on Environment and Development (WCED). *Our Common Future.* New York: Oxford University Press, 1987.

MARIAROSA DALLA COSTA

Some Notes on Neoliberalism, on Land and on the Food Question

THE PROBLEM of the growing degradation of the food system owing, among other things, to its genetic manipulation, relates to research technology directed at enhancing nature's productivity and has as its counterpart the expropriation and privatization of land and the development of agrarian reforms aimed at re-stratifying labour worldwide.

These measures seek to impose in an increasingly pervasive way class relations and models of production that are peculiar to today's concept of development. Thus, agrarian reforms and policies implemented in the twentieth century have guaranteed better nutrition to a few, malnutrition or hunger to many, and in particular, have been used as a powerful tool to disrupt organizational networks that various sections of the world's population have created in their struggle to assure themselves better nutrition and a better life. We, therefore, fully agree with the assertion that food crises are fundamentally products of the political economy of capitalism (Cleaver).

This is also true of "technological miracles" concerning food production. On one hand, as they simulate the source of abundance, they destroy the biodiversity and the reproductive powers of nature, the only real source of abundance (Shiva). On the other hand, through the genetic manipulation of food and the industrial and commercial policies that sustain it, they make food increasingly inaccessible to the vast majority of humanity.

This leads not only to a progressive destruction of nature's reproductive capacity, but also to the progressive annihilation—through wars, repression, epidemics, and hunger—of populations rendered superfluous by the expropriation and poisoning of land due to the use of pesticides or landmines. The uprooting, "ghettoization," and enclosure of populations, deprived of their fundamental means of subsistance—above all, land—and ultimately confined to slums, refugee camps, and jails, have as their counterpart the "enclosure" of food. Food is, in fact, already inaccessible to many because of the combined policies of land expropriation, technological innovation in agricultural methods, and the relationship between prices and wages (when there is one). In addition, food is always more subject to further manipulation,

189

made unavailable for use by privatization, monopolization, or technological patents.

But, what role do policies play regarding land and food in the so-called new globalization of the economy (Wallerstein; Mies)? It is necessary to clarify some premises. The neoliberalism that characterizes the latest phase of accumulation, contrary to what is often assumed, is not a spontaneous process where the productive forces of the economy are simply set free to compete among themselves. In reality, neoliberalism is a capitalist strategy planned as much as the Keynesian economic strategy was. Its planning resides in that gigantic operation of underdevelopment of social reproduction represented by the policies of structural adjustment. Such policies were implemented in substantially identical ways around the world during the '80s and '90s. They were intended to clear the way for the unfolding of neoliberalism. The institutions assigned to "plan" this underdevelopment of reproduction, which above all is an attack on labour and on the struggles of women, are the International Monetary Fund (IMF) and the World Bank (WB). Today, these institutions represent the government without borders of international capital. If the former presides over the formulation of directives regarding adjustment policies, the latter launches development projects which are their corollary.

The current phase of accumulation rests in fact on two fundamentals. The first consists of the new international division of labour, which concerns not only the sphere of production but also reproduction (Federici). As a result, more Third World women than ever perform domestic work for the first world, either by remaining in their countries of origin or by emigrating to so-called advanced nations. Such a division and restructuring of labour would not occur if adjustment policies, with the dramatic poverty which they provoke, did not lead to the migration of many. The second fundamental consists of the new economic liberalism, which in seeking the deregulation of labour to allow increased corporate competition in the new globalized economy, assumes that reduced contractual power is a result of increasing poverty caused by adjustment policies.

However, the underdevelopment of reproduction created by such policies, the foundation on which international division of labour and economic neo-liberalism rests, resulted in the international cycle of struggles that unfolded in the 1960s and 1970s. From the '80s onward, structural adjustment policies have contributed to widespread misery and become the terrain for growing struggles and rebellion (George; Midnight Notes Collective; Dalla Costa and Dalla Costa 1995, 1996).

Paradoxically, in particular in Italy, the political debate, whether institutional or not, does not usually mention adjustment policies, thereby hiding how continuing cuts in public spending for social consumption and privatizations belong to a concerted strategy at the international level. But to an even lesser extent does the debate address the privatization and expropriation of land, which are at the heart of the underdevelopment of reproduction and which constitutes the main source of world hunger and of policies of annihilation and enclosures of always larger sectors of population. From my point of view, the other side of the hidden attack on social reproduction is the progressive poisoning of the land. This is because land, ever further outside the control and knowledge of local populations, must guarantee an always higher productivity and always higher profit for the international food industry. In the same way the expropriations of land and forced migration of populations (to which improbable resettlements are promised), play a central role in the various programs of the World Bank, and have remained unmentioned in the Italian debate.

If *these operations on the land* and consequently *on the populations,* are *crucial constants* in the policies by which the IMF and World Bank, as institutional summits of international capital, guarantee the further expansion of capitalist relations that leads to the increasing encroachment on and devastation of the reproductive powers of nature, what are the implications for us? I will mention here only a few points while directing your attention to a more detailed study elsewhere (Dalla Costa M. 1996).

Because the expansion of capitalist relations leading to the commodification of every form of life constitutes a state of siege that threatens us all, such operations must be *at the center of our political thinking and activity.* These operations continually restructure class relations around the world, thus, to express an anti-capitalist resistance capable of confronting this new phase of accumulation, to defend ourselves as working class of the global economy means, first of all, supporting the struggles over land in ever more regions of the planet, and developing a political reunification around this question (of the land) in all its varied aspects at the international level.

In this sense, it is fundamental to learn and tell others about the struggles against this process all over the world, and to act in support of them. This may help to dam an overflowing river rushing towards us. We need to spread word of the victories that have already occurred. It helps us to shake the belief in the inevitability of capitalist development. Above all, it is of fundamental importance that we pose ourselves the question (even in advanced nations) of how we relate to the land/earth.

Lessons from Indigenous and women's movements in the South have revealed that there are no mechanical or chemical short cuts, to say nothing of biotechnological ones, when it comes to the land. There are no simple technological solutions to guarantee the fruits of the earth and the renewability of its forms of life. The earth needs reproductive work—it is necessary to care for it through human presence and activity and it is necessary correspondingly to give back as much as is taken. This is just as true for human beings who are, after all, a part of the life of the earth. Technology in both cases can only perform a marginal role. It can serve to cut grass in the same way that a washing machine can do the laundry but not to raise a child. This understanding compels us to rethink the working day, just as we do when we take into account the reproductive work involving human beings. The lack of any serious response on this issue, combined with the lack of any serious response over the question of land, can only render even more tragic the difficulty of human reproduction. But if the technological approach is not the solution, then liberation from agricultural work based on technological advancement is a false liberation. This false liberation should have resulted in a labour force that on one hand is unemployed, and on the other, supposedly free for more intensive use on other fronts. Yet, to re-localize development here means, above all, to restore a human presence which, beginning with new relations among humans and between humans and nature, will also be able to invent a technology appropriate to the new relations between living things. The abandonment of the countryside by women in Italy was not only a refusal to do hard work but also of hierarchical control by the elderly and by men in the isolation of the village life. Today more and more women and men all over the world are experimenting with practical alternatives in land-use, beginning with practical alternatives among themselves and within a context rich in potentialities for communication and exchange without frontiers. In this sense also, the rising in Chiapas (Esteva) has constituted a great laboratory.

But the question of what kind of relation with the land/earth, according to the Indigenous lesson, forces us to address the problem of what are in effect our commons, commons that we want to preserve or reconquer. In my opinion, they are the earth as public space (against policies that increasingly restrict space for collective activity), the earth as source of biodiversity, and the earth as source of natural evolution.

The struggle over time and wages, so much in discussion in recent years in the advanced countries,[1] is myopic if it is not linked to the land question and attempts to change current agricultural policies, including those regarding animal husbandry, in a way that preserves the biodiversity, integrity, and renewability of nature. If not linked to all these questions, the victory on the struggle for higher wages will leave in our hands only the possibility to buy more poison and with it our extinction. The reproductive powers of nature and its biodiversity, as Indigenous communities teach, multiply instead of reducing our possibilities of life, making them always more monster-like, as is increasingly happening. The development of practical alternatives must gain strength from the struggles, refusals, and protests against current policies.

It is important to know that these practices are developing with many articulations even in the advanced nations, as in, for instance, in the United States. While the waged economy, through a growing unemployment, dooms ever more women and men to live on the street without food or hope, those seeking alternative solutions to feed themselves and have a roof over their heads are discovering new social relations that put into place other economies and other relations with the land. I am alluding to those movements and those initiatives which we can group under the name "social ecology," "bioregionalism," or "community economy" (Dalla Costa M. 1996). Here the need to assure one's own nutritional requirements is linked to attempts to re-localize development not only to keep at the local level the availability of the land, but also the guarantee of healthy food, work skills, and financial resources without letting them be devoured by the uncontrollable reign of the global economy.

One of the more meaningful examples is the city of Binghamton in the State of New York. Of 40,000 inhabitants, 15,000 were fired by IBM, a firm which had never before fired large numbers of people, but which was transferring production to the Third World. A short time later, the supermarkets also closed. This collapse corresponds to what has happened in many other U.S. cities hit by high unemployment. One safety valve for the community, to be able to eat and live, was to rediscover the land, to create at the borders of the city community biological gardens that could count also on an internal market. On the basis of the recovered time and land, people could build new relationships and elaborate a new culture with nearby Native communities and reservations. This experience with community gardens following factory closings has happened on a larger scale in the former automobile capital of Detroit.

These are only two examples. But many others are developing and becoming widespread. Cities and communities are also constructing alternative circuits of local money, organizing, on a large-scale, alternative networks of labour and professional exchange. There are also movements, as in Minnesota, Wisconsin, and Vermont, around the question of bovine growth hormone, uniting animal rights activists, ecologists, and family farmers against agro-business. The abuse of animals is also the abuse of small-scale economies and the environment. In Arizona, the question of land has for the first time united family farmers and Native Americans against agri-business that wants farm land and against mining companies that want the uranium, coal, and oil underneath Native reservations.

These examples, from my point of view, are very significant and full of implications, which will become clearer in the near future. They are examples to which we will turn in our search for alternative economies and struggles. What is certain is that our planet, the Earth, under a multiplicity of perspectives, is emerging as an increasingly important issue capable of uniting in a powerful circuit of struggles her many diverse children.

This paper was presented at the session "Feminist Critique of the Food Globalization, Production and Trade" held at the "Women's Day on Food" alternative conference at the Fao Summit held in Rome, Italy, the 15th November 1996.

This article originally appeared in Italian with the title "Neoliberismo, terra e questione alimentare" in Ecologia Politica *1 (1997). Reprinted with permission.*

Mariarosa Dalla Costa, Professor at the University of Padua, has been at the forefront of the international feminist movement since the beginning of the 1970s, when she initiatedthe debate on women's unpaid work in the home and on women as reproducers of labour power. Her best known book, Famiglia, welfare e stato tra Progressismo e New Deal *(1983), will soon available in English. Since the 1990s, her research has focused on the issues of the Earth/land, movements for sustainable agriculture and fishing, and alternative food policies. Her work has been translated into six languages, including Japanese. Among her books in English, she is the author of* Gynocide: Capitalist Patriarchy and the Medical Abuse of Women *(2007); and editor of, with Giovanna F. Dalla Costa,* Women, Development and Labor of Reproduction *(1999); and with Monica Chilese,* Nostra madre oceano: Questioni e lotte del movimento dei pescatori *(2005) (forthcoming in English, Our Mother Ocean: Questions and Struggles for the Fishers' Movement).*

[1]See the appeal of 35 intellectuals published in the newspaper, *Il manifesto,* the 27 of October 1996. To this matter, I dedicated further considerations in my article, "L'indigeno che è in noi, la terra cui apparteniamo."

REFERENCES

Cleaver, Harry. "Food, Famine and the International Crisis." *Zerowork: Political Materials* 2 (1977): 7-69.

Dalla Costa, Mariarosa. "Sviluppo e riproduzione." *Donne, sviluppo e lavoro di riproduzione. Questione delle lotte e dei movimenti.* Eds. M. Dalla Costa and G. F. Dalla Costa. Milano: FrancoAngeli, 1996. 21-56.

Dalla Costa, Mariarosa. "L'indigeno che è in noi, la terra cui apparteniamo." *Vis a Vis* 5 (1997): 73-101. ("The Native in Us, the Land We Belong To." *The Commoner* 6 (Winter 2003). Web.)

Dalla Costa, Mariarosa and Giovanna F. Dalla Costa, eds. *Donne e politiche del debito. Condizione e lavoro femminile nella crisi del debito internazionale.* Milano: FrancoAngeli, 1993. (*Paying the Price: Women and the Politics of International Economic Strategy.* London: Zed Books, 1995).

Dalla Costa, Mariarosa and Giovanna F. Dalla Costa, eds. *Donne, sviluppo e lavoro di riproduzione. Questione delle lotte e dei movimenti.* Milano: FrancoAngeli, 1996. (*Women, Development and Labor of Reproduction: Struggles and Movements.* Lawrenceville, NJ: Africa World Press, 1999).

Esteva, Gustavo. "The Revolution of the New Commons." Unpublished paper. 1994.

Federici, Silvia. "Riproduzione e lotta femminista nella nuova divisione internazionale del lavoro." *Donne, sviluppo e lavoro di riproduzione. Questione delle lotte e dei movimenti.* Eds. M. Dalla Costa and G. F. Dalla Costa. Milano: FrancoAngeli, 1996. 57-90.

George, Susan. *A Fate Worse than Debt.* Harmondsworth, UK: Penguin Books, 1988.

Manifesto (Il), October 27, 1996.

Midnight Notes Collective, ed. *Midnight Oil: Work, Energy, War, 1973-1992.* New York: Autonomedia, 1992.

Mies, Maria. *Patriarchy and Accumulation on a World Scale: Women in the International Division of Labour.* London: Zed Books, 1986.

Shiva, Vandana. *Staying Alive.* New Delhi: Kali for Women, 1988.

Wallerstein, Immanuel. *The Modern World System.* New York: Academic Press, 1974.

NANCY C. M. HARTSOCK

Women and/as Commodities

A Brief Meditation

I WOULD LIKE TO BEGIN this article with a brief feminist mythic story derived from the Ancient Greek tragedy, *Oedipus Rex*:

> One day, towards the end of his rather miserable life, the old blind hero of the tragedy sensed the presence of the Sphinx. He asked her why things had turned out so badly for him. "Well," the sphinx explained, "your answer to the riddle was only partially correct." "Wait a minute," he said. "You asked me, 'what walks on four legs in the morning, two at noon, and three in the evening?' I answered Man—who crawls as a child, walks upright as an adult, but upon reaching old age must use a cane. That's a perfectly good answer." "Well," said the Sphinx, "what about Woman?" "Come on," said Oedipus, "when you say Man, of course that implies Woman too. Everyone knows that." The Sphinx smiled as she replied, "That's what you think." (Rukeysan qtd. in Folbre 1992: xxiii)

I want to suggest here that attention to the question, "What about women?" can provide important insights for understanding the operation and trajectories of global capitalism. Even more than that, I want to suggest that the situation of women in the new global economy—especially third world and migrant women—may hold the key to understanding political economy and capital/ labour dynamics—but only insofar as we begin theorizing from women's lives.

Women have been both included and excluded in different ways in different locations. To the extent that they have been drawn into wage labour the conditions and structure of their work have been systematically different from that of men. In the new global economy, however, these conditions are being generalized to more and more workers. That is, the global labour force is being feminized in several ways. First, more women are working for wages. Second, more men are being subjected to the kinds of labour discipline initially practiced on women. Third, there are changes in the structure of labour itself—i.e., many work processes are becoming more like the work women have done in the past

195

This strategy and argument runs counter to most of the literature on globalization and the new economy. The literature on globalization, whether influenced by Marxism or not, has failed to make of central consideration the roles of women and how women are both included and excluded. Thus, Michael Hardt and Anthony Negri's book *Empire* includes no index entry for women. This is not an isolated instance. Overall, at the macro or grand theory level, economic discourse on globalization erases gender as integral to the social and economic dimensions of globalization. Thus, in asking the question, "what about women?" I want to raise broader questions about how feminist analyses which begin from attention to women's lives can clarify and contribute to an understanding of the processes involved in global political economy and I want to make the implicit suggestion that beginning from women's lives can contribute to making feminist change.

In *Capital*, as Karl Marx develops his account of commodity production and his theory of surplus value, he focuses solely on the male worker who buys commodities in the market to reproduce himself for labour the next day. The work that goes into preparing these commodities for consumption and the non-waged labour which is essential to reproducing the worker is not attended to. In this he appears to follow Adam Smith in the *Wealth of Nations,* who in writing about the importance of self-interest stated, "It is not from the benevolence of the butcher, the brewer, or the baker that we expect our dinner, but from regard to their self-interest" (9). But Nancy Folbre is clear to say "just a minute. It is not usually the butcher, the brewer, or the baker who fixes dinner, but his wife or mother" (Folbre 2001: 11).

I propose to begin an account of women's structural roles in globalized capitalism by looking specifically at how women's lives interact with the production and circulation of commodities.[1] Marx begins Volume I of *Capital* with an account of commodities and their circulation, at the end of which he concludes that while commodities may seem to be simple things an analysis demonstrates that they abound in metaphysical subtleties and theological niceties. I want to suggest that the story is in fact more complicated than his account allows for—because he begins with men and not women.

The story he tells goes like this:

1. The market appears to be the fundamental institution of social life —the exchange of commodities. Since the fall of communism, we have seen the growth of the faith that the introduction of markets will bring prosperity, democracy, and all the good things of life).
2. Social relations both appear to be and are about the exchange of commodities.
3. Commodities have both use values and exchange values.

Marx argues that this story is in error because commodities have to be recognized as, or are really in fact, labour in its crystallized or congealed form.

Once we recognize that commodities are really labour and labour time, and the status of the object as commodity is a purely social construct (not an atom of matter goes into its construction as commodity), we are in a position to understand the ways in which this story is at once fictional, distorting, and foundational. But since we now know the story should really be about labour we are in a position to tell a different story—the story Marx tells about the importance of producing subsistence, and the consequences of alienated labour. This shift of focus from commodities to labour enables Marx to demonstrate both how misleading and harmful commodity production and exchange in capitalism is and to envision more humane social relations.

So here I want to return to the epigraph with which I began and ask again, "what about women?" What happens when we start from commodity production and circulation by beginning with women? There is way too much to do here, so I will start with a meditation on the concept of the commodity—beginning with women's lives (an overly universalist project, but at this very general level, hopefully it can be more useful than distorting (because it *will* distort).

Women's relation to commodities, and women's entanglement with commodities, is more complicated than men's since women are both more and less involved in the production and exchange of commodities. There are several relations:

1) Women's formal waged work has the same—or at least similar—dynamics to men's. They produce commodities with both use values and exchange values.

2) Women's production work in the informal economy and especially household economies are such that they produce use values directly and these are consumed *as* use values, for example, food, clothes, services, etc. Women are less involved in the capitalist market than men. They have less access to money, less involvement in the market, and less involvement with commodity production and exchange. In the informal sectors, their products are often appropriated by the men in the household who take them to market, exchange them, and often keep the proceeds.

3) Women contribute to the reproduction of labour power on a daily and (and long-term) basis—i.e., working up the commodities necessary to sustain the male worker—or engaging in such activities as subsistence farming, reproductive labour and childrearing.

4) Women *are* commodities in ways that few men are. They possess, like other commodities, use values and exchange values. Men, and women as wage workers, possess a commodity, labour power—with a use value and an exchange value. But men are not themselves commodities. The labourer, unless a slave, is not himself a commodity. He exists to at least some extent as a man with at least potential access to species being, that is, carrying possibilities or exercising all his human faculties.

Women are commodities in obvious ways: most of the women in the world are disposed of and controlled by others. But women, like other commodities have both exchange values and use values. There is, of course, the worldwide trafficking in women and girls, now said to be the one of the three most important sources of income for organized crime. And there are practices such as bride prices, and also dowries. Lest we are tempted to dismiss these as practices of "primitive" societies, we should remember the figure of the executive's trophy wife in advanced capitalism, a woman whose exchange value depends on the fact that she is beautiful, blond, thin, and 20.

But women also have use values and are consumed, used up like other commodities. Women are consumed physically by enforced childbearing. The leading cause of death for women around the world is still pregnancy and the complications of childbearing. Women are also consumed emotionally in the form of the caring labour they do.[2]

Women also work for wages—wages which for the majority of women are controlled by men. Those involved in various development strategies (e.g., micro-lending) have long recognized that a woman's income is a source of income for the household as a whole while a man's wage is often his alone.

What are the consequences of existence as a commodity as well as the possessor of at least one commodity? Commodities do not control their own destinies, do not decide (yet) when to come to market. As exchange values they have no past and no future. Most fundamentally agency, subjectivity, and history disappear from view. Thus, women are often not thought to have (and in many cases don't experience themselves as having) goals and purposes and interests other than those dictated by custom and assumed to be unchanging. Or rather, there is no place in this story for women to recognize their own species being or potentials.

A second consequence is that women's labour becomes invisible and devalued. Housework appears to many not as work but as an expression of love. Moreover, women's caring labour both disappears as work and, when done for wages, can be paid at very low rates. One reason for these outcomes is that when looked at in a formal sense, commodities as such don't labour, they are exchanged and used/consumed.

In sum, then, unlike male workers and male capitalists, who are involved in only one circuit—and that one not involving every minute of every day, women are involved in four. These circuits in traditional Marxist political economy involve commodities such as: (C) labour power, food, housing; (M) money; (UV) use values and (LP) labour power; but these categories are not sufficient to understand women's relationships to the circuits of commodities. I propose to rewrite the original account of the labourer's involvement—C-M-C—the exchange of labour power for money with which to buy the commodities necessary for life into the following four circuits:

First, women, like men, have a commodity, their potential for work, which they sell for money in order to buy other commodities which will allow them to return to the market to sell their capacity to labour yet again.[3]

Second, women are more involved in the production of use values which are directly consumed rather than being first exchanged. Third, women are the major producers of the unique commodity: labour power, broadly conceptualized under the heading of social reproduction which includes the biological reproduction of the species, the reproduction of the labour force—which involves education and training, and the reproduction of provisioning and caring needs (see Bakker and Gill 11).[4]

Fourth, women *are* commodities—therefore both are and are not people/ human subjects with potentials for expansion of their subjectivities and the possibilities for creating more humane communities.[5]

The structures of circuits two, three, and four depend on forms of domination outside the circuits of commodities. Thus, marginalization is important—it leads to women's invisibility as actors. The invisibility also contributes to the ability of societies to maintain a series of fictions by means of which women's activities can be devalued. Women's lack of power is also at work in structuring women's participation in these circuits. Women are kept in all these circuits by being forced to see themselves through the eyes of others: consider for example the ideal of thinness and its devastating physical consequences for many young women in the West. Finally, women as a group are kept in "their place" by the threat and actuality of systematic violence.

I think that for feminist scholars there are several things central to a critical understanding that begins from examining women's places in the circulation of commodities. In this task we can get some guidance from Marx, but only some. Thus, Marx found his subject matter in labour, which allowed him to focus on agency, activity, processes, history. Feminist scholars however, have been clear that labour as a category comes from attention to men's lives, includes a labour/ leisure distinction, and is too narrow. It doesn't map well onto the activities women engage in. Perhaps we would be better off to start with the term "life activity."

A second and related question is that of what dynamics allow for women to become commodities. Or, put differently, what is it about women's life activities that allows them to be distorted in these particular ways? Part of this understanding will be an account of how women's dynamic life activity can be distorted so that women become commodities, and how the four circuits with which women are involved both reinforce and contradict each other. For example, women's household work—caring labour, production of specific use values, is replicated in their waged work—the jobs they have, the segregated labour market, and the specific industries that disproportionately employ them.

Moreover, it is important to ask what contradictions grow out of both being a commodity and producing them. What openings for change can be seen? And also what new possibilities for abuse/domination/exploitation emerge as women move from producing for domestic "markets" within the family and producing for international and "public" markets.

This is all very partial and incomplete—but hopefully several implications for theorizing women's lives become visible. Just thinking about commodities from a feminist standpoint a number of categories become evident as inadequate. To begin with just three:

1) The terms labour/labour power a) fail to capture what women actually do; b) fail to provide an account of processes of reproduction and also for possibilities for change; and c) raise questions about whether there really is abstract human labour. Perhaps all human activity must be re-understood as carrying marks of gender, race, and/or sexuality.

2) The concept of alienation has enabled a powerful account of the consequences of the separation of the worker from his labour power in both its form as activity and its form as product. Women are separated from their humanity in different and perhaps more thorough and thoroughgoing ways. Yet for women this is a contradictory situation, since at the same time as they are treated as commodities themselves, they are also involved in the direct provisioning of human needs outside the market. This situation could allow for a much more complex understanding of the concept of alienation.

3) Attention to women's several relations to the production and circulation of commodities might be the basis for a different understanding of the fetishism of commodities—i.e. the arguments that what should be relations between people become (and are conducted in the market) as relations between their things— their commodities. But what if some people are themselves commodities? How exactly does this distort human relations?

By beginning with the circuit of commodities in an account that begins from women's lives we can see the need to tell a much more complicated story than political economists have given us. Beginning from women's lives, we might be able to develop a more complex account of the processes of globalization at work in the world.

Nancy C. M. Hartsock is Professor Emerita of Political Science at the University of Washington. She is the author of Money, Sex and Power: Toward a Feminist Historical Materialism *and* The Feminist Standpoint Revisited and Other Essays. *She is currently at work on a book-length project on retheorizing women and globalization.*

[1]Here I take some inspiration from the beginning of Marx's Volume I of *Capital.*
[2]This is Nancy Folbre's central argument in her book, *The Invisible Heart.*
[3]In this circuit, they are involved in the circuit, C-M-C, or perhaps better, C-M minus-C in recognition of the fact that the wages they receive exchange for the labour power they possess are lower than those men receive. Thus, they have a commodity, their potential for work, which they sell for money in order to buy other commodities which will allow them to return to the market to sell their capacity to labour yet again.
[4]Here the circuit might be described as LP-LP'-LP2. to indicate that women's labour produces the commodity labour power, which has the capacity to produce more than its cost (value) of reproduction. At the same time LP needs the continuous and ongoing work of women to sustain it.
[5]This circuit might be described as WC-M (where M can stand for either money

or marriage)—MPP (male pleasure and power). Thus women as commodities are exchanged for marriage and/or money and this in turn produces and reproduces male pleasure and power.

REFERENCES

Bakker, Isabella and Stephen Gill. *Power, Production, and Social Reproduction.* New York: Palgrave MacMillan, 2003.

Folbre, Nancy. "Introduction." Nancy Folbre, Barbara Bergmann, Bina Agarwal, and Maria Floro, eds. *Women's Work in the World Economy.* New York: New York University Press, 1992.

Folbre, Nancy. *The Invisible Heart.* New York: The New York Pres, 2001.

Hardt, Michael and Aanthony Negri. *Empire.* Cambridge: Harvard University Press, 2000.

Marx, Karl. *Capital.* Volume I. New York: International Publishers, 1967.

Smith, Adam. *An Inquiry Into the Nature and Causes of the Wealth of Nations.* 3rd Edition. Volume I. Edinburgh: Mandel, Pig and Stevensen, 1989.

MARILYN WARING

The Invisibility of Women's Work

The Economics of Local and Global "Bullshit"

I HAVE WATCHED WOMEN in many parts of the world following herds of
animals to scoop up steaming dung in their bare hands, placing it in woven
baskets which they then hoist onto their heads and carry. The loads they
bend for, lift, and carry are very heavy, and the work is very tiring. In the context
of the lives of these women, access to dung is a matter of daily survival. In
addition to providing fertilizer, it is a primary source of cooking fuel and is also
used as a building material and plaster. When used as organic manure, the dung
must be dried for several months and then carried to the households' farming
plots. These are seldom contiguous, and may be several kilometres from the
household. I recall images of women walking bare-footed along rough narrow
paths on the sides of steep hills, for example, in Indonesia or Nepal. Entire days
are spent carrying on their heads baskets full of fertilizer for the small family
plots before ploughing.

In many places in the developing world, livestock are held in a small enclosure
immediately next to the home, since the pressure on land use means that, with
a few seasonal and agro-ecological exceptions, fewer livestock are allowed to
wander freely or are herded. Gathering fodder for the animals and then bringing
them water become more arduous tasks for women and children, with longer
and longer walks. At least the dung is closer to the household.

In parts of Africa and Asia, dung is also used as a basic material for building
construction, maintenance, and decoration. Adobe houses are covered with
a mixture of mud, dung, and straw and replastered several times a year. The
mixture is spread by hand, and only women do this work. In some villages, the
plaster is mixed with coloured pigments, and spectacular decorative patterns
often adorn the outside of the houses.

As a result of forest depletion, women increasingly need dung to burn as an
alternative to wood fuel. After collection, they mix it with straw and water and
make it into flat cakes. Then it is dried, usually in the sun, and the women need
to turn each cake several times in this process before it is dry enough for storing.
Making dung cakes can take up to two hours a day and, when the cakes are stacked,
there is the further process of thatching and sealing the pile to keep out the rain.

Making dung cakes to be used as fuel appears to me to be an entire manufacturing process, with clear inputs and outputs of an economic nature. In mining or gas extraction, for example, paid workers harvest the primary resource. Machines transport it to processing plants. The raw material is refined, the product manufactured. It is sold, then consumed. The traditional economic model is followed: workers process raw materials for the market. This counts. But when dung, the "non-product," is carried as a "service" by "housewives," to sustain land, dwellings, and households, then, according to the economic model, nothing happens. There is no economic activity. But dungwork is only women's work, so it is a safe assumption that in the official definitions of productive work it will be invisible.

The area of human activity generally excluded from economic measurement is household activities, the products of which are seldom or never marketed, i.e. the unpaid services of housewives and other family members, household maintenance, subsistence agriculture performed by children or "housewives," voluntary work, and reproductive work: most of the work that most of the people do most of the time.

"Growth" figures register "market" activities, i.e. cash-generating activities, whatever the nature of that activity and regardless of its legal status. In New Zealand, companies dry dung products and sell them in pelletized form for the home gardener. The process is called manufacturing. The results are marketed. The workers are paid. When the rural women of the developing world recycle dung, nothing in the process, the production, or the labour has an economic value.

The value of this most primary of all forms of production, and its links with women's unpaid work, raise crucial policy questions which have seldom, if ever, been contemplated by the arbiters of what does and does not count. As a consequence, much of the rhetoric intended to ensure continuing exclusion of these activities, and large amounts of women's other work, from measurement is made on the basis that all this has little or no effect on most micro and all macro economic activity.

Yet the consequences for micro and macro policy planning are immense. While dung can be a replacement fuel for scarce wood, and therefore ease the rate of deforestation, this use is a major loss in terms of soil conservation and fertility. For example, it is estimated that in Nepal eight million tonnes of dung are now burnt each year, equivalent to one million tonnes of foregone grain production (World Bank). At the same time, the use of dung as a fuel is a major instance of import substitution, and is a national saving in terms of the debts that would be incurred through the importation of fuel if resourceful women had not processed the alternative.

THE RULES OF WORK

Any economic report of the World Bank, the International Monetary Fund (IMF), United Nations (UN) agencies, or national governments, is based on national account statistics. The UN uses these figures to assess annual contributions, and to appraise the success of regional development programs. Aid donors use the United Nations System of National Accounts (UNSNA) to identify deserving cases, "need" being determined by "per capita gross domestic product" (GDP). While the most in "need" would tend to register low growth figures, donors prefer to invest in countries showing high rates of growth, paving the way for their own exports and investment opportunities. In the same way, the World Bank uses these figures to identify nations that most urgently need economic assistance, but prefers those with higher rates of growth, making it easier for multinational corporations to use the same figures to locate new areas for overseas investments. The availability of IMF loans and loan rollovers comes with contingencies to force changes in government economic policies to increase growth rates based on these figures. Companies in turn use these national accounts projections to project the markets for their goods and to plan their investment, personnel, and other internal policies.

Resources are mined, skies are polluted, forests are devastated, watercourses are turned into open sewers and drains, whole populations are relocated as valleys are flooded and dammed, and labour is exploited in chronically inhumane working conditions. The statistics record economic growth. It is claimed that national accounting provides factual information. As I have demonstrated, dung cakes are a manufactured product that requires hours of labour. And that is a fact. But not according to the UNSNA, where facts are carefully selected in a way that predetermines public policy.

Cooking, according to the UNSNA is "active labour" when cooked food is sold and "economically inactive labour" when it is not. Housework is "productive" when performed by a paid domestic servant and "nonproductive" when no payment is involved. Those who care for children in an orphanage are occupied; mothers who care for their children at home are "unoccupied."

The authors of the UNSNA boast that per capita GDP in any country is a measurement of the well-being of its citizens. A major reason that only cash-generating activities are taken into account is to ensure that countries can determine balance of payments and loan requirements--not as a comparative exercise, but as a controlling exercise. Those to whom money is owed (first world governments, multinational banks, and multilateral agencies) are primarily interested in gauging the cash generating capacity of the debtor countries, not their productive capacity.

Women have argued against this myopic approach to production for decades. In 1900, Charlotte Perkins Gilman wrote: "the labour of women in the house, certainly, enables men to produce more wealth than they otherwise could; and in this way women are economic factors in society."

Following the calls made by women at their successive United Nations world conferences in Mexico City and Copenhagen, the final document of the End of Decade Conference for the United Nations Decade for Women, held in Nairobi in 1985, included this paragraph:

The remunerated and in particular the unremunerated contributions of women to all aspects and sectors of development should be recognized, and appropriate efforts should be made to measure and reflect these contributions in the national accounts and economics statistics and in the Gross Domestic Product. Concrete steps should be taken to quantify the unremunerated contributions of women to agriculture, food production, reproduction, and household activities.

Dung, whether as a fertilizer, cooking fuel, or building material, should be quantified. But, in official statistics, women's contribution to both productive and subsistence.[1] agricultural production anywhere has been poorly estimated or ignored. Where women's contribution has been noted, arbitrary demarcations between formal and subsistence production have been imposed, never reflecting the blurring of such distinctions in the working day of the hundreds of millions of women concerned.

Because definitions used in national surveys and censuses have relentlessly excluded the great bulk of work performed by women, women's productivity has been assumed to be pitifully low. This is especially so in agriculture and in work in rural areas, where the majority of women on the planet are to be found. Whether we like it or not, this is the basis for policy decisions in key economic sectors.

NON-ORGANIC DAILY BULLSHIT

As we see, it is impossible to talk about women without talking about the processes occurring throughout an economy. Yet planners usually talk about the economy without talking about either the value of what women produce or the specific effects on women. The direct discrimination against women is both overt and covert and exacts major economic costs. There are the opportunity costs, of ignoring constraints women face and of failing to provide women with improved opportunities to participate fully in the development process. There are the costs of gender stereotyping in major labour-market and home-maintenance activities. There are the costs of refusing to recognize women by claiming that the household is the unit of economic analysis, but then failing to analyze the household as a business enterprise of interdependent workers, contributing to two sub-systems of production with different skills, potentials, knowledge bases, and rights to resources. There is the inefficient use of resources, poor targeting, and mal-investment by men's deliberate obstruction of women's access to land titles, credit, knowledge, extension services, appropriate technology, and a wide range of other services, all of which hinder a nation's development and growth statistics. And all the above accumulatively contribute to the inter-generational costs incurred through poor nutrition, overpopulation, and poverty.

In such a context, women are not just another category to be met in macro-economic policy (though they are seldom considered in that context).

Trade, transnational corporations, commercial lending, and aid are the four dominant channels through which international economic relations manifest themselves and affect national macroeconomic policies. Usually, the policy strategy mix advocated to generate a high growth rate in the GDP increases poverty, inequality, and unemployment. Low-income groups suffer the most, and women suffer more than men. When powerful macro forces are working against the poor, special micro measures such as a few income-generating projects will not bring about any significant improvement in the well-being of women.

Equity and efficiency are not mutually exclusive outcomes. Women are not a problem for the economy. On the contrary, meeting the challenges of survival depends more than ever before on women's organizational, management, ecological, and productive skills. That women have been, through direct discrimination, denied both opportunities to influence the adjustment process and their share of benefits brought by structural change means that they are the least-dependent resource in the community. They are, therefore, the group most likely to respond to inputs leading to self-reliance.

It does not require years as a policy planner or a degree in economics to observe that an extremely effective way to increase the time women have available for income-generating or productive activity is to introduce appropriate technology to save their time spent in hours of repetitive drudgery necessary for the survival of the household. Simone de Beauvoir wrote in *The Second Sex*, "Few tasks are more like the torture of Sisyphus than housework, with its endless repetition: the clean becomes soiled, the soiled is made clean, over and over, day after day." In fact, technology inputs in the name of economic progress, overwhelmingly directed at males, have frequently had the effect of increasing the working day of women even more. Studies by the International Rice Research Institute in the Philippines demonstrate conclusively that the increase in rice production in Asia increased the work traditionally done by women twofold, while the money from the twice-yearly harvests went to the men because the land was in male names. Labour-saving technology was applied to men's tasks (land clearing, ploughing), while women's planting, weeding, harvesting, and storage work doubled with increases in crops and production.

It should be noted that the female activities in this production arrangement constitute the bulk of the labour requirement for these crops. Regardless of such evidence, throughout the region men have higher levels of input in the early stages of agricultural production, such as field preparation, and monopolize most mechanical-technical inputs. Ploughing or threshing, by either animal- or fuel-powered machines, is done by men, while hand threshing is a female, labour-intensive activity. Driving tractors is reserved for men, and all the menial agricultural tasks of the region—seed preparation, weeding crops, transplanting rice, picking cotton or tea, raising silk worms, and cocoon reeling—are overwhelmingly women's work, and have the fewest technological inputs.

In a comprehensive study of farming women in New Zealand, Deirdre Shaw found that 88 percent view themselves as being in the farming profession, seeing their role as physical, decisional, administrative, economic, supportive, and organizational. Ninety-nine percent were involved in horticultural or stock work, yet felt that little was done to enable them to participate in discussion groups, field days, and farm visits, due both to lack of child care and, at times, to attitudes.

Women who have the opportunity or flexibility to make choices about their treatment by governments change their votes. And, in the marketplace, they deliver their judgements in an equally appropriate way. Forty-one percent of the women in the study make it clear that companies in the rural service industry will, and do, lose their business if women are not treated as equal and knowledgeable partners. At the same time, interviews with people in the rural service industry revealed that 82.5 percent first thought of a farmer as being male. Less than half felt that a woman's role on the farm was a partnership, with one-third seeing women in a "farmer's wife/support" role. It also revealed that, while the majority of men interviewed saw women as being in a partnership, they also considered women to be farmers only when farming on their own.

The market is as tardy as governments to respond. The New Zealand Agricultural Field Day is held annually in the middle of winter at Mystery Creek, Hamilton. Billed as the largest single annual event in the country and attracting 140,000 people, it is seen by the suppliers of equipment, information, and services to the industry as "the window for our products for the year." One-hundred and twenty-six million dollars is reported to have been spent in four days on the product lines on display in 1994, and millions more is spent subsequently as a direct result of the visits of farmers to the event. For a number of years I lived directly across the road from the site, which was in my constituency, so I have had the opportunity to observe its growth and its shortcomings.

In New Zealand, women play an increasing role in the financial administration of farms. They are frequently the bookkeepers, planners, data-entry specialists. There is evidence that they generally, in Australia perhaps more markedly than in New Zealand, have higher educational qualifications than their husbands. They furnish the accountants with the materials for taxation returns, pay the accounts, and are active partners in designing the cropping or breeding policies for the year and in setting the production targets. But all of this seems lost on the marketeers at this biggest event of the year. There is no provision of on-site quality child care facilities. Equity questions aside, I consider this a major marketing blunder. No one can concentrate on making decisions about equipment worth thousands of dollars with a toddler demanding attention.

Whether markets or governments dominated by men can face it, the fact is that an increasing proportion of agricultural production, food security, environmental protection, nutrition, and animal health depends on the efforts of women, who work the longest days, at the most activities, with the least financial rewards and minimal economic recognition.

The role and work of women on the planet are intimately related to the goal of comprehensive socio-economic and political development. This work is vital for the development of all societies and for the quality of life on our planet. The manner in which high growth-rate activities are pursued increasingly sees escalating import volumes, environmental plundering, repatriation of profits, and little evidence that skills and technology are transferred, especially to rural women. In the key issue of agricultural trade in the Uruguay round leading to the General Agreement on Tariffs and Trade (GATT), Asian members of the Cairns group, which included Indonesia, Malaysia, the Philippines, and Thailand, had assiduously pursued the policy of restoring free trade to agriculture, with no evidence that any planning had been done to assess the socio-economic impact on the majority of the rural population, namely women and children.

The textbook World Bank and IMF formula for structural adjustment is argued frequently in the context of "political stability." The emphasis is on the deregulation of finance, capital, and labour, and a reorientation towards exports, along with a downward adjustment of exchange rates. Throughout this period, the developed countries have manipulated the system of exchange rates in order to maintain favourable terms of trade for themselves.

These policies for "political stability" have been policies for corruption, for unfair taxes, and for food shortages. They have seen rural revolts over expropriation of land. They have threatened food security and in their concentration on mono-cropping for export, have inflated basic food prices in the developing countries and vitally affected basic nutrition with the loss of land and resources for subsistence agriculture. A poor crop or harvest failure has not infrequently provoked armed conflict on a national or international level. Not only does food become a weapon of war, but the conflict causes extensive environmental degradation and population displacement—a most unstable situation.

Throughout the world there are political movements of people concerned about their own impoverishment, social disadvantages, and the misuse of national resources. It is a conscious struggle by women from all classes, castes, and nations against their inequitable burdens, their exclusion from political power, the lack of autonomy over their own bodies and, for too many rural women, a struggle for the lives of themselves and their children. And it has not escaped the observation of these women that their subordination is continually imposed on them, willingly and unwillingly, by men in a multitude of guises and in a multitude of ways. Women understand "agency," that they do not live as passive victims: that men have complicitly and explicitly denied their options.

This article has been excerpted, with permission of the author from Three Masquerades: Essays on Equality, Work, and Human Rights *(1997).*

Marilyn Waring is Professor of Public Policy at AUT University in Auckland New Zealand. She is a feminist political economist and environmental and human rights activist. She is the author of Counting for Nothing/If Women Counted; Three

Masquerade: Essays on Equality, Work, and Human Rights; In the Lifetime of a Goat; 1 Way 2 C the World *and co-author of* Who Cares? The Economics of Dignity, *about the 24/7 work of caregivers of those living with HIV and AIDS.*

[1]To be pedantic, a subsistence household or unit is one that does not carry out economic transactions with other units but exists completely on what it produces. To be realistic, exchange activities with the rest of the economy do occur, but they are infrequent and do not represent the basic elements of the unit's or person's economic life. In practice, where most production is intended for own use, the term used to describe this is subsistence.

REFERENCES

Asian Development Bank. *Women in Development: Nepal.* Manila, Philippines: Asian Development Bank, 1987.

de Beauvoir, Simone. *The Second Sex.* Trans. H. M. Parsley. London: Jonathan Cape, 1953.

Shaw, Deirdre. "The Work of Farming Women." M.A. Thesis. University of Waikato. Hamilton, New Zealand, 1993.

United Nations. "Report of the World Conference to Review and Appriase the Achievements of the United Nations Decade for Women: Equality, Development, and Peace." New York: United Nations, 1986.

World Bank. *Nepal: Poverty and Incomes: A Joint Study, World Bank and United Nations Development Program.* Washington: World Bank, 1991.

VANDANA SHIVA

The Seed and the Earth

The Colonization of Regeneration

SEEDS AND THE EARTH are central to the life-support of our planet. The seed symbolizes the biological richness of life in its regenerative power, and the earth symbolizes the living fertility from which all life derives nourishment and growth. Nature's fertility has been represented since ancient times through the symbolism of the earth Mother. The seed and the earth have been perennial symbols for the reproduction of society, of the human species.

Patriarchal world views in all their variation, from the ancient to the modern, from east to west, share one assumption—they are based on the removal of life from the earth, on the separation of the earth from the seed, and on the association of an inert and empty earth with the passivity of the female. The seed and the earth symbolism undergoes a metamorphosis when put into a patriarchal mould; and with it gender relations are restructured. This non-ecological view has formed the basis of patriarchal perceptions of gender roles in reproduction across religions and across ages.

The continuity between regeneration in human and non-human nature that was the basis of all nature-religions has been broken. Human beings have been separated from nature. Creativity is now the exclusive monopoly of men who are seen to be engaged in "production." Women are engaged in mere "reproduction" or "procreation," and nature has become inert, a mere "resource."

WOMEN AS NON-CREATIVE NATURE

Woman, earth, mother—these have been the symbols of creation—but not according to patriarchy. For patriarchy, creation takes place *ex nihilo* (to produce where nothing was before, to form out of nothing). Everything else is procreation (to beget, engender, generate, to produce offspring). Creativity is reserved for God in a male image. Pro creativity is the lot of women, nature, and god as nature personified. As a result, in the patriarchal paradigm, only "god-like" men can aspire to creativity. This devaluing of regeneration and the relocation of creativity from the regeneration of life to production of industrial commodities simultaneously devalues women and nature.

210

The assumption that male activity is true creation because it takes place ex nihilo is ecologically false. No industrial commodity is "formed out of nothing," no industrial process takes place "where nothing was before." Nature and its creativity is consumed at every level of industrial production—as "raw material," as "energy," for "waste" disposal. The assumption that only such production is truly creative because it produces from nothing hides the destruction that accompanies it. The patriarchal creation boundary allows ecological destruction to be perceived as creation, and ecological regeneration and creation to be perceived as non-creation. This devaluing of regeneration underlies the ecological crises and the crises of sustainability. To sustain life involves, above all, to regenerate life. But in the patriarchal view, to regenerate is not to create, it is merely to "repeat."

The assumption of creation ex nihilo is also false because no regeneration is mere repetition. Each child born, each plant renewed is a novel and creative experience. Each offspring, while maintaining the continuity of regeneration is "new" and different. This is how diversity is produced and renewed. While no industrial process takes place ex nihilo, the creation myth of patriarchy is particularly unfounded in the case of biotechnologies where life forms become the "raw material" for industrial production. Yet creation myths continue to create values that deprive all prior regeneration of value as "pure repetition."

FROM TERRA MATER TO TERRA NULLIUS

Constructing nature as lifeless matter was essential to the destruction of all prior value and rights. Non-European societies were viewed as not fully human when Europeans colonized them in a process that will soon be 500 years old. Being animals, the original Australians, Americans, Africans, and Asians possessed no rights as humans. They could, therefore, be ignored as people and exterminated. Their lands could be usurped as "terra nullius"—lands empty of people, "vacant," "waste," "unused." The morality of the missions justified the military takeover of resources all over the world to serve imperial markets. In a state of nature, everything is considered worthless as it is not serving human needs—earthly phenomena become valuable only after human lab our and machine technology transform them into useful material.

The making of terra nullius (the empty earth) from terra mater (the earth mother) is probably the most significant shift induced by modern patriarchy. The reductionist mechanistic metaphor simultaneously creates the measure of value and the instruments for destroying that which it does not value. It creates the possibility to colonize and control everything that is free and self-generative. Through reductionist science, technological development proceeds steadily from what it has already transformed and used up, toward that which is still untouched. is in this sense that the seed and women's bodies as sites of regenerative power are, in the eyes of capitalist patriarchy, among the last colonies. These sites of creative regeneration are turned into "passive" sites where the export "producers" produce and add value. Nature, women, and non-European people merely provide "raw" material. The devaluation of contributions from women and nature goes hand-in-hand with the value assigned to acts of colonization as acts of development and improvement. Separation, which should be a sign of alienation, is transformed into a means of ownership and control. The act of removal thus becomes the act of owning, and it is for the ability to remove, separate, and fragment that capital depends on science and science-based technologies. However, ownership through removal and "mixing with lab our" denies that in situ existence does involve prior lab our. There is no clear divide between nature and human lab our in the cultivated seed and the human offspring.

THE COLONIZATION OF HUMAN REGENERATION

The process of birth has always been at the centre of all images of creativity and fertility, and the mother has been the source of that creativity. However, old patriarchal beliefs, combined with the new technologies, reinforce the image of women as empty vessels and men as the creators.

When women have children, they are viewed less as sources of human regeneration than as the "raw material" from which the "product," the baby is extracted. In these circumstances, the physician rather than the mother comes to be seen as having produced the baby. In the case of IVF, an expert committee sees doctors not only as "enablers" but as "taking part in the formation of the embryo itself."

Whereas the focus was formerly on the mother, and the organic unity of the mother and the baby, it is now cent red on the "fetal outcome" controlled by doctors. Women's wombs have been reduced to mere containers and their passivity has been constructed along with their ignorance. The direct organic bond with thefetus is substituted with knowledge mediated by men and machines.

With the new reproductive technologies, the shift in power from the mother to the doctor, from women to men is accentuated. Singer and Wells in *Having Babies* have suggested that the production of sperm is worth a great deal more than the production of eggs. They conclude that sperm vending places a greater strain on the men than egg "donation" does on women, in spite of the chemical and mechanical invasion into the woman's body. Further, IVF and other technologies are currently offered for the "abnormal" cases of infertility, but the boundary between normal and abnormal is as fluid as the boundary between nature and non-nature. When pregnancy was first transformed into a medical disease, professional management was limited to abnormal cases, while normal cases continued to be looked after by the original professionals, the midwife. While 70 percent of childbirths were thought normal enough to be delivered at home in the 1930s, 70 percent were identified as abnormal enough to be delivered in the hospital in the 1950s. As Ann Dakly has stated in Captured Wombs, "The wombs of women are containers to be captured by the ideologies and practices of those who do not believe that women can take care of themselves."

An article called "A Revolution in Making Babies" in *Time* magazine describes techniques to cross the "barrier" that menopause poses to pregnancy. The article states that "new findings suggest that these women may be infertile not because their uterus are too old but because their ovaries are." It systematically interprets the body's rhythms as technological barriers. Crossing these barriers involves fragmenting the organism, in the mind and materially. In fact, reducing organic wholes into fragmented, separable or substitutable parts has been the reductionist way of breaking out of nature's limits.

The rise of the western medical profession is in essence the rise of male control over women's knowledge and women's bodies. Patriarchal science and patriarchal laws have worked hand-in-hand to establish the control of professional men over women's lives.

Recent work on surrogacy and new reproductive technologies reveals how women's knowledge, contributions, and rights are being forced to disappear. Women's regenerative capacities have been substituted by doctors as "producers" and rich infertile couples as "consumers." The woman whose body is being exploited as a machine is not seen as the one who needs protection from exploiting doctors and rich couples. Instead, the "consumer" needs protection from the biological mother who has been reduced to a surrogate uterus.

The earlier stages of the patriarchal division of labour and the creation boundary had created a gendered dualism between production and reproduction, creation and procreation, with reproduction and procreation being exclusively female activities. With the new biotechnologies, reproduction too is moving out of women's control. Gena Corea projects that by the year 2050, women:

> will be divorced from their own procreative power as we (in our generation) are divorced from our sexuality.... These will be women who, from their earliest days, grew up with the reality of IVF, embryo transfer, surrogate motherhood, artificial wombs, and sex predetermination technology. From childhood, these women will have watched television news reports involving the "Storage Authority," that is, the board in charge of frozen sperm, eggs, and human embryos.

This, then might be the reproductive consciousness of our daughters in the twenty-first century: "Reproduction is a complicated, intellectual and technical feat performed by teams of highly skilled men who use, as raw material for their achievements, the body parts of a variety of interchangeable females."

The new reproductive technologies allow for new levels of invasion into the processes of childbirth. Yet it is the old metaphor of women as passive vessels that is renewed with the new technologies. Medical developments have simply allowed contemporary scientific rhetoric to reassert an enduring set of deeply patriarchal beliefs that women are passive containers in the renewal of life. This idea of woman as vessel, and the fetus as "created" by the father's seed, and owned by patriarchal right goes hand-in-hand with breaking the organic links between the mother and the fetus which is part of her body. Recent work on children and the environment has reduced the mother to a factor in the child's environment. And "fetal rights" and "fetal protection policies" tend to treat mothers as the biggest threat to the fetus instead of the very condition for its life. Since women are not unknowing matter, and since their knowledge is often at variance with the knowledge of "medical experts,"women's attempts to make decisions about their bodies (and fetuses as an organic part of their bodies) are viewed as a threat, and are therefore criminalized; even though it is the doctor who is often the criminal in insisting on the use of violent invasive technologies against the knowledge of women.

THE COLONIZATION OF PLANT REGENERATION

Plant regeneration is based on maintaining the cycles of fertility—in the earth, and in the seed. However, agricultural development in the patriarchal world view sees cycles of fertility as limits that need to be broken, and sees breaking these limits as symbols of transcendence and power.

Sustainable agriculture is based on the recycling of soil nutrients. This involves returning to the soil part of the nutrients that come from it and that support plant growth. The maintenance of the nutrient cycle and the fertility of the soil is based on this inviolable law of return. The Green Revolution paradigm, however, substitutes the nutrient cycle with linear flows of purchased chemical fertilizers from factories (inputs), and marketed agricultural commodities (outputs). The Green Revolution is essentially based on "miracle seeds" which need chemical fertilizers and which do not produce any "outputs" which could be returned to the soil. The earth is again viewed as an empty vessel which can be filled with irrigation water and chemical fertilizer. The only "activity" is in the "miracle seeds" which transcend nature's own fertility cycles.

However, ecologically, the earth and the soil are not empty, and plant growth of Green Revolution varieties does not take place ex nihilo with the seed fertilizer packet. The development of soil diseases and micro nutrient deficiencies are indicators of the invisible demands the new varieties are making on the fertility of the soil. The desertification of soils is also an indicator of the broken cycles of soil fertility caused by plant breeding which produces plant outputs only for the market, not for the soil.

Technologies are not a substitute for nature, and they are not able to work outside nature's ecological processes without destroying the very basis of production. Nor can markets provide the only measure of "output" and "yields." The Green Revolution creates the perception that soil fertility is produced in chemical factories, and that agricultural yields are measured only through marketed commodities. Crops like pulses which fix the nitrogen in the soil have therefore been displaced. Millet, which produces high yields from the perspective of returning organic matter to the soil, has been rejected as a "marginal" crop. Biological products not sold on the market but used simply to maintain soil fertility are totally ignored in the cost-benefit equations of the Green Revolution miracle. They are not purchased, and they are not sold. Yet what is "unproductive" and "waste" in the commercial context of the Green Revolution is now emerging as productive in the ecological context and as the only route to sustainable agriculture. By treating essential organic inputs that maintain the integrity of nature as "waste," the Green Revolution strategy ensures that fertile and productive soils are actually laid waste. The "land-augmenting" technology has proved to be a land-degrading and land-destroying technology. With the greenhouse effect and global warming, a new dimension has been added to the ecologically destructive effect of chemical fertilizers. Nitrogen-based fertilizers release nitrous oxide into the atmosphere which is one of the greenhouse gases causing global warming. Chemical fertilizers have thus contributed to the erosion of food security through the pollution of the land, water, and atmosphere.

While the Green Revolution is based on the assumption of the inert earth, the biotechnology revolution robs even the seed of its fertility and self-regenerative capacities. The colonization of the seed reflects the patterns of the colonization of our bodies. Profits and power are behind the invasion into all biological organisms. There are two major routes to the commodification and colonization of the seed. The first is through technical means, the second through property rights.

The hybridization of seed was an invasion into the seed. It broke the unity of the seed as grain and the seed as means of production. In doing so, it created the opportunity for capital accumulation that private industry needed in order to put down firm roots in plant breeding and commercial seed production. And it became the source of ecological disruption by transforming a self-regenerative process into a broken linear form of supply of raw material and a reverse flow of commodities.

Modern plant breeding is primarily an attempt to remove the biological obstacle to marketing the seed. The seed which reproduces itself stays free, a common resource and under the farmers' control, especially women farmers. The corporate seed has a price and is under the control of the corporate sector or under the control of agricultural research institutions. The transformation of a common resource into a commodity, of self-regenerative resources into mere "input" changes the nature of the seed and of agriculture itself. Since it robs peasants of their livelihood, the new technology becomes an instrument of poverty and under development.

The decoupling of seed from grain also changes the status of the seed. From being a finished product, nature's seeds and people's seeds become raw material for the production of the corporate seed as commodity. The cycle of regeneration of biodiversity is therefore replaced by a linear flow of free germ plasm from farms and forests into labs and research stations, and flow of modified uniform products as priced commodities from corporations to farmers. Diversity is destroyed by transforming it into mere raw material for industrial production, which necessarily displaces the diversity of local agricultural practice.

This change in the nature of the seed is justified by creating a framework that treats self-regenerative seeds as "primitive" and as "raw" germ plasm, and the seed that is inert and non-reproducible as a finished product. The whole is rendered partial, the partial is rendered whole. The commoditized seed, however, is ecologically incomplete and ruptured at two levels: 1) it does not reproduce itself, even though by definition, a seed is a regenerative resource. Genetic resources are thus transformed through technology from renewable into non-renewable resources. 2) it does not produce by itself. It needs the help of inputs, such as chemical fertilizer. As the seed and chemical companies merge, the dependence on these inputs will increase, not decrease. And whether a chemical is added externally or internally, it remains an external input in the ecological cycle of the reproduction of the seed. It is this shift from the ecological processes of reproduction to the technological processes of production that underlies the problems of dispossession of farmers and of genetic erosion.

Farmers' seeds are rendered incomplete and valueless by the process that makes corporate seeds the basis of wealth creation. The indigenous varieties, evolved through both natural and human selection, and produced and used by ThirdWorld farmers worldwide are called "primitive." Those varieties created by modern plant breeders in international research centres or by transnational seed corporations are called "advanced" or "elite."

The issue of patent protection for modified life forms raises a number of unresolved political questions about the ownership and control of genetic resources. The problem is that in manipulating life forms, you do not start from nothing, but from other life forms which belong to others—maybe through customary law. Secondly, genetic engineering and biotechnology do not create new genes, they merely relocates genes already existing in organisms. In making genes the object of value through the patent system, a dangerous shift takes place in the approach to genetic resources.

Most Third World countries view genetic resources as a common heritage. In most countries, animals and plants were excluded from the patent system until recently, with the advent of biotechnologies. With the new biotechnologies, life can now be owned. The potential for gene manipulation reduces the organism to its genetic constituents. Centuries of ongoing innovation are totally devalued to give reproductive technologies—new boundaries are being drawn between what is nature and what is not nature, what is a right and what is not a right.

The U.S. international trade commission has estimated that U.S. industry was losing between 100 to 300 million U.S. dollars due to the absence of "intellectual property rights." The institutioning of this regime of "rights" demanded by the U.S transfers of these extra funds from the poor to rich countries and exacerbates the Third World crisis ten times over.

The U.S. has accused the Third World of "piracy." The estimates provided for royalties lost are 202 million dollars in agricultural chemicals, and $2,545,000 for pharmaceuticals. However, as the team at the Rural Advancement Fund International has shown, if contributions of Third World peasants and tribals are taken into account, the "pirate" roles are substantially reversed. The U.S. owes hundreds of millions for royalties in agriculture and thousands of millions for royalties in pharmaceuticals. In other words, in these two biological industry sectors alone, the U.S. owes billions to the Third World.

It is to prevent the accounting of these debts that the creation boundary is being set up through intellectual property rights. Without it, the colonization of regenerative processes of life is impossible. Yet, if this last colony is allowed to be carved out in the name of patent protection, innovation, and progress, life itself will have been colonized. And that colonization will herald the ultimate ecological crisis in which cycles of regeneration are torn apart, and forced into non-renewable linear flows of raw materials and commodities. The colonization of life will be complete when we allow the technological mind set to colonize our minds and allow technological means to be viewed as ends of human choice. In biotechnology, the science of means is being pushed into the "womb and seed pool" to transform the conception of life itself.

Protection of life in this age of pervasive and invasive technologies requires, above all, that we do not slip into viewing technique and know-how as values and ends in themselves. It requires that we keep alive in us a capacity to make ethical choices about what is good and valuable, and subject technological means to those ethical ends. Else we will have foreclosed our options to celebrate life in its spontaneity, diversity and renewability.

This article is excerpted from the author's testimonial to the World Women's Congress for a Healthy Planet, Miami Florida, November 8 to 12, 1991. For more recent comments on these issues by Vandana Shiva see "Vandana Shiva on the Problem with Genetically Modified Seeds", podcast of an extended interview with Bill Moyers aired on July 13, 2012. <http://billmoyers.com/video>.

Vandana Shiva is an internationally renowned activist for biodiversity and against corporate globalization, and author of Stolen Harvest: The Hijacking of the Global Food Supply; Earth Democracy: Justice, Sustainability, and Peace; Soil Not Oil; *and* Staying Alive.

HELEN FORSEY

GMOs

Globalizing Male Omnipotence

A S A WOMAN who loves life, eats food, and works with farmers, I have watched the public debate over Genetically Modified Organisms (GMOs) with the keen interest of a participant-observer. After all, the issue of genetic manipulation touches multiple aspects of our lives—the safety and quality of our food, the health and stability of the environment, the on-going contest between the public good and private globalized corporate interests. Whether and how we as humans manipulate the stuff of life profoundly affects both the present and the future of our own and other species on this planet.

Everyone who is concerned about the rapid advance of genetic biotechnology pretty well agrees on that much. But in almost all the discussions, there is a gaping hole. Through all the talk of butterflies and bacteria, profits and preferences, nutraceuticals and novel foods, margins and marketability, almost no one seems to have noticed that the whole GMO enterprise reeks of patriarchy.

It is a hard thing to say in mixed company, but I am convinced that genetic engineering represents the culmination of the perverse but pervasive masculine quest for control. I trust that the reader will give me the benefit of the doubt and allow me to skip the ritual prefatory explanation of why this claim does not constitute "an attack on men," so as to get on with the real discussion.

Admittedly, some of the connections between GMOs and male dominance may not be immediately obvious. Nonetheless, if you look beneath the surface, GMO technology itself, its ownership aspects, the way it is being introduced and promoted in the context of globalization, and even much of the controversy surrounding it, all demonstrate a fundamentally patriarchal mind-set. In this article I want to substantiate this claim, and address the problem this situation represents for women, other human beings, and the planet.

THE ILLUSION OF "CONTROL"

For years, men have fought wars, built empires, colonized whole continents, taken over corporate rivals, and penetrated outer space as they compete for mastery of the universe. Now, with the tools of biotechnology, they are invading what Indian physicist and activist Vandana Shiva (1997) calls the "inner spaces" of the living cell, trying to take possession of its DNA, the very stuff of life. The space may be different, but the mentality of conquest is the same.

The patriarchal illusion of control is one of the hallmarks of a globalized culture where "masculine" values predominate. Descartes' famous declaration about becoming "the masters and possessors of nature" encapsulated this mechanistic mentality in 1636, and as Carolyn Merchant, Brian Easlea and others have noted, the same attitude has largely shaped scientific endeavour ever since.

This mentality and its corresponding practice are clearly linked today with the neo-liberal ideology of global capitalism, in which giant transnational corporations, almost always headed by powerful white men, seek to consolidate their ability to exploit other human beings and the earth. The World Trade Organization (WTO), international trade agreements, and specific agreements like the one on Trade-Related Intellectual Property (TRIPs)—basically, the patenting of life—embody that ideology and enable the corporate elites to pursue their goal of dominance, free of any constraints that might be imposed by local or national governments or by communities of people defending their human rights and their place on the planet.

Key to this on-going corporate endeavour is biotechnology, at once an extreme expression of the mechanistic world view and, together with the "intellectual property rights" that accompany it, a powerful practical tool for imposing that worldview on societies and environments across the globe. Those of us who have watched how patriarchy operates in other contexts recognize the familiar patterns and have little trouble connecting the dots. Unfortunately, however, most well-known critics of global devastation have failed to notice the role patriarchy plays at the source of the problem. Leading spokespeople in the environmental movement continually make statements like: "We have long thought of ourselves as masters of the natural world, but now that drive to dominate and control is having dangerous consequences." Or: "Much of the planet is dying, and we are, all of us, the cause." This language neatly avoids requiring anyone to confront the gender dimension of the domination mentality. It thereby also short-circuits a deeper analysis, which is needed if we are ever to truly understand our predicament and move through and beyond it.

When we do take the gender dimension seriously, we become aware that seeing human beings as "masters of the natural world" is significantly and specifically a view of reality as men experience it under patriarchy. Most women find it hard enough to imagine ourselves as "masters" of anything, and that is not a mere quibble over a choice of words. Man's "drive to dominate and control" has always been dangerous to women, to children, and to other living things; but we have regularly been ignored, ridiculed, and silenced—often brutally—for daring to try to point this out.

Feminists like Elizabeth Dodson Gray, Dorothy Dinnerstein, and Vandana Shiva (1989) have noted that patriarchal societies have long identified women with "nature" and have sanctioned the all-out exploitation of both, at the same time colonizing or destroying earth-based cultures which honour the feminine principle and the natural world.

Meanwhile, women's social conditioning and actual life experience tend to make us somewhat more skeptical of mastery and conquest, less obsessed with ownership, perhaps more respectful of natural processes. Someone who lives in a woman's body and has to cope every day both with her own biology and with a whole range of male attempts at control, is less likely to fall for the dangerous illusion that "we" can (or should) ultimately manage everything.

GMOS AND THE MASCULINIZATION OF AGRICULTURE

In the specific context of the current genetic engineering debate, these gender-related realities make a difference at many levels. As female human beings, women are generally less apt to be entranced by a philosophical concept based on mastery of nature, less likely to be aroused by the prospect of exerting ultimate control over life. Women farmers and gardeners tend to be somewhat less susceptible to the pro-biotech ads in the farm press promising "More Bottom Line Power" or proclaiming "Just the Facts" about GMO seeds. As preparers of food, many women are suspicious of government and corporate propaganda aimed at denying them informed choice through mandatory labelling of GMO foods. And, as the majority of the world's poor, women are less willing to be taken in by promises of "happy-ever-after" in a brave new world run by the same technocrats and free-traders who have always exploited and impoverished them.

Of course it would be simplistic to suggest that the dispute over GMOs splits neatly along gender lines. Many men as well as women oppose the patriarchal values of dominance and control, and are valiantly resisting the onslaught of the biotech giants. Unfortunately there are also many women who have bought into the corporate pro-GMO line. This issue is not a case of men versus women, it is a clash of world views. If we are to adequately address the pro-GMO position, it is essential that we understand its inherently patriarchal nature.

In an article entitled, "Monocultures, Monopolies, Myths and the Masculinization of Agriculture," Vandana Shiva pleads for recognition of this crucial element. She points out that in most of the world, "women farmers have been the seed keepers and seed breeders over millennia," practicing a subsistence agriculture which feeds masses of people. "In this woman-centered agriculture," she says,

> knowledge is shared, other species and plants are kin, not "property," and sustainability is based on renewal of the earth's fertility and regeneration of biodiversity. There is no place for monocultures of genetically engineered crops and monopolies on seeds.

Shiva's (1998) vision contrasts sharply with the current picture she paints of "corporate men investing in theft and biopiracy [who] present themselves as creators and owners of life."

Again, this male compulsion to own and control the life force itself feels eerily familiar to feminists. Some years ago, I heard Geraldine Finn speak at Carleton University about the way male science has attempted, through computer technology, to appropriate the creation of human intelligence. She held up a newspaper advertisement showing a computer in a baby carriage, and wondered rhetorically what the psychological appeal might be.

Others around the world, observing men's pervasive habit of claiming ownership of women and children and the key role in reproduction, have identified "womb envy" as a male phenomenon that transcends cultures. It seems reasonable to suggest that the same dynamic might be at work in the field of genetic engineering.

Shiva's writings repeatedly point out that even as the biotechnology corporations push a myriad of species and millions of peasant farmers to extinction, they persist in calling themselves "the life sciences industry." I would add that this corporate abuse of the term "life sciences" parallels the use of the phrase "pro-life" by the opponents of reproductive choice. Both are patriarchal appropriations of life-affirming values—traditionally seen and experienced as women's values. Appropriation twists the values and then tries to use them for anti-life, anti-choice, anti-female purposes.

THE FEMINIZATION OF RESISTANCE

Another example of the neglected gender dimension of the GMO debate is the patronizing attitude of biotech proponents in the corporations and in certain corporate-oriented farm groups towards consumers who oppose them. The superior, condescending tone of much of the industry talk about "educating consumers" comes at least in part from a very male place, and is directed towards a mass of the population which is generally perceived as female.

Think about it: what image does the word "consumer" conjure up? A guy in a suit with a briefcase? A man in a hard-hat with a hammer, or in a checked shirt driving a tractor? Not likely. The typical image is one of a woman, pushing a shopping cart through a grocery store with small children in tow. Against a cultural backdrop which still too often paints women as light-weight, "emotional," beings who can be easily hoodwinked by "scare-mongers," the GMO pushers can indulge in paternalistic little homilies about "the customer" always being right, even though she may be "scientifically" wrong.

These people give no real credence to the possibility that all those consumers out there just might have good reasons for wanting to avoid genetically modified products. By disregarding the potential validity of women's concerns, they can dismiss the widespread public opposition to GMOs as merely the "emotional" reaction of ignorant and gullible housewives to technological innovation. In the arrogance of this mentality, which is given considerable play in the mainstream farm press, consumer resistance is viewed as nothing more than a marketing challenge that the corporate PR and marketing people have to solve.

What is really happening in consumerland is, of course, quite different. The widespread and increasing opposition to genetically-modifiied foods from both female and male consumers is an informed and conscientious response to an unproven and risk-laden technology. Women in particular have been targeted too often by marketing experts intent on selling the latest in food additives or pharmaceutical products, and we have good reasons for being wary. For most of us, concerned about our own and our families' health, the Precautionary Principle is the intuitive starting point from which we enter the GMO arena.

One of the most hopeful and inspiring examples of resistance to GMOs as harbingers of corporate globalization is the decade-long battle to ban Bovine Growth Hormone (BGH) from Canada. In the 1990s, this genetically engineered "production aid" was Monsanto Corporation's flagship product, introduced with great fanfare to demonstrate the marvels of GM technology.

Since injections of BGH force dairy cows to produce up to 20 percent more milk—and burn them out in the process, one would think Monsanto would have realized the folly of trying to promote such a technology to anyone with mammary glands. Moreover, use of the genetically engineered hormone presents possible human health risks, and raises economic as well as animal welfare concerns at the farm level.

Canadian farmers, consumers, scientists, health activists, and others mobilized in an unprecedented and persistent opposition to this intrusive drug, forcing the government in 1999 to impose a permanent ban on the sale of BGH in Canada. (The ban does not, however, cover its use, and cross-border shopping for the drug is not unknown.)

I would maintain that a non-patriarchal society could never have come up with anything resembling BGH. Feminist culture has deep roots in nature and in the spiritual and moral values of humility and wonder, caring and respect.

It is not surprising, then, that women are the backbone of the increasing world-wide opposition to GMOs. Except for the minority who have been bought or hoodwinked by industry interests, women—and the increasing numbers of men who are open to women's perspectives—are generally unwilling to ignore the risks or to disregard the enormous unknown potential impacts of this technology on human beings and the Earth.

By contrast, the guys with the briefcases claim to know the facts, and they reassure us with all the confidence that their big salaries and sparkling career prospects bestow. "Not to worry, folks," they say. "We're managers. We'll manage the risk, manage nature, manage the earth. There's no problem when we're in charge."

How far will they go with their "management?" One of the largest biotech companies is reportedly on record as wanting to make all crops transgenic so that people will have no choice but to consume them. This outrageous, ultimate, "obey or starve" scenario is conceived in a place where the brown, the black, the poor, and the female are despised—and can therefore be manipulated or destroyed with impunity.

The issues in this struggle go deeper than even many activists realize. Like the movement for peace, like the movement to save the Earth, the resistance to the patenting and manipulation of life urgently needs the understandings we have as women and as feminists. Let's make sure it gets them. At stake is nothing less than the future of life itself.

Helen Forsey is an Ottawa Valley writer and activist. Her books include Circles of Strength: Community Alternatives to Alienation (1993), The Caboose at the Cape: A Story of Coming Home *(2011), and* Eugene Forsey: Canada's Maverick Sage *(2012).*

REFERENCES

Dinnerstein, Dorothy. "Survival on Earth: The Meaning of Feminism." *Healing the Wounds: The Promise of Ecofeminism.* Ed. Judith Plant. Toronto: Between The Lines Press, 1989.

Dodson Gray, Elizabeth. *Green Paradise Lost.* Wellesley, MA: Roundtable Press, 1979.

Forsey, Helen, "Back into the Quagmire: Linking Patriarchy and Planetary Destruction." *Alternatives* 19 (3) (1993): 47-49.

Easlea, Brian. *Fathering the Unthinkable: Masculinity, Scientists and the Nuclear Arms Race.* Pluto Press, London, 1983.

Merchant, Carolyn. *The Death of Nature: Women, Ecology and the Scientific Revolution.* San Francisco: Harper and Row, 1980.

Ontario Farmer. Volumes 33 and 34. London, Ont., 2000-2001.

Shiva, Vandana. *Biopiracy: The Plunder of Nature and Knowledge.* Toronto: Between The Lines Press, 1997.

Shiva, Vandana. "Development, Ecology and Women." *Healing the Wounds: The Promise of Ecofeminism.* Ed. Judith Plant. Toronto: Between The Lines, 1989. 80-90.

Shiva, Vandana. "Monocultures, Monopolies, Myths and the Masculinization of Agriculture." International Conference on Women and Agriculture, Washington, DC, June, 1998.

Shiva, Vandana. "The Seed and the Earth: Biotechnology and the Colonization of Regeneration." *Close To Home: Women Reconnect Ecology, Health and Development Worldwide.* Ed. Vandana Shiva. Gabriola Island, BC: New Society Publishers, 1994. 128-143.

Western Producer. Volumes 78 and 79. Saskatoon, Sask., 2000-2001.

ANA ISLA

The Struggle for Clean Water and Livelihood

Canadian Mining in Costa Rica
in the Era of Globalization

> *I want you to tell Canadians that here [Costa Rica] there is a town
> (Miramar) that struggles against the big powers, that we are fighting
> desperately to eradicate Canadian powers from our lands.*
> —Alexander Flores Aguero (1999, Traditional Popular Culture
> National Award)

"SAY YES TO LIFE, No To Mining!" was the slogan of a protest against the
Canadian firm Vanessa Ventures Ltd in Costa Rica on March 22, 2002.
Thousands of Costa Ricans took to the streets in Ciudad Quesada to
battle the decision of their national government to grant a permit for open pit
gold mining to another Canadian mining corporation.

Why are Costa Ricans fighting Canadian mining firms? The answer involves
forests, pollution, debt, water, local livelihoods, and globalization-related
national policy changes. Women are central in the mining protests, both as
leaders and as those whose lives are most affected.

Two periods built the Costa Rican resistance: the globalization of the debt
crisis, in the 1980s, that brought International Monetary Fund (IMF) and World
Bank (WB) policies (stabilization and structural adjustment) to Costa Rica's
doorstep to facilitate entry of foreign investment; and the globalization of the
environmental crisis, in the early 1990s, that brought corporate environmental
NGOS to Costa Rica's forest to expedite enclosure.

Costa Rica—which has one of the highest per-capita debts in Latin
America—has been experimenting with sustainable development in the form of
conservation areas as part of its overall strategy of retiring foreign debt through
debt-for-nature swaps (Isla). The Sistema Nacional de Areas de Conservacion
(SINAC) has divided the country into eleven Conservation Areas under the
supervision of MINAE (the Ministry of Environment and Energy). MINAE has
taken the right to land ownership away from owners of small- and medium-
sized farms and placed it in the hands of the government in order to promote
biological corridors in the conservation areas.

224

In 1991, the World Wildlife Fund-Canada (WWF-C) and MINAE (Ministry of Environment and Mining) drafted the first step of a management plan, *El Plan General de Uso de la Tierra* (The General Land Use Plan) for the Arenal-Tilaran Conservation Area (ACA). This plan regulated land access and use. According to the WWF-C Canadian director (interview, summer 1998), the *Land Plan* in ACA was based on the characteristics of the territory and its biophysical potentialities, and it identified the limits of acceptable human intervention for the sustainability of the area. The area is called "Costa Rica's gold belt" due to fairly large deposits of buried alluvial gold which are found there. The gold belt includes the towns of Montes del Aguacate and Cordillera de Tilaran, in the mining district of Abangares. The towns of Libano, Miramar and Montes del Aguacate (Biamonte 1999) also belong to this district.

The Arenal-Tilaran Conservation Area extends over 250,561.5 hectares (ha) of land. Out of this total, the *Land Plan* document recommended protecting 116,690.2 ha for sustainable development, including a research program, ecotourism and global air market (selling CO_2). But by 1993, a large part of these territories had been designated for mineral exploration (*Plan General de Uso de la Tierra*). A pamphlet entitled, "Description of the Arenal-Tilaran Conservation Area" (made available by ACA-Tilaran's central offices), clearly underlines this contradiction: the pamphlet decries the destruction of the rain forest but also encourages transnational corporation (TNCs) investments in farming, wood and forest activities, environmental services, and the extraction of earth minerals in ACA. By 1998, at least eight Canadian mining firms were operating more than twelve gold mines in the Arenal area.

COSTA RICA'S GOLD BELT

Open pit mining in Costa Rica now uses the extremely toxic cyanide lixiviation technique, which has led to severe pollution and consequently to organized resistance among local communities. Women and men are concerned that an increase in strip mining can further destroy local rivers and lakes. The resistance to mining is therefore a struggle not only for clean water but also for the preservation of livelihoods. The government has tried to sell sustainable development as "environmental preservation" in the name of ecological conservation. However, communities in the "gold belt" understand that the "national" government cannot protect their interests and their livelihoods, because it cannot protect their environment. For instance, on the Pacific coast, MINAE granted twenty concessions to transnational mining corporations that exploit 11,697 hectares of land, while a further eleven concessions are still under negotiation. The indebted Costa Rican government's abandonment of land to mining corporations has led to the expropriation of 16,097 hectares of land from local communities. In many cases, communities have been forcibly evicted (Isla).

On the Pacific coast, the following Canadian mining companies are already in operation:

1) Las Lilas Mining Project in *Quebrada Grande de Liberia,* owner of the subsidiary Tierra Colorada S.A of Barrick Gold, a Canadian company;

2) Mining Rio Chiquito de Tilaran, owned by Corporation Minerals Mallon S.A, a subsidiary of the Canadian Mallon Minerals. Newmont Mining was also involved in exploring the property (*Mining Magazine,* March 1992:179);

3) Mining La Union, in La Union of Montes de Oro, owned by Minerales La Union S.A, a Canadian subsidiary;

4) Mining Beta Vargas in La Pita de Chomes, Puntareanas and San Juan of Abangares-Guanacaste, owned by the subsidary Novontar S.A of Lyon Lake Mines of Canada;

5) Ariel Resources Ltd, in La Junta de Abangares, the oldest Canadian mining in Costa Rica, extracts gold through three subsidiaries:

a) Mining Tres Hermanos, operated by el Valiente Ascari;

b) Mining San Martin, operated by Mining of Sierra Alta S.A; and,

c) Mining El Recio, operated by Minera Silencio S.A.

Ariel Resources Ltd has been operating in the area since 1986. In November 2000, it disappeared from Costa Rica, leaving debts with the Costarican Hydro Institute (ICE) and with its workers, who presented complaints at Cañas Tribunal against one of Ariel Resources subsidiaries (Torres 2000).

Women and men in the area wrote a Position Paper in 1999 in which they highlighted their concern with the inadequacies of MINAE. The paper describes their distress with mining and the problems that have been created in the area:

•The displacement from traditional ways of life and livelihood to give space to mining. "We were expelled from Rio Chiquito in Tilaran to make room for mining, because they claimed that we were causing damage to flora and fauna, water and soil";

•The suffering of women, men and children when water contamination forces them to emigrate

•The grief and hardship due to the openings of hollows in the soil where their cattle fall and die;

•The disruption to their culture and relationship with nature by the elimination of recreation spaces; consequently, drug-addiction, alcoholism and prostitution become more significant.

The Position Paper concludes with incredulity about the promise of job creation and mistrust that MINAE and its partners can confront the ecological crisis while simultaneously supporting the mining industries. Community members's experience has shown that the only outcomes are destruction and illusory benefits that disappear immediately once the mine closes, leaving only devastation.

Mining corporations raise significant funds in the stock markets to begin production. These are for the most part mutual funds, which collect money deposited by individuals and invest it in an array of financial assets; and pension funds, which are huge pots of retirement savings under professional investors" management. Thus, a significant number of middle-class Canadians with investments in these types of funds are implicated in the exploitation of Costa Ricans and other Latin Americans where mining has been unleashed.

ORGANIZING AGAINST GOLD MINING: THE CASES OF ARIEL RESOURCES LTDA AND MINA MACONA

Costa Ricans are organizing and resisting in the face of these threats. In 2001, I interviewed forestry engineer Sonia Torres, who states:

> *We welcome investments, if they respect our identity as agricultural people and our wish to live in peace and harmony with nature. But we won't accept projects we have not asked for, we do not want them. If foreign investors want to invest here, they must accept people's participatory processes, because we won't accept projects that conspire against our well-being, even if they were accepted by the "national" government. We already have our own development based on land, clean water and air, community, and solidarity.*

Sonia Torres was the coordinator of the National Front Against Gold Mining between 1999 and 2000. Torres and the National Front described the struggle against gold mining, using two examples to illustrate the disaster brought by mining to their water and their lives. Both examples involve Canadian-owned mines.

The Canadian firm Ariel Resources Ltd. operated for twelve years and its subsidiaries extracted gold in La Junta de Abangares. The subsidiaries are located on a hillside, where gravity helps to draw the mining contaminants toward the rivers and the areas modest homes. In this case, the gold mining is underground, and the material is extracted mechanically through tunnels developed along the gold and silver bearing quartz vein. The extraction is done by a process called cyanide lixiviation, which involves dissolving the metals using sodium cyanide. The process implies health risks for the workers in many ways, and it is deadly for the environment and local communities.

Despite the concern of local communities, the mines continue to leach cyanide into the river, streams and soil. At the urging of women, men and children, organized by the National Front, in 2000, a socio-environmental impact study documented the alteration and destruction of the land, biodiversity, scenery, water, air quality and human health, including evidence that underground water was also being contaminated. Despite the analysis, the Health Minister declared there was no contamination. Torres (2002) states that the local river also contains

800 times more iron than normal. As we stood outside of the "Cuatro Vientos" mine, which was abandoned by a Canadian company, we viewed the one main street of the town of Las Juntas de Abangares. It is still covered with rocks and yellow water which leaked from a chemical dump site. Torres stated that in addition to the destruction created while the company was in operation, neither the government nor the company was held responsible once the contract ended.

The destruction of the natural resources of local communities has impoverished community members at every level. They have lost fertile land to erosion and their water supplies are contaminated. *Campesinas/os* have been forced to abandon their *fincas* (farms) and emigrate to shanty towns or to the capital city of San Jose and into destructive ways of life (Torres 2001). While walking through this land of desolation, Torres points out many dried-up mountain streams surrounding the mine. Water pollution and mines treated with cyanide have also been deadly for fauna and flora, and for mangrove swamps, essential to maintain biological diversity. The worst effects can be seen in the water of the *Agua Caliente* river, which is now yellow and fetid with the odours of the chemicals used in mining (Gamboa). The *Agua Caliente* is a hot river due to geologic activity, and in the past it was used for recreation, therapeutic treatment and as a source of food. It is now terribly polluted. Local community members continued to use the waters because they didn't know about the mine discharges. As a result of the poison, aquatic life has been exterminated and community health has been undermined. According to Elizabeth Pizarro, from the Ministry of Health of Abangares, the local population has been experiencing rising illnesses, such as asthma, allergies, skin irritation, gastritis, and neurological disorders. But the most affected have been women, who suffer a high rate of miscarriages. The contamination of the water and air in the area has created much grief for rural women, who have to cope with high levels of birth defects and child mortality. Abangares child mortality is higher (15.2 percent) than in other parts of the country (12.5 percent), and the number of children with Down Syndrome is double that in other areas.

A second example of mining's effects in Costa Rica involves the Macacona mine in Esparza, Puntarenas (Fundacion Coyoche), known also as the Mondongo mine. It was the first open pit or strip mine in Costa Rica and was owned by the Canadian Barranca Mining subsidiary of Hearne Ltd. It controlled 200 hectares of land, and the mine covered 20 hectares. Open pit mining has many impacts on the environment and the social and cultural aspects of local communities. The first clear threat is that it eliminates the forest and any vegetation in the area, creating conditions for mudslides, while removing enormous quantities of soil in a short period of time. At Macacona, strip mining was done for seven years until the community closed the mine down at the end of 1989. However, twelve years later, the hectares operated by the mining company are still lifeless. The forest and its wildlife that had existed on the higher ground were removed in order for the company to made a vertical cut 150 meters deep, breaking the underground aquifer stratum for 925 metres (Fundacion Coyoche). The cyanide and other toxins used in the process of mining the gold killed the forest and contaminated the mountain streams of Turbina, Rio Paires, Rio Jesus Maria, and the mangrove swamps of Tivives and the Gulf of Nicoya. The pollution killed fish, wildlife, cattle and even people. Franklin Casares Villalobos drank water in Turbina and died instantly. Land sediments still contain cyanide and the destruction continues when the rain washes down the poison and the wind disseminates it throughout the surrounding areas; however, no one has been held responsible.

People have never received compensation for the destruction of their health, loss of life or for the degradation of the environment on which their livelihood depends. No amount of money could recompense the losses to these communities. However, Sonia Torres states that "The lies are the same, that we should sacrifice our quality of life for job creation. That was never the case, because mining produces few jobs for the locals. One characteristic of mining is that the operation is short-lived (a period of ten years on average), but its environmental and social implications are permanent. Local communities are contaminated, during the operation and long after a mine company leaves, since the abandoned infrastructure continues the contamination because of tanks and deposits of acid left behind" (Torres 2001).

These catastrophic experiences have led to resistence against mining among local communities. At the same time the Costa Rican government wants to impose a new round of strip gold mining projects in Miramar, Abangares, Puntarenas San Carlos and Liberia.

RESISTANCE IN THE ARENAL CONSERVATION AREA: THE CASE OF THE BELLAVISTA MINING PROJECT

Costa Rican Mining Rio Minerales S.A. and Metales Procesados M.R.W.S.A., subsidiaries of the Toronto-based Wheaton River Minerals, operate the Bellavista mine in the Arenal Conservation Area, two kilometres north of Miramar de Montes de Oro, Canton 4 in the province of Puntarenas. They signed a contract for exploration, granted by MINAE, and they also received the approval of SETENA, the Costa Rican agency which approves environmental impact assessments and establishes the monetary guarantees. The corporation has special Free Zone status and is thus exempt from taxes for imports (machinery, etc.) and exports including profit remittance. Consequently, local communities both subsidize and pay the full price of the mining corporation's destruction.

In 1996, the Pacific Regional Front of Opposition to Gold Mining initiated a campaign against Bellavista Mining, which was then owned by the Canadian mining company, Rayrock Corporation. Fuelled by opposition to the use of cyanide in lixiviation tanks, the campaign made public the following information:

We are opposed to mining in Bellavista, because it could:
• damage 12 water springs that are used for human consumption;

•destroy 117 *manzanas* of secondary forest;
•spoil *La Plata* and *Agua Buena* mountain streams;
•cause landslides that could deposit more than 35 million tons of material;
•contaminate fish with heavy metals, producing cerebral damage and malformation;
•cause an overflow of one million, seventeen thousand cubic litres of water contaminated with cyanide."(Pacific Regional Front, written on T-shirts)

Following this campaign, the Rayrock Corporation sold the project. In 1999, the Canadian company, Wheaton River Minerals Ltd., obtained a licence to operate the Bellavista mine. According to Sonia Torres, the government granted Wheaton River an even bigger area than before, so that the impact will be massive. According to the Pacific Regional Front, despite the fact that the project covers an area of 172 hectares, 473 hectares of surrounding land are directly affected, while an area of 6,172 hectares, which includes the watershed of the Ciruelas River, is indirectly affected. The project has already begun its destruction by cutting trees with the authorization of MINAE.

The community has to confront powerful interests in its demands for the protection of local water and subsistence. Since 1996, the Canadian mining establishment and its figureheads in Costa Rica, Rio Minerales S.A. and Metales Procesados M.R.W.S.A., have used different strategies to harass local community members who are opposed to their project. One of these instruments is the use of legal intimidation. In 1997, Sonia Torres was taken to court by Galaxie S.A. (POGGSA), a subsidiary of the Canadian firm Rayrock which then owned Bellavista.

In 2001, Wheaton River (through its figurehead Rio Minerales) accused Marta Blanco, a teacher and municipal councillor, of defamation. Wheaton River, in alliance with three MINAE officials who assisted the corporation as witnesses, accused Marta of falsely claiming that thousands of trees had been cut down for the Wheaton River project. at a special municipal meeting on September 18, 2000. Blanco denied the accusations. Blanco stated that for years, "the mining company has been sending lawyers and other contracted individuals with tape recorders to every municipal meeting to intimidate the members. They pressure the municipality to keep silent about the problems they are creating. On the day of our meeting where garbage collection was discussed, a lawyer of the company was there." Blanco adds,

On one occasion, I said that strip mining projects are synonymous with the total destruction of nature, because they cut down thousand of trees. For these words, I was taken to court, despite the fact that I did not refer to the Wheaton River Minerals project. The company claims that I lied that it had cut down thousands of trees and, furthermore, that it operates with MINAE and SETENA permits; therefore, I was making false statements, since the project is operating legally. We went to a conciliation meeting, at the Puntarenas Court. At the court, the lawyer for the company told me that the conciliation consisted in my resignation from the municipal post. The conciliation should be seen as a warning to the municipal office to stop speaking about their project. I made it explicit that my position was not going to change and that I was not going to resign.

Blanco was then taken to court by the corporation. In October 2001, the Puntarenas court, under Judge Antonio Rodriguez Rescia's direction, declared Marta responsible for defamation of Rios Minerales S.A and ordered her to pay the equivalent of CAD$ 3,250 in fines, damages, and court costs.

Blanco, with the support of the municipality and the Front Committee of Opposition to Mining in Miramar (Miramar Front), appealed this decision to a final constitutional court of appeal, and won. On March 1, 2002, Judges Javier Llobet Rodríguez, Fernando Cruz Castro and Rafael Sanabria Rojas, rejected the previous verdict, finding a lack of grounds for the corporation to accuse Marta Blanco who, as a municipal councillor, was only carrying out her responsibilities and her rights to defend the environment.

THE CASE OF VANESSA VENTURES LTD

On March 16, 2002, the Northern Front in Opposition to Mining in Cielo Abierto (Northern Front) called a press conference to announce a protest to be held in Ciudad Quesada on March 22, 2002. It demanded that the national government "Say yes to life, no to mining." The reason for the protest was another agreement between MINAE, the Costa Rican government, and another Canadian corporation. This time Infinito Industry S.A., a subsidiary of Vanessa Ventures Ltd. of Vancouver, had received a ten-year licence to mine in Las Crucitas, obtaining approval for a 1000- hectare exploitation area.

The Crucitas Project is located in Alajuela Province, Canton San Carlos, District of Cutris, 95 km. north of Ciudad Quesada and 20 km northeast of Coope Vega community. The San Carlos Municipality had rejected the idea of mining in Las Crucitas de Cutris de San Carlos, on September 11, 1995. When it became known in January 2002 that MINAE had approved the Crucitas mine the previous December, students from elementary schools, high schools and universities; teachers, members of unions, ecologists, *campesinas/os*, officials of the Catholic church, women's groups, members of parliament, and municipal governors took to the streets of Ciudad Quesada to say "No to mining." Balbina Gonzales, a *campesina* from San Carlos, demanded that water be protected. She stated "I would rather live without electricity or roads in good condition, but I cannot live with mining because it will destroy the water, which is vital for life and livelihood" (personal communication). She also demanded the protection of her subsistence economy. In addition she denounced the blackmail by this corporation in her town and manifested her decision to fight hard to defend her and her family's livelihood (Hernandez).

LOCAL MUNICIPALITIES VERSUS NATIONAL GOVERNMENT

Since 1996, led by affected women and men who have seen their health and their lives damaged, local municipalities have increasingly rejected mining projects in open confrontation with MINAE and its environmental approvals branch SETENA. Abangares Municipality in a historic special session in October 1998, made the decision to oppose strip mining in open confrontation with the national government (Frente del Pacífico ""Empresa Minera Obtiene"; "Municipalidad se Opone"). In that session, the municipal government lamented the loss of lives of community members caused by the greed of the transnational companies operating in the area, supported by a few local miners and greedy politicians.

The Abangares Council stated that it:

• is against every practice of mining exploitation whether strip, tunnel or gallery mining in Abangares and in the entire country;
• encourages similar statements by other municipalities in the country; authorizes communities and members of the National Front in Opposition to Strip Mining to release media communiqués;
• approves the initiative to translate the decision into many languages and to distribute them nationally and internationally;
• promotes an Action Plan to socio-economically transform Abangares.

One by one, municipalities that have experienced the devastating activities of mining have gained courage and rejected mining in their territories. Since 1996, local municipalities are fiercely fighting against the immiseration of the people and ecological destruction in Costa Rica's gold belt. The following municipalities have rejected mining projects:

• September 11, 1995: San Carlos Municipality rejected the exploitation of mining in Las Crucitas de Cutris de San Carlos;
• September 16, 1995: Sarapiquí Municipality repudiated strip gold mining in the country, in particular in Arenal Huetar Norte;
August 1996: Montes de Oro Municipality opposed the Bellavista Mining Project;
• June 26, 1997: Abangares Municipality requested Puntarenas Municipality to nullify the permit to Beta Vargas Mining;
• September 10, 1997: Puntarenas Municipality countered gold strip mining;
• March 27, 1998: Abangares Municipality declared itself against all practices of mining exploitation, metallic stockpiling, and underground

and tunnels in Abangares and any part of the country;

•July 14, 1998: Puntarenas Municipality ratified the opposition to Beta Vargas Mining and solicited authorization from the Supreme Court of Justice to immediately stop the mine;

•August 13, 1998: Montes de Oro Municipality rejected Bellavista Mining exploration and exploitation in Bellavista and other parts of the Canton;

•October 1, 1998: Abangares Municipality vetoed metallic strip mining in its territory;

•October 29, 1998: Montes de Oro Municipality declared foreign and national mining corporations *"persona non grata"*;

•November 2, 1998: Liberia Municipality rejected Las Lilas Mining;

•March 24, 1999: Tilaran Municipality, requested examination of Rio Chiquito Mining;

•July 24, 1999: Montes de Oro Municipality repeated its disapproval of Bellavista Mining and warned and denounced the work of the corporations;

•January 2000: Montes de Oro Municipality declared its solidarity with the North Zone Municipalities opposing metal mining in Crucitas;

•February 22, 2000: Upala Municipality requested that the Central government stop providing permits and confront the pressure for mining the area;

•September 4, 2000: San Carlos Municipality rejected gold mining in Crucitas and Conchito.

CONCLUSION

Costa Ricans have been living with the devastating consequences of an experiment in sustainable *corporate* development, in which nature is controlled and managed for profit in conservation areas and biodiversity preserves. The Costa Rican government has allowed mining to be carried out everywhere in the Arenal Conservation Area, despite the knowledge that mining destroys nature and people. The government further knows that women and men are fed up with it's compromise with capital, in which open pit mining in conservation areas is called "sustainable development." Costa Rican state officials receive international prizes recognizing them as top-rate "conservationists." At the same time, mining project approvals have been kept secret from the local Costa Rican population as well as from the international public. But the effects of mining cannot be kept secret from the communities who are expropriated and burdened with ill health and degraded environments.

Costa Rican women and men, with the support of local municipalities, are no longer silent. They are on the streets, defending their rights to clean water and a secure livelihood. In their battle against mining, women have uncovered the colonial relations of sustainable development in the alliances between their "national" government and international mining capital. At the same time, women have shown that politics is not separate from subsistence and everyday life. By confronting corporations" harassment and court actions, women active against mining have empowered and united local community members as well as local municipalities against the perpetrators of grievous wrongdoing. Costa Rican women's courageous confrontation against Canadian mining corporations suggests to us that local and international communities can be united against corporate globalization. Internally, women are building resistance. Internationally, they request solidarity from Canadian women, especially middle class women whose stocks, mutual funds and pension funds directly contribute to the exploitation of nature in Costa Rica. By pressuring investors in Canada, by writing to the Canadian government and by exposing the fallacy of "sustainable development," Canadian women can join their Costa Rica sisters in their struggle for a just and healthy planet.

Ana Isla is an Associate Professor at the Department of Sociology and the Centre for Women's and Gender Studies, Brock University. She is an active member of Women for a Just and Healthy Planet.

REFERENCES

Frente del Pacífico de Oposición a la Minería de Oro. "48 Sesiones de la Municipalidad de Abangarees. 26 de Febrero 1998 aa 25 de Enero de 1999." Resumenes de Actas, 1999.

Frente del Pacífico de Oposición a la Minería de Oro. "Empresa Minera Obtiene Estatus de Zona Franca en Costa Rica." Pamphlet, July 30, 2001.

Frente del Pacífico de Oposición a la Minería de Oro. "Inicia Juicio de Empresa Minera Contra Regidora Municipal." Pamphlet, August 13, 2001.

Fundacion Coyoche. "Mina Macacona: Un Libro Abierto que Todos Debemos Leer." September 1997.

Hernandez, Carlos. "Sancarlenos repudiaron la mineria." *La Nacion* March 23, 2002.

Isla, Ana. *An Environmental Feminist Analysis of Canada/Costa Rica Debt-for-Nature Investment: A Case Study of Intensifying Commodification.* Unpublished dissertation, OISE/University of Toronto, 2000.

"Municipalidad se Opone a Mineria de Oro." *La Voz de la Pampa* October/November 1998.

Plan General de Uso de la Tierra. Vol. II. *Sintesis, Diagnosticos and Pronosticos Sectoriales.* Prepared by Arenal Conservation Area, 1993.

Pizarro, Elizabeth. "Impactos de la Mineria en la Salud. Ministerio de Salud, Área Rectora de Abangares." Speech, San Carlos, November 25, 1998.

Position Paper. "Posicion de las comunidades costarricenses afectadas y amenazadas por la mineria del oro." Frente Nacional en contra de la Minieria de Oro, 1999.

Torres, Sonia. Personal interview, July 2001.

Torres, Sonia. Personal interview, July 2002.

Torres, Sonia. "Proyecto Minero Crucitas." Press Release. Coordinadora Frente Nacional de Oposicion a la Mineria, 2000.

Torres, Sonia. "El Proyecto Minero Bellavista." Press Release. Coordinadora Frente Nacional de Oposicion a la Mineria, 1999.

WENDY MILNE

Changing Climate, Uncertain Future

Considering Rural Women in
Climate Change Policies and Strategies

THERE IS UTTER UNCERTAINTY about what the future will look like in the age of climate change. Just a handful of the anticipated social, economic and environmental costs of climate change—drought, extreme weather, flooding, fires, disease, starvation, resource depletion—foretells disaster for people and ecosystems around the world. There will be little shelter from the fallout of a changing climate. And there is no doubt that it is the world's poor and marginalized, the people who have had the smallest role in creating climate change and who are the least able to shape responses for adaptation and mitigation, that are the most vulnerable to climate destabilization.

Canadians are witnessing that even the subtlest changes in the climate has the potential to affect our daily lives. From households to workplaces, across urban, rural, and remote landscapes, there is a budding recognition that the climate is changing. Yet, even with the increasingly visible evidence of the force of climate change there is negligible public debate and citizen action, and only restrained policy and strategic responses from municipal, provincial, and federal governments. Even more marginalized is dialogue on how to protect people and ecosystems that are the most vulnerable, and make certain that all public interests and social locations, and not just a select few, are considered in climate change policies.

Ultimately, equitable responses to climate change require informed citizens and democratic approaches that do not leave communities, regions or segments of the Canadian population out of the negotiations. This article explores the affects of climate change from the typically marginalized experiences of rural communities and rural women. Examining climate change from rural and gendered perspectives gives context to the problem and provides directions for including the experiences of rural women in climate change polices and strategies.

CANADIAN CLIMATE CHANGE POLICY DIRECTIONS

Since the late 1990s successive Canadian governments have moved from resistant to denial toward offering policy directions that fully address primary causes of climate change: including unjust economic relations and unsustainable consumption patterns fueled by fossil fuels. Instead, Canada's current Conservative government, has responded to the global challenge of climate change by, at best, supporting only market-based principles to guide international negotiations that protect the global north's interests and priorities, and, at worst, obstructing any national or international agreements and dialogue.

The lack of federal response and the silencing of opposition voices on the issue have translated into limited public engagement in response to the growing threat of climate change. As well, the abstract science, economic language, and trading mechanisms that dominate discussions of climate change marginalizes other forms of knowledge (Holloway) and is outside the learning approaches of most citizens (McBean and Hengeveld). These technical responses have contributed to a public that is concerned about climate change, yet not able or even encouraged to translate this concern into action, especially when it comes to energy conservation and changing consumer patterns (Kasemir, Swartling, Shule, Tabara and Jaeger; Plotnikoff, Wright and Karunamuni).

Citizen engagement is critical to ensure equitable responses to climate change. Currently, climate change approaches are incapable of recognizing differential impacts, the inherent power imbalances in responsibility taking and decision-making, the marginalization of local knowledges, and the unequal risks based on social and geographic locations. Turning a feminist lens on climate change policies and strategies, and in particular viewing the changing climate from rural women's experiences, offers some direction for dismantling imbedded biases, increasing understanding of the full range of gender-based inequities, and encouraging the participation of women who are the most vulnerable to the impacts of climate change.

CHANGING CLIMATE IN RURAL COMMUNITIES

Across the vast, sparsely populated, rural landscape of Canada, are communities in the throws of a wide range of social, economic and environmental changes. There has been job cuts in the forestry, fishing, mining and food producing sectors, a downsizing of government support, and a growing gap between the "haves" and "have-nots" (Shortall and Bryden). Family farms are on the decline (Sumner), resource communities are experiencing boom-and-bust cycles of growth, stagnation and decline (Reed), and rural communities dependent on multinational manufacturing and industries have lost in aftermath of free trade and restructuring by losing plants to lower wage communities (Winson and Leach).

The prospect of climate change increases the vulnerability of these rural communities, consequently threatening the very foundation of Canada's social, economic and environmental well-being. Already in rural and remote parts of Canada reports of floods, forest fires, drought, shrinking glaciers, and shorter ice seasons are indicators of a changing climate (Lemmen and Warren).

Agricultural production, crucial for feeding Canadians, has had signs of things to come. The extreme drought and heat that plagued much of Canada in 2001 resulted in some prairie provinces having lowered crop yields and threatening the availability of water and feed for livestock (Lemmen and Warren). And in Canada's north the impacts of a changing climate has resulted in shorter winter seasons and unpredictable ice conditions that has compromised the safety of traditional hunting and fishing practices, has undermined traditional knowledge of living with the land and resources, and made ice roads unreliable (CCME).

Clearly, the remaking of rural Canada has been occurring in a manner that raises uncertainty about the agency of rural people, and the ability to have equitable input into local, regional, and national policy and strategic development. Climate change is only increasing the likelihood of conflict in rural areas that will make it extremely difficult for working collectively toward viable solutions (Pendergraft). Too often, all levels of urban-centric policy development is based on assumptions that rural communities are stagnant, homogeneous, pastoral places empty of multiple identities, oppressions or acts of resistance (Sachs 1996) where everyone lives in harmony with nature (Li 1996) and where there is a presumed lack of difference and implied consensus and agreement on practices and ideology (Abowitz). In fact, rural areas are places where dominant groups exercise control over meaning (Dupuis and Vadergeest), there are increasing inequalities (Scott, Park and Cocklin), and where issues of most concern to women are often subservient to community issues (Li 1996).

Ensuring an equitable policy process, and in particular a rural policy process, requires recognition of the power relations that allow the structural exclusion of women (Shortall). To confront power relations that exclude the experiences of rural women it is imperative to shape an understanding of the gender and rural dimensions of climate change.

RURAL WOMEN AND CLIMATE CHANGE: POLICY CONSIDERATIONS

Researchers argue that rural women, particularly in the South, will be especially vulnerable to the effects of climate change (Denton; Dankleman). In wealthier societies, like Canada, there is likely to be less gender differentiation from the effects of climate change (Skutsch). However, in a context where changes in rural Canada has led to the reorganization of government work and plant closures, where the necessity of off-farm labour and relocation has increased women's isolation, limited women's ability to find paid work, and reduced access to needed social services and health care (Leach; Shortall), it can be concluded that women will be unjustly exposed to the pressures of climate change.

Margaret Skutsch argues addressing rural women and gender concerns in climate change policies will increase the efficiency of climate change responses, and ensure that work toward gender equity will not be threatened. Clearly, feminist research and advocacy on climate change in general, and rural women in particular, needs to do more to develop comprehensive knowledge to direct equitable and gender-sensitive policy development, as well as to contribute to energy efficiency, and mitigation and adaptation strategies being planned to respond to climate change. Situating Skutsch's argument within a Canadian context, and recognizing that there is no one rural women's experience, the following discussion outlines how rural women, already experiencing disparity, will be further vulnerable if policy development in areas as diverse as health, agriculture, natural resources, energy conservation, technology, and transportation continue to neglect gender and rural inequalities.

Health

Health Canada's Climate Change and Health Office predicts that the increased smog episodes, heat waves, water and food borne contamination, vector borne diseases, stratospheric ozone depletion, and extreme weather events that result from climate change will compromise the general health and well-being of Canadians. The impact of these changes will be adversely experienced by the most vulnerable of our society. Most affected will be the elderly, children, immuno-compromised individuals, and the poor and Aboriginal populations (see also Lemmen and Warren) with the elderly and women experiencing the most morbidity from heat waves (WHO). And undoubtedly, "some communities will be more vulnerable than others, for geographic reasons, due to health status or because of limited resources" (Climate Change and Health Office 1).

Women who live in rural areas already have limited health resources as current systems for health information are poorly coordinated and inadequately promoted, and health services are often infrequent, irregular and limited (Centres of Excellence for Women's Health). The ongoing lack of health services, combined with state-introduced cutbacks, means that rural women have even more responsibility for caring for dependents, both young and old (Winson and Leach). Combined with the increased levels of illness, as well as responding to food shortages, nutritional problems, and food and water shortages because of climate change women's burden will likely increase exponentially (Villagrasa; Wamukonya and Skutsch).

Agriculture Production

Agricultural sectors are seeing the impacts of warmer temperatures, moisture loss, and extreme weather conditions affecting soils, livestock, pests and weeds, and water resources (Lemmen and Warren). Despite the extreme vulnerability of agriculture to climate change, scientists continue to construct debates in such a way as to marginalize other forms of situated knowledge and practices about farming (Holloway). Lewis Holloway argues that to respond to climate change

> recognition must be given to the way that the environment is constructed in locally specific ways by farmers through their experiences of physical and biological processes understood within particular social, economic and cultural contexts. (2030)

Women, while active in all aspects of agriculture, are even more marginalized and underrepresented in decision-making about agricultural policy and global issues (Angeles). Therefore, scientists and climate change adaptation specialists must also strive to include the situated experiences of rural women in polices and strategies. Carolyn Sachs (1996) argues that the concept of situated knowledges proves particularly useful when grappling with issues and questions related to rural women. Including the situated knowledges of rural women provides access to disaggregated information into the decision-making process within the household on farm production choices and strategies, offering a rethinking of how local knowledge can be used to organize alternative approaches to agriculture (Feldman and Walsh).

NATURAL RESOURCE MANAGEMENT

In Canadian society, rural women's dependence on natural resources is practically invisible. While fewer women work directly in natural resource extraction, women and their families livelihoods depends on their labour in after-extraction processing, and in most of the general support services in local communities. The invisibility of women's role in natural resources, compounded by women's relatively low organizational status in North America natural resource management, has meant that women have had little influence in decision-making and in public forums (Davidson and Black). For example, in the Atlantic fisheries women have been excluded from decision-making about their future (Christiansen-Ruffman) and in British Columbia forestry 'planning initiatives and transition programs first segregated issues into gender categories and second assign the greatest need for and support of interest attributed to men" (Reed 190).

Including women's perspectives in natural resource management provides access to a "wholistic approach to problems—considering family, community and environment—as their starting point" (Christiansen-Ruffman 60) and a broader understanding of how land and resource use is linked to daily life of production, reproduction, and community caregiving (Reed). As climate change responses in rural areas will involve comprehensive land and resource use solutions, gender-sensitive approaches in the design and implementation are important for enabling populations to survive inevitable changes in the climate (Skutsch).

Household Energy Conservation

Women, as primary caregivers of the household, are often placed in a position to reduce household energy consumption and teach children how to conserve energy. However, the feminization of poverty has resulted in single women, senior women, and women-led families spending at least 20 percent of their income on heating and electricity, especially since poverty is linked to less energy-efficient housing and reliance on older inefficient appliances (Clancy and

Roeher). Specifically, in rural areas, women have unique housing issues related to affordability, suitability, maintenance, and property management that have been ignored in housing policies (Steele). The only conclusion that can be drawn from this situation is that if women are being put in a position to contribute to stabilizing the levels of greenhouse gases in the atmosphere than women should clearly be in a position to be active participants in determining energy conservation policies and strategies.

Technology

Strategies to respond to climate change are currently not about reducing production and economic growth, but aimed toward the adoption of clean, green, and renewable energy technology. Historically, households, farms and communities in rural areas have experienced that advances in technology have uncoupled production from employment (Reed) and increased women's domestic workload (Riney-Kehrberg). Gender imbalances related to technology had "clearly done more to alleviate the workload in the barn than in the farm" (Fleming 32) confirming that "technology merely served as a tangible, countable symbol of women's secondary status on the family farm" (Jellison 183). This trend continues today where technology development is still aimed toward men, as they are considered the decision-makers and users of the technology (Skutsch). Women's role in technology is largely overlooked resulting in many technological innovations that are inappropriate for women's lives (Cecelski). Working toward gender-sensitive policies in technology development have the potential to include women as active participants and promoters of sustainable technologies and challenge dominant technological practices (Milne 2003b).

Transportation

Climate change will likely affect roads, rail, air, and water transportation corridors (Lemmen and Warren), while responding to the Kyoto Protocol will change the way we currently use and design transportation systems. Rural areas already have significant transportation problems. Most areas are not serviced by public transport, and travel is often on treacherous roads that may be unpaved (Reed). Rural women have to travel long distances to access employment, healthcare, and other necessities. There are extreme financial, emotional, and social costs of living without adequate transportation services. For example, being away from the family, especially during a health crisis, where basic travel costs may not be covered is very stressful (Centres of Excellence for Women's Health). Transportation is already an obvious barrier to rural women's equality and will need to be considered in climate change policy development.

CONCLUSION: ENGAGING RURAL WOMEN IN CLIMATE CHANGE

Climate change is not gender, class, race or geo-political neutral. Therefore, all international, national and local polices and strategies need to consider equitable approaches to reducing greenhouse gases and responding to changes in the climate. To ensure a more gender-sensitive approach there is a need for more women on the various commissions within the climate change policy development process, and gender considerations need to be included in future policy formulations and activities (Villagrasa). Specifically, as Njeri Wamukonya and Margaret Skutsch argue, rural women should be targeted and included as active participants in policy decision-making, mitigation activities, vulnerability studies, projects for adaptation, technology transfer and capacity-building.

Engaging rural women in climate change policy and strategy development will require working through conflicts, diversity, and entrenched interests. While some rural women are very active in maintaining the status quo in rural areas and frequently fight environmental activism that threatens traditional ways of life (Brandth and Haugen; Reed) other rural women are at the forefront of environmental activism and social change (Sachs 1994). However, there is also precedence in rural areas of women working across vast differences, learning from each others experiences, and working collaboratively in the interests of the community. As Margaret Grace and June Lennie argue, including rural women in problem-solving and decision-making processes provides alternative and innovative perspectives.

> The diversity of rural women's personal identities, skills and knowledge, and in terms of the wide range of issues they bring to public forums, is one of the their greatest strengths and needs greater recognition ... rural women bring a holistic and future-oriented perspective to complex social, environmental and economic issues. We would argue that such a perspective is necessary in our rapidly changing world where innovative solutions to problematic issues is urgently needed. (366)

There is little doubt that climate change is the most complex social, economic, and environmental problem that will be faced this century. Including rural women in the climate change policy and strategy process not only ensures equity, innovation, and access to situated knowledges, but it goes a long way toward ensuring the very health of rural communities and peoples across the planet.

Wendy Milne has a Ph.D. in Rural Studies. She is a researcher/consultant and part-time educator on gender, renewable energy, environmental justice, energy literacy, and sustainable rural communities.

REFERENCES

Abowitz, K. K. "Reclaiming Community." *Educational Theory* 49 (2) (1999): 143-159.

Angeles, Leonora C. "Reflections on Feminist Policy Research on Gender,

Agriculture and Global Trade." *Canadian Woman Studies/les cahiers de la femme* 21/22 (4/1) (2002): 34-39.

Centres of Excellence for Women's Health. Rural, *Remote and Northern Women's Health: Policy and Research Directions*. Winnipeg, 2004.

Brandth, B. and M. Haugen. "Rural Women, Feminism and the Politics of Identity." *Sociologia Ruralis* 37(3) (1997): 325-344.

Canadian Council of Ministers of the Environment (CCME). Climate, Nature, People: Indicators of Canada's Changing Climate. Winnipeg: CCME.

Cecelski, Elizabeth. *The Role of Women in Sustainable Energy Development*. Golden, Colorado: National Renewable Energy Laboratory, 2000.

Christianson-Ruffman, L. "Atlantic Canadian Coastal Communities and the Fisheries Trade: A Feminist Critique, Revaluation And Revisioning." *Canadian Woman Studies/les cahiers de la femme* 21/22 (4/1) (2002): 56-63.

Clancy, Joy and Ulrike Roehr. "Gender and Energy: Is there a Northern Perspective?" *Energy for Sustainable Development* 7 (3) (2003): 44-49.

Climate Change and Health Office. *Climate Change and Health and Well-Being: A Policy Primer*. Ottawa: Health Canada, 2001.

Dankleman, I. "Climate Change: Learning from Gender Analysis and Women's Experience of Organizing for Sustainable Development." *Gender and Development* 10 (2) (2002): 21-29.

Davidson, Penny and Rosemary Black. "Woman in Natural Resource Management: Finding a More Balanced Perspective." *Society and Natural Resources* 14 (2001): 645-656.

Denton, Fatma. "Gender and Climate Change: Giving the 'Latecomer' a Head Start." *IDS Bulletin* 35 (3) (2004): 42-49.

Denton, Fatma. "Gender Impact of Climate Change: The Human Security Dimension." *ENERGIA News* 3 (3) (2000): 13-14.

Duncan, C. M. and N. Lamborgini. "Poverty and the Social Context in Remote Rural Communities." *Rural Sociology* 59 (3) (1994): 437-461.

Dupuis, M. E. and P. Vandergeest. *Creating Countryside: The Politics of Rural and Environmental Discourse*. Philadelphia: Temple University Press, 1996.

Feldman, Shelley and Rick Welsh. "Feminist Knowledge Claims, Local Knowledges, and Gender Divisions of Agricultural Labor: Constructing a Successor Science." *Rural Sociology* 60 (1) (1995): 23-43.

Fleming, K. *Power at Cost: Ontario Hydro and Rural Electrification, 1911-1958*. Montreal and Kingston: McGill-Queen's University Press, 1992.

Government of Canada. *Project Green, Moving Forward on Climate Change: A Plan for Honouring our Kyoto Commitment*. Ottawa, April 2005.

Government of Canada. *Climate Change: Achieving our Commitments Together. Climate Change Plan for Canada*. Ottawa, November 2002.

Grace, Margaret and June Lennie. "Constructing and Reconstructing Rural Women in Australia: The Politics of Change, Diversity and Identity." *Sociologis Ruralis* 38 (3) (1998): 351-370.

Holloway, L. "Understanding Climate Change and Farming: Scientific and

Farmers' Constructions of 'Global Warming' in Relation to Agriculture." *Environment and Planning A* 31 (1999): 2017-2032.

Jellison, K. *Entitled to Power: Farm Women and Technology, 1913-1963.* Chapel Hill: University of North Carolina Press, 1993.

Kasemir, B., U. Swartling, A. G. Shule, D. Tabara and C. Jaeger. "Citizens Perspectives on Climate Change and Energy Use." *Global Environmental Change* 10 (3) (2000): 169-184.

Leach, Belinda. "Transforming Rural Livelihoods: Gender, Work and Restructuring in Three Ontario Communities." *Restructuring Caring Labour: Discourse, State Practice and Everyday Life.* Ed. S. M. Neysmith. Toronto: Oxford University Press, 1999. 209-225.

Lemmen, Donald and Fiona Warren. *Climate Change Impacts and Adaptation: A Canadian Perspective.* Ottawa: Natural Resource Canada, Government of Canada, 2004.

Li, Tania M. "Images of Community: Discourse and Strategy in Property Relations." *Development and Change* 27 (1996): 501-527.

McBean, G. and H. Hengeveld. "Communicating the Science of Climate Change: A Mutual Challenge for Scientists and Educators." *Canadian Journal of Environmental Education* 5 (2000): 1-19.

McLeod, Brenda. "First Nations Women and Sustainability on the Canadian Prairies." *Canadian Woman Studies/les cahiers de la femme* 23 (1) (2003): 47-54.

Milne, Wendy. "Energy and Sustainable Communities: Women Shifting Power." *Women and Environments International Magazine* 62/63 (2003b): 38-39.

Pendergraft, C. A. "Human Dimension of Climate Change: Cultural Theory and Collective Action." *Climate Change* 39 (1998): 643-666.

Plotnikoff, Ronald, Mary-Frances Wright and Nandini Karunamuni. "Knowledge, Attitudes and Behaviours Related to Climate Change in Alberta, Canada: Implications for Public Health Policy and Practice." *International Journal of Environmental Health Research* 14 (3) (2004): 223-229.

Reed, Maureen G. *Taking Stands: Gender and the Sustainability of Rural Communities.* Vancouver: University of British Columbia Press, 2003.

Riney-Kehrberg, Pamela. "Women, Technology, and Rural Life." *Technology and Culture* 38 (4) (1997): 942-953.

Sachs, Carolyn. *Gendered Fields: Rural Women, Agriculture and the Environment.* Boulder, CO: Westview Press, 1996.

Sachs, Carolyn. "Rural Women's Environmental Activism in the USA." *Gender and Rurality.* Eds. Sarah Whatmore, Terry Marsden and Philip Lowe. London: David Fulton Publishers, 1994. 117-134.

Scott, K., J. Park and C. Cocklin. "From 'Sustainable Rural Communities' to 'Social Sustainability': Giving Voice to Diversity in Mangakahia Valley, New Zealand." *Journal of Rural Studies* 16 (2000): 433-446.

Skutsch, Margaret. "Protocols, Treaties and Action: The 'Climate Change

Process' Viewed Through Gender Spectacles." *Gender and Development* 10 (2) (2002): 30-39.

Shortall, Sally. "Gendered Agricultural and Rural Restructuring: A Case of Northern Ireland." *Socioligia Ruralis* 42 (2) (2002): 160-175.

Shortall, Sally and Bryden, John. "Rural Restructuring: Causes, Consequences and Opportunities." *Changing Rural Institutions.* Ed. R. C. Rounds. Brandon: Canadian Rural Restructuring Institute, 1997. 239-248.

Steele, Margaret. *Housing Options for Women Living Alone in Rural Areas.* Ottawa: Canadian Mortgage and Housing Corporation, 2002.

Sumner, Jennifer. *Sustainability and the Civil Commons: Rural Communities in the Age of Globalization.* Toronto: University of Toronto Press, 2005.

Suzuki Foundation. *Briefing Notes on Canada's Climate Change Plan.* April 13, 2005a.

Suzuki Foundation. *Climate Change Plan Lacks Teeth.* April 13, 2005b.

Villagrasa, Delia. "Kyoto Protocol Negotiations: Reflections on the Role of Women." *Gender and Development* 10 (2) (2002): 40-44.

Wamukonya, N. and M. Skutsch. "Gender Angle to the Climate Change Negotiations." *Energy and Environment* 13 (2002): 115–124.

Winson, A. and B. Leach. *Contingent Work, Disrupted Lives: Labour and Community in the New Rural Economy.* Toronto: University of Toronto Press, 2002.

World Health Organization (WHO). *Climate Change and Human Health: Risks and Responses.* 2003.

III. Displacement, Migration and Violence

VANDANA SHIVA

Our Violent Economy is Hurting Women

VIOLENCE AGAINST WOMEN is as old as patriarchy. Traditional patriarchy has structured our worldviews and mindsets, our social and cultural worlds, on the basis of domination over women and the denial of their full humanity and right to equality. But it has intensified and become more pervasive in the recent past. It has taken on more brutal forms, like the murder of the Delhi gang rape victim and the recent suicide of a 17-year-old rape victim in Chandigarh.

In India, rape cases and cases of violence against women have increased over the years. The National Crime Records Bureau (NCRB) reported 10,068 rape cases in 1990, which increased to 16496 in 2000. With 24,206 cases in 2011, rape cases jumped to incredible increase of 873 percent from 1971 when NCRB started to record cases of rape. And Delhi has emerged as the rape capital of India, accounting for 25 percent of cases.

We need to see how the structures of traditional patriarchy merge with the emerging structures of capitalist patriarchy to intensify violence against women. The movement to stop this violence must be sustained until justice is done for every one of our daughters and sisters who has been violated. And while we intensify our struggle for justice for women, we need to also ask why rape cases have increased 240 percent since 1990s when the new economic policies were introduced. Could there be a connection between the growth of violent, undemocratically imposed, unfair economic policies and the intensification and brutality of crimes against women?

I believe there is. I am not suggesting that violence against women begins with neoliberal economics. I am deeply aware of the deep gender biases in our traditional cultures and social organizations. I stand empowered today because people before me fought against the exclusions and biases against women and children: My grandfather sacrificed his life for women's equality, and my mother was a feminist before the word existed.

The economic model focusing myopically on "growth" begins with violence against women by discounting their contribution to the economy. Violence against women has taken on new and more vicious forms as traditional patriarchal

249

structures have hybridized with the structures of capitalist patriarchy. We need to examine the connections between the violence of unjust, unsustainable economic systems, and the growing frequency and brutality of violence against women. We need to see how the structures of traditional patriarchy merge with the emerging structures of capitalist patriarchy to intensify violence against women.

Our society has traditionally had a bias against the girl child. But the epidemic of female feticide and the disappearance of 30 million unborn girls has taken that bias to new levels of violence and new proportions. And it is into this context of the dynamics of more brutal and more vicious violence against women (and multiple, interconnected forms of violence) that the processes unleashed by neoliberalism are contributory factors.

First, the economic model focusing myopically on "growth" begins with violence against women by discounting their contribution to the economy. The more the government talks ad nauseum about "inclusive growth" and "financial inclusion," the more it excludes the contributions of women to the economy and society. According to patriarchal economic models, production for sustenance is counted as "non-production." The transformation of value into disvalue, labour into non-labour, and knowledge into non-knowledge is achieved by the most powerful number that rules our lives, the patriarchal construct of GDP—Gross Domestic Product—which commentators have started to call the "Gross Domestic Problem."

When economies are confined to the marketplace, economic self-sufficiency is perceived as economic deficiency. National accounting systems, which are used for calculating growth as GDP, are based on the assumption that if producers consume what they produce, they do not in fact produce at all, because they fall outside the production boundary.

The production boundary is a political creation that, in its workings, excludes regenerative and renewable production cycles from the area of production. Hence, all women who produce for their families, children, community, and society are treated as "non-productive" and "economically inactive." When economies are confined to the marketplace, economic self-sufficiency is perceived as economic deficiency. The devaluation of women's work, and of work done in subsistence economies of the Global South, is the natural outcome of a production boundary constructed by capitalist patriarchy. The resource grab that is essential for "growth" creates a culture of rape.

By restricting itself to the values of the market economy, as defined by capitalist patriarchy, the production boundary ignores economic value in the two vital economies which are necessary to ecological and human survival. They are the areas of nature's economy, and sustenance economy. In nature's economy and the sustenance economy, economic value is a measure of how the earth's life and human life are protected. Its currency is life-giving processes, not cash or market price.

Second, a model of capitalist patriarchy which excludes women's work and wealth creation in the mind, deepens the violence by displacing women from their livelihoods and alienating them from the natural resources on which their livelihoods depend—their land, their forests, their water, and their seeds and biodiversity. Economic reforms based on the idea of limitless growth in a limited world, can only be maintained by the powerful grabbing the resources of the vulnerable. The resource grab that is essential for "growth" creates a culture of rape—the rape of the earth, of local self-reliant economies, and of women. The only way in which this "growth" is "inclusive" is by its inclusion of ever larger numbers in its circle of violence.

I have repeatedly stressed that the rape of the Earth and rape of women are intimately linked, both metaphorically in shaping worldviews, and materially in shaping women's everyday lives. The deepening economic vulnerability of women makes them more vulnerable to all forms of violence—including sexual assault. The economic model shaped by capitalist patriarchy is based on the commodification of everything, including women.

Third, economic reforms lead to the subversion of democracy and privatization of government. Economic systems influence political systems. The government talks of economic reforms as if it has nothing to do with politics and power. Leaders talk of keeping politics out of economics, even while they impose an economic model shaped by the politics of a particular gender and class. Neoliberal reforms work against democracy. We have seen this recently with the Indian government pushing through "reforms" to bring in Walmart through FDI in retail. Corporate-driven reforms create a convergence of economic and political power, a deepening of inequalities, and a growing separation of the political class from the will of the people they are supposed to represent. This is at the root of the disconnect between politicians and the public that we experienced during the protests that have grown throughout India since the Delhi gang rape.

Worse, an alienated political class is afraid of its own citizens. This is what explains the increasing use of police to crush nonviolent citizen protests, as we have witnessed in Delhi. A privatized corporate state must rapidly become a police state. This is why the politicians must surround themselves with ever increasing VIP security, diverting the police from their important duties to protect women and ordinary citizens.

Fourth, the economic model shaped by capitalist patriarchy is based on the commodification of everything, including women. When we stopped the WTO in Seattle, our slogan was, "Our world is not for sale." An economics unleashed by economic liberalization—an economics of deregulation of commerce, of privatization and commodification of seeds and food, land and water, women and children—degrades social values, deepens patriarchy, and intensifies violence against women. Economic systems influence culture and social values. An economics of commodification creates a culture of commodification, where everything has a price, and nothing has value.

The victim of the Delhi gang rape has triggered a social revolution. We must sustain it, deepen it, expand it.

The growing culture of rape is a social externality of economic reforms. We need to institutionalize social audits of the neoliberal policies which are a central instrument of patriarchy in our times. If there was a social audit of corporatizing our seed sector, 270,000 farmers would not have been pushed to suicide in India since the new economic policies were introduced. If there was a social audit of the corporatization of our food and agriculture, we would not have every fourth Indian hungry, every third woman malnourished, and every second child wasted and stunted due to severe malnutrition. India today would not be the Republic of Hunger that Dr. Utsa Patnaik has written about.

The victim of the Delhi gang rape has triggered a social revolution. We must sustain it, deepen it, expand it. We must demand and get speedy and effective justice for women. We must call for fast-track courts to convict those responsible for crimes against women. We must make sure laws are changed so justice is not elusive for victims of sexual violence. We must continue the demand for blacklisting of politicians with criminal records.

We must see the continuum of different forms of violence against women, from female feticide to economic exclusion and sexual assault. We need to continue the movement for the social reforms needed to guarantee safety, security, and equality for women, building on the foundations laid during India's independence movement and continued by the feminist movement over the last half-century. The agenda for social reforms, social justice, and equality has been derailed by the aganda of "economic reforms" set by capitalist patriarchy.

And while we do all this we need to change the ruling paradigm that reduces society to economy, the economy to the market, and is imposed on us in the name of "growth."

Society and economy are not insulated from each other. The processes of social reforms and economic reforms can no longer be separated. We need economic reforms based on the foundations of social reforms that correct the gender inequality in society, rather than aggravating all forms of injustice, inequality, and violence.

Ending violence against women needs to also include moving beyond the violent economy to nonviolent, sustainable, peaceful, economies that give respect to women and the Earth.

This article was posted on YES!Magazine.org on January 18, 2013. Reprinted with permission of the author.

*Vandana Shiva is an internationally renowned activist for biodiversity and against corporate globalization, and author of S*tolen Harvest: The Hijacking of the Global Food Supply; Earth Democracy: Justice, Sustainability, and Peace; Soil Not Oil; *and* Staying Alive. *The last section of this essay was adapted by the author from "Forest and Freedom," written by Shiva and published in the May/June 2011 edition of* Resurgence *magazine. Shiva is a YES! contributing editor.*

RATNA KAPUR

The "Other" Side of Globalization

The Legal Regulation of Cross-Border Movements

THE CURRENT MOMENT of globalization is witnessing an extraordinary movement of people, legitimate and illegitimate, across national and international borders. These movements are exposing the porosity of borders, the transnational reality of subaltern existence, and the contingent foundations of international law. And this global movement of people has created a panic across borders—a panic which is manifesting itself in the strengthening of border controls, tightening of immigration laws and casting of the "Other" as a threat to the security of the (First World) nation-state. In this essay, I discuss how the issue of cross-border movements is being displaced onto a first world/ third world divide, designed to keep the "Rest" away from the "West," and premised on liberal exclusions and understandings of difference. I also examine how laws encounter with these constitutive "Others," quite specifically the transnational subaltern subject, disrupts and disturbs the universalist premise of international law.

This essay is divided into two sections. In the first section, I discuss how the global economic processes have triggered a contemporary wave of migration, legal and illegal, and the international and domestic responses to this phenomenon. In the second section, I discuss how recent legal responses to cross-border movements have been informed by the "War on Terror," which has converged with the discourse of the conservative Right building on the xenophobia pre-dating September 11, and turned it into a hostile antagonistic fear of the "Other" who is threatening the security of the nation (Human Rights Watch).[1]

My analysis exposes how the political and legal agenda that is currently being pursued in relation to cross-border movements is diametrically opposed to women's rights and others who cross borders in their capacities as migrants, refugees or asylum-seekers. The legal interventions in the lives of the "transnational subaltern subject" are being articulated primarily from the perspective of the host country and within the overarching concern for the security of the nation.

Throughout this text I use the term "transnational subaltern subject." In using the term "subaltern" I borrow from the insights of postcolonial theory and the subaltern studies project which have highlighted the fact that certain voices have been excluded from the dominant narratives and telling of history.[2] The subaltern studies project regards hegemonic history as part of modernity's power/knowledge complex, which in the context of colonialism, was deeply implicated in the "general epistemic violence of imperialism" (see, for example, Spivak; Otto). It reads the official archive against the grain and focuses on "listening to the small voice of history" including peasants, women, and even religious, sexual, and racial minorities (Guha 1996; Ahmad).

The history of subaltern studies is neither linear nor consistent. It is an area of scholarship that has undergone several permutations and transformations. The project was initially launched in Britain in the 1960s when Gramsci's writings exercised a significant influence on the shape of English Marxism. This period triggered an analysis of peasant societies based on the position and location of the subaltern subject—that is the location of the peasant. This project of writing history from below was subsequently taken up within postcolonial contexts, including in India.[3] Although the project was initially grounded in historical materialism and a search for an essential peasant consciousness, for some, this approach seemed too limited and restrictive for contesting the Eurocentric, metropolitan and bureaucratic systems of knowledge. The influence of Michel Foucault came to affect the subaltern project, producing subaltern critiques, which challenged scholarship and political activism that continued to adhere to the "Enlightenment ideals." The project splintered into those who continued to write histories from "'below" and those who adopted a more Foucauldian analysis (Chakrabarty). The new tradition that emerged was concerned with challenging all traditions and disciplines that were defined within the logic and rationale of the Enlightenment project. This dimension of the scholarship was concerned with unmasking the universal project spawned by the Enlightenment—its focus on reason, the atomized, ahistorical subject of liberalism, and the idea that history was a linear movement of progress emanating from the metropolis that spread across the globe. It shifted away from economic analysis as the primary zone of power, and began to unpack the multiple sites and locations of power through a discursive and textual analysis. Subaltern studies no longer remained preoccupied with the idea of a peasant rebel as an autonomous political subject who wrote his/her own history. The project did however continue to adopt the rich tradition of historical materialism that was spawned in its earlier incarnation. The scholarship expanded and began to address and challenge the neo-imperialism of the late twentieth century and problems of agency, subject position, and hegemony in an era of globalization.[4] In this essay, I draw on the insights of the subaltern studies challenge to the assumptions about universality; neutrality, and objectivity on which legal concepts are based, exposing such concepts to be products of the ruptures produced in and through the colonial encounter (Mehta; Anghie; Darien-Smith & Fitzpatrick). Quite specifically, I reveal how the legal regulation of cross-border movements is contingent on law's understanding of and engagement with difference.

THE CONTEXT

Nearly 150 million migrants are crossing borders in our world today—from rural towns to urban centers, from the periphery into the metropolis, from the global south into the global north (IOM). And these crossings are profoundly challenging our most basic notions of women's reproductive labour, family, community, nation, culture, and citizenship. Transborder and in-country movements and migrations are occurring for a plethora of reasons: the reconfiguration of the global economy, the ability to travel, displacement and dispossession of marginalized populations, the awareness through consciousness raising that there are better options elsewhere, armed conflict and of course the basic human aspiration to explore the world.

A growing number of floating migrants are squatting on "global borderlands" having been forced from their own homelands by powerful forces of exclusion and disadvantage (Sanghera). Countries of the global north and the global south are pockmarked with these global borderlands and their alien inhabitants are practically invisible to those who reside in and manage the business and defense of homelands (Sanghera). And these inhabitants are gendered subjects, consisting of large numbers of young women and adolescent girls.

Globalization is invariably used to refer to the free flow of capital, deemed as critical to the efficiency of the market and intrinsic to the globalization process. It is a ubiquitous process that has challenged the fixed borders of the nation state and the autonomy of the sovereign subject. The market also triggers a global flow of labour, yet the free flow of labour is not addressed within the discourse of market management. It is addressed in and through the international legal order by initiatives dealing with trafficking, human smuggling, border controls, terrorism, and sexual morality. The impact of these different initiatives on cross-border movements is mediated by gender, class, religion, sexual, and marital status.

What remains to be addressed in these responses is how countries of origin and destination stand to gain in significant economic ways from migration, including from clandestine migrant-mobility. In the context of globalization, migrations do not just happen—they are produced. The countries of destination and the sites of employment are determined by the demand on the part of the market and capital for an increased rate of profit. This demand is partly fulfilled by depressing the wages of labour and decreasing the costs of production. The specific demand for an abundant supply of low wage labour and a shrinking supply of a local workforce especially in the global North also helps to sustain the economy of the global metropolises and the continuing processes of migration. At the same time, remittances in the form of gifts and cash remittances to countries of origin have registered extraordinary increases over recent years. Estimates of migrants' remittances have been recorded at over one hundred billion U.S. dollars of which 60 percent goes to developing countries (Buch, Kucklenz and Le Manchec). Some studies reveal that over the last decade, remittances have actually provided a larger source of income for developing countries than official development assistance (Hamburg World Economic Archives). They also appear to be a more stable source of income than private flows, which can be volatile and only flow into a limited number of countries. A good portion of these remittances are invisible as they do not flow through regular channels of the economy. Yet some studies in the Asia-Pacific reveal that the remittances flow back through informal and underground conduits, and sustain household, community, and sometimes even local and national economies.[5]

Although migration is a fact of a globalized economy, the response of the international legal order to what is cast as the *migration dilemma* is either incomplete, or one that aggravates the situation of those who cross borders. The issue is a politically charged one as it exposes the porosity of national borders, and reveals the "other" side of globalization. In recent years the avenues for regular, legal, and safe migration have decreased worldwide, due to increased border controls, and restrictive migration and immigration policies adopted in countries of transit and destination. This phenomenon has given rise to a growing market for clandestine migration services under the migrant-mobility regime (Sanghera). The clandestine regime is produced in part by a legal structure that fails to recognize the need for marginalized groups to migrate on the one hand and the demand for cheap, exploitable labour, on the other. The regime that has emerged consists of providing a host of "services" to those who cross borders, including the facilitation of smuggling, illegal migration and underground travel, and the provision of false passports, visa permits, and identity papers. The presence of this regime constantly threatens to rupture and force the rearticulation of the nation-state and the uniformity of the liberal subject. The regulatory edifice of the law with its punitive consequences is being confounded by the emergence of this clandestine migrant-mobility regime.

GENDERED ALIENS

The response to migration is highly gendered. Female migration is not addressed within the framework of the global economy, the search for better economic opportunities or the demand for women's reproductive labour. Women's cross-border movements continue to be addressed primarily through anti-trafficking discourse at the international, regional, and domestic level. Under these initiatives, a woman's consent is irrelevant and her subjectivity denied. She is addressed primarily as a victim, to be rescued, rehabilitated, and repatriated. At times her consent is acknowledged only to implicate her in the discourses of immorality, (for such migration is consistently and erroneously conflated with sex work), and criminality, to be penalized together with traffickers, and terrorists for exposing the porosity of borders and the vulnerability of the nation-state. These responses do not engage with the premise that migration is a manifestation of globalization—that it is indeed globalization. The responses are constructed along the binaries of the "West" and the "Rest." And women, especially from the postcolonial world, are cast as either victims, incapable of decision-making or consenting, sexual deviants, disrupting the moral and social fabric of the sexually sanitized West and/or dangerous "Others," threatening the security of the nation state (Kapur).

Women are the primary squatters of the new global borderlands that constitute part of the contemporary transnational, transmigratory world. Half of nearly all migrants are women and girls, and many of these are migrating independently rather than as part of a family (Sadiqu).[6] The process of women's movement is determined by a number of factors that render them amenable to migration and vulnerable to human rights violations. Women move and are moved with or without their consent for a variety of reasons. The insecurity of food and livelihood and the growing economic reliance of households on earnings of women and girls; the erosion of social capital and the break down of traditional societies; the transnationalization of women's labour in sectors which do not comply with labour or human rights standards and often rely on exploitative labour, forced labour, and slavery like practices (Sanghera). And this movement is rendered vulnerable as a result of several normative assumption about gender and sexuality, quite specifically, the normative assumption that women's primary work is in the home, underscored by the sexual division of labour. The fact that women's movement is impelled by a number of economic push and pull factors remains largely unaddressed in schemes that focus on anti-trafficking, restrictive immigration regulations at borders, and the penalizing, criminalizing, and deportation of alien migrants as a response to the growing "problem" of transnational migration and trafficking. Closing doors to keep the individual migrants out by resorting to the tools of deportation or incarceration, ignores the economic engine that drives transborder and female migration.

Women migrants constitute a substantial pool of workers, offering their reproductive labour in the form of work in the sex trade, domestic work, and/or marital bliss. And she becomes more attractive to the global economy if her status as a migrant is illegal, in which case her social and economic options and demands are constrained. The disadvantaged migrant woman becomes the *ideal worker* from the standpoint of capital and integral to sustaining the current structure of the economy. This situation of illegality and disadvantage also renders migrant women vulnerable to exploitative and forced labour like conditions of work.

The choice of the female migrant to cross borders is conditioned by the push and pull factors that induce movement. This choice is neither facilitated nor protected by international legal mechanisms, which are triggered once she steps across the line that separates "here" from "there."

Equating trafficking with migration leads to simplistic and unrealistic solutions—in order to prevent trafficking there is a conscious or inadvertent move to stop those who are deemed vulnerable from migrating. Even when curbing migration is not a stated programmatic focus, an inadvertent impetus is to dissuade women and girls from moving in order to protect them from harm. Conflating trafficking with migration results in reinforcing the gender bias that women and girls need constant male or state protection from harm, and therefore must not be allowed to exercise their right to movement or right to earn a living in the manner they choose.

Secondly, curbing migration will not stop trafficking, but merely drive the activity further underground, and make it more invisible. This lesson has been learnt from states who have proceeded to enforce increasingly stringent immigration controls as a response to heightened trafficking in persons and narcotics. Borders cannot be impermeable, and stricter immigration measures have resulted in pushing the victims further into situations of violence and abuse.

Thirdly, when no clear conceptual or operational distinctions are drawn between migration and trafficking, and in fact, when migration is considered equal to trafficking, then it logically follows that the number of victims of trafficking is equal to the number of those who have migrated voluntarily. This logic operates particularly in the case of adolescent girls and women migrants, and not in the case of men. This practice has resulted in an extremely flawed methodology for conducting baseline surveys on trafficking in "risk-prone" and "affected districts" in different South Asian countries. Absence of women or girls is routinely considered tantamount to "missing persons," and therefore, trafficked. This logic has resulted in the viewing all consensual migrant females as trafficked.

The focus of ant-trafficking initiatives at the domestic, regional, and international level rarely focus on providing women who move with human rights—the tools that are critical to fighting abuse, violence, and harm they may experience in the course of movement. Instead, some of these measures are morality measures that conflate women's cross-border movement with sexual corruption and contamination. Other initiatives assume that the problem exists over "there" in the "third world" or postcolonial world and suggest strategies that reinforce the image of a truncated seriously battered, culturally constrained, and oppressed subject that needs to be rescued and rehabilitated by a civilizing west (Mohanty). More recently, trafficking initiatives have been obscured by an overarching concern with security, particularly on the part of the industrial world, which perceives the "outsider" as dangerous, from which the nation must be protected.

MIGRATION AND TERRORISM

The issues of trafficking and migration are now being taken up within the overarching concern with security of the nation and the global "War on Terror." The War on Terror has acquired a supernatural life and existence outside of the international legal order, while simultaneously pursued in and through the processes and institutions of the international regime. The Security Council and the General Assembly have been deployed to foreground the security and sovereignty of some nation-states through the abrogation of the security and sovereignty of other nation-states. The legal mechanisms endorsed in pursuit of this endeavor have resulted in the enactment of laws at the domestic and international level that have further cauterized cross-border movements, and justified going after anything and anyone one does not like.

Globally, we are witnessing a heightened anxiety about the "Other," who is perceived as a threat or someone who is dangerous to the security of the nation. The boundary line of difference is being redrawn along very stark divides—between friend and enemy, those who are good and those who are evil. Although these concerns are most explicitly voiced by the extreme right or religious right, less noticed is the more uniformly pervasive emergence of similar forms of conservatism within mainstream discourses. The "alien migrant" has become one of the primary casualties of the failure to define either the purpose or limits of the War on Terrorism. And this failure forces migrants to continue to move through illicit channels, and remain vulnerable, stigmatized and illegitimate.

Across Europe and North America, the conservative voice is building on the fear of the "Other" crossing borders, the threat they pose to the nation-state and the values of "western civilization." Pat Buchanan voices this fear when he predicts the death of the west from immigrant hoards amongst others in his book the *Death of the West*. He argues that the very survival of the west is under threat, as a result of depopulation, surrender of nationhood, and the flood of Third World immigration.

> Now that all the Western empires are gone, Western Man, relieved of his duty to civilize and Christianize mankind, reveling in luxury in our age of self-indulgence, seems to have lost his will to live and reconciled himself to his impending death. Are we in the twilight of the West? Is the Death of the West irreversible? (1)

And these fears have been accentuated post-September 11th. Buchanan argues that the events of September 11th exposed a new divide.

> Suddenly we awoke to the realization that among our millions of foreign-born, a third, are here illegally, tens of thousands are loyal to regimes with which we could be at war, and some are trained terrorists sent here to murder Americans. (2)

There is the fear of some fanatical, uncontrolled migration from places that have nothing in common with America's history (all 200 years of it), heroes, language, or culture And there are some specific races or ethnic groups that are particularly averse to changing, or assimilating. And that "Other" is mostly "Arab looking" and Muslim. Their cultures are constantly essentialized and pitted against universal norms and values such as freedom or liberty.[7]

The new War on Terrorism has created space for a more strident and alarming response to the global movements of people, reducing it at times to nothing more than an evil threat. If terrorism is defined as a transnational crime, then by

259

merely committing the crime of seeking illegal movement and illegal entry these people could be defined as terrorists. Because the smugglers offer travel services to illegal migrants, they would easily fall within the category of transnational organized crime, criminals, and potential terrorists. At the very worst they are terrorists and at best they are criminals who have sought to cross the border illegally. These simple equations again led to a disjuncture between reality of the illegal migrant and the issue of terrorism. The conflation of the migrant with the terrorist is not new, but it has received greater attention since September 11.[8] It has afforded more space for the representation of the "Other" as a fanatic and dangerous and opposed to freedom (Porras).

The mass movements of people have produced responses at the international and domestic level that fail to account for the factors that have triggered such movements. At the international level, cross-border movements have been addressed within the framework of trafficking and smuggling. This approach has had a particularly adverse impact on women pushing them further into situations of violence and exploitation. At the domestic level, these movements have been addressed through appeals to assimilation and tests of fealty to the nation,[9] through the criminal law and the othering of the "alien migrant," who fails to assimilate and continues to enter countries through illegal means. Since September 11th, security has become the overarching concern, and enabled some governments to use the fear of threats to the nation to detain the "Other" in ways that fan the flames of hatred and intolerance and fail to make a distinction between the migrant, terrorist and trafficker (Volpp).

These responses fail to engage with the transnational, transmigratory processes that have been triggered by new global processes. Cross-border movements have become a feature of the contemporary moment and an integral aspect of globalization. Although a new legal arrangement has been established to deal with and facilitate the cross-border movement of capital, there has not been a simultaneous movement to deal with the concomitant cross-border movement of people and labour through legal processes that accommodate this new reality. Instead states have sought refuge in traditional notions of nation-state identity and sovereignty to resist cross-border traffic. And this assertion of national identity is being constituted and buttressed through assimilationist moves as well as through the creation of fear of the "Other" as a threat to the nations security.

The War on Terror has resulted in legal reforms that alienate those who have been cast as the "new enemy" and justifies the resort of punitive measures on the grounds that these people are evil or dangerous and not entitled to due process or rights. The recourse to border controls, ethnic purity, cultural values and nationalism, are constructed along the anxieties of dealing with difference and serve to stigmatize, penalize and criminalize those who cross borders. These responses push us further away from addressing the complexity of cross-border movements and the equally complex legal and political responses required to address the issues raised by such movements.

The space for the migrant is being eroded through the discourse of trafficking and through the discourse of terrorism and threats to the security of the nation. Both justify initiatives designed to keep the "Rest" away from the "West." This shift is troubling given that movement and migration is partly a phenomenon of the current phase of globalization and hence it is and will continue to be a feature of our transnational world. Criminalizing or victimizing those who cross borders forces these people to continue to move through illicit channels, and remain vulnerable, stigmatized and illegitimate. It seems unlikely that the security of what's left of the nation-state can be achieved at the cost of the security of the alien migrant. Indeed it will only serve to encourage the construction of a paradox, where the security of the alien migrant is perhaps less threatened by people smugglers than by the current international system of protection offered to people who move as migrants, refugees, or asylum-seekers.

RE-CONFIGURING RESPONSES TO CROSS-BORDER MOVEMENTS

The legal interventions in the lives of the alien migrant have been articulated primarily from the perspective of the host country. The subaltern voices are omitted from these conversations and yet these are the voices that can assist in untangling the conflations and confusions that are taking place between trafficking, migration and terrorism in the international and domestic legal arenas. The voice of the subaltern needs to be in the foreground—not as a terrorist, nor as a victim, but as a complex subject who is affected by global processes, and seeking safe passage across borders. They are exposing the need to think about international law and rights in ways that are not confined to the boxes of sovereignty, the nation state and the autonomous subject of liberal rights discourse. Their stories provide a very different narrative about why people move and how to accommodate that movement. For example, as Saskia Sassen has demonstrated, the evidence indicates patterns in the geography of migration, and receiving countries get migrants from countries and places that form or did form a part of their zone of influence (Sassen). This would explain some of the patterns of migrations to the United States and the United Kingdom. It is partly an outcome of the actions of a government's foreign policy and their economic involvement in countries of origin. Earlier colonial patterns also inform current migration patterns, captured in the slogan, "We are here, because you were there." One of the most obvious ways in which to alleviate the injustices and harms that occur during the course of movement is to alter immigration laws in order to accommodate these cross-border movements. The fear of a flood of "Others" is neither grounded in statistics nor a self-evident negative process. The fear of change or survival of one's culture and identity is based on a false assumption that cultures are static and fixed and frozen in time (du Gay and Hall). Yet the colonial encounter is evidence of the fact that a return, the retrieval of a pristine and culturally authentic space is not possible (Grewal and Kaplan).

Yet the legal reform of immigration laws is neither adequate nor sufficient to address the broader concerns I have set out in this article. The transnational subaltern subject also brings a normative challenge—to the porosity of national borders, the notion of fixed, stable, autonomous, sovereign subject, and the emergence of non-state entities as a significant force in the international arena. The sovereign state and the sovereign subject are being laid bare through the challenges posed by the worlds constitutive "Others." The liberal state and the liberal subject are based on the idea of fixed borders, with clearly identifiable interests and identities. They are imbued with the power to decide, choose, and act autonomously. Yet globalization, which produces the challenge of migration and non-state actors to the legitimacy of the borders of the sovereign state and the autonomous subject, indicates otherwise. The complexity of new global formations and the dynamic character of transnational subaltern subjects, challenge any notion that the state and individual are hermetically sealed and capable of exercising control through self-contained power (Brown). The inability to distinguish those who constitute national subjects from those who are alien or foreign is blurred reflecting the uneasy location of a distinct national entity with distinct borders and a distinct, clearly delineated national subject. The legitimizing tools of cohesion, unity and sovereignty become blunt in the face of a more complex and integrated world and global economy and the challenge posed by the transnational subaltern subject.

The role of law, at the international and domestic level, should be to address how broader transnational processes affect flows or movements of people and are an integral feature of globalization. And this in turn requires radical rethinking. As long as these issues are not viewed through the complex lens of globalization, market demand and the in/security of the nation-state, the rights and legitimacy of these people will remain unaddressed or compromised, and contribute to the growing instability of both the host country and this itinerant population. Cross-border movements have been caught within the framework of a "War" fought along the simple binaries of good versus evil, civilization versus barbarism. A response to border crossings cannot be adequately addressed through such binaries. Indeed this myopic response will do little to discourage the illegal crossing of borders or the determination of those who want to move.

The agency of women also needs to be foregrounded. She is currently invoked as either a victim in need of rescue from the conniving, manipulative, culturally primitive subaltern family or is herself equated with the demonized or contaminating "Other." Her complex subjectivity remains unaddressed in the legal and policy approaches being pursued at the national and international levels. Women's choice or agency remains either non-existent, questionable or tainted. Her choice to move must be distinguished from other situations where her consent is absent or her movement is compelled by strife or conflict.

Women's choices to cross borders need to be viewed within the context of empowerment and their search for better economic market opportunities. Their consent must be located in the matrix of the global economy, market demand, and cross-border migrations. Currently, their cross-border movements are largely located and addressed within normative understandings about women's sexuality, the security of the nation, and the criminal law. Her choice is reconfigured through international legal processes, and she is either rendered a victim, to be repatriated to her home country, or as a criminal, a trespasser, to be prosecuted along with traffickers and terrorists for having exposed the porosity of national borders. Legal barrier methods fail to attend to the complex factors that induce migration, and instead, target the individual, as being exclusively responsible for the problem of transnational migration. The receiving country is not implicated in this migration phenomenon, and is justified in resorting to methods of containment and confinement. These punitive measures constitute migrant women as outlaws, and compel them to live illegal lives. The international legal order has failed to facilitate women's freedom of mobility and safe migration, especially though not exclusively, from the south to the north. Her consensual movement is rendered illegal, through the foregrounding of the security of the nation-state, the conservative sexual morality that often informs anti-trafficking laws, and the xenophobic responses to global movements that increasingly inform immigration laws. These "overground" legislative measures are supplemented by a parallel "underground migrant-mobility regime," where travel agents and transporters, complete with route maps, directions, and a list of the least vulnerable points of entry, negotiate how their human cargo will cross borders, avoiding apprehension by state agents and border patrols.

Regardless of why women move, their assertion of the right to mobility, self-determination and development, must not be confused with the violence, force, coercion, abuse or fraud that may take place in the course of migration or transport. The crime rests in the elements of abuse and violations, which are committed against women along the continuum of women's migration and not because of the movement or mobility per se.

In order to address the issue of cross-border movements, we cannot simply remain confined to the domestic arena, where regulatory enforcement is focused on the individual and the border. Nor can this process be addressed in the international legal arena purely in terms of criminality or trafficking. These responses fail to understand the global context in which such movements are occurring. In order to understand and respond to the relationship between such global movements and the law, it is necessary to revisit this issue as not one that is cast in terms of binaries—the security and cohesion of the state, versus the invasion of hoards of "Others." It must be addressed against this broader canvass of transnationalism. Transnational movements require a transnational response and analysis—they cannot be caught within older frameworks. We need to complicate the global-local, center-periphery, which is based on a purely locational politics. The transnational subaltern subject is living the global reality and evidence of the fact that global and cultural flows are neither unidirectional nor uniform. They reverse and displace the original aims of most legal responses, which are directed at securing and policing the borders of the nation state, and the stability of the sovereign subject. The transnational subaltern subject is exposing the unstated norm from which such responses are emanating, and returning the gaze in a way that forces us to revisit current legal responses to cross-border movements, and to acknowledge the fact that people will move illegally if legal means are not made available to them.

The transnational subaltern subjects are moving—across national regional and international borders. And they are simultaneously drawing attention to the disparate arenas of power with which we must engage in order to understand the global movement of people and the normative and political significance of the transnational subaltern subject.

> Before professors in business schools were talking about global economics, illegals knew all about it.... The illegal immigrant is the bravest among us. The most modern among us. The prophet.... The peasant knows the reality of our world decades before the Californian suburbanite will ever get the point. (Kumar xiv)

Ratna Kapur is the Distinguished Global Professor of Law, Jindal Global Law School, Sonepat (Delhi), and also on the Faculty of the Geneva School of Diplomacy and International Relations. She is also the co-founder and titular head of the Centre for Feminist Legal Research, New Delhi.

[1]Some of this fear or aversion is expressed in the enactments of anti-terrorist legislation around the globe which are vaguely drafted, over inclusive and are likely to be use to target protest which is legitimate but may be disapproved.
[2]See, for example, Guha 1982a, 1982b, 1997; Guha and Spivak; Chaturvedi; Beverley; Chakrabarty. See also Chatterjee 1983, 1986.
[3]See also Sarkar's *A Critique of Colonial India* who best represents the focus of the earlier efforts of subaltern studies. Sarkar argues in favor of a theoretical framework capable of capturing the nuances of the agency of the colonized by foregrounding the spaces of resistance in the colonialist-nationalist discourse.
[4]The subaltern project took on several other incarnations. In North America, it became influential partly because it coincided with the emergence of multiculturalism, but more importantly, because it converged with postcolonial theory (see Said). The project in merging somewhat with postcolonial scholarship continued to challenge the metaphysical foundations of the Enlightenment, and highlighting the production of knowledge through the relationship of power— that is—through moments of crisis, ruptures, fractures and conflict
[5]There are equivalents of the well known hawala system in all regions of the world. The hawala system, emanating out of Inida, is a massive and efficiently organized system within the undergound parallel economy that specializes in money transfers within and across borders. It is also one of the many informal systems targeted by the "War on Terror."
[6]See Lim and Oishi's article "Interantional Labour Migration and Asian Women: Distinct Characteristics and Policy Concerns," where the authors state that in most countries of Asia, the transnational migration of women has increased

from 15 percent to 27 percent, resulting in Asian women outnumbering Asian men as overseas migrants (87).

[7]In his address to the nation on September 11th, President Bush concluded that the U.S. had been attacked by "evil" because "we're the brightest beacon for freedom and opportunity in the world" (President George W. Bush, Statement in Address to the Nation, Sept. 11, 2001, available from Office of the Press Secretary, The White House). "This will be a monumental struggle of good versus evil. But good will prevail" (President George W. Bush, Remarks Following Meeting with National Security Team, Department of State 12 September, 2001, available at www.usembassy.org.uk/bush73 visited on 28th of August). The Italian Prime Minister, Silvio Berlusconi, is reported to have "praised Western civilization … as superior to that of the Islamic world and urged Europe to reconstitute itself on the basis of its Christian roots" (Erlanger A8). "I think the world increasingly will understand that what we have here are a group of barbarians.… So it's an attack not just upon the United States but upon, you know, civilized society.… We also have to work, through, sort of the dark side, if you will… That's the world these folks operate in, and so it's going to be vital for us to use any means at our disposal, basically to achieve our objective. And I think we have to recognize we are the strongest, most powerful nation on Earth" (Vice President Cheney, Text of Remarks on Meet the Press, 17 September, 2001, on file, http://www. whitehouse.gov/vicepresident/news-speeches/speeches/vp20010916.html). See also recent comments by religious right leader Pat Robertson describing Islam as a violent religion that seeks "to dominate and then if need be destroy" ("Islam is violent in nature ").

[8]The broad scope and breadth of the legislation that has been enacted by some states attests to the fact that they are using the legislation for purposes other than merely targeting terrorism. See especially Human Rights Watch, World Report. The report criticizes legislation enacted immediately after the September 11th attacks, as being over inclusive and compromising on civil liberties. For example, it states that the emergency legislation rushed through the U.S. Congress, the so-called *USA Patriot Act*, permits the indefinite detention of non-deportable non-citizens once the attorney general "certifies" that he has "reasonable grounds to believe" that the individual is engaged in terrorist activities or endangers national security. These broad and vague criteria could allow the attorney general to certify and detain any alien in the United States who had any connection, however tenuous or distant in time, with a group that had once unlawfully used a weapon to endanger a person" (xxiv). The report is critical of several other measures by governments in different parts of the world that feed an anti-immigrant agenda rather than an anti-terrorist concern. Similar human rights compromises could be found in other aspects of the global response to terrorism. Australian Prime Minister John Howard, stoking post-September 11 fears of foreigners, built his candidacy for re-election in November around his summary expulsion, in blatant violation of international refugee law, of asylum-seekers who had reached outlying Australian territory. Proposed European Union-wide security measures

included a broad definition of terrorism that threatens freedom of association and the right to dissent; a European arrest warrant to facilitate transfer of terrorist suspects without fair-trial safeguards; and a "re-evaluation" of the right to seek asylum in Western Europe in light of new security considerations. Proposals by the British government would permit the prolonged arbitrary detention of foreigners suspected of terrorist activity and severely curtail the right to seek asylum. The Indian government used the new focus on terrorism to push for sweeping new police powers of arrest and detention—powers last used to crack down on political opponents, social activists, and human rights defenders. The U.S. government detained over 1,000 suspects following the September 11th attacks, but threw a shroud of secrecy over the cases that made it impossible to determine whether criminal justice powers were being appropriately applied.

⁹See White Paper of the British Government, Safe Borders Secure Haven, February 2002, proposing that people who want to become UK citizens take a compulsory English language test and an exam on the ways of British life, British society, and British institutions. The sole previous requirement was just a passport. They will also be required to take a citizenship pledge. These measures are justified by the home secretary in the following terms: "Our future social cohesion, economic prosperity and integrity depends on how well we rise to the global challenge of mass migration, communication and flight from persecution." Some of these measures have been incorporated into the recently enacted *British Nationality, Immigration and Asylum Act*, 2002.

REFERENCES

Ahmad, Aijaz. "Fascism and National Culture: Reading Gramsci in the Days of Hindutva." *Lineages of Present: Political Essays*. New Delhi: South Asia Books, 1996.

Anghie, Anthony. "Franscisco de Vitoria and the Colonial Origins of International Law." *Social and Legal Studies* 5 (3) (1996): 321-336.

Beverley, John. *Subalternity And Representation: Arguments In Cultural Theory*. Durham, NC: Duke University Press, 1999.

Brown, Wendy. *Politics Out of History*. New Jersey: Princeton University Press, 2001.

Buch, Claudia M., Anja Kucklenz and Marie-Helene Le Manchec. *Worker Remittances and Capital Flows*. Kiel Institute for World Economics, Working Paper No. 1130. 2002.

Buchanan, Pat. *Death of the West: How Dying Populations and Immigrant Invasions Imperil Our Country and Civilization*. New York: St. Martin's Press, 2002.

Chakrabarty, Dipesh. "Radical Histories and Question of Enlightenment Rationalism: Some Recent Critiques of Subaltern Studies." *Mapping Subaltern Studies and the Postcolonial*. Ed. Vinayak Chaturvedi. London: Verso, 2000. 256-280.

Chatterjee, Partha. "More on Modes of Power and the Peasantry." *Subaltern*

Studies II: Writings on South Asian History & Society. Ed. Ranajit Guha. Delhi: Oxford University Press India, 1983. 311-349.

Chatterjee, Partha. *Nationalist Thought and the Colonial World: A Derivative Discourse?* London: Zed Books, 1986.

Chaturvedi, Vinayak. Ed. *Mapping Subaltern Studies And The Postcolonial.* London: Verso, 2000.

Darian-Smith, Eve and Peter Fitzpatrick. Eds. *Laws of the Postcolonial.* Ann Arbor: University of Michigan Press, 1999.

Du Gay, Paul and Stuart Hall. *Questions of Cultural Identity* London: Sage Publications Reprint Edition, 1986.

Erlanger, Steven. "Italy's Premier Calls West Superior to Islamic World." *New York Times* 27 September 2001: A8.

Grewal, Inderpal and Caren Kaplan. "Introduciton: Transnational Feminist Practices and Questions of Postmodernity." Eds. Inderpal Grewal and Caren Kaplan. *Scattered Hegemonies: Postmodernity and Transnationbal Feminist Practice.* Minneapolis: University of Minnesota Press, 1994.

Guha, Ranajit. "On Some Aspects of Historiography in Colonial India." *Subaltern Studies I: Writings on South Asian History & Society.* Ed. Ranajit Guha. Delhi: Oxford University Press India, 1982a. 1-9.

Guha, Ranajit. "Preface." *Subaltern Studies I: Writings on South Asian History & Society.* Ed. Ranajit Guha. Delhi: Oxford University Press India, 1982b. vii-viii.

Guha, Ranajit. "The Small Voice of History." *Subaltern Studies IX.* Eds. Shahid Amin and Dipesh Chakrabarty. Delhi: Oxford University Press India, 1996.

Guha, Ranajit. Ed. *A Subaltern Studies Reader 1986-95.* Minneapolis: University of Minnesota Press, 1997.

Guha, Ranajit and Gayatri Chakravorty Spivak. Eds. *Selected Subaltern Studies.* New York: Oxford University Press, 1988.

Hamburg World Economic Archives-IDP. Migration and Remittances, Dossier No. 3, April 2003.

Human Rights Watch, *World Report 2002.* Web. Retrieved August 28, 2002.

International Organization of Migration (IOM). *World Migration Report,* 2000.

"Islam is violent in nature." *New York Times* 23 February 2002: A8.

Kumar, A. *Passport Photos.* Los Angeles: University of California Press, 2000.

Kapur, Ratna. "The Tragedy of Victimization Rhetoric: Implications for International/Postcolonial Feminist Legal Politics." *Harvard Human Rights Journal* 15 (1) (2002).

Lim, Lin Lean and Nana Oishi. "International Labour Migration and Asian Women: Distinct Characteristics and Policy Concerns." *Asia Pacific Migration Journal* 5 (1) (1996).

Mehta, Uday Singh. *Liberalism and Empire: A Study in Nineteenth Century British Liberal Thought.* Chicago: University of Chicago Press, 1999.

Mohanty, C. Talpade "Under Western Eyes: Feminist Scholarship and Colonial Discourses." *Third World Women and the Politics of Feminism.* Eds. Chandra

Talpade Mohanty, Lourdes Torres and Ann Russo. Indiana: Indiana University Press, 1991.

Otto, Diane. "Subalternity and International Law: The Problems of Global Community and the Incommensurability of Difference." *Social And Legal Studies* 5 (3) (1996): 337-364.

Porras, Ileana. "On Terrorism: Reflections on Violence and the Outlaw." *Utah Law Review* 119 (1994).

Sadiqu, Nafis. "Undocumented and Irregular Migration in the Asia-Pacific Region." United Nations Population Fund, Paper presented at the International Symposium on Migration, "Towards Regional Cooperation on Irregular/ Undocumetned Mirgation." Bangkok April 21-23, 1999.

Said, Edward. "Foreword." *Selected Subaltern Studies*. Eds. Ranajit Guha and Gayatri Chakravorty Spivak. New York: Oxford University Press, 1988. v-x.

Sarkar, Sumit. *A Critique of Colonial India.* Calcutta: Papyrus, 1985.

Sanghera J. "Enabling and Empowering Mobile Women and Girls: Strategy paper on the Safe Migration and Citizenship Rights of Women and Adolescent Girls," ASEM meeting on "Gender, Migration and Trafficking," sponsored by Swedish Department for International Cooperation and UNIFEM, Bangkok, October 2002.

Saseen S. *Globalization and Its Discontents: Essays on the New Mobilitiy of People and Money.* New York: The New Press, 1998.

Spivak, Gayatri Chakrovorty. "Three Women's Texts and a Critique of Imperialism." *Critical Inquiry* 12 (1) (1985): 243-261.

Volpp, Leti. "The Citizen and the Terrorist." *University of California Law Review* 49 (1575) (2002).

AUDREY MACKLIN

Women as Migrants

Members in National and Global Communities

THE RIGHT TO RESTRICT the entry of non-citizens to one's territory is considered the *sine qua non* of sovereignty.[1] When it comes to immigration, international law accepts more or less uncritically the characterization of states as private clubs and migrants as membership applicants. The major exception to that principle is the UN *Convention Relating to the Status of Refugees,* but it should not escape notice that virtually all major countries of asylum, including Canada, expend considerable energy on "non-entrée" mechanisms to prevent asylum seekers from getting to the clubhouse door.[2]

Women migrants often embody—literally—the absence, the breakdown, or the inequities of the international Legal regime. War, global economic restructuring, human rights abuses, the persistence of gender oppression all over the world each play a role—alone, in combination, or alongside other factors—in propelling many women to depart their countries of nationality and seek new lives in Canada. International law directly impacts Canadian immigration law and policy; and in this sense, women migrants (and migrants generally) *are* the impact of international law on CanadaCanadian immigration law is what the state does to either deflect, minimize, or harness that impact in the service of domestic interests. It does this through creating categories into which it classifies those for whom the accident of birth did not confer Canadian citizenship: legal or illegal; immigrant or refugee; citizen, permanent resident, or visitor; independent or family class. Canada does not directly control the conditions of women's lives leading up to their departure, but the category into which it sorts a woman will become another force affecting that woman's life and her experience of migration. Her migration status may have a liberating effect, it may compound existing constraints, it may do some of each. In this sense, Canada may be held directly accountable for the impact domestic immigration law has on the migrant.[3]

TRAFFICKING IN GENDER ROLES

The exploitation of migrants as cheap labour is a gender-inclusive phenomenon. Both male and female migrant job ghettos exist in the Canadian marketplace one need look no further than to the identity of the women cleaning our rooms in this hotel, or the men driving the cabs in this city to find evidence of this. It is not uncommon to refer to this phenomenon as using immigrants to do our "dirty work"—the work Canadians are unwilling to do. What is distinctive, in my view, is the extent to which certain women are imported to perform as women. The insertion of female migrants intogender-specific roles is not a by-product of their immigration, it is the very reason for it. Being a traditional female is a job desired by fewer Canadian women these days, so women with fewer options in their lives are imported to do the women's work. What are those traditional female gender roles? Stripped down to the crudest form, they are sex, child rearing and elder care, and domestic labour. Packaged for transnational trade, these services are embodied as sex-trade workers, domestic workers, and so-called mail-order brides. The first provide sex, the second perform child care and housework,[4] and the third are meant to furnish all three.

To its credit, the Committee on the Elimination of All Forms of Discrimination Against Women (CEDAW) candidly acknowledges the conceptual links between the global traffic in women as sex-trade workers, domestic workers, and "mail-order brides," underscoring the fact that the "push" factors propelling women into the global market, and the "pull" factors creating the demand for them, are similar across categories. Another important characteristic of this trafficking in gender roles is the sexualization of the "race," ethnicity, or culture of the woman. By this I mean that the cultural, racial, or ethnic origins of the women are used to construct a "super-feminine" version of a woman who is sexually insatiable, docile, a natural housekeeper, obedient, undemanding, loves children, and is otherwise more "feminine" than her Canadian counterpart. As bell hooks writes:

> When race and ethnicity become commodified as resources for pleasure, the culture of specific groups, as well as the bodies of individuals, can be seen as constituting an alternative playground where members of dominating races, genders, sexual practices affirm their power-over intimate relations with the Other. (qtd in Chun 1208)

Of course, most sex trade workers are born in Canada, most childcare is still performed by Canadian women, and most women who enter into marriage in Canada are citizens. For present purposes, the questions I wish to consider in relation to these activities are as follows: what difference does the fact of migration across international frontiers make? Further, what difference does the immigration status of a minority of women who occupy these fields make? Finally, what does international law have to say about any of this?

SEX WORKERS

By migrant sex workers I include women who strip, lap/ table dance, or exchange sex for money. Many of women in this occupation in Canada are migrants from poorer regions of the world, especially Southeast Asia andEastern Europe. Some women are explicitly recruited as strippers in Canadian clubs. As early as 1997, it came to media attention that, for several years, so-called "brokers" had been taking advantage of a 1978 loophole in Canadian immigration law exempting "exotic dancers" from the employment validation process required to issue a temporary work visa to a non-citizen or permanent resident. This meant that women with valid job offers from strip club owners could appear at the border and obtain a temporary work visa as "exotic dancers." (Ordinarily, one must apply for a work visa at a Canadian mission abroad, where visa officers can assess the validity of the employment contract and query whether the employer could locate Canadians who were, or could easily become, qualified to do the work.)

Insufficient numbers of Canadian or permanent resident women are willing to endure the wages and working conditions of legal sex work, and so club owners demand that the state subsidize their industry by importing women on temporary work permits to do the work for the wages and under the working conditions that employers are prepared to offer. Apparently, the employment validation exemption for strippers spawned a burgeoning and highly profitable racket of importing foreign women. Because exotic dancing is part of a spectrum of sex work that crosses the border between legal and illegal, the transborder trade in exotic dancers, unsurprisingly, was predictably accompanied by abuse, extortion, and/or forcible prostitution of the women involved. Women could be pressured, induced, coerced, or forced to engage in types of sex work in or outside the clubs that was not legal, but which earned their employers more revenue. Men will pay more to do things to women, or to make women do things to themselves or to other women, than they will pay for lawful acts. Club owners systematically neglect the health, safety, or fair treatment of sex workers, and this is mirrored in the state's disinterest in protecting sex workers qua workers under occupational health and safety law, or employment standards legislation. For those who actually worked as "exotic dancers," the ever-present threat of deportation operated as a powerful tool of exploitation. For those forced into prostitution, the threat of deportation is a double-edged sword. One might suppose that a woman who has been tricked, beaten, and raped into prostitution might prefer to be "caught" by authorities and repatriated rather than prostituted. But in practice, the woman may also legitimately fear reprisals against herself or her family at home if she seeks assistance from Canadian authorities. Also, the stigma of returning home as a prostitute may mean that the life she left behind is no longer available to her.

To the extent that this work to be the least worst option in their lives, individual women's decisions to engage in sex work as the exercise of autonomy under conditions of constraint, in much the same way as workers in many 4D jobs (dirty, dangerous, difficult or degraded)can be described as consenting to exploitative work. Of course, many women in sex work may in fact be misled, deceived or coerced into doing work or enduring conditions of abuse, overwork, under or non-payment, that they neither expected nor agreed to; again, sex work is not unique in this. In saying this, I am siding with those who do not regard sex work's unique features as rendering sex work so distinct from other forms of labour that it demands an utterly separate normative analysis or qualitatively unique policy prescriptions.

Still, there is little doubt that for many women (and all girls) today, migration into sex work is not a door opening to a better life. Migration simply signifies another mechanism of subordination and control. Whether it involves moving Canadian girls between Halifax and Toronto or transporting Thai girls to Vancouver, , pimps everywhere know that isolating a young woman from her home, her family, and her support network will render her frightened, helpless, and less able to escape. Crossing international frontiers makes the strategy all the more potent. Many of the women do not speak the language, do not understand the culture, have no idea where to turn for help, and have no money to return home. Indeed, their families may have borrowed money from smugglers to pay the cost of passage, and the women are effectively indentured to repay that money through sex work. Their families depend on them to send remittances home to support those left behind. The woman's "foreignness" only adds to her vulnerability, which in turn is packaged and sold as a sexual enticement to the clients who consume her.

Trafficking in women and children has long attracted the attention of the international community. It is directly prohibited by various international treaties and ILO Conventions.[5] As early as 1904, the *International Agreement for the Suppression of the White Slave Traffic*[6] expressed the international communities' concern about the sale of women into prostitution in Europe. Of course, the title of the treaty betrayed the racist focus of reformers concerns,[7] though by 192 1 the terminology shifted to "trafficking in women and children." In 1949, the fledgling United Nations consolidated four earlier treaties on the subject into the *Convention far the Suppression of the Traffic in Persons and of the Exploitation of the Prostitution of Others.*

The contemporary international legal response to human trafficking takes the form of a protocol to the 2000 United Nations Convention on Transnational Organized Crime. The title of the supplementary Protocol to Prevent, Suppress and Punish Trafficking in Persons, Especially Women and Children, reveals its preoccupation (though not exclusive focus) on women and children. The Protocol defines trafficking as follows:

> "Trafficking in persons" shall mean the recruitment, transportation, transfer, harbouring or receipt of persons, by means of the threat or use of force or other forms of coercion, of abduction, of fraud, of deception, of the abuse of power or of a position of vulnerability or of the giving or receiving of payments or benefits to achieve the consent of a person having control over another person, for the purpose of exploitation. Exploitation shall include, at a minimum, the exploitation of the prostitution of others or other forms of sexual exploitation, forced

labour or services, slavery or practices similar to slavery, servitude or the removal oforgans.

The definition is ambiguous about whether prostitution is intrinsically exploitative, reflecting an ongoing debate inside and outside feminist circles about the character of sex work.

Other provisions in the Protocol encourage states to regard trafficked persons as victims, and to provide them with various forms of assistance and support. Article 7 invites, but does not require, states to adopt "legislative or other appropriate measures that permit victims of trafficking in persons to remain in its territory, temporarily or permanently, in appropriate cases."

The Trafficking Protocol has no enforcement mechanism, but the United States assumed the role of global anti-trafficking sheriff when it launched the annual Trafficking in Persons Report in 2001. The TIP reports rank states in accordance with the severity of trafficking problems in that state and the extent to which, in the U.S.' view, the state is taking appropriate steps to address the phenomenon. Like the Trafficking Protocol, the U.S. TIP regime has been the subject of much commentary and controversy regarding its scope, objectives, method and effects.

Canada, like most other countries of the global north, regards trafficking through the fetishizing of foreign women and female sexuality. The iconic trafficked person remains the virginal girl abducted into sexual slavery and not, for example, the exploited male migrant agricultural worker. For all the lurid focus on sex trafficking, the measures allegedly adopted to capture and prosecute traffickers virtually never materialize into 'rescue' and protection of trafficked persons, or apprehension or prosecution of traffickers. But to the extent that trafficking is bound up with transborder movement in the popular imagination, the state can deploy measures designed to enforce borders and exclude female migrants, and package them as humanitarian anti-trafficking measures.

The government's first move in the late 1990s was to close the loophole that made it possible to obtain exotic dancer visa work permits at the border. The Adult Entertainment Association, a lobby group of club owners, embarked on an elaborate regulatory tango with the government, in which the club owners tried to ensure a supply of temporary foreign workers, while the government used low visibility bureaucratic tactics to retain access in law, while sharply reducing the number of permits actually issued. The pressure on Canada to cease an immigration program that appeared to make the government a party to sex trafficking collided with the insistence of Canadian employers that they were entitled to the same beneficial access to temporary foreign workers as any other industry. -

Early in 2012, the government revealed its perfected anti-trafficking regulatory tool: Section 30 of the *Immigration and Refugee Protection Act* authorizes immigration officers to deny a work permit to someone otherwise qualified and already approved for that permit in order to "protect foreign nationals who are at risk of being subjected to humiliating or degrading treatment, including sexual exploitation" (Bill C10, 2012, s. 206). In other words, Canada will protect foreign women from the horrors of trafficking by barring them from entering Canada. The same logic might support protecting Canadian women from sexual harassment by barring them from the paid workforce. Indeed, Canada's stated commitment to international efforts to combat the global trafficking in women thus provide a moralizing discourse for yet more discretionary and restrictive border control. However, closing the door to legal entry of women who work in the sex trade does not necessarily sponsored reduce the number of women working in the sex trade (even in Canada), or diminish their vulnerability to exploitation by brokers. Like virtually all other countries in the world today, Canada simply cannot seal its borders against the inflow of people anymore than it can seal its borders against the outflow of capital. Closing off a legal channel may divert the flow of trafficked women to other countries, but it will probably also divert many of those women into the category of illegal migrants. And if there is one group of people who are even more vulnerable to abuse and exploitation than temporary workers, it is illegal migrants.

FOREIGN DOMESTIC WORKERS

Many migrants work as live-in child care providers. The dynamics giving rise to this phenomenon are complex (see Macklin 1992). First, the demand emanates from Canada's politically powerful middle class; second, the supply is claimed as a necessary incident to Canadian women's access to the professions, thus allowing some proponents to stake their claim on feminist terrain; third, the government needs a safety valve to diffuse public protest over its persistent refusal to invest in universal, affordable child care. The resistance to change in the organization of the professional workplace, the identity of child care and domestic labour as "women's work," and the neo-liberal divestment of government from sustaining a social safety net are thus sustained in part on the backs of foreign domestic workers.

The Live-In Caregiver Program (LCP) is the current incarnation of Canadian government-sponsored programs to provide middle-class families with cheap child care, elder care and domestic labour. Women from poor countries have been migrating to Canada to work *as* "domestics," "nannies," or "servants" since before Canada had immigration legislation. By the 1950s, the national origin of many of these women had shifted from Europe to the Caribbean, and along with this shift came restrictive immigration rules designed to confine them to domestic labour and expel them when they were deemed no longer useful.

Up until the late 1970s, most of the women entering Canada as domestic workers originated from the Caribbean; today, most are Filipina, though I have heard anecdotally that East European women are also entering the market. Racialized stereotypes have accompanied each successive wave, rationalizing the role of women of colour as domestic workers, be it as the black "Mammy" figure, or the submissive, nurturing Filipina girl/woman. It will be interesting to discover what stereotypes crystallize around East European women should their numbers increase.

In the 1970s, women were only admitted as domestic workers on temporary work visas, much like the system described above with respect to sex trade workers. Effective political organizing by domestic workers led to the 1981 program known as the Foreign Domestic Movement (FDM). After two years as a live-in domestic worker, the worker could apply from within Canada for permanent resident status ("landing"), which then put her on the road to formal citizenship. If the woman did not complete two years of live-in service, she would be treated like a migrant worker, meaning that she had no protection against removal. The successor Live-In Caregiver Program preserves this two-year live-in requirement, but alters the criteria for selection and ultimate landing. At the risk of oversimplification, the LCP has made it more difficult to be selected, but easier to get landed. Thanks to litigation, the government has finally been forced to make the anomalous status of domestic workers explicit in legislation. Compared to the horror stories emanating from Singapore or the Middle East, the plight of domestic workers in Canada appears relatively good.

It cannot escape notice that the profound inequality of power along the axes of wealth, citizenship, race, and knowledge between employers and employees gives employers a significant advantage over workers. The point is not that all domestic workers are exploited, but rather that domestic work, occurring in the unregulated environment of the home, performed under the perpetual spectre—real or not—of deportation, potentiates exploitation. Should employers choose to take advantage of their employees' vulnerability, there is good reason to think they can "get away with it." As activist and former domestic worker Pura Velasco puts it, the combination of "temporary immigration status and compulsory living-in make the employers believe that they own the workers" (161).

From an immigration perspective, the centrepiece of the Live-In Caregiver Program is the mandatory two-year live-in requirement, in exchange for which foreign domestic workers is almost certain to acquire permanent resident status. Normally, persons with skills in short supply in the Canadian labour force are permitted to immigrate as permanent residents without being put on "probation" for two years. Why is that not so for domestic workers? The short answer is that permanent residents are legally entitled to do whatever work they choose once they enter Canada. Parents and policy makers feared that if given the same liberty as other permanent residents to choose their employment, women would get out of live-in domestic work as soon as possible. Holding the stick of deportation (or, if you will, the carrot of future permanent residence) in front of domestic workers to confine them to live-in work is the only way to keep them in the job. If the trafficking in women for sex is a contemporary form of enslavement, then the LCP is a form of government-enforced indentured labour.

The United Nations, addresses the issue of exploitation and abuse of female migrant workers worldwide. The Commission on the Status of Women, the

Commission on Human Rights, the Commission on Crime Prevention and Criminal Justice, the ILO, the Secretary-General, the various treaty bodies of the UN human rights system, and the Special Rapporteur on Violence Against Women, dertaken initiatives in relation to female migrant workers. Among the products have been a report of the Secretary-General on violence against women migrant workers,[9] examination by the Special Rapporteur on Violence Against Women, and an expert group meeting convened by the Division for the Advancement of Women on Violence Against Women Migrant Workers.

Two General Assembly resolutions[10] condemn violence against women migrant workers and call on Member States to take various measures to promote the rights and welfare of women migrant workers. Both resolutions encourage Member states to consider signing and ratifying the 1990 *International Convention on the Protection of the Rights of All Migrant Workers and Members of their Families*[11] as well as the 1926 *Slavery Convention*. In his report to the General Assembly on the Traffic in Women and Girls, the Secretary-General also indicated that the concept of trafficking articulated in the 1949 *Convention* "has been expanded to include trafficking for the purpose of other forms of exploitation of women" including forced labour and forced marriage.[12] The Secretary-General also quotes approvingly comments by CEDAW to the effect that importing foreign domestic labour is another form of sex exploitation.

To date, no source country for migrant workers has been able to wrest from host countries adequate and effective protection of their nationals abroad. The former all depend on the foreign remittances sent back by migrant workers, and lack either the political will or political clout to jeopardize that income by potentially antagonizing employer states.

The *International Convention on the Protection of the Rights of All Migrant Workers and Members* of *Their Families*[13] represents the most direct attempt to elevate the plight of migrant workers from a matter of foreign relations between individual states to the domain of the international community. Not surprisingly, several of the eleven countries that have signed or ratified the *Convention on Migrant Workers* are major source countries of migrant workers.[14] None are major employer states. Canada has neither signed nor ratified the instrument.

Roughly speaking, the *Convention on Migrant Workers* confirms migrant workers' entitlement to the same employment, civil, and political rights and responsibilities accorded to nationals, except those related to permanent residence and voting. It expressly forbids "torture or cruel, inhuman or degrading treatment or punishment" (Article 10), guarantees that no migrant worker shall be held "in slaveryor servitude" (Article 11 (l)), or be required to perform "forced or compulsory labour" (Article 11 (2)). It entitles migrant workers to state protection from *inter alia,* "violence, physical injury, threats and intimidation, whether by public officials or private individuals" (Article 16 (2)), extends to migrant workers the same protections owed to nationals respecting employment and labour standards (Article 25), and expressly forbids confiscation of passports (Article 21).

The *Convention on Migrant Workers* does not explicitly address the particular vulnerabilities or concerns of women migrant workers, such as the danger of sexual abuse and sexual exploitation, however these omissions can be overcome by a gender-sensitive interpretation of existing provisions.

Though not a signatory to the *Convention on Migrant Workers,* Canada has an interest in appearing to conform with its provisions. After all, the *Convention* is meant to embody minimum standards of decent and fair treatment. Thus, Canada indicated in a report to the UN General Assembly that, consistent with Articles 25 and 40 of the *Convention on Migrant Workers,* "no distinction was drawn between national and foreign workers insofar as the protection afforded by labour laws was concerned.[15] Of course, this is technically true: no employment or labour statute explicitly excludes foreign workers from its ambit; rather, several just happen to exclude domestic work—the very sector dominated by foreign women—from some or all protection.[16] In practice, the *Convention* i guarantee of equality of treatment with nationals amounts to an empty promise when the occupation has historically been excluded from employment and labour protection (Hune), an exclusion which derives largely from it's denigrated status as "women's work" belonging to the unregulated "private sphere." Canada's claim to fulfilling the antidiscrimination provision in the *Convention* is a rather cynical attempt at obfuscation.

There are other provisions of the *Convention on Migrant Workers* that Canada could not claim to fulfill with respect to foreign domestic workers. Article 39 guarantees to migrant workers "liberty of movement" and the "freedom to choose their residence" in the employer State. Clearly, domestic workers admitted to Canada under the Live-In Caregiver Program do not enjoy this freedom insofar as they are obliged to live in the employer's home in order to retain their immigration status.

In my view, the real reason that the *convention on Migrant Workers* has so little impact on Canadian law is that its fundamental premises-that migrant workers should not be exploited, and that exploitation can be prevented by entitling migrant workers to the same legal protection as nationals-misses the whole point of migrant labour. Countries import migrant labour for two reasons: either their own labour force genuinely lacks the technical or professional skills required to do the job, or else the local labour force is unwilling to do the work for the price and under the working conditions employers wish to offer. I believe that foreign domestic workers fall into the latter category. The very purpose of institutional, long-term migrant labour arrangements of this sort is to enable employers to subject workers to wages and working conditions that citizens and permanent residents consider unacceptable. We deny this by insisting that the appropriate comparators are the wages and working conditions available in the State of origin rather than those guaranteed to Canadian workers; we rationalize it by pointing to the dearth of adequate, affordable, universal daycare in Canada, and the various time and financial stresses on Canadian working parents (read: mothers);[17] and we excuse it by offering permanent residence as the reward for two years of indentured service. Whichever of these explanations we find compelling, any international instrument which fails to grasp this essential nature of migrant labour arrangements is doomed to irrelevance.

INTERNET BRIDES

If you have not heard about the thriving international mail-order bride industry, you need look no further than the hundreds of websites on the internet. Eastern European states, as well as the the Philippines is a major supplier country.[18] As is well known, the historical presence of American military bases in that country was accompanied by the sexual colonization of the local women. The bases may have closed, but American men took away with them a certain nostalgia for the benefits they reaped from the racial, sexual, and economic exploitation of the women they left behind. Both sex tourism and the mail-order bride industry deliver these benefits to men through other means. Just as the pressures wrought by economic collapse has put East European women's bodies on the international market as sex-trade workers and domestic workers, so too has it propelled them into the international marriage market. Why are male customers looking abroad for marriage partners? Christine Chun summarizes the consumer-husband's motivation:

> Marriage brokers rely upon the consumer-husbands' dissatisfaction with American women and the Women's Movement. According to most of the men who seek mail-order brides "American women are too aggressive, too demanding [and] too devoted to their own careers." Marriage brokers recognize that '[t]he mail order bride business has been stoked by a backlash against women's liberation and the feeling of the "subscribers [that] American women are aggressive and selfish." (1176)

Agencies that traffic in mail-order/internet brides accommodate consumer preferences by selling a "gender role fantasy" of Filipina and East European women "to men who blame their failed relationships on American women" (Chun 11 76). Thus, the Asian woman is constructed as docile, subservient, sexually available, and devoted to domesticity. As Renee Tajima puts it:

> Images of Asian women ... have remained consistently simplistic and inaccurate.... There are two basic types: the Lotus Blossom Baby (aka China Doll, Geisha Girl, shy Polynesian beauty) and the Dragon Lady (Fu Manchu's various female relations, prostitutes, devious madames).... This view of Asian women has spawned an entire marriage industry. (qtd. in Chun 1208)

The stereotypes of Russian women emerging from the communist era may seem, at first glance, less attractive to male consumers disgruntled with "strong" women. Nevertheless, marriage brokers such as Eugene Kantor assert that while an Asian woman allegedly subscribes to a role that is "not servitude, necessarily, but a certain position in the family structure" a Russian woman is not as "drastic" in her views, but nonetheless insists that she "should cook, do the laundry, etc., even if she works the same amount of hours (outside the home) as the man." Kantor then zeroes in on the real "advantage" of Russian women over Asian women from a marketing perspective:

> Russian women, are—how shall I put this?—racially they are of different stock [than Asians]. The reality of life, again, is such that not every white man is looking for an Oriental woman, necessarily, a white woman would probably be a better candidate for them. (qtd. in Weir 40-42)

What are women looking for in the consumer-husband? Away out of grinding poverty, a future in a country of opportunity, and possibly a means of providing financial support via remittances to family members at home.

If a Canadian man marries a non-citizen woman abroad, he can sponsor his wife as a spouse, in which case she will arrive in Canada as a permanent resident. Under an impending regulatory change to Canadian immigration law, that spouse will enter Canada on a two year "conditional" permanent resident visa. If, at the end of two years, the state is satisfied that the marriage is genuine, the sponsored spouse will acquire secure permanent resident status. During the two year limbo, the sponsored woman's immigration status is dependent on her relationship with her husband. If he rejects her or if she leaves him, her immigration status will be revoked and she will be deportable. The ostensible purpose of this two year probationary period is to discourage the incidence of "marriage fraud," in which a naïve Canadian is duped into marrying a duplicitous foreigner. The foreign spouse then abandons the Canadian spouse immediately after arriving in Canada. Many countries other than Canada impose a probationary period on sponsored spouses, although there is no evidence that this actually reduces the incidence of "marriage fraud." As with foreign domestic workers, the precarious immigration status of a spouse may exacerbate her vulnerability to abuse. Reports of physical, emotional, and sexual abuse of women who migrate under these conditions are not uncommon. A few women have been killed. Given the attitude and expectations that many consumer-husbands bring to the marriage, it is hardly surprising that some would exploit the obvious inequalities of power between themselves and their wives. How does Canadian immigration law figure into this equation? In essence, the man can hold over his wife the threat that if the woman objects to his treatment of her, he will report to immigration authorities that the woman deceived him about her motives, and was only using him as a mechanism to immigrate to Canada, rather than marrying with the intention of residing with him permanently. In other words, he can claim that he was duped into a marriage of convenience.

International law has little to say explicitly about the mail-order bride industry. No international instrument directly addresses the phenomenon, and to my knowledge, it has not yet been the focus of scrutiny by any UN body. Of course, one could address it within the context of the anti-discrimination provisions of the CEDAW, the UN Declaration on All Forms of Violence Against Women, and the comments by the Committee in respect of organized marriages indicates a receptiveness to that.

Insofar as immigration law is concerned, however, there is no political will as yet to protect mail-order brides from potential abuse by conducting background criminal checks on the sponsor-husband (instead of only on the applicant-wife), regulating the "brokers," or providing the applicant-wife directly with information about her rights, her entitlements, and sources of assistance should she require it.

CONCLUSION

There is an international traffic in women to meet the demands of western men for sex, for child care, and for housework. This suggests that the decline in the number of western women willing to serve traditional roles has not altered the demand for those services, only the identity of those who are sought to perform them. There is no shortage of poverty-stricken men in countries like the Philippines and Russia, yet there is no market for "mail order grooms," or male prostitutes for women.[19] While there is a growing number of male elder care workers, the proportion remains very tiny overall.

Trading in women's work is big business. Whether one speaks of pimps, marriage brokers or nanny agencies, the fact is that someone else is making a lot of money off the fact that mostly poor, mostly young, foreign women are a bargain for certain Canadian johns, parents, and single men. The extent of international law's concern for the plight of these women seems to vary in accordance with the perceived legitimacy of the demand for their services in wealthier countries. The impact of international law on domestic immigration law thus seems more rhetorical than real: invoking international law's condemnation of trafficking in women for sexual exploitation is mainly useful for buttressing a decision to exclude sex workers, rather than a commitment to protecting their rights and interests as workers in Canada. Concerns about exploitation and trafficking do not figure in the discourse about Canada's legislated scheme of indentured labour in relation to live-in domestic workers. The possibility that women (and men) view migration via marriage as a chance to improve their life circumstances is channeled into a narrative about innocent Canadians duped by marriage fraudsters, which in turn sustains legal reforms that intensify the vulnerability of immigrant spouses to domination and abuse.

As the female migrant's role moves from the "public sphere" of commercial sex work, to the liminal zone of live-in care work, to the "private sphere" of the spousal relationship, the choices made by domestic policy are revealing about who is regarded as needing and deserving the law's protection, and what that protection entails. The notion that Canada protects women from trafficking by excluding them, or protects citizen spouses by making their foreign spouses more vulnerable, suggests that international human rights norms sometimes have as difficult a time crossing the Canadian border as do female migrants.

This article first appeared in the Canadian Council on International Law 1998 Annual Proceedings. It is reprinted with permission, and has been modified slightly to bring it up to date with subsequent legal developments .

Audrey Macklin teaches, researches, and advocates in the area of immigration and refugee law. She wrote this article while on faculty at Dalhousie Law School (1991-2000), and is also a former member of the Refugee Division of the Immigration and Refugee Board. Feedback and comments are welcome, and can be addressed to a.macklin@dal.ca.

[1]See *Chiarelli* v. *Canada (MEI)*, [1 9921 2 SCR 71 1].

[2]For a discussion of women as refugees, see Macklin (1995).

[3]1t is arguable, of course, that Canada is also indirectly accountable for migration from other countries by virtue of its role in creating or sustaining the global inequities that often propel people to leave their countries of origin.

[4]Domestic workers may also be subject to sexual harassment and violence, indicating that some employers believe sex to also comprise part of the domestic worker's informal job description.

[5]The description of international law in relation to the sex trade contained in this section draws heavily on the information contained in Farrior.

[6]May 18, 1904, 35 Stat. 426, 1 LNTS 83.

[7]See Demleitner. In a recent newspaper article, a journalist reports on the number of Nigerian, Polish, and Albanian women working as prostitutes in Italy. While explicit attention is given to how many European women are abducted and violently forced into prostitution, there was no discussion of how the "statuesque young African women dressed in little more than lingerie" ended up being prostituted in Italy. See Hooper.

[8]If the woman is indigent, the host country and country of origin are to share the cost of repatriation.

[9]E/CN.4/1998/75.

[10]GA Res A/RES/51/65 28 January 1997; GA Res A/RES/52/97 6 February 1998.

[11]GA Res 45/158, annex, 45 UN GAOR Supp. (No. 49A) at 262, UN Doc. (1990).

[12]A/51/309 27 August 1996.

[13]GA Res 45/158, annex, 45 UN GAOR Supp (No. 49A) at 262, UN Doc. A/45/49 (1990).

[14]As of 31 March 1998: Bosnia and Herzegovina, Cape Verde, Colombia, Egypt, Morocco, Philippines, Seychelles, Sri Lankaand Uganda (ratified); Chile and Mexico (signed).

[15]UN GA A/52/356, 17 September 1997.

[16]I suggest that the rationale behind the exclusion of domestic work from employment protection is inextricably linked to the fact that it has been conceptualized as the "private sphere" of "women's work; as a sub-category, live-in domestic labour has shifted into the realm of "foreign" women's work. For a discussion about the efforts of Ontario domestic workers to acquire collective bargaining rights, see Fudge at 119-145.

[17]Hong Kong city councillor Jennifer Chow recently advocated a 20 percent cut in salaries of domestic workers in that city on the grounds that the economic crisis in Asia meant that middle-class Hong Kong couples could no longer afford to pay domestic workers as much money. The alternative to slashing domestic workers' salaries would be doing without them, leaving middle class couples with the "appalling prospect of having to do their own housework." (Source: website *Aviva* at www. aviva.org, original article appearing in *The Guardian* (European Edition).

[18]In 1993, almost 30 percent of Filipino emigrants (19,000 out of 64,000) did so on the strength of fiancée or spousal sponsorship. See Chun. I believe it is safe to assume that most were women.

[19]There are, of course, thousands of boys from poor countries who are prostituted to men from Europe, North America, and Australia.

REFERENCES

Chun, Christine. "The Mail Order Bride Industry: The Perpetuation of Transnational Economic Inequalities and Stereotypes." *University of Pennsylvania Journal of International and Economic Law* 17 (1996): 1155-1208.

Demleitner, Nora. "Forced Prostitution: Naming an International Offense." *Fordham International Law Journal* 18 (1994): 163-197.

Government of Canada. *Safe Streets and Communities Act.* SC 2012, c.1, Royal Assent, 13 March 2012. Web.

Hooper, John. "Anti-vice drive arouses passions." *Guardian Weekly* 30 August 1998: 7.

Hune, S. "Migrant Women in the Context ofthe International Convention on the Protection of the Rights of All Migrant Workers and Members of Their Families." *International Migration Review* 25 (1991): 800-818.

Farrior, Stephanie. "The International Law on Trafficking in Women and Children for Prostitution: Making it Live Up to its Potential." *Harvard Human Rights Journal* 10 (1997): 213-255.

Fudge, Judy. "Little Victories and Big Defeats: The Rise and Fall of Collective Bargaining Rights for Domestic Workers in Ontario." *Not One of the Family: Foreign Domestic Workers in Canada.* Eds. Abigail B. Bakan and Daiva Stasiulis. Toronto: Univerity of Toronto Press, 1997. 119-145.

Macklin, Audrey. "Foreign Domestic Worker: Surrogate Housewife or Mail-

Order Servant!" *McGill Law Journal* (37) (October1992): 681-760.

Macklin, Audrey. "Refugee Women and the Imperative of Categories." *Human Rights Quarterly* 17 (May 1995): 213-277.

Macklin, Audrey. "At the Border of Rights: Migration, Sex-Work and Trafficking." *On the Margins of Globalization: Critical Perspectives on Human Rights.* Lanham: Lexington Books, 2004. 161-191.

Velasco, Pura. "'We Can Still Fight Back: Organizing Domestic Workers in Toronto." *Not One of the Family: Foreign Domestic Workers in Canada.* Eds. Abigail B. Bakan and Daiva Stasiulis. Toronto: University of Toronto Press, 1997.

Weir, Fred. "Imperialism of the Heart." *Canadian Dimension* 24 (6) (September 1990): 40-42.

PURA VELASCO

Migrant Workers Amidst Globalization

T HE IMPACT of economic globalization on the lives of poor Filipinos is so devastating, and the need for jobs so pressing, that despite the horrifying stories of injustices suffered by Filipino migrant victims, Filipino workers cannot be dissuaded from leaving the country in search of overseas employment. In my particular case, the threat of living in perpetual poverty, unemployment, and misery drove me to leave my own family in 1981 to work in Saudi Arabia. Today, many years later, these are still the same threats that push a lot of us to brave the violence against migrant workers abroad just to have the chance to find these better albeit elusive opportunities.

Since the beginning of American neocolonial control of the Philippines in 1901, our natural and human resources have been reserved for American businesses and their partners to use and expropriate. Every time our laws are changed to accommodate foreign business interests, the Philippine government and its transnational partners come up with promises of jobs and progress for the Filipino people. But our experience tells us that these were not the real goals of government and corporations. We have opened and continue to open our doors wide to foreign firms so that at present, our forests, minerals, and other natural resources are almost depleted. Rural and urban poor communities with no sanitation, health, education, and social services are experiencing the devastating impact of "fast-tracked" development projects by foreign corporations. Time and again, communities of the poor are demolished by private armies and by the military, and such brutal use of force and intimidation does not exclude arson and murder. Agricultural and forest lands have been converted to open pit mining, agri-business and industrial peace zones or export processing zones. These areas are called industrial "peace" zones because unions and strikes are not allowed. Workers are routinely required to get recommendation letters from public officials, and parish priests or pastors certifying that they are not members of unions or activist organizations and will not participate in union and strike activities.

Foreign companies are welcome to expand their business—whether it be in agriculture, mining, real estate, logging, fishing, communication, energy, financial management or in the pharmaceutical industries.

Vancouver-based Placer Dome Mining Company is a good example of the many foreign companies that create havoc in the lives of poor working class Filipinos and which have connections with corrupt government officials who very often have business interests. In the '60s it started its partnership with the former dictator Marcos' mining company, Marcopper, the biggest gold and copper mining company in the Philippines. Placer Dome massively displaced thousands of rural folks in Marinduque when its mine tailings polluted and destroyed the sources of food and livelihood of the community. These displaced communities are now considered internal refugees in urban cities and have joined the growing number of unemployed migrant workers. The President at that time, Gloria Arroyo, repeatedly ignored the pleas of the Marinduque people for her to intervene in their case against Placer Dome by bringing their case to the attention of Prime Minister Chretien. Later, when the Placer Dome executives absconded from the Philippines right after they were found guilty of polluting and, in effect, killing the Boac River and the Calacan Bay by a congressional investigation, she still maintained her hands-off policy. She even chose to ignore the advice of her Minister of Agriculture and Environment, who, together with the Chairperson of the congressional investigation, recommended that she bring up this issue during her official visit to Ottawa. However, the strong protests by Filipino migrant workers and their supporters from Vancouver, Toronto and Ottawa forced President Arroyo's hand, and for her Ottawa meeting with Chretien, she invited both her Minister of Agriculture and Environment as well as the chair of the congressional investigation of the Placer Dome environmental disaster to present this case.

What happened to the people of Marinduque is not an isolated case. It is also happening to many other communities in the Philippines especially now that the government has joined the bandwagon of the anti-terrorist campaign initiated by the Bush government. The truth is, the American troops now in Mindanao are not really there to weed out the Al-Queda/Abusayaf bandits-for-ransom group. They are in these vast and fertile lands to protect transnational businesses— Dole is just one of them—and and enable them to continue their land-grabbing activities by driving away indigenous communities and small farmers from their lands. President Akino's successor, President Benigno Aquino III, knows that he needs the U.S. military to control Mindanao since many hinterland communities are now organized and continue to defend their ancestral lands, forests and farms from rapacious transnational companies and their local partners in crime.

The Philippines is rich in natural resources, and the economy is essentially agrarian and lacks basic industries. It does not have a national industry. It is a country where multinational companies from the U.S., Japan, Canada, and Europe are active in keeping the country as an infantile economy: an amazingly cheap source of raw materials and a willing dumping ground for surplus products. As a result of this set-up we have a semi-feudal and semi-colonial political economy unable to provide meaningful employment and social services to our people. Our currency is tied to the U.S. dollar and continues to devalue so that we can no longer afford to pay the price of basic goods and services. We used to be number four in food production worldwide, but now we import rice, meat, milk, soap and a lot of our basic necessities. Our production is focused on exportable products such as, bananas, cashew, pineapple, and asparagus.

The International Monetary Fund/World Bank imposition of structural adjustment programs in the Philippines has also intensified the misery of our people with deathly poverty and massive unemployment. Our government institutions such as schools, hospitals, and public utilities are very inefficient and beyond the reach of the majority of our people. Most of our institutions are privatized, and those that are publicly funded are run by corrupt bureaucrats and politicians, and so everywhere you turn, the patronage system is rampant. It compounds the problem of access to training and employment. Filipinos, who are mostly poor, would offer gifts to their patrons just to maintain their connections. Workers would resort to personally paying to do volunteer work and to get reference letters from some bureaucrats and public officials. So, given these difficult economic and employment situations, our workers are conditioned and oriented to become so-called "docile, cheap and exportable labour"—and this is the kind of labour that is attractive to labour-receiving countries like Canada.

The Philippines, according to an International Labour Organization (ILO) study, has remained the number one source of migrant workers all over the world, followed by Sri-Lanka, Bangladesh, and Thailand. We are now seven million Filipino migrant workers involved in the nation building of 168 countries other than the Philippines. Our host countries benefit greatly from us. We are recruited at the prime of our lives. Seven million of us are like a nation by itself and our number is increasing as overseas employment has become an indispensable component of the Philippine government's Comprehensive Employment Plan. The Philippine government has no new solution to the high rate of unemployment and underemployment in the Philippines under the neo-liberal policies of deregulation, liberalization and privatization. Labour export has shifted from being a temporary solution to becoming a permanent policy with increasing government aggressiveness in marketing the Filipino as a global worker and in marketing the Philippines as a human resource center. For many years now the Comprehensive Employment Plan has meant more Filipinos employed overseas than it has meant an increase in local employment. For example, in the year 2001 alone, some 842,000 workers were deployed abroad, while local employment went down by 290,000 (which is the recorded number of laid-off workers).

Labour export remains an attractive business enterprise despite the persistent feedback from Filipino migrant workers that it is a source of national shame because of massive abuses to Filipinos by foreign employers. It remains lucrative because it generates foreign exchange—about seven billion dollars annually; generates revenue for government and "creates" employment by exporting people. Labour export means survival for every Philippine administration, great income for bureaucrats and politicians and easy money for the private profiteers. It is no wonder that our government has failed to protect Philippine domestic workers around the world. Most notoriously, for instance, the government did criminally little to prevent Flor Contemplacion, a Filipino domestic worker being hanged for the wrongful conviction of killing her friend Delia Maga, also a domestic worker, and the little son of Ms Maga's employer.

The Philippine government and the labour-receiving countries have found productive milking cows in the migrant workers—amassing large revenue from workers' employment and immigration processing fees like visas, passport, head tax, professional license, etc. A study by the Philippine government revealed that the documentation process for overseas deployment involves 76 signatures. This means that a worker has to pay the total cost of 15,400 pesos for signatures and stamps on their documents. This is only for the authentication segment of the application part of the process. We are not yet talking about the major fees. The second time I departed the Philippines for work abroad, I decided not to go through the formal channel set up by the Philippine government because I could not afford it.

It also costs a lot to settle abroad. Some years ago, in Canada it cost me about 4,000 dollars to process my papers under the Foreign Domestic/Live-In Caregiver Program until I got my landing papers. But do we get our money's worth? Many of us are not sure about this. On the contrary, governments keep on creating policies that are oppressive to poor migrant workers, such as, Immigration Canada's head tax and bond system in sponsoring family members and the proposal not to grant automatic Canadian citizenship to children born in Canada by parents who are not landed immigrants or citizens of Canada. Of course, we should not forget the racist and discriminatory Foreign Domestic Movement Program(FDMP) which is now called the Live-In Caregiver Program (LCP). Governments often set up agencies or offices that are allegedly, following policy, responsible for managing labour. However, they merely turn out to be efficient revenue centers.

Canada, as an advanced capitalist country, has used immigration policies to recruit skilled cheap labour in time of economic need. It also closes its door in time of economic crisis.

In the 1960s and '70s many of those recruited by Immigration Canada were Filipino health professionals, teachers and garment workers. An estimated 70 percent of this immigration wave were women. Most of them were sent to settle in areas like Newfoundland, Labrador and Winnipeg. But since the 1980s and '90s, thousands of Filipino women have entered as domestic workers under the Foreign Domestic Movement Program now known as the Live-In Caregiver Program.

Canada refuses to sign the International Convention for the Protection of Migrant Workers[1] on the pretext that it has the Live In Caregiver Program (LCP), which according to the government is a program that protects foreign domestics from abuse and exploitation. In reality, the LCP's mandatory requirement for domestic workers to live with their employers for close to three years without landing rights is exploitative and puts the workers in vulnerable conditions. This federal program traps our women in exploitative and oppressive situations. With low wages and long working hours, the workers are ghettoized on the lowest economic and political rung of Canadian society. Domestic workers are brought in to the country under a federal program, but the workers work under provincial jurisdiction. So nobody pays attention to the Employment Standards except the workers.

Also, domestic workers who are in a live-in condition find it difficult to demand their rights because they are afraid to lose their jobs, thus putting in danger their immigration status. They could also be barred from the place where they live and work. They routinely experience sexual harassment, violation of employment contracts, and other forms of abuse, but often they just suffer in silence. The Canadian government and our employers see us as mere slaves or vacuum cleaners that can be discarded. But there is also that unseen violence of not caring whether or not we suffer from a permanent deskilling because we have become mere chattel, even after we are Canadian citizens.

After many years of struggling economically, many are trapped in domestic work, or other jobs that resemble domestic work, in factories, homecare, and service industries. We think it is high time that the Canadian government perceive the shamefulness of shifting the burden of providing universal childcare and elderly care from society to the backs of Third World domestic workers. We also think that the LCP is a tragic waste of rich human resources and has to be scrapped! Immigration officials, like the former Immigration Minister Eleanor Caplan keep on saying that Canada should bring in the best and the brightest immigrants and yet they will not allow Filipino nurses to practice their profession even if they have passed the nurses licensure exams in British Columbia (despite the nursing crisis there). They want to keep skilled and talented immigrant women in a trap, where their labour remains cheap and flexible. In short, they want to maintain the discriminatory regulations within the LCP.

In Metro Toronto and other major cities of Canada, the segregation of the Filipino women workers into low paying jobs is clear. They are concentrated in the homecare, laundry, janitorial, telemarketing, data entry services, and factory work. The few nurses and medical technologists who have upgraded themselves are part-time or contract workers working for private agencies. Yes, they are mobile, working in three or four jobs, with a larger income than most Filipinos, but they have no access to upward advancement in their respective professions. And although the Canadian government acknowledges that we are one of the most highly educated of all immigrant groups, we also remain one of the lowest paid. Such low wages necessitate long working hours and extra jobs—so that ironically, this system deprives our own families of that nurturing and care that Filipino domestic workers are required to provide for others.

The impact of this oppressive system continues to worsen, despite all hope and good intentions. I remember in 1990 when I arrived in Toronto with 209 other domestic workers from my town, we were very hopeful that things would be better for us here. It was difficult to engage my compatriots in a conversation on the possible impact of the global economic restructuring that Canadians had started to talk about at that time. When I mentioned that we might experience the impact of structural adjustment programs for the second time, and in Canada, my friends told me that Canada was an independent, strong country and its government would never bow down to the pressure of the free market. They also advised me to be a good domestic worker and to focus my energy in acquiring citizenship papers as it would free me from doing domestic work, and would help me get fair and decent treatment in Canada. Well, it has been decades since our arrival. I still receive the regular invitations to social events from friends. But the invitations are more urgent and not the usual social and recreational events, but meetings organized by parents, churches, and the youth.

A lot of discussions are focused on the incalculable social cost of migration and the impact of flexible work situations on our families and the community in general. These discussions gradually make us aware of broad and encompassing problems. For one, we become aware that the LCP, a program for domestic workers, is just an "entry point" for us—to go into that enormous stream of work that is the dirty, cheap, and undesired jobs. Slowly we understand that it was the bait we snapped at, and now we have to remain in these jobs that are essentially domestic servitude. We discover that this systematized compartmentalization into "jobs for people of colour" wherein we suffer the disappearance and devaluation of our skills and experience, is the almost unseen weapon of discrimination that can annihilate our spirit. We know that this is all about institutionalized racism and other forms of discrimination.

We begin to see other broad and encompassing problems. We are worried that our youth are now being recruited as a second generation of marginalized labourers. Many of our youth in Canada are not able to handle the pressure from family reunification and settlement concerns. The difficulties in family reunification are compounded by the length of separation, which is a result of many factors: a restrictive immigration policy; the exorbitant head tax, the landing fee, and numerous employment fees as well as the income requirement to sponsor. Such is the low quality of life among these troubled families, that it is often marked by social and health problems like the high incidence of tuberculosis, teen pregnancy, increasing number of high school drop-outs, suicides, addiction, and domestic violence.

We are also alarmed by the increasing number of undocumented workers and mail-order brides in our community who are in very precarious situations exploited by their employers, brokers and partners.

Our community is frustrated with the fact that we have remained at the fringes of Canadian society. We are frustrated with the constant reminder from the federal and provincial governments that they no longer have enough money for social programs and services, We know that most of us handle two, three or more jobs—and most of them are part-time jobs—just in order to stay afloat. In fact, in this way, we have an income to be able to pay our taxes, and yet we are often blamed for using social programs that we paid for. To us that is evading the real issue, that jobs and social services are being stolen from us in the name of profit for a few.

However, this is the case whether we are in Canada or in the Philippines. We have been supporting this global economic system whose main beneficiaries are the elite. We, who are deprived but are courageous, are going to follow and settle where the resources are. We are aware that the privileged few will always create barriers that would prevent us from having decent lives. We will not surrender to these barriers. We have traveled this far, and have given up so much that we can only continue to grapple with and confront them.

On March 17, 1995, Flor Contemplacion, a Filipino domestic worker was hanged in Singapore for the wrongful conviction of killing her friend, Delia Maga, also a domestic worker, and the little boy in Maga's care.

The travesty of Flor Contemplacion's wrongful conviction and hanging generated massive protests organized by Filipino migrants and their supporters all over the world against the Philippine and the Singaporean governments. The Singaporean government's arrogant refusal to stay the execution despite evidence of Ms. Contemplacion's innocence, and the restrained action by the Philippine government in her defence showed us that our interest and welfare did not rest in the hands of our government nor the host countries' governments, but in our own hands. We took this opportunity to expose the plight of poor migrant workers to the international consciousness of people. It also gave us the opportunity to strengthen the overseas organizing drive started by Migrante International, an alliance of Filipino migrant workers organizations. A few months after the death of Flor Contemplacion on March 17, 1995, Migrante International coordinated the successful campaign to stay the execution by musketry of Sarah Balabagan, who was then a 16-year-old Filipino domestic worker convicted of stabbing her rapist, a United Arab Emirate employer.

In Canada, we continue to mount campaigns to fight for the rights and welfare of Filipino migrants. We mounted a national campaign to stay the deportation of Leticia Cables, the nanny from Edmonton, Alberta who was considered to have violated the LCP regulation when her employer—a lawyer—shared Leticia's service with another family since she could not afford to pay her full salary. We fought hard when Melca Salvador, the nanny from Montreal, Quebec was being deported with her Canadian-born son when she did not complete her LCP in the required three years because she got pregnant. Leticia Cables was able to come back to Edmonton and Melca Salvador won her fight to stay in Canada with her son. Our network of Filipino migrants has staged many demonstrations, protests, and deputations directed at the Canadian government for the restrictive and discriminatory regulations embedded in the LCP and the *Immigration Act*. Our national network across Canada has established peoples' organizations in Vancouver, Winnipeg, Toronto, Montreal, and Ottawa. We also belong to Migrante International, which is an alliance of Filipino migrant workers organizations. When Migrante International[2] had its international conference in November 2001, in the Philippines, it was attended by migrant organizers from all over the world. At a later conference in Japan, a network was created of Asia-Pacific migrant organizers supporting each other's work in organizing migrant workers from the different countries of the Asia-Pacific region.

As Filipino women workers, we are proud of the long history and vibrancy of our efforts to educate, organize and mobilize ourselves to address the roots of our problems in Canada and in the Philippines. We contribute at the local, national, and international levels of the women's movement. We recognize the need to deepen our understanding and organizing among specific groups of Filipino women in Canada: the migrant workers and the young Filipino-Canadian women.

The Filipino workers are like bamboo trees. We are very flexible. We don't break easily. We develop informal networks that help us to survive difficulties when we move from job to job, border to border. I have personally experienced these informal networks which helped me circumvent discriminatory rules at the borders or twist these ridiculous rules that the system imposes on us. But more important than little personal "rebellions" like this, we have learned over the years that formal and solid organizing is more effective in protecting ourselves and our rights. Finally, it is critical that we not only focus on the immediate problems that migrant workers presently face, but address the root causes of migration—poverty and unemployment.

Pura Velasco came to Canada as a domestic worker in 1990. She is currently coordinator of an Alzheimer's Adult Day Program at the Woodgreen Community Centre in Toronto. She is an active member of the Philippine Solidarity Group and the Migrant International Organization. She was President of the Toronto Organization for Domestic Workers' Rights (INTERCEDE) from 1990 to 1993.

[1]See the Intrernational Protocol for the Protection of All Migrant Workers and their Families at <www.bayefsky.com/general/cmw_sp_sr_2_2005.pdf>.
[2]See the Migrante International web site <http://migranteinternational.org>.

KERRY PREIBISCH

Gender Transformative Odysseys

Tracing the Experiences of Transnational Migrant
Women in Rural Canada[1]

EVERY YEAR, close to 28,000 men and women from Mexico and the Caribbean come to rural Canada to work as agricultural workers under a temporary employment authorization program known as the Seasonal Agricultural Worker's Program (SAWP). The SAWP has greatly expanded since its inception in 1966, when some 264 Jamaican men were authorized to work in southern Ontario. Despite the fact that the SAWP is highly gendered— over 97 percent of the migrant workforce is male—scholarly attention to the incorporation of foreign labour in Canadian agriculture has largely neglected to incorporate gender analysis when examining this phenomenon and has used women's numerically small presence to justify all-male samples. It is only very recently that the growing numbers of women and their increasing visibility in rural spaces have instigated the study of women's experiences of migration and the tabling of gender analysis in the debate (see Barndt 2000; Barrón; Becerril). This article contributes to efforts to bring to light the experiences of Mexican migrant women in rural Canada and further theoretical understandings of how and why women and men experience migration differently.

BACKGROUND

The federal government issues some 28,000 temporary employment visas to migrant workers destined for agriculture every year under the SAWP. The visas allow these non-citizens to stay in Canada for up to eight months, but their permission to work is tied to a single employer. The government refers to the program as a "labour mobility program," but in fact, workers are denied labour mobility. It is precisely this element, made possible by the citizenship status migrant workers are granted, that constitutes these workers as a highly vulnerable labour force. Since workers are in effect tied to their employers and cannot move to more attractive work sites, they have limited bargaining power to press for improved working or living conditions.[2] Employers also have the right to dismiss, and therefore deport, workers at will.[3] Since workers have been repatriated for falling ill, refusing unsafe work, or making complaints related to housing, the threat of repatriation itself constitutes an effective mechanism of control.

The SAWP operates in nine Canadian provinces, but over two-thirds percent of workers are concentrated in Ontario. Although the SAWP is carried out under the federal *Immigration Refugee and Protection Act and Regulations* and implemented within bilateral frameworks of agreement between Canada and the labour source countries,[4] it is governed by provincial statutes with regard to employment standards, labour and health (Verma). Since it is illegal in the province of Ontario for agricultural workers to unionize, the vast majority of Canada's SAWP workers are thus unable to seek the support of labour leaders to represent them before their employers. They are able, however, to contact home country designates, but worker assessments of their representatives have been less than favourable, if not damning (Basok; Binford; Preibisch 2000, 2003; Verduzco). While this may suggest incompetence, labour supply countries are limited in their capacity to represent workers' interests by the very structure of the SAWP that allows employers to choose, on an annual basis, the countries that will supply them with labour, a privilege that disempowers the participating labour-exporting states and leads to heavy competition between them to deliver productive, disciplined workers (Preibisch 2004). Within the current global economy, remittances represent an integral source of foreign exchange for all labour supply countries in the SAWP.

The racialized process of labour replacement can be observed over the SAWP's history that began in 1966 with an international agreement between Jamaica and Canada. Trinidad-Tobago and Barbados became participants a year later, and in 1974 the program was extended to Mexico. Although Mexico was a latecomer, it now accounts for the majority of labour placements, some 68 percent in 2011. The incorporation of migrant workers in Canadian agriculture is not only highly racialized, involving countries in the global south with large populations in moderate to extreme poverty, it is also highly gendered. Women were excluded from the program until 1989, when employers were allowed to hire female candidates and in general, choose the gender of their workers. Today, women—primarily from Mexico—represent approximately three percent of the workforce. The role of gender in shaping the incorporation of migrant workers is evident in women's relative absence but also their specific insertion in the production process (e.g. packing, canning, pruning) and their concentration within particular commodities (e.g. floriculture, fruit, and food processing).

The incursion of women into a formerly male sphere evokes a number of issues, including gender as a basis for labour incorporation, gendered experiences of migration, and the implications of transnational livelihood strategies for gender relations, concerns that formed the basis of our research agenda. To explore these, we employed a range of ethnographic methods including lengthy, in-depth interviews with a non-probability sample of over 32 women in 2002. Interviews with men, employers, and community groups were also conducted. All interviews were conducted in Spanish, tape recorded, and reconstructed through transcription, and later coded and analyzed using qualitative software.

In 2012, there were 17,926 Mexicans working in Canada under the SAWP, 662 of whom were women, just over 3.75 percent. Although recruitment in Mexico is broadening to include workers from throughout the republic, most of the women come from five key states within close of Mexico City: the State of Mexico, Tlaxcala, Puebla, Guanajuato, and Morelos. Approximately 42 percent of women are employed in the province of Ontario, predominantly in fruit packing, vegetable greenhouses, and canning/food processing. They are therefore concentrated around the town of Leamington (Essex), the greenhouse capital of North America, and Niagara-on-the-Lake, in the province's fruit belt. Although both of these towns lie within regions of high migrant worker concentration which acts to minimize the social isolation that they experience, transportation in rural areas is very expensive. Furthermore, there are a number of women working far from the main catchment areas with little social contact outside the farm.

ENGENDERING MIGRATION STUDIES

Feminist scholars have made important gains in revealing how multiple systems of oppression based on social difference—in which gender is but one relation of power—organize the movement of people (Hondagneu-Sotelo 2003; Pessar). In their attempts to engender migration studies, researchers have exposed the importance of gender expectations and responsibilities on migrants' decisions to move (Hondagneu-Sotelo 1994; Kanaiaupuni), the gendered nature of social networks in migratory destinations (Goldring 1996; Hondagneu-Sotelo 1994); gender differences in the use of remittances (Goldring 1996); and the growing labour demand for migrant women in post-industrial capitalist economies (Bakan and Stasiulis; Chang; Salazar Parreñas). Further, feminists were among the first critics of "liberal understandings of citizenship ... based on notions of gender-neutral, racially neutral and regionally homogenized individuals who are strangers to each other, rather than differently empowered, positioned and interrelated individuals and communities" (Baines and Sharma 88).

Using this social relational focus, feminists have argued that in the context of growing North/South inequalities, the granting or withholding of citizenship rights serves as a mechanism by which high-income states determine incorporations in labour markets and society in general, including the creation of cheap, vulnerable, and socially excluded workers (Baines and Sharma; Stasiulis and Bakan 1997; Ball and Piper). High-income nation-states not only enjoy the hegemonic authority to selectively bestow mobility rights, but also to make discriminations based on gender, age, or national origin (Stasiulis and Bakan 2003). Under Canada's immigration system, migrant farmers seeking to work in agriculture may qualify as immigrants and enjoy full citizenship rights if they can prove they have the means to purchase and manage a farm, while those who can demonstrate they are land-poor from designated countries in the South may qualify for temporary wage labour without labour mobility. Predictably, those comprising the former category originate primarily from high income European nations where farmers enjoy considerable state support, while the latter originate from poor countries in the South where neoliberal restructuring has eroded rural livelihoods.

Scholarly efforts to shed light on women's migratory experiences and theorize the role of gender have focused on gendered labour markets in which women predominate. Consider, for example, the sizeable literature dedicated to migrant women and employment in domestic work and caregiving, particularly within Canada (e.g. Arat-Koc and Giles; Bakan and Stasiulus; Chang; Hondagneu-Sotelo 2001; Pratt; Salazar Parreñas). This is not the case for agriculture, a male-dominated occupation, despite the compelling argument in favour of gender analysis to understand the restructuring of agriculture, production relations, and labour flexibility in light of an increasingly globalized food chain (Barndt 2000; Barrientos, Dolan and Tallontire; Lara; Pearson; Raynolds). Deborah Barndt (1999) has argued that the face of the proletariat of the global food system is predominantly female, where women constitute the majority of workers serving agribusiness and food processing industries in the South, and conversely supermarkets and fast food restaurants in the North. Although the "faces" of migrant labour in Canadian agriculture are largely masculine, gender analysis can explore how social relations of power shape and organize migration, work, and agriculture in a global context, the concern to which I now turn.

GENDERED EXPERIENCES

The thousands of migrant men and women coming to rural Canada every year share a number of experiences as non-citizen agricultural workers. The jobs they fill are generally dirty, difficult, and dangerous. Yet in Ontario, as mentioned previously, both foreign and domestic agricultural workers are excluded from several key labour and employment-related statutes designed to protect workers (Verma). Further, research on the quality of non-citizen migrants' working and living conditions has found enormous variation between farms, indicating weak regulations and poor enforcement (Preibisch 2003). The significant work-related health and safety risks all agricultural workers face may be greater for migrant workers because they work longer hours, often do not report illnesses/injuries to avoid deportation or losing pay, and do not always receive prompt medical attention when they do report their health concerns (Preibisch 2003). SAWP workers' wages, between $9.75 and $13.60 in 2012, are also subject to a series of deductions, including their airfare, visa, and those deductions Canadian workers normally incur. They also face living expenses that can total up to $120 per week (Carvajal). Migrant workers therefore work longer hours to accumulate greater earnings, an estimated 40 to 70 hours per week, six to seven days per week (Preibisch 2003). As Olivia,[5] stated: "I'd like to work more [than ten hours a day] but my body can't do it. It's because we want to take as much advantage of being here as we can in order to save enough and not have to come back."

While most migrants claim that they voluntarily work their allocated hours, a 2003 survey found that over a fifth of workers felt that on occasion they had been asked to work too much (Verduzco). According to Olivia, "we have to work as long as our employers want. Canadians finish work when they say 'I'm going home now,' and don't have any problems. We can't do this or they'll send us home."

Although men's and women's experiences of labour migration may be shared in the sense that they are non-citizens from the South and farm workers, they differ in significant ways. To begin with, women constitute a very small minority as a result of their historical exclusion and the persistence of gender ideologies in both Canada and the labour exporting countries that define agricultural work (and international migration) as male pursuits. It is not surprising that many women reported initial, intense resistance from their families and communities. As Soledad recalled, "[my family] put a very tough obstacle in my path. My brothers and one of my sons said, "if you go, don't come back. You will not be able to enter your own home."

Similarly, Canadian employers' perceptions of women's suitability for agricultural work conform to an agrarian patriarchal culture, in which women are seen as unable to carry out heavy work but suited to those tasks requiring a gentle touch, patience, and greater care.

Secondly, most of the women face very different material realities than their male counterparts. The women who enter the SAWP are often sole heads of households, owing in part to the fact that Mexican civil servants recruited only single mothers (widowed, separated or divorced) prior to 1998. Single mothers perceived that male migrants derived higher economic benefits because of the support from non-migrating female partners, who take responsibility for the family, social networks, the farm and/or business in the migrant's absence. As Micaela stated:

> It is easier for men because they always have the pillar in their house that is their wife. They come, they work, they send money to Mexico and the wife there is the one that takes responsibility for everything. They have land, animals, or they have a store, a business, and the woman works there and they work here. But in the case of women [coming to Canada], the majority of us are single mothers who do not have this opportunity. For us, money sent is money spent because we send money only for the daily expenses of our children and there is no one that supports us economically there.

Migrating to Canada allowed women to earn substantially more than they would in Mexico, where occupations open to poor women are usually highly contingent, poorly rewarded, and where the social costs of neoliberal restructuring have been borne disproportionately by them. Women's Canadian earnings allowed them some measure of economic independence and, for some, the opportunity to buy land, build homes, or finance small businesses.

Further, women cited that the key difference in men's and women's experience was that migrant men leave their children in the care of their wives, while women must leave their children with their mothers, female kin, a neighbour, or at times, an older sibling. Leaving their children engendered significant emotional strain for both men and women. An estimated 40 percent of Mexican workers spend a larger part of the year working in Canada than in their home communities (FARMS). While all workers spoke of the pain of family separation, women's experiences were perhaps more acute considering that to some degree within all classes in Mexico, and especially in low-income groups, motherhood is the assumed primary adult gender role and carries enormous symbolic power (Logan). While for men, engaging in transnational livelihoods means fulfilling their primary gender role as breadwinners, for women it implies deserting theirs, as it has been traditionally defined. One woman felt that she has not been "a 100 percent mom" to her child. Another stated that "I've always told myself that my first responsibility is my children, and in that sense I feel that I am not fulfilling it because I'm not with them. This depresses me." Community groups and health professionals working with the migrant community reported high rates of mental health issues, particularly among women (Preibisch 2003). Citlali, a woman working in Canada for eight months of each of the last five years, said: "sometimes I think that I am of no use to [my children], that they just say, 'she is the one sending us money from there, she is the one giving me everything,' like an object." This sentiment illustrates a fundamental anxiety the transnational mothers (and fathers) we interviewed experienced, that their migratory periods abroad were negatively affecting their relationships with their children and their children's socialization.

While women expressed considerable anxiety with regard to leaving their children, they were firm in the belief that their decisions were in their children's best interests. In particular, women wanted to provide their children with an education so they would have more choices than they did. Citlali stated: "as a woman, alone, you have to fight for your children. In Mexico it is very difficult to raise children, and on your own, it is always very difficult. You have to find a way."

Thus while women agonized over their decisions to migrate and leave their children, they also saw themselves as fulfilling their gendered responsibilities. Indeed, the women engaging in transnational livelihoods are reinventing gendered expectations of what it means to be a good mother. Similarly, Pierrette Hondagneu-Sotelo and Ernestine Avila report from their research with domestic workers in the U.S., "given the uncertainty of what constitutes 'good mothering,' and to defend their integrity as mothers when others criticize them, transnational mothers construct new scales for gauging the quality of mothering" (335).

Another key difference in women's experiences as non-citizen agricultural workers is in terms of their sexuality. Their scant representation among a sea of men means that on the one hand, they have their choice of intimate partners and perhaps greater bargaining power within these relationships than in Mexico, while on the other, they are subject to tremendous efforts to control that power. To explain further, we found that migrating women experienced greater latitude in choosing an intimate partner and more freedom to pursue a relationship than in their home communities, where they have to more carefully abide by the cultural expectations of their gender. Also, women's spatial separation from the full gamut of gendered responsibilities associated with social reproduction was experienced by some women as liberating, as it enabled them to spend their brief off-work periods on themselves, including the occasional night out dancing. According to one woman: "in Mexico women have to be more tied to their children: to take them to school, to wash clothes, to iron. But here you just apply yourself to the job and after work you do what you like. There is more freedom." Furthermore, women who had formed relationships in Canada, reported that these relationships were more equitable than those with their former male partners in Mexico, although there was evidence that this was not always the case.

Increased ability to exercise a social life or pursue an intimate relationship is not without high social costs. Our research found that migrant women are considered to be sexually available and are stigmatized within the migrant community in Canada and their own communities. Another woman reported that in Mexico "they think the women that go to Canada are here to prostitute ourselves. They judge us very poorly." Indeed, women's participation in transnational migration involves breaking strict gender norms regarding their women's roles and mobility:

> When men come north and leave their families in Mexico … they are fulfilling familial obligations defined as breadwinning for the family. When women do so, they are embarking not only on an immigration journey but a more radical gender-transformative odyssey. They are initiating separations of space and time from their communities of origin, homes, children, and sometimes, husbands. In doing so, they must cope with stigma, guilt, and criticism from others. (Hondagneu-Sotelo and Avila 321)

While in most rural Mexican communities, women face rigid social barriers to leaving their localities unattended or talking to men other than their husbands, women exercising transnational livelihoods in Canada get on a plane, travel thousands of kilometres, and spend eight months unattended and unsupervised. As mentioned, women's decisions to work in Canada were often met with resistance by their families, including one woman's brothers who accused her of abandoning her children. Mexican men and women's own families are not alone in seeking to control women and their sexuality; employers also actively do so. For example, some employers abuse a provision in the SAWP allowing them to set down "farm rules" outlining care of the property and the use of amenities by including rules that forbid female workers to leave the farm, prohibit visitors of the opposite sex, or establish a curfew. These measures work to reduce non-citizen migrants' social commitments and further discipline the workforce.

CONCLUSION

This article provides some insight into the experiences of the Mexican migrant women working in rural Canada, focusing on how experiences of migration are gendered. Although this subject is worthy of more exhaustive treatment, the article serves to further empirical and theoretical understandings of international migration and shed light on women's livelihoods under contemporary global restructuring within a traditionally male-dominated occupation. In particular, it adds to debates concerning the extent to which the new livelihoods women are engaging in within the contemporary world economy—whether these are found in global factories or the fields of global agriculture—are both emancipating and subjugating, as well as arguments concerning how transnational migration can transform gender relations in unexpected ways. Perhaps as importantly, and for the purposes of this volume, it draws our attention to a group of women who are often absent from our considerations of rural Canadian landscapes.

Kerry Preibisch is associate professor in the Department of Sociology and Anthropology at the University of Guelph. Her areas of interest are gender, race, class and citizenship; temporary migration programs, migrant rights, and development; and labour regimes in globalized sites of food and agricultural production

[1]The first portion of this title is a quote from Hondagneu-Sotelo and Avila. An expanded version of some of the arguments and data presented here is in Preibisch (2006). I would like to acknowledge the research role of Luz Maria Hermoso in this study and the use of the data that was jointly collected.

[2]Under the SAWP, employers must provide housing at no cost for their workers in either privately-owned or rented accommodation (except British Columbia).

[3]The disincentive to employers of dismissing workers is the costs of bringing a new worker to the farm (employers are responsible for a portion of the airfare) and sending the dismissed worker home if the employer claims responsibility for the dismissal.

[4]Jamaica (1966); Trinidad and Tobago, Barbados (1967); Mexico (1974) and the member states of the Organization of Eastern Caribbean States (1976).

[5]All quotes from have been translated from Spanish and in some cases, paraphrased for clarity. All names are pseudonyms.

REFERENCES

Arat-Koc, S. and Giles, W. *Maid in the Market: Women's Paid Domestic Labour.* Halifax: Fernwood Publishing, 1994.

Baines, D. and Sharma, N. "Migrant Workers as Non-Citizens: The Case Against Citizenship as a Social Policy Concept." *Studies in Political Economy* 69 (2002): 75-107.

Bakan, A.B. and Stasiulis, D. "Foreign Domestic Worker Policy in Canada and the Social Boundaries of Modern Citizenship." *Science and Society* 58 (1) (1997): 4-37.

Ball, R. and Piper, T. "Globalisation and Regulation of Citizenship: Filipino Migrant Workers in Japan." *Political Geography* 21 (2004): 1013–1034.

Barndt, D. *Tangled Routes: Women, Work, and Globalization on the Tomato Trail.* Oxford: Rowman and Littlefield Publishers, 2000.

Barndt, D. *Women Working the NAFTA Food Chain: Women, Food and Globalization.* Toronto: Second Story Press, 1999.

Barrientos, S., C. Dolan and A. Tallontire. "A Gendered Value Chain Approach to Codes of Conduct in African Horticulture." *World Development* 31 (9) (2003): 1511–1526.

Barrón, A. "Condiciones laborales de los inmigrantes regulados en Canadá." *Comercio Exterior* 50 (4) (2000): 350-53.

Basok, T. *Tortillas and Tomatoes.* Montreal: McGill-Queens University Press, 2002.

Becerril, O. "Relación de género, trabajo transnacional y migración temporal: trabajadores y trabajadoras agrícolas mexicanos en Canadá." Paper presented at the Primer Coloquio Internacional sobre Migración y Desarrollo: Transnacionalismo y Nuevas Perspectivas de Integración, City of Zacatecas, Mexico, October 23-25, 2003.

Binford, L. "Social and Economic Contradictions of Rural Migrant Contract Labor Between Tlaxcala, Mexico and Canada." *Culture and Agriculture* 24 (2) (2002): 1-19.

Carvajal Lidia. *The Farm-Level Impacts in Mexico of the Participation in Canada's Seasonal Agricultural Workers Program (CSAWP).* Unpublished dissertation, University of Guelph, 2008.

Chang, G. *Disposable Domestics: Immigrant Women Workers in the Global Economy,* Cambridge, MA: SouthEnd Press, 2000.

Foreign Agricultural Resource Management Services (FARMS). *Statistical Reports for 2002.* Mississauga: Foreign Agricultural Resource Management Services, 2003.

Goldring, L. "Gendered Memory: Constructions of Reality Among Mexican Transnational Migrants." *Creating the Countryside: The Politics of Rural and Environmental Discourse.* Eds. E. M. DuPuis and P. Vandergeest. Philadelphia: Temple University Press, 1996. 303-329.

Hondagneu-Sotelo, P. "Gender and Immigration: A Retrospective and Introduction." *Gender and U.S. Immigration: Contemporary Trends.* Ed. P. Hondagneu-Sotelo. Berkeley: University of California Press, 2003. 3-19.

Hondagneu-Sotelo, P. *Doméstica: Immigrant Workers Cleaning and Caring in the Shadows of Affluence.* Berkeley: University of California Press, 2001.

Hondagneu-Sotelo, P. *Gendered Transitions: Mexican Experiences of Immigration.* Berkeley: University of California Press, 1994.

Hondagneu-Sotelo, P. and E. Avila. "'I'm Here, But I'm There': The Meanings of Latina Transnational Motherhood" *Gender and U.S. Immigration: Contemporary Trends.* Ed. P. Hondagneu-Sotelo, Berkeley: University of California Press, 2003. 317-340.

Kanaiaupuni, S. M. "Reframing the Migration Question: An Analysis of Men, Women, and Gender in Mexico." *Social Forces* 78 (4) (2000): 1311-1348.

Lara F. S. *Nuevas experiencias productivas y nuevas formas de organización flexible del trabajo en la agricultura mexicana.* Mexico City: Juan Pablos Editor, 1998.

Logan, K. "Women's Participation in Urban Protest." *Popular Movements and Political Change in Mexico.* Eds. J. Foweraker and A. Craig. Boulder: Lynne Rienner Publishers, 1990.150-159.

Pearson, R. "Moving the Goalposts: Gender and Globalisation in the Twenty-First Century." *Gender and Development* 8 (1) (2000): 10-19.

Pessar, P. "Engendering Migration Studies: The Case of New Immigrants in the United States." *Gender and U.S. Immigration: Contemporary Trends.* Ed. P. Hondagneu-Sotelo. Berkeley: University of California Press, 2003. 30-42.

Pratt, G. "Is this Canada? Domestic Workers' Experiences in Vancouver, B.C." *Gender, Migration and Domestic Service.* Ed. J. Momsen. London: Routledge, 1999. 23-41.

Preibisch, K. "Migrant Agricultural Workers and Processes of Social Inclusion in Rural Canada: Encuentros and Desencuentros." *Canadian Journal of Latin American and Caribbean Studies* 29 (57-58) (2004): 203-240.

Preibisch, K. *Social Relations Practices between Seasonal Agricultural Workers, their Employers, and the Residents of Rural Ontario.* Research report prepared for The North-South Institute, Ottawa, 2003.

Preibisch, K. "Tierra de los no-libres: Migración temporal México-Canadá y dos campos de reestructuración económica." *Conflictos migratorios transnacionales y respuestas comunitarias.* Eds. L. Binford and M. D'Aubeterre. Puebla: Benemérita Universidad Autónoma de Puebla, 2000. 45-65.

Preibisch, K. "Engendering Labour Migration: The Case of Foreign Workers in Canadian Agriculture." *Women, Migration and Citizenship: Making Local, National and Transnational Connections.* Eds. E. Tastsoglou and A. Dobrowolsky, London: Ashgate Press, 2006. 107-130.

Raynolds, L. "Wages for Wives: Renegotiating Gender and Production Relations in Contract Farming in the Dominican Republic." *World Development* 30 (5) (2002): 783-798.

Salazar Parreñas, R. *Servants of Globalization: Women, migration and domestic work.* Stanford, CA: Stanford University Press, 2001.

Stasiulis, D. and A. Bakan, *Negotiating Citizenship: Migrant Women in Canada and the Global System.* New York: Palgrave Macmillan, 2003.

Stasiulis, D. and A. Bakan. "Negotiating Citizenship: The Case of Foreign Domestic Workers in Canada." *Feminist Review* 57 (1997): 112-139.

Verduzco Igartua, G. *Mexican Workers' Participation in CSAWP and Development Consequences in the Workers' Rural Home Communities.* Ottawa: The North-South Institute, 2003.

Verma, V. *CSAWP Regulatory and Policy Framework, Farm Industry-level Employment Practices and the Potential Role of Unions.* Research report prepared for The North-South Institute, Ottawa, 2004.

RICHARD POULIN

Globalization and the Sex Trade

Trafficking and the Commodification
of Women and Children

C APITALIST GLOBALIZATION TODAY involves an unprecedented
"commodification" of human beings. In recent decades the rapidly
growing sex trade has been massively "industrialized" worldwide (Barry;
Jeffreys 2009). This process of industrialization, in both its legal and its illegal
forms, generates profits amounting to billions of dollars. [1] It has created a
market of sexual exchanges in which millions of women and children have been
converted into sexual commodities. This sex market has been generated through
the massive deployment of prostitution (one of the effects of the presence of
military forces engaged in wars and/or territorial occupation (Strudevant and
Stolzfus) in particular in the emerging economies, the unprecedented expansion
of the tourist industry (Truong), the growth and normalization of pornography
(Poulin 2000), and the internationalization of arranged marriages (Hughes).

The sex industry, previously considered marginal, has come to occupy a strategic
and central position in the development of international capitalism. For this
reason it is increasingly taking on the guise of an ordinary sector of the economy.
This particular aspect of globalization involves an entire range of issues crucial to
understanding the world we live in. These include such processes as economic
exploitation, sexual oppression, capital accumulation, international migration,
unequal development and such related conditions as racism and poverty.

INDUSTRIALIZATION AND GLOBALIZATION OF THE SEX TRADE

The industrialization of the sex trade has involved the mass production of
sexual goods and services structured around a regional and international
division of labour. These "goods" are human beings who sell sexual services.
The international market in these "goods" simultaneously encompasses local
and regional levels, making its economic imperatives impossible to avoid. [2]
Prostitution and related sexual industries—bars, dancing clubs, massage
parlours, pornography producers etc.—depend on a massive subterranean
economy controlled by pimps connected to organized crime. At the same
time businesses, such as international hotel chains, airline companies, and the

tourist industry, benefit greatly from the sex industry.

This industry is now an important economic power. It constitutes five percent of the GDP of the Netherlands (Dusch), 4.5 percent of South Korea (Conseil économique et social), three percent of Japan (Kirby), maybe six percent of China (Bentor) and, in 1998, prostitution represented 2 to 14 percent of all the economic activity of Indonesia, Malaysia, the Philippines, and Thailand (Lim). According to a study conducted by Ryan Bishop and Lilian Robinson, the tourist industry brings four billion dollars a year to Thailand. It is not without reason, then, that in 1987 the Thai government promoted sexual tourism through advertising "The one fruit of Thailand more delicious than durian [a local fruit], its young women" (Hechler).

The industrialization of the sex trade and its globalization are fundamental factors that make contemporary prostitution qualitatively different from the prostitution of yesterday. "Consumers" in the economic North now have access to "exotic" and young, very young, bodies worldwide, notably in Brazil, Cuba, Russia, Kenya, Sri Lanka, Philippines, Vietnam, Nicaragua, and, given the trafficking of children, in their own countries. The sex industry is diversified, sophisticated, and specialized: it can meet all types of demands.

Another factor, which confers a qualitatively different character on the current sex trade, is the fact that prostitution has become a development strategy for some countries. Under obligations of debt repayment, numerous Asian, Latin American, and African States were encouraged by international organizations such as the International Monetary Fund (IMF) and the World Bank (WB) to develop their tourism and entertainment industries. In each case, the development of these sectors engendered the development of the sex trade (Hechler).[3] In certain cases, as in Nepal, women and children were put directly on regional or international markets (notably in India and in Hong-Kong) without the country experiencing a significant expansion of local prostitution. In other cases, as in Thailand, local, regional, and international markets developed simultaneously (Barry).

We can see that, in every case, the "goods" in this market move trans-continentally and transnationally from regions with weak concentrations of capital toward regions with stronger concentrations. According to different international organizations, at the beginning of the millennium, four million women and children were victims, each year, of international trafficking, 90 percent for purposes of prostitution. A database established in the framework of the International Program against the Trafficking of Persons of the United Nations Office on Drugs and Crime (UNODC), which gathers information from more than 500 sources, estimates that 92 percent of victims of trafficking were used in prostitution and that 48 percent of the victims were children, especially girls. Moreover, the database included 127 States as originating countries and 137 as destination (Kangaspunta). The main destination countries were the major capitalist countries or those that constituted an important regional centre. The main "issuing" countries were those on the capitalist periphery. The global hierarchy was clear as were the regional hierarchies.

For example, over ten years, 200,000 Bangladeshi women and girls were the object of trafficking to Pakistan (CATW), and we find that between 20,000 and 30,000 Thai prostitutes are from Burma (CATW). A good part of the migratory stream makes its way towards industrialized countries.[4] Foreign women are generally at the bottom of the prostitution hierarchy, are socially and culturally isolated, and work in the worst possible conditions.

Part of the traffic is legal. That is the case for countries, such as Switzerland, Cyprus,[5] Japan, South Korea, Thailand, Luxemburg,[6] Panama (International Human Rights Law Institute), etc., that issue many thousands of "artist" visas each year for the men's "entertainment" industry. In 2004, Swiss embassies issued 5,953 visas of this type (Joz-Roland). The same year, Slovenia issued 650, of which a large part went to Ukranian women, Luxembourg about 350 (Reseau), Cyprus 1200 (Gautier) and Canada 500 to Romanian women[7] (more if other nationalities are counted).[8] In 2004, the Japanese government issued 71,084 visas to Philippinas (Nuqui). Several Caribbean countries (Saint Lucia, Bahamas, Jamaica, Surinam) issue such visas. That is also the case for the Dutch Caribbean where prostitution is regulated, notably St. Marten, Curaçao and Bonaire (IOM). Because it is a legal activity, these numbers are not counted in statistics of human trafficking.

In 2005, the International Labour Organization (ILO) estimated that 2.45 million persons were victims of trafficking each year (Lim 2010). This estimate is quoted by the majority of international organizations and also by the U.S. Department of State (Department of State). However, this figure comes from a study on trafficking for the purposes of "forced work," which includes only "forced prostitution," which represents 43 percent of cases, or 1.39 million persons. It does not take into account the whole of trafficking for purposes of prostitution. The same year, the Office to Monitor and Combat Trafficking in Persons estimated that sexual exploitation was the objective of about 75 percent of human trafficking (Office to Monitor and Combat Trafficking). In 2010, according to the UNODC, 84 percent of victims of human traffickers in Europe were prostituted.

PROSTITUTION INEQUALITY AND POWER

Any political economic analysis of prostitution and trafficking in women and children must take into account structural discrimination, uneven development, and the hierarchical relationships between imperialist and dependent countries and between men and women. In recent years under the impact of structural adjustment and economic liberalization policies in numerous countries of the Third World, as well as in the ex-USSR and Eastern Europe, women and children have become "new raw resources" within the framework of national and international business development. Capitalist globalization is more and more characterized by a feminization of migration (Santos). Women of ethnic minorities and other relatively powerless groups are particularly exploited. So, the internal traffic of Thai females consists mostly of 12-16 year olds from hill tribes of the North and the Northeast. In Taiwan, 40 per cent of young prostitutes in the main red light district are aboriginal girls (Barry 139). At the world level, the customers of the North abuse women of the South and of the East as well as local women from disadvantaged groups. From an economic point of view, these "goods" are doubly valuable because bodies are both a good and a service. More precisely, we have seen a commodification not only of the body, but also of women and children as human beings. This has led many to see this trafficking in women and children as a form of slavery (CATW).

Kidnapping, rape, and violence continue to act as midwives of this industry. They are fundamental not only for the development of markets, but also for the "production" of these "goods," as they contribute to making them "functional" for an industry that requires a constant supply of bodies. Research has shown that between 75 and 80 per cent of women in prostitution were sexually abused in their childhood (Satterfield; Chaleil).[9] More than 90 per cent are controlled by a pimp (Silbert and Pines 1982; Barry). A study of street prostitutes in England established that 87 per cent had been victims of violence during the previous 12 months and 43 per cent suffered from grave physical consequences of abuse (Raymond). An American study showed that 78 per cent had been victims of rape by pimps and customers, on average 49 times a year; 49 per cent had been victims of removal and transported from one state to another and 27 per cent had been mutilated (Raymond). The average age of entrance into prostitution in the United States is 14 years (Silbert and Pines 1981; Giobbe).

Only 15 per cent of women in prostitution in the United States have never contracted a venereal disease (Leidholdt). Fifty-eight per cent in Burkina Faso have AIDS, as have 52 per cent in Kenya, about 50 per cent in Cambodia and 34 per cent in the North of Thailand. In Italy, in 1988, two per cent of the prostituted women had AIDS, compared to 16 per cent ten years later (Leidholdt; Mechtild). One of the reasons customers give for sexually exploiting children is to avoid sexually transmitted diseases. But the data show this is no protection. For example, in Cambodia there are between 50,000 and 70,000 prostitutes. More than a third of them are less than 18 years old and about 50 per cent of these young people are HIV positive (Véran). In the industrialized countries, 70 percent of female infertility is caused by venereal diseases caught from husbands and partners (Raymond). Given such conditions, it is hard to understand how some researchers can continue to treat "sex work" as predominantly and simply a freely chosen occupation/activity.

PROSTITUTION AND TRAFFICKING

Over the last four decades, most of the countries of the Southern Hemisphere have experienced a phenomenal growth of prostitution. For two decades, this has also been the case for the countries of the ex-USSR and Eastern Europe. Millions of women, teenagers, and children thus live in the red-light districts of the urban metropolises of their own countries or in those of the nearby countries. Two million women prostitute themselves in Thailand (Barry 122), 400,000 to 500,000 in the Philippines (CATW), 650,000 in Indonesia (CATW), about ten million in India (of whom 200,000 are Nepalese) (CATW), 142,000 in Malaysia (CATW), between 60,000 and 70,000 in Vietnam (CATW), one million in the United States, between 50,000 and 70,000 in Italy (of whom half are foreigners, most notably from Nigeria), 30,000 in the Netherlands (CATW), 200,000 in Poland (Opperman). In Germany, in 1992, sexual services are sold to 1.2 million "customers" per day (Opperman; Ackermann and Filter). It is estimated in 2012 that 66 percent of German men have paid for sex.

UNICEF (2003) estimates that a million children are brought into the sex industry every year. The industry of child prostitution exploits 400,000 children in India, 100,000 children in the Philippines (CATW), between 200,000 and 300,000 in Thailand (Oppermann), 100,000 in Taiwan (UNICEF 2001) and in Nepal (ECPAT), 500,000 children in Latin America, and from 244,000 to 325,000 children in the United States. If one includes children in all the sex industries, the U.S. figures climb to 2.4 millions (UNICEF 2001). In the People's Republic of China, there are between 200,000 and 500,000 prostituted children. In Brazil, estimates vary between 500,000 and two million (UNICEF 2001). About 35 per cent of the prostitutes of Cambodia are less than 17 years old (CATW). Some estimates are that during one year, the prostituted "sexual services" of one child are sold to 2,000 men (Robinson).

Just as the development of local prostitution is tied up with rural migration towards cities, hundreds of thousands of young women are moving internationally towards the urban areas of Japan, Western Europe, and North America. These rural migrations towards close or distant urban areas show no sign of slowing down (Santos). On the contrary, everything indicates that it is continuing and that traffic in women and children is widespread. The women and children of South and Southeast Asia constitute the most important group: 400,000 persons a year are objects of the aforementioned traffic. Russia and independent states from the ex-USSR constitute the second most important group (175,000 persons a year) followed by Latin America and the Caribbean (about 100,000 persons) and Africa (50,000 persons) (UUSC).

The number prostituted from the Philippines, Taiwan, Thailand, and Russia installed in Japan is estimated at 150,000 (CATW). About 50,000 Dominicans prostitute themselves abroad, notably in the Netherlands, where they were found to make up 70 per cent of the occupants of 400 Amsterdam sex-shop "windows" (Guéricolas 31). About 500,000 women of Eastern Europe and between 150,000 and 200,000 women of the countries of the ex-USSR prostitute themselves in Western Europe. Of these, it is estimated that 150,000 are in the red-light districts of Germany—a country where 75 per cent of the prostitutes are foreign (Oppermann). About 40 per cent of Zurich's prostitutes are from a Third World country (Oppermann). About 50,000 foreigners arrive each year in the United States to supply the prostitution networks (O'Neill).

Every year, nearly a quarter million women and children of Southeast Asia (Burma, Yunnan province in China, Laos and Cambodia) are bought in Thailand, a transit country, for a price varying between 6,000 and 10,000 U.S.

dollars. In Canada, the intermediaries pay 8,000 dollars for a young Asiatic from the Philippines, Thailand or Malaysia whom they resell for 15,000 dollars to a pimp. In Western Europe, the current price of a European woman from the former "socialist" countries is between 15,000 and 30,000 USD. On their arrival in Japan, Thai women have a debt of 25,000 USD. The bought women have to work for years to pay off "expenses" incurred by the pimps (CATW).

Sex tourists do not limit themselves to poor countries. Hamburg's Reeperbahn, Berlin's Kurfürstendamm and the red-light districts of Amsterdam and Rotterdam are well known destinations. In countries that have legalized prostitution or where it is tolerated, prostitution has become an important tourist draw. Non-governmental organizations from these countries are actively lobbying at the European and international levels for the recognition of prostitution as simply "sex work," an occupation like any other.

The growth of sexual tourism over the last 30 years has entailed the "prostitutionalization" of the societies involved. In Thailand, with 5.1 million sexual tourists a year, 450,000 local customers buy sex every day (Barry 60). The now massive South East Asian sex industry began with the Vietnam war. The U.S. government stationed servicemen not only in Vietnam, but also in Thailand and the Philippines (Jeffreys 1997), these last two countries serving as rear bases in the fight against the Vietminh. The resulting increase in local prostitution established the infrastructure necessary for the development of sexual tourism. The presence of the military created an available work force. More importantly the military presence also provided opportunities for contact with foreigners and the social construction, through pornography, of an exotic sexual image of young South Asian women. Government policies favourable to sex tourism contributed to the explosion of this industry. Between 1937 and 1945 the Japanese army of occupation exploited between 100,000 and 200,000 Korean women imprisoned in "comfort stations" (Barry 128). After the Japanese defeat, the Association for the Creation of Special Recreational Facilities, financed indirectly by the U.S. government, opened the first comfort station for U.S. soldiers. At its height this association exploited 70,000 Japanese women (Barry 129). More recently, 18,000 women served 43,000 U.S. servicemen stationed in South Korea (Barry 139). Today these numbers continue to swell and include women from the Philippines, Russia, and other countries in sex industries around the U.S. bases (Moon).

THE LIBERALIZATION OF THE SEX INDUSTRY

In 1995, during the United Nation's Fourth World Women's Congress in Beijing, the concept of "forced" prostitution appeared (UN). This was the first time the term "forced prostitution" was used in a UN document. This created a special (presumed minority) category of prostitution that could be opposed without opposing the sex industry as such. Constraint/force was identified as the problem rather than the sex trade itself. The way was opened for the normalization and legalization of the industry.

In 1997, at the Hague Ministerial Conference on Private International Law, when the European ministers attempted to draw up guidelines harmonizing the European Union's fight against trafficking for the purposes of sexual exploitation, their definition of trafficked women included only those women who were being trafficked against their will. In 1998, the International Labour Organization (ILO) called for the economic recognition of the sex industry on the grounds that prostitutes would then benefit from workers' rights and protections and improved working conditions that it presumed would follow (Lim 1998). In June 1999, the ILO adopted an agreement on unbearable working conditions for children, the Convention Concerning the Prohibition and Immediate Action for the Elimination of the Worst Forms of Child Labour. The agreement provides a long list of the work children do, including prostitution. This is the first time in an international text that sex work is presented as simply a job.[10] The United Nations' Special Rapporteur on Violence against Women was at pains in her report to the UN Human Rights Committee in April 2000 in Geneva, to distinguish trafficked women from "clandestine migrant sex professionals."

All these statements and agreements tend to undermine the struggle against the growing sex industry and the system of prostitution which is at its heart, for they shift opposition from the system itself, to the use of force/constraint within the system. They aim to protect only women who have not agreed to their exploitation and *can prove this,* placing the burden of proof on already vulnerable women. In attempting to regulate this fast growing area of the economy these approaches are tending to regularize it. For instance, when the European Union declares its opposition to the illegal traffic in persons, it implies that there is a "legal" traffic. Thus, as Marie-Victoire Louis has pointed out, such initiatives transform the struggle against the commodification of women and girls into its legitimization. She states:

> *[Toutes ces politiques entérinent] l'abandon de la lutte contre le système prostitutionnel [et] confirme[nt] la légitimation de la marchandisation du système prostitutionnel, au nom de la mise en oeuvre de certaines modalites de sa regulation.* (131) ([All these policies endorse] the abandonment of the struggle against the prostitution system [and] confirm the legitimacy of the commodification by the prostitution system in the name of the implementation of certain modalities of its regulation.)

CONCLUSION

The globalization of prostitution has created a vast market in sexual trade, where millions of women and girls are converted into sexualized merchanidise. Over the last decades years, we have seen an extremely profitable "sexualization" of many societies based on social domination. We have witnessed the industrialization of prostitution, of the traffic in women and children, of pornography, and of sexual tourism. This once marginal market is an increasingly central aspect of current capitalist globalization. Sex multinationals have become independent economic forces (Barry) quoted on the stock exchange,[11] sexual exploitation is more and more considered to be an entertainment industry (Oppermann), and prostitution a legitimate job (Kempadoo; Dorais).

The increasing size and centrality of the global sex industry helps explain why so many groups and agencies are adopting normalizing regulatory approaches in their attempts to address its harms. However, this strategy is deeply flawed. The rapidly expanding international sex market exploits above all women and children, especially members of marginal and minority groups in the Third World and in the former "socialist" countries. This "leisure industry" is based on the systematic violation of human rights, for it requires a market in commodified human beings and the complicity of pimps and clients who are prepared to buy and sell women and children.

The commodification at the heart of the growing sex industry is only one among many varied instances of the commodification of all of life that is a defining characteristic of current neo-liberalism. Patents are now issued on genetic life forms (including human genomes) and all forms of traditional knowledge (Shiva 1997, 2000). Water is being privatized (Barlow). In the name of environmental protection and sustainable development, markets have been created for trade in CO_2 and emissions credits (the right to pollute) (Kyoto Protocol). The apparent "normalcy" of trade in human beings in this period has led to misguided regulatory approaches in some quarters. Yet this very "normalcy" is what makes refusal of the sex industry as such, so essential. In this context, resisting or struggling against the commodification of women and children in the sex industry becomes a central element in the struggle against capitalist globalization. Anything less is complicity.

Richard Poulin est professeur émérite au département de sociologie et d'anthropologie de l'Université d'Ottawa et professeur associé à l'Institut de recherches et d'études féministes de l'UQAM. Il s'intéresse aux questions relatives à l'exploitation et à l'oppressions sexuelle depuis plus de 25 ans, domaine dans lequel il a publié plusieurs livres, dont Pornographie et sexualisation précoce *(2009) et* La mondialisation des industries du sexe *(2005 et 2011).*

[1]According to Chulalungkborn Political Economy Center at the University of Thailand, in 1993 worldwide the sex industry generated incomes of between 20 and 23 billion USD (ECPAT Australia 29). Other estimates put incomes from the legal sex industry at 52 billion dollars (Leidholdt).

[2]Barry reports that as a result of globalization, complete fishing villages in the Philippines and Thailand have been transformed into service providers (126).

[3]In Cameroon, in 2006, an official explained on the radio that it was necessary "to encourage the national prostitution industry to support the development of lasting tourism" (cited in "Crime organisé..." 56).

[4]For example, the majority of New Zealand's prostitutes are from Asia (CATW).

[5]Cyprus ended this programme in 2009.

[6]Luxembourg ended this programme in 2004. In 1999, women from Eastern Europe received 88 percent of the work permits the country issued for "artists" (Réseau).

[7]After political scandal Canada "suspended" this programme in 2004.

[8]More than one thousand permits of this kind were issues each year in Canada. (McDonald, Moore and Timoshkina).

[9]These figures confirm the findings of my research (2004) with escort dancers.

[10]Countries, such a France, although ratifying this Convention, have underlined that their ratification in no way recognizes prostitution as work.

[11]The most important bordello in Melbourne, Australia, "The Daily Planet," is now quoted on the stock exchange (Jeffreys 1999: 185).

REFERENCES

Ackermann L. and C. Filter. *Die Frau nach Katalog*, Freiburg: Herder Verlag, 1994.

Barlow, M. *Blue Gold: The Battle Against the Corporate Theft of the World's Water*. Toronto: Stoddart, 2002.

Barry, Kathleen. *The Prostitution of Sexuality*. New York: New York University Press, 1995.

Bentor, Teresa M. "Chine: la prostitution à tous les coins de rues." *Chine Information*, 28 décembre 2008.

Bishop, R. and L. Robinson. *Night Market. Sexual Cultures and the Thai Economic Miracle*. New York, Routledge, 1998.

Chaleil, Max. *Prostitution: Le désir mystifié*. Paris: Parangon, 2002. Print.

Coalition Against Trafficking in Women (CATW). *Factbook on Global Sexual Exploitation*. Manila: CATW, 2001. Web.

Conseil économique et social. Nations Unies. *Compte rendu analytique de la 14e séance: Republic of Korea*, 18/05/2001. E/C.12/2001/SR.14 (Summary Record), 18 mai 2001.

Convention Concerning the Prohibition and Immediate Action for the Elimination of the Worst Forms of Child Labour (ILO No. 182), 38 I.L.M.1207 (1999).

"Crime organisé, trafic des migrantés et traite des êtres humains." *Nouveaux Cahiers du socialisme* 5 (2011): 56.

Dorais, Michel. *Travailleurs du sexe*. Montréal: VLB, 2003.

Dusch, Sabine. *Le trafic d'êtres humains*. Paris: PUF, 2002.

End Child Prostitution, Child Pornography, and Trafficking of Children for Sexual Purposes (ECPAT) – Australia. *ECPAT Development Manual*. Melbourne: ECPAT, 1994.

Giobbe E. "Juvenile Prostitution: Process of Recruitment." *Child Trauma I: Issues and Research*. New York: Garaland Publishing, 1992.

Guéricolas, Pascale. "Géographie de l'inacceptable." *Gazette des femmes* 22 (1) (mai-juin 2000): 27-31.

Hechler, David. "Child Sex Tourism." 1995. Web.

Hughes, Donna M. "Rôle des agences matrimoniales dans la traite des femmes." *L'impact de l'utilisation des nouvelles technologies de dommunication et d'information sur la traite des êtres humains aux fins d'exploitation sexuelle.* Bruxelles: Conseil de l'Europe, 2001. 4-16.

International Human Rights Law Institute. *In Modern Bondage: Sex Trafficking in the Americas.* Chicago, DePaul University College of Law, 2005.

International Organization for Migration (IOM). *Assessment of Trafficking in Persons in the Caribbean Region.* Washington: IOM, 2005.

Jeffreys, Sheila. "Globalizing Sexual Exploitation: Sex Tourism and the Traffic in Women." *Leisure Studies* 18 (3) (July 1999): 179-186.

Jeffreys, Sheila. *The Industrial Vagina : The Political Economy of the Global Sex Trade.* New York, Routledge, 2009.

Joz-Roland, Emmanuelle. "Bienvenue dans la Suisse des cabarets." *Solidarités*, n° 43, 6 avril 2004.

Kangaspunta, Kristiina. "Mapping the Inhuman Trade: Preliminary Finding of the Database on Trafficking in Human Beings." *Forum on Crime and Society* 3 (1-2) (2003): 81-103.

Kempadoo K and J. Doezema. *Global Sex Workers.* New York: Routledge, 1998.

Kirby, Steve. "Asie-sida-société, la menace du sida en Asie aggravée par la banalisation de la prostitution." *Agence France-Presse* 13 août 2001.

Kyoto Protocol. *United Nations Framework Convention on Climate Change.* Web.

Leidholdt, Dorchen. *Position Paper for the Coalition Against Trafficking in Women.* Eds. Donna M. Hughes and Claire M. Roche. Kingston, RI: CATW 2001. Web.

Lim, Lin Lean. *The Sex Sector: The Economic and Social Bases of Prostitution in Southeast Asia.* Geneva: ILO, 1998.

Lim, Lin Lean. «Traite, demande et marché du sexe.». dans Jules Falquet *et al., Le sexe de la mondialisation. Genre, classe, race et nouvelle division du travail*, Paris: Presses de la Fondation nationale des sciences politiques, 2010.

Louis, Marie-Victoire. « Pour construire l'abolitionnisme du XXIᵉ siècle. *Cahiers marxistes* 216 (juin-juillet 2000): 123-151.

McDonald, Lynn, Brooke Moore et Natalya Timoshkina. *Les travailleuses migrantes du sexe originaires d'Europe de l'Est et de l'ancienne Union soviétique : le dossier canadien.* Condition féminine Canada, novembre 2000. Web.

Moon, K. *Sex Among Allies: Military Prostitution in U.S.-Korea Relations.* New York: Columbia University Press, 1997. P

Nuqui, Carmelita G. *Combating Human Trafficking: The Philippine Experience.* Novembre 2005. Web.

Office to Monitor and Combat Trafficking. *Collecting Data on Human Traffickin.* Washington. 16 March 2005. Web.

O'Neill Richard, Amy. *International Trafficking in Women to the United States: To Contemporary Manifestation of Slavery and Organized Crime.* Washington, DC: Center for the Study of Intelligence, 1999.

Oppermann M. "Introduction." *Sex Tourism and Prostitution: Aspects of*

Leisure, Recreation, and Work. Ed. M. Oppemann. New York: Cognizant Communication Corporation, 1998. 1-19.

Poulin, Richard. *La violence pornographique, industrie du fantasme et réalités*. Second edition. Yens-sur-Morges: Cabédita, 2000.

Poulin, Richard. *Le sexe spectacle, consommation, main-d'œuvre et pornographie*. Hull/Ottawa: Vents d'Ouest/Vermillion, 1994.

Raymond, Janice. *Health Effects of Prostitution*. Kingston: University of Rhode Island, 1999. Web.

Report of the Special Rapporteur on Violence Against Women. Intergration of the Human Rights of Women and the Gender Perspective: Violence Against Women. Commission on Human Rights, 56th Session. E/CN.4/2000/68: 29 February 2000.

Réseau U.E. d'experts indépendants en matière de droits fondamentaux. *Rapport sur la situation des droits fondamentaux au Luxembourg en 2004*. CFR-CDS/LU/2004. 3 janvier 2005. Web.

Robinson, L. N. *The Globalization of Female Child Prostitution*. Bloomington: Indiana University, 1998. Web.

Santos, Aida F. *Globalization, Human Rights and Sexual Exploitation*. Kingston, RI: University of Rhode Island, 1999. Web.

Satterfield, S. B. "Clinical Aspects of Juvenile Prostitution." *Medical Aspects of Human Sexuality* 15 (9) (1981): 125-132.

Shiva, V. *Biopiracy: The Plunder of Nature and Knowledge*. Boston: South End Press, 1997. Print.

Shiva, V. *Stolen Harvest: The Hijacking of the Global Food Supply*. Cambridge: South End Press, 2000.

Silbert, M. and A. M. Pines. "Entrance in to Prostitution." *Youth and Society* 13 (4) (1982): 471-500.

Silbert M and A. M. Pines. 1981. "Occupational Hazards of Street Prostitutes." *Criminal Justice Behaviour* 195 (1981): 395-399.

Strudevant, S. P. and B. Stolzfus, eds. *Let the Good Times Roll. Prostitution and the U.S. Military in Asia*. New York: The New Press, 1992.

Truong, T. D. *Sex, Money and Morality: Prostitution and Tourism in Southeast Asia*, London: Zed Books, 1990.

United Nations (UN). *Report of the Fourth World Conference on Women*. Beijing, 4-15 September 1995. Conf.177/20, 113b. Web.

UNICEF. *Child Trafficking Statistics*. New York: UNICEF, 2003. Web.

UNICEF. *L'Unicef demande l'élimination de l'exploitation sexuelle des enfants à des fins commerciales*. New York: UNICEF, 2001. Web.

United Nations Office on Drugs and Crime (UNODC). *Trafficking in Persons to Europe for Sexual Exploitation*. 2010. Web.

Unitarian Universalist Service Committee (UUSC). *The Modern International Slave Trade*. Cambridge, MA: UUSC, 2001. Web.

Véran, Sylvie. « Cambodge. Vendue à 9 ans, prostituée, séropositive », *Nouvel Observateur* 3-10 août 2000: 10-11.

LEE LAKEMAN

Linking Violence and Poverty in Canadian Restructuring

The CASAC Report

ANADIAN ASSOCIATION of Sexual Assault Centres (CASAC) Links is a project in which ten anti-rape centers each allocated one staff and gathered ten callers to participate in a five-year research and development project. In examining the application of legal and feminist concepts of equality to the legal cases of women complaining of violence, we found ourselves up against not only the law but also the regressive changes to our country's social safety net and to global economic relations. We have tried here to connect our crisis calls to those other grave considerations. What follows is several small parts of our national CASAC Links report: *Canada's Promises to Keep: The Charter and Violence Against Women.*

SOME EFFECTS OF RESTRUCTURING CANADA ON THE NATURE, SEVERITY AND INCIDENCE OF VIOLENCE AGAINST WOMEN

"The poor will always be with us," "prostitution is the oldest profession," and "men are just naturally that way." These stereotypical assumptions and essentialist positions or attitudes are not promoted in CASAC centres.[1] Rather, we see that each corporate move, social policy, and interaction of the state with its subjects moves us toward or away from the desired future. Class, race, and gender division and domination are social and economic constructions always in the making, as is equality.[2]

The end of the welfare state and the social welfare it sometimes provided is part of the globalization process in which Canada has played a role and that has engulfed women living in Canada. We have rarely had the opportunity to express, in our own way, the connections we live daily between those international economic forces, federal laws and policies, and what is happening in anti-rape centres. Rare indeed is our opportunity to express the *link* between global/federal forces and our advocacy supporting women, especially those violated women trying to engage the power of the state against the power of their male abusers.

The CASAC Links project offered possibilities for renewing our alliances with

313

other anti-rape centres and for speaking out together about the lives of women; but in any case we were compelled to do so by the changes in our daily work brought by the changes in Canadian society.

We are not the best ones to articulate, and there isn't space in this report to fully express, the devastating impact on Canadian women of the loss of public sector jobs and services.[3] But from our point of view, it is clear that there are few women who have not been made more vulnerable to criminal sexual assault. Every form of criminal violence against women in Canada has been aggravated. There is no liberatory and/or ameliorative process affecting violated women that has not been damaged and undermined.

CASAC's goal of a social economy that values women's labour and fairly shares wealth with women has been drastically set back. The trajectory of reforms toward those ends that had been won by our grandmothers, mothers, and ourselves—from the vote to unemployment insurance, from pensions to childcare, from self-determination to settling land claims, from welfare to more humane immigration policies, from criminalizing sexist violence to the inclusion of women in a living Charter of Rights and Freedoms—has been reversed in the service of grotesque individualism and corporate wealth.

CASAC wishes to express our understanding of those effects which we have encountered *most often* in our crisis work during this five-year research and development period (1998-2003), and which affect anti-violence work most profoundly: the loss of women's welfare, the promotion of prostitution and the use of the *Divorce Act* in such a way as to uphold the permanence of the patriarchal family, and the restructuring of Canada (from the shape of the justice system to the structure of civil society). These effects appear to CASAC to amount to a refusal by our national government to apply the Charter of Rights and Freedoms. To apply the Charter would require a diligent application of the current knowledge of women's oppression and an appropriate commitment to women's advancement.[4]

There are those who see it differently.[5] We have had to defend our positions rather rigorously in the last few years. The government has applied only formal equality when attending to equality at all. It has sometimes ignored both the Supreme Court rulings against formal equality and the reverse impact of the application of these polices. Huge economic and political forces have been mounted to oppose any government role beyond armies and prisons. Sometimes we have found ourselves reeling from many simultaneous blows.

At the same time, there was a big push, supported by government, to promote the rights of victims, even a possible new national victim's association. (The government was referring here to the rights to information about upcoming hearings, the rights to be notified if an offender is released from jail, etc.; what might in general be considered politeness and consideration.) The government promotion of the notion of "victim" as a legal policy category plus the changes to community policing, sentencing changes, to confinement in the home rather than jails, and the promotion of prostitution, opened up a number of key questions within criminal justice: for instance, who defines community and how? And who is considered part of the community? What is the relationship between the state and the community? What is the relationship between women's antiviolence groups, social change, and the state? [6]

We were interested in those conversations that might affect our understanding of our options as the nature of the Canadian state changed.

THE BOTTOM LINE: THE LOSS OF THE WOMEN'S WELFARE

Most members of the community realize that we are contending with mean-spirited welfare reductions and restrictions that make life more difficult for the poor. No government declared honestly to its citizens before election either the nature of welfare cuts it intended or the further feminization of poverty that would be imposed by those cuts. It is simply not true that Canadians voted for those attacks on the poor.

And no government within Canada has been given a mandate to end welfare. Any such mandate would be legally questionable in any case, given the Charter and human rights law and conventions. This is perhaps why no government makes public those whom it is refusing subsistence. But CASAC women are witness to the fact that women across the country have no guaranteed, or even likely, access to a promised minimum standard of living. No matter how poor, women have no guarantee of welfare in any form. As women consider their options for improving their lives they certainly learn this, and so do we.

We have lost a small but significant recognition and amelioration of the historically disadvantaged economic condition of women's lives. But as predicted in feminist accounts of the end of Canada Assistance Plan (CAP) funding and as recorded in our alternate reports to the oversite committee of the United Nations Convention on the Elimination of All Forms of Discrimination Against Women (CEDAW), women in Canada have also lost what application we had of this encoded economic human right. (Brodsky and Day). CASAC is most concerned that we are losing this benchmarked recognition of the economic oppression and redistribution of income toward equality.

In each province and community the attacks and erosion have been different, ranging from workfare to "man in the house" rules, age limitations, rate decreases, time limited access, lifetime bans, immigration and settlement restrictions, punishment bans after and through criminalization, to bans based on health requirements.

Not only has the formal policy been degraded, but the positive discretionary power in applying procedures and enforcing regulations has also been curtailed. Management and sometimes the remaining staff too often interpret rules with the same anti-entitlement attitudes.

The abdication of the federal role in assuring women and others who need a guaranteed dignified income is plain and it is Canada-wide. This includes the downward pressure of shrinking transfer payments and block funding without national standards (Brodsky and Day). That abdication encourages provinces to set social welfare, education, and health needs of the community against the needs of business for roads and bridges, to ship goods, and transport tourists. We don't win.

Transition houses too were funded under the same mechanisms of the CAP program. They were one of the permissible ways that social welfare dollars could be spent by the provinces.

Transition houses in Canada emerged partly to deal with the limits that existed in the welfare policy of the 1970s. Welfare departments would refuse to grant women welfare cheques when they came to the state for assistance in dealing with abusing husbands. Welfare workers were directed to tell women that the state could not be responsible "for the break-up of families" (Lakeman). If a woman left and established residency on her own, then welfare might be granted since it was an assumed economic right of Canadians to not starve or be homeless. Since they usually had no money, women moved to transition houses, where they didn't need rent or deposits, not only for immediate safety, but to establish a separate residence to prove to the state that they had left the marriage/family/couple. During their stay with us, they qualified for welfare.[7]

Women still come. Transition houses are full. Shelters for the homeless and other emergency facilities are also full. But now these women "qualify" for welfare less and less often, and they do not ordinarily receive benefits without aggressive advocacy from someone independent of government. They are told constantly that it is not a right and cannot be relied on. Welfare, they are told, can be reduced, withdrawn, and denied temporarily. A woman could be banned for life.[8]

While we are focused here particularly on social welfare payments to single and single-parent women, the colloquial understanding of the women who call us and the women who work in our centers is of a human right to a dignified minimum income that might be delivered as unemployment insurance, minimum wage, old age or disability pension or welfare but was in their minds entitlement by law to every resident to an economic share that could ensure survival and dignity.

Women, especially poor women, have always had to make extra-legal deals with the men in their lives. When ex-husbands or lovers are taking a kind of responsibility by sliding women money under the table for childcare, we are all glad. But in women's position of extra dependence created by the state withdrawal, sometimes those deals are dangerous underground contracts, which the women cannot enforce, and which subjugate them to the very men they are trying to leave for the sake of themselves and their children.

Any welfare granted currently is so inadequate and insecure as to force the women into subsidizing it with an informal economy: house work for others, childcare for others, personal health care for others, food preparation and production for others, drug sales, and/or prostitution.[9] Subsidizing legally is either clawed back through mechanisms that "allow" recipients to keep only pittance earnings above the welfare check or the subsidizing activity itself is illegal. To be poor is to be criminalized.

In our CASAC report we are most concerned with what happens to women under these conditions trying to report sexual violence. Women who complain to the state of rape, sexual harassment, incest, sexual exploitation, and trafficking face the denial of security: no exercisable right to welfare. If by some cleverness, accident, or kindness a woman gets welfare and is subsidizing it to get by, she is vulnerable to blackmail by her attacker. If she reports criminal sexual abuse, she will quickly be threatened (directly and indirectly) by the defence bar. Exposure can cause either a loss of informal income or the loss of her credibility as a complainant. She can and will be painted as a liar, thief, con, drug dealer, prostitute, unworthy of the protection of the law.

The 14- or 18-year-old incest victim leaving home, the worker on minimum wage or making her way in the informal economy, the dislocated woman pulled from her small town or reserve into the city for work or education, the immigrant woman struggling to survive or trying to transition into lawful citizenship and a reasonable life—all are frustrated. If the normalcy of male violence against women were not known, one might think this was something other than state collusion with violence against women.[10] Access to the rule of law and equal protection under the law become meaningless.

In anti-rape centres we now face daily many women who judge that they simply cannot leave or escape men who criminally abuse them: husbands, fathers, bosses, pimps, johns, landlords, and sometimes social or welfare workers.[11] Since they cannot afford to actually leave, they cannot afford to effectively stand up to their abusers either. Those that do leave those economic positions are on their own with their children, and they know it.

A GLOBAL ECONOMY: THE PROMOTION OF PROSTITUTION

Can anyone still believe that there is no connection between the economic redistributive functions of the state, including within the social safety net, and the staggering increase in the informal economy? The economic division of the peoples of the world is staggering. The economic division among Canadians is growing exponentially.

Child and street-level prostitution and the so-called "adult entertainment" industry are booming. This is globalization being brought to Canada. Drug trafficking and prostitution are replacing welfare, health care, and education as the hope of the destitute.

Professor Dara Culhane at Simon Fraser University describes "a process that moves women farther and farther out from under whatever small protections working people and women have been able to construct within the state."[12] While they have been for many years prey to the law-and-order agenda and remain so, at the same time some are now moving out past the reach of law to the no-woman's land of the urban and suburban informal economies.

Aboriginal women have been talking about this for years as a factor in violence against women on and off reserve. We remember Teresa Nahanee at an Ottawa Legal and Education Access Fund (LEAF) conference in the early 1990s describing the condition of Aboriginal women in many parts of Canada as having to live without any basic rule of law. Now these are the conditions for many women in every major Canadian settlement.

Many women are being driven into the hands of global traders in labour, flesh, and drugs. They are trafficked into and throughout Canada by those global traders on the one hand and, on the other, within Canada by Canadian gangs, particularly the motorcycle gangs.[13] As protection we are offered racist immigration practices that jail the people trafficked and legalization of the prostitution industry. Of course, we don't want the criminalization of the victims, including all those at the bottom of these rigid hierarchies.[14] But surely we are all aware now that this multi-billion dollar prostitution industry is actively involved not only in the trade itself, but also in the promotion of the legalization of the trade in women and drugs.[15]

As with our struggles against the rest of the inhumane multinational trade agenda, we must expose, confront, and interfere with the managers, owners, profiteers, and consumers. The leadership of Sweden in this matter of human rights and women's rights is impressive and hopeful.[16] Sweden has criminalized the seller and begun to protect the victimized.[17] It regards prostitution as violence against women. It is no accident that Sweden is not building an economy on tourism or the sex tourism that goes with it.

To ignore women's equality aspirations and the current unequal status of women in Canada and in the world will undermine any progressive efforts to protect prostituted women from criminalization. Naive good intentions to protect the individual women should not be used to tolerate the development of this grotesque industry. In our efforts to address the needs of women trafficked into and throughout Canada, CASAC has come to the conclusion that we can only serve them by protecting their gender rights, their status as women, and the status of all women. No one is disposable or worthy of any lesser rights.

In our centres we are contending with women trafficked from abroad as indentured labour, mail order brides, domestic workers, and street-level prostitutes. Sometimes we are asked to support beaten and raped exotic dancers, as well as women working in "escort" services and "massage" parlours. Daily we are dealing with women dislocated from remote territories within Canada and trying to make their way in the cities. We are taking calls from, housing, and referring women who have been supplementing their incomes with prostitution and who want protection, both legal and political, from their pimps, johns, boyfriends, lovers, and fathers, and sometimes from the government officials to whom they try to report incidents of violence.

The public provision of exit services to women leaving prostitution is inadequate. From our centres in the early 1980s we supported the development of both The Alliance for the Safety of Prostitutes (ASP) and Prostitutes and

Other Women for Equal Rights (POWER) networks.[18] Both were spin-offs, in both membership and politics, of anti-rape centres that wanted to specialize in serving women prostituted.

During this project we participated in Direct Action Against Refugee Exploitation (DAARE)[19] and have supported financially and politically Justice for Girls[20] and many other initiatives across the country. But we remain convinced that to use the easier provision of services as an argument for legalization is misguided. As Cherry Kingsley says:

> If we want to set up areas to protect women, to give women dignity and
> police protection, appropriate childcare, housing, and job training, and
> so on, then we should do that. Why should women have to service men
> sexually to be offered those things needed by all women?[21]

Certainly among the women who call us and come to us, most do not choose prostitution except as a highly available way to survive. We speculate that the few women in the world who do choose it are short-time participants with privileges that allow them to leave. The provision of services specific to women trapped in or wanting to leave prostitution is inadequate everywhere. But to think that such services alone will curtail the harm of prostitution in the midst of this economic agenda is ridiculous. And for the federal government to refuse to try to curtail the domestic and international prostitution of women is barbarous.

The recognition of the so-called "rights of prostitutes" or the new talk of decriminalization (meaning legalization) is a self-serving policy ploy.[22] It legitimizes men's right to abuse women and also legitimizes Canada's refusal to redistribute income to women, some of whom are the most needy women, both within her borders and in the international community.

Predictable access to welfare was a power used by more than the destitute. It was a power in the hands of all women: the knowledge that we could (in a very modest amount) pay for food and shelter for ourselves and our kids by right. It was a power used to fend off attackers and to take advantage of opportunities. It was a basis on which to build one's self respect. The organizing in the 1930s, resulting in the legislation of welfare rights, had declared that everyone in Canada was entitled to at least this minimal share in the community and in the commonwealth.

We have no romantic memories of the days when welfare was great. We learned early in our herstory, and as we discussed our lived experiences, a critique of the welfare state as social control, especially of women.[23] We needed much more income redistribution and much less regulation of women's lives (Sidel). Still, we share with many second and third-wave feminists[24] a critique of the dismantling of the welfare state and the social safety net that it sometimes provided.[25]

Canadians have been deceived and manipulated to achieve this reversal of social policy. Clearly national standards are necessary as are achievable protections for women across the country.

When we redesign "welfare," as we surely will, we must start by acknowledging everyone's right to an adequate income. We must revive the Guaranteed Annual Income concepts that generated welfare reforms from the 1930s to 1975. Feminists must not tolerate going back to notions of family income or of the worthy and unworthy poor, to disentitling immigrant workers, divisions of minimum wages from disability rights, disassociated child poverty, or to mothers' allowances, Aboriginal disentitlement, forced work camps, or age restrictions even when disguised as age entitlements. We will certainly not tolerate going back to the intrusive state supervision of the private lives of women.

In this desperate time for so many women, perhaps we should take heart that most Canadians have not yet realized our loss of welfare and will surely rise to the occasion.

The CASAC Links Report, Canada's Promises to Keep, is available online at <www. casac.ca>.

Lee Lakeman lived for years on welfare raising her son. She has worked for over 30 years as an anti-violence activist beginning in Woodstock, Ontario. Currently, she is a member of the collective operating Vancouver Rape Relief and Women's Shelter. www. rapereliefshelter.bc.ca

[1]We are saying that there is nothing intrinsically different about the women and children who end up poor or violated. And the men who violate them are not biologically compelled; they make choices to do so.

[2]Professor Dorothy Smith's work has helped us to keep seeing this. Her early analysis of the United Way struggle in Vancouver from the 1970s to 1990s was followed by conversations with us about class and the women's movement over the years.

[3]We have learned a lot from Penni Richmond, Madelaine Parent, Sharon Yandel, and Linda Shuto, and suggest their bodies of work as a source of that history and its importance to women.

[4]According to our Supreme Court Rulings that support both substantive equality approaches rather than merely formal equality (a notion that sometimes treating unequal groups exactly the same way causes more inequality) and support contextual understandings.

[5]The Social Union Framework Agreement has not been an improvement on the Meech Lake Accord or the lost CAP and Health regimes. It has left women totally vulnerable in every way. The process has barred non-government involvement. We have no reassurance either that our particular identities will be recognized or that our collective or universal needs and entitlements will be met. While there seems to be some consensus that the framework can be adjusted to serve us as citizens and specifically as women, we should not be satisfied with less than the language that encodes those promises in enforceable national standards and oversight mechanisms.

[6]In their 1992 book, *Women, Violence and Social Change*, Dobash and Dobash present the results of a respectful examination of the ways in which anti-violence groups have analyzed and affected the state by comparing the movement in Britain where a welfare state was in place to the U.S., where a constitutional rights-based approach was more common.

[7]Between 1975 and 1995 it was rare for women to have trouble getting welfare after living in a transition house.

[8]In both B.C. and Ontario, lifetime bans have been imposed. Temporary refusals have been instituted. Time limits—for instance, of only being eligible for two years out of five—have been imposed. Health criteria have been imposed. Rate reductions have been imposed.

[9]All welfare rates as well as minimum wage rates in the country are below the poverty line.

[10]Federal-Provincial-Territorial Ministers Responsible for The Status of Women. (2002).

[11]Welfare workers and social workers are sometimes reported to us as abusers of their clients. They have much more power to abuse if the women know they have no enforceable right to welfare: they are dependent on the discretion in his hands.

[12]Personal communication, October 2001.

[13]In our work we have become aware of the ownership and prostitution dealings of (at least) The Hell's Angels in every province except the Maritimes, the Big Circle Boys gang, the Lotus gang, Fukianese, the Russians, the Mafia-related gangs, and the Vietnamese gangs.

[14]Most of the Canadian women's movement has agreed that prostitutes and low-level drug dealers should not be jailed or even criminalized. We have also agreed that those women trafficked as indentured labour or sex slaves should not be criminalized or deported. Our debates are about how to deal with the men and how to interfere with the trade.

[15]Gunilla Eckberg, personal communication, September 2003. She is special advisor to the government of Sweden on prostitution.

[16]For instance, see Lakeman, Lee and Jay, in particular, page 216.

[17]And here we mean the pimps. We rarely see the women as the sellers.

[18]See online: <http://wwwrapreliefshelter.bc.ca/herstory/rr_files86.html>.

[19]The extra A is because the cookie company DARE threatened women organized under that name with lawsuits if we used their trademark name, although the police have a drug abuse program with the same name.

[20]Justice for Girls is a group focusing on feminist intervention against the exploitation of young women.

[21]Cherry Kingsley, personal communication, October 2001. Cherry Kingsley escaped prostitution and often speaks as a woman who has experienced these conditions. She works in the International Centre to Combat Exploitation of Children.

[22]Decriminalization used to mean preventing charges against the women. Now

it is shorthand for the legitimating of the trade. We continue to stand with the women and against the trade.

[23]See CASAC newsletters (1978-1982) available at Vancouver Rape Relief library.

[24]Such as the member groups of FAFIA and the B.C. CEDAW group.

[25]See online <http://www.fafia-afai.org/index_e.htm>

REFERENCES

Brodsky, G. and S. Day. *Canadian Charter Equality Rights for Women: One Step Forward or Two Steps Back?* Ottawa: Canadian Advisory Council on the Status of Women, 1989.

Dobash, E. and R. Dobash. *Women, Violence and Social Change.* London and New York: Routledge, 1992.

Lakeman, L. *99 Federal Steps Toward an End to Violence Against Women.* Toronto: National Action Committee on the Status of Women, 1993.

Lakeman, Lee, Alice Lee and Suzanne Jay. "Resisting the Promotion of Prostitution in Canada: A View from Vancouver Rape Relief and Women's Shelter." *Not for Sale : Feminists Resisting Prostitution and Pornography.* Eds. Rebecca Whisnant and Christine Stark. North Melbourne, Vic.: Spinifex Press, 2004.

Sidel, R. *Keeping Women and Children Last: America's War on the Poor.* New York: Penguin, 1996.

Part Two:

Organizing for Another World

JOAN GRANT-CUMMINGS

The Global Capitalist Economic Agenda

Impact on Women's Human Rights

THE GLOBALIZATION of the capitalist economic system through structural adjustment programs in the South (Asia, Africa, Latin America, the Caribbean) as well as economic restructuring in the North has wreaked havoc in the lives of most women and devastated our communities. Its proponents—largely the business and corporate elite, supportive governments, and right-wing followers—have in the last two and a half decades sought to eradicate all other economic systems and devastate the social economy.

As a consequence the human rights of women and workers—including migrant workers and the unemployed, people living in poverty, Indigenous peoples, people with disabilities, and people of colour—have been violated in some way, shape, or form. In every category women's rights and conditions have been the most adversely impacted. This globalized capitalism, more so than ever before, relies increasingly on the exploitation of women's unpaid work for its survival. This is the most important indicator of the inherent anti-woman, anti-feminist, discriminatory principles along which capitalism is constructed. For women, in particular feminist women, feminism is, therefore, an important antidote to eradicate this global capitalist beast.

Feminism is a woman-led revolutionary imperative to make changes from an equality-seeking framework; changes that will reframe the "global family" from a human rights perspective, ensuring that women, men, and children are equal in all societies. Of course, women as a group are not homogeneous. Some groups of women who clearly identify themselves as part of the feminist movement, have to consider not only the context of their own lived experiences within their communities and globally, within movements of liberation such as feminism, but also the fact of their oppression within other arenas. Specifically, the lives of Aboriginal women, Black women, women of colour, lesbians, women with disabilities, women living in poverty, immigrant women, refugee women, and women who work at the bottom of the corporate heap differ greatly from the "average" Canadian woman, whoever she may be.

This leads many to frame feminism within the context of their complete identities and the different revolutionary struggles they simultaneously engage in and experience. Their knowledge-base and full experiences challenge feminism to incorporate an integrated analysis of equality.

It is important to enunciate our definition of feminism as it will inform the actions we will or must take to ensure our society is a place where human rights and equality rights are guaranteed and protected. While human rights are our birthright and it is the responsibility of our governments to ensure that they are not violated, feminists know that they are violated daily: male violence against women and other forms of sexism; racism; lesbophobia and homophobia; ableism; ageism; lack of access to health care; bias in the justice system; xenophobia; bias in the education system; poverty; forced migration; inequity in our workplaces and our homes; sexist media portrayals; etc., are ways that the rights of women are impacted upon daily. On top of this, the new economic world order has rapidly created the greatest economic apartheid we have ever seen.

The globalization of the capitalist economic system is not an accidental phenomenon or a natural course of events. This is a well thought-out and orchestrated plan by the corporate capitalist business elite. In 1976, the Business Council on National Issues (BCNI) was formed in Canada, with a membership of 150 corporate giants. They developed a long-range plan of how Canada (along with its G-7 partners) (now G-8) could actively support the plan of corporations largely from the G-7 nations, with the aim of fully integrating them nationally, and to thus internationalize capitalism. In other words, destroy or discredit any other economic systems, control all markets, and control the agenda.

One major component was to silence, isolate, and discredit the voices of the social justice movements that they saw as "too influential" on government. Of course, this included the feminist movement. The other "culprits" in their books are the labour movement, environmentalists, human rights activists, anti-racist groups, and other anti-discriminatory movements.

SOME FEMINIST HISTORY

To adequately deal with this issue, some global feminist history is necessary. The 1960s and the '70s were different years for feminists in the South from those of feminists in the North. The restructuring of the capitalist economy had already been implemented in the South by the time feminists in the North caught up in the 1980s and '90s. The analyses of structural adjustment programs (SAPs) by feminists in the South has thus been instructive for many feminists in the North and furthered our understanding of the latest make-over of the capitalist beast (DAWN). Simply put, G-7 countries like Canada, thinking about how to maximize profits with little cost, saw the South as a haven for cheap labour. They influenced governments by offering them major loans and dollars to "develop." This development included the building of factories, agressive mining, logging, agribusinesses, etc. Using the International Monetary Fund (IMF), and the World Bank (WB), countries in the South were convinced to "develop" and "liberalize."

Let us look at the results through southern women's eyes: the destruction of women's own markets; the destruction of women's own economic systems; reduced or no land ownership; loss of Indigenous lands without compensation or restitution; destruction of traditional farming practices and their subsequent replacement with cash crops; the underdevelopment of health, education, and social service systems; disappearance of traditional social and cultural ways of community development; disappearance of traditional diets and eating patterns; increase in women's poverty, under- and unemployment; trafficking in women and girls; the phenomenon of the feminization of migration of our communities for economic reasons; increased civil rights violations and a loss of democratic structures within societies; widespread abuses and inequities in workplaces; the phenomenon of the urban poor and the homeless who were displaced peoples from Indigenous lands; the feminization of poverty (DAWN).

I grew up in Kingston, Jamaica when all of this was occurring. The profits made by the higglers-women and street sellers within their own markets literally paid off Jamaica's IMF loans when the elite and the business barons siphoned their profits from the suffering of the poor—largely women—into U.S., Canadian, and other foreign banks. There are always those who reap benefits from the suffering of the people, especially under the IMF and the WB. You see, the IMF and the WB loans demanded that none of the money borrowed be put towards Indigenous farming practices. All food production from these loans must be put towards export markets. Still today, in many countries of the South, two-thirds of the goods in the marketplaces hail from the North, and are not Indigenous to the land. In the face of this, how then can governments in the South truly develop health, education, and social development systems? It is a testament to the tenacity, resistance, and abilities of the people of the South that there still remain today any traditional cultural practices, foods, social systems, identities, etc. and that resistance to global capitalism is actually growing.

In Canada, in the 1970s and '80s, feminists, armed with recommendations from the Royal Commission on the Status of Women, were pushing and pressuring governments to make changes for employment rights; state funded daycare; anti-violence programs; changes to the justice system; a women's equality fund; changes in the economic policies; changes to the Immigration Act; etc. Word had started to spread about the structural adjustment programs and their impact on the political, economic, and social life of countries in the South. Yet northern feminists for the most part did not see or understand the threat to the North. It was not until the end of the '80s and the beginning of the '90s that northern feminists realized we needed to look at what was transpiring in our own backyard.

Simultaneously, within the feminist movement the work to deal with racism was also beginning to take root. Women of colour and Aboriginal women had started to openly and publicly challenge white sisters in the movement. The struggle was public, vocal, and instructive in terms of organizational change and made a major contribution to Canadian feminism's international work and understanding of the capitalist economic restructuring process. A feminist analysis, in the North, of the capitalist economic restructuring process, in fact, eventually included an anti-racist analysis of globalization, exposing the racism implicit in globalization. Additionally, work with women from the South took the form, not of patronizing instructive feminism, but of an anti-racist, equality-seeking feminism, where the analysis of women from the South was valued and fully integrated in any economic analysis for women in the North. Developing our analysis of the federal government's policies and programs from an anti-racist feminist perspective, broadened feminism's ability to communicate with women nationally and globally and to have an understanding of the government's and the corporate elites' agenda that was more inclusive of a broader-based population of women.

THE ALPHABETIZATION OF OPPRESSION

The marker most activists use for Canada's active involvement with the makeover of the capitalist beast is the negotiation and signing of the North American Free Trade Agreement (FTA)—a process that began in in the mid 1980s and culminated in 1994 when the agreement was finally ratified. The FTA was ratified despite the major public outcry and foretold what could be expected from subsequent governments—despite public opposition, the corporate agenda will prevail. The new economic world order involved a re-regulation (some say de-regulation) that favoured the business elite, the right-wing, and political elites. In order to actualize this new economic world order some things had to happen: money had to be found to fuel it; it had to be sold to the public; and opposition had to be dimmed or squelched.

The government for its part came up with the deficit dragon. Trade agreements and international investments along the lines that capitalists dreamed of meant the lowering of corporate taxes and tariffs to "allow the free flow of capital and goods" (Asia Pacific Economic Cooperation Business Committee). What our government and corporations neglected to tell us is that by lowering corporate taxes and tariffs (taxes on goods for export and import), the government loses revenues. What Canada really had was a revenue-generating problem, not a deficit problem! The creation of the deficit dragon and the making of the deficit slayer had begun. The Liberal federal finance minister would prove to be the noble knight designated for this adventure. He would take us into the black.

But how did he choose to take us into the black? Well, we cut social spending, destroyed the social economy, cut health care, welfare, education, public and social services. "The women will pick up the slack" seemed to be the refrain of our governments and the capitalist giants. After all, women love volunteering in our communities. "Welfare bums; power-hungry feminists; greedy union bosses; irresponsible students; single mothers; those pesky immigrants and refugees; gays and lesbians—family destroyers; and 'lying' environmentalists" became the scapegoats for the revenue shortfall.

Public and private sector downsizing—massive layoffs that disproportionately affected women, people of colour, Indigenous peoples, and people with disabilities became the order of the day to maximize profits and to pay for the new global economy. The 80 or so rightwing think-tanks employed by the business elite and the corporate media were used to sell the message that globalization is here to stay and that it is good for us.

For women specifically, the cost of globalization has been great. Through the eyes of Canadian women this is a snapshot of the price we are still paying:

> •increased poverty for women of all ages—the feminization of poverty;
> •increased migration of women: from the South to the North; within the South; within the North—(as migrant workers, temp workers, domestic workers, refugees, immigrants);
> •an increase in the wage gap between men and women;
> •backward steps regarding pay and employment equity;
> •reduced access to postsecondary institutions due to rising tuition costs;
> •increase in labour-intensive and part-time jobs;
> •destruction of social services, public services, health and education systems;
> •loss of employment and under-employment;
> •increased trafficking in women and girls;
> •a whopping increase in women's unpaid work—in the home, community, and paid workforce;
> •an attack on public pensions that women rely on more than men;
> •an increase in racism, lesbo-phobia, xenophobia, and the ever present feminist backlash;
> •the de-funding and increased under-funding to equality-seeking women's groups and women's service organizations.

The extent of the anti-feminist backlash is broad and far-reaching, as is the erosion of some of the gains made. The de-funding and under-funding of feminist organizations has resulted in the silencing of women's voices in many places, and affects our ability to do feminist research, advocacy, lobbying, and to have an impact on government polices and programs.

WHAT KIND OF SOCIETY ARE WE BUILDING?

Capitalism is not a sustainable economic policy or development policy. It exploits rather than protects the guaranteed human rights of the population. It only guarantees the wealth of 20 percent of the population. It is rooted in racism, white supremacy, sexism, and other oppressions. Why do we continue to support a system that is biased towards and exploitative of at least 80 percent of the world's population?

CHALLENGING THE CAPITALIST BEAST

Globally, most of us form the opposition. This is why building a globalized resistance and creating alternatives has taken root in the international feminist movement. Women around the world are challenging trade agreements, trading blocs, and the "alphabets": the Multilateral Agreement on Investment (MAI) now the World Trade Organization (WTO); the General Agreement on Tariffs and Trades (GATT); the Asia Pacific Economic Cooperation (APEC); the Association of South East Asian Nations (ASEAN); the Southern Africa Developmenet Community (SADC), the Free Trade Agreements of the Americas (FTAA) etc. These acronyms stand for trading and economic systems that are biased against women, and are definitely not gender neutral, especially when considering that women control only ten percent of the world economy, own only one percent of the world's land, yet perform over 66 percent of the world's work (United Nations)! Women are only 52 percent of the world's population.

It is important for us to challenge our governments to divest from these trade agreements and blocs in as many public forums as we can and put forward alternatives rooted in a people-first before economics framework. We must form our own think-tanks and reclaim our own markets. Women's groups, by teaming up with labour movements, environmentalists, human rights activists, anti-poverty groups, peasant-farmers, health-care workers, educators, gay and lesbian organizations, and grassroots anti-violence movements, can challenge this new corporate, global beast. A more international activist movement is taking root. The women's movement in Canada has to increasingly solidify its own activism at a global level.

Excerpted from a speech given at the University of Toronto for International Women's Day, March 8th, 1998.

In Canada, Joan Grant Cummings was actively involved in a number of Black community organizations, as well as feminist organizations. She worked with the Jamaican Canadian Association, was on the board of INTERCEDE, the Executive Director of Women's Health in Women's Hands, and the President of the National Action Committee (NAC) on the Status of Women in Canada. She was the returned to her native Jamaica in 2000 and is currently a researcher/consultant as well as a volunteer with the Women's Resource and Outreach Centre (WROC).

REFERENCES

Asia Pacific Economic Cooperation Business Committee. "The Report of the Asia Pacific Economic Cooperation Business Committee."

DAWN. "Women Reclaim the Market." Paper presented at NGO Forum, World Summit for Social Development. Copenhagen, Denmark, March 8, 1995.

United Nations. *1996 United Nations Human Index Report*. New York: 1996.

JOYCE GREEN

Resistance is Necessary

C ANADA HAS LIVED with neoliberalism for about four decades. It has also lived with the Charter of Rights and Freedoms and our renewed Constitution for most of the same period. The impulses in the Charter are not those of capitalist accumulation and the monetization of everything. Rather, the Charter speaks of rights for those who are vulnerable, against the oppression of governments. As the great Black American legal scholar Patricia Williams wrote, "in law, rights are islands of empowerment."

It was post-World War II international politics that gave the world the Universal Declaration of Human Rights, and it's Covenants on Civil, Political, Social, Cultural and Economic rights. Those documents formed the basis for other rights claims at international law, and importantly, they informed Canadian law. As signatory to these international laws, Canada agreed to be bound by them. But states do not have to be signatory to be bound by international law: Westphalian assumptions aside, the principle of law is that it applies regardless of the agreement of those to whom it applies.

Thus, in the same era that the welfare state was being replaced by the neoliberal state and national economic policies were being supplanted by the structures of globalized capitalism (such as "free trade" and the discipline of transnational market and capital imperatives), Canadians retained some political commitment to the virtue of democracy, of community, of solidarity and of equality. In 2013, four decades and counting later, we can assess how well we are doing both in the context of our neoliberal state, and relative to democracy and justice.

Back in the 1970s, when constitutional negotiations preoccupied the political class, gays and lesbians were mostly closeted, lest they be fired, harassed, or beaten up. Bisexual and transgendered people weren't even on the agenda. Indians struggled through the National Indian Brotherhood to get rights issues on the national agenda, against premiers who denied, smirked, and opposed (for a good example of this, view the National Film Board video, *Dancing Around the Table*); and a prime minister who had brought forward the 1969 White Paper "Choosing a Path," calling for the elimination of treaties, status, reserves, and the notion of rights (eerily replicated in contemporary federal proposals for privatization of reserve land). Metis struggled to be recognized at all—first through the Native Council of Canada, and then through the new Metis National Council. Women who took a feminist analysis worked through the National Action Committee on the Status of Women (NAC) and its, literally, hundreds of local groups; and through the Native Women's Association of Canada (NWAC) and the Women's Legal Education and Action Fund (LEAF) (Rebick 2005b). Abortion was illegal—as indeed it appears that Conservative MP Brad Trost would prefer to have it again (Payton)[1]—and birth control had barely been legalized. Women still found it difficult to get credit in their own right, as some lenders would ask for a husband or father to co-sign a loan application. Native women worked through the NWAC as well as with NAC, particularly on native women's equality rights and Aboriginal rights. The voices of Canadians who had suffered legislated oppression, such as Japanese, Chinese, the disabled, the poor, and Aboriginal peoples, were rarely heard in public space by white affluent Canadians.

The operating assumption of our governments, our media, and most Canadians was that the experience and expectations of privileged white men was good enough to provide political representation and opportunity for others. Those who argued for rights were criticized for whining, and for being "special interests," thus damaging the implied "general interests."

The negotiations leading up the Charter's 1982 inclusion in the constitution of Canada were polarized, with some (like the late Alan Blakeney, then-Premier of Saskatchewan) arguing that it would hamstring governments, removing their legislative and policy flexibility; and that it was inconsistent with the British constitutional traditions which are the basis of Canadian ones.[2] Others, however, pointed to Canada's spotty history of racism, colonialism, and sexism delivered through public policy and law, and argued that our history demonstrated the need for rights protections (Green 2005a, 2005b, 2011).

And most of you will know that despite the Charter, many of these issues continue. For example, the long list of missing and murdered Aboriginal women in Canada continues to grow (FAFIA; Amnesty International); free speech is more difficult to exercise without fear of political blowback; and free assembly by citizens is increasingly attended by police and by political monitors, as was seen most shockingly in the police force used against citizen protests at the G8/G20 meetings in Toronto in June 2010 (Seglins 2012a, 2012b). Those speaking for protection of our ecosystems are maligned as "eco-terrorists" by our current federal government (McCarthy). Claims of a need for "security" are used to limit free speech, free association, free movement, and even, in the case of Abousfian Abdelrazik, the right to return home.[3] Post 9/11, our rights have been compromised in return for the promise of security. I leave it to you to decide if we are more secure because of this.

Neoliberalism is not, in my view, a beneficial transformation for the majority of Canadians. The environment is treated as a resource for an economy in which corporate elites conspire with neoliberal governments to maximize the profitability of the former and the political hegemony of the latter. Citizens are treated (and treat themselves) as private economic actors, not as guardians of the public space for community and democracy. Hostile governments have attacked civil society communities who disagree with them: feminists, Indigenous organizations and movements, anti-globalization activists, environmentalists, and scholars and activists in what is called, for shorthand, "the Left." The achievement of the Charter is an important but insufficient condition for the protection of the rights and freedoms that, mostly, were already promised to us at international law. And the Charter itself is based on this international law.

The questions for us as citizens and democrats include: How, then, can we actually enjoy our rights? How can we support others to enjoy their rights? Because my rights are never secure if your rights are insecure. That is a lesson for the security wonks to learn.

Rights are never "given" to people. They are won through political struggle by informed and committed citizens. This has been true since the Magna Carta— not granted by the Crown to the nobles, but wrested from it. Hold that thought.

The First Ministers—that group of premiers and the then-prime minister who negotiated the Charter—did not really want a Charter that would limit governments. Rights are shields against government abuse. The First Ministers had to be convinced of the need for the Charter, and citizens did the convincing. The politicians did not "give" women and Aboriginal people rights recognition. They were actually opposed to recognizing those rights. The women's movement, especially the National Action Committee on the Status of Women and the Native Women's Association of Canada, organized nationally to convince Canadians and thus, the First Ministers, that there could be no equality of rights without recognition of women's rights (Kome; Green 1993, 2007; Rebick 2005a, 2005b, 2009). Women and men live in a society that treats them differently, and treats women worse on economic, social, and political measures. Moreover, biology means we have different life experiences and opportunities. Equality means recognizing the real life experiences of men and women, not by treating them all as (white) men.

And the First Ministers certainly did not want to recognize something that Canada had always denied—Aboriginal and treaty rights. These important rights challenge the legitimacy of the Canadian state and invoke our usually sanitized history of colonialism and oppression (Green 2005a, 2005b, 2011). Note please: these rights are NOT in the Charter, but are recognized and affirmed in the 1982 Constitution Act. My point here is that it was Aboriginal people, organized and politically active, together with their allies, who traveled to London, England and lobbied the British Parliament to hold up the Canadian Constitution until their rights were recognized. The First Ministers agreed only because they had to do so to accomplish their other constitutional goals.

So is Canadian democracy a failure?

Only if we are failures as citizens.

The Charter begins by guaranteeing all the contained rights and freedoms "subject to such limitations as are justifiable in a free and democratic society." Our Constitution assumes that it is our political Prime Directive: a free and democratic society, shaped by rights protections and with basic freedoms for citizens. Who decides on contested issues, when rights are claimed but not respected? The courts decide.

And who can afford to go to court? Are the courts well educated on especially the political realities of our most marginal citizens? Can they make remedies that governments will be forced to respect?[4] Always remember, as a citizen you have rights, and governments MUST justify any limitation of them, before the courts. And the Charter is a list of rights, but not an exhaustive list. The courts can "read in" analogous rights, which is what they did in order to protect gays and lesbians. This is part of our constitutional process.

Citizen action in communities (such as the iconic Idle No More movement) has transformed our Constitution and our political culture. It must continue to do so, because while some court protection for some rights and a measure of justice has been obtained, there is much injustice remaining in our communities. Most of those who are oppressed are not in a position to litigate, and only through collective political action can we provide a voice to those who are otherwise voiceless. For example, there may come a time when a court "reads in" constitutional limitations on governments not only as a consequence of the Charter, but of the framework of international law on human rights. That moment, however, will only come when many of us stand in solidarity with Indigenous people who are resisting various forms of oppression and occupation by the colonial state.

The price of a free and open democratic society is individually informed, collectively engaged citizens. Information and activism take time and commitment. That is the flip side of rights: we have *responsibilities* to each other and to our communities and environment. Many of us do not even get off the couch to vote—in what is a highly undemocratic electoral system. Most of us don't appear to know the electoral system is undemocratic. Many of us only think individually—what is good for us—rather than in relation to our community—what is good for all of us. But as the late great Rosemary Brown, a former NDP MLA and then MP, and the first Black woman to so serve, said: "none of us has made it until all of us have made it."

My mother used to say to me, "Dear, they only do what you let them do." Mom was right. Our governments only violate rights when they think there will be few or no repercussions. For example, consider: the federal government's fight against adopting the UN Declaration on the Rights of Indigenous Peoples; and the failure of all orders of government to put in place the conditions for the minimums of human health and security for poor people, prisoners, homeless people, racialized people and those suffering from mental health afflictions and addictions. Marginalized people are pretty much abandoned as objects of solidarity by us, through our governments. Notice how the political issues are also economic ones, and the political response is now thoroughly neoliberal.

Our governments only do what we let them do.

If we are responsible citizens, we will learn about the lives and dreams of people like us, but also of people not just like us. We will be committed to everyone's best interests, not just to our own. That is, we will care about community and relationship. We will speak in public places, and at kitchen tables, about our rights and about our dreams. We will support others. We will support governments who are concerned about all of us, not just about markets, capital, and their political base. We will consider our wants and needs in the context of ecosystems with their own needs calculus. We will demand the media be more balanced, less biased. We will never stop working for justice, because it is always a goal, never completely achieved.

The feminist movement brilliantly conceptualized transformation as process rather than goal: it is in our search that we make political community and measures of justice. We always begin as individuals, but in the context of history, culture, economic class, geographical territories, and so on. This produced another brilliant feminist analysis that remains our political mantra: the personal is political. By understanding our lives and our difficulties personally, and then as shared with others, we move to seeing ourselves as political subjects and citizens. We move to analysis and action rather than helplessness.

The price of justice is vigilance. The price of citizenship is engagement. The price of apathy is oppression. Resistance is necessary.

Joyce Green is a Professor of Political Science at the University of Regina, where she teaches Canadian politics, critical race and post colonial theory, and the politics of decolonization in Canada. She is the editor of Making Space for Aboriginal Feminism *(2007).*

[1]Judy Rebick (2005b) writes that the Charter's Section 7 was successfully argued by Henry Morgentaler at the Supreme Court of Canada in 1993, effectively producing a women's right to reproductive choice. See also *R. v. Morgentaler.*
[2]See, for example, Johansen and Rosen; Topp.
[5]See, for example <http://en.wikipedia.org/wiki/Abousfian_Abdelrazik>.
[4]There is much concern that the politicized and untransparent judicial appointment process, which produces fairly homogeneous and arguably at least implicitly politically compromised judicial benches, makes it difficult for courts to adequately assess the above questions. The education of lawyers, who become judges, is a form of intellectual hegemony that discourages critical thinking about the legal system's assumptions. Moreover, even in the case of the most enlightened judicial outcomes, courts may not compel governments to spend money or take positive action. Finally, the structural and philosophical nature of the legal system, in the context of the colonial state, makes deference to and protection of the state a most common component of constitutional and related judicial decisions

REFERENCES

Amnesty International. *No More Stolen Sisters: The Need for a Comprehensive Response to Discrimination and Violence Against Indigenous Women in Canada*. London: Amnesty International Publications, 2009.

Feminist Alliance for International Action (FAFIA). "Disappearances and Murders of Aboriginal Women and Girls in Canada." Submission to the United Nations on the Elimination of Racial Discrimination, January 2012.

Green, Joyce. "Constitutionalising the Patriarchy: Aboriginal Women and Aboriginal Government." *Constitutional Forum* 4 (4) (Summer 1993).

Green, Joyce. "Self-determination, Citizenship, and Federalism: Indigenous and Canadian Palimpsest." *Reconfiguring Aboriginal-State Relations*. Ed. Michael Murphy. Kingston: Institute of Intergovernmental Relations, School of Policy Studies, Queen's University, 2005a. 329-352.

Green, Joyce. "Towards Conceptual Precision: Citizenship and Rights Talk for Aboriginal Canadians." *Insiders and Outsiders: Alan Cairns and the Reshaping of Canadian Citizenship*. Ed. Gerald Kernerman and Philip Resnick. Vancouver: University of British Columbia Press, 2005b. 227-241.

Green, Joyce. 2007. "Balancing Strategies: Aboriginal Women and Constitutional Change." (Revised). *Making Space for Indigenous Feminism*. Ed. Joyce Green. Halifax: Fernwood Press, 2007. 140-159.

Green, Joyce. 2011. "Canada the Bully: Indigenous Human Rights in Canada." *Prairie Forum* 38 (2011): 9-32.

Johansen, David and Philip Rosen. "The Notwithstanding Clause of the Charter." Library of Parliament Research Publications, Background Paper No. BP-194-E. 16 October 2008. Revised May 17, 2012. Web.

Kome, Penny. *The Taking of 28*. Toronto: The Women's Press, 1983.

McCarthy, Shawn. "Ottawa's new anti-terrorism strategy lists eco-extremists as threats." *The Globe and Mail* 6 September 2012. Web.

Payton, Laura. "Government apathetic on abortion, Tory MP Trost says." *CBC News* 28 September 2011. Web.

R. v. Morgentaler. [1993] 3 S.C.R. 463.

Rebick, Judy. *Ten Thousand Roses*. Toronto: Penguin Canada, 2005a.

Rebick, Judy. "The Political Impact of the Charter." *Supreme Court Law Review* (2005b) 29 S.C.L.R. (2d): 85-91. Web.

Rebick, Judy. *Transforming Power*. Toronto: Penguin Canada, 2009.

Seglins, Dave. "G20 charges coming against Toronto police commanders." *CBC News* May 17, 2012a. Web.

Seglins, Dave. "G20 report slams police for 'excessive' force." *CBC News* May 16, 2012b. Web.

Topp, Brian. "Allan Blakeney: Deftly Navigating Thunderstorms." *Policy Options/Options Politiques* (June-July 2012): 42-48.

Williams, Patricia J. *Alchemy of Race and Rights*. Cambridge, MA: Harvard University Press, 1992.

I. UN Decade for Women and Beyond

Development Crisis and Alternative Visions

Third World Women's Perspectives

WE BELIEVE that women's experiences with the development process, as researchers, activists and policy-makers, brought us to a range of common understandings despite different starting-points. The hopes raised by the UN Decade for Women made these experiences possible. But as the Decade draws to its close, we have also become more aware not only of the success and failures of the last ten years, but of the need to question in a more fundamental way the underlying processes of development into which we have been attempting to integrate women. In many of the discussions and actions generated throughout the Decade, there has been an implicit belief that women's main problem in the Third World has been insufficient participation in an otherwise benevolent process of growth and development. Increasing women's participation and improving their shares in resources, land, employment and income relative to men, were seen as both necessary and sufficient for dramatic changes in their economic and social position. Our experience now leads us to challenge this belief.

Although dissonant voices questioning these assumptions could be heard very early in the decade, it is only in the last two or three years that they have begun to coalesce with vigour. We can no longer simply assume that development as it has evolved in most Third World countries is a process inherently benign to the people living there. The consequences of long-term economic processes which are often inimical, or at best indifferent, to the interests and needs of poor people, are being felt through interlinked crises or massive and growing impoverishment and inequality; food insecurity and unavailability; financial and monetary disarray; environmental degradation; and growing demographic pressure. Nations and the international polity have tended to react to these pressures through increased militarization, domestic oppression, and foreign aggression. There is a growing sense of hopelessness, even lack of concern, about the Third World's poor in international donor and agency circles. This is compounded by the shift to bilateralism in aid and the cutbacks in contributions to multilateral institutions by some of the richest, most powerful, and most militaristic nations.

The nations of the Third World are increasingly being forced to rely upon internal resource mobilization to make up for sharp reductions in the availability of external resources. While creating serious hardships for the poor and middle income earners, such pressures may prove a blessing in disguise if they lead to policies that are more self-reliant and more geared to meeting the survival and subsistence needs of people. Women, in this context, are not only among the needy. More importantly, they offer strategic leverage for tackling the crisis of survival, since they constitute the crucial human links in the ongoing reproduction of people.

New strategies for survival cannot succeed, however, if women are continuously squeezed, as they are now being, in the pincers of scarcer access to resources and greater demands on their labour time. The vision and methods needed to empower women to draw themselves and the poor out of impoverishing economic and social structures are the subject of our document. But we have no wish to see women crushed further under the burden of their traditional work in unchanging divisions of labour. Rather, we wish to argue that, if the survival of human beings is now the most pressing problem in the world, and if women are the crucial human links in that survival, then the empowerment of women is essential if new, creative and cooperative solutions to the crisis are to emerge.

As part of this process of empowerment, we feel a need to reaffirm and clarify our understanding of feminism. Throughout the decade the women's movement has debated the links between the eradication of gender subordination and of other forms of social and economic oppression based on nation, class or ethnicity. The time has come to articulate the position that feminism cannot be monolithic in its issues, goals and strategies since it is the political expression of the concerns and interests of women from different regions, classes, nationalities and ethnic backgrounds. There is and must be a diversity of feminisms, responsive to the different needs and concerns of different women, and *defined by them for themselves*. This diversity builds on a *common opposition to gender oppression and hierarchy* which, however, is only the first step in a political agenda.

For many women in the world, problems of nationality, class and race are inextricably linked to their specific oppression as women. Their definition of feminism includes the struggle against all forms of oppression: it is both legitimate and necessary. In many instances, gender equality cannot come without changes on these other fronts. On the other hand, the struggle against gender subordination can not be compromised in the struggle against these other forms of oppression, or be relegated to a future when they maybe wiped out.

Many women from the Third World are acutely conscious of the need for this clarification and self-affirmation. Throughout the decade they have had to face accusations from two sides. On the one hand, there are those who dismiss them as not being truly feminist because of their attempts to link the struggle against gender subordination with that against other oppressions. On the other, there are those who accuse them of being divisive within class or national struggles. This is why we feel the need to affirm that feminism allows for the broadest and deepest development of society and human beings free of all systems of domination. Such a vision has been articulated before, particularly at Bangkok in 1979 and at Stony Point in 1980. This document is an attempt to build on those earlier initiatives, to sharpen our analysis and strengthen our attempts at change. While we refer to this as a "Third World" perspective, it is inclusive of all who share in the vision outlined above, whether from the South countries, from oppressed and disadvantaged groups within the North, or all others who share in and are committed to working towards its fulfilment.

In this context we believe that it is from the experience of the most oppressed women who suffer on account of class, race and nationality—that we can most clearly grasp the nature of the links, and the kinds of action we must take.

Such a perspective would imply that a development process that shrinks and poisons the pie available to poor people, and then has women scrambling for a larger relative share, is not in women's interest. We reject the belief, therefore, that it is possible to obtain sustainable improvements in women's economic and social position under conditions of growing relative inequality, if not absolute poverty, for both women and men. Equality for women is not made visible within those existing economic, political and cultural processes that separate resources, power and control from large sections of people. But neither is development possible without greater equity and participation for women.

Our vision of feminism, born of our experience as activists and analysts, has at its very core a process of economic and social development geared to human needs through wider access to economic and political power. Equality, peace and development by and for the poor and oppressed are inextricably interlinked with equality, peace and development by and for women.

Our main audience in this document is women—those who have, through this past decade and longer, attempted in practical and analytical ways to come to grips with the implications of such a vision. Indeed, the actions undertaken by women themselves, individually and through organizations, have provoked the most exciting and potentially most promising events of the last decade. Women have come together in organizations, networks, and movements. They have sought to tackle problems of income and employment, and to alter the ways in which society, governments, international institutions, men and women themselves, evaluate women's works. They have struggled to bring the basic survival of human beings and the right to live in dignity to the forefront of consciousness, to organize against military repression and militarization, and in a host of other ways. It is women, therefore, who have been the catalysts behind many of the actions of governments, agencies, and others during the last ten years.

It is important for us in the women's movement to understand and acknowledge our own achievements and strengths. We are living in a time when the ideological climate and mood are more gloomy regarding the prospects for peace and for genuine human and economic development than they were at the start of the decade. It is easy to be pessimistic about the concrete achievements of the past years in improving women's economic and social position. They appear to have been as meagre as the resources that agencies and governments have actually directed to women. But why not look at our experiences in another way? We know now from our own research how deeply ingrained and how far back historically the subordination of women goes. What we have managed to do in the last few years is to forge *worldwide* networks and movements as never before to transform that subordination and in the process to break down other oppressive structures as well. Only women know how hard they have had to struggle within their own families and communities to achieve the personal autonomy that fuels and builds upon wider socio-economic change. Starting from little knowledge and training, and having to challenge the full social, economic, and psychological weight of gender (and often class, national, and ethnic) oppression, we have acquired skills and self-confidence, and the capacity for change.

While it is to such a process of ongoing self-empowerment that this document is dedicated, many of the issues raised here, the analysis, and strategies proposed are for the consideration and action of agencies and governments as well. But we realise from our experiences of the past decade that the political will for serious action by agencies is contingent upon women organising to promote change. We need, therefore, to clarify our role in affecting the major social and economic issues of our times, and to assess the successes, failures and potential of our organizations. We do this with the recognition that few large movements of our times have the mass potential, the freshness of vision, the courage to experiment with new methods for action, and the respect for adversity and challenge that the women's movement does. It is time for us to assert with clarity, rigor and passion.

Summary of paper presented by DAWN at the NGO Forum '85. The full text of this presentation was written by Gita Sen with Caren Grown. Collaborating agencies and organizations in the DAWN project include the African Association of Women for Research and Development (AAWORD), Dakar, Senegal; the Women and Development Unit at the University of the West Indies (WAND), Barbados; the Asian and Pacific Development Centre (APDC), Malaysia; and the Chr Michelsen Institute (CMD), Norway.

DAWN stands for Development Alternatives with Women for a New Era, an inspiring network of Third World women's groups, working for alternative and more equitable development processes. DAWN began as Third World feminist initiative in Bangalore, India, in August 1984. The Bangalore meeting decided to produce a paper outlining their consensus of thought on women and development, which grew into its NCO Forum contribution.

JANICE WOOD WETZEL

The World's Women Unite in Diversity

Report on Nairobi

UCH HAS BEEN WRITTEN by many concerning the UN Decade for Women Conference held in Nairobi, Kenya in July of 1985. Most of the reports have focused on the official governmental meeting, with occasional colourful forays into Forum '85, the non-governmental organizations' peripheral conference. There has been an essential perspective missing from the scene—a view that suggests that the sideshow may have been the main event, a kind of participatory community theater that promises to play to standing-room only crowds for decades to come. I suggest that what happened at Forum '85, in contrast to the official governmental conference, is worthy of concentrated attention. The implications are far-reaching as it becomes clear that the women of the world are united in their intent and perception. The official governments of the world, by contrast, stand out in bas-relief against a backdrop of obfuscation and rhetoric. The United States is the leading player, the protagonist in what would be an international farce were it not so deadly serious. To clarify my critique, let me first provide some historical background information.

In 1972, the United Nations proclaimed 1975 an International Women's Year to be held in Mexico City. At that initial conference, a document called "The Declaration of Mexico, 1975" was drawn up by an informal working group of the nonaligned countries. In a revolutionary statement, the declaration began by recognizing the oppression of all women everywhere, linking oppression with inequality experienced globally by women; with underdevelopment due to unsuitable national structures, as well as a profoundly unjust world economic system; and the absence of rights concerning women in family matters in regard to choosing whether or not to marry or to have children; and mandating the elimination of violence against women such as rape, incest, forced prostitution, physical assault, mental cruelty, and coercive and commercial marital transactions. Men were called upon to participate more responsibly, actively and creatively in family life.

This landmark document was adopted together with a "World Plan of Action" by majority vote, to be implemented by each nation. As a result, 90 percent of the world's governments today have some sort of organization promoting

343

women's advancement. But the reality is that few have acted upon, much less implemented, any part of Mexico City's declarations or plans. A mid-decade international conference for women held in Copenhagen in 1980 produced yet another document (similar to Mexico City's) called the "Programme of Action."

However, the official conference must be viewed realistically. It is a meeting dominated by the men of the world who are in power. Out of 18 people presented on the opening dais at the official plenary, only four were women. In one country, only men were delegates. In all countries, delegates are selected by their leaders because their ideology is congruent. Should it in any way differ, they are not allowed to say so. The official conference is programmed to be sure. That an ideological forward-looking global agenda for women was consensually agreed upon at that meeting is to their credit, whether or not the world's governments again choose to ignore the document. But the indirect impact of the Decade of Women's unofficial NGO conference, Forum '85, has proven to be even more phenomenal. It is no wonder that governments are threatened. This meeting was *real,* not just ideological posturing.

To attend Forum '85 was to experience an extraordinary event. Eleven thousand women from over 150 countries came together at Nairobi University in a very literal sense. Unlike the previous international meetings, both official and unofficial, this one was marked by unity. Women gathered in Asian kimonos, in Indian saris, African khangas and Arabic chadors and veils. They were joined by colorful Latinas as well as relatively bland Europeans and North Americans. Fifty percent were black Africans and 30 percent were Asians. There were Indigenous women who spoke only Swahili, middle-class professionals, religious sisters, the able bodied and physically impaired. There were punk youth, elite intelligentsia, the politically astute, the apolitical, articulate orators, quiet-spoken poets and silent meditators. The women of the left and right from both rural and urban communities were represented well. From youth to old age—black, brown, red, yellow, white and all the shades between—came together to discuss in 1000 formal workshops (and I daresay probably one billion informal conversations) the issues that confront women everywhere.

By the third day, preconceived expectations of hostile confrontations dissipated. The word began to spread of the unity present among the women—acknowledged between workshops at breaks in the quadrangle, at small tables at lunch in the cafeteria, waiting in lines, on buses, or sipping tea at the nearby Norfolk Hotel. Then unity became part of the dialogue of workshop participants and presenters alike, Betty Friedan's following under the Fig Tree, and finally reported in the daily conference paper, *The Forum.* Journalists called their publishers excitedly. The typical response was "Yes, but isn't there anything *sensational?*" "This *is* sensational!" they replied. Too often the real historic message went unpublished, invisible and unsung, true to cliché. Despite differing ideology, geography, race, culture, colour, or age; despite their national differences that would polarize the delegates at the official conference, these women were in agreement concerning the situation of women in the world. They stood united in diversity.

The Reagan government in the U.S. disallowed a final plenary at Forum '85. The administration had the power to disallow as well a formal agenda or final document. Despite these constraints, the unifying issues emerged. At an informal "plenary" spontaneously called by the women of a dozen countries, the issues were highlighted by one speaker after another. It would seem that the Declaration that was conceived in Mexico City in 1975 had gone through a ten-year melding process. Mexico City has been called "the greatest consciousness-raising event in history." Copenhagen, with all its apparent conflict, set in motion the most intricate mechanism of women ever recorded. Women began to realize that *collective action* was the key to their power and effectiveness. Solidarity links forged over the decade have turned out to be stronger bonds than ever imagined. Forum '85 is just the beginning of an unbreakable chain of women throughout the world dedicated to healing and liberating themselves, their children, and in turn their men and their nations.

The women of the world in large numbers appear to agree:

•that women's universal oppression and inequality are grounded in the patriarchal systems that ensure the continuance of female subservience and secondary status everywhere;
•that women do two-thirds of the world's work, yet two-thirds of the world's women live in poverty. Their work usually is unpaid, underpaid and invisible. Their fiscal dependency is perpetuated despite the fact that they do almost all of the world's domestic work plus working outside the home and growing one-half of the world's food;
•that women are the peace makers, yet war takes its heaviest toll on them as they hold their families intact, struggling for physical safety and sustenance;
•that there is universal sexual exploitation of girls and women, often resulting in sexual domination and abuse throughout their lives;
•that women provide more health care (both physical and emotional) than all the world's health services combined; that they are the chief proponents of the prevention of illness and the promotion of health. Yet they have fewer health care services, are likely to experience chronic exhaustion due to overwork, and to be deprived emotionally and physically by their men, their families, their communities and their governments;
•that women are the chief educators of the family, yet outnumber men among the world's illiterates at a ratio of 3:2; that even when educated, they generally are not allowed to lead.

The scenario shifts culture by culture, but the story line remains the same. The common condition of women must be changed. And with such change a more humane world will evolve.

There was a general sense of agreement at the informal "plenary" that the three-pronged purpose of the Decade for Women—Equality, Development, and Peace—would never come to be without mutuality and justice. The restructuring of society - the recognition of and full compensation for women's work and men's equal sharing of family responsibility and commitment, once derided notions relegated to avant garde feminist ideology, have emerged as basic universal mandates among vast numbers of seemingly disparate women of all cultures. Many women take great risks when they stand up to be counted. Some risk abuse, even torture, within the family; others risk governmental abuse and imprisonment. The courage of these women is remarkable and is in proportion to the seriousness with which they weigh their situations. By way of example, church representatives asked us to come home and report the fact that Kenyan women who spoke out were threatened with imprisonment. Their pictures were taken when they did so in Nairobi. (That I can attest to.) It is hoped that publicity will lessen the likelihood of repercussion.

The governments of the world may continue to ignore women's documents. They may continue to disallow those events that they cannot control. Still the work will go on in rural villages and urban settings, in remote corners of the earth and in highly populated regions. The momentum is there. The commitment is firm. The global connections are in place. Prediction: the end of the Decade of Women marks the beginning of an international women's movement the world has yet to experience. The women of the world are organizing. They are thinking and communicating and supporting one another. They have seen themselves mirrored in the faces of their sisters. I have not felt this hopeful for women and for the world—ever.

Janice Wood Wetzel is a former Dean and Professor Emerita of Social Work at Adelphi University in Garden City, New York. She has served as the Main United Nations Representative in New York City for the International Association of Schools of Social Work since 1988. Dr. Wetzel is a well-published international educator and researcher who has specialized in the human rights, mental health and advancement of women from a global perspective for more than 40 years.

MARGARET FULTON

Peace is the Way to Peace

Peace Tent at Nairobi

EMBRACING, DANCING, QUILTING, making banners and singing slogans were as much a statement of the United Nations Women's Conference held in Nairobi in July 1985 as were the actual workshops, seminars, lectures, discussions, affirmations, and resolutions. Women of the world had gathered together for the third time in ten years: the greatest of all "happenings" of this century occurred.

In Mexico City in 1975 the theme of the first ever international women's conference was established: Equality, Development, Peace. While the many aspects of "equality" and "development" formed the basis of the majority of the discussions in 1975—and again in Copenhagen at the Mid-Decade Conference in 1980—it was clear that "peace" was the central theme and the central issue in Nairobi. None of the multitude of problems facing women can be solved until a climate of peace stabilizes our global society. Workshop after workshop— whether designed to discuss issues related to equality, economics, health, agriculture, education, literacy, religion, sexuality, political structures, refugees, technology, or ecology and the environment—invariably concluded that, until the threat of nuclear war is removed from the planet, until the militarization of the globe is stopped, until the institutionalized violence against women and our environment is ended, any efforts to bringing about real social change would be superficial at best, and meaningless at worst.

Although no formal agendas were established for the Forum, an examination of workshop, seminar, and forum titles indicates that despite the tremendous number and variety of workshops scheduled, all discussions took on an urgency because of a shared awareness that not only women, but all people in our multi-cultural world civilization face total destruction. Group discussions on any topic seemed to stem from three common assumptions: 1) destruction of the planet through nuclear war; 2) destruction of ourselves through genetic engineering and manipulation; 3) destruction of the delicate ecology of the planet through pollution, acid rain, or other careless handling of toxic wastes.

The underlying sense of imminent destruction unless things change informed every meeting. The linking threads in all discussions wove a pattern of awareness

347

best described by Sister Rosalie Bertell in her book *No Immediate Danger? Prognosis for a Radioactive Earth:*

> The global sickness has a name. It is called violence, whether manifested within a nation or between nations. Its presence puts a premium on strength and makes 'blooming' an expendable luxury. It rears its head at the devaluation and distortion of women, either through virtual slavery, exaggerated equality with males (military services, heavy manual labour) or rape. It leads to rape of the land, violence towards the poor, oppression of the weak. It thrives on feats of extraordinary, power, megaprojects, technological egotrips and requires the passive co-operation of the weak and ignorant. It is unable to survive in the face of truth, human solidarity, compassion and non-violent action. (313)

In the midst of Forum '85 on the University of Nairobi campus stood a "Peace Tent," the ultimate symbol of "truth, human solidarity, compassion and nonviolent action." The activities coordinated within the tent became the focus of both the NGO and the official government conference. Outside the big blue and white tent was a huge globe symbolizing our world, our planet. On top of it was the symbol of the UN Women's Decade, and prominently displayed in the many posters and banners hung without and within the tent was the dove of peace. The concept and genius behind the "Peace Tent" (and a full credit for its implementation, programming and staffing) goes to a growing network of international women's peace groups—a network that had begun to build before 1975, and which had strengthened sufficiently during the decade to become the centre of the global consciousness permeating not only the thinking and activities of those representing non-governmental organizations, but also affecting the mindset of the official government delegations. As workshop after workshop documented the spread of the many forms of violence around the globe, violence so well described by Rosalie Bertell, the peace tent activities communicated a sense of hope against the inevitable—a hope summarized as women's alternatives to violence women's ability to heal, to nourish, and to use Sister Rosalie's phrase "to bloom" again.

Canadian women have worked constructively to create a new belief in alternative action. Our presence and activities in Nairobi contributed to an awareness not only that Canadians have given leadership in the past, but also that Canadians must assume even more leadership responsibilities in the future. We are a rich nation, and we are perceived by many nations as a neutral power. While our government does not accept that we are a neutral power, it does at least contend that we are a non-nuclear power. Although many Canadians accept the government's position on neutrality and therefore continue to perceive us as being puppets of the United States, unable to make any decisions independent of American approval, many other people—both in Canada and from a wide number of other nations—perceive us as ideally situated to lead a third group of nations anxious to form an alternative to the world being divided into the confrontational blocks of those aligned with the USA and those aligned with the USSR.

Over and over again women stated the need to go beyond political ideologies, beyond national and racial differences, beyond religious creeds, beyond commercial and economic interests—indeed, beyond all forms of power that dominate, oppress and repress—in order to find alternative systems to those presently propelling us toward disaster. Alternatives can be found, and Canadian women are leading the way.

At Nairobi, Canadian delegates made three very specific contributions. At the NCO levels significant involvement occurred in:

•the Peace Tent and other workshops connected with the final pre-Nairobi Women's International Conference held at Mount Saint Vincent University, Halifax, Nova Scotia on June 5-9, 1985, "The Urgency for True Security: Women's Alternatives for Negotiating Peace";

•in all aspects of women's studies through the distribution of the "International" issue of *Canadian Woman Studies* (Vol. 6, No. 1) at the official UN Conference, and;

•our Canadian delegates to the official UN Conference, led by Maureen O'Neil (Co-ordinator of Status of Women Canada), gave outstanding leadership on the "Forward Looking Strategies" strategies which reflect belief in the capability of the human race to find alternatives, to go beyond negative power struggles.

There was reason for considerable national pride the day the Honourable Walter McLean, Secretary of State, visited the Peace Tent and formally presented Dame Nita Barrow, the Forum Convenor from Barbados, with the statement on peace written and agreed upon by the 350 delegates from 33 countries present at the Women's International Peace Conference in Halifax in June, 1985. This statement reads as follows:

We 350 women of the world community, from 33 countries, meeting at the Women's International Peace Conference in Halifax, Canada, June 5-9, 1985, affirm the overwhelming need and desperate urgency for peace, which we believe is both the process we live and the goal for which we work. At this conference, women from diverse racial, cultural, ethnic and political backgrounds representing different sides of conflict areas, came together as a living example of women negotiating peace. Some of us compromised our own safety to make this commitment.

Although women's voices have not been heard and women have not participated equally in peace negotiations or in formulation of the institutions and the cultural fabric in which we live, we are more than half the world's population; we do have power; and we are shaping it for peaceful living.

We reject a world order based on domination, exploitation, patriarchy, racism and sexism. We demand a new order based on justice and the equitable distribution of the world's resources.

We condemn militarism. Militarism is an addiction that distorts human development, causing worldwide poverty, starvation, pollution, repression, torture and death. Feeding this habit robs all the world's children and future generations of their inheritance.

We all live in the shadow of the threat of nuclear war. We demand an end to research, testing, development, and deployment of all weapons of mass destruction, to the militarization of space and to all forms of violence. As a first step, we call for a comprehensive test ban treaty.

We support the rights and the efforts of all peoples to self-determination and to freedom from military and economic intervention. As an example, we cite Nicaragua as a new kind of society, and as a symbol of hope which must be allowed to live.

We will continue to communicate and join with women all over the world in our struggle for peace. As a result of this conference, we are developing a worldwide women's peace network. Our first act has been to pledge our vigilance in monitoring the ongoing safety of our sisters who are at risk as a result of attending this conference.

We are committed to acting globally, nationally, locally and individually for peace. We will not compromise our commitment to the survival and healing of this planet. We affirm the right of every human being to live with dignity, equality, justice and joy.

While this statement lacks any official Canadian government approval, it is certainly becoming the basis of similar statements coming from the international peace networks. Initiative for the Halifax Conference came largely from the Canadian Voice of Women, who formed a coalition of Canadian women to sponsor the Conference. While Murial Duckworth, Ursula Franklin, Marion Kierans, Kay MacPherson, and many others primarily responsible over the years for women's peace networking in Canada were unable to be in Nairobi, Barbara Roberts, Alice Wiser, and numerous newer peace workers kept alive in Nairobi the fundamental search for alternatives begun at the Halifax Conference. Shelagh Wilkinson distributed hundreds of copies of *Canadian Woman Studies* and the contents of this "International" issue formed the basis of ongoing discussion.

Dorothy Rosenberg from Montreal was indefatigable in her organization of a panel discussion, which I chaired, on "Women's Education for Policy Change Towards Peace and Development." Our three-hour session attracted over 350 delegates who listened attentively (many of them using ear-phones which picked up translations in five languages—English, French, German, Spanish and Swahili). Panelists included the well-known Norwegian feminist Birgit Brock-Utne, peace researcher and educator. Lyse Blanchard, Director of the Women's

Programme for the Government of Canada and without whose help many of us would not have been in Nairobi, gave a feminist's examination of systems analysis on the decision-making process and military thinking. Anne Sisson Runyan, who has also devoted herself to researching international peace issues from a feminist perspective, and Dorothy Rosenberg addressed themselves to questions of how to bring about policy changes, particularly in regard to economic conversion of military budgets to spending on social developments. Carmencita Hernandez spoke for immigrant women and exposed their exploitation in the spiralling militarization of the globe.

Keeping in mind that the world spends one trillion dollars a year on the arms race, it was not surprising that workshops dealing with women's strategies to divert military spending to the basic needs of women and children for clean water, adequate food and shelter were well-attended. Nor is it surprising that more women the world over are coming to realize that educating women just to participate in and become part of the patriarchal and hierarchical structures which are now reinforced by science and technology, will change nothing. Those who espouse a feminist ideology of equality which demands a woman's equal right along with men to a combat role in the military are only assisting in retrenching the militaristic goals of domination which threaten the survival of the planet. Such women are only supporting male systems of violence. Violence used in an effort to stop violence will only breed worse forms of violence. Violence is embedded in much of our modern technology, and the ultimate mega-project, as Ursula Franklin has pointed out, is war. War supposedly is designed to bring about peace, but only new and more sophisticated forms of violence result.

Out of the many heated discussions on the issue of male dominance and male power structures—symbolized by the mega-projects of the multinationals, the banks, and the politically powerful groups—came this growing awareness that if the world is to survive, women must go beyond all political or religious ideologies to form a new kind of world order, one based on a sense of nurturing and conserving, collaboration and cooperation, and not on competitiveness and conquering. As Solange Vincent from Montreal has so clearly stated, "the way ahead for women is not to join in the oppressive structures, but to fight the militaristic aspects of society." According to Mme Vincent, feminists who promote a philosophy of education that supports individual achievement within the concept of the survival of the fittest only fall into the trap of the current male systems. If any policy changes for peace and development, or any alternatives to existing systems of international negotiations are to be found, then women must be educated and given management training that will promote the collective interests of women, and that will espouse values designed to transform society by sharing the world's resources, rather than exploiting them for privilege, power, and profit.

By no means were all of the discussions on peace held in the peace tent, and by no means were they all peaceful. The somewhat turbulent history of the tent began, ironically, over a battle for space. It seems that Coca Cola had determined to set up their red and white tent in the space allocated to the organizers of the

Peace Tent. When the dove of peace flag finally flew *Credit: Nikita A. Crook* over the blue and white peace tent, it signalled that women can negotiate for space and win even against the multi-nationals. At times the debates were so heated that the tent was being dubbed the "war tent," and some Iranian national delegates (well coached by their male attendants) determined to post their banners declaring war as their guiding principle for life. Their war cries interrupted more than one peace session, but their shouts were often drowned out by song and their posters replaced by banners declaring "Women Unite:"

> *And they shall beat their pots and pans into printing presses*
> *And weave their cloth into protest banners*
> *Nations of women shall lift up their voices with nations of other women*
> *Neither shall they accept discrimination any more*
> (Mary Chagnon)

The sense that peace is a subversive activity, however, was apparent by the number of CIA and KGB representatives who seemed always to be lurking nearby. They were in particular evidence when the Russian women debated with the American women. Indeed, the Kenyan Government officials became so nervous of an international incident developing that they determined to close the tent. Dame Nita Barrow demonstrated her metal by declaring that if any such action were taken, she would close the Forum. Peace networking and planning continued without further harassment. Russian and American delegates pledged to work together for joint peace demonstrations.

Edith Ballantyne, General Secretary of the Women's International League for Peace and Freedon (WILPF) stressed the fact that women were the initiators of many new forms of action, such as peace marches, peace camps, schools of peace, and peace studies and research. The Scandinavian women have initiated and organized international peace marches to Paris, and from Stockholm to Moscow and Minsk. In Nairobi the UN Secretary-General Mr. Perez de Cuellar met with women who had participated in "The Great Peace Journey" and encouraged their efforts and plans to visit as many UN countries as possible in 1986 during the UN-sponsored "International Year of Peace." It is most important for women in all countries to support those peace initiatives. They are a genuine alternative to arms talks. The NGOs in the world can create a new basis for international negotiations for disarmament and development. In the long run, the purpose of the peace marches is to create a new security system and a world where nobody goes hungry because we spend millions on armaments.

Women are becoming more comprehending, more conscious. We want to be heard, and that in itself is very different to what has gone on in the past when only men held arms talks behind closed doors. Women must be included on government negotiating teams. Only when women are included at the United Nations and the Geneva talks will a true alternative for negotiating peace emerge. Women are the catalysts for bringing about change, but if we are not heard, not included at international meetings, there will be no change. And as women in the Peace Tent stated over and over again, the real alternative to violence and nuclear war is not to commit such acts.

One of the last major sessions in the Peace Tent was chaired by Fran Hosken, the editor of *WIN* (parts of this session are included in the Autumn 1985 issue, Vol. 11, No. 4). The discussion confirmed that the Peace Movement, the Ecology Movement, and the Feminist Movement are all parts of a fundamental social revolution which is really the only true revolution because women are involved: it is a genuinely different revolution because it is bloodless. No group has done more to demonstrate the effectiveness of non-violent action that the Greenham Common women. The women gathered in Nairobi were there to learn and to share with each other, not to compete with each other. Women's studies and peace studies are opening up new concepts of conflict resolution and demonstrate the need for alternative educational programs at all levels. Non-military solutions to international conflicts must be learned. Much of what was said by Ursula Franklin at the Halifax Conference in June about alternatives was repeated by other women present in Nairobi. Hilkka Pietila, the Secretary-General of the Finnish United Nations Association, reminded us that we must renew efforts to make the UN work:

> *This year we are celebrating the fortieth anniversary of the UN, which provides a good opportunity. We do not need all kinds of additional agreements—all the negotiations about disarmament and arms reductions have only led to increases in the arms race. Peace is the way to Peace, not discussions about arms. The women's peace movement needs to get back to basics; we should not get involved in complicated discussions about different kinds of armaments. That, as the record shows, does not lead to peace. Peace is the only way to peace.*

It is up to women to find the way to peace. What made the experience at Nairobi so exciting and so positive was that the Conference took place in Africa. The women of the world were together for the first time. The Conference in many ways belonged to the African and Asian women. They were there in great numbers, and their rejection of sophisticated Western technology as being of little use in solving their needs, became their statement on peace. Women need good garden tools, not computers. Having their land turned into cash crops—which are used in turn to buy military goods—in no way serves their needs to find nutritious food for their children. As women from all parts of the world shared their problems in Nairobi, the sense of sisterhood and solidarity strengthened. The women of the world were at peace with each other; they can and will find the way to peace for the planet.

Margaret Fulton was a feminist peace activist and President of Mount Saint Vincent University in Halifax.

SARI TUDIVER

Women and Health

A Summary Report From the UN End of Decade for
Women Conference held in Nairobi, Kenya, July 1985

M Y GOALS IN ATTENDING FORUM '85, the non-governmental parallel
event to the UN Conference, were to learn more about the quality
of health care for women in various countries; about how women
are organizing new or alternative services and the problems they face; and to
discuss strategies for lobbying governments to improve legislation and services.
I was attending the Forum on behalf of the Manitoba Council for International
Cooperation (MCIC), a provincial coalition of organizations involved in
international development and social justice work, with a strong commitment
to gender equity. In addition, I was to be the Canadian delegate to Health
Action International (HAI), a network of consumer, development and women's
health groups based in The Netherlands, which promotes the rational use of
pharmaceuticals. I joined a group of women trying to have some small impact
on the official conference through redrafting a section of the Forward-looking
Strategies for the Advancement of Women Document.

THE OFFICIAL CONFERENCE

Amendments to the Forward Looking Strategies Document (FLS) could be
proposed by organizations with observer status at the UN; representatives from
observer NGOs could also speak briefly to an amendment. The International
Organization of Consumers Unions (IOCU), a sponsoring organization of HAI,
was able to put forward our proposals and those of the International Baby Food
Action Network (IBFAN).

I met several times with women from WEMOS (Women and Pharmaceuticals
group from The Netherlands), with IBFAN representatives from Kenya, Trinidad
and Tobago, with women from the Australian Women's Health Network,
Pesticides Action Network, IOCU and others to develop our strategy. Almost
no one had seen a copy of the FLS document prior to coming to Nairobi. We
reviewed the relevant sections pertaining to women's health and the use of
pharmaceuticals in particular.

Paragraph 153 fused trafficking in drugs with therapeutic uses of drugs that, we felt, left the intention ambiguous. Through collective effort we came up with an alternate version. As well, major amendments were proposed for Paragraph 159 that pertained to fertility control methods. We then passed these proposed amendments to members in our official delegations. In my case, I spoke with Muriel Smith, Manitoba Minister Responsible for the Status of Women, and explained the rationale behind our amendments. The proposals were taken to the appropriate committee for consideration, with some success for Paragraph 153 and considerably less for Paragraph 159. The process of trying to change even one paragraph was time-consuming and somewhat frantic. Our proposals would have benefitted from a review of the FLS Document prior to coming to Nairobi. At the same time, the experience was an intense course in identifying key issues, sharpening lobby skills and gaining added insights into the process of compromise and nuance so integral to UN conferences. As a document to which all participating member states gave consensus, the FLS became a useful tool for lobbying national governments and for heightening public awareness on specific issues addressed within it.

FORUM '85 —HEALTH ISSUES

Health was one of the sub-themes of the Decade for Women and a variety of workshops addressed family planning methods; trends in the development of the new reproductive technologies; quality and safety of reproductive health care; primary health care and training of women; maternal and child health; nutrition; women and mental health; traditional practices affecting women and children in Africa; and women and pharmaceuticals (for example, the harms caused by diethylstilbestrol (DES), a drug taken during pregnancy; and by the injectable contraceptive Depo-Provera). Other workshops focused on organizing international women's health networks and coalitions such as the International Baby Food Action Network (IBFAN) and Health Action International. The relations between health and peace were raised, for example, in sessions on the health effects of violence against women and on the impacts of nuclear testing in the Pacific on women's reproductive health. Unfortunately, only a few workshops pertained to women and occupational health.

Health-related workshops which I attended focused on the Quality of Reproductive Health Care (organized by health professionals from Asia, Latin America and Africa); Women and the Pharmaceutical Industry (led by a Norwegian pharmacist); The Uses of Estrogen/Progesterone Drugs Internationally (WEMOS–The Netherlands); Women as Consumers (IOCU and IBFAN); and Building an International Feminist Health Network (Boston Women's Health Collective and ISIS). Other workshops organized by DAWN (Development Alternatives With Women for a New Era) on development strategies also addressed reproductive choice and the links between population and development. In Nairobi I spoke with organizers from DES Action groups and with several doctors and other health workers from Bangladesh, India and Kenya. At the invitation of a Manitoba doctor, I spent several hours visiting a clinic where health workers monitor and treat sexually transmitted diseases among prostitutes. This clinic, located in a poor area of Nairobi, was part of a collaborative study between Kenyatta Hospital and the University of Manitoba focusing on heterosexual transmission of HIV/AIDS.

In this report, I highlight some major areas of concern raised by women in the workshops I attended and some of the initiatives that women are taking to address their health needs:

1) *Women consistently expressed concern about inadequate information on drugs, the inability to make informed choices or a lack of choice at all concerning contraceptives.* Women from the South wanted to have information on what current medical opinion is in countries where drug approval regulations are more stringent and to know what is NOT approved for use elsewhere. They discussed double standards in marketing practices, unethical advertising on the part of pharmaceutical companies, and the drain of precious resources to purchase nonessential drugs or partial doses of essential antibiotics. Women shared stories about increasing use of tranquillizers in their countries and multiple prescriptions. A woman from Senegal spoke of the "good doctor" as one who is seen to prescribe the most medication.

2) *Many women were involved in organizing the delivery of women-centred health services.* Discussion often centred on the need to address the root causes of ill health in poverty and inadequate public health measures. In the last five years women in various countries had organized services to provide better quality care and counseling. While these were isolated efforts, they reflect the attempt of an international women's movement to organize alternative services and develop models of what women would like to see as the norm. The following are a few examples shared by the women:

•A doctor from the Bangladesh Women's Health Coalition described the establishment of six clinics (rural and urban) for women that offer individualized attention and confidentiality, including counseling; take detailed personal histories; provide information on birth control methods and their possible side effects; and use women paramedics. They also help women secure employment. These clinics receive government and NGO funds; some charge modest fees.
•A woman from Colombia discussed how her group organized services for abused women living in slum areas to provide legal advice, family planning information, and help accessing doctors, including those who perform abortions.
•A midwife from Senegal runs a clinic where, she emphasized, "women are treated with respect and have their problems listened to." Young unmarried women can come for information about family planning. There are group meetings to talk about common problems and help

women gain employment. She discussed the special problems of a largely rural country with a very high fertility rate.

Women talked about these initiatives, compared situations, funding problems, community access to services and raised questions about why these projects/services are so marginalized and precarious. They asked: How do women gain access to national planning and priorities regarding health care in order to ensure that their experiences and expertise are taken into account?

3) *The strengths of the Nairobi conference were the possibilities for sharing information and strategies across continents.* Links were formed among groups such as DES Action-Canada, DES-Netherlands and information about DES passed on to women in Latin America and other parts of the world. Information about estrogen/progesterone drugs being used as a supposed abortifacient drew many examples of its use in Europe, Japan, and countries of the South. Information on the recall of the Dalkon Shield intrauterine device and the legal suits brought against its manufacturer A. H. Robins were widely distributed. The fact that Depo Provera was not yetnapproved for use as a contraceptive in the U.S., but was used coercively in South Africa in black women highlighted the political aspects of fertility control.

By 1985, many national and international women's health networks had formed. Of particular note are the Latin American and Caribbean Women's Health Network based in Santiago, Chile; ISIS International, and Women's Global Network on Reproductive Rights, originally based in Amsterdam (now in Manila). Women's health networks in Australia, India, Bangladesh, the UK, U.S. and Canada are particularly active. In addition, Health Action International (www.haiweb.org) has lobbied at the World Health Organization (WHO) for a Code of Marketing Practices for the Drug Industry and in support of extending the WHO Action Programme on Essential Drugs and Vaccines. HAI has a strong focus on women and pharmaceuticals. The Nairobi Conference provided an opportunity to extend these networks and plan further strategies.

Lessons were shared from the successful Nestle boycott and IBFAN campaign that resulted in the WHO International Code of Marketing of Breast-milk Substitutes, approved in 1981. Women at the Forum emphasized that monitoring of the WHO Code and of national practices and policies must continue in order to ensure that the Code is effective in promoting breastfeeding and limiting the marketing of breast milk substitutes.

The women identified strategies of empowerment—how to lobby and exert pressure on politicians and how to mobilize women to deal with health and consumer issues affecting themselves and their families. Hazel Brown, from Trinidad and Tobago, was particularly inspiring:

> *Women have power they don't use. We called ourselves the Housewives Association—what could be more innocent and non-threatening than that? Housewives are not supposed to interfere—right! They are the lowest*

common denominator—a judge and a house worker can be housewives....
In our group, women come in as housewives and go out more aggressive and
knowledgeable about what affects their lives.

Her advice about strategy has relevance for all women working for improved
health care for women:

•Know your facts: sit down in small groups and inform yourselves about
milk, contamination, nutrition; try and link up with experts who can
prove something is wrong.
•Build solidarity among the groups and go after the key man. Make sure if
you plan to hold out outside someone's office that you know who will stay
with all the kids. Track down who the key person is - you always have some
contacts that are useful: someone went to school with his wife or his child
or works for him.
•Build one issue on the other and build on your victories.
•Use different kinds of strategies with different groups. Don't be afraid to ask
and challenge. [They persuaded an ad agency to produce breastfeeding
campaign materials for their group; it became a model campaign.]
•Share your information with others, exchange ideas. [It was in this
way, through contacts with American, Kenyan, and other groups that
lobbying was organized for the WHO Code on Breastmilk Substitutes.]
•If you want to change the world, you have to start with yourself.

Sari Tudiver is a cultural anthropologist with a long-standing passion for improving
women's health. She has worked in academic settings, for international development
and women's health organizations and for the Canadian federal government in health
policy and remains fascinated by the differences in discourse among these sectors. She
was a founding member of the Canadian Women's Health Network and is a board
member of Inter Pares, the Canadian international development NGO. She works as
an independent researcher and writer in Ottawa.

BONNIE KETTEL

Women's Action Agenda 21

New Approaches to Sustainable Development

VANDANA SHIVA SUGGESTS that "maldevelopment" is an inevitable outcome of the "masculine" view of nature that emerged along with the "patriarchal project" of modern science (14-15). My argument draws on the work of John Livingston, who argues that maldevelopment in the South—and over consumption in the North—are the inevitable outcome of a view of nature that he refers to as "resourcismo." The phrase is apt: "resourcismo" refers to an outlook on the natural world that places profits, technology, and men's interests at the centre of development (Kettel; Stamp 1989).

Implicit in this view is the assumption that the significance of nature rests in its exploitation, and that the environment, the life space surrounding us, consists of a multiplicity of resources destined for use in a worldwide quest for economic growth. Evernden points out that, "resources are ... human categories, indices of utility to industrial society." Yet, the predominance of resourcism tempts us to adopt its language and thereby to "enslave" nature and to treat people as "what the bureaucrat unashamedly calls a 'human resource'." Evernden challenges us to critique the assumption that "only utility to industrial society can justify the existence of anything" (10-11).

WOMEN, NATURE AND DEVELOPMENT

The first World Conference on Environment and Development's (WCED) report, Our Common Future, was published in 1987. As a basis for a women, environment, and development research and policy analysis, the approach to sustainable development put forward in the report is a subterfuge. The view that nature—and women—can be "managed" with greater efficiency is central to its sustainable development agenda. The primary goal of Our Common Future is a "new era of economic growth, one ... based on policies to sustain ... the environmental resource base" (WCED 1). The measure of sustainable economic growth is improved "per capita income growth" which has two essential elements: more efficient economic growth and lower population growth. However, the imperatives for sustainable development set forward in Our Common Future are different for the North and the South. The message for the North is to develop "greater efficiency in using materials and energy" (WCED 50-51). The message for the South, for Asia, Africa, and Latin America, where "population growth is now concentrated," is to have fewer children (WCED 99).

With the publication of Our Common Future, women and the environment became an urgent topic for development policy analysis. In response, the United Nations Environment Programme (UNEP) set up a Senior Women's Advisory Group on Sustainable Development (SWAG or SWAGSD).[1] At the same time, funding institutions such as the World Bank (Stone and Molnar), the Food and Agriculture Organization (FAO), and the Canadian International Development Agency (Thompson) began to develop women and environment perspectives and programmes.

These official policy initiatives often reflect the influence of the WCED approach to sustainable development and funder approaches to women and the environment. Indeed, Stone and Molnar speak of "women and resource management." For these authors, the solution to women and the environment issues is increased participation of women in existing programme and project initiatives. Policy initiatives conceptualized through the WCED approach, however, tend to "manage" women as a "human resource" for "sustainable development." One of the African projects presented as a success at the Global Assembly of Women and Environment described later offers an example:

> With the assistance of village leaders, the project was organized ... with mostly young people and women participating.... The project involved the collection of stones to fill the gullies, and the planting of trees and grass to prevent erosion.... The projects are accomplished in a very orderly fashion. The Chief beats the gong to inform citizens about the prevailing problem.... Decisions made are channeled through unit leaders.... Unit leaders inform their people of the days set for communal labour.... Deviant citizens are fined. The most beneficial aspects of this project are that it prevents buildings from collapsing and helps maintain the fertility of the soil.... (UNEP and WorldWIDE)

But what does this apparently successful environmental rehabilitation project, that makes efficient use of women's labour, contribute to women's personal benefit, or authority as environmental decision-makers? My view is that, without explicit support for women and their legitimate environmental interests, no initiative or activity should be funded or recognized as a "women and environment" project.

In the 1980s, women and environment became an important focus for broader feminist participation in policy formulation and political action. The Women in Development and Environment WorldWIDE Network was founded in 1982 as an international non-governmental organization (NGO) made up of women "concerned about environmental management and protection," and the education of "the public and its policy makers about the vital linkages between women, natural resources and sustainable development" (WorldWIDE, 1991a: 7, 8). Together with SWAG, WorldWIDE organized four regional assemblies in Harare, Tunis, Bangkok, and Quito on women and the environment in preparation for the 1992 United Nations Conference on Environment and Development (UNCED, also known as the Earth Summit).

The policy dilemmas inherent in a resourcist approach to women and the environment were apparent at the African Women's Assembly in Harare. The impetus and organization for the event stemmed ultimately from UNEP and SWAG, with the assistance of WorldWIDE, and personnel from the International Union for the Conservation of Nature (IUCN). The event was also supported by the Zimbabwe Ministry of Natural Resources, which was at that time led by Minister Victoria Chitepo, a prominent member of SWAG. Each of the agencies participating at the Assembly had its own agenda for the meeting, which overlapped only partially with those of the other organizers. This ambiguous, top-down approach had the goal of empowering African women, especially rural women, in the quest for sustainable development.

Not surprisingly, given its UNEP-SWAG origins, the Assembly's deliberations were organized by a resourcist view of the sustainable development agenda. Workshops, which included members of SWAG, representatives of various donor institutions, women and environment consultants and advocates, and a number of village women from rural Zimbabwe, were based on resource zones or sectors: Forests and Woodlands, Deserts and Arid Lands, Rivers and Lake Basins, and Seas (Loudiyi, Nagle and Ofosu-Amaah). As a result, issues arising from women's involvements with the natural environment were marginalized and distorted. The overall result was confusion and contradiction in the structure of the Assembly, the discussions at the workshops, and the initial outcome of the workshop deliberations.

The four regional assemblies led to the "Global Assembly of Women and the Environment," held in Miami in 1991. The Global Assembly, which was jointly sponsored by UNEP and WorldWIDE, was part of the official background deliberations for UNCED. It focused on 218 success stories of women's grassroots involvements with regard to four key environmental concerns: water, waste, energy, and environmentally-friendly technology. Despite the resource frame that limited the organization and much of the dialogue of these assemblies, they were crucial in the emergence of feminist environmentalism at a global level. They brought women together, regionally and internationally, and provided a forum for discussion of women's environmental dilemmas and insights. They also provided visible recognition of the leadership role that women from the South, including women from rural communities, have to play in challenging the maldevelopment of the present and reformulating policy for the future. Stressing that women's full participation is essential for achieving sustainable development, the Global Assembly recommended that "the needs and views of women must be incorporated in the establishment of priorities in the management of human and natural resources" and that "women should also be involved in setting priorities..." (WorldWIDE 1991b: 5-6).

Many of the most active feminist participants in the Global Assembly also participated in the unofficial World Women's Congress for a Healthy Planet,which was held immediately afterward in the same city to take advantage of the funding that brought so many activists together for the global assembly.

The second gathering was organized autonomously by feminist non-governmental groups and global networks led by the Women Environment and Development Organization (WEDO). It brought together 1,500 participants from 84 countries around the world. The conference dialogue and decisions reflected and consolidated a deeply transformative women-centred consensus that had been developing among women over previous decades of regional and issue based networking and United Nations gatherings. The "Women's Action Agenda 21", produced following the conference as a collective statement and preparatory guide for engagement with the UN Conference on Environment and Development (UNCED) coming up in Rio de Janeiro in 1992, pledges the participants to "the empowerment of women, the central and powerful force in the search of equity between and among the peoples of the Earth and for a balance between them and the life support systems that sustain us all" (WEDO 16). It is a call for feminist collaboration in environmental action that goes far beyond the scope of the women and environment agenda established within the institutional policy framework for sustainable development put forward by WCED or by the UNCED. The inspiring Preamble of "Women's Action Agenda 21" opens this volume, Vandana Shiva's statement at the Congress, "The Seed and the Earth," appears in Part I and Statements produced by the Southern, Indigenous and North American caucuses at the Congress follow this article.

At the Global Forum, an international gathering of environmental activists and NGOs held in Rio de Janeiro in parallel with the official UN Conference on Environment and Development, the official UNCED position on sustainable development was roundly criticized. Several alternative NGO treaties and points of view were proposed, but "the most striking area of common ground" was "the strong criticism of the existing models and practices of development" and "the broad agreement that current strategies of development were unjust, inequitable and unsustainable" (ING 2). The official global action plan adopted at UNCED in Rio de Janeiro in 1992, is titled "Action Agenda 21." Its position on women and environment is contained in Chapter 24 (WorldWIDE 1992:5-7). Chapter 24 was a great leap forward for the institutionalization of women and environment policy internationally, and nationally on the part of signatory governments. Nevertheless, it is limited by the resourcism of the WCED approach to sustainable development, and also by the structural inertia of official policy formulation. Thus, one of the objectives proposed for national governments is "to consider developing and issuing by the year 2000 a strategy of changes necessary to eliminate constitutional, legal, administrative, cultural, behavioural, social and economic obstacles to women's full participation in sustainable development and in public life" (WorldWIDE 1992: 5). Without local and international organization and collaboration, how many signatory governments will move forward with this objective?

In this context, the significance of the "Women's Action Agenda 21" is the potential it represents for collaborative support, within nations and globally, not only for the implementation of Chapter 24, but also for a vibrant new feminist environmentalism. The Women's Action Agenda 21 is the manifesto for an emerging political alliance among feminist environmentalists at a variety of institutional levels: political activists, NGO workers, scholars and policy analysts, and women from nations and local communities across the planet. Within this new alliance, there is one immediate task: the elaboration of a conceptual framework that will facilitate well-informed policy and programme support for the goals of the "Women's Action Agenda 21."

CONCLUSION

The WCED approach to sustainable development is centred in a view of nature that is implicitly culture-bound and male-biased. Although Our Common Future and the UNCED Agenda 21 do represent an important opening for policy initiatives addressing secure livelihoods and the protection of biodiversity, these documents, and the policy approaches that stem from them, fail to challenge our view of nature as a "resource" to be "managed" for the pursuit of profit in global development. A central task for women and environment research, I suggest, is to document women's landscapes and the challenges to women's images of the natural environment and styles of environmental decision-making that are implicit in externally-imposed agendas, even in the guise of sustainable development.

It is in this context of practical environmental interests that women mobilize their styles of environmental decision-making and develop particular strategies for environmental use and protection. As for issues, the co-ordinators of twelve women, development and environment networks who met in Amsterdam following the UNCED Conference agreed to focus their future collaborative efforts on alternative economics, the protection of biodiversity, climate change, and global trade as key policy arenas for women, environment, and development in the lead-up to the 1995 World Women's Congress in Beijing. As the Canadian Coordinator of one of the twelve networks, I add a final note: there is no hope in subterfuge.

This article was written following the World Women's Congress for a Healthy Planet held in Miami in 1991.

Bonnie Kettel is now an Associate Professor Emeritus of the Faculty of Environmental Studies at York University. She was the Canadian Co-ordinator for the Women, Environment and Development Network (WEDNET), a large scale research initiative focusing on African women's Indigenous knowledge of natural resource management. Subsequently she became the first Co-ordinator of the Gender Advisory Board of the UN Commission on Science and Technology for Development. Most recently, she participated in the founding of the York Climate Consortium, including the development of a research proposal for an interdisciplinary approach to satellite-based Arctic climate assessment.

[1]SWAG included members from Kenya (Margaret Kenyatta and Wangari Maathai), Somalia (Hawa Aden), Zimbabwe (Victoria Chitepo), France (Simone Veil), Finland (Air a Kalela), Hungary (Eva Szilagyi), UK (Fiona McConnell), Colombia (Margarita Marina deBotero), Ecuador (Yolanda Kakabadse), Egypt (Shafika Nasser), Jordan (Eideh Mustapha Mutlag Qanah), Tunisia (Hedia Baccar), India (Sheila Dikshit), Indonesia (Soepardjo Roestam), Phillipines (Veronica Villavicencio), and Thailand (Khunying Ambhorn Meesook). Joan Martin-Brown of UNEP was an ex-officio member of SWAG.

REFERENCES

International NGO Forum (ING). Abstract of the Treaties. Rio de Janeiro: ING, June 1992.

Loudiyi, Dounia, B. Nagle and W. Ofosu-Amaah. *The African Women's Assembly: Women and Sustainable Development.* Washington: WorldWIDE, 1989.

Stone, Andrew and Augusta Molnar. "Issues: Women and Natural Resource Management." Paper presented to the Work Program on the Economics of Resource Management. Washington, DC: World Bank, August 1986.

Thompson, Patricia. "Environment and Women: Opportunities for Improved Development." Paper for the Environment Sector. Ottawa: CIDA, 1987.

United Nations Environment Program (UNEP) and WorldWIDE. Global Assembly of Women and Environment: "Partners in Life." Washington, DC: WorldWIDE, 1991.

Women's Environment and Development Organization (WEDO). *Official Report: World Women's Congress for a Healthy Planet.* New York: WEDO, 1992.

World Commission on Environment and Development (WCED). *Our Common Future.* Oxford: Oxford University Press, 1987.

WorldWIDE, "Interview with Joan Martin Brown." WorldWIDE News 9 (2) (1991a): 1, 7-8.

WorldWIDE. Global Assembly of Women and the Environment. Final Report. Washington, DC: WorldWIDE, 1991b.

WorldWIDE. "Gender and Environment: Beyond UNCED." Global Assembly of Women and the Environment. Special Report No. 3.

INTERNATIONAL INDIGENOUS WOMEN'S CAUCUS STATEMENT

As Indigenous people our lives are intertwined with the natural world. Our creation stories tell of our emergence in traditional homelands, which continue to nurture and give meaning to our lives. We are inseparable from the lands in which as we as peoples were created.

We view our responsibilities to care for the Earth as our mother. As Indigenous peoples, we are witnessing the destruction of our sacred Mother earth. She is being raped as the forests are clear-cut, gouged in the search for minerals, poisoned by radioactive and chemical waste, and we as her children are being destroyed in the ruthless search to seize her precious gifts for human consumption. The suffering and pain of Mother Earth is felt by us as if it were our own. She is being destroyed, as we are being destroyed, at a rate in which it is impossible for healing and renewal.

As Indigenous peoples, we have lived in our traditional homelands for tens of thousands of years in harmony and balance with all of the natural world. We believe that all living things were given life by the Creator, and such we are all co-equal beings sharing the gifts of our sacred Mother Earth. We are dependent upon her for our sustenance, interdependent on one another for the fulfillment of our lives, and interconnected with each other spiritually and physically. The Creator gave us natural laws to instruct us in the way in which we must live in harmony and balance with all of life, taking only what is required for our survival and acknowledging these many gifts of life which were given so that we might live.

Today we face the destruction of the human spirit and the consequent destruction of the natural world. In order to cease this destruction, it is incumbent upon all human beings to:

•Recognize that all human actions, laws, and policies must be informed by an ethic based upon adherence to the laws of the natural world that govern creation and which are embodied in the spiritual traditions of Indigenous peoples;

•Include a long-range perspective in our ethic that insures a positive impact on the next generation of all living things;

•Recognize that honouring and protecting the diversity of life must include not only the plant and animal world but also the diversity of peoples and the spirituality, cultures, and ways of life inherent within;

•Recognize that all of life is sacred, co-equal, and entitled to existence apart from any relationship to human beings;

•Protect the rights of Indigenous peoples to our homelands and ways of live to insure our continuation as peoples living in the manner in which we were instructed by the Creator;

•Reflect the love of the creator in our lives, be mindful of our impact upon all living things and make clear choices that support life rather than destroy it.

The true challenge of human beings it to place our full attention upon ways in which we can live upon Mother Earth in a manner consistent with natural law and in peace, harmony, and a balance with all things.

Regional Caucus Statement from the World Women's Congress for a Healthy Planet (reprinted from "Women's Action Agenda 21," the Congress Report).

STATEMENT FROM THE WOMEN OF THE SOUTH CAUCUS

We, the women of the South, affirm that equity and justice must be the guiding principle between men and women, among communities and among nations, for a healthy people and a healthy planet.

We believe that people have the right to sustainable livelihoods: material, spiritual, cultural, ecological and political.

We condemn the alienation of people from land, especially the Indigenous peoples, the poor and women.

We recognize the overconsumption, which underpins the lifestyles of the North and the elite of the South, is a central element of the Western development model. Further, that this overconsumption reinforces poverty in the South and is a major factor in the degradation and depletion of the earth's resources, which are finite. We demand an end to overconsumption.

We take cognizance of the fact that the debt burden imposed by the North through the IMF, the World Bank and other international financial agencies imposes crippling conditions on the poor of the South, of whom women are the majority. Furthermore, it exacerbates environmental degradation. We demand an end to the debt burden. We further condemn the "debt-for-nature" swap which gives the North the rights to control the natural resources of the South.

We recognize that the present imbalances in international trade must be rectified. We reject all attempts to patent the genetic resources of our earth and attempts to claim monopoly rights over them.

We condemn the present structural adjustment policies dictated by the North, which have intensified poverty in the South and increased the burdens on women and the poor.

We condemn coercive population control strategies which violate both women's bodies and their human rights.

We affirm the need for peace and disarmament and an end to militarism as essential requirements of a healthy planet. Military and nuclear testing, which is often carried out in the South, and in regions of marginalized people in the North, must end.

We demand an end to the dumping of hazardous and toxic wastes, unsafe pharmaceutical and agricultural and consumer products by countries in the North to those in the South.

We urge greater South-South dialogue and cooperation, particularly among women of our countries, in the search for common solutions to common human and environmental problems.

Long live solidarity of Women of the World.

Regional Caucus Statement from the World Women's Congress for a Healthy Planet (reprinted from "Women's Action Agenda 21," the Congress Report).

NORTH AMERICAN REGIONAL CAUCUS REPORT

We North American women are living in nations in which overconsumption by some co-exists which poverty and social deprivation for many and ecological degradation for all; and in which women and children everywhere are threatened physically as well as economically.

We join with our sisters from the South in rejecting the world market economic and social order, which is promoted, protected and sustained by both military might and military protection.

We particularly support changes which contribute to:

•An equalizing redefinition and redistribution of power and resources within and between nations and regions;

•A shift in the exploitative and hierarchical relations among and between peoples and the planet;

•A basic redefinition of such concepts as power, human rights, wealth, work and progress, in terms which recognize and reaffirm the value of women, nature and indigenous peoples;

•The demilitarization of our economies and our cultures in order to free our creative genius for a more humane and renewable planet.

We see all these as necessary parts of a process in which the knowledge, values, wisdom and vision of women around the world can shape the priorities of ways of being in the world.

The following is a partial list of the issues and action proposals of the North American Caucus as presented by Dianne Dillon-Ridgley at the final plenary session of the World Women's Congress:

•We pledge mutual support to stop all forms of genocide among indigenous people and recognize all aboriginal and indigenous rights to land and sovereignty.

•We vigorously oppose "Free Trade Agreements" that destroy the environment and exploit cheap labour and natural resources. We will work to hold transnational corporations liable for damage to our environment in our courts.

•We call for mutual cooperation among all UNCED participants to ensure that the safety of street children in Brazil will be in no way jeopardized by our presence there.

•We vigorously call for an end to environmental racism, which is the dumping, siting or placement of environmentally hazardous substances or facilities in the communities of colour in North America and around the world, primarily because of race and powerlessness of peoples in those communities.

•We call for immediate, negotiated, Comprehensive Test Ban Treaty.

Regional Caucus Statement from the World Women's Congress for a Healthy Planet (reprinted from "Women's Action Agenda 21," the Congress Report).

CHARLOTTE BUNCH, MALLIKA DUTT AND SUSANA FRIED

Beijing '95

A Global Referendum on the Human Rights of Women

ONE OF THE MOST STRIKING ASPECTS of the Fourth World Conference on Women in Beijing was the way in which it focused world attention on the human rights of women. Women's human rights permeated debates at both the official United Nations inter-governmental Conference and at the parallel non-governmental organizations (NGO) Forum held 80 kilometres away in Huairou: in the speeches given by many heads of delegations, including Hillary Rodham Clinton's adoption of the theme "women's rights are human rights"; in the vehement opposition on the part of some governments to what they called the "creation of new rights" in the Platform for Action; in the many workshops and demonstrations at the NGO Forum and in the efforts of the Chinese security to contain that event.

That global focus on women's human rights was accompanied by an insistence that all issues are women's issues and that women's equality, development, and peace cannot be discussed in isolation from the global economic, political, and cultural forces rapidly re-shaping the world. Thus, as a "post-Cold War" conference, major divisions that had marked earlier women's conferences, such as divisions between northern and southern women over what were women's issues or over Israel and Palestine, were replaced by political differences over issues like the global economy or the role of religion. And these debates crossed geographical and cultural boundaries.

The challenge for women's movements in Beijing was to forge a coherent approach that would both accommodate a range of diverse views and provide enough unity to face down those who sought to utilize the event as a way to counter feminism and the growing influence of women in global debates. The idea that this Conference was about defending and promoting the human rights of women provided just such a cohesive umbrella for many. That women succeeded not only in holding the line on gains from previous world conferences but also in advancing on some issues and in creating new networks and strategies in the process is a testament to the fortitude of women. It is also a sign of hope for the future. That we succeeded in the face of well-financed opposition from major religious forces, indifference, and lack of adequate funding on the part of the UN, a host country uncomfortable with non-governmental organizations, frequent competition among NGOs, and some governments that were either antagonistic or seeking to co-opt women is almost a miracle.

But this miracle did not come out of nowhere. In the ten years between the World Conference on Women in Nairobi in 1985 and Beijing, the global women's movement has become a force to contend with. At the Nairobi Conference, women from third world countries demonstrated that they were creating vibrant local feminist movements offering new perspectives on many issues which also provided the basis for solid global networks to develop. This networking has forcefully emerged in the cross-cultural alliances formed to influence recent UN world conferences.

In 1992 at the Rio Earth Summit, women won acknowledgment of their critical role in sustaining the environment. In Vienna in 1993, at the World Conference on Human Rights, women gained recognition of women's rights as human rights and of violence against women as a human rights issue. At the Cairo International Conference on Population and Development in 1994, women confronted abusive population policies and lobbied for a Declaration that recognized the centrality of women's empowerment in population and development policy. At the 1995 World Summit on Social Development in Copenhagen, women forced governments to acknowledge the devastating impact of economic policies on women and to commit to involving them in efforts to eradicate poverty.

Participation in international arenas has enabled women from diverse regions to define common agendas and to formulate coordinated strategies for lobbying governments. Corresponding dialogue at the NGO Forums has intersected with lobbying strategies and allowed women to air differences, to elaborate new ideas, and to deepen links with one another. Women have also strengthened networks through electronic mail, newsletters, telephones, faxes, meetings, and other events—all of which have been used to expand alliances, negotiate differences, mobilize coordinated actions, and confront governments and international institutions.

The connections made among women from 1985 to 1995 were reflected in women's actions even before they arrived in Beijing. For over two years, women organized at the local, national, regional, and international level to influence this Conference. In unprecedented numbers, they participated in regional preparatory meetings, held numerous NGO events, and formed coalitions to give voice to diverse concerns. At the two UN international preparatory meetings held in New York, caucuses formed on topics ranging from human rights to peace and economic justice as well as around constituencies like lesbians and older women. Many of these caucuses included networks with experience at previous world conferences. They converged in the Linkage Caucus, a sort of caucus of caucuses, which sought to develop agreed upon NGO proposals for the Platform.

The world learned about the strength of women's global connections when the Chinese government moved the NGO Forum out of Beijing and sought to isolate it in Huairou. UN Secretary-General Boutros Boutros-Ghali's office was flooded with calls, faxes, petitions, and letters from around the world. Women engaged in a global conversation about strategies to ensure an adequate site while simultaneously debating whether to boycott the Forum. The alacrity with which women responded to calls for action and the numbers who entered the debate reflected how seriously women took this event. Understanding the need for global solidarity, women decided to show strength of the movement by attending, in spite of the obstacles posed by the site. Over 38,000 people registered for, and at least 30,000 attended the Forum, making this the largest UN gathering in history.

NGO FORUM

Women's determination to do their work was reflected in the dialogue and networking that took place in Huairou despite logistical problems created by rain, the Forum's disorganization, harassment by Chinese and other government agents, and the overwhelming size of the event. The story that too often did not make it into the press was how, despite difficult conditions, women succeeded in holding their events, learning from each other, and building their movements.

The Forum included a plethora of some 3,000 events that served to educate, involve, and inspire at many levels. Women's rights as human rights was a palpable presence throughout. Banners and posters demanding recognition of women's human rights were visible at every turn, and the program listed hundreds of workshops related to the topic. Panels encompassed the human rights dimensions of everything from structural adjustment programs to education, health, sexuality, and violence against women. Migrant women highlighted human rights violations by countries of the North; comfort women demanded increased accountability from the Japanese government for World War II human rights abuses; lesbians insisted on recognition of the human right to control one's sexuality; and women from East Timor, Tibet, Rwanda, and the former Yugoslavia utilized human rights concepts to describe violations of women in conflict situations. Sessions also addressed international legal instruments and UN agencies and mechanisms, examining their utility in advancing women's human rights.

Among the multitude of issues discussed, certain themes resonated across regions. The prevention of violence against women in all its forms was clearly of great urgency as was advancing women's health and reproductive rights. Other priorities included reversing the negative impact of international economic policies, countering the rise of religious and secular conservatism, and giving women a greater voice in policy making.

The global dialogue about violence against women ranged from discussions of private acts of incest and domestic abuse to state violence in conflict situations and military prostitution. Women's determination to end all forms of violence is reflected in the transformation of this issue from Nairobi to Beijing. Ten years ago, governments had only begun to acknowledge domestic violence and rape as social problems in the Forward-Looking Strategies. By the 1993 World Conference on Human Rights, women had organized a global campaign and tribunal that politically positioned violence against women in its many forms squarely on the international human rights agenda.

Tribunals, panels, workshops, and demonstrations held at the Forum revealed the enormous burden violence places on women's lives and how different constituencies like immigrants and refugees, or ethnic, racial, and religious minorities, Indigenous, lesbian, disabled, or older women experience specific forms of violence. Thus, women have moved from making this issue visible to demanding accountability for it from governments and the UN. As Pierre Sane, Secretary-General of Amnesty International and one of the Judges at the Global Tribunal organized by the Center for Women's Global Leadership in Huairou put it,

> What we want for governments is not simply to give their assent to the need to protect and promote women's human rights in yet another piece of paper. If it is to achieve anything, the Beijing Conference must be ... a genuine catalyst for action and the swift delivery of real protection. (Global Tribunal on Accountability for Women's Human Rights)

The pressure that women's organizing in this area has put on governments was evident when it emerged as a priority at all the regional preparatory meetings. In the Beijing Platform, the eradication of violence against women was one of the least controversial objectives and governments acknowledged that it was a state responsibility which called for more action. A Worldwide Campaign to End Violence Against Women was launched by the United Nations Development Fund for Women (UNIFEM) with several NGOs and a number of governments who made concrete commitments to work on this issue. Many agreed to meet with NGOs when they return home to develop national plans of action against gender-based violence.

The impact on women of the globalization of the world economy was another central concern at the Forum. Women from North America and Western Europe discussed economic restructuring with its cutbacks in social services and health care in ways that echoed the devastation of structural adjustment policies described by women from the Third World. And the new voices of women from Eastern Europe and the former Soviet Union that emerged at this Conference also reported their negative experiences in the transition to market economies. In sharp contrast to Nairobi where this issue was divided more on North-South lines, women from all regions saw international economic and trade policies as placing increasing burdens on them. Still, women from the South tended to understand the economy as connected to other problems like violence against women, while northern women more often approached these as separate issues.

Despite broad consensus among many NGOs and documentation of how economic globalization is harming women, governments were not willing to address this topic substantially. The Beijing Platform does acknowledge the negative impact of structural adjustment and calls for recognition that women's unwaged work constitutes a large percentage of national economies. But no effort was made to address the causes of these problems and governments remain engaged in practices that perpetuate them.

Another issue that resonated with women from all over the world was the danger posed by the backlash against feminism and the growing power of secular and religious conservatism. Discussion of how to counter these forces politically was interwoven with intense conversation about culture, religion, ethnicity, and nationality in women's lives. While there was resistance to the ideologies of religious fundamentalists and the secular right, passionate debates took place about whether women should organize within religious frameworks or from entirely secular space.

Such questions of identity politics formed a sub-text throughout the Forum. Many wanted to affirm their distinct identities around race, ethnicity, nationality, religion, age, sexual orientation, disabilities, etc. and to identify areas where their perspectives or problems were often ignored. Some of the tents based on region and diverse identities became lively arenas serving this purpose. Of particular note was the mobilization of disabled women who faced extraordinarily difficult conditions at the Forum and utilized these to educate women about the issue. Nevertheless, many did not want to be isolated in a group based only on identity and sought to bring identity based perspectives into other issues. The struggle to recognize differences while also finding areas of commonality was a recurring theme throughout the Forum, as it is in women's movements locally.

Women from regions torn by ethnic or religious warfare discussed their responsibilities in the conflicts and often sought to go beyond nationalistic divisions. For example, feminists from countries of the former Yugoslavia met frequently, ate, sang, and protested together; then they formed a network to continue contact across national divisions even though the war often makes this difficult. The Women in Blackvigil at the Forum spoke loudly with its large numbers of diverse women—often from countries at war with each other— gathered together in silence to protest male warfare and domination around the world. Again, the transformation of the movement from Nairobi to Beijing was evident. In Nairobi, conflicts between women often degenerated into screaming matches. In Beijing, many women negotiated painful divisions with respect, even if not agreement, which underscored the urgent need for more women in positions of power if the world is to move toward peace.

Sessions at the Forum dealt with many other topics, such as political participation, health and reproductive rights, literacy and women's studies, media and communications, appropriate technologies, etc. Many of these included human rights questions, such as what conditions are necessary for women to be able to fully exercise their human rights and how to establish government accountability in a time of growing privatization. Overall there was recognition that women must address all aspects of life, not just woman-specific topics as some had argued in previous UN women's conferences. Indeed many sought transformation of the global debates of our day, building on women's organizing at the Rio, Vienna, Cairo, and Copenhagen Conferences. In part, this requires that women both enter mainstream debates, such as that represented by the government Conference, as well as challenge its premises. Many who attended the governmental Conference, which began midway through the NGO Forum, sought to bring the challenging discussions and the strength of women's presence in Huairou to that arena in Beijing.

THE UNITED NATIONS INTER-GOVERNMENTAL CONFERENCE

The governmental Conference in Beijing was mandated to produce a consensus Platform for Action that would implement the goals set forth in 1985 in the Nairobi Forward-Looking Strategies and advance the Conference themes of "action for equality, development, and peace." Over 4,000 NGO delegates who were accredited to that Conference lobbied, as many had at the regional and international preparatory meetings, to get our perspectives reflected there. Human rights language permeated both the Beijing Declaration and the Platform for Action agreed to by all 189 governments present.

The women's human rights caucus was a collaboration of NGOs who lobbied government delegates around human rights throughout the negotiations on the Platform for Action. The caucus grew out of the success of the Global Campaign for Women's Human Rights at the 1993 World Conference on Human Rights in Vienna and built on both global and regional alliances developed with other caucuses in Cairo and Copenhagen, as well as during the two-year preparatory process for Beijing. In addition, a number of governmental delegations included feminists and women involved in both health and human rights networking over the past few years who promoted these concepts from the inside. The distance from the NGO Forum in Huairou made it difficult for many women who wanted to lobby during the first week to get to the government Conference. Nevertheless, caucus efforts were strengthened by the high visibility of women's human rights activities at the NGO Forum and especially by activities that brought the spirit of the Forum to Beijing, such as the delivery to the UN High Commissioner for Human Rights of over one million signatures to a world-wide petition demanding that the UN act urgently to promote and protect women's human rights.

The combined effect of all these activities was a groundswell of support for making the entire Platform a document about the human rights of women, including women's right to education, food, health, and freedom from violence, as well as to the exercise of citizenship in all its manifestations. Previous UN women's conferences were seen as primarily about women and development or women's rights rather than being about human rights. This expansion of what is generally considered to be "human rights," and its usage to frame a wider set of women's concerns reflects organizing done over the past several years.

In this sense, Beijing saw the mainstreaming of women's human rights. Previously, women had to make the case that our issues are a legitimate part of the international human rights agenda. In Huairou and Beijing, this legitimacy was assumed. The incorporation of human rights language into their work by governments and women's organizations from all regions indicates more than a rhetorical gesture. It signals a shift in analysis that moves beyond single-issue politics and identity-based organizing, and enhances our capacity to build global alliances based on collective political goals and a common agenda. Moreover, since human rights has legitimacy amongst many governments, the appeal to human rights agreements and international norms can fortify women's organizing.

Overall, the Platform asserted the universal and holistic nature of the human rights of women. Specific language and commitments that human rights advocates gained in Beijing include the reaffirmation and extension of commitments to promote and protect women's human rights, including the right to be free from violence, the right to sexual and reproductive health free from discrimination or coercion, access to information about sexual and reproductive health care, equal rights to inheritance for women and girls—although not the "right to equal inheritance," and the obligation of governments to pursue and punish perpetrators of rape and sexual violence against women and girls in situations of armed conflict as war crimes. Universal government ratification of the Convention on the Elimination of All Forms of Discrimination Against Women (CEDAW) and limiting reservations to it were urged, along with consideration of an optional protocol to strengthen its implementation. In this process, commitments to women from previous conferences were maintained, and even expanded in the cases of: protection of human rights activists; the acknowledgement that systematic rape during armed conflict is a war crime, and in some cases a crime against humanity; the recognition of the right of women to have control over their sexual and reproductive health; that parental rights must be qualified to ensure they respect privacy and access to information by adolescents and children; and the importance of system-wide integration of women's human rights throughout the UN.

However, clear gaps remain in the official Platform for Action. This is most evident in the lack of strong interaction between development and human rights discourses. As the sub-group on women's economic rights noted, the human rights section of the Platform reflects largely a concern for women's individual rights rather than the collective, systemic, or development rights associated with women's economic concerns, particularly around globalization, economic restructuring, and structural adjustment. Similarly, there is not adequate discussion of the relationship between human rights and peace and militarism. Even within the standard rubric of human rights, there were some disturbing losses: no explicit reference to sexual rights or sexual orientation; the replacement of explicit references to race and ethnicity with "demographic factors" in some sections; the use of "Indigenous people" rather than the term "peoples"; and weak language about the various form of "family."

Some major controversies illustrate both what women gained and the limitations of the Platform. For example, in the contested area of sexual rights, many thought it could not be won and the phrase per se was rejected. However, these boundaries were expanded in the health section of the Platform which states in Paragraph 97 that the human rights of women include their right to have control over and decide freely and responsibly on matters related to their sexuality, including sexual and reproductive health, free of coercion, discrimination, and violence.

Similarly, explicit support for the rights of lesbians and the term "sexual orientation" were excluded from the document in final late night negotiations. Nevertheless, the door was opened with this first open discussion of the issue in the UN, which also exposed the virulence of homophobia among those who manipulate it to oppose women's human rights generally. At least some governments in each region supported the issue, and a number stated that their interpretation of the prohibition of discrimination on the basis of "other status" in several human rights documents applies to lesbians and gays.

Another major debate centred on the term "universal" and the use of religion and culture to limit women's human rights. Women sought to maintain the Vienna World Conference on Human Rights' recognition that women's human rights are universal, inalienable, indivisible, and interdependent. The Vatican, its supporter states, and some Muslim governments attempted unsuccessfully to limit the extent of universal application of women's human rights. However, they used this debate to claim that there is a feminist imperialism that reflects disrespect for religion and culture, an over-zealous individualism, and an effort to impose western values which destroy the family and local communities. This isn't a new debate, but more thought must go into how to argue for universality of rights without implying homogenization, especially around religion and culture, aspects of which can also be positive for some women.

Of course, each movement forward for women was met with resistance. For instance, 19 states entered reservations to text that was not in conformity with Islamic law, particularly references to reproductive health and rights, inheritance, sexuality, and abortion. The Holy See put forward their interpretation of much of the Platform, especially the Health and Human Rights sections, as expressing "exaggerated individualism." The extensive reservations on religious and cultural grounds reflect ongoing debates about the human rights of women which could not have been resolved in Beijing but they do lay out the contours of future collaborations and confrontations.

In the critical area of implementation and resources, the promises of the Platform are not backed up with adequate commitments from either governments or the UN. While the Platform includes strong language about gender integration and coordination within the UN, these are rarely assigned to specific agencies or actors, and there is little clarity about which institutional tasks are the responsibility of whom. The idea of making this a conference of commitments was proposed by Australia and promoted by many NGOs, but did not get widespread government acceptance. NGOs nevertheless kept track of commitments referred to in government speeches, and these can form a basis for demanding accountability from our governments.

Throughout the Platform, paragraphs call for re-evaluation of all policies using gender analysis which might ultimately lead to a fundamentally different way of constructing programs, and certainly provides guidance for action. Paragraph 297 notes that states should, as soon as possible, develop strategies to implement the Platform. Member states should be reminded of this as the next stage begins of translating the Platform into concrete strategies and ensuring that its promises are carried forward. How much the Platform for Action advances women's human rights ultimately depends on how much women are able to use it to further their efforts to influence policy and action at all levels from the local to the global. For now, it provides us with a global affirmation that the rights of women are human rights and that they are in urgent need of world attention.

This article has been reprinted with permission from the Women's Health Journal, *Numbers 3,4 (March-April 1995) (Santiago, Chile). Reprinted with permisson.*

Charlotte Bunch, Founding Director and Senior Scholar, Center for Women's Global Leadership (CWGL), Rutgers University, is an author and organizer in feminist and human rights movements. Distinguished Professor in Women's and Gender Studies, she directed CWGL for 20 years, leading their path-breaking work on women rights as human rights, the 16 Days of Activism Against Gender Violence Campaign, Women's Global Leadership Institutes, and advocacy at the United Nations including the GEAR Campaign for the creation of UN Women.

Mallika Dutt is the Founder and Director of Breakthrough for Human Rights based in India and the United States.

Susana Fried works for the United Nations Development Program HIV/AIDS office.

REFERENCES

Global Tribunal on Accountability for Women's Human Rights. NGO Forum. Sept. 1995.

United Nations. Nairobi Forward-Looking Strategies for the Advancement of Women as Adopted by the World Conference to Review and Appraise the UN Decade for Women: Equality, Development, and Peace, Nairobi, Kenya, 15-26 July 1995.

United Nations. Platform for Action and the Beijing Declaration as Adopted by the World Conference on Women, Beijing, China, 4-15 Sept. 1995. New York: United Nations Dept. of Public Information, 1995.

LINDA CHRISTIANSEN-RUFFMAN

Pages from Beijing

A Women's Creed and the NGO Declaration

THE BEIJING CONFERENCE was surrounded by billions (no trillions) of pages of documents. At the Conference itself, thousands of the world's media churned out stories for television, radio, newspapers, and magazines. These stories appeared around the globe via media and the internet. Other reporters produced pages of daily news and fliers that announced events for conference participants in several languages at both the UN NGO Forum and the official UN conference. Lots of the pages were part of both official and informal educational and decision-making processes discussed below. From all of these pages, this chapter shares gems of artistic and strategic wisdom that I found in this UN process and the circumstances of their production.

HISTORICAL OVERVIEW AND REFLECTION

The title of this article, "Pages from Beijing," reminds us of the wealth contained in words that resonate through time and space. It is also an historical description, a grounded feminist analysis, and a record of women's collective thinking. In 1995, an incredible diversity of the world's women came to Beijing, China, the site of this Fourth United Nations (UN) Conference on Women: Action for Equality, Development and Peace. They came from many places and spaces to participate in this UN conference that was also at the intersection of two UN sets of conferences—the UN conferences on women (1975-1995) and a whole series of other important UN conferences in the 1990s.

The first UN conference on Women (1975 in Mexico City) was a sound conceptual and policy step and a celebration of women and International Women's Year. As a result of further pressure from women's movements from many nations, the year turned into the UN Decade for Women, further marked by UN conferences in Copenhagen (1980) and Nairobi (1985). Prior to the 1995 Fourth World Conference on Women that was held in Beijing, feminist leaders such as Bella Abzug from the USA, founder of the global network WEDO (the Women's Environment and Development Organization), and Peggy Antrobus from the Caribbean, Coordinator of the Third World women's network DAWN (Development Alternatives with Women for a New Era), encouraged women's presence at upcoming UN conferences. The so-called "Conferences of the '90s" included: the Rio Conference on Environment (1992), the Vienna Conference on Human Rights (1993), the Cairo Conference on Population and Development (1994) and the Copenhagen World Summit for Social Development or WSSD (March 1995) as well as this Women's Conference (August 1995) at Beijing.[1] Unlike the dominant scholarly and policy conventions of those times, women were present as engaged actors, both physically and politically. Outcomes from these UN conferences illustrate the importance that women's movements had in shaping the agenda to equate women's rights and human rights and to focus on the centrality of women's reproductive rights for population and development, the role of women in poverty eradication, and "the need to put people [diverse women and men] at the centre of development." At WSSD in 1995, world leaders with, and in response to, wide NGO and social movement support and pressure, "pledged to make the conquest of poverty, the goal of full employment and the fostering of social integration over-riding objectives of development."

At the many local, state, national, regional, global, and various sectoral meetings and discussions around these conferences and their preparatory meetings (PrepComs), women were insisting upon policy spaces by, for, about and with women. Women were developing, broadening, deepening and consolidating diverse and holistic global feminist analyses that engaged women's social realities and conceptions of social development. These analyses were critical of the harm to women, the planet, and all living beings being created by patriarchal assumptions and policies shaped through the faulty contemporary patricentric paradigm and models of wealth.[2] They sought alternative assumptions and development models based on social needs, human rights, equality and social justice. They respected evidence-based empirical findings that explicitly included women in all their diversity and used feminist, holistic and multi-faceted approaches. They welcomed research that articulated visions of real alternatives.

Historically at the same time, and consistent with WSSD's relative political invisibility,[3] many of us also recognized that economic fundamentalist and neo-patriarchal processes from the so-called "Washington consensus"[4] were trumping equality, democracy and social justice in other arenas. In Canada, this general process began more slowly than in the U.S. and England, partly because of Canada's discussions around the introduction of its Charter of Rights and Freedoms in the early 1980s in which Canadian women were successful in achieving equality rights. In 1987 and 1988, when the first free trade agreement was being negotiated with the United States (agreed October 1987), it was the subject of intense debate and election maneuvering, especially in Canada, as well as protest by the National Action Committee on the Status of Women (Canada's coalition of women's groups) and other progressive groups. The public protests in Canada were more muted with different levels of political maneuvering when the North American Free Trade Agreement (NAFTA) was being negotiated and launched on January 1, 1994 among Canada, U.S. and Mexico. In 1994, the secret negotiations on the Multi-lateral Agreement on Investment or MAI which prioritized trade over social needs were successfully stopped by international protests including Canadians. Such corporate-driven trade talks and agreements, and the establishment of the World Trade Organization (WTO) in 1995, were being conducted in secret by governments, even unbeknownst to other government representatives negotiating agreements reflecting much different social priorities at the World Summit for Social Development.

This changing and competing global political context of the mid-1990s is another reason to revisit these pages. They brought forth the, by now familiar, critique of neo-liberal and neo-patriarchal assumptions that legitimized exploitation, competition, and supported militaristic values and predatory development. Contrary to the WSSD approach, people did not matter in this growing neo-liberal and globalized world that celebrated death over life, profit over people, greed over cooperation, celebrity over equality, and violence over peace. In Canada, neo-patriarchy's hierarchies were intensifying and narrowing women's spaces everywhere, but the focus was not directly on women. The secretive, undemocratic trade agreements plus government reactions to the attack on the World Trade Centre on 11 September 2001, and lack of government transparency allowed for a reign of economic fundamentalist conservatism that ever since has damaged men as well as women and the environment while further taking poverty and women off the political agenda.

In 2011, the Arab Spring and the Occupy movement again drew attention to increasing inequalities and the interests of 99 percent of the world's population as opposed to the one percent who benefit from neo-liberalism and many governments' inadequate complicit responses to economic crisis. In addition to the exploitative and unjust economic system, they criticized top down patriarchal hierarchies and modeled new democratic ideas and forms. Similar alternative foci characterize the multi-month 2012 student protest in Quebec (sometimes called Solidarity and other times the "red square" movement) which started as a student protest against a rise in tuition fees and advocated for free tuition and the right to democratic protest. They are also reflected in Idle No More, First Nations' resistance to the Canadian federal government's attack on life, land, liberty and First Nations sovereignty. Thus, the alternative ideas in WSSD and Beijing resonate now more generally than when written.

Another reason for the relevance of these reflections today is that the UN is currently embarked on a new round of UN Conferences marking the twentieth anniversary of the Conferences of the 1990s. Moreover on International Women's Day (March 8, 2012), the President of the UN General Assembly (Mr. Nassir Abdulaziz Al-Nasser) and the UN Secretary General (Mr. Ban Ki-moon) announced a Fifth UN Conference on Women for 2015. There is not unanimous support within the global women's movement for the idea of a Fifth World Congress. Some critics point to rampant conservatism in some countries and to historically patriarchal formations of governments that no longer suit contemporary times. Moreover, the Commission of the Status of Women meeting in March 2012 at the UN in New York was unable to reach consensus among national governments. These points and the 2013 resignation of the head of UN Women raise uncertainties about when a Fifth World Conference of Women will be convened. The concepts of Equality, Development and Peace that have been part of the titles of the four World Conferences on Women have untapped potential for the UN, as discussed in the conclusion.

Part of my inspiration for writing the first version of this article in 1995 (see Christiansen-Ruffman 1996) grew from reflections while observing the UN official site after most governmental delegates had left their paper trails. While I remember bemoaning the waste and number of trees that were required to support the negotiations in 1995, several of us also reflected on the importance of documentary messaging and a preference for sustainable resources over much more polluting and harmful military ways of resolving world issues. Inspired by powerful insights from an Indigenous woman whom I met as we both used available computers to draft documents, I remember taking time to honour the wealth of women's knowledge and wisdom that was present in these pages. This wealth was not only a product of Beijing but of the global women's movement's engagement over time along with other activists and intellectuals.

Paper pages were an important part of the participatory process. Ideas, drafts and pages were generated, shared, revised and circulated in Beijing, with on-site copiers, computers and line-ups providing hubs of information and socio-political faces. It will be interesting to see if such faces remain central to future UN gatherings, and if not, how this changes participatory processes. When I wrote the first version of this article years ago in 1995, "page" and "pages from Beijing" conveyed the miraculous ability of individuals to put symbols and letters on paper (and on a computer screen) to make words that conveyed meaning and wisdom to share with others. Perhaps it was partly inspired by this phrase from *A Women's Creed*: "The magical skill that reads marks into meaning." From the gathering at Beijing, I wondered, which of the trillions of pages that surrounded this event would most resonate at that time, as well as over time, with my friends and with the world's diverse peoples? I decided then on the three documents introduced here—the official Beijing *Platform for Action* of the United Nations, *A Women's Creed*, and the *NGO Beijing Declaration*, and I would make the same choice today. These documents focus not only on women's attempts to end discrimination against women, but also on women's articulated solutions to the local and global world crises and critiques of anti-human, anti-social and anti-planet "solutions" that international financial institutions of northern or western governments were beginning to impose as structural adjustment policies on the economic south, and on its own citizens under other labels such as debt reduction (see Christiansen-Ruffman 1995). They reflect the developing feminist consensus and holistic, change-oriented analysis that was emerging in the diverse global women's movement and that also attracted the attention and acceptance of male colleagues.

THE BEIJING *PLATFORM FOR ACTION*

The goal of the official Conference was for the governments of the world to reach agreement on a final wording for the official *Platform for Action* (*PFA*).[5] Essential to this task were the pages of reports and proposals leading up to Beijing as well as alternative drafts, lobby documents and reflections produced during the event. At Beijing, delegates and representatives from governments and non-governmental organizations (NGOs) each formed caucuses by issue areas, identity categories, and regions which worked to influence the document, as well as one another. Pages of suggested "language," position papers, and press releases were produced within NGO caucuses. Official country negotiators worked from myriads of their own country's documents, as well as a plethora of expert reports from the many United Nations agencies, think tanks, and NGOs. They drafted and redrafted position papers on paragraphs under dispute within successive versions of the *Platform for Action*. The search for compromise language produced more pages of communication from other members of the negotiating team, other country delegations, accredited NGOs, NGO caucuses, to say nothing of the pages of communication being circulated among country officials "at home," within, and between policy branches of the many relevant government departments. At the conference centre in Beijing, government delegates laboured within working groups, drafting committees, and other (more or less) informal groups, day and night, to produce the final pages of text.

On the last day of the official Conference in Beijing, countries reached consensus on the 362-paragraph *Platform for Action* and its accompanying official *Beijing Declaration*. The Beijing *Platform for Action* provides the UN's plan for women's "full participation on the basis of equality in all spheres of society, including participation in the decision-making process and access to power" (par. 13). Agreed to by the governments of the world, it provides policies for government action toward equality. The *PFA* is useful to groups within countries who wish to hold their governments accountable for implementing policies supportive of women.[6] It remains the main reference document at the annual Commission on the Status of Women meetings in New York.

UN PROCESSES AND THE WOMEN'S MOVEMENT

The documentation processes in preparation for Beijing have been helpful to the global women's movement. They have put and kept women's issues on national and international political agendas and have provided research and documentation on the status of women. Years before Beijing, research organizations, governments, and groups within the women's movement began their research and policy development related to this Fourth World Women's Conference. Governments monitored progress toward equality in their countries, sometimes in consultation with women's groups and also suggested future strategies. In Canada, Status of Women Canada released its plan: *Setting the*

Stage for the Next Century: The Federal Plan for Gender Equality (August 1995). After Beijing, women in many countries began to document their country's implementation of the promises made in the documents signed at these official women's conferences.

Canada was one country in which women and their NGOs focused on Beijing over several years. The Canadian Beijing Facilitating Committee (CBFC) was formed to share information and coordinate activities among NGOs and in August 1994 held an issues-identification conference in Winnipeg. By October 1994, Canadian NGOs were both attending the regional preparatory conference in Vienna and organizing at the local level. In January 1995, the CBFC identified "lead groups" to correspond with each of the 12 major topics in the *Platform for Action* (see footnote 5). Before the New York preparatory meeting in March 1995, these "lead groups" established networks to read the *Draft Platform for Action* and suggest amendments by adding or deleting "language." After that process, the networks each came up with their own more visionary ideas and "wish lists" for a feminist agenda for equality, development and peace. These suggestions were put together in a document for NGOs to take to Beijing. After Beijing, the "lead groups" and their networks reviewed the official *Platform for Action* and selected five priority clauses or sections from this document that they considered to be especially useful for action in Canada. The result is the 184-page document: *Take Action for Equality, Development, and Peace: A Canadian Follow-Up Guide to Beijing '95* (CBFC). For each of these areas, this document describes what the *Platform* says, what this means for women, and how women locally can take action to address this issue. Thus many pages of documents were produced by Canadian NGOs around the Beijing process. They contributed both to visionary and strategic analysis within the local and global women's movement and to governmental discussions within the United Nations.

The official Conference adopted mainly a set of mainstreaming "solutions" that aim to fit women into current institutions in equal numbers with men. For example, an exclusive mainstreaming agenda would encourage equality of women in the military rather than changing the patriarchal assumptions of violence on which contemporary nations have been built. A mainstreaming agenda would not focus on articulating and building peaceful alternative assumptions and institutions.[7] Many women and their NGOs at Beijing knew that the mainstreaming solution did not go far enough. They also wanted major changes to existing unjust and inequitable institutions. Their more visionary feminist thinking about ways to transform contemporary institutions was often not accepted into the official *Platform for Action*. Some was.[8] The more creative thinking happened around the edges. In retrospect, pages from the *PFA* portray the official mainstreaming agenda while the alternatives are less visible to those who were not there.

The remainder of this chapter discusses two group-produced statements of alternatives, introduces one, and briefly describes the networking circumstances under which both were created. Their continued use suggests their effectiveness.

They are particularly appropriate as globalization processes undermine collective ideals, and as feminist analyses are increasingly critical of the global patriarchal processes of austerity, "economic fundamentalism" and "political impotence."[9] The local and global women's movement is increasingly recognizing these structural features as key impediments to a socially and economically just, equitable, and sustainable future. NGO participants in Beijing affirmed the feminist consensus that fundamental changes are needed if thriving, healthy, ecologically friendly, and sustainable societies are to be achieved. These pages are, in my estimation, some of the most important pages of the Beijing process, even though they are not credited as such by officialdom.

A WOMEN'S CREED

A Women's Creed grew out of synergies between Beijing and the UN World Summit for Social Development (WSSD) process. By December, 1994 when A Women's Creed was collaboratively written, the women's caucus at the WSSD had already shown evidence of analytic, political, organizational and symbolic strength within the WSSD preparatory meetings or PrepComs.[10] From a handful of participants at its first meeting, co-organized by DAWN and WEDO, the women's caucus grew to become a centre of women's energy and analysis during the PrepComs and at the Summit itself. Its early morning meetings were an invaluable source of information and women-centered analysis, and eventually a part of the daily schedule of male and female allies as well. Bella Abzug of WEDO created an effective Caucus strategy that relied heavily on document production and lobbying. Current drafts were reproduced with textual improvements that were politically good for women highlighted as either added—or deleted— words, phrases, and new clauses. We found that considerable changes could be made by the addition and deletion of words. Since our goal was to make a difference, we sometimes held back. But in our surrounding discussions, our global alternative analysis developed and collective imaginations flourished. In addressing economic and social injustices, the Caucus was both visionary and practical. We worked politically to improve the wording of documents both by lobbying governments on specific clauses and by articulating our alternative and critical analysis/vision for ourselves, our progressive male colleagues and individuals and organizations in the global women's movement.

We also worked in ways that were building on and building an international feminist movement. Around the boundaries of the UN conferences and the Women's Caucus spaces that we created there, including at the PrepComs, we gathered to share ideas and information and to build collective understandings, analyses, strategies and praxis. The 1990s UN Conferences and their PrepComs provided occasions when the Third-World women's network, DAWN (Development Alternatives with Women for a New Era), held workshops of its own and with its "northern partners" to build shared analysis of macro social, economic and political processes. DAWN, the network of feminist researchers

A WOMEN'S CREED

We are female human beings poised to transform the world. We are the majority of our species, yet we have dwelt in the shadows. We are the invisible, the illiterate, the labourers, the refugees, the poor.

And we vow: *No more.*

We are the women who hunger—for rice, home, freedom, each other, ourselves.

We are the women who thirst—for clean water and laughter, literacy, love.

We have existed at all times, in every society. We have survived femicide. We have rebelled—and left clues.

We are continuity, weaving future from past, logic with lyric. We are the women who stand in our sense and shout *Yes.*

We are the women who wear broken bones, voices, minds, hearts—but we are the women who dare whisper *No.*

We are the women whose souls no fundamentalist cage can contain.

We are the women who refuse to permit the sowing of death in our gardens, air, rivers, seas.

We are each precious, unique, necessary. We are strengthened and blessed and relieved at not having to all be the same.

We are the daughters of longing. We are the mothers in labour to birth new politics for the twenty-first century.

We are the women men warned us about.

We are the women who know that *all* issues are ours, who will reclaim our wisdom, reinvent our tomorrow, question and redefine everything, including power.

We have worked now for decades to name the details or our need, rage, hope, vision. We have broken our silence, exhausted our patience. We are weary of listing refrains on our suffering—to entertain or be simply ignored. We are done with vague words and real waiting; famished for action, dignity, joy. We intend to do more than merely endure and survive.

They have tried to deny us, define us, defuse us, denounce us; to jail, enslave, exile, gas, rape, beat, burn, bury—and bore us. Yet nothing, not even the offer to save their failed system, can grasp us.

For thousands of years, women have had responsibility without power—while men have had power without responsibility. We offer those men who wish being brothers a balance, a future, a hand. But with or without them, we will go on.

For we are the Old Ones, the New Breed, the Natives who came first but lasted, Indigenous to an utterly different dimension. We are the girl child in Zambia, the grandmother in Burma, the women in El Salvador and Afghanistan, Finland, and Fiji. We are whale-song and rain forest; the depth-wave rising huge to shatter glass power on the shores; the lost and despised who, weeping, stagger into the light.

All this we are. We are intensity, energy, the people speaking—who no longer will wait and who cannot be stopped.

We are poised to move forward—ruin behind us, no map before us, the taste of fear sharp on our tongues.

Yet we will leap.

The exercise of imagining is an act of creation.

The act of creation is an exercise of will.

All this is political. And possible.

Bread. A clean sky. Active peace. A woman's voice singing somewhere, melody drifting like smoke for the cookfires. The army disbanded, the harvest abundant. The wound healed, the child wanted, the prisoner freed, the body's integrity honoured, the lover returned. The magical skill that reads marks into meaning. The labour equal, fair, and valued. Delight in the challenge for consensus to solve problems. No hand raised in any gesture but greeting. Secure interiors—of heart, home, land—so firm as to make secure borders irrelevant at last. And everywhere laughter, care, celebration, dancing, contentment. A humble, earthy paradise, in the now.

We *will* make it real, make it our own, make policy, history, peace, make it available, make mischief, a difference, love the connections, the miracle, ready.

Believe it.

We are the women who will transform the world.

A Women's Creed *was written by Robin Morgan, in collaboration with Mahnaz Afkhami, Diane Faulkner, Perdita Huston, Corrine Kumar, Paola Melchiori, Sunetra Puri, and Sima Wali at the Women's Global Strategies Meeting, November 29 to December 2, 1994, sponsored by the Women's Environment and Development Organization or WEDO.*

from the economic south, had made one of the most important contributions to the Nairobi Conference on Women in 1985 with its platform document and book, *Development Crises and Alternative Visions: Third World Women's Perspectives.*[11] Indeed, in 1985, with little notice and only a hope of a place to stay, I flew to Nairobi to attend this Third UN Conference on Women because I had read a draft of the DAWN document that I considered to be such a brilliant holistic feminist analysis (see excerpt on page 353 of this volume).

In preparation for Beijing, Peggy Antrobus (coordinator of DAWN) took steps to collaborate with "northern partners" in order to build a more global critique. At the UN Conference on the Environment in Rio in 1992, she called together specific feminists with an alternative analysis who could represent NGOs such as the Canadian Research Institute for the Advancement of Women (CRIAW/ICREF), Women in Development Europe (WIDE), Alternative Women in Development (ALT-WID), and Society for International Development (SID) to discuss collaborative possibilities in working toward Beijing by bringing women's voices to the other UN conferences as well as Beijing. For the NGO program associated with the PrepComs on Population and Development and on Social Development, "DAWN and its northern partners" planned educational programs and seminars to develop a more global feminist analysis. We called ourselves by a series of names, including Alianza at the WSSD Summit. In Beijing we presented panels and workshops as the Women's Global Alliance for Alternative Development; later we became the Women's International Coalition for Economic Justice (WICEJ).[12]

We also talked about linking The World Summit for Social Development with Beijing to bolster the international feminist movement. In order to give concerted attention to strategic thinking, WEDO planned the Women's Global Strategies Meeting (November 29-December 2, 1994). Some of the 148 women from 50 countries in attendance planned the "180 Days, 180 Ways" Campaign to link International Women's Day (March 8) at the UN World Summit for Social Development (and its strong feminist alternative analysis) with Beijing and to give visibility to the many activities of women's groups around the globe. Others participated in an envisioning exercise that produced *A Women's Creed* adopted by the assembly and circulated widely since then.[13] By the time of Beijing, it had already been translated into Arabic, Chinese, French Persian, Russian and Spanish by the Sisterhood is Global Institute. Over the years, I have watched how this feminist vision has resonated and been appreciated by students, colleagues, international and local acquaintances and friends—both male and female.

THE *NGO BEIJING DECLARATION*[14]

The official UN *Platform for Action* negotiated in Beijing did not express the new analysis or vision contained within *A Women's Creed*. Although the *Platform for Action* remains a useful resource to hold governments accountable, and the women of the world would be better off if it were fully implemented, mainstreaming women into the existing unjust system is not enough. Growing bodies of research and increasing numbers of women's voices have recognized the negative consequences of the patriarchal global system for women. The women's movement, the UN women's conferences, and other UN conferences have sparked feminist analysis that has stimulated: (1) an exploration of women's specific experiences, as women, coming as they do from diverse circumstances throughout the world; (2) an exploration of different forms of patriarchy, discrimination and oppression against women; and (3) an exploration of ways to envision and to create a transformed world. At Beijing, many women wanted to use this alternative analysis to discuss topics not on the official agenda.

As far as I know, no one went to Beijing with plans to write the alternative declaration which came to be known as the *NGO Beijing Declaration*. The seed for this alternative document had formed within the Women's Caucus at WSSD and gained strength from the disjuncture between our feminist analysis and that contained within the official *Platform for Action*. The *Platform for Action*'s mainstreaming strategy helped to exclude most clauses relevant to economic justice and the macro socio-economic context. The last of these were negotiated away in New York from July 31 to August 4, 1995, in often closed sessions at a little-publicized "Intersessional."[15] Thus when we arrived in Beijing, the official *Beijing Declaration* was almost the only place where NGOs in the Economic Justice Caucus might insert our analysis into the official documentation.

Immediately before the UN Conference began, NGOs held a number of meetings both in Beijing and Huairou (the site of the NGO Forum) to discuss what we would like to see in the official *Beijing Declaration*. To maximize our chances of having an influence, we started with a current Draft Declaration, and then suggested clauses to be added. With input from a number of NGOs, the Economic Justice Caucus prepared to participate in the official drafting process. But the inter-governmental committee at Beijing that was assigned to write the official *Declaration* prohibited NGOs from even entering the room. We had to send our suggestions in through individual delegates and acquire new drafts and progress reports from them. We watched from the outside with dismay as governmental representatives rushed to agree to language in each paragraph without our suggested additions. We heard of celebrations by delegates whose agendas coincided with those of multinational corporations.

The writing of an alternative declaration was a collaborative process in response to this exclusion among NGOs and a growing consensus that alternative ideas were needed to solve the problems facing women and the world. Despite almost unimaginable obstacles from inadequate infrastructure and unfamiliar computers, languages, and cultures, drafts were energetically produced and modified. Enthusiastic feminists insisted on signing even during the editing process as this document was being produced for the scheduled final day of September 15. Individuals representing NGOs from all around the world and some Parliamentarians signed onto this *NGO Beijing Declaration* with incredible speed.

The document was finalized with signatures of participants and supporters, and it was also conceived by participating NGOs as an interim document to enable more time for discussion and sharing around the world. A more long-term, democratic and sustained process of document review and renewal was proposed to accommodate the need for some feminist group representatives to take the document to their groups for ratification and/or amendment. Developing and increasingly reliable electronic communication technologies will enable more adequate consultation and participation at UN conferences between feminists at the conferences and those following from their home bases.

CONCLUSION

None of what I have called "gems" of literary and strategic wisdom highlighted here would likely have happened without the Fourth UN World Conference on Women in Beijing. Nevertheless, in many ways that conference alone would not have been able to produce them. The wisdom and visions emanating especially from the alternative documents reflect the increased sophistication of the global feminist movement and its many diverse associated organizations and individuals at that time. Feminist analytic sophistication had developed at the three previous UN women's conferences on Equality, Development and Peace, at the so-called UN conferences of the 1990s of which Beijing was part, and at the many global, international, national, regional and local movement venues where diverse women worked toward building collaborative understandings and a holistic, change-oriented and strategic analysis.

Of the UN-associated venues, almost no feminist who attended several UN conferences would likely have picked Beijing as the most productive. In comparing Beijing with Nairobi, the Third World Congress on Women held ten years earlier, for example, we find many similarities as well as significant differences. The presence of many pages of paper and the process and lengthy negotiations to achieve consensus were similar. Government agreement was reached on both the Beijing *Platform for Action* and the 1985 Nairobi *Forward Looking Strategies* after a late night meeting negotiated by government officials in the presence of NGO observers. In Nairobi, the focus of the accompanying NGO forum was full of alternative feminist analysis and visions, unofficially led in part by DAWN, the network of feminists from the economic south mentioned above. Another centre of women's alternative space at the Nairobi Forum was the Women's Peace Tent, which Margaret Fulton describes in this volume.[16] Located at the centre of the venue, its discussions were full of forward-looking ideas and peaceful, life-affirming and holistic visions, and its processes promoted conflict resolution practices of "true listening" and speaking respectfully across differences. Despite concerted efforts, such deliberately created feminist spaces were not central at the NGO Forum in Huairou, China. As suggested above, the official mainstreaming agenda as well as the twelve specific issue areas tended to fracture, compartmentalize and depoliticize the discussion compared to the more holistic, visionary analysis of Nairobi and the other conferences of the 1990s. The mainstreaming in the Beijing process seemed almost designed to close down discussions of alternatives. As well, bureaucratic ways of organizing and highly restrictive processes at the official UN conference in Beijing (and to a lesser extent at the NGO Forum) limited activities of NGO representatives. Two more specific examples are the aforementioned exclusion from the agenda in Beijing of all items related to the economy and economic justice and particularly secretive and exclusionary government negotiations relating to the *Beijing Declaration*.

In preparatory meetings leading up to Beijing there was a strong, organized anti-feminist presence, This atmosphere led some feminists to feel under siege and to adopt a limited, defensive strategy of "no retreat" from gains made earlier and elsewhere. Some women felt intimidated and silenced by the power of male-led women with clear financial resources amidst growing neo-patriarchal and conservative world rhetoric.[17] Those of us at the WSSD were disappointed and/or troubled by the relatively diminished space for feminist engagement, change-oriented feminist analysis and alternative thinking. In a self-destructive patriarchally-structured society, disengagement for women has never been a viable option. In these times of crisis, women's leadership is clearly necessary, now more than ever before.

Despite these disappointments about the women's conference at Beijing, and, ironically, perhaps because of them, the three sets of pages highlighted here all remain significant. The official *Platform for Action* still offers promise of equality by governments of the world to women that are useful for making changes through lobbying on issues of equality in the current system. The *NGO Beijing Declaration* continues to offer a women's transformative strategic analysis, and *A Women's Creed* still offers a holistic feminist analysis with vision and inspiration to supporters of women's movements. The *NGO Beijing Declaration* and *A Women's Creed* name the effects of our "failed system" on women and all life. They make alternatives seem "real," "political" and "possible," stimulating minds, actions and hopes. They show the potential power of women's imaginations and feminist analyses that value genuine peace, social development and respect for each other, the earth and the diversity of life.

The two documents that look toward an alternative future may well be useful as we prepare for the UN's post-2015 agenda and Beijing+20 or the Fifth World Women's Conference. A continued focus on the concepts of Equality, Development and Peace (that have been named in each of the women's conferences to date) have untapped UN potential. Feminist thinking about these three concepts has come a long way since 1975. At that time, as Antrobus points out, these three words reflected contributions and important issues from geo-political blocks of the period before Mexico City (1975)—"equality" from the so-called developed "first world," "development" from the so-called "Third World" or economic south, and "peace" from the Soviet or communist-led "second world." Perhaps because of these world divides, their potential ideological over-politicization and their hierarchies, these concepts were not as central as they could have been in

Beijing or in the other women's conferences. Nevertheless, the diverse women of the world in Beijing were clearly articulating and demanding alternatives with their eyes on the whole world and its failed institutions.

Since Beijing, economic, ecological and social crises and their analyses both reveal and confirm that our "civilization's" existing patriarchal paradigm, one based on hierarchies, exploitation and violence, is no longer viable. During this period, the concepts of Equality, Development and Peace have been emergent in the analytic thinking of many women's groups, some grounded locally such as Indigenous women and elders' groups, and some started or situated at the global level such as WEDO, DAWN and Feminists for a Gift Economy. The Conferences of the '90s and the growing critique of outdated assumptions have nurtured years of transformative thinking and practice. Brought together with attention to diversity, new understandings are collectively generated in what might be called "thinking women's workshops" (see, e.g., the Pictou Statement on p. 513). Feminist critiques of the patriarchal definitions of Equality, Development and Peace have become more clear and sophisticated, and alternative conceptualizations are broader, ecological, life centered, people-friendly, and focus more on relationships. They build on a culture of peace, social security, equality, and social justice that is viable for women and men in the new millennium.

The need for new thinking has been recognized by the UN's post-2015 planning agenda. Given the outstanding contributions of women to the Conferences of the '90s, has the UN ensured women's equal participation at all levels and stages of UN planning processes? The anti-social and anti-ecological paradigm will continue to harm life on this planet without feminist leadership to challenge its patriarchal assumptions. Transformative change in these circumstances requires women's holistic socio-ecological analysis, both inside and outside of the UN. This shifting of priorities may be even nearer than we have dared to dream. Indigenous women's inspiring leadership of Canada's Idle No More movement, honouring the earth and its generations of life, offers hope for a new feminist-inspired knowledge, culture, economics and politics for this millennium.

Linda Christiansen-Ruffman is Professor Emerita at Saint Mary's University where she co-founded Women's Studies and the inter-university graduate program. She is a founding member of many organizations, for example, Women's Action Alliance for Change Nova Scotia, Nova Scotia Women's FishNet, and International Feminist University Network. She presided over both CRIAW/ICREF and Canadian Sociology Association and their local counterparts and received recognition awards from them and from Canada's Feminist Alliance for International Action (FAFIA).

[1]Of the eight UN conferences in the two sets leading to Beijing, I attended half of them. I also participated in all of the New York preparatory meetings for WSSD and in 1995 for Beijing as well as some annual follow-up meetings in subsequent years such as the UN Commission for Social Development (CSocD) and the UN Commission on the Status of Women (CSW). The generalizations

in this article are drawn from all these events.

[2]For a definition of patricentric, see Christiansen-Ruffman (1989). The significance of historical patricentrism and patriarchy is confirmed by more recent macro historical research that focuses on the exclusion of women in the last millennium from key social assets such as land, inheritance and higher education and from important positions in the hierarchies of church, state, and the economy, and also by my research on women's political involvement not usually captured by more institutionalized models common in scholarly research.

[3]WSSD never had any visibility in Canada. Our Prime Minister was one of the few Heads of States who did not attend the Copenhagen Summit of World leaders, and potential headlines on the Summit's conclusion were displaced by a Canada-initiated fish war. Opposing policies were being implemented by the Canadian government. More globally, as a sign of WSSD invisibility and neo-liberal reassertion, within just a few years, the initials WSSD came to stand for the 2002 World Summit of Sustainable Development, held in South Africa, ten years after Rio. In this article, WSSD refers to the World Summit for Social Development.

[4]See Antrobus for a historical overview that is especially relevant to this analysis.

[5]The "1995 Beijing *Platform for Action"* is available from the web by this extended title and at both the UN Women and the UN sites. It focuses on 12 issue areas, namely Women and Poverty, Education and Training of Women, Women and Health, Violence against Women, Women and Armed Conflict, Women and the Economy, Women in Power and Decision-making, Institutional Mechanism for the Advancement of Women, Human Rights of Women, Women and the Media, Women and the Environment, and the Girl-child. Overall its aim is to mainstream women in policy and to garner resources to do so.

[6]For information on how well Canada had lived up to its previous UN obligations, see the work of Canada's Feminist Alliance for International Action (FAFIA). Established by feminists at the Canadian Research Institute for the Advancement of Women (CRIAW/ICREF) after Beijing to bring Quebecois, First Nations and other Canadian women together. FAFIA uses international instruments to influence Canadian domestic ideas and policies. While I was on FAFIA's Steering Committee between 2000 and 2007, I came increasingly to lend support to the Human Rights Framework contained in the Convention on the Elimination of All Forms of Discrimination Against Women (CEDAW). I had been part of a successful lobby in Nova Scotia and Canada for ratification of that convention between 1979 and 1982. Before and during the 1980s, I was able to take my human rights as a woman for granted in Canada, but it was not long before neo-patriarchal forces began to reappear and the Canadian Supreme Court began to pass decisions which violated women's rights, reversing earlier decisions that had been supportive of women. To raise awareness, feminist lawyers rewrote these problematic Supreme Court decisions in response to what "Canadian feminist/equality/Charter activists, lawyers, and academics" described as the "sorry state of equality jurisprudence under s.15" (section 15 of the Canadian Charter) in the introduction to their rewriting the arguments of six supreme court decisions in

Canadian Journal of Women and the Law (2006, volume 18, no. 1). *The Women's Court of Canada* is also available electronically to the wider legal community and public at <www.TheCourt.ca/decisions-of-the-womens-court-of-Canada>, where their feminist alternative arguments were posted, starting from 2008-2010.

[7]An analysis that centres women's multiple realities and is holistic, multi-faceted, multi-leveled and transformative has the most potential to change the present world social system based on violence.

[8]In the Canadian example above, it is significant that some women returning from Beijing, who were often part of the lead groups, consciously selected both mainstream and alternative clauses in their post-Beijing review of the PFA.

[9]When I first wrote this, "political impotence" referred to the apparent inability of politicians to deliver on promises made to address real social needs such as safe water for all, clean air, shelter, and food and their inability to stop violence against women and establish real peace in the world. Since then, we have seen successive efforts to identify millennium development goals (MDGs), the struggles required to ensure women were included in these new global objectives, and then the apparent inability to even reach these few modest goals. Since then, we have also seen the new phase of economic fundamentalism in Canada displacing social responsibility and goals such as equality. It was not only a social but a political coup. Through free trade agreements, negotiated in secret, political institutions were relinquishing democratic power to the WTO. I understand these processes as the increasing embeddedness of patriarchal historical solutions in the current structure, culture and processes of nations on many levels and continued patriarchal responses to crises. For example, governments articulated that economic might is right when banks were seen "as too big to fail."

[10]I participated in all three two-week PrepComs for WSSD (January 31-February 11, 1994, August 21-September 2, 1994 and January 16-28, 1995), an informal intersessional (October 24-28, 1994) and the official Copenhagen Summit of national leaders (March 5-12, 1995).

[11]An Indian edition of this book by DAWN, published in Delhi, was sold at Nairobi in 1985, and an edited version, by Gita Sen and Caren Grown, was published in 1987 by Monthly Review Press. See Antrobus and Christiansen-Ruffman for a discussion of this book's methodological and theoretical feminist importance and Antrobus for her analysis and personal reflections on these UN events and on the changes over the decades.

[12]This little-known associational history explains why Riddell-Dixon's book could erroneously identify me in Beijing as a member of DAWN. I was part of a DAWN network and partnership, working as an ally with DAWN members but not as a member.

[13]At the WEDO conference one evening, I had a memorable feminist discussion with many of the *Creed's* drafters and then heard its first public reading by Robin Morgan. Shortly after, I received a paper copy and have subsequently photocopied and distributed it following the oral agreement of wide distribution and encouragement of translated versions. Subsequently, I have heard it read by

an Indigenous woman from another province at a Sisters in Spirit October 4 vigil for missing and murdered Indigenous women, in a memorial service for a male student from the economic south after being found on his bulletin board, and by students at ceremonies related to violence against women.

[14]A full text is available at: <www.vrouwen.net/vweb/wcw/ngodec.html>. See Christiansen-Ruffman (1996) for a print copy of the *NGO Declaration*.

[15]As one of the few NGO representatives present at this intersessional meeting, I was dismayed to notice an inverse relationship between what I thought were important clauses to retain and the amount of time that such clauses were under consideration at this intersessional meeting.

[16]The Peace Tent in Nairobi was organized by women from various groups, and individuals including Canada's Barbara Roberts in whose memory the Canadian Research Institute for the Advancement of Women administers a scholarship. The tent was funded by an anonymous donor, later identified as Genevieve Vaughan, a peace activist and an important thinker on the gift economy.

[17]The anti-choice rhetoric and violent imagery on posters and pamphlets created a toxic environment at the March 1995 preparatory meeting in New York.

REFERENCES

Antrobus, Peggy. *The Global Women's Movement: Origins, Issues and Strategies.* London: Zed Books, 2004.

Antrobus, Peggy and Linda Christiansen-Ruffman. "Women Organizing Locally and Globally: Development Strategies, Feminist Perspectives." *Feminists Doing Development: A Practical Critique.* Eds. Marilyn Porter and Ellen Judd. New York: Zed Press, 2000. 175-189.

Canadian Beijing Facilitating Committee (CBFC). *Take Action for Equality, Development, and Peace: A Canadian Follow-up Guide to Beijing '95.* Ottawa: Canadian Research Institute for the Advancement of Women, 1996.

Christiansen-Ruffman, Linda. "Canada, Social Development and the Debt Crisis: A Feminist Revaluing and Reconstruction." *Development: Journal of the Society for International Development* 1 (1995): 41-44.

Christiansen-Ruffman, Linda. "Inherited Biases Within Feminism: 'The Patricentric Syndrome' and the 'Either/Or Syndrome' in Sociology." *Feminism: From Pressure to Politics.* Eds. Angela Miles and Geraldine Finn. Montreal: Black Rose Press, 1989. 123-145.

Christiansen-Ruffman, Linda. "Pages from Beijing: *A Woman's Creed* and the *NGO Declaration*." *Canadian Woman Studies/les cahiers de la femme* 16 (3) (1996): 35-41.

Christiansen-Ruffman, Linda. "Women, Knowledge and Change: Gender Is Not Enough." *Resources for Feminist Research/Documentation sur la recherche féministe* 32 (1/2) (2007): 114-138.

Riddell-Dixon, Elizabeth. *Canada and the Beijing Conference on Women: Government Politics and NGO Participation.* Vancouver: UBC Press, 2001.

MARY SILLETT

Ensuring Indigenous Women's Voices Are Heard

The Beijing Declaration of Indigenous Women

WOMEN FROM 189 NATIONS met in Beijing from August 30 to September 8, 1995 for the NGO Forum on Women '95. They gathered to lobby the United Nations Fourth World Conference on Women held simultaneously to define agendas for the twenty-first century that would chart a course for the future of women around the world. The NGO Forum on Women builds on the three previous Women's Forums and UN Conferences that marked the Decade for Women: the first in Mexico (1975); the second in Copenhagen (1980); and the third in Nairobi (1985). This Forum, unlike the others, also builds on the major issue-based world conferences that took place since that time: the UN Conference on Environment and Development (1992); the World Conference on Human Rights (1993); the International Conference on Population and Development (1994) and the World Summit for Social Development (1995). Recognizing these issues and forging critical links between the conferences, women became central players on the international stage. Their activities at the conferences now affect the lives of women globally.

The NGO Forum at Huairou had a number of different processes occurring simultaneously and in the middle of the Forum, the United Nations Conference officially began, which further complicated the processes. At the Forum, I concentrated on the daily Indigenous Caucus sessions and when time permitted, I attended workshops. The UN Conference also had an Indigenous Working Group and in the final days of the NGO Forum, there was discussion between the two groups. This discussion was absolutely essential so that the Indigenous persons at the UN Conference could represent the positions developed by the NGO Indigenous Caucus.

PAUKTUUTIT'S POSITIONS FOR THE NGO FORUM

Before going to Beijing as a representative of Pauktuutit, a national organization representing the interests of Inuit women, I was asked to focus on the following issues: 1) The Inuit Circumpolar Conference (ICC) has worked extensively within international forums to have Inuit and other Indigenous peoples' collective and individual rights recognized as essential components of international human rights work. 2) Of particular importance is the establishment of a permanent forum for Indigenous Peoples in the United Nations system and the need to continue to change and strengthen the institutional framework of the UN to recognize the increasing paramountcy of the issues affecting Indigenous Peoples. 3) On November 4, 1991, the Council of European Communities adopted EEC Regulation No. 325491. The Regulation not only prohibits the use of leghold traps in the EEC, it bans the import of the fur products of 13 species from countries which either employ leghold traps or utilize trapping methods which do not meet international humane trapping standards.

The Regulation took effect on January 1, 1995. The Regulation provided a "year of grace" if the EEC determined that by July 1, 1994, sufficient progress was being made in developing humane methods of trapping. This "year of grace" expired on December 31, 1995. Twelve of the species listed in the Regulation are trapped in Canada. Hunting and trapping is a way of life for tens of thousands of Aboriginal peoples across Canada. A ban on the import of wild fur into the EEC is not just a matter of economics or the maintenance of a standard of living. It is a question of human rights. Aboriginal peoples harvest twelve of the species on the EEC list and many of them have already suffered from the downturn in the hunting and trapping economy.

In Canada, an Aboriginal Task Force was created to look into the issue. Amongst their recommendations, they felt that at the international level, the following issues must be addressed: work towards gaining a "year of grace" from the Regulation; ensure that Aboriginal interests are adequately represented in the entire decision-making processes; develop a long-term strategy to deal with the EEC Regulation and related initiatives, including communications programs; ensure that there is permanent and accountable representation in Europe to communicate and provide current information on issues related to the fur trade; ensure a united front at the political level; develop alternative markets; and ensure EEC compliance with the Regulation.

And, 4) since the creation of the United Nations, there has been an ongoing debate about which term should be used to refer to Indigenous Peoples. We insist on the usage of Indigenous Peoples (with an "s") because under international law, "peoples," not people, have the right to self-determination. Peoples have collective rights. People have individual rights. Some nations, including Canada, have refused to recognize this language.

THE BEIJING DECLARATION OF INDIGENOUS WOMEN

The Indigenous Women's Caucus held daily sessions at the Huairou site where groups of Indigenous women from over 30 countries worked on a draft declaration to influence the UN Platform for Action—a strategic plan which guides the long-term activities of the UN. The collective effort of our group resulted in the Beijing Declaration of Indigenous Women which covers the issues of concern to Indigineous peoples around the world: self - determination, land and territories, health, education, human rights violations, violence against women, intellectual property rights, biodiversity, the Human Genome Biodiversity Project, and political participation.

We agreed the two most important things were the issues of self-determination and the need to voice strong objection to the patenting of Indigenous genetic materials through the Human Genome Diversity Project.

On the first issue, we stated that the UN must recognize Indigenous Peoples with an "s" as peoples with the right to self-determination granted them under international law and as peoples with collective rights, not as people with individual rights.

On the second issue, the Human Genome Diversity Project (HGDP), which is an international consortium of scientists, universities, governments, and other interests in North America and Europe organized to take blood, tissue samples (cheek scrapings or saliva), and hair roots from hundreds of so-called "endangered" Indigenous communities around the world, the Caucus called upon all to oppose the project. On the assumption that Indigenous peoples are facing extinction, scientists are gathering DNA samples from living peoples. Genetic manipulation raises serious ethical and moral concerns with regard to the sanctity of life. The Caucus opposed the patenting of all genetic materials and urged the international community to protect all forms of life from genetic manipulation and destruction.

The Beijing Declaration of Indigenous Peoples was given to Madeleine Dion-Stout, an Indigenous representative at the UN governmental conference so that she could use it in attempts to influence the drafting sessions of the Platform for Action. As well, the Indigenous Caucus drafted a message to the G-7 which concentrated on the themes that we are peoples with the right of self-determination, that we have rights and responsibilities to protect theearth, and that we need economic justice based on Indigenous values—not on western values.

WORKSHOPS

In addition to the Indigenous Caucus sessions, I was able to attend, among others, a workshop on the struggle for recognition of Aboriginal rights. The facilitators from the Frog Lake Indian Band in Alberta were unable to attend so two other women from Canada actually led the workshop. There were two issues which clearly dominated this session. One was the Indigenous Peoples with the "s" issue and the other was whether or not there should be separation of women's issues from Indigenous Women's issues.

There was general agreement that the UN must recognize the self-determining and collective rights of Indigenous peoples. It was acknowledged that Canada was not a supporter of that position and that efforts have to be made domestically and internationally to change that position.

Two participants (out of about 40) felt that we must struggle to achieve fundamental human rights for women worldwide because women's issues are the same everywhere. Women worldwide want to be free from inequality, underdevelopment, war, and oppression, and we should not underestimate this effort by dividing women into different categories such as women, Indigenous women, displaced women, immigrant women, etc. Debra Harry, an Indigenous woman from the United States led the other side of the argument (which was widely supported by the rest of the participants) stating that there was a need in all forums to recognize the special circumstances of Indigenous peoples. Indigenous peoples, unlike others, have been objects of legislation; have been colonized; have been treated like minorities, displaced, insular objects, and never like peoples with human rights, with self-determining rights, with any rights at all, and it is, for these reasons she believes, that Indigenous women need extraordinary recognition.

Another workshop was on sustainable development and biodiversity by Indigenous women from South America. This workshop was given by a speaker with a translator. She talked about the traditional Indigenous knowledge of her people and how this knowledge has been exploited by outsiders for profit. She was very detailed in her presentation about the knowledge and medicines of her peoples and she expressed anger at outsiders who, instead of respect, showed disrespect for the contributions they have made to the world.

This issue was frequently raised by many Indigenous women throughout our gatherings and its obvious importance is highlighted in the intellectual property sections of the Indigenous Declaration.

CONCLUSION

The "peoples" issue was one identified by all the participants in the Indigenous Caucus and it is well represented in all of the documents resulting from the Forum. The fur issue is reflected in the subsistence issue of the Declaration. In the fall of this year, the European Parliament will be voting to see if they will accept the report done by experts from different countries regarding a process to determine "humane trapping standards." The outcome of this vote will determine international humane trapping standards and the regulations with respect to the import of wild fur products.

Excertped from a report prepared for Pauktuutit Inuit Women's Association.

Mary Sillett was born in Hopedale, Labrador, and graduated in 1976 with a Bachelor of Social Work from Memorial University of Newfoundland. She has worked on Inuit and Aboriginal issues in community, regional, provincial, national, and international settings. She is a past President of the Inuit Women's Association of Canada and was a Commissioner on the Royal Commission on Aboriginal Peoples. She was also the Interim President of the Inuit Tapirisat of Canada.

SHELAGH DAY

Women's Sexual Autonomy

Universality, Sexual Rights and Sexual Orientation at the Beijing Conference

WOMEN'S RIGHT to make autonomous decisions about their sexuality was recognized for the first time at the Fourth World Conference on Women, and the debate on the inclusion of "sexual orientation" turned out to be pivotal in securing this. In the course of the debate in Beijing, three issues became linked: the universality of women's human rights, women's right to make uncoerced choices regarding matters related to their sexuality, and women's right to be free from discrimination based on sexual orientation.

At regional conferences, the Preparatory Meetings in New York, and the Beijing Conference, there was a new push to secure the acknowledgement that the human rights of women include the right to decide freely on matters related to their sexuality, as well as their reproduction. Conservative delegations, who took exception to this, fought to weaken the language in the Platform for Action regarding the universality of human rights, and to assert that women's human rights, particularly as they relate to matters of reproduction and sexuality, are subject to national laws, and to religious and cultural values.

Sexual orientation became a bargaining chip used by the contending forces. Progressive delegations argued that sexual orientation should be mentioned in the document, at least as one of the additional grounds on which women experience discrimination, and they insisted, until the last minute, on keeping it in. Meanwhile, conservative delegations would not countenance its inclusion, and refused to agree to language regarding the universality of women's human rights until "sexual orientation" was taken out of the text.

Because of the intensity of the struggle over these issues they were not finally decided until 4:30 a.m. on September 15, the last day of the Conference, after the first debate ever held in a United Nations forum on the subject of sexual orientation.

The result was that "sexual orientation" was dropped from the Platform, but new language on women's right to make free and uncoerced decisions regarding their sexuality was included. Since it will be important for women to build on this new language regarding sexuality, and to continue the struggle for explicit recognition of the rights of lesbians, this article examines the positions of both the proponents and the opponents of women's sexual autonomy, and provides a detailed description of the final debate on universality, sexual rights, and "sexual orientation."

THE PROPONENTS OF WOMEN'S SEXUAL AUTONOMY

It was clear to human rights activists concerned with women's sexual rights that it was necessary to work on all three of these issues—universality, sexual rights, and sexual orientation—together at the Beijing Conference, because they were connected and each would be key to any advancement.

For the lesbians among these activists, of whom I am one, it was particularly important to work on all three issues. The fight for recognition of women's right to sexual autonomy encompasses the particular forms of oppression experienced by lesbians within the general problem of the sexual coercion faced by all women. Women's vulnerability to sexual coercion is a critical dimension of women's inequality. When women's sexual autonomy is not recognized, women are not recognized as fully independent human beings.

Many women are coerced into having unwanted relationships and unwanted sex with men by religious, cultural, and economic pressures, and by means of violence. Women who live alone because they are widowed, divorced, or because they do not marry are penalized socially and economically in many societies. Simultaneously, women are penalized for having relationships with women. The network of coercive forces that deny women the freedom to determine their sexual relationships with men, including whether to have lesbian relationships, are enforced by legislation ranging from under inclusive social and economic benefit schemes that are reserved for heterosexual couples, to government and police inaction to prevent women from being beaten and killed for being lesbian, or for leaving their husbands. Women will not have full human rights until they have autonomy over their bodies, their sexuality, and reproduction, including the freedom to have sexual relationships with women, and to bear and raise children without men.

The value of the lobby for recognition of women's sexual autonomy cannot be underestimated, since this is a threshold requirement for women's equality in every society. However, for lesbians, a drawback is that the right to sexual autonomy can be discussed as though it pertains only to heterosexual women, and lesbians can remain entirely invisible. Indeed, some member states were only prepared to talk about women's sexual autonomy in the context of heterosexual marriage, where, presumably, it means to them that a woman should, in certain circumstances, be allowed to refuse to have sex with her husband. The forces that make heterosexuality compulsory, and, in particular, the penalties that lesbians experience for resisting the social imposition of heterosexuality, and for rejecting patriarchal forms of family life, can be left out of the debate.

By contrast, in the debate in Beijing over the inclusion of "sexual orientation" in the Platform for Action lesbians were highly visible. The drawback here, however, is that the issue is characterized as the need to protect the members of a vulnerable and despised minority. Lesbians are treated not as women, but as some not quite defined, but aberrant and endangered, life form. The fact that lesbians and heterosexual women are all oppressed by the presumption that male-dominated heterosexuality is "normal," and by the social coercion involved in keeping this presumption in place, is lost.

For lesbians, it was important to lobby for the more incisive feminist analysis inherent in the right to sexual autonomy, and, as well, to have the visibility provided by the debate over "sexual orientation."

The issue of universality was important to both the sexual autonomy and "sexual orientation" issues. Should culture and religion trump women's human rights, so that women's right to sexual autonomy, or lesbians' right to live without discrimination and persecution, are defined and determined by each religion or culture? Human rights activists who organized and participated actively in the lobby on these issues were concerned about being sensitive to cultural differences, but in the mouths of the anti-feminist forces in Beijing, religion and culture were mere code for retaining the right to subordinate women. Given this opposition, universality was a key issue, with women trying to retain the recognition won at the Vienna World Conference on Human Rights in 1992 that women's human rights are universal, inalienable, indivisible, and interdependent.

THE OPPONENTS OF WOMEN'S SEXUAL AUTONOMY

The debate in Beijing revealed clearly that, among the member states of the United Nations, there is a group that is opposed to women's advancement, particularly if it means that women will enjoy sexual and reproductive autonomy. This group is composed of countries that are religion-based states, such as the Holy See and Iran, and states where the Holy See, or some strain of religious fundamentalism, has a strong influence. It includes Guatemala, Honduras, Malta, Côte d'Ivoire, Belize, Sudan, Jordan, Benin, Libya, and Syria, among others. This group of states also enjoys the active support of nongovernmental organizations (NGOs), such as the Catholic Campaign for America, Focus on the Family, and Canada's R.E.A.L. Women.

Many feminists now think of this group of states and NGOs as the international religious right. They are a serious threat to women's advancement, and a part of a political backlash that is keeping women isolated and endangered in many countries of the world (Manier). They are the organized opposition to the fledgling international women's movement.

The Holy See, whose positions on women are typical of the delegations of the religious right, stated in a Report prepared for the Beijing Conference that women and men have "equal dignity in all areas of life," but they do not have "an equality of roles and functions" (Report of the Holy See 2). "True equality between women and men ... will only be attained if the specificity of women is safeguarded" (8). This "specificity" of women is their "particular relationship with everything that concerns the gift of life" (21).

For these delegations, women's role in the family and society is defined by their reproductive capacities. Some fundamentalist Muslim states argued for the use of the word "equity" instead of "equality," in order to indicate that women need not be given access to the same social and political power and economic resources as men, because of their different roles. However, other delegations took the path of the Holy See, not openly rejecting the language of women's equality, but defining it in a way that upholds male supremacy and patriarchal family models, and keeps women categorized as "different," inferior, and subordinate.

This group of member states and NGOs is not unschooled in feminism. It has paid attention to feminist writing, and deploys against feminists some of our principles and concerns. For example, feminists have argued that women cannot obtain equality simply by being treated the same as men, and consequently have argued in some circumstances for differential treatment in order to overcome women's subordination. The Holy See uses this to bolster and legitimize its argument that women are "different" and should be treated differently, even though, in its mouth, this is simply an endorsement of male supremacy.

Beginning in the regional conferences, continuing through the March 1995 New York Preparatory Meeting and following through to Beijing, the Holy See, and the states and NGOs that form the international religious right, opposed many elements in the PFA, and the feminists whom they view as the force behind them. Throughout the process, members of this group claimed that the Draft Platform reflected hostility to marriage, motherhood, men, and the family; that it portrayed motherhood as repressive; suggested that the family is a cause of inequality and a site of violence; attempted to redefine gender as something fluid, socially constructed, and changeable; and sought to eliminate the natural differences between men and women (see NGO Coalition for Women and the Family; Catholics for Free Choice). In June 1995, Navarro-Valls, the spokesman for the Holy See, said in a press conference that the Draft Platform was too much about "gender" and "sexuality" and not enough about "motherhood." He called for laws that would "guarantee women the fundamental right to be mothers" and "promote motherhood" (Catholics for a Free Choice 1995a, 6).

In addition, these states and NGOs claimed that the Draft Platform defended and promoted sexual license under the guise of sexual and reproductive health because it condoned sex for unmarried individuals and adolescents; because it favoured "western-style, childless, and deviant" families; because it "overemphasized" women's participation in the labour market; because it made abortion "a keystone" to the Platform; because it contained the word "gender" which could lead to the endorsement of five genders—masculine, feminine, lesbian, homosexual, and transsexual; because it reflected "western ultra feminist" values; and because it included "sexual orientation" which would lead to endorsing "depraved sexual behaviour, including homosexuality, pedophilia, bestiality, and sodomy."[1]

Also, after putting up such an intense fight at the Cairo International Population and Development Conference in 1994, it was not surprising that these delegations demanded inclusion of a restrictive footnote to the Health Section during the Preparatory Meetings for Beijing, which would make all of the rights in the Health Section of the Platform subject to national laws, and to religious and cultural values. It is the Health Section of the *PFA* that contains references to women's reproductive rights, to access to birth control and family planning measures, and to eliminating unsafe abortion, female genital mutilation, son preference, early marriage, sexual exploitation, sexual abuse, and discrimination against girls and women in the allocation of food. Commitment to many of these elements was hard-won in Cairo in 1994. These delegations attempted to pull back from what was agreed to in Cairo by trying to weaken language regarding the universality of women's human rights and by inserting the footnote to the Health section.

On the three issues—universality, sexual rights, and sexual orientation—the position of the religious right was vehement opposition to the four modest references to "sexual orientation" and to the delineation of sexual rights, and support for the weak wording about universality in Paragraph 9 of the opening section of the Platform and for the restrictive footnote to the Health Section. The final hours of debate at the Beijing Conference took place against the backdrop of their intense, protracted, and organized opposition to women's social, sexual, and reproductive equality, and, in particular, to the recognition of women's sexual autonomy.

THE PRE-BEIJING TEXT

The Draft Platform for Action that went to Beijing for final negotiation was developed through five regional conferences for Latin America, Africa, Asia, Western Asia, and Europe/North America. Each of these regional conferences produced an official document and these were integrated by the United Nations Conference Secretariat to produce the Draft Platform. At the Preparatory Meetings held in New York in March and July 1995, some text was agreed to, and it appeared unbracketed in the Draft Platform that went to Beijing; text that was not yet agreed to appeared in brackets.

In the Draft Platform,[2] the three issues that became linked—universality, women's right to sexual autonomy, and sexual orientation—appeared in this way:

Universality
Paragraph 9 of the Draft Platform read as follows:

> The Platform for Action is drawn up in full conformity with the purposes and principles of the Charter of the United Nations and international law. It is recognized that the formulation and implementation of strategies, policies, programmes, and actions in all

areas of concern are the responsibility of each country, with full respect for the various [religious and ethical values, cultural background, and philosophical convictions of all its people] and in conformity with all [universal] human rights and fundamental freedoms.[3]

The footnote to the whole of the Health Section of the Draft Platform for Action read:

The implementation of the actions to be taken contained in the section on health are the sovereign right of each country, consistent with national laws and development priorities, with full respect for the various religious and ethical values and cultural backgrounds of its people and in conformity with universally recognized international human rights.

Women's Sexual Rights
Paragraph 97[4] in the Health Section read:

Sexual rights include the individual's right to have control over and decide freely on matters related to her or his sexuality, free of coercion, discrimination, and violence. Equal relationships between women and men in matters of sexual relations and reproduction, including full respect for the physical integrity of the human body, require mutual consent and willingness to accept responsibility for the consequences of sexual behaviour.

In addition, Paragraph 232(f) in the Human Rights Section called on governments to:

Take action to ensure that women's [sexual and] reproductive rights are fully recognized and respected.

Sexual Orientation
There were four references in the Draft Platform to sexual orientation. Two appeared in "diversity" paragraphs (48 and 226) which simply included sexual orientation in a list of factors which pose additional barriers to women's enjoyment of their human rights.

Paragraph 226 in the Human Rights Section, which is typical of this "diversity" language, read:

Many women face additional barriers to the enjoyment of their human rights because of such factors as their race, language, ethnicity, culture, religion, [sexual orientation,] disability, or socio-economic class or because they are Indigenous people, migrants, including women migrant workers, displaced women, or refugees. They may also be disadvantaged and marginalized by a general lack of knowledge and of recognition of their human rights as well as by the obstacles they meet in gaining access to information and recourse mechanisms in cases of violation of their rights.

In addition, Paragraph 180(b) would have required governments to prohibit discrimination in employment based on sexual orientation, as well as sex and parental status, and Paragraph 232(h) would have required governments "to consider what legal safeguards may be required to prevent discrimination on the grounds of sexual orientation...."

None of this text regarding universality, sexual rights, and sexual orientation was agreed to when the Draft Platform for Action went to Beijing.

THE FINAL DEBATE

Throughout the two weeks of the official Conference these issues were fought over in two Working Groups, and in informal "contact groups" convened on specific issues. United Nations Working Groups operate on a consensus model, adopting text when the Chair can determine that there is a broad measure of agreement, even if there is not unanimity. Votes are never taken. When a text could not be agreed to after some discussion in a Working Group, it was taken off the floor for lengthier negotiations, often with one member state being asked to convene a contact group, and with those states which had particular disagreements being asked to participate.

By September 14 a new text for Paragraph 97 (now Paragraph 96), the sexuality paragraph, had been adopted.

Unfortunately, the reference to "sexual rights" was gone; but the revised text importantly rooted women's right to control and decide on matters related to our sexuality in the already established scheme of women's human rights. The new text read:

> The human rights of women include their right to have control over and decide freely and responsibly on matters related to their sexuality, including sexual and reproductive health, free of coercion, discrimination, and violence. Equal relationships between women and men in matters of sexual relations and reproduction, including full respect for the integrity of the person, require mutual respect, consent and shared responsibility for sexual behaviour and its consequences.

The day before the Conference was to end, however, key issues were outstanding. Working Group II, which was dealing with the Human Rights Section of the Platform—and issues considered related to it—till had not resolved the contentious matters of 1) the universality paragraph and the footnote to the Health Section; 2) Paragraph 232(f), which would insert a reference to the reproductive rights and the sexual rights of women articulated in the Health Section into the Human Rights Section, and require governments to take action to ensure that these rights are respected; and 3) the four references to sexual orientation, which were all still in brackets.

On this last working day of the Conference, September 14, Working Group II was expected to reconvene at 3:00 p.m. to finish negotiations and adopt the text for these last crucial items. But delegates did not return at 3:00 or at 6:00, or at 9:00 though announcements were made that sessions would start at each of these times. Finally at midnight, the delegates came back into the room. This delay was a clear signal that informal negotiations had been difficult and protracted.

Some time after midnight, Working Group II began its consideration of the universality paragraph and the footnote to the Health Section. Word circulated that a deal had been struck: the text of Paragraph 9 had been renegotiated with the understanding that delegations would then agree to drop the footnote to the Health Section, since Paragraph 9 would apply to the whole text of the Platform. At the invitation of the Chair, the package was proposed from the floor.

A number of delegations indicated that they approved, including major groups of delegations, such as the European Union and the group of 77 non-aligned nations. It seemed as though, finally, there was agreement. But then some delegations—the Holy See, Iran, Egypt, Kuwait, Malta—began to indicate that while they would accept the language for Paragraph 9, they wanted to keep the footnote to the Health Section. The package deal was coming unstuck on the floor. After some confusion, the Chair decided that the delegations were not ready to deal with this issue yet, and took it off the floor.

It was now 3:00 a.m. and the next issue on the agenda was sexual orientation. And there ensued an historic debate. Three o'clock in the morning, September 15, 1995, was the first time that the issue of sexual orientation had ever been debated in any official United Nations forum.

At the beginning, those on the supporting side of the debate lacked passion. They were tired and they considered this issue a loser even though, at least for bargaining purposes, they had supported it, and had kept it alive until the end. The following contains segments from this historic debate.

Canada opened with a very short statement:

> Many countries who participated in a contact group on this issue support the inclusion of sexual orientation in the Platform. Canada supports retaining the words.

Then the opposition delegations began to take the floor and the following debate ensued:[5]

Benin: Benin does not have the same information as Canada. This is a non-subject for this Conference. This Conference on women has three goals:

equality, development, and peace. We do not want this Conference to go down as the conference on the sexual revolution, but as a conference for women who have responsibilities for development and peace. We are not here for a sexual revolution. This phrase should be deleted. We want a dignified historical Platform.

Egypt: Egypt objects to the inclusion of sexual orientation in 48, 180(b), 226, and 232(h). We want it deleted from all of these Paragraphs. This phrase contains behaviour that is contrary to our cultural and religious values. This is a forum for dealing with women's problems, not a conference to introduce new concepts that do not respect the feelings of the overwhelming majority of delegates in this Conference. The notes of the Conference should reflect this fully.

Iran: After several days of work, we have a Platform that can support women. We appeal to the delegates not to bring up an issue that will overshadow the dignity of this Platform. This phrase is ambiguous and totally unacceptable to most of us. It should not be brought up at all in this Platform.

European Union (15 countries): The European Union supported inclusion of the references to sexual orientation from the outset. We regret that there is no consensus on this. We hoped that this language would have been retained.

Ecuador: It is too bad that we have spent so much time on this subject. Ninety nine percent of women do not want this in. It should not appear in the Platform.

Libya: Libya urges all delegations to show flexibility and agree to the deletion of sexual orientation. Libya cannot accept its inclusion in any circumstance. It is completely against our cultural values.

New Zealand: New Zealand strongly supports retention of the phrase sexual orientation. This is about full equality and what it means for women. We are dealing with discrimination, and the right to be free from discrimination in all circumstances. The reference to sexual orientation is a recognition of this right.

Chair (Patricia Licuanan): I have twenty-eight speakers on the list.

Israel: Paragraph 48 deals with issues of discrimination against women, listing factors which can cause discrimination. In Israel we have passed anti - discrimination laws that prohibit discrimination based on sexual orientation. This does not indicate approval or disapproval. It merely shows that it exists. We support lifting the brackets and keeping the text.

Switzerland: Switzerland supports lifting the brackets. This is necessary to complete the list of groups that are discriminated against. It is a question of equality. It is time for sexual orientation to be protected. Deleting the reference to sexual orientation will not delete the people it is intended to protect. This affects the same proportion of people in every country. It is a question of human rights.

Syria: Millions of women are watching. Why are we harming other important causes and looking for exceptions. We should delete this language so that we can go back home to our countries with the equality and dignity of human rights. This is against our ethics and morals.

Jordan: This is totally contrary to our values and traditions. We insist on its deletion from the Platform and we want our statement to be included verbatim in the records of the Conference.

Uganda: Uganda does not understand this reference. This has nothing to do with the subject matter of this Conference. Also, these words may counter our religion and culture. It is the role of family, marriage, and motherhood that should be supreme. These words should be removed altogether.

Belize: There arises a question of materiality and statistics. Race has a meaning to us. Also the number of women who are single mothers is large. Also refugees. This delegation is unaware of the size of the population of disadvantaged people referred to here. Until we know this we cannot support it.

South Africa: After the long history of discrimination in South Africa, we decided that when we were the government we would not discriminate against any group of persons, no matter how small their proportion in the population. We understand discrimination, and we do not have short memories. To demonstrate this, our constitution has a non-discriminatory clause, and discrimination on the basis of sexual orientation is prohibited. Though the number of people may be small, we do not discriminate against them, as we do not discriminate against anyone. We support the inclusion of sexual orientation in the Platform.

Kuwait: We cannot accept sexual orientation in any paragraph. Maybe we can solve this problem out of the hall....

Senegal: For my delegation, this is not a matter dealt with in our constitution, and it is not accepted in our culture, tradition, or religion. So we are not yet able to support legislation regarding the institutionalization of sexual orientation. It is our people who decide. Therefore we should delete this phrase....

Slovenia: This is a question of a woman's basic right to freely decide for herself regarding her body and her sexuality. Today's debate shows us that this is a crucial issue of women's human rights, and it must be in the Platform.

Ghana: Sexual orientation should be deleted from the Platform.

Australia: Listening to my colleagues this evening shows why sexual orientation should be included. I support South Africa. I am very concerned if we are only here to support the majority of women. Those whose orientation is difficult for the majority should be protected from discrimination.

Bangladesh: Sexual orientation has a hidden meaning. In future this will open the floodgates to many behaviours that we cannot accept. Trying to glorify such behaviour offends our ethical and aesthetic sense. The whole dignity of the document and of women throughout the world may be washed away. We should delete this expression.

Cuba: Cuba opposes all forms of discrimination and serious violations of human rights. Inclusion of the reference to sexual orientation in the Platform is proper.

Côte d'Ivoire: The majority of women have real problems. Sexual orientation only concerns western women who have no problems. This is contrary to universal nature and morality. It should be deleted.

Algeria: Algeria does not believe that this should be in the text. It does not conform to the agenda of this Conference.

Sudan: Speaking about priorities and the difficulties women face, it is enough that we had a long wrangle a few days ago over an attempt to introduce new rights. It is difficult in English and in Arabic to define what this means. This is something unnatural. Instead of wasting our time trying to bring here new terminology, if we speak about priorities, the majority of women of the world are expecting us to deal with poverty, and disease. People might see sex and not development. This is unnatural behaviour and is repugnant to my culture and to the majority of people around the world. We object to the presence of this term. This is a refusal, not a reservation.

United States: Some speakers say that discrimination is a non-subject. We say it is the subject of the Conference. When one person's human rights are violated we are all diminished. We support the inclusion of the term.

Nigeria: What is the definition of sexual orientation. How does sexual orientation facilitate empowerment and peace. It is not moral to legalize illegality and to glorify what should not be glorified. There should be a definition. Let's call a spade a spade. How can this help development and peace for women. Or equality. Sexual orientation should be kept in a cooler.

Guatemala: This text is hard to accept. Our priorities are based on the majority of women who are experiencing other forms of discrimination. Why do we have to talk about this. It does not belong here.

Barbados: This is about equality, development, and peace. Equality is an essential element for development and peace. We should ensure that no women will be discriminated against. No women should be discriminated against because of sexual orientation. We should unbracket this text everywhere in the Platform.

Chair: This debate is very important. It is the first time it has been talked about at the United Nations. It is clear to me that more discussion is warranted. However, we have a divided room. There is no consensus. Therefore, for the time being, I have no alternative but to delete the bracketed text. Sexual orientation will be removed from the Platform.

The Chair banged her gavel, indicating that the issue was decided.

A number of countries then took the floor to make interpretive statements, indicating how they would apply the text in their jurisdictions. Canada was the first to speak.

Canada: We wish to make an interpretive statement. The inclusion of sexual orientation would have created no new rights, but rather recognized that human rights must be respected. We interpret references in the Platform for Action to prohibitions against discrimination based on "other status" to include a prohibition against discrimination based on sexual orientation.

Chile, New Zealand, Latvia, Israel, Australia, Jamaica, Brazil, Columbia, South Africa, the European Union, Bolivia, Norway, the United States, and the Cook Islands all spoke to say that they regretted the omission of the references to "sexual orientation" and would interpret "other status" as including "sexual orientation." Slovenia stated that it would interpret a woman's right to control her body and freely decide on matters related to her sexuality as including a woman's right to decide freely regarding her sexual orientation.

Ghana, Syria, Yemen, Belize, and Venezuela stated that they supported the Chair's ruling and were pleased that "sexual orientation" was dropped from the Platform.

THE OUTCOME

Immediately after this debate and the deletion of "sexual orientation" from the Platform, the Chair returned to the issue of universality. This time the package deal went through, virtually without discussion. The new Paragraph 9 was accepted and the footnote to the Health Section dropped. The final adopted text on universality, is repetitive, if not byzantine in its wording, and not very strong. It reads:

> The objective of the Platform for Action, which is in full conformity with the purposes and principles of the Charter of the United Nations and international law, is the empowerment of all women. The full realization of all human rights and fundamental freedoms of all women is essential for the empowerment of women. While the significance of national and regional particularities and various historical, cultural, and religious backgrounds must be borne in mind, it is the duty of States, regardless of their political, economic, and cultural systems, to promote and protect all human rights and fundamental freedoms. The implementation of this Platform, including through national laws and the formulation of strategies, policies, programmes, and development priorities, is the sovereign responsibility of each State, in conformity with all human rights and fundamental freedoms, and the significance of and full respect for various religious and ethical values, cultural backgrounds, and philosophical convictions of individuals and their communities should contribute to the full enjoyment by women of their human rights in order to achieve equality, development, and peace.

Last but certainly not least, Working Group II adopted Paragraph 232(f) which carries over into the Human Rights Section of the Platform the references from the Health Section to women's reproductive rights and the right to sexual autonomy, and instructs governments to take action to ensure that these human rights are fully respected and protected.

It was clear that once "sexual orientation" was off the floor, the delegations of the religious right were prepared to accept the package deal on universality, and the inclusion of the reference to women's sexual autonomy in the Human Rights Section. Working Group II adjourned at 4:30 a.m. on September 15.

CONCLUSION

How should we look at this? Though I sometimes wondered in Beijing about the usefulness of these intense struggles over words and phrases, my conviction was reinforced that the recognition of women's sexual autonomy is a threshold requirement for women's equality. I conclude that though the negotiation of text can seem picayune and remote from the oppressive conditions of women's live, it is nonetheless vital to take every political opportunity open to us to push forward women's human rights. The debate in international fora about the critical dimensions of women's inequality that are related to sexuality has been opened, and it cannot be closed down again now.

I also saw first-hand that the opposition to women's equality is determined, organized, and powerful, and that women around the world are facing growing fundamentalist forces that are using religion and culture to legitimize subordinating and oppressing women. The weak language on universality in the Platform for Action is a significant indicator of the fragility of women's human rights. Some commentators have noted that no United Nations document has more references to religion than the Beijing Platform.

Of course, the lesbian caucus and every woman who worked on this issue was disappointed that the references to "sexual orientation" did not make it out of brackets. Lesbians were also, however, exhilarated. We were more visible in Beijing than at any previous United Nations Conference, and had many more supporters. Palesa Beverly Ditsie, a black woman from South Africa, was the first "out" lesbian to ever address a United Nations Plenary session, and she gave a riveting speech. The debate reported here was also a landmark in United Nations history. It revealed disturbing bigotry. But it also revealed that there is support for recognizing the human rights of lesbians in many regions of the world, and enough support to make "sexual orientation" a bargaining tool in a very important triangle of issues—in a triangle of issues to which it is integrally, not accidentally, connected.

From my engagement in the debate in Beijing I also learned that the issues in this triangle—universality, sexual autonomy, and sexual orientation—illuminate each other. Together, they force us to ask the broadest questions. Are all women included within the sphere of human rights application, or are some excluded because they belong to a despised or unrecognized minority? Is the content of women's right to sexual autonomy defined openly enough to deal with all the manifestations of sexual oppression that women experience? The early morning debate in Beijing over "sexual orientation" shows that too many governments openly admit that they will deny human rights to women who do not conform to religiously or culturally approved sexual and reproductive behaviour, or to women whom they consider an unpopular minority. It also underscores the fact that women will not enjoy equality until all women have the right to make autonomous decisions about their sexuality, free from coercion, discrimination, and violence.

Shelagh Day is an expert on human rights, with many years of experience working with governments and non-governmental organizations. She was the Director of the Saskatchewan Human Rights Commission, the first President of the Women's Legal Education and Action Fund, and a founder of the Court Challenges Programme of Canada. Currently she is a Director of the Poverty and Human Rights Centre, and the Chair of the Human Rights Committee of the Canadian Feminist Alliance for International Action. She was awarded the Governor General's medal in commemoration of the Person's Case in 2008 to honour her contributions to the advancement of the rights of women in Canada.

[1]These phrases are quotes from leaflets handed out by the NGO Coalition for the Family at the Preparatory Meetings and the Beijing Conference, and from Catholics for Free Choice's "The Campaign for a Conservative Platform: A Chronology of Vatican and Allied Efforts."

[2]The text that is quoted here is taken from the Secretariat Reference Copy of the Draft Platform for Action, Incorporating the results of the informal consultations found in document A/CONF. 177/L. 3, dated 16 August 1995.

[3]The bracketing here indicates that the whole paragraph was not agreed to, and in addition, particular parts of the paragraph, namely the reference to "religious and ethical values, cultural background and philosophical convictions of all its people" and the use of "universal" as a descriptor for human rights and fundamental freedoms, were not agreed to.

[4]In the final Platform for Action, because of renumbering, this became the text of Paragraph 96.

[5]This record has been produced from notes taken by the author and by a minute taker from Earth Negotiations Bulletin, a bulletin providing daily summaries of events of the Conference. Both individuals were present during these deliberations.

REFERENCES

Catholics for Free Choice. "Campaign for a Conservative Platform: A Chronology of Vatican and Allied Efforts." The Vatican and the Fourth World Conference on Women. New York: Catholics for Free Choice, 1995a.

Catholics for Free Choice. "Distortion of the Draft Platform for Action." The Vatican and the Fourth World Conference on Women. New York: Catholics for Free Choice, 1995b.

Manier, Benedicte. "When God Enters Politics." *Living Differently: Beijing '95.* Paris: ENDA, 1995.

NGO Coalition for Women and the Family. The Beijing Platform for Action Reflects a Dangerous and Flawed Philosophy. Pamphlet handed out by NGO Coalition for Women and the Family at the Beijing Conference, 1995.

The Holy See. *Report of the Holy See in Preparation for the Fourth World Conference on Women.* n.p.: n.d.

KAREN PEDERSEN

Putting Agriculture on the Agenda

Representing Farm Women in Beijing

GRICULTURE WAS NOT EVEN MENTIONED in the Canadian submission to the UN Conference on Women. Therefore, it is not surprising that agriculture was only mentioned twice throughout the original draft Platform for Action. I felt it was important that if we were going to talk about women's equality that we talk about all women equally. I went to Beijing to put agriculture on the agenda.

I participated at the NGO Forum in Huairou as Youth President of the National Farmers' Union. I left my honey farm during harvest to represent farmers across Canada who could not leave. I went to make sure the voices of all the women working on and off the farm would be heard.

In developing countries, they [women] produce, process, and market up to 80 percent of the food (Status of Women Canada 66), yet, in Beijing, agriculture was not considered a women's issue. Where our food comes from and how it is produced should have been an integral part of the themes addressed at the Conference, in particular its impact on the economy, the environment, women's health, and youth.

The Women, Food, and Agriculture Working Group (WFA) was formed specifically to make agriculture an integral part of the Platform for Action. It was an international group that collectively made decisions, held workshops, and lobbied delegates. By not covering the workshops organized by the Women, Food, and Agriculture Working Group and other such groups, the media missed the most important happenings in Beijing. In one workshop sponsored by Philippine women, the media would have seen 100 or more women huddled under a small canopy tent, with those standing on the outside edges soaked by the pouring rain. In other workshops where the organizers did not show up, women on the floor took over, making the workshop a forum for all. None of the women would leave because as they shared the stories of their own lives, they discovered common elements whether they were from developing or industrialized countries.

Agriculture is becoming agribusiness. As food production is being changed into a commodity-focused business, those who grow and eat the food are being

412

hurt. Food is being grown where it is cheapest, regardless of detriment to the land or to the people who produce and consume it.

Corporations who move food commodities around the world can only afford to do so if they are paying low commodity prices while charging high consumer prices. While commodity prices fluctuate, corporations continue to skim profits off the top as producers average a price below their cost of production. Most food commodities are sold while prices are low because producers need the money to pay bills. When the prices go up there is little commodity left to be sold, yet consumer prices are raised to pay for supposedly higher commodity costs.

Land ownership is a problem for many women. Many countries do not allow women to own land, even though they are the producers of food on that land. In countries where the laws do allow women to own land, other factors make ownership impossible. The cost of land is usually high due to tourism, industry, or inflated prices. Credit is difficult to attain. For those that do attain credit, a situation like the one that exists in Canada is likely to arise. The first generation finally finishes paying off their loans on the land just prior to retirement. To be able to retire they must sell their land to the next generation who then spend the rest of their lives paying the debt until it is transferred once again. In reality, the producer never owns the land.

Once a producer has land to grow food on, what to produce and how to produce that food become the next questions. Often producers are limited in their choices because of the need for ready cash. Globalization pressures them to grow "cash" crops such as cotton, canary seed, coffee, bananas, wheat, and potatoes, which are not necessarily food nor good to the land. Keeping the balance sheet in mind, many producers abuse their land with excessive clearing and improper crop rotation. Growing only one or two specialized crops makes them prime targets for disease. Producers then become dependent on artificial fertilizers and chemicals in attempts to remedy the situation.

Developing countries need more technology. That can simply mean having the instructions for a chemical in their own language or the knowledge of which chemicals are banned in industrial countries. Industrialized countries have too much technology. Hybrid seeds in which yields outweigh disease resistance are common, requiring the use of more chemicals for production. Bigger equipment requires a larger land base to be efficient. Producers know which technologies best lend themselves to sustainable food production yet the balance book often has more weight during the decision making. For instance, artificial hormones such as recombinant Bovine Growth Hormone (rBGH) for dairy cows are being forced on producers. Much like chemical use, once multinational corporations like Monsanto have convinced governments to allow new technology like rBGH, the balance book pushes farmers into using the product to attain a competitive edge. Unfortunately, this creates a dependence on the drug and that whole way of producing. Once farmers are hooked they have usually lost their competitive edge and do not have the capital to stop the dependence by switching the whole premise of their production. In the end, the cash crisis felt by farmers the world over requires more economic efficiencies and more technology, and therefore fewer farmers and less environmental protection.

Once the food is produced, farmers need to market and transport it. Long distances from markets make for high transportation costs. Cash crops are often moved internationally to a market that will pay the highest consumer price. There are only so many means of efficient transportation which makes producers captive shippers. Small pockets of producers, such as the banana producers in St. Lucia, are limited by both markets and transportation. Only one company will buy and transport their bananas so they must accept whatever price that company will give.

One wonders how producers survive at all. Many do not, which is why there is a mass exodus to urban areas. As more people leave the farm, the small supporting communities die. In Canada many of the producers survive by working long hours both on and off the farm. Unemployment rates rise as the exodus to urban areas continues and those that stay on the farms take urban jobs.

The women at the Conference discovered that many of their problems were shared internationally and therefore set to working on common solutions. Producers wanted co-operatives in many aspects of their operation. Working co-operatives would give them control in accessing credit, labour, information, and sharing costs. They wanted land restructuring laws for public ownership of land which would allow access to women. They wanted a return on their labour and investment which would cover their costs of production. Orderly marketing, through supply management[1] and single desk selling,[2] was proposed as a means to eliminate the many transaction costs created by inefficiencies in the open market.

I found the solutions ironic as I sat and listened. We had already developed these structures in Canada. Many co-ops are currently in the process of being privatized. We have the Canadian Wheat Board and many other examples of orderly marketing. Yet Canadian producers' initiatives are being dismantled in the name of globalization and market freedom. The international trade agreements are destroying the structures that producers have created. Perhaps that was why the Canadian government did not want to tackle agriculture in Beijing. It would be difficult to defend signing two international agreements, the General Agreement on Tariffs and Trade (GATT) and the Platform for Action, with diametrically opposed principles.

Women left the workshops of the WFA organized and energized. They had more information and more contacts through which they could channel information. I was able to let people know about Via Campesina, a global movement of farmers' organizations. Through these workshops and the united effort of the WFA, agriculture was integrated into the document. It did not go far enough, but it was a big improvement from the two clauses in the original draft. We succeeded in having economic methods of food production recognized as an important aspect of people's nutrition and health, the environment, and the future of youth.

The Fourth UN Conference on Women is over. We, the participants, have a responsibility to continue the work of Beijing. We need to work towards ensuring governments do not ghettoize women's issues. That means they must be an integral part of any signed UN agreement. At the November 1996 International Food Security Conference in Rome, it was important that women be recognized as the majority of the world's producers and dealt with appropriately.[3]

It is also our responsibility to hold our governments accountable to the Platform for Action. This document will mean nothing if we do not force governments to live up to their obligations. Finally, it is necessary that we bring home our enthusiasm as well as our knowledge from Beijing. We will only achieve equality if we are united and excited.

Karen Pedersen is a honey producer from Cut Knife, Saskatchewan. She farms collectively on a small family farm with her extended family while acting as International Program Committee representative for Saskatchewan for the National Farmers' Union (NFU) and as La Via Campesina's co-chair of the North American Women's Commission. She was past Youth President and Women's President of the NFU. In those roles, she was responsible for organizing young farmers and women and ensuring that young farmers' and women's voices are heard on issues which affect them. Over the past several years she has had the opportunity to farm in the United States, Denmark, Grenada, and New Zealand increasing her understanding of global agriculture.

[1]Supply management controls supply of the product so that producers and consumers are assured of a stabilized reasonable price with excellent quality. In Canada, eggs, poultry, and dairy are currently governed by supply management. If supply management were lost the economy would suffer tremendously and the direct impact on consumer prices would only be a savings of $0.50 per $100 basket of goods (see Bromfield, Jenness, and Justus).

[2]Single desk selling is the precept of all producers marketing their product collectively through one agency. This agency allows them to share the cost and risk of marketing and returns the profit from marketing their product to the producers. Organized into a large body, they have the power to ask for a higher price than they would receive on the open market. Without single desk selling, producers are price takers on the open market bearing all the risks individually while middlemen retain the profit. The Canadian Wheat Board is an example of single desk selling. In 2011, Prime Minister Harper announced that he would remove the single desk from the Canadian Wheat Board by Aug 1, 2012 despite farmers' wishes on the issue.

[3]It was in Rome that the idea of "food sovereignty" was introduced by Via Campesina. Food sovereignty is the right of peoples to healthy and culturally appropriate food produced through sustainable methods and their right to define their own food and agriculture systems. It develops a model of small scale sustainable production benefiting communities and their environment. It

puts the aspirations, needs and livelihoods of those who produce, distribute and consume food at the heart of food systems and policies rather than the demands of markets and corporations.

Food sovereignty prioritizes local food production and consumption. It gives a country the right to protect its local producers from cheap imports and to control production. It ensures that the rights to use and manage lands, territories, water, seeds, livestock and biodiversity are in the hands of those who produce food and not of the corporate sector. Therefore the implementation of genuine agrarian reform is one of the top priorities of the farmer's movement.

Food sovereignty now appears as one of the most powerful response to the current food, poverty and climate crises. The concept of food sovereignty has grown into a worldwide movement that challenges power structures at every level and therefore recognizes that patriarchy cannot exist with food sovereignty.

REFERENCES

Bromfield, Geoff, Robert Jenness, and Martha Justus. *NAFTA TRO Panel Economic Impact Analysis*. Ottawa: Informetrica, 1995.

Saskatchewan Agriculture and Food. *Stat Facts* 12.07.1996.

Status of Women Canada. *Setting the Stage for the Next Century: The Federal Plan for Gender Equality*. Ottawa: Status of Women Canada, 1995.

II. Rights and Reform

CHARLOTTE BUNCH

Feminism, Peace, Human Rights and Human Security

G ENERALIZATIONS ABOUT WOMEN and peace are difficult, especially for a white U.S. American who has not experienced war first-hand, but whose government has conducted countless military operations around the globe. What I do hope to do here is to raise some questions that come from struggling from that location to be simultaneously a feminist, human rights and anti-war/anti-imperialist activist.

Acknowledging when and where we enter is a central tenet of feminist inquiry. Questions of women and peace/war are very particular, having to do with the specificity of each conflict—of time, place, race, ethnicity, class, religion, and other discrete circumstances—as well as related to various social constructions of gender, of masculinity and femininity. In that sense peace and the relation of women to war is a very local issue. And yet, women and war/peace is also a very universal subject discussed in a variety of ways for centuries. Throughout the twentieth century, and especially with the intensification of globalization and the rise of religious and ethnic fundamentalisms, feminists have found it useful to make cross-cultural comparisons, to share analysis and strategies, as well as to build international solidarities for peace.

There is a dynamic tension between the universality of this subject and the need for global action by feminists on the one hand, and the necessity of being grounded in the particulars of each situation and not overlooking real differences among women on the other.

PEACE, HUMAN RIGHTS, AND GENDER

First, what do we mean or expect when we talk about peace? Most women's peace activism springs up around particular conflicts and does not begin with a plan for world peace. But we must ask what are the conditions necessary for a permanent peace to be achieved. We should look at the existing regional and international structures for peace making and peace keeping, like the UN, and at the assumptions of the men who created them to see if those assumptions—like the emphasis on national sovereignty—are a sound basis for peace. We must ask what it will take to en-gender these structures and transform them into more effective vehicles in the quest for peace, security and human rights for all. Otherwise, women will always be re-acting to patriarchal wars.

We face these questions today in a difficult context, made more complex by the events of September 11 in the U.S. and their aftermath. We have seen the most extensive development of nuclear, biological and other weapons of mass destruction in the last half century that would seem to serve as a sufficient argument for why global structures to ensure peace are now a necessity for human survival rather than just a desirable vision. But rather than being more peaceful, we entered the twenty-first century with many unresolved civil and ethnic conflicts, and an increasingly militarized daily life where the lines between civilians and combatants seem ever murkier. We have sophisticated local and global terrorisms, a rise in the political use of religious extremism, an expanding arms trade led by the world's one remaining super-power, and the structural violence of the widening economic gap between haves and have-nots.

Indeed, one compelling argument for women playing a greater role in peace building and governance today is the perception that women could hardly make a bigger mess of the world than male leadership has done over the past centuries.

In this turbulent time, what then do women make of peace? The first aspect of peace is an end to violent/armed conflict—the absence of war—or what is called "Negative Peace." But this is not enough to ensure that armed conflict will not arise again nor does it address questions of what is needed to end all forms of violence—militarization, the structural violence of racial and economic injustice, or the ongoing violence against women in daily life.

"Positive Peace," on the other hand, is a term used to describe an "alternative vision" that leads to the reduction of all forms of violence in society and moves toward the "ideal of how society should be" (Women Building Peace Campaign of International Alert cited in Pankhurst and Anderlini). It is also concerned with justice and the larger dynamic of domination or power over "the other" as a mode of human interaction.

Indicators of the conditions of justice and equity that comprise positive peace are spelled out in the UN Universal Declaration of Human Rights, whose framers in 1948 saw the promotion and protection of human rights as critical to preventing genocide and war in the future. The UDHR spells out broad principles of both political/civil rights and socio-economic human rights that constitute a considerable commitment to justice, development and equality as the basis for positive peace. While we know these rights are not the world reality and their pursuit has been misused, nevertheless, movements seeking justice around the globe have continued to utilize the concept of human rights and the vision embodied in the UDHR as standards that their governments and the international community should uphold.

Feminist perspectives of positive peace build on the expanding world of human rights concepts and practice. Demanding the protection and promotion of the human rights of all as a central tenet of peace-building helps to ensure that inequities must be addressed and that peace should not be purchased at the price of simply allowing the prevailing military powers to have their way. Human rights principles also demand that the pursuit of justice not allow for the impunity of war criminals after a peace accord is reached.

Central to feminist conceptualizations of peace and human rights is the recognition of a continuum of violence against women, in which all forms of violence are seen as interrelated. The institutionalization of male dominance is maintained by violence and the threat of violence and leads us to question whether the term "peacetime" provides an accurate description of the lives of most women. As two South Asian feminists noted when responding to the question of whether feminism disrupts 'peaceful' homes, "one person's peace can be another's poison" (Bhasin and Khan).

War and armed conflict bring additional violation to women's lives, but these are linked to the gender-based violence and abuse of women in "normal" life. Thus, violence against women in war brings together the subordination of females with their membership in other targeted groups, expresses women's status as the property of the men in her community, and reflects social acceptance of violations of women more generally.

Further, when violence is tolerated in an everyday way in the family at the core of society, children come to see violence as an inevitable part of conflict and a natural way to deal with differences in all areas of the social order. Thus ending the violence of militarism, war and racism is tied to ending violence in the home. These are mutually reinforcing forms of violence that must be challenged simultaneously.

While it is primarily women activists and feminist theorists from all regions of the world who have pioneered work on the gendered nature of war and conflict (e.g. Elise Boulding, Jacklyn Cock, Cynthia Enloe, Ritu Menon, Betty Reardon, Simona Sharoni, Yayori Matsui, etc.), one "scientific" study by a male political scientist is of interest here. Joshua Goldstein has sought to show why there is so much cross-cultural consistency in gendered war roles, even when there is great diversity of cultural forms of both war and of gender roles when considered separately. He concludes what many feminists have contended that gender and war are inextricably linked: "Gender roles adapt individuals for war roles, and war roles provide the context within which individuals are socialized into gender roles. For the war system to change fundamentally, or for war to end, might require profound changes in gender relations. But the transformation of gender roles may depend on deep changes in the war system" (Goldstein 6-11).

HUMAN SECURITY VS. NATIONAL SECURITY

The term "human security" has come into greater use recently as a way to describe an integrated vision of positive peace, human rights, and development. The United Nations Development Program (UNDP) Human Development Report, as well as United Nations Secretary General Kofi Annan in his

Millenium Report, speak of security less as defending territory, more in terms of protecting people. Non-govermental organizations (NGOs) have called for redefining security in terms of human and ecological needs instead of national sovereignty and borders. This requires a new social order that ensures the equal participation of marginalized groups, including women and Indigenous people, restricts the use of military force, and moves toward collective global security (Hague Agenda for Peace and Justice in the 21st Century cited in Hill and Ranson). Rita Manchanda notes:

> the human security discourse has come up from below, from peoples and groups excluded from the national security debate, defined and articulated by civil society groups, social movements and marginal groups, especially women. (1)

This term has emerged as an alternative to the state centered concept of "national security," rooted in the military security-defense domain and academically lodged with "realists" in the field of International Relations.

Feminists challenge the military paradigm by asking questions about whose security does "national security" defend? For example, in looking at East Asia, some have concluded:

> The security treaties ... that provide for U.S. bases, military operations, and port visits in South Korea, Japan, and the Philippines also compromise the security of local people. Negative social effects of the U.S. military presence on host communities include military prostitution, the abuse of local women, and the dire situation of mixed-race children fathered by U.S. military men. (Kirk and Francis 229)

Wider acceptance of the paradigm of human security holds promise for women, but we know how easily feminist perspectives can become marginalized as a concept becomes more mainstream. For example, a Joint Proposal to Create a Human Security Report from Harvard University and the United Nations University presented in May of 2001 outlined an ambitious plan to create a report that would map key systemic causes of armed conflict and violent crime as well as a human insecurity index. Yet, while no group lives in greater insecurity than females around the globe, the proposal *never* once mentions women, gender, masculinity, rape, violence against women or any other concept that has emerged out of several decades of feminist work. A similar absence was reflected in a call from *Human Rights Dialogue* for essays on "Human Rights and Public Security." Much of the feminist discourse on these issues has never been read by men in the field and can still be overlooked unless women are vigilant about ensuring that the evolution of this concept fully encompasses the female half of humanity.

Efforts to advance peace and the concept of human security were set back by the events of September 11th and the ensuing resurgence of the masculine dominated discourse on defense. Media response to this crisis proved a rude reminder that when it comes to issues of terrorism, war, and national security, feminism is not on the map. There was rich discussion about these events among women on the internet, but public commentary in the Western media was dominated by male "authority" figures. Even the UN High Commissioner for Human Rights, Mary Robinson, one of the first to frame a response to 9/11 from the perspective of international law by suggesting justice for this act of terrorism be pursued internationally as crimes against humanity, rather than as a call to war, was quickly side-lined by the U.S. and the UN.

It is women who have been targeted by fundamentalist terrorism in many places from Algeria to the U.S., and it is mostly feminists from all parts of the world who have led the critique of this growing problem globally. Nevertheless, only when it became convenient for military purposes to discuss the rights of Afghan women did the issues of women and fundamentalism surface in the mainstream media. However, this discussion has not been extended to the rights of women in other conflicts, and non-Islamic fundamentalist attacks on women like those in Gujarat, India or the Democratic Republic of Congo are not being highlighted. Thus, what could have led to an examination of threats to women's human rights posed by political fundamentalism, terrorism, and armed conflict in many guises was used instead by the U.S. and other western powers to demonize the "Islamic other" and to justify more militarization of society.

The justification of fighting against "terrorism," has been used to curtail human rights both in the U.S. and elsewhere. It has also led to a continuing increase in defense budgets in many countries over the past year from the U.S. and Israel to Colombia and the Philippines. Meanwhile, the donor countries pledges at the UN Financing for Development World Conference (March 2002) have fallen far short of what is needed to even begin to fulfill the millennium goals for advancing human security. Thus, human security as a guiding global principle is far from being embraced as a replacement for the nationalist security paradigm.

Since September 11th, governments in all parts of the world have used terrorism as an excuse to jettison commitment to some human rights in the name of fighting terrorism or providing for national or public "security." Thus, recognition of women's rights as human rights, including rape as a war crime, which is not yet deeply entrenched, is jeopardized by the increasingly militaristic national security discourse and the accompanying eclipse in commitment to human rights. The need for articulating an approach to global security that ensures human rights and human security for all is more urgent than ever in the post-September 11th world.

WOMEN'S ROLE IN PEACE-BUILDING

One of the areas in which there is the greatest agreement among feminists is about the gendered character of war, militarism, and armed conflict and the harm it causes women. Even where there is considerable diversity in the construction of sex roles, what is remarkable is the way in which war still operates in very specific gendered ways, and military forces use and rely on women as critical parts of the war process even as they privilege masculinity. In short, gender matters to war makers and what happens to women is not just an accidental byproduct of war or biology. Nowhere is this clearer than in the violence that women experience in war and conflict.

Since militarism is clearly gendered and women are victimized by war, does this mean that women are more peaceful or that peace is feminine? Images of women advocating for peace as those who are more nurturing and non-violent abound from the early twentieth century to the Madres of Plaza de Mayo in Argentina or the Russian Mother's movement. While such images may serve a useful purpose for women in a particular time or place—particularly when these are the only roles in which society gives them legitimacy, they pose a number of problems for feminists claiming equality and agency. Since the human species has experienced so many centuries of social construction of roles based on gender, especially in relation to war, it is probably not possible to determine conclusively whether such traits are inherently biological or not. Therefore, rather than trying to prove or disprove a biological argument, it is more useful to look at the issue of what women bring to peace-building in other ways.

Women play many roles in armed conflict—not only as peacemakers or victims but also as perpetrators and supporters of war. There is a growing body of work addressing the complexity of women's relationships to war and militarism (e.g., Moser and Clark; Enloe; Turshen and Twagiramariya). Too many women commit acts of violence and support men who do so, whether in war or in the family, to say that women as a group are innately non-violent. However, it is also true that men commit the vast majority of acts of violence in the world, both against other men and against women and children—as armed forces, agents of the state and in the private sphere. Therefore it would also be absurd to claim that women and men are equally violent, or that women as a group do not have any proclivities toward resolution of conflicts non-violently—at least within the constraints of a patriarchal world where gender roles equate "manhood" with toughness under fire and female violence is generally discouraged.

While not all men are violent nor all women peaceful, a world structured by gender has produced real differences in how most men and most women experience war and violence—both as victims and as perpetrators. These gender differences are further complicated by the particularities of each culture and community, making universal generalizations about them difficult, but this does not make "women" as a political category useless. As Cynthia Enloe observes:

> To avoid seeing all women as natural allies simply because they are women, then, is crucial for building reliable causal analyses and for crafting effective strategies. However, arriving at this conclusion does not require a person to lose all confidence in the belief that "women" is

an authentic political category useful in making sense of the causes and consequences of militarization. (297)

Women peace activists have made creative use of women as a constituency to have significant impact on ending armed conflicts and have courageously intervened between groups of warring men, from Ethiopia and Somalia to South Asia. Having different life experiences than men means that women bring different issues to the table and bring awareness of different needs and different possible solutions to the process. A number of studies have begun to document the specific ways in which women generally have a more cooperative and less hierarchical approach to solving problems and are more inclusive in bringing others into the process, which can lead to giving more people a stake in the peace agreements and compromises reached (Anderlini; Boulding; Cockburn; Moser and Clark).

While women should be part of all aspects of peace processes because of the specific life experiences and perspectives they bring to the table, we must be aware that women are not all the same. Since women's lives are affected by their race, ethnicity, class, religion, history and culture and other factors, as well as gender, it is important to ensure that women are more than a token presence and that those involved represent diversity in background. From the research that has been done, having more women involved in decision-making does usually matter in the results that will be achieved especially if a critical mass of at least about 30-35 percent is reached. However, it also matters where those women come from, what their commitment is to women's rights, and what are their overall politics.

The need for women to be part of all aspects of the peace-building process should be self-evident and does not rest on claims to their being innately more peaceful. This is a right that rests on the simple but profound principles of justice and democracy. As half or more of humanity, women have the right to be part of the decision-making on all critical activities that deeply affect their lives. Gender balance, as a democratic principle, should apply to the full range of peace-building activities.

WOMEN'S PEACE ACTIVISM

Women's activism around peace takes many forms, often depending on a group's politics as well its values and life circumstances. In looking at examples of such activism, a variety of dilemmas and questions that feminists concerned with peace face are raised: Are feminists pacifists or do we believe in just wars and liberation struggles? Does holding military forces accountable to the rules of war and integrating women into military forces only strengthen them and reinforce social acceptance of military solutions? Do mother's movements necessarily reinforce gender stereotypes? What actions can feminists take when society is polarized around male-defined or nationalistic options none of which we want to support? How do feminists who usually create non-formal and often marginal ways of working for peace get taken seriously in the formal peace-making processes?

One of the most significant forms of feminist peace organizing in the last two decades is embodied in efforts by women to cross national and ethnic lines and reach out to women of the "other" side, as well as to critique their own government or community's position. The issues of nationalism or communalism can be difficult for feminists. Some may feel that their own community oppresses women, but they may still be torn by loyalties to that community in the face of its domination by other forces or simply by virtue of being part of it. The nationalist/communitarian forces will certainly pressure or even try to force women to be loyal, often as symbols of the culture. In some cases, women feel that being a fighter for their group can be a way to prove themselves as political actors with agency. However, for women to play a significant role in ending conflict usually requires standing aside and being critical of nationalism, or at least of how the warring parties are manipulating it. There are a number of examples of women's peace initiatives that have taken this step—in Northern Ireland, Cyprus, Mali, the former Yugoslavia, the Middle East, and across the India-Pakistan border—to name a few. Central to such efforts is women's rejection of the nationalist project of dividing groups along racial/ethnic, religious, and/or cultural lines and dehumanizing "the other." In refusing this logic, activists often face violence, repression, or rejection from members of their own communities for being traitors.

Let me end with a few comments about women's global networking for peace. International solidarity has played an important role in sustaining many feminist peace activists, especially when they challenge the dominant nationalist or communalist discourse. Women have supported each other through keeping lines of communication open and accurate information flowing, with money and care packets, with counseling and hand holding, with assistance in escaping difficult situations and finding asylum, with petitions to governments, the UN, and other bodies. Global networking has also achieved a number of important gains in relation to war and armed conflict at the international level.

In past decades, women's efforts at the UN, have led to more attention to women and armed conflict, which became a full chapter of the Beijing *Platform for Action* and received considerable attention at the Beijing Plus Five Review in 2000. Women raised the profile of sexual violence in war in the Ad Hoc Tribunals on the former Yugoslavia and Rwanda and made certain that issues of gender-based violence and persecution were incorporated into the Statute of the International Criminal Court. Another major breakthrough was the passage of UN, Security Council Resolution 1325 on Women, Peace and Security in October of 2000, which mandates the inclusion of women in all of the peace processes as well as gender mainstreaming into all these activities. The dilemma posed by global networking at the UN is how to ensure that such gains are not simply rhetorical and that they are implemented effectively in a gender and culture specific way at all levels.

This leads back to the importance of making sure that *women's peace activism is both local and global*, and that the dynamic tension between the universality and specificity of this work is recognized and grappled with continuously. Only through such a process can women's peace activism not only respond to the needs of each situation but also impact the larger global structures creating many of these conflicts so that we can move toward a pro-active vision of positive peace with human rights and human security at its core, rather than continue to be called upon to clean up after the endless succession of male-determined armed conflicts.

This article is adapted from a paper written for the "Women and Peace Panel" at the "Women, Peace Building and Constitution-Making International Conference," 2-5 May, 2002, Colombo, Sri Lanka.

Charlotte Bunch, Founding Director and Senior Scholar, Center for Women's Global Leadership (CWGL), Rutgers University, is an author and organizer in feminist and human rights movements. Distinguished Professor in Women's and Gender Studies, she directed CWGL for 20 years, leading their path-breaking work on women rights as human rights, the 16 Days of Activism Against Gender Violence Campaign, Women's Global Leadership Institutes, and advocacy at the United Nations including the GEAR Campaign for the creation of UN Women.

REFERENCES

Annan, Kofi A. *"We the Peoples": The Role of the United Nations in the 21ˢᵗ Century.* The Millenium Report of the United Nations Secretary General. New York: United Nations, 2000.

Anderlini, Sanam. *Women at the Peace Table: Making a Difference.* New York: United Nations Development Fund for Women, 2000.

Bhasin, Kamala and Nighat Khan. *Feminism and its Relevance in South Asia.* New Delhi: Kali for Women, 1986.

Boulding, Elise "Feminist Interventions in the Art of Peacemaking: A Century Overview." *Peace and Change* 20 (4) (October 1995).

Cock, Jacklyn. *Colonels and Cadres: War and Gender in South Africa.* Oxford: Oxford University Press, 1991.

Cockburn, Cynthia. *The Space Between Us: Negotiating Gender and National Identities in Conflict.* London: Zed Books, 1998.

Enloe, Cynthia. *Maneuvers: The International Politics of Militarizing Women's Lives.* Berkeley: University of California Press, 2000.

Goldstein, Joshua S. *War and Gender.* London: Cambridge University Press, 2001.

Hill, Felicity and Pam Ransson. *Building a Women's Peace Agenda.* Hague Appeal for Peace, ed. New York: New York Gender Focus Group of the Hague Appeal for Peace, 2001.

Kirk, Gwyn and Carolyn Bowen Francis. "Redefining Security: Women Challenge U.S. Military Policy and Practice in East Asia." *Berkeley Women's Law Journal* 15 (2000): 229-271.

Manchanda, Rita. "Redefining and Feminizing Security." Unpublished manuscript, 2001.

Matsui, Yayori. *Women in the New Asia*. London: Zed Books, 1999.

Menon, Ritu. "Borders and Bodies: Recovering Women in the National Interest." *Common Grounds: Violence Against Women in War and Armed Conflict Situations*. Ed. Indai Lourdes Sajor. Quezon City: Asian Centre for Women's Human Rights, 1998.

Moser, Caroline O. N. and Fiona C. Clark, eds. *Victims, Perpetrators or Actors? Gender Armed Conflict and Political Violence*. London: Zed Books, 2001.

Pankhurst, Donna and Sanam Anderlini. *Mainstreaming Gender in Peacebuilding: A Framework for Action*. London: International Alert, 2000.

Reardon, Betty. *Women and Peace: Feminist Visions of Global Security*. Albany: State University of New York Press, 1993.

Sharoni, Simona. *Gender and the Israeli-Palestinian Conflict: The Politics of Women's Resistance*. Syracuse: Syracuse University Press, 1995.

Turshen, Meredeth and Clotilde Twagiramariya, eds. *What Women Do in Wartime: Gender and Conflict in Africa*. London: Zed Books, 1998.

United Nations Department of Public Information. *The Beijing Declaration and The Platform for Action: Fourth World Conference on Women, Beijing, China, 1995*. New York: United Nations, 1996.

United Nations Development Program (UNDP). *Human Development Report 1994*. New York: Oxford University Press, 1994.

Women Building Peace Campaign of International Alert, 2000.

MARILOU MCPHEDRAN

Creating Trialogue

Women's Constitutional Activsim in Canada

> *We now have a Charter that defines the kind of country in which we wish to live, and guarantees the basic rights and freedoms which each of us shall enjoy as a citizen of Canada. It reinforces the protection offered to French-speaking Canadians outside Quebec, and to English-speaking Canadians in Quebec. It recognizes our multicultural character. It upholds the equality of women, and the rights of disabled persons.*
> —Pierre Elliott Trudeau (1982)[1]

WOMEN'S CONSTITUTIONAL EQUALITY rights have evolved from decades of women's activism, drawn up from the grass roots of the daily lives of women and children, reaching into the exclusive corridors of malestream[2] political and legal institutions, to impact on constitution-making and constitution-working. In the past 25 years, the world's strongest, clearest articulations of commitment to equality-based democratic rights and freedoms have been developed—including Canada's *Constitution Act* 1982.[3] Intensely focused women's activism during negotiations over text yielded substantive amendments in our much heralded constitution. Yet women's constitutional activism has often been treated as a "sidebar" in mainstream accounts of these formative periods in democratic evolution. Official records have little on Canadian women's influential contributions in those intensely political arenas—at each drafting stage and, as integration of the constitution proceeded, to the country's legal system, thereby affecting national aspirations for this constitutional democracy.[4] Before returning to Canada to enter politics, Michael Ignatieff observed how Canadian constitutional development accommodated diversity,

The rights revolution makes society harder to control, more unruly, more contentious. This is because rights equality makes society more inclusive, and rights protection constrains government power.... What makes the Canadian political story so interesting is the way in which women's organizations, Aboriginal groups, and ordinary citizens have forced their way to the table and enlarged both the process of constitutional change and its results.[5]

WOMEN'S ACTIVISM AND CONSTITUTIONALISM

From the early 1980s through the mid 1990s, the crumbling of the Berlin Wall released a flood of newly independent states embarked on constitution-making, South African apartheid officially ended when the interim constitution was put in place, and the Canadian constitution was "patriated"—following the prime minister's promise to "bring the constitution home"[6] from under England's authority. While the last mentioned event was hardly on the same scale of human upheaval as the first two, they are all examples of the progression of constitutionalism and constitution-making around the globe, including Afghanistan, Brazil, Eritrea, Nicaragua, Rwanda and Uganda.[7] Women mobilized on every continent, around their vision of women's constitutional equality rights, as a means to live their rights.

Questions about both sides of women's constitutional activism arise—one side being women's impact on constitution-making and thus on final constitutional text; but the other side being the impact of constitution-making on women and their social movements. In the hope that this article will be a useful contribution to the rather sparse discourse on women's activism and democratic reform, observations are prompted by the following four practical questions.[8]

1. What conditions generated women's readiness for constitution making; what characteristics influenced the nature of women's constitutional activism?

2. What was wrong with early draft equality provisions; how did women activists succeed in attaining amendments?

3. What kinds of engagement (alliances) proved effective in the social movement toward the best textual protection possible; were strategies time limited, were alliances sustained?

4. What about "results"—what was generated from activism that had a demonstrated impact on the constitutional drafting / amending / follow-up / processes?

PUTTING WOMEN ON THE CONSTITUTIONAL AGENDA

The following is a brief summary of key events and indicators from the decades of activism that rolled up to the crucial moments of influence when the constitution of Canada was finally constructed as the 1970s slid into the 1980s.

> *Whenever I don't know whether to fight or not, I fight.*
> —Emily Murphy[9]

The "Famous Five" Persons

In 1928, five women[10] collectively petitioned the Supreme Court of Canada, to ask: Does the word "person" in Section 24 of The *British North American Act* include female "persons?" Chief Justice Anglin answered for a unanimously negative Supreme Court of Canada.[11] The five petitioners had to choose between strategies, to a) convince the government to legislate in their favour or b) litigate further to the Judicial Committee of the Privy Council of England. The Five opted to appeal, but could not afford to be present.[12] On October 18, 1929, Lord Chancellor Sankey of the Privy Council, provided the English lords' unanimous answer,[13] "...and to those who would ask why the word [persons] should include female, the obvious answer is, why should it not?"[14]

Litigation was a strategic choice that few Canadian women of the time could have made. Long years of women's rights activism, relatively advantaged social positions and political access made such high impact litigation possible for these five activists.[15]

Building National Women's Rights Machinery

In 1967, decades after the Persons Case, responding to pressure from disgruntled women's groups, a *Royal Commission on the Status of Women* was mandated to "inquire into the status of women in Canada and to recommend what steps might by taken by the Federal Government to ensure for women equal opportunities with men in all aspects of Canadian identity."[16]

But a year into the Commission's mandate, Pauline Jewitt queried why governments were avoiding the public hearings, "They [commissioners] know that a basic re-examination of the role of men in the status of women problem, while it may terrify the men, does not terrify the women. And they know the hearings, far from being a catharsis, have given women a new determination to ensure that they may yet be treated, in dignity and worth as equals of men."[17]

Dissatisfaction with the Commission's 167 final recommendations culminated in April 1972, when hundreds from across the country gathered to form a new non-governmental, activist umbrella organization—known as NAC—the National Action Committee on the Status of Women.[18] A year later the federal government established the Canadian Advisory Council on the Status of Women (CACSW), then several provinces appointed women to advisory councils, which became crucial in family law reforms that moved to centre-stage in the 1970s, when the Supreme Court of Canada made decisions under the *Canadian Bill of Rights* that spoke volumes to Canadian women about the difference between "justice" and the "law."[19]

READINESS—WOMEN LOST EVERY BILL OF RIGHTS CASE

Aboriginal Women and Children

With their appeals heard together and rejected by the Supreme Court, Jeanette Lavell and Yvonne Bédard, Aboriginal women who had married non-Aboriginal men, argued that s.12 (1)(b) of the federal *Indian Act* discriminated against women of Indian status making them lose that status upon marriage to a non-Indian, when Indian men could extend status to non-Indian wives, and in turn, their children.[20] This loss under the Bill of Rights prompted national concern—and a dramatic activist response by a group of Aboriginal women, who took their small children, fathered by non-status men, to walk in protest from the Tobique reserve to the federal capital of Ottawa. One of their leaders, Sandra Lovelace (appointed to the Senate of Canada in 2005), successfully petitioned the United Nations Human Rights Committee[21] alleging violations by Canada under the *Optional Protocol to the International Covenant on Civil and Political Rights*.[22]

Just a Wife

In dismissal of her lifetime of work in ranching with her husband for more than 25 years, the Supreme Court awarded Irene Murdoch just two hundred dollars a month, agreeing with the trial judge that her "routine" work of "any ranch wife"[23]—was insufficient to create a legal claim to the matrimonial property.[24] Irene Murdoch's loss galvanized family law reform in every province and territory for the rest of the 1970s.

No Protection for a "Pregnant Person"

Stella Bliss was fired because she was pregnant. After her baby was born, she sought, but did not find, appropriate employment, but the Unemployment Insurance Commission turned down her application—because she had been pregnant when she lost her job and she did not meet the more stringent criteria applied to pregnancy benefits. Canadian courts found no sex discrimination, because all pregnant women were equally denied regular unemployment benefits, the proper comparitor was not men, but rather women—pregnant and non-pregnant persons.[25]

Thus, the platform for constitutional activism had been framed-in by repeated judicial denial of discrimination rampant in Canadian women's daily lives. Plus, the federal government had not followed the recommendation that the CACSW should report openly to Parliament. Unwittingly, governmental preference for less accountability set the stage for a political standoff that triggered women's constitutional activism in the 1980s.[26] When the government cancelled the CACSW women's constitutional conference, the high stakes were widely understood by Canadian women.

> The issue—whether women would have a share in the future of the nation—knit up all kinds of raggedy ends.... "A lot of us sensed it and not just in the organized women's movement. It had been building.... this shoddy treatment of a strong and honest woman [Doris Anderson] at the same time as denying us our rights as citizens.... Boom."[27]

FIVE YEARS OF CONSTITUTION-MAKING: 1981-86

The Shift to Constitution-Focused Women's Activism
Executive Constitutionalism v. Canadian Women

Dissent in any form, whether it touches on practical governance or not, can appear to herald the withdrawal of consent to legitimate authority; which makes legitimate authority very nervous…. Ordered use of the power to disbelieve, the first power of the weak, begins here, with the refusal to accept the definition of oneself that is put forward by the powerful.[28]

On the anniversary of the Persons Case in 1980, the federal minister responsible for the status of women in Canada[29] gave a dinner speech to women activists, who had just attended a CACSW study day on the proposed constitutional text,[30] learning that it was as weak as the existing *Canadian Bill of Rights* when it came to protecting women,

> When carefully coiffed matrons banged their fists on tables in response to Lloyd Axworthy's remarks, and the Ad Hoc Committee on Women and the Constitution was born to fight for women's right to be included in the Constitution, this first step was taken. Once the weak learn to distrust the reality defined by their rulers, Elizabeth Janeway points out that the way is open for them to bond together, to organize and to act. This is precisely what the Ad Hoc committee did in networking with women's groups across the country.[31]

Only weeks later, some of the women who had surprised themselves by shouting at a cabinet minister that October night were presenting before a hastily convened special joint parliamentary committee reviewing the draft constitution. Representing the largest national women's NGO, the NAC spokeswoman reminded parliamentarians that Canada had just signed the United Nations Convention on the Elimination of all Forms of Discrimination Against Women (CEDAW),[32] then she cautioned that,

> Women could be worse off if the proposed Charter of Rights and Freedoms is entrenched in Canada's Constitution. Certainly the present wording will do nothing to protect women from discriminatory legislation, nor relieve inequities that have accumulated in judicial decisions.[33]

Women's activism shifted into even higher gear when the media reported how the senator co-chairing the special joint committee said, to the NAC spokeswomen after they finished their presentation,

> I want to thank you girls for your presentation. We're honoured to have you here. But I wonder why you don't have anything in here for babies or children. All you girls are going to be working and who's going to look after them?[34, 35]

Kome reviewed women's groups' presentations on the draft constitutional text, finding: "Efficient coordination ensured they would not contradict each other…. Most attention was paid to Clause 15, concerning "Non-discrimination Rights.""

...Women wanted the section renamed 'Equality Rights,' to emphasize that equality means more than non-discrimination."[36]

Amendments suggested by women's groups were incorporated, to a considerable extent, in the next draft of the constitution, released January 1981. As assessed by Manfredi, this success before the special joint committee represented "only the first stage in the feminist effort to redesign Canadian institutions through constitutional modification.[37]

For most of 1981—primarily through the new grassroots alliance known as the Ad Hoc Committee of Canadian Women on the Constitution—thousands of women in Canada mobilized to respond to the cancelled women's constitutional conference and to push for amending the equality rights provisions in the draft constitution. Newly minted women lawyers volunteered to lobby federal politicians in Parliament, while crowds of angry women joined government appointed women's advisory council members in confronting political leaders at home, on the steps of their legislative buildings—laying claim to a place in Canadian constitutional history in headlines of the time. Nevertheless, most Canadian historians and mainstream media commentators paid little attention to women's constitutional activism in retrospective accounts.[38]

But by the end of 1981, Attorneys-General of the national and provincial governments moved back behind closed doors, responding to the Supreme Court of Canada's constitutional reference decision that summer, which encouraged the federal government to redress its unilateral constitutional process.[39] However, the amended constitutional text had passed both the House of Commons and the Senate before the Supreme Court reference. This left thousands of women, who had mobilized across Canada, thinking that a significant political and legal victory had been secured by amendments to the Charter, including the last-minute insertion of s.28—an Equal Rights Amendment (ERA) fought for by Canadian women's constitutional activists—heightened by awareness of the American ERA campaign being lost during this time. "Section 28. Notwithstanding anything in this Charter, the rights and freedoms referred to in it are guaranteed equally to male and female persons."[40]

In those closed federal/provincial negotiations an optional override on certain rights was proffered. Women constitutional activists described the override as surtax on their hard won constitutional rights.[41] The Ad Hoc alliance re-mobilized against the "taking of twenty eight," the s.33 override was lifted from s.28, but not from s.15.[42] The grassroots battle for s.28 was validated by legal commentary of the time, which anticipated it would serve as a protective legal tool for women.[43] "Section 28 should not be dismissed as being a "mere application" of section 15. The principle of sexual equality is now a legal standard of the highest priority."[44]

But as the '80s closed, little could be seen of the protective potential in s. 28. Indeed, as South Africa prepared for Mandela's release from prison and South African women activists were on a cusp, Canadian feminist constitutional experts were becoming more concerned. In November 1990, the University of the Witwatersrand in Johannesburg hosted a South African women's pre-constitutional conference, organized by Lawyers for Human Rights—entitled "Putting Women on the Agenda," inviting speakers from other countries—Zimbabwe, Namibia, Botswana, and Canada—so as to "empower women to participate in all the crucial aspects of the transformation...."[45]

Invited to reflect on the decade since Canadian women had negotiated constitutional amendments, Elizabeth Sheehy cautioned her African colleagues, "Lessons from ... Canada may be helpful for the negotiations over women's equality rights, but women must conserve their energy and resources. Long term struggle lies ahead in fighting off 'rights' challenges to women's few and fragile gains...."[46]

WOMEN'S GLOBAL CONSTITUTIONALISM

Intersectionality

In today's context, it is difficult to answer—which organization or individual women's rights leader could legitimately claim to speak for an Aboriginal woman or a woman living with a disability in Canada? All the executive members of NAC who testified before the joint constitutional committee in November 1980 were white women (including myself as an advisor) who differed in age, socio-economic status and faith, concerned that differences "between the life patterns of women and men have not been considered by the drafters of the proposed Charter" but they made no distinctions among women.[47] Twenty years later, in her comparsion of feminist constitutional rights discourse in Canada and South Africa, Murphy cautioned,

> But regardless of the issue, a theory of women's rights is deployed to protect or challenge measures on the basis of the impact on women's lives.... I believe that even a cursory study of different women's movements can serve to warn against any sort of constant narrative about women's rights that will work wherever women are.[48]

Murphy criticized the Canadian constituional activists of the '80s, many of whom went on to found LEAF and other women's NGOs focussed on systemic change driven by constitutional equality values, and in her judgment,

> The continuing insistence in Canada on the theoretical and strategic coherence of women's rights in the early 1990s had very different effects (overwhelmingly negative) than the same insistence in South Africa at the same period of time (overwhelmingly positive).[49]

Murphy's criticism is thought-provoking—always a good thing. Indeed, criticism of this nature was encouragement for writing this article—specifically on activism, informed by 30 years of feminist activist legal and political

435

human rights work. Is there a fundamental incompatibility between reliance on accessing rights through law—one component of constitutionalism—and actually attaining justice that impacts positively on women's and girls' lives?

Globally, women's rights activists are "voting" with their inquiries—and the fact is that inquiries, often followed by international aid agency-funded delegations, now come to LEAF from all over the world. Like the thousands of Canadian Ad Hockers in 1981 and the estimated milions of women in South Africa who mobilized around the *Women's Charter for Effective Equality* a decade ago, women are not prepared to risk being left out of new legal sysytems. Concerns have been raised internationally about state-centered law reform, which Stephen Golub has termed "rule of law (ROL) orthodoxy."[50] Didi Khayatt, formerly the director of York University's Centre for Feminist Research, has written of being raised in a privileged Egyptian home and how the relative lightness of her skin and her advantaged upbringing shielded her from "the anguish of discrimination ... or the experience of being silenced"—concluding that she could not therefore assume the label "woman of colour" and the oppression that the term implies. "Rigid definitions of race and ethnicity which do not account for fluidity of the categories are not useful in that they mask the differences of class and location."[51]

WOMEN AMID GROUP DIFFERENTIATED RIGHTS

Aboriginal Women in Canada

Before South Africa became a constitutional democracy, a cabinet minister from the Apartheid regime held a press conference in Canada to describe the similarities between the *Indian Act* and Apartheid principles, a furor in Canada ensued.[52] He had a point.

As a definable racial group, Aboriginal women in Canada have the most in common with the oppressioon lived by colonized and racialized women in South Africa. Aboriginal women activist lawyers have taken different points of view on seeking or relying on constitutional protections for Aboriignal women's equality rights. Before her judicial appointment, Mary Ellen Turpel questioned why non-Aborignal women would strive to attain a legal form of "equality" when the standard to be achieved was in fact the white woman's equivalent of the lived privileges of white men.

> I do not see it as worthwhile and worthy to aspire to, or desire, equal opportunity with White men, or with the system that they have created. We do not want to inherit their objectives and positions or to adopt their world view.[53]

Constitutional amendment negotiations in Canada continued long after the patriation of 1982. The promised negotiations on Aboriginal rights, to be added to the Constitution, began soon after patriation in 1982. Attempts were made to craft an equality guarantee specifically for Aboriginal women. Spokeswomen for the largest Aboriginal women's organization, Native Women's Association of Canada (NWAC), took the position that white men's model of patriarchy so pervaded Aboriginal communities, on and off-reserve, that Aboriginal women needed to rely on their constitutional rights. But NWAC leaders were acutely disappointed with what was enacted to address their rights in the 1983 amendments—specifically (s.34(4)). Faced with the weak wording in the Constitution, NWAC developed a constitutional litigation strategy, as one means of attempting to secure stronger protections for Aboriginal women. By the '90s, NWAC had sued the prime minister and the federal government over exclusion of Aboriginal women from yet another round of constitutional negotiations.

> Aboriginal women have been legally, politically and socially subordinated by the federal government and by Aboriginal governments..... We have been shut out from our communities because they do not want to bear the costs of programs and services to which we are entitled as Indians.... Under sections 15, 28 and 35 (4) of the *Constitution Act, 1982,* women are entitled to substantive equality rights.[54]

THE "DOUBLE WHAMMY" OF WOMEN'S CONSTITUTIONAL ACTIVISM

Women's activism changed final constitutional text on equality—and vice versa. Commentators differ; a "plus" from one perspective is sometimes assessed as a "minus" from another. Of a number of early thought-provoking observations made by Canadian commentators, in addition to those already mentioned earlier, Andrew Petter,[55] was representative of the sceptical—at best, guardedly optimistic—predictors about the impact of the *Charter* for women. Petter, like Turpel, raised the question of using men as the equality standard, pointing out that the "LEAF victory" in the girl-gets-to-play-hockey case only applied to a very limited number of girls and did not really celebrate girls' hockey skills or approach to the sport. Perhaps best known is the Gwen Brodsky and Shelagh Day finding (based on only the first three years of Charter litigation) that sex equality cases accounted for a mere ten percent of the equality cases.[56] Sherene Razack questioned channelling resources into high impact constitutional equality litigation and raised concerns about the exclusionary nature in the founding of the chief women's equality litigant, LEAF, in its early years of operation.[57]

But another perspective as to the value of Canadian women's constitutional activism can be seen in the writing of South African lawyer, Beth Goldblatt,

> [In the United States] [s]ince women and men both benefited where there was temporary disability, pregnancy was not regarded as a ground of sex-based discrimination as there was no male comparator. Women were expected to bear the costs of their pregnancy. This approach to pregnancy could not occur under our [South African] anti-discrimination clause since pregnancy is specifically listed as a ground of

discrimination. Nevertheless, a similarly conservative approach might be taken towards childcare unless our anti-discrimination jurisprudence is clearly defined. The more progressive approach is to be found in the European Court case of *Dekker* v *Stichting Vormingscentrum voor Jong Volwassenen* (VJV Centrum Plus) [1992 ICR 325] and the Canadian Supreme Court case of Brooks v Canada Safeway Ltd. [1989] 1 S.C.R. 1219] The court in Brooks recognised that "since pregnancy and childbearing are fundamental social needs... it was discriminatory to place the whole burden on only part of the population." It is this argument which needs to inform the use of s 9(3) [of the South African Constitution] in advocating a right to child care.[58]

CONCLUSION

Much of this article has looked at the "what" and "how" of women's consitutional activism. In conclusion, let's glimpse briefly toward "what next" and "what if"— as courts deliver decisions interpreting constitutional equality that surprise, confuse, please and disappoint. There is no doubt that academic discourse on the detriments and benefits generated by women's constitutional activism will only expand, particulary as the many constitutions forged over the past decade— in diverse countries such as Ukraine, Afghanistan, and Rwanda—mature and retrospectives elongate.

Academic Criticism of Activism

Frankly, I am concerned that much of academic discourse may not be helpful in supporting and nourishing the women who bend to the much messier task of constitutional activism and democratic reform. Hindsight is a luxury activists seldom have and academics can be helpful in bringing perspectives forward that help to hone strategies. Participatory action research can be a powerful tool for women's rights, fought for by ordinary women who want to be able to live their rights, and, as is so often the primary driver for women, to build a place for their children and grandchildren to live their rights. But resources to compensate for inadequacies of communication or production can seldom be accessed by activists. In Canada, after exhausting months of political battle all through 1981, described earlier, women were faced with the s. 28 sex equality ERA disappearing under the s.33 override, so activists fought for it—substantially and symbolically.

> [T]he battle began all over again.... Said Gerry Rogers, one of the Newfoundland activists—in a phrase that applies to so much of the work of democracy—"It's sort of like doing dishes—they're never done. There's *always* another dirty dish."[59]

Writing more than 20 years later, the value of the activism on s.28 has been disappeared. Diana Majury was not optimistic, "There has been no engagement in the decisions of the Supreme Court of Canada with the question of what, if anything, section 28 adds in terms of equality protection for women (or for men)."[60]

In contrast to Majury, Beverley Baines[61] wrote in 2005, that s.28

> ...may yet prove multifunctional, capable of working strategically against, or substantively with, section 15. Thus I'm hoping for another defining moment in which scholarship and jurisprudence collude to recognize a purposive interpretation of section 28 that will sustain the intentions of its feminist drafters.[62]

By 2006, purposive interpretation for s.28 as the Canadian "ERA" had not been seen, and, of the five sex equality appeals litigated by women to the Supreme Court of Canada, all were lost.[63]

In *R. v. Kapp,* in 2008, although giving a minority opinion, Supreme Court Justice Bastarache acknowledged the protective nature of s.28, "Is this shield absolute? Obviously not. First, it is restricted by s.28 of the Charter which provides for gender equality '[n]otwithstanding anything in this Charter'."[64]

Both of Sharon McIvor's grandmothers were status Indians, but her grandfathers were not. After 17 years, McIvor's case finally reached the British Columbia Supreme Court (BCSC) in 2006.[65] The BCSC agreed with McIvor that the *Indian Act* contravened the *Canadian Charter of Rights and Freedoms* as well as international conventions on human rights, women's rights and children's rights and concluded that the offending section 6 of the *Indian Act* was of no force and effect. However, the Federal Government appealed the decision to the British Columbia Court of Appeal (BCCA), and, while the BCCA ruled against McIvor and did not rely on s.28, it acknowledged its prophylactic function:

> Section 28 is a provision dealing with the interpretation of the Charter. It does not, by itself, purport to confer any rights, and therefore cannot be "contravened". Further, the equality rights set out in s.15 explicitly encompass discrimination on the basis of sex; they are incapable of being interpreted in any manner which would be contrary to s.28.[66]

Parliament proposed changes to the *Indian Act (Bill C-3* received royal assent in December 2010*)* that failed to address fully the sex discrimination embedded in the *Indian Act.* McIvor did not stop—she presented her case to the United Nations Human Rights Committee in 2011 using The First Optional Protocol to the *International Covenant On Civil And Political Rights.* She has stated:

> Many people in Canada, Aboriginal and non-Aboriginal, recognize that this long-standing discrimination against Aboriginal women and their descendants is wrong and should end. Before me, Mary Two-Axe Early, Jeanette Corbière Lavell, Yvonne Bedard, and Sandra Lovelace [now

Senator Sandra Lovelace-Nichols] all fought to end sex discrimination against Aboriginal women in the status registration provisions in the *Indian Act*. I will continue, with the same determination they had, until Aboriginal women enjoy equality.[67]

The LEAF model, while respectful of the Rule of Law, grew directly from women's constitutional activism—interdisciplinary, intergenerational, evidence-based advocacy, incorporating high impact litigation and other strategies to attain lived rights. Golub takes a similar approach to legal empowerment, against "Rule of Law orthodoxy."

Numerous studies by academics and development organizations highlight the importance of building the capacities, organization, or political influence of civil society—all of which legal empowerment contributes to—in improving the lives of the disadvantaged. A growing array of qualitative and quantitative research more specifically suggests that legal empowerment has helped advance poverty alleviation, good governance, and other development goals.[68]

For all the differences and disappointments that are woven within the small and not-so-small victories that strengthen good governance in the constitutional venues inhabited by women—in South Africa, Canada, and so many other countries, such as Afghanistan and Rwanda, where women's activism has also changed constitutional text and machinery—let's acknowledge the imperfect, courageous work of ordinary women and adopt the invocation of South African women activists:

Malibongwe Igama Lamakhosikazi
Let the name of the women be thanked.[69]

Aspects of this article can be found in "Gender Democracy and Canadian Constitutional Trialogue" in Lessons from Europe's and Canada's Constitutional Experiences, *John Erik Fossum (ed.), (ARENA Centre for European Studies, University of Oslo, Norway, April 2011), "Women's Constitutional Activism in South Africa and Canada," with Susan Bazilli, in the* International Review of Constitutionalism, *Volume 9, 2009, No. 2, "A Truer Story: Constitutional Trialogue,"* Supreme Court Law Review, *2007, and "The Impact of s.15 on Canadian Society: Beacon or Laser?" in the* National Journal of Constitutional Law, *Volume 19, 2006.*

Marilou McPhedran is the Principal (Dean) of The University of Winnipeg Global College, was the Chief Commissioner of the Saskatchewan Human Rights Commission and held the Sallows Chair in Human Rights, College of Law, University of Saskatchewan in 2007 and 2008 and was the founder and Co-director, International Women's Rights Project, Centre for Global Studies, University of Victoria, 2003-2006. Appreciation is expressed to my activist colleagues and to my LL.M. advisor, Professor Bruce Ryder of York University's Osgoode Hall Law School, for his encouragement to share my reflections as a feminist activist lawyer, based largely on the model I now teach—"evidence-based advocacy"—grounded in skills learned as a lawyer and strategist doing considerable pro bono work, including co-founding several grassroots non-governmental organizations with missions to address root causes of women's inequality, including LEAF—the Women's Legal education and Action Fund—an internationally recognized pioneer in high impact litigation strategies for women's rights.

[1] Pierre Elliott Trudeau, "Remarks by the Prime Minister at the Constitutional Proclamation Ceremony on April 17, 1982" (Library and Archives Canada: 1982), Online <www.lac-bac.gc.ca>.

[2] Radha Jhappan, "Post-Modern Race and Gender Essentialism or a Post-Mortem of Scholarship," *Studies in Political Economy*, Fall 1996, 15 at 20.

[3] *Constitution Act*, 1982, being Schedule B of the *Canada Act* 1982 (U.K.), c.11 [hereinafter, the "Canadian Constitution" or if referenced in a section focused only on Canada, the "Constitution"].

[4] Author's note: The Canadian Broadcasting Corporation (CBC) featured the twentieth anniversary of the Charter of Rights and Freedoms in 2002, quoting only experts who happened to also be white men, making no mention of how the social movement of women shaped Canadian constitutional principles of equality. My review of archival websites for the Government of Canada yielded not a single feature on women's role in constitution-making—no mention of the national ad hoc women's constitutional coalition that numbered in the thousands, no mention of the Native women's rights lobby and, for Doris Anderson, who was a pivotal and prominent media presence in the constitutional battles of 1981—there was one radio clip, from 1970, on a different topic.

[5] Michael Ignatieff, *The Rights Revolution*, (House of Anansi Press Ltd., 2000) at 6-7.

[6] Peter Hogg, "Patriation of the Canadian Constitution" (1983), *8 Queen's L.J.* 123 at 126.

[7] Alexandra Dobrowolsky and Vivien Hart, "Introduction: Women, New Politics and Constitutional Change," in Alexandra Dobrowolsky and Vivien Hart, eds., *Women Making Constitutions—New Politics and Comparative Perspectives* (Palgrave Macmillan, 2003) at 1,2.

[8] A few notable exceptions in Canada being Penney Kome, Katherine de Jong, Chaviva Hôsek in the 1980s and, more recently, Alexandra Dobrowolsky.

[9] Nancy Millar, *The Famous Five—Emily Murphy and the Case of the Missing Persons*, (Western Heritage Centre, 1999) at 9-15. In 1916, Emily Murphy (not a lawyer) presided over the new Women's Police Court as the first women police magistrate in the British Empire, was widely read under her popular pen name "Janey Canuck" but was less popular under her own name—Judge Emily Murphy—as the author of *Black Candle* in 1922, about addiction to opium and cocaine in Canada. Judge Murphy was indisputably the leader in the "Persons Case," who called the other four together to have tea on her verandah and to sign the petition to the Supreme Court of Canada in August 27, 1927. Judge

Murphy paid legal costs that the other women did not, and was principally responsible for navigating the lawsuit through the courts. In 1907, as a young pastor's wife in Edmonton, who had grown up protected by the customs of privilege in Ontario, she was shocked to hear poor women describe how they were not protected by custom or by law and so she went to the legislative library to find out for herself that property laws did not protect a wife's interest in the family home. These inquiries led to her connection with Henrietta Muir Edwards (whose name became the lead citation for the Persons Case, of Fort McLeod, Alberta, the "convener of laws" for the National Council of Women, then Canada's largest women's NGO. The *Supreme Court of Canada Act* provided for government funding of significant questions of constitutional law. The Famous Five petitioned for an interpretation of section 24 of the *British North America Act*, renamed the *Constitution Act 1867,* when the constitution was patriated and the *Constitution Act* 1982 was enacted.

[10]Emily Murphy, Nellie McClung, Henrietta Muir Edwards, Louise Crummy McKinney and Irene Parlby, now known in Canada, as the "Famous Five" For more information: <http://www.famous5.org>.

[11]*Reference as to the Meaning of the Word "Persons' in Section 24 of the British North America Act, 1867,* [1928] S.C.R. 276. "…women are not eligible for appointment by the Governor General to the Senate of Canada under Section 24 of the British North America Act, 1867, because they are not 'qualified persons' within the meaning of that section."

[12]Millar, above, p. 45, describes how the Five lost control over the question that had been put to the Supreme Court of Canada. The *Supreme Court Act* allowed costs of the petition and appeal to be covered by the government if the issue was considered by the government to be of sufficient national importance, but it also gave the Attorney General and his government lawyers' *de facto* control over the case. Never presented to the court, the two questions drafted by the Five, in which they purposely omitted use of the word "persons', were: "Is power vested in the Governor general of Canada or the Parliament of Canada, or either of them, to appoint a female to the Senate of Canada?" and "is it constitutionally possible for the Parliament of Canada, under the provisions of the *BNA Act*, or otherwise, to make provision for the appointment of a female to the Senate of Canada?" Their government funded lawyer, Newton Rowell, travelled to London in July of 1929 to argue their appeal, paid by the Government of Canada.

[13]October 18th is now officially celebrated in Canada as "Persons Day" commemorated by the annual awarding of a Governor General's medal to five long-time activist women, and one young woman leader.

[14]Reference as to the Meaning of the Word "Persons" in Section 24 of the British North America Act, 1967, [1928] S.C.R. 276, rev'd *Edwards v. Canada* (A.G.), [1930] A.C. 124 (P.C.) For different perspectives on this historic case, see also: D. Bright, "The Other Woman: Lizzie Cyr and the Origins of the "Persons Case" (1998) 13(2) *Can. J. of Law & Soc.* 99; and K. Lahey, "Legal 'Persons'

and the Charter of Rights: Gender, Race and Sexuality in Canada" (1998) 77(3) *Canadian Bar Rev.* 402.

[15]Nellie L. McClung, "Women are Discontented," *The New Citizenship,* as reprinted in Cook and Mitchison, *The Proper Sphere,* at 288-289. As Nellie McClung, one of the Famous Five, and a life-long activist author, noted, "The women who are making the disturbance are women who have time of their own…. Custom and conventionality recommend amusements, social functions intermixed with kindly deeds of charity… while women do these things they are thinking, they wonder about the causes, the underlying conditions—must they always be."

[16]CBC Radio and Television Archives, "Equality First: the Royal Commission the Status of Women" Accessed online Aug.20.04 ,www.archives.cbc.ca>. Author's note: Based on the account of Laura Sabia, a Toronto city councilor, president of the Canadian Federation of University Women, the first president of the National Action Committee on the Status of Women (NAC) and a chair of the Ontario Advisory Council on the Status of Women. Laura Sabia convened the first meeting, to which she invited "young" feminist lawyers (myself among them), to discuss litigation strategies using the constitution.

[17]Pauline Jewitt, "Where were the MEN when Canada set out to find what makes life tough for its women?" *Macleans Magazine,* January 1968, p.12. Jewitt became a Member of Parliament who strongly supported the women's constitutional activists during the drafting negotiations in 1981.

[18]Lorna Marsden, "The Role of the National Action Committee on the Status of Women in Facilitating Equal Pay Policy in Canada" in R. S. Ratner, ed., *Equal Employment Policy for Women* (Temple University Press, 1980) 242 at 244; *Status of Women News,* Vol. 6 no. 2, Spring 1980 [the now defunct quarterly newsletter from NAC].

[19]*Canadian Bill of Rights,* S.C. 1960 c.44 [still in force, but subject to the Constitution Act 1982]

[20]*A.G. Canada* v. *Lavell* [1974] SCR 1349 [hereinafter Lavell]

[21]*Lovelace v. Canada* (1981) Report of the Human Rights Committee, GAOR 36th Sess., Supp. No.40 (AQ/36/40), Annex XVIII, 166. The UN Human Rights Committee held that Canada had violated Article 27 of the *International Covenant on Civil and Political Rights.*

[22](1966) G.A. Res. 2200 (XXI), 21 U.N. GAOR , Supp. (no.16) at 59, U.N. DOC.A/6316 (1966). In force for Canada 23 March 1976. As the constitutional activism of the 1980s started to roll—almost ten years after the march from Tobique—the Government announced partial redress, giving discretion to band councils to ask the government to exempt them from s.12 (1) (b)—a change that perpetuated inequity and division among many Aboriginal communities, to this day.

[23]*Murdoch* v. *Murdoch* [1975] 1 S.C.R. 423. Beth Atcheson *et al.* noted that Ernest Shymka of Calgary represented Mrs. Murdoch on a contingency basis, but in the end was not paid fees or disbursements. When asked to describe the

nature of her work, Mrs. Murdoch replied "Haying, raking, swathing, moving, driving trucks and tractors and teams, quietening horses, taking cattle back and forth to the reserve, dehorning, vaccinating, branding, anything that was to be done." When asked if her husband was ever away from their properties, she replied, "Yes, for five months every year" at 443.

[24]Murdoch *supra*. Note: the monthly $200 stipend was supplanted later by a "lump sum" settlement of $65,000 without the monthly payments.

[25]*Bliss* v. *A.-G. Canada*, [1979] 1 S.C.R. 183.

[26]Author's note: When constitutional reform re-surfaced on the government agenda in 1979, the CACSW, largely due to the initiative of its new president, Doris Anderson, engaged in a national public education campaign on women's constitutional rights. In the 1970s, there was only one widely circulated Canadian women's magazine, Chatelaine, which had a women's rights editorial policy, largely due to Anderson's years as editor, making her a trusted and credible spokeswoman for women all over the country. It was the very public dispute between Anderson and the federal Cabinet's Minister Responsible for the Status of Women, when she resigned over government cancellation of the CACSW women's constitutional conference, that triggered formation of the grass roots ad hoc women's constitutional coalition.

[27]Anne Collins, "Which Way to Ottawa? A Special Report on the Women's Conference on the Constitution," *Homemaker's Magazine,* Holiday 1981 11 at 22. Author's note: the comment is attributed to Linda Nye, who co-chaired the women's constitutional conference in 1981 and was a leader in the Ad Hoc Committee of Canadian Women on the Constitution.

[28]Elizabeth Janeway, *Powers of the Weak* (New York: Alfred A. Knopf, 1980) at 166-7. Just as Parliament confirmed in Canada's national anthem that "true patriot love" would "in all our *sons* command," Elizabeth Janeway described women's unused political potential as power of the weak.

[29]The Hon. Lloyd Axworthy, who in later years proved often to be a strong ally on human security and international women's rights, particular when the Taliban regime was oppressing women in Afghanistan in the 1990s.

[30]The October 1980 wording on "equality rights" (not a term being used at that time by the government) was: "The Canadian Charter of Rights and Freedoms guarantees the rights and freedoms set out in it subject only to such reasonable limits as are generally accepted in a free and democratic society with a parliamentary system of government.

15.(1) Everyone has the right to equality before the law and to the equal protection of the law without discrimination because of race, national or ethnic origin, colour, religion, age or sex."

[31]Elizabeth Janeway, *Powers of the Weak* (Random House of Canada Ltd., 1980) in Judith Finlayson "Women and Power: Part 5—Power in the Public Sphere," *Homemaker's Magazine,* November 1982, 50 at 59. See also Anne Collins account of the dinner in Appendix.

[32]G.A. Res. 34/180, U.N. GAOR, 34th Session, Supp. No. 46, at 193, U.N. Doc. A/

RES/34/180 (1980) Canada acceded in 1981; South Africa in1995.

[33]The October 1980 wording on "equality rights" (not a term being used at that time by the government) was: The Canadian Charter of Rights and Freedoms guarantees the rights and freedoms set out in it subject only to such reasonable limits as are generally accepted in a free and democratic society *with a parliamentary system of government.*

15.(1) Everyone has the right to equality before the law *and to the equal protection of the law* without discrimination "because of race, national or ethnic origin, colour, religion, age or sex.[emphasis added]." Also of significance to what transpired, the precursor to s.25 on Aboriginal rights and s.24 on what is now attacked under the final version of the Charter as the anti-democratic "activist" judicial power to order remedies such as "reading in" was worded in 1980 as follows: "Undeclared Rights and Freedoms. The guarantee in this Charter of certain rights and freedoms are not be construed as denying the existence of rights or freedoms that exist in Canada, including or freedoms that pertain to the native peoples of Canada."

[34]Penney Kome, *The Taking of Twenty-Eight: Women Challenge the Constitution,* 1983 (Toronto: Women's Educational Press). Available now online http://tinyurl.com/yfvw5x p. 36.

[35]During the negotiations on constitutional text, unguarded comments by male authority figures (in this case, Sen. Hays) acted as a catalyst because the media treated it as "news' and thus the information spread across the country—at no cost of time or money to the women activists, other than interviews. The special joint committee was composed of Members of Parliament and Senators, co-chaired by MP Serge Joyal from Quebec and Senator Harry Hays from Alberta. With increasing corporate concentration of media ownership seldom held by socially progressive owners, my observation is that neither of these responses to women occur much anymore—officials are very careful with public statements and women's issues in Canada are generally not considered "news' plus neo-conservative women columnists are now the most widely read.

[36]Kome, p. 35

[37]Christopher P. Manfredi, *Feminist Activism in the Supreme Court: Legal Mobilization and the Women's Legal Education and Action Fund* (Vancouver: UBC Press, 2004) at 48

[38]Some exceptions being Ramsay Cook, The Proper Sphere, Catherine L. Cleverdon, *The Woman Suffrage Movement in Canada: The Start of Liberation* (2nd ed.) (Toronto: University of Toronto Press, 1978), Patrick Watson and Benjamin Barber, *The Struggle for Democracy* (Lester & Orpen Dennys Ltd, 1988) 141-169. Penney Kome entitled a chapter of her book on Canadian women's constitutional activism, "The Invisible Woman" and documented examples of exclusionary reporting. Kome gave as an example, that Canada's "national" newspaper, *The Globe and Mail,* devoted 453 column inches to the "Native lobby" compared to 143 column inches to the women's rights lobby. This comparison does not come out of a constitutional rivalry between Native

leaders and women, though some journalists erroneously reported that, and Premier Blakeney of Saskatchewan did make support for both a condition of his endorsement of the women's position. Author's note: the broader-based women's lobby argued for "Indian rights for Indian women." In 1982, when *The Globe and Mail* published a special supplement on the constitutional negotiations and final text, women's activism was not listed among the major influences of outcome. In Michael Valpy and Robert Sheppard's book, *The National Deal: The Fight for a Canadian Constitution*, 1982 (Toronto: Macmillan of Canada), the Ad Hoc constitutional conference was omitted from the authors' appended chronology of significant events shaping the constitution.

[39]At this point, the author must become narrator. Steno pad notation [with my added explanations for the purpose of this article written 25 years later, in square brackets]: "Mon. 9 Nov/81 Laura Sabia: jumping the gun on [holding a women's protest] public forum. Flora [McDonald—then the senior Progressive Conservative women MP, having been in Joe Clark's cabinet] says 0 in writing yet & not till the 20th. [Referring to the Nov.5.81 Accord to which premiers agreed "in principle" but the drafting was done by officials, after the politicians had gone home] Advises MP lobbying as best tactic."

[40]Canadian Charter of Rights and Freedoms, part I of the Constitution Act 1982, being Schedule B of the Canada Act 1982 (UK), c.1

[41]Kome, in *Taking of Twenty-Eight*, p.90, noted that Alberta's Premier Lougheed was the first to agree to lifting the s.33 override from s.28, referencing the Alberta women who won the "Persons Case" in 1929.

[42]Kome, p.90.

[43]N. Colleen Sheppard, "Equality, Ideology and Oppression: Women and the *Canadian Charter of Rights and Freedoms*" (1986) 10 *Dal. L. J.* 195 at 222. Mary Eberts, "Sex-based Discrimination and the Charter" in Anne F. Bayefsky & Mary Eberts, eds., *Equality and The Canadian Charter of Rights and Freedoms* (Toronto: Carswell, 1985) 183; Catharine A. MacKinnon "Making Sex Equality Real" in Lynn Smith, ed., *Righting* the *Balance: Canada's New Equality Rights* (Saskatoon: Canadian Human Rights Reporter, 1986) 37 at 41, in Majury at 307-8. "Colleen Sheppard saw this in relation to the enhancement of section 7 rights for women: "The radical potential of this section [28] becomes apparent if we contemplate the notion of equal liberty or security of the person for women and men." Mary Eberts argued that s.28 "should ... lead a court to require a high level of justification [under section 1] for any sex-based distinction." Rosalie Abella postulated that section 28 "means that in interpreting the onus on a respondent to justify the reasonableness of a limit to an otherwise guaranteed right, gender equality is an immutable right." According to Catharine MacKinnon, "Anti-subordination could be the distinctive guiding interpretive principle of section 28."

[44]Katherine J. de Jong, "Sexual Equality: Interpreting Section 28" in Bayefsky & Eberts, at 528.

[45]Bazilli, Preface, *Putting*.

[46]Elizabeth A. Sheehy, "Women and Equality Rights in Canada: Sobering Reflections, Impossible Choices' in Susan Bazilli ed., *Putting Women on the Agenda*, (Johannesburg: Ravan Press, 1991) 262 at 272

[47]Author's personal copy, National Action Committee Archives, Toronto, Ontario, Canada.

[48]Ronalda Murphy, *supra* note at 23

[49]Murphy, *supra* note 136 at 34

[50]Stephen Golub, "Beyond Rule of Law Orthodoxy: The Legal Empowerment Alternative," *Rule of Law Series Working Paper 41*, Washington, DC: Carnegie Endowment 2003). <http://www.ceip.org/files/pdf/wp41.pdf>.

[51]Didi Khayatt, "The Boundaries of Identity at the Intersection of Race, Class and Gender" *Canadian Woman Studies*, 1994, Vol.14, No. 2, at 8.

[52]CBC Radio and Television Archives <www.archives.cbc.ca>.

[53]Mary Ellen Turpel, "Patriarchy and Paternalism: the Legacy of the Canadian State for First Nations Women" (1997) *Can. J. of Women and the Law*, 180.

[54]National Speaker of NWAC, Gail Stacey-Moore, "Aboriginal Women, Self Government, The Canadian Charter of Rights and Freedoms, and the 1991 Canada Package on the Constitution," an address to the Canadian Labour Congress, December 3,1991

[55]Andrew Petter, "Canada's Charter Flight: Soaring Backwards into the Future," *J. of Law & Society*, 16(2), 1989, 51

[56]Nine of the 52 claims were made by women, with about a 50 percent rate of success, but this was before the *Andrews* decision in 1989. In *Canadian Charter Rights for Women: One Step Forward or Two Steps Back?* Published in 1989 by the CACSW, authors Gwen Brodsky and Shelagh Day did not dismiss the Charter outright but they certainly sounded the alert, pgs.118-119.

[57]Sherene Razack, *Canadian Feminism and the Law: the Women's Legal Education Fund and the Pursuit of Equality*, 1991 (Toronto: Sumach Press).

[58]Beth Goldblatt, "Litigating Equality — The Example Of Child Care" in Saras Jagwanth and Evance Kalula (eds.), *Equality Law—Reflections from South Africa and Elsewhere* (Juta Law, 2001) 8 at 20.

[59]Patrick Watson and Benjamin Barber, *The Struggle for Democracy*, (Lester & Orpen Dennys Ltd, 1988) at 166.

[60]Diana Majury, "The *Charter*, Equality Rights, and Women" (2002) 40 *Osgoode Hall Law Journal* 3&4, 298-335, at 307-309. "It is interesting to speculate why this happened-whether section 28 was seldom invoked and accordingly has languished forgotten and untested; whether groups were unable to come up with a distinctive section 28 argument; whether it was eclipsed and made redundant by stronger section 15 jurisprudence than was anticipated; whether judicial discomfort and/or uncertainty about section 28 led to its abandonment; or whether women's groups developed discomfort about the apparent privileging of sex discrimination claims over other forms of discrimination."

[61]Author's note: Professor Baines was the principal academic advisor to the Ad Hoc Committee of Canadian Women on the Constitution during the drafting

negotiations in 1981.

[62]Beverley Baines, "Section 28 of the Canadian Charter of Rights and Freedoms: A Purposive Interpretation," 2005, Vol.17 *Canadian Journal of Women and the Law*, 1, 2005, 45-70. "However, time has yet to reward section 28's promise. In fact, section 28 is seriously compromised by arguments that relegate it to impractical strategic domains, or worse, fail to address its substantive interpretation."

[63]Beverley Baines, "Equality, Comparison, Discrimination, Status' in F. Faraday, M. Denike, M. K. Stephenson (eds.), *Making Equality Rights Real: Securing Substantive Equality Under the Charter* (Toronto: Irwin Books, 2006) p.78. As of September 2006, the five Canadian appeals lost are: *Symes* v. *Canada* [1993] 4 SCR. 695; *Native Women's Association of Canada* v. *Canada* [1994] 3 SCR. 627; *Thibaudeau* v. *Canada* [1995] 2 SCR. 627; *Vancouver Society of Immigrant and Visible Minority Women* v. *Canada* [1999] 1 S.C.R. 10; *Newfoundland (Treasury Board)* v. *Newfoundland and Labrador Association of Public and Private Employees* (NAPE) [2004] 3 S.C.R. 381.

[64]*R. v. Kapp*, [2008] S.C.J. No. 42, (para 97 per Bastarache, J for the minority)

[65]<http://www.canlii.org/en/bc/bcsc/doc/2007/2007bcsc827/2007bcsc827.html>.

[66]*McIvor v. Canada* (Registrar, Indian and Northern Affairs) [2009] B.C.J No. 669 (par 64 BCCA).

[67]<http://www.fafia-afai.org/en/news/2011/sharon-mcivor-petitions-un-human-rights-committee>.

[68]Golub, Rule of Law Orthodoxy, above, Legal empowerment differs from Rule of Law [ROL] orthodoxy in at least four ways: (1) attorneys support the poor as partners, instead of dominating them as proprietors of expertise; (2) the disadvantaged play a role in setting priorities, rather than government officials and donor personnel dictating the agenda; (3) addressing these priorities frequently involves nonjudicial strategies that transcend narrow notions of legal systems, justice sectors, and institution building; (4) even more broadly, the use of law is often just part of integrated strategies that include other development activities. Numerous studies by academics and development organizations highlight the importance of building the capacities, organization, or political influence of civil society—all of which legal empowerment contributes to—in improving the lives of the disadvantaged. A growing array of qualitative and quantitative research more specifically suggests that legal empowerment has helped advance poverty alleviation, good governance, and other development goals.

[69]Albertina Sisulu, "Preface" in Gertrude Ntiti Shope, ANC, *Malibongwe, Celebrating Our Unsung Heroines* (Jet Park South Africa: Teamwork Printers, 2002), p.6.

CYNTHIA D. STIRBYS

Gender-Based Analysis and Indigenous Worldviews

G ENDER-BASED ANALYSIS (GBA) according to the Status of Women Canada
(SWC) is a process that assesses the differential impact of proposed and/or
existing policies, programs and legislation on women and men. It makes
it possible for policy to be undertaken with an appreciation of gender differences,
of the nature of relationships between women and men and of their different
social realities, life expectations and economic circumstances. It is a tool for
understanding social processes and for responding with informed and equitable
options (2001: 1). Therefore, GBA is an analysis that is intended to reduce or
eliminate gender bias in policies, programs, and services, but is it appropriate
to be applied to the First Peoples of Canada? Status of Women Canada[1] is the
branch within the federal government that initially developed the GBA training
curriculum "using a policy and program development framework familiar
to most policy analysts" (Neville 7) that prepares them to address inequities
between men and women. But it is not necessarily an approach that takes other
worldviews into consideration and, for this reason, a GBA lens applied to First
Nations communities can do more harm than good when policies are not relevant
to their life experience and circumstances. This article will discuss the federal
government's perspective on equality and its inability to achieve it, first for women
in general and then specifically for First Nations women in Canada. And, despite
commitments to international conventions, the federal government fails in its
approach to GBA. In addition, the federal government lacks an understanding
of the differential impacts that colonization has had on First Nations people, as
demonstrated by its own contradictory policies and legislation to the detriment
of First Nations people and their culture.[2] Additionally, factors involved in the
differing worldviews between First Nations culture and the federal bureaucratic
culture will be discussed as a means to re-creating a GBA framework that reflects
the real needs of First Nations (and Aboriginal) people.

WHERE CANADA IS AT WITH GBA

Gender-based analysis is not a new initiative. In fact, it has been discussed in

449

various provincial and federal government departments since the 1970s when the Canadian International Development Agency (CIDA) first introduced the idea of GBA (Williams). In the 1980s and 1990s, the government of Canada adopted the principles of GBA, and by 1995 after the Fourth United Nations World Conference on Women, adopted the *Beijing Platform for Action*. The commitment extended to the "effective integration of a gender perspective throughout their operations, policies, planning and decision-making" (Neville 2). Canada presented its *Federal Plan for Gender Equality* that called for the implementation of GBA throughout all federal departments and agencies to inform and guide the federal legislation and policy-making process. This demonstrated Canada's commitment to act on its endorsements of agreements that also include: the *Universal Declaration of Human Rights;* the *Convention on the Elimination of All Forms of Discrimination Against Women* (cedaw); and, the *United Nations Declaration on Violence Against Women*. It was intended that gender-equality analysis automatically become a part of the lens in which future policies are developed for non–Aboriginal and Aboriginal populations in Canada.

Although Canada's federal departments have a GBA strategy in place, the further development of policies using this tool is almost non-existent. Aboriginal Affairs and Northern Development Canada (AANDC) previously known as Indian and Northern Affairs Canada (INAC) has had a Gender Equality Assessment Policy (GEA) in place since 1999. In the last few years, a substantial amount of effort has been made by the INAC Women's Issues and Gender Equality (WIGE) Unit to support staff so that they can conduct a GEA on their own policies, however, implementation has been slow and in some cases absent. Member of Parliament Anita Neville has noted that the status of implementation of gender-based analysis throughout the federal government differs significantly between departments and agencies. Overall, even when gender-based analysis does exist, few staff and few resources are available in the lower ranks of the bureaucracy, having minimal or no mechanisms for ensuring that GBA is actually achieved (Neville 33). Although some in government have been focused on applying the tools and techniques of GBA for many years, implementation has been met with resistance in many government departments. According to the Standing Committee on the Status of Women, inequalities still exist in Canada as women have been disproportionately affected by the lack of economic opportunity, whilst experiencing higher levels of poverty and domestic violence. Yet inequalities are that much greater for Aboriginal women in Canada. The need for GBA continues, to determine whether programs, policies, and laws work for equity, and whether these programs, policies, and laws work as well for women as for men (Neville 2005: 1). Yet there is uncertainty as to whether equality can be achieved in Canada given there is no political will to do so. In less than one year since being elected, Prime Minister Stephen Harper broke his election campaign promise to the Canadian Feminist Alliance for International Action (FAFIA) "to improve the situation of women's rights in Canada." According to a FAFIA media release dated January 18, 2007, the operating budget of the SWC was reduced by $5 million dollars (43 percent of its budget) resulting in "the closure of 12 of its 16 regional SWC offices, the elimination of the Court Challenges Program, the termination of funding for all advocacy related work by women's groups and the removal of the word *equality* (author's emphasis) from the mandate of SWC's Women's Program."

Program funding cuts like this impact the ability to do further research. Research is required to determine the diversity of women and whether or not this diversity of women's experience is reflected in new policies or programs. This is especially important since gender alone is not reflective of women's lives and experiences. Throughout Canada, diverse groups of women, including Aboriginal women, women with disabilities, and lesbian women have continued to argue that their experiences, needs, and interests have not been adequately represented or taken up by social service providers, by educational and research institutions, or by governments. For example, in the area of health policy, women from various communities have argued for relevant data disaggregated by gender, racial background, sexual orientation, disability, and Aboriginal status (Teghtsoonian). As a result, funding cuts would not allow government departments to respond to the health (and cultural) needs of diverse groups of women despite SWC's original mandate to address the "different social realities, life expectations and economic circumstances" (SWC 2001: 1). For example, SWC could not provide training to assist in the development of a "culturally-affirming framework" for First Nations women.[3] Therefore, some additional funding would be necessary to conduct research in order to integrate the analysis developed in Aboriginal communities. GBA that includes multicultural and disability factors must also be applied in policy and decision-making processes with the central business of government.

HISTORICAL ROLES OF FIRST NATIONS WOMEN

This section will look at the historical roles of First Nations women to show how equality and balance were the norm before contact (colonization). The basic premise of this section acknowledges that First Nations have vast and diverse cultural background and histories and because of this First Nations, Inuit, and Métis women do not comprise one homogenous Native group (Beaver 2001). In many First Nations cultures, the "social makeup [was] based on equality and respect towards all life, including that of the sexes"; in some languages, there are no words that can be translated "to describe genders as in the case of he/she" (Beaver 2001: 7). For example, the Micmac language "does not distinguish between male/female; the distinction is between animate/inanimate."[4] Gender equality (inequality) was not an issue during pre-contact eras because each person was valued and held an important role within the community: men, women, elders, and children (Beaver 2001: 7). Jeanette Armstrong shows that in traditional societies, women held "immense power" as it was they who "shaped the thinking of all its members in a loving, nurturing atmosphere within the base family unit. In such society, the earliest instruments of governance and law to ensure social order came from the quality mothering of children" (ix).

Darrah Beaver states, "equality-based communities in which Aboriginal Peoples once lived, were rooted in the wisdom of the women" (8). One nation that was predominantly matriarchal was the Iroquoian society that centred its "familial, social, and political organization of the communities" on women (Beaver 2001: 10). It was the women in Iroquois society who "managed the land, the crops, the longhouses, and women were essential to both the tribal economy and political organization, as demonstrated by their clan systems" (Beaver 2001: 11). Within the clan systems, the women of the long house never moved out like the men. When it was time to marry, the woman and her husband were expected to reside in the long house with her birth family, clan relatives, and clan mother. The ordering of this kin relationship was to ensure that the women of the long house eventually would gain "the prestigious roles of some day becoming clan mothers themselves" (Beaver 2001: 11). George Beaver (1997) explains the role of the clan mothers was that of decision-maker for her longhouse and governing the community:

> The leading women in villages, as the heads of lineages, exerted their influence through a variety of means, from using their right to appoint, chastise, and dethrone peace chiefs from among a group of eligible hereditary candidates, to demanding that war chiefs avenge the deaths of family members, and to pressing their views in councils, particularly at the lineage and village levels, either directly or through male representatives. (43)

Women created the balance in the leadership and were the "direct representatives of the members of their clans and longhouses, their role on the council of chiefs assured that every citizen was equally represented. In this way, women governing created balance and social order within their society without gender bias" (Beaver 1997: 12).

DIFFERENCE IN WORLDVIEWS IMPACT FIRST NATIONS WOMEN'S REALITY

While GBA is seen as a tool to combat gender bias, GBA as it stands is a western paradigm that may not be appropriate to ensure the re-balancing of roles between First Nations men and women. Why? There are differences in worldviews where western society is trying to achieve something that they have never achieved (equality), whereas First Nations (Aboriginal) societies are attempting to reclaim their egalitarian ways and undo the damage done by colonizers. That is why "GBA" is more meaningful to First Nations if it is considered a *Gender Balancing Analysis* or a *Re-balancing* initiative. For First Nations, GBA is political in nature given the historical injustices and the legacy of colonization. First Nations are addressing Canada's discriminatory policies and legislation such as the *Indian Act*, Bill C-31 and Matrimonial Real Property Rights that we currently live by. In this way, politics cannot be avoided when First Nations must live by a separate rule of law imposed by the government, resulting not only in different life experiences but the expectation that First Nations must live a lower quality of life compared to other Canadians.

Evelyn Zellerer's research shows that conflict began in Canada when new settlers brought with them a new worldview that opposed the First Nations worldview:

> Traders, missionaries, settlers, and government officials brought with them values from a patriarchal, capitalist society which often conflicted with the cultural values of Aboriginal Peoples. For example, traders had difficulty dealing with Aboriginal women who, in some societies, were in charge of furs and whose consent was required before men could complete bargains. Missionaries tried to instill values of a nuclear family with a husband as the authority and where children and wives are to be disciplined. This contrasted with the values of Aboriginal extended families and closely knit clans where individual autonomy was respected and children were sacred. (11)

With the advent of Christianity and colonization in the seventeenth century, the Huron-Montagnais, by taking on a foreign worldview, transformed their society in less than 30 years (Anderson). The Huron-Montagnais society had maintained "egalitarian relations between the two sexes" before the Jesuits arrived (5). The differences between men and women were seen as "both significant *and* complementary" and Huron-Montagnais society did not, and could not, "exist without the contributions of *both* sexes" (Anderson 5). That changed however, when the Jesuits were able to transform the delicate balance of society where "women and men, for the most part, occupied different roles, but retained equal capacity to exercise power" to the European worldview that saw women as "inferior" (Anderson 7, 12). The French imposed their Christian doctrine that determined a First Nations woman's sexuality made her a "[s]eductress, emissary from hell, [and] temptress" since this "posed a threat to the very power relations the Jesuits hoped to instil" (Anderson 86). Jesuits saw First Nations women's "[f]reedom of sexual expression" as "a lack of control, a certain wildness that appeared to threaten civilization itself" (Anderson 86). Therefore, in order to gain control over the Native populations, the Jesuits targeted the most intimate form of relations and in this way ensured their form of "hierarchal ordering of societal relations" as part of the conversion process (Anderson 86). As such, the Jesuits expressed their authority over women and convinced First Nations men that First Nations women were "of a lesser worth than men, more susceptible to influences of evil, weaker in every way and in need of men's guidance" and "assured women a position of greatly reduced powers and rewards, compared to those granted to men" (Anderson 6).

The contradiction in worldviews becomes very apparent when we recognize that Canada was built on the notion of inequality right from its beginning. For example, Duncan Campbell Scott, Deputy Superintendent of Indian Affairs, pursued the "idea of a 'monolithic identity' for Canada; the idea of a 'white, male, Eurocentric' society that would eventually emerge and Canadians would 'never have to apologize again'" (qtd. in Stirbys 15). He ensured the "inherited policy" of assimilation that came before him would become more "repressive" during his tenure (1879-1932) (Stirbys 3, 14). For example, Scott stood by the *Oliver Act* of 1911 that used the government's "powers of coercion" to amend the *Indian Act* to take Indian lands "without surrender for roads, railways, and other public purposes" (Stirbys 14). The Indians could be removed at any time for any purpose and Scott saw that while building a new nation, "the government must do what they must do in the name of progress and 'Indian rights ... should not be allowed to interfere with those of the whites'" (Stirbys 14).

Scott's legacy continues today as shown in attitudes toward women in which "wifely obedience" is a "key nugget of wisdom contained in the old Christian marriage rites. Unambiguously, a man is told to love his wife, and his wife to obey her husband" ("You've Come a Long Way ... Maybe"). This attitude can only presume the patriarchal notion that many women's needs are denied in favour of serving her husband. Also recall Harper's massive cuts to any organization that advocates on behalf of women. This decision will have an even greater effect on First Nations (and Aboriginal) women who are said to be "the doubly denied or the forgotten minority" and suffer not only discrimination on the basis of race and gender, but are also neglected by both Aboriginal and non-Aboriginal society (Beaver 2001: 2). Compare the clan mothers who represented their longhouses and communities and held prestigious and respected positions to that of a First Nations woman today who is discriminated against because she is forced to live under imposed legislation and policy. First Nations women were greatly impacted by section 12 (1)(b) of the *Indian Act* due to the fact that if they marry non-Indian men, they lost their status but when an Indian man marries a non-Indian woman, his wife gains status. Kathleen Jamieson in "Indian Women and the Law in Canada" outlines the consequences of the *Act:*

> The woman, on marriage, must leave her parents' home and her Reserve. She may not own property on the reserve and must dispose of any property she does hold. She may be prevented from inheriting property left to her by her parents. She cannot take any further part in band business. Her children are not recognized as Indian and are therefore denied access to cultural and social amenities of the Indian community. And, most punitive of all, she may be prevented from returning to live with her family on reserve, even if she is in dire need, very ill, a widow, divorced or separated. Finally her body may not

be buried on the reserve with those of her forebears (qtd. in Beaver 2001: 18).

The federal government in recognizing the discriminatory aspects of the *Indian Act*, instituted Bill C-31 to make changes to the *Act* which followed in 1985. Prior to the revisions however, First Nations women were forced to give up "their cultural ties to their families, land and communities and dictated who was an Indian for the purposes of the *Indian Act*" (Beaver 2001: 22). The new bill did not result in equality for First Nations women, since the new *Act* "worked to instill a system of patriarchy in the governance system that went with it" (Beaver 2001: 23). Bill C-31 was to ensure that women who had lost their status under s.12 (1)(b) along with those who had been involuntarily enfranchised would be reinstated. However, sexual discrimination continues today despite the passing of Bill C-31 since the Bill C-31 reinstatee cannot pass her own status onto her children unless born to a father with Indian Status (Beaver 2001: 24). Bill C-3 received Royal Assent and came into effect as of January 31, 2011 to amend the registration provisions in the *Indian Act* (AADNC 2013). But many believe that Bill C-3 is no different from Bill C-31(Gabriel 2010) and it may be too soon to realize whether discrimination will end for First Nations women. In essence, First Nations women continue to be denied their basic human rights by not allowing them to practice their cultural matrilineal right to pass descent through the mother. According to Darrah Beaver, claims for the existence of matriarchy are based on three conditions: societies in which women make the major contribution to subsistence; societies in which descent is traced through women (i.e., matrilineal); and, myths of ancient rule by women (11).[5]

A First Nations woman wanting to pursue a human rights complaint, was denied yet again since under the *Canadian Human Rights Act*, Section 67 "restricts the ability of people living or working in communities operating under the *Indian Act* to file complaints of discrimination if the discrimination they are complaining about is related to the *Indian Act*" (Canadian Human Rights Commission 2). Although section 67 was repealed in 2008, and the CHRA now applies to First Nations on reserve there are still concerns in how First Nations human rights will be addressed given the complexity of on-going legal, social, economic and political issues. A main concern is that the CHRA is based on a western legal system (NWAC 2011). According to the Native Women's Association of Canada (NWAC) what is required is an "intercultural" human rights approach to bridge First Nations and Western knowledge systems and legal traditions consistent with solving conflicts based on equality rights and not gender alone (2011: 7). For example, the Canadian Research Institute for the Advancement of Women (CRIAW) states that "Prioritizing one ... entry point (gender) or one relation of power (patriarchy) to the exclusion of others, (race and class), misrepresents the full diversity of [First Nations] women's realities, applying only one entry point into analysis simplifies and reduces what are actually very complex systems of oppression" (cited in NWAC 2011: 4).

GBA, according to the *Status of Women Handbook* (2001), is about fairness and justice for both men and women; it is a tool to redress past and systemic discrimination, ensure a relational approach and an accountable process, and of course to legally ensure the human rights of all (23-26). In other words, GBA is a tool to ensure that policies, programs, or legislation does not perpetuate or increase gender inequities. Clearly one may observe that the federal government has developed opposing policies and legislation for First Nations to the extent that it not only increases the gender inequalities but that it absolutely contributes to marginalizing and reducing the quality of life for many First Nations women and their children. And, this is the main reason GBA in its current form should not be applied to First Nations. GBA overlooks the on-going colonization that is reflected in the discriminatory policies, programming, and legislation designed specifically for First Nations people since before Confederation.

WHERE ABORIGINAL ORGANIZATIONS ARE AT WITH GBA

Many non-governmental and Aboriginal women's organizations are in the process of developing their own culturally-affirming approaches.[6] The Assembly of First Nations (AFN), the national organization representing First Nations citizens in Canada has developed a framework that they consider a teaching and decision-making tool. This tool is meant to be used to revive the complementary roles of men and women that once made First Nations families strong and their nations vibrant (AFN 2009: 27). What sets AFN's GBA apart from federally instituted GBA's is that gender is not seen as a binary western concept. Instead, gender is more reflective of the roles and responsibilities to family and community. For example, the "Winkte" is a name given to someone who may be physically a man but dresses as a woman and is valued for his/her gift and sacred role in community (AFN 2009: 32). Historical discrimination has contributed to devaluing the unique roles of contemporary Winktes. AFN is working from a First Nations cultural worldview as a means to "restore and remember historical gender-balanced concepts and working with First Nations to further develop new concepts and mechanisms of gender balancing" in a modern context that includes complex realities.[7] The AFN Gender Balanced Analysis Framework has six main steps and begins with: 1) Understanding and Recognition of Traditional Values and Ways of Balance; 2) Identifying and Defining Issues and Desired Outcomes; 3) Identifying Information Needs, and Conducting Research and Analysis; 4) Implementing Decisions; 5) Monitoring and Evaluation of outcomes. The intent of the development of the framework was to do training with First Nations communities, to guide AFN's own policies and processes, and to guide those federal departments that develop policy and services for First Nations people. However, implementation has been challenged by the lack of funding resources.[8] The AFN Gender Balancing Analysis is currently used in limited ways to address policy in such areas as tobacco, diabetes, and FASD.

Other non-governmental organizations like the Native Woman's Association of Canada (NWAC) have incorporated a "culturally-relevant GBA" (CR-GBA) intended to support the development of appropriate policies and programs that are effective, equitable, and challenge "preconceived notions of culture and gender" for Aboriginal women (2010: 2). In addition, NWAC has developed a culturally-relevant gender application protocol (CRGAP) workbook that guides the user through four sections employing a process of asking specific questions within each principle of the CRGAP. The four sections within each principle ask about: the actions that are required of policy makers; what tracking and performance measures have been put in place; what are the outcomes; and what are the best practices and lessons learned? The three main principles support the full participation of Aboriginal women and other sectors in community by aiming to: 1) achieve *equity in participation* by addressing obstacles women may experience and what measures were taken to eliminate these obstacles; 2) *balance communication* by indentifying the facts and using the data/information to inform what the gender differences are; and 3) achieve *equality in results* by asking what actions need to be taken to improve the process and how many programs have resulted in creating positive change. Through the promotion of Aboriginal women's perspectives on different policy issues, the CRGAP is intended to be an educational and awareness raising tool. This tool is meant to challenge and shift the on-going stereotypical attitudes that can make a difference in elevating the opportunities and quality of life for Aboriginal women (NWAC 2010).

Pauktuutit, a national organization representing Inuit women reported the need for a GBA framework that reflects an Inuit perspective i.e. "the Inuit Way" (Guillou and Rasmussen). To date, there has been little or no research done to show the interaction between gender roles and health of Inuit. For example, regarding the indicators related to food security (diet) and gender: do gender roles make a difference for how often Inuit women have access to and consume country food? And does an increased consumption of country food protect women from developing diabetes? The proposed model for an Inuit GBA Framework focuses on the interactions of four domains: 1) The Inuk woman, her family, and community; 2) Elders, culture and language; 3) Land and country food; 4) Euro-Canadian economy, institutions and government (Guillou and Rasmussen). Within these domains there is a four step gender analysis to further consider the relationship between traditional and contemporary influences, current issues and the *Inuit Way* (Pauktuutit 2009). The two top reasons preventing the implementation of the Inuit GBA include a lack of: gender-specific data necessary to carry out a proper analysis (Pauktuutit 2008) and human resource capacity.[9]

The Aboriginal Women's Health and Healing Research Group (AWHHRG),[10] the former national network of First Nations, Métis, and Inuit women researchers interested in community-based research focused on the health of Aboriginal women, their families and communities, held their inaugural meeting to discuss GBA in February 2007. The intent of the meeting was to begin a dialogue to assess what a "culturally-affirming framework" might entail. Is a "culturally-affirming framework" different from being culturally-sensitive? However defined, the framework must be built on "fundamental values and principles … of Aboriginal peoples" that includes policy and legal issues (AWHHRG). The group also wanted to redefine or clarify terms currently used in describing GBA, such as "equality, equal outcomes, and equity" (AWHHRG). Knowing the impacts when applying GBA would be beneficial when considering research, politics, and leadership; collective versus individual rights; policy and program development; changing roles and parenting; relationships (two-spirited, male-female, children, and elders); Aboriginal identity and cultural roles; socio-economic conditions; and, community safety (violence prevention). The group took a broad perspective on GBA and questioned whether a foreign concept should be adapted or "Indigenized" for Aboriginal people.[11] No definitive answers emerged. But it might be in the best interests of First Nations and Aboriginal communities to begin developing their own frameworks since "working within the same framework and mindset that caused the problem in the first place" cannot solve current problems of injustice.[12]

CULTURAL DIFFERENCES IN TERMS AND DEFINITIONS

GBA currently uses terms that do not incorporate a First Nations cultural context. For example, the word "gender" only takes in the western worldview that has a meaning of male/female only. Sexuality in a First Nations context considers multiple genders, "at least three, but up to six" which includes male, female, and not-male/not female (or two-spirited) (Cameron). Michelle Cameron states that the term "two-spirited" is a part of the "counter-hegemonic discourse and reclamation of [Aboriginal peoples'] unique histories" (123). Aboriginal communities embraced two-spirited members who were seen as "integral parts of the community, occupying positions of honour and communal value" (124). Two-spirited people were respected for having a third perspective other than those held by either a man or a woman.

The western paradigm of GBA does not consider a First Nations concept of gender when they define it as "the culturally specific set of characteristics that identifies the social behaviour of women and men and the relationship between them" (SWC 2001). The "modern constructs of gay/lesbian/bi … are based on sexual orientation, whereas two-spiritedness is based on gender orientation" (Cameron 124). In Aboriginal culture sexual orientation and gender orientation are defined in two separate categories. A First Nations (Aboriginal) context sees that sexual orientation "is based on physical sex characteristics" and gender orientation "is not based on physical sex characteristics, but rather on the roles the person chooses to align with" (Cameron 124). Cameron uses herself as an example to make the distinction. She states that whether she chooses to be with a man or a woman, in the context of the original term "two-spirited," she would still be considered two-spirited despite her "male" choice of gender role. But in a western sexual dichotomy, she would be considered homosexual (124).

Sexuality (or the sex of the person) in a western binary concept refers to the "biological classification of an individual into either 'male' or 'female' based on chromosomes, genitalia and secondary sexual characteristics" (see http://gendertree.com/WhenDoesItHappen.htm). And it is the "religious dogma" of the residential school system that two-spirited people were come to be seen in the "same light as sin and sexual abusers" (Cameron 124). But those survivors who may have been sexually abused by a pedophile have not come to recognize that this is not the same as being "gay, lesbian, bi, or two-spirited and that, in fact, most child molesters identified as heterosexual men" (Cameron 124). Therefore, in a First Nations or Aboriginal paradigm, culture, sexual orientation, gender orientation, and the impacts of colonization (intergenerational traumas) must be dealt with concurrently. Any separation of these characteristics is otherwise an attribute of the dominant (Christian) white culture. According to Cameron, two-spirited Aboriginals do not subscribe to or fit into the western dichotomies of human sexuality. She states that "[w]e are not either/or; we are neither/nor" (124). The GBA framework as it stands, is not an "adequate framework for the complexities involved in two-spiritedness" (Cameron 124).

CONCLUSION

GBA as it is currently defined by the SWC Handbook is adequate in that it addresses the inequalities between men and women. Yet, it is not enough for those working in First Nations (Aboriginal) policy development to use GBA as it currently stands. Civil servants cannot give due diligence to their First Nations clients without knowing the historical and political context of many of the socio-economic hardships especially for First Nations women and their children. It is imperative to have a firm grasp of what a culturally-affirming approach is and how it is defined, otherwise the process becomes meaningless. Challenges remain when a GBA considers homogeneity an ideal by only focusing on one worldview, in addition to the lack of political will to ensure equality in Canada. These approaches must take into account the needs, concerns, and voices of First Nations (Aboriginal) men, women, youth, elders, and two-spirited individuals in relation to cultural diversity; accommodation of colonial impacts; new concepts and terminology to ensure cultural appropriateness (in whatever way this is defined by First Nations and Aboriginal groups); and legal arguments to remove discriminatory and opposing polices and legislation. These considerations can only strengthen the approach. Many non-governmental and Aboriginal women's organizations are currently working together to develop their own unique approaches. However, given the richness of First Nations and Aboriginal culture, the opportunity is open for Canada to work with these diverse groups and cultures to become a world leader in developing a *culturally-affirming gender re-balancing* framework that combines worldviews.

Cynthia D. Stirbys, a Saulteaux-Cree from Cowessess First Nations earned a Masters Degree in Conflict Studies, Saint Paul University, Ottawa, Ontario. She is currently doing her Ph.D. at the Institute of Women's Studies, Ottawa University. Her research examines the experiences of female Indian residential school survivors which align with her strong interest in First Nations health and gender re-balancing issues. She would also like to acknowledge and thank Jennifer Blomqvist, Chelsea Gabel, and Erin Corston for their contributions and constructive feedback based on their research and/or health field experiences.

[1]The SWC are the official trainers in GBA for all federal departments in Canada.

[2]The catalyst for writing this article was in the development of a First Nations culturally-affirming framework. Although there are common concerns around GBA between the three constitutionally-recognized groups—Inuit, Métis, and First Nations—it should not be assumed that these groups fit into one "homogenous" cultural model. First Nations is the group referred to unless stated otherwise.

[3]Author's personal experience with SWC. The SWC representatives became uncomfortable stating that to do so would "mess with their marketing" of GBA. Although they could not accommodate the request, the group participated in a regular SWC GBA training workshop.

[4]A First Nations participant noted this at the awhhrg GBA Workshop held February 19, 2007.

[5]See also <http: //www.encyclopedia.com/articlesnew/081999.html>.

[6]Author has worked with three groups (AFN, NWAC, and AWHHRG) on GBA between (2006-2007).

[7]As stated by the AFN representative when presenting the Gender-Balancing Framework at Trent University, March 17, 2007.

[8]In personal communication with AFN staff (M.F.H.), September, 2011.

[9]Personal communication with Executive Director, Pauktuutit, September, 2011.

[10]Although the organization has since closed down, the second GBA report is available at <http://www.awhhrg.ca/home.php>.

[11]From the final report of the inaugural meeting, "Beginning the Dialogue on Defining a Culturally-Appropriate GBA Framework," Vancouver, BC, March 2007.

[12]As stated by Taiaiake Alfred at a luncheon at Saint Paul's University, September 21, 2004.

REFERENCES

Aboriginal Affairs and Northern Development Canada (AANDC). "Registration Process for Bill C-3 Applicants." March 2013. Web.
Aboriginal Women's Health and Healing Research Group. Web.
Assembly of First Nations. "Gender Balancing: Restoring Our Sacred Circle."

Assembly of First Nations Gender Balanced Analysis Framework. Ottawa: Assembly of First Nations, July 2009.

Anderson, Karen. *Chain Her By One Foot: The Subjugation of Native Women in Seventeenth-Century New France.* New York: Routlege, 1991.

Armstrong, Jeanette. "Invocation: The Real Power of Aboriginal Women." *Women of the First Nations: Power, Wisdom, and Strength.* Eds. Christine Miller and Patricia Chuchryk. Winnipeg: University of Manitoba Press, 1997.

Beaver, Darrah. "Doubly-Denied: A Look at Canada's Aboriginal Women." Unpublished research paper, Carleton University, Ottawa, 2001.

Beaver, George. *Mohawk Reporter: The Six Nations Columns of George Beaver (Iroquois Reprints).* Ohsweken: Iroqrafts Publications, 1997.

Cameron, Michelle. "Two-Spirited Aboriginal People: Continuing Cultural Appropriation by Non-Aboriginal Society." *Canadian Women's Studies/les chahiers de la femme* 24 (2,3) (2005): 123-127.

Canadian Human Rights Commission. "A Matter of Rights. Special Report of the Canadian Human Rights Commission on the Repeal of Section 67 of the Canadian Human Rights Act." Ottawa: Minister of Public Works and Government Services, 2005.

Feminist Alliance for International Action (FAFIA). 2006. "All Party Leaders Have Signed the CEDAW Pledge! View the Responses." Web.

Government of Canada. House of Commons. Standing Committee on the Status of Women. *Gender-Based Analysis.* 39th Parliament, 1st Session. Issue No. 2, May 16, 2006.

Gabriel, Ellen (March, 2010). "Politics: re: Bill C-3 An Act to promote gender equity in Indian registration by responding to the Court of Appeal for British Columbia decision in *McIvor v. Canada* (Registrar of Indian and Northern Affairs) Amendments." Web.

Guillou, Jessica and Rasmussen, Derek. "Inuit Gender-based Analysis Framework: Excerpts from a Report on the Health of Pauktuutit Inuit Women of Canada." September, 2011. Web.

Indian and Northern Affairs Canada (INAC). *Gender Equality Analysis Policy.* Ottawa: Status of Women Canada, the Department of Justice and Human Resources Development, 1999.

Indian and Northern Affairs Canada (INAC). "Gender Equity in Indian Registration Act." 2010. Web.

Neville, Anita. "Gender-Based Analysis: Building Blocks for Success." Report of the Standing Committee on the Status of Women. Ottawa: Government of Canada, 2005.

Native Women's Association of Canada (NWAC). "The *Canadian Human Rights Act* and Aboriginal Women Executive Summary Report and Focus Groups Recommendations." Ottawa: Native Women's Association of Canada, March 2011.

Native Women's Association of Canada. "GBA: A Culturally Relevant Gender Application Protocol." Ottawa: Native Women's Association, June 2010.

"Platform for Action." Fourth World Conference on Women, Beijing, 1995. Division for the Advancement of Women Online: <http://www.un.org/womenwatch/daw/beijing/platform/>.

Pauktuutit. "Inuit Gender-based Analysis Framework: Culturally Relevant GBA in an Inuit Context." Powerpoint Presentation. Wendake, QC. September, 2008.

Pauktuutit. "Inuit Gender-based Analysis and the Food Mail Program Final Report of a Case Study." Ottawa: Pauktuutit Inuit Women of Canada Report Prepared for Indian and Northern Affairs Canada, March 2009.

Stirbys, Cynthia. "The Policy of Hegemonic Structures in Aboriginal Country and the Paradox of Altruism and Fear." Unpublished Master's research paper, Saint Paul's University, Ottawa, 2004.

Status of Women Canada (SWC). "Gender-based Analysis Policy Training: Participant Handbook." Ottawa: Status of Women Canada, 2001.

Status of Women Canada (SWC). "Gender-based Analysis: A Guide for Policy-Making." Ottawa: Status of Women Canada, 1998. Web.

Teghtsoonian, Katherine. 1999. "Centring Women's Diverse Interests in Health Policy and Practice: A Comparative Discussion of Gender Analysis." Paper Prepared for "Made to Measure: Designing Research, Policy and Action Approaches to Eliminate Gender Inequality," National Symposium, Halifax, Nova Scotia. 3-6 October.

Williams, Wendy. 1999. "Will the Canadian Government's Commitment to Use Gender-based Analysis Result in Public Policies Reflecting the Diversity of Women's Lives?" Paper Prepared for "Made to Measure: Designing Research, Policy and Action Approaches to Eliminate Gender Inequality", National Symposium, Halifax, Nova Scotia. 3-6 October, 1999.

"You've Come a Long Way ... Maybe." *Citizen's Weekly* 28 January 2007: B6-B8.

Zellerer, Evelyn. 1993. *Violence Against Aboriginal Women.* Ottawa: Royal Commission on Aboriginal Peoples, 1993.

CYNTHIA L. COOPER AND MARGIE KELLY

Life, Interrupted

Reproductive Damage from Chemical Pollutants –
Alarm Growing Since Rio

arm to human health, and especially to women's reproductive health, is moving up quickly on the scale of environmental concerns. This development, based on a growing understanding of the harm from small amounts of pollutants, reverberates with fundamental values of women's lives, human rights, and also may become a galvanizing issue for environmental activists.

In 1992, Agenda 21, the blueprint for global environmental action created for the United Nations Earth Summit in Rio, paid only passing attention to the damaging effects of chemical contamination on human health, including reproductive health. Instead, it emphasized the need to manage risks to the environment associated with chemical use. Nations were urged to "strengthen international risk assessment" of chemicals and "produce guidelines for acceptable levels of exposure" for a greater number of toxic chemicals (UN 1992).

Ten years later at the Johannesburg Summit, priorities shifted. This time, the document developed by conference participants focused less on risk assessment and more on people's health, setting goals for 2020 "to use and produce chemicals in ways that do not lead to significant adverse effects on human health and the environment" (UN 2002).

What happened during that decade to raise alarm about toxic chemical pollution as a major threat to human health and sustainability of the planet? In short, environmental scientists showed that dangerous chemical contamination is interfering with human reproduction. Extensive chemical usage threatens the ability of women and men to bear children and to raise healthy children (Colburn, Dumanoski and Meyers).

Procreation is a fundamental human right, and is among the most momentous rights and life activities of women and men. Interference with that right through the involuntary exposure to chemicals threatens basic assumptions about human existence and sustainability. Recognizing that environmental contamination by toxic chemicals is compromising the ability to reproduce, women's reproductive rights advocates and environmentalists are establishing new alliances to confront the growing threat to the right to bear children and to bear healthy children.

THE PROBLEM: HORMONE DISRUPTION AND REPRODUCTION

In January, 2003, the U.S. government released startling results from the largest survey of its citizens' body burden of environmental chemicals. The Centers for Disease Control (CDC) studied toxic chemicals in the bodies of ordinary people in the U.S. and found a wide array of toxic chemical contaminants and hormone disrupters (CDC 2003a).

Confirming the results of an earlier, smaller analysis issued by the CDC in 2001, the report explained that every single person studied bore measurable levels of pesticide products. Mercury, a toxin, was found in women of childbearing age, along with disturbing amounts of the plasticizers and phthalates, which are associated with developmental damage in animals and found in products such as cosmetics, perfume, and car interiors. Yet, the study analyzed only 116 of over 70,000 synthetic chemicals in commercial use (CDC 2003b). And no one knows the consequences to human health of combining a chemical potpourri of toxins.

The CDC study came in the wake of new attention to the hormone-disrupting properties of chemicals. Hormone disrupters are human-made substances that interfere with the body's hormone system, upon which healthy reproduction depends (Thornton 2000). Hormones also affect human growth, development, and intelligence. The list of synthetic chemicals that cause hormone disruption is long: dioxin, PCBs (now banned but still bioaccumulated in the environment), phthalates, organochlorines, mercury, and pesticides. These chemicals can be found in food, water, building materials such as vinyl pipes and flooring, and household products, ranging from tuna to drinking water, from soft plastic bath toys to plastic food wrap, from nail polish to carpeting (Colburn et al.; Schettler, Solomon, Valenti and Huddle).

So drenched is the environment with these chemicals—air, water, and soil— that, according to Joe Thornton, author of Pandora's Poison, all persons (and animals) on the planet have now absorbed some chemicals into their systems, and normal bodily systems cannot break them down (Thornton 2002). They are literally inescapable. Neither social status nor geographic location nor personal precaution will fully protect a person from exposure to these contaminants (Thornton, McCalley and Houlihan).

Environmental scientists are discovering that even at very low levels of exposure, hormone disrupters can cause infertility, low sperm count, birth defects, second generation childbearing problems, early puberty, and a host of other serious medical conditions and diseases (Ford; Schettler et al.; Colborn; NIEHS). Among the first scientists to propose the connection between environmental contamination and breast cancer were Devra Lee Davis and Mary Wolff (Davis et al.; Wolff et al.). Previously, analyses of environmental harms focused on cancer and diseases caused by major exposures; new studies look at the long-term degradation of human and animal life from minor exposures (Colborn; Steingraber; Thornton, Pandora's Poison).

The conclusion: reproduction suffers.

Minuscule amounts of chemicals may act as hormone disrupters, and the harm may be discovered only years later to children born of unsuspecting parents. For example, offspring of rodents exposed to phthalates, a very common element in consumer products, experience reduced sperm counts and altered sexual characteristics (Myers). Low levels of exposure of laboratory animals in utero to another compound, bisphenol-A, a chemical used in polycarbonate plastic, causes a lowering of the age of puberty of offspring (Myers).

Even though there is universal exposure to this potentially devastating and untested cauldron of chemicals, they are absorbed involuntarily. No one agrees to participate in a grand experiment with synthetic chemicals, or even knows that she is participating. Exposure to and bodily absorption of these chemical contaminants are not done willingly, voluntarily or by consent of those affected.

A REPRODUCTIVE RIGHTS APPROACH TO ENVIRONMENTAL CONTAMINATION

Reproductive rights inherently encompass the right to choose to bear children, as well as the right to decline childbearing. Advocacy organizations have outlined the rights of childbearing women as including healthcare prior to pregnancy and childbirth, a healthy delivery, postnatal care, and informed consent in decisionmaking ("The Rights of Childbearing Women"). Some have called for "freedom from reproductive hazards" within the environment, workplace and home (Kolbert 306).

Existing laws and documents on reproductive rights have not yet grappled with the specific issues raised by environmental factors that cause harm to reproduction. But rights articulated both internationally and in the U.S. provide an important framework for reproductive freedoms, including the right to bear children.

INTERNATIONAL HUMAN RIGHTS

International human rights documents recognize the right to bear children and the responsibility of governments to provide enabling conditions to do so in safety, according to Laura Katzive, an international lawyer formerly with the Center for Reproductive Rights in New York. The Universal Declaration of Human Rights, a primary international human rights document, adopted by the nations of the world in 1948, explicitly identifies the basic human right of every man and woman to "found a family" (Art. 16.1).

The Declaration further states that all people are entitled to live in a "social and international order in which their rights can be realized" (Art. 28). This affirmative right, says Katzive, can be seen as extending the obligations of governments beyond merely refraining from interfering with the right to bear children to an active duty to ensure that healthy conditions exist in which all people can exercize the right.

465

In addition to elaborating on the right to attain the highest standards of sexual and reproductive health, language in international documents also emphasizes "safe motherhood," a term used to underscore the importance of the right to bear children under healthy conditions (Centre for Reproductive Rights). The definition of "safe motherhood includes the reduction of pregnancy-related deaths and ill-health in infants, as well as the alleviation and elimination of environmental health hazards that affect the ability to bear children" (World Health Organization qtd. in Boland 23-24). When applied to the problem of hormone-disrupting chemicals, the concept of "safe motherhood" serves to highlight the rights of women and men to bear children in a healthy, enabling environment.

COUNTRY LAWS: THE UNITED STATES AS AN EXAMPLE

As far back as 1942, the U.S. Supreme Court stated that the right to bear a child is a central liberty—"one of the basic civil rights of man," the Court wrote in *Skinner v. Oklahoma*. Any action by the government that would impinge on the right to bear children must meet the strictest standards of scrutiny, the Court said. The right to bear children is part of a zone of privacy, which includes the right to use contraception and the right to make decisions about abortion. The U.S. Supreme Court acknowledged these as an integral part of the U.S. Constitution. The right to privacy protects citizens from governmental intrusion in decisions to bear children, just as it protects citizens from governmental intrusion in decisions not to bear children.

Although the U.S. Supreme Court has recognized that the right to bear children is "fundamental" (*Carey v. Population Services International*), hormone-disrupting chemicals pose a somewhat different challenge in the law. The production of the potentially-damaging chemicals is largely undertaken by corporations and, as such, does not generally involve an action by the government which can give rise to constitutional scrutiny under the scheme of law in the U.S. system. But it is legitimate to inquire whether the government has taken sufficient steps to prevent women and men from serious reproductive harm or abrogation of the right to privacy, and to insist that corporations have a legal and moral obligation to prevent harm to the fundamental right to bear children.

Taken together, international doctrines provide valuable guidance for framing a pro-choice position on the rights of women and men who desire to procreate. They appropriately place the emphasis on the adult right to reproduce and to bear healthy children. The reproductive rights and women's rights movements worldwide have been in the forefront on these topics.

DES: CONSEQUENCES OF HORMONE DISRUPTION FOR WOMEN'S REPRODUCTION

The problems associated with DES (diethylstilbestrol), a chemical compound prescribed to pregnant women in the 1950s and 1960s to prevent miscarriage, has a terrifying connection to the litany of adverse effects on reproduction from hormone disrupters, as shown in wildlife populations. DES, while a pharmaceutical, had hormone-disrupting properties, and the experience and study of it provided much information and alarm about environmental hazards. In the case of DES, many of the daughters of the women who took that drug were unable to bear children, and are at higher risk of developing breast cancer due to in utero exposure to hormone disrupters (Palmer et al.). Scientists studying hormone disruption report similar incidences of sterility and deformed genitalia in the offspring of fish and birds exposed to synthetic chemicals (Colborn et al.; Schettler et al.). The same mechanism of hormone disruption is at work, and the results are alarming prognosticators for women facing harmful chemical exposures.

When Valerie DeFillipo, then a senior director at Planned Parenthood Federation of America in Washington, DC, attended a conference on environmental contamination and hormone disruption, she saw the links. DeFillipo said she began to understand how what is put into the environment enters your body and affects reproduction, and realized its importance to the reproductive rights community in the future (see, also, Cooper). And a solid alliance between environmentalists and reproductive rights advocates could change the hearts and minds of policymakers, said Patricia Waak, former director of the National Audubon Society's Population and Habitat Program.

A PRECAUTIONARY APPROACH TO CHEMICALS

Among environmental scientists, there is a growing consensus that supports a shift in the way chemicals are released into the environment. They believe that it is no longer appropriate to assume that a chemical is safe and then later to ban it or limit its usage when it is proves to cause severe damage. A "dirty dozen" of especially persistent chemicals have been targeted for complete elimination in an international treaty of 127 nations, known as the Persistent Organic Pollutants (or POPs) treaty (Reuters). But these chemicals have already caused significant harm to human health and the environment. Instead of permitting the release of chemicals, whose harm may not be known for years or decades, environmental scientists are recommending that the "precautionary principle" should be implemented. According to the precautionary principle, chemicals would be tested prior to their release, and only upon receiving completely clean results would they be released. Scientists also encourage searches for safe alternatives to existing chemicals that cause harm (Thornton 2002, 2000; Myers).

Sweden is the first nation in the world to adopt fully the precautionary principle, calling for the introduction of new goods free of hormone-disrupting chemicals and for the phase-out of harmful human-made chemicals (Swedish Government).

CONCLUSION: A CRITICAL OPPORTUNITY TO WORK TOGETHER FOR ENVIRONMENTAL SUSTAINABILITY, BETTER HEALTH, AND GREATER REPRODUCTIVE FREEDOM

Contamination from chemicals, without the knowledge or consent of the individuals who absorb them, unquestionably violates reproductive rights. Reproductive rights clearly include the fundamental right of women and men to have children if they so desire, and to have children whose health is not irrevocably compromised by environmental contaminants.

The effects of hormone disrupters concern people from varied backgrounds, diverse economic strata, and all geographic locations. Men as well as women are threatened by the harms caused by hormone disrupters. Reproductive rights advocates and environmentalists are natural allies, as are those in the growing environmental health movement, such as activists concerned about the environmental causes of breast, ovarian and prostate cancer.

Environmentally-conscious women's organizations and reproductive rights activists could bring new support and political clout to secure this solution to prevent future chemical contamination of the earth.

This collaboration could also be a powerful antidote to the efforts of the anti-choice movement to weaken reproductive rights by promoting "fetal rights," giving a fetus rights that are independent of, and in some cases superior to, those of the pregnant woman and virtually eliminating her rights. In the area of hormone disrupters, pro-choice thinkers can preempt any anti-choice assertions that focus on endangerment to the right-to-life of the fetus, rather than on the rights of the pregnant woman. Toxic chemicals do their harm by destroying an adult's ability to bear healthy children, and their children's ability to lead healthy lives, including healthy reproductive lives. The anti-choice arguments are neither appropriate nor necessary. At this stage of the debate, an opportunity exists to head off a dangerous dynamic by avoiding the model that blames and punishes mothers for their behavior during pregnancy. Individual women should not be blamed for the damage their children suffer from toxic pollutants in their food and water (Brody).

In addition, although the "common ground" with anti-choice groups is, indeed, slender in most areas, reproductive rights organizations can take the lead in challenging them to stand up against environmental toxins that affect the well-being of all persons desiring to become parents. For example, several Catholic healthcare organizations that are generally opposed to abortion and contraception have become leaders in demanding substitutes for medical products, such as mercury and plastic tubing, that damage the environment and may interfere with reproduction. Working with environmental organizations like Health Care Without Harm, many hospitals are now committed to eliminating dangerous materials, products, and processes to improve patients' health and future well-being (Leciejewski).[1]

The understanding of such rights that pro-choice advocates bring to this emerging issue can provide the framework for promoting change. And by focusing on this vital environmental concern, together environmental and reproductive rights advocates can broaden the definition and application of reproductive rights as fundamental human rights. Women's lives, and the future of the planet, may depend on it.

Cynthia L. Cooper is a lawyer, journalist and author of several nonfiction books on justice topics. She has written or worked for several nonprofit organizations in the U.S., including Center for Reproductive Rights, Religious Coalition on Reproductive Choice, Amnesty International USA, The Parenting Project, Open Society Institute, and the Ford Foundation.

Margie Kelly is a communications strategist with experience in public education, media relations, online advocacy, and program management. She has collaborated with non-profit organizations and community groups across the U.S., pioneering social media strategies to build successful public information and legislative campaigns. Previously, Kelly worked for Safer Chemicals, Healthy Families, a coalition of environmental and health groups, the Center for Reproductive Rights in New York City, and Greenpeace USA.

[1]See www.chw.edu and Healthcare Without Harm at www.noharm.org.

REFERENCES

Boland, Reed. "Promoting Reproductive Rights: A Global Mandate." New York: Center for Reproductive Rights: 1997.

Brody, Charlotte. Former President of Health Care Without Harm, Personal Interview, July, 2002.

Carey v. Population Services International, 431 U.S. 678, 686 (1977)

Centers for Disease Control (CDC). "Second National Report on Human Exposure to Environmental Chemicals." 2003a. Web.

Centers for Disease Control (CDC). "National Report on Human Exposure to Environmental Chemicals." 2003b Web.

Center for Reproductive Rights. "A Human Rights Approach to End Maternal Mortality." June 6, 2010. Web..

Colborn, Theo, Dianne Dumanoski, and John Peterson Myers. *Our Stolen Future.* New York: Plume/Penguin 1997. Web.

Cooper, Cynthia L. "Enviros and Pro-Choicers Join Forces." Aug. 1, 2002. Web.

Davis, D. L., H. L. Bradlow, M. S. Wolff, T. Woodruff, D. G. Hoel, and H. Anton-Culver. "Medical Hypothesis: Xeno-estrogens as Preventable Causes of Breast Cancer." *Environmental Health Perspectives* 101 (1993): 372-376.

DeFillipo, Valerie. Personal Interview, July 2002.

Ford, Gillian. *Listening to Your Hormones.* Rocklin, CA: Prima Publishing, 1997.

Katzive, Laura. Personal Interview, April, 2003.

Kolbert, Kathryn. "Developing a Reproductive Rights Agenda for the 1990s." *From Abortion to Reproductive Freedom: Transforming a Movement.* Ed. Marlene Gerber Fried. Boston: South End Press, 1990. 297-306.

Leciejewski, Mary Ellen. Ecology Program Coordinator, Catholic Healthcare West, Personal Interview, April 2003.

Myers, J. P. "Transcript: Environmental Threats to Reproductive Rights." National Family Planning and Reproductive Health Association (NPHJRA), 2000. Web.

National Institute of Environmental Health Sciences (NIEHS), National Institutes of Health. "Endocrine Disruptors." Web.

Palmer, J. R. et al. "Risk of Breast Cancer in Women Exposed to Diethylstilbestrol in Utero: Preliminary Results (United States). 2002. Web.

Reuters. "127 Nations Adopt Treaty to Ban Toxic Chemicals." May 22, 2001. Web.

"The Rights of Childbearing Women." Maternity Center Association, 1999. Web.

Steingraber, Sandra. *Living Downstream: An Ecologist Looks at Cancer and the Environment.* Reading, MA: Addison Wesley, 1997.

Thornton, Joe. *Pandora's Poison: Chlorine, Health, and a New Environmental Strategy.* Cambridge MA: MIT Press. 2000.

Thornton, Joe. Personal Interview, April 2002.

Thornton, Joe, Michael McCally, and Jane Houlihan. "Biomonitoring of Industrial Pollutants: Health and Policy Implications of the Chemical Body Burden." *Public Health Reports* (July-August 2002): 315-323.

Schettler, Ted, Gina Solomon, Maria Valenti, and Annette Huddle. *Generations at Risk: Reproductive Health and the Environment.* Cambridge, MA: MIT Press, 1999.

Skinner v. Oklahoma ex rel. Williamson, 316 U.S. 535 (1942).

Sweden. The Government's New Guidelines on Chemical's Policy. Web.

ESTHER THARAO AND NOTISHA MASSAQUOI

Black Women and HIV/AIDS

Contextualizing Their Realities, Their Silence and Proposing Solutions

I N THE YEARS SINCE the emergence of the HIV/AIDS epidemic, the disease has become endemic in many developing countries especially in Sub-Saharan Africa and the Caribbean, fuelling a fear of the spread of HIV/AIDS across borders. This factor alone has numerous implications for Black women living in Canada and other industrialized nations. Labels, cultural meanings, and interpretations about the disease formed since its emergence continue to influence both the discourse on HIV/AIDS and the access to programs and services geared to its control for those most vulnerable to or at risk of infection. In the mid-'80s as the discourse unfolded, we, as African women living in Canada, were not so much concerned with contracting the HIV virus as we were with the racist undertones of media reports depicting HIV/AIDS as just another tragedy that was plaguing the poor, the powerless, and those living on the margins of society, namely Africans, IV drug users, and gay men. The total absence of any consideration of the social and political realities that left African people so devastated by this disease, coupled with the calculated correlation between the magnitude of the infection rates and the ascription of the exact origins of the disease, created an emphasis on the duality of "us" versus "them"—a discourse informed by centuries of mistrust based on our historical experiences of colonization and slavery.

Our focus was on refuting racist suppositions including the notion that Africans brought AIDS to the world, that Africans engaged in sexual activity with monkeys, that Africans performed barbaric rituals involving the drinking of human blood, that Africans' immoral sexual practices and polygamous family structures were going to be our own downfall. Instead of trying to kill the snake that had just entered into the house, precious time was wasted on futile debates about its origins. We can no longer afford to expend our energy refuting the racist speculation about the origins of HIV/AIDS. As African women living in Canada, it is quite clear that our communities here and globally are dealing with a crisis of major proportions—a reality clearly supported by available global statistics and those emerging in developed countries including Canada.

Despite the fact that Black communities in general, and Black women in particular, represent a significant element of the HIV epidemic, researchers and policy makers have largely ignored them. The absence of Black women in the HIV arena is especially evident in accessing prevention, treatment, support, and care initiatives is especially evident. They usually appear only in terms of staggering numbers of those infected either in epidemiological updates or in reference to prenatal HIV transmission and prevention. There is an urgent need for further research in this population to better understand the psychosocial,cultural and structural determinants of HIV risk.

THE ROOTS OF VULNERABILITY TO HIV/AIDS FOR BLACK WOMEN IN CANADA

That HIV/AIDS continues to pose a considerable threat for African and Caribbean women including married women, young women, and girls is not a result of individual risk-taking or lives filled with sexual adventures. Their vulnerability is not only biological like all other women but also unique and deeply rooted in socio-cultural and structural factors that intersect with gender, race, class, and political and economic conditions Lack of economic opportunities which increases dependency on men; deprivation of rights to autonomy and sexual control over their bodies create an environment of possible gender based violence; cultural practices that increase risk of infection such as genital mutilation, vaginal cleansing, and limited educational opportunities leading to misinformation about the epidemic are all factors many Black women continue to experience in Canada, a country to which they had migrated in search of a better life for themselves and their families. An understanding and documentation of these factors is imperative if efforts to improve access to services and ensure the involvement of Black women in prevention, treatment, support, and care programs are to be successful (Tharao and Massaquoi 2000; Massaquoi and Lala).

In Canada, healthcare delivery is directed toward the achievement of improved health by preventing diseases, addressing injury, controlling threats to one's life and influencing social conditions in order to ensure the realization of optimal health and quality of life for the community at large. This model of service delivery also guides healthcare professionals in the provision of health programs and services most appropriate for the clients they serve. However, in reality, the healthcare environment in which African and Caribbean communities seek assistance is one that imposes substantial barriers that hinder access to health services. Many of the communities' needs do not conform to North American systems of healthcare delivery, systems based primarily on a bio-medical, monocultural model (Massaquoi and Lala). Consequently, Black communities tend to utilize healthcare services less and receive critical diagnosis and treatment significantly later than other populations due in large part to the cultural, linguistic, racial, gender, and class barriers embedded within the system.

This understanding, coupled with staggering epidemiological reports encouraged us over a decade ago to investigate the contextual realities and barriers faced by African and Caribbean women and their vulnerability to HIV infection. The voices of 65 African and Caribbean women, and of the service providers working with them, were heard through focus groups and key informant interviews conducted by Women's Health in Women's Hands Community Health Centre[1] in 1999. We have drawn on the experiences of these informants, and our own years of experience in community education, support, and care of African and Caribbean women infected and affected by HIV/AIDS to develop the understanding of the issues impacting on Black women and the HIV/AIDS epidemic we present below. It is our hope that this knowledge will illuminate the realities still faced by African and Caribbean women in relation to HIV/AIDS, highlight the cultural context into which epidemiological data should be fitted, and propose some viable solutions to deal with the issues.

ECONOMIC MARGINALIZATION

Due to lack of employment opportunities, many Black women live beneath the poverty line, making it impossible for them to afford the amenities that only money can buy. As we are all aware, employment is the cornerstone of good health and when this is threatened all other determinants of health are destabilized as well. People living in poverty are less likely to seek early treatment for HIV infection, are more likely to have been less healthy when they contracted the virus and are more likely to have more advanced symptoms when they present themselves for treatment. Consequently they tend to die sooner from AIDS.

Economic marginalization presented itself as one of the most powerful social barriers to HIV prevention for African and Caribbean women. Most of the women who participated in the focus group discussions were either unemployed or employed in minimum wage jobs. This compounded their social conditions as well as their personal levels of stress.

I have to worry about feeding, clothing and housing my children. I don't have time to think about AIDS.

I work three jobs, I don't have time for anything else.

Economic marginalization further offsets the imbalance in gender relations within the women's lives and their decision making power including sexual decision making power.

I never go anywhere by myself, I am not allowed. He takes me to all the places I need to go. He has to know I am looking for information [HIV information]. I don't need that.

With this kind of control, women are not in a position to insist on fidelity, demand condom use, or refuse sex with their partner even when they suspect or know that their partner is already infected. Women often lack the economic power to remove themselves from relationships that carry major risks. HIV/AIDS and the risk of infection for Black women is not solely an individual behavioral problem and the extent to which poverty and employment risk factors need to be considered in proposed interventions and programs cannot be underestimated (Tharao and Massaquoi 2000).

RACISM AS A DETERMINANT OF HEALTH

There is growing evidence that the experience of racial discrimination can have a pervasive and devastating impact on the health and well being of communities of colour (Randall). Racism in Canada has caused distinct barriers to accessing healthcare services. It has created an environment within which quality healthcare is a commodity that has become socially, economically and politically unattainable by particular members of our society. One factor that has been implicated in the exacerbation of this impact is the current inadequacy in the provision of culturally-appropriate, anti-racist, inclusive healthcare services for all individuals. This inadequacy is particularly apparent in the context of the need for sensitive and appropriate care for Black women who face multiple oppressive forces of racial and sexual discrimination. Racist experiences with healthcare providers and the healthcare system was one of the primary reasons why Black women reported a reluctance to access healthcare services including HIV/AIDS education, prevention, testing, treatment, support and care. Women's personal experiences of racism included:

•Negative stereotypes about Black women and women of colour:
I went to a clinic to have an abortion, it was a traumatic event in my life, they treated me very coldly and the only thing I remember the doctor saying to me was "Do you know who the father is?" My white friend went to the same clinic and received all kinds of counseling and support.

•Practitioners dismissing health concerns as not important
...It took a year to finally find out what was wrong with me. My doctor kept saying it was all in my head and my people tended to worry too much and he never really took me seriously. Finally I got a new one who cared. I think if I was white things would have been better.

•Lack of sensitivity when dealing with issues of cultural differences, acculturative stress and racism.
Having my first child in Canada was a scary thing. I didn't speak the language and did not have any family here. When I went for my first prenatal examination the Doctor gasped and said "Oh my God." He had

never examined someone who had undergone female genital mutilation. I felt humiliated and very exposed. When I went to the hospital to deliver my baby the Doctor called all his colleagues to look at me without my permission. This is not a human way to treat people.

LACK OF CULTURALLY AND LINGUISTICALLY APPROPRIATE PRIMARY PREVENTION INFORMATION

Ensuring access for all to primary prevention HIV/AIDS information and services in formats and languages that people can understand, and are comfortable with, is a fundamental requirement if HIV/AIDS is to be prevented. Access to primary prevention ensures that individuals and communities are equipped with skills to prevent infection, promote safer sex and responsible sexual behaviours, and ensure that women have the necessary skills and tools to enable them to act on the prevention information provided to protect themselves. There are very few prevention programs and educational resources targeted specifically to Black women. This means that most Black women have very little knowledge of HIV/AIDS, modes of transmission and how it can be prevented. Most significantly, they lack an understanding of their own risk:

I never thought I was at risk, I was married, I did not use drugs and I was not gay. From all the things I saw on TV or in the paper it looked like a very white thing. In my mind there was no risk of infection for me.

Very few educational resources such as pamphlets, posters or booklets—the most popular of the HIV/AIDS social marketing tools—have visual representation of Black women or cultural imagery nor are they translated for an audience which does not speak English as its first language. Often times the primary prevention messages are inappropriate for particular groups, for example, encouraging condom use as an HIV prevention method without addressing gender power imbalance, cultural, and social barriers. Such messages are futile for women who do not hold any sexual decision making power within their relationships.

The need for target specific resources became an urgent issue for us when the policy on HIV testing during pregnancy, was announced without any culturally appropriate and language specific resources developed for Black women as a part of the program. Women's Health in Women's Hands could not deliver the program effectively without appropriate resources to supplement the information women were getting from providers. The Centre developed "Healthy Options for Women," an HIV-prevention and education resource targeted to Black women. The images in the booklet are of Black women, the information is tailored to meet the needs of Black women in relation to HIV/AIDS, and the booklet is translated into several languages spoken by African/Caribbean women. The importance of targeted information in relation to HIV/AIDS cannot be overemphasized as indicated by the quote:

> *Personally, when I look at HIV pamphlets or material it does not deal with my issues as a Black woman.*

It is clear that, in the case of Black women, there is a lack of readily available basic information on HIV prevention. This creates a situation whereby women do not understand and cannot accurately assess their own risk of being infected. Consequently they are not prompted to seek information and services. Most still think HIV/AIDS is someone else's problem. This lack of information creates a false sense of safety and reduces the riced or the urge to learn more about HIV/AIDS, how it is transmitted and strategies for its prevention.

LIMITED CULTURALLY APPROPRIATE AND LANGUAGE SPECIFIC HIV/AIDS PREVENTION, SUPPORT AND CARE PROGRAMS

In-depth interviews with service providers working in AIDS Service organizations and HIV clinics in Metropolitan Toronto revealed that most HIV/AIDS programs are delivered within mainstream settings which often lack the capability or the inclination to provide culturally-appropriate and language-specific services and/ or information to meet the hiv/aids needs of Black women (Women's Health in Women's Hands). Culturally-sensitive programs ensure comfortable environments where issues can be discussed openly without anyone feeling uncomfortable, offended or excluded. Information can be conveyed in so many different ways but only some of these ways are appropriate for specific cultural groups.

> *Have a discussion about sex in a group, no way; this is not our way. Why are we changing what we grew up with just because we are in a new country?*

When it comes to ensuring that women receive HIV/AIDS information in the languages they are comfortable speaking, the use of translators or cultural interpreters more often than not creates a barrier to service. Many Black women acknowledge openly that they do not want anyone from their community knowing about their HIV status. They are fearful that confidentiality will be broken and their community will find out about their status.

> *White organizations are a problem especially when you don't speak English ... they use translators from your community and then word gets around.*

Some women would prefer to struggle and get limited information in English or to have no information at all rather than to use a translator/interpreter who is, in most cases, a person from their community. The need for confidentiality often supercedes the need for information.

> *If people found out I may be rejected by my family and my community....*
> *This is worse for me than to find out that I had AIDS.*

Women are also worried about what people will think if they are seen looking for information. One woman summarized it:

> *Going to an AIDS service organization means either of two things. You are HIV positive and are seeking support or you are looking for prevention information hence your sexual behaviors are questionable.*

As a result of the stigma associated with HIV/AIDS, many women will not want to be linked to an agency providing HIV/AIDS services. This sentiment was also expressed with regard to the practice of designating a specific staff person to address HIV/AIDS issues within a multi-service agency.

> *If you have specific staff people assigned to work with HIV positive women, everyone knows your status as soon as you walk into their office. I would rather not go.*

SOCIO-CULTURAL ISSUES AND PRACTICES THAT INCREASE THE RISK OF INFECTION FOR BLACK WOMEN

Most of the service providers interviewed acknowledged that they experienced multiple challenges in their efforts to provide services for Black women. Lack of knowledge and understanding amongst service providers about cultural practices, norms, and values and how these practices increase the risk of HIV transmission further reduces the effectiveness of programs. Practices such as female genital mutilation and vaginal cleansing, issues many healthcare workers in Canada are unaware of, have direct correlations with increased rates of infection and should be part of risk assessment for women (Tharao and Massaquoi 2001; Tharao, Calzavara, and Myers). To accurately assess the risk of HIV infection for African and Caribbean women, an understanding of these practices is essential.

Religious and health-related beliefs, values, and norms further compound the issue. Most Black women come from settings where healthcare is accessed only when one is ill. Health promotion is a North American concept that has to be understood and accepted before it can be adopted. Religion also plays a central role in the lives of many Black women. Though some religious groups support HIV/AIDS prevention work, others have not acknowledged that it is an issue of concern and continue to portray it as an issue of immorality, hence a punishment from God for those who are infected. This poses a major dilemma since any prevention initiatives are seen to contradict religious beliefs and to go against the will of God or Allah. Given a choice, many women elect to follow what is prescribed by their religion thereby greatly limiting their access to information, prevention tools, support and care. The quotation below is an indication that the concept of prolonging life as a result of treatment is seen by some to contradict religious belief.

If it is the will of Allah for me to die tomorrow, no treatment on this earth can change that, so why try?

FEARS ASSOCIATED WITH BEING HIV POSITIVE AND ITS IMPLICATIONS

The stigma associated with HIV/AIDS and the social construction of the disease has created a distancing effect in the communities that have long been blamed as its originator. Stigma, with its subjective notions of shame, disgrace, and cultural misinterpretations that result in a "spoiled identity" (Williams and Goffman) have all greatly influenced how those most at risk react to the threat of the epidemic. AIDS-related stigma is further complicated by other socially discrediting characteristics of the groups most affected by it.

Visible minority group membership, homosexuality, drug use, commercial sex, and poverty are all characteristics that carried significant negative social implications prior to the epidemic and have now become associated with HIV/AIDS. The racist discourse that dominated the first decade of HIV/AIDS and personal experiences with racism remain major factors in the continuing silence and the increase in HIV infection among Black women and their communities. Once diagnosed with HIV/AIDS one cannot escape the socio-cultural interpretations attached to it creating negative implications for the individual, for their social interactions and for their relationships. Commonly believed images, stereotypes, and attitudes about the disease itself, compounded by constant anxiety about what others think or feel about them determines whether people seek and/or access services. People are shamed, condemned, and ostracized because of their HIV status or perhaps false perception of it.

Personally, I don't want to know. I couldn't deal with a positive HIV status, the devastation and shame. Leaves people wondering how you got it

There is an under-representation of Black women and Black communities in general in the utilization and access to HIV testing information and testing services. Information from service providers and preliminary results obtained from a study being undertaken by the University of Toronto, "HIV/AIDS in East African Communities Living in Toronto" indicate that fear of HIV, testing and being alienated from one's community and the impact of an HIV positive test on immigration status and/or ability to sponsor family members are definite reasons for the underutilization of HIV testing services (Tharao and Massaquoi 2000; Calzavara, Myers and Tharao; Tharao, Calzavara, Myers 2001).

The fear of testing HIV positive and its implications are a reality many Black women do not want to entertain. The shame, stigma, and discrimination associated with the disease makes women look at HIV diagnoses as something they would be better off not knowing. This limits access to testing services, early diagnosis, and early access to treatment and service for those who may be infected. For immigrant and refugee women, their reality includes the fear that a positive test might result in deportation, losing their children to child protection services, or the possibility of being unable to sponsor other family members to Canada (Tharao and Massaquoi 2000). Currently, there are restrictions on the immigration of HIV positive persons to Canada. Those who are HIV positive are considered "medically inadmissible" and are denied permanent resident status on the grounds that they would place an excessive burden on Canadian health and social services (Canadian HIV/AIDS Legal Network).

> *Once immigration knows you are sick, what chance do you have of sponsoring family and what happens to your children?*

Due to the economic marginalization of African and Caribbean women, a positive HIV test result would be just another issue in the long list of daily hurdles these women must contend with and many would prefer not knowing instead of adding to their burden.

> *Why would I want to know if I was HIV positive, I don't have OHIP and I could not afford medicine or pay for my doctor?*

For other women, the fear of stigmatization for the community as a whole as opposed to personal stigma was a deterrent for testing.

> *Stigma and discrimination against the whole community will increase if the public becomes aware of increasing rates of infection in communities of colour.... More positive results would lead to more strict immigration policies harming us all.*

HIV prevention strategies traditionally address issues of personal safety, personal choice, and individual rights. For women who are raised in communally-oriented societies, the well being of the family and the community supercedes all rights of the individual. Successful strategies and programs for many communities must be adjusted in order to address this reality. Individual strategies should be complemented with strategies targeted to whole communities in order to modify cultural values, beliefs, norms, and practices that increase risk of Black women to HIV infection.

CONCLUSIONS

If we are to develop an effective strategy to reduce the increasing rates of HIV/AIDS amongst Black women living in Canada, we must base programs and services on the realities of Black women's lives. Historical perspectives such as the long-term effects of colonization and slavery and their role in the interpretation of the epidemic need to be understood and taken into consideration in any strategies developed to deal with the epidemic.

Socio-cultural and economic factors such as poverty, unemployment, gender-based violence such as sexual abuse and rape, harmful cultural beliefs, values, norms, and practices further compounded by racism and other types of discrimination that further increase the risk of HIV infection must to be addressed in programs targeted to Black women.

Finally, the lack of involvement of Black women in the development, implementation, delivery, and evaluation of HIV/AIDS programs and services targeted to them is still an issue that demands attention. Black women's involvement in decision-making roles in organizations providing services to them is paramount if their silence is to be broken and their distance from the issue dealt with effectively. They must be part of the solution.

Most Black women in Canada find about their HIV status late in the stages of infection; those who are likely to be infected have not been diagnosed hence only limited numbers can benefit from available services and treatment therapies (Tharao and Massaqoui 2000). Eliminating barriers to HIV prevention, support, treatment and care information, and services is crucial in addressing HIV/AIDS for African and Caribbean women. Tailoring programs to identified needs within the context of language, culture, gender roles, socio-economic status and creating policies that support the efforts that we as activists are making will increase the numbers of those accessing prevention, testing and care services and hence will increase access to treatment.

Improving quality of care is critical to improving Black women's health and well being. Black women are suffering unnecessary mortality and morbidity resulting from disease prevalence due to HIV infection. Multi-disciplinary research is still needed into Black women's health so that an intersectional gender and race perspective may be incorporated into health policies and programs. The existing lack of race and sex-disaggregated data and information in Canada hinders the ability of decision-makers to develop effective, inclusive HIV/AIDS policies and programs. Adequate institutional mechanisms and resources are required for the successful achievement of inclusive health policies and programs to reduce the high rate of HIV infection amongst Black women.

Esther Tharao has been involved in HIV/AIDS work in Canada for over ten years and currently works at Women's Health in Women's Hands in Toronto as a health promoter. She is considered one of Canada's primary voices on HIV/AIDS issues facing Black communities and has presented on this subject at many conferences. She is a member of the Ontario Advisory Committee on HIV/AIDS, the Ontario HIV Endemic Task Force, and the Ministerial Council of the Canadian HIV/AIDS Strategy. She is also involved in several community-based HIV/AIDS research projects at Women's Health in Women's Hands.

Notisha Massaquoi has been an advocate for women's healthcare globally for the past 25 years. She is currently the Executive Director of Women's Health in Women's Hands Community Health Centre which provides primary healthcare prioritizing racialized women in Toronto. She is also a lecturer for the faculties of social work at York University and Ryerson University. Her previous publications include the co-edited anthology entitled Theorizing Empowerment: Canadian Perspectives on Black Feminist Thought.

[1]Women's Health in Women's Hands is a Community Health Centre for women of diverse backgrounds in Metropolitan Toronto and surrounding municipalities. Our mandate is to provide community, mental and clinical health promotion support from an inclusive feminist, pro-choice, anti-racist, anti-oppression, and multilingual participatory framework prioritizing women from the Caribbean, African, Latin American and South Asian communities. We believe that women have the right to receive quality health care and to make informed choices about their health. We work towards enhancing our sense of well-being and health by placing women's health into women's hands. We are committed to being advocates for change in our communities.

REFERENCES

Calzavara, L., T. Myers and E. Tharao. "Influence of Immigration and Country of Origin on Uptake of HIV-Related Services and Programs: East African Communities in Toronto, Canada." Poster Presentation at the Ninth Annual Canadian Conference on HIV/AIDS Research. Montreal, April 27-30, 2000.

Canadian HIV/AIDS Legal Network. "HIV/AIDS and Immigration: A Discussion Paper." Montreal, October 2000.

Health Canada. "HIV and AIDS in Canada, Surveillance Report to December 31, 2000." Health Canada: Ottawa, April 2001.

"HIV/AIDS in East African Communities Living in Toronto: A Proposal for Developmental Funding. Final Report." Prepared for the AIDS Program Committee, Positive Action Fund. Research team: Liviana Calzavara, Ted Myers, and Esther Tharao. December, 2000.

Massaquoi, N. and A. Lala. "Women's Health in Women's Hands: An Integrated Approach to Health Care for Black Women and Women of Colour." Presentation at the 2nd International Primary Health Care Conference. Melbourne, Australia, April 2000.

Randall, R. Vernillia "Racist Health Care: Reforming an Unjust Health Care System to Meet the Needs of African-Americans." *Health Matrix* (3) (Spring 1993): 127-194.

Tharao, E., L. Calzavara and T. Myers. "To Test or Not to Test: Factors Influencing HIV Testing in East African Communities in Toronto." Paper Presented at the 10th Annual Canadian Conference on HIV/AIDS Research. Toronto, Canada, May 3-June 3, 2001.

Tharao, E., L. Calzavara and T. Myers. "What Service Providers Need to Know to Provide Effective HIV/AIDS Programs and Services for African Immigrants in Canada: East African HIV/AIDS Study." Oral/Poster Presentation, 13th

International AIDS Conference, Durban, South Africa. July 9-14, 2000.

Tharao, E. and N. Massaquoi. "Factors Limiting Access to AIDS Treatment for Black Women and Women of Colour." Paper Presented at the Ninth Annual Canadian Conference on HIV/AIDS Research. Montreal Canada, April 27-30, 2000.

Tharao, E. and N. Massaquoi. "Building Effective HIV/AIDS Initiatives for Immigrant/Refugee Women Living in Developed Nations: A Canadian Experience." Presentation at the Forty-Fifth Session of the Commission on the Status of Women, United Nations. New York, April 2001.

Williams, S. and S. Goffman. "Interactionism and the Management of Stigma in Everyday Life." *Sociological Theory and Sociology.* Ed. C. Scambler. Tavistock: London and New York, 1987. 134-64.

Women's Health in Women's Hands. *HIV/AIDS Initiative: Women's Health in Women's Hands.* Annual Report. Toronto, 2000.

Women's Health in Women's Hands. "Healthy Options for Women." Toronto: 2000.

MARTHA FRIENDLY

Why Women Still Ain't Satisfied

Politics and Activism in Canadian Child Care

I T IS NOW more than 40 years since the Royal Commission on the Status of
Women first recommended a *National Day Care Act* (1970) and more than
20 years after Judge Rosalie Abella called child care "the ramp that provides
equal access to the workforce for mothers" (Royal Commission on Equality
in Employment). Sixty-five years have passed since women organized to fight
closure of Toronto's wartime day nurseries (Prentice 1996) and almost three
decades since the inspired day care activism of the 1970s and 1980s put child
care on Canada's political map to stay (Rebick).

Yet Canada has not achieved the "free, non-compulsory, publicly-funded, non-
profit, 24-hour national day care system" promoted by Toronto's Action Day
Care in the 1970s and 1980s. Indeed, although in most modern countries the
idea that high quality child care and early childhood education are synonymous
and a benefit to young children is well accepted (OECD 2006; UNESCO), the
very idea of early learning and child care is under attack by the religious right
in Canada (McDonald) and by the federal government. In the words of the
Honourable Diane Finley, Federal minister responsible for child care: "There
have been many studies that show that the best people to raise children are the
parents" (CTV News). At the same time, the idea that child care is an issue of
special interest to women is disparaged by the right, as, for example,

> Child care, caregiving and poverty are not just women's concerns but
> the problems of the Canadian family. To ghettoize them ... does a
> disservice to others in the game including men, children and extended
> family members. (Kheiriddin[1])

This suggestion that in the twenty-first century "women's priorities are
everybody's priorities" and that gender wars over issues like child care are "old
wars" is consistent with the statement of the Honourable Bev Oda, then-
Conservative Minister responsible for women's issues, that "We don't need to
separate the men from the women in this country"[2] (qtd. in "An agency well
pruned").

Nevertheless, research shows that while both mothers (including employed mothers) and fathers devote more time to their children than previously (Gauthier, Smeeding and Furstenberg Jr.), women still carry the major responsibility for children in a variety of ways—taking parental leave (available to either parent) at a considerably higher rate (Friendly, Beach and Ferns), working a "double day" (Gauthier, Smeeding and Furstenburg Jr.) and—if they are lone-parents—claiming the very lowest incomes among family types (Statistics Canada).

Most early childhood educators and child care workers—a notoriously underpaid group—are women as well (Beach, Bertrand, Forer, Michal, and Tougas). And over the years, organizing and activism for child care has been primarily by women (Prentice 2001). While now there are undoubtedly more men—fathers, child care workers, trade unionists, politicians, economists—who are essential and dedicated players in the Canadian fight for child care, by and large, the social movement that has long fought for child care is still mostly made up of women.

THE CURRENT CHILD CARE SITUATION IN CANADA

In 1986, a federal Task Force on Child care concluded that "sound child care and parental leave programs can no longer be considered a frill but are, rather, fundamental support services needed by all families in Canada today" (Cooke, London, Edwards and Rose-Lizée iii). But Canada has made little or no progress towards this system at the national level or—outside Quebec[3]—in any of the provinces.

Canadian women with young children have joined the paid labour force in ever-increasing numbers for the past three decades. By 2009, their labour force participation rate had risen from 61 percent (1995) to 69 percent for mothers whose youngest child was 0-2 years, 75 percent for those youngest was three to five years and 84 percent with a child 6-15 years (Friendly, Beach and Ferns). Canadian mothers' employment rates are high among OECD countries, higher than those in France, Denmark, Hungary, the U.S., the UK, and others (Friendly 2006a).

In its review of Canada undertaken as part of its twenty nation comparative study of early learning and child care, the Organization for Economic Co-operation and Development (OECD) commented that:

> national and provincial policy for the early education and care of young children in Canada is still in its initial stages. Care and education are still treated separately and coverage is low compared to other OECD countries. (2004: 6)

Canada's child care lags not only when compared to western Europe but even to the Anglo-American nations and even some developing countries (OECD 2006; UNESCO). As the OECD's (2006) analysis showed, Canada was the lowest spender in the OECD at 0.25 percent of GDP (compared to Denmark, the highest spender, at two percent of GDP), had very high costs to parents relative to most other OECD countries and had very low rates of access both for children aged 0-3 and aged 3-6 years (Friendly 2006a).

No province/territory provides space for anywhere close to a majority of young children. There are no national standards or approach and while each province/ territory has regulated child care centres, part-day nursery schools, regulated family day care (in private homes) and public kindergarten, the range, quality and access to early learning and child care programs varies considerably by region and circumstance. Funding in all provinces except Quebec still relies heavily on a residual welfare model—fee subsidies for eligible low-income families—which by no means suggests that all low-income families can access a subsidized place. As a result, high user fees for regulated child care—required to support most of the cost of program operations—are a main barrier to access for modest and middle-income families.

And while there has been growing recognition—based on child development research—that learning begins at birth, that young children learn through play, that development in the early years forms a foundation for the future, and that early childhood education programs have an important role to play in how all young children develop, research shows that the quality of Canadian child care programs are more likely to be mediocre than excellent (Goelman, Doherty, Lero, LaGrange, and Tougas).

THE POLITICS OF CHILD CARE: 2003-2011

Following the activism for child care throughout the 1980s, child care mostly remained off national policy agendas until 2003 when the Multilateral Framework on Early Learning and Child Care was put in place by Federal Human Resources Minister Jane Stewart who called it, "the beginning of a very solid national daycare program for Canadians" (Lawton). Then, in the 2004 election campaign, the federal Liberals under Paul Martin promised to build on this commitment to begin developing a national early learning and child care system based on four principles—Quality, Universality, Accessibility and Developmental [programming] (QUAD). After the Liberals won the 2004 election with a minority government, they committed $5 billion over five years (new dollars) to begin to build the system. In 2005, the federal government came to agreements-in-principle with all provinces based on only two conditions[4]—that the federal funds be used for regulated child care programs based on provincial/ territorial "action plans" and that there would be regular reporting on how the funds were used.

This marked the first time that a Canadian government had followed through with an election commitment at the national level to improve child care through—as Canadian constitutional arrangements require—provincial/ territorial implementation. While there was considerable variation in the provinces' directions, in coming to agreements-in-principle with the federal government, provinces committed to detailed action plans specifying how the federal transfer funds would be spent. On the federal side, the federal government promised five year funding upon production of the action plans.[5] Unlike previous agreements about children's issues, all provinces and territories including Quebec participated.

In the 2006 election campaign, the Conservatives under Stephen Harper made child care one of their five priority election issues, vowing to reverse the processes set in motion by the Liberals. The Conservatives' intention was to cancel the agreements; to send all families a monthly check for $100 (taxable) to promote "choice in child care"; and to set out capital incentives to encourage employers to establish child care programs (Conservative Party). Following the January 2006 election of a minority Conservative government, the new government's first announcement after officially taking office was that the funding agreements would be terminated and—as per the legalese in the agreements—would get federal funding for just one year. Thus, all federal funds for the nascent national, provincially-executed child care program were to end March 31, 2007.

The Conservative government put the individual cash payment—called, at that time, the "Choice in Child care Allowance" (later renamed the Universal Child Care Benefit [UCCB])—in motion on July 1, 2006. It is a payment to all parents with children under age six of $1,200 a year, taxed on behalf of the lower-income spouse (including a spouse not in the labour force, who would pay no tax). In addition, the Conservatives said that they would "help employers and communities create child care spaces in the workplace or through cooperative or community associations by establishing a tax credit" of $10,000 per space (Conservative Party,).

In 2011, the UCCB has been in place for five years. While growth in public funding for high quality regulated child care has become as scarce as hens' teeth, the UCCB costs an estimated $2.5 billion annually and has cost approximately $12.5 billion in public funds (Child Care Advocacy Association of Canada). Yet even in a recessionary fiscal environment featuring significant public service and program cuts, there has been no assessment of whether the UCCB meets the needs of families and children. Or even on what it is spent. Mothers continue to enter the paid labour force but expansion of regulated child care has slowed down considerably; in some regions, existing child care is in crisis as public funding fails to cover ongoing costs and centres close or fees increase. Increasingly, "the market" and for-profit child care have become a substitute for public policy solutions featuring accessible high quality child care.

Between the 2006 election and 2011, child care remained a public issue. The federal New Democrats' Olivia Chow introduced a private member's bill to limit federal child care funding to high quality non-profit and public child care but the bill was not supported by the Conservatives. Child care was a significant issue in the 2011 federal election as the Liberal Party promised to deliver a national program to provide "early learning and child care for every child who needs it"

("The child-care challenge").

In response to these efforts by the opposition parties, Human Resources Minister Diane Finley articulated what the Toronto Star called Conservative "disdain" for a national child care plan, declaring that such a plan would interfere with parents' "choice", "forcing [them] to have other people raise their children" ("Minister Finley"). A firestorm of criticism countered Finley's pronouncement but the Harper government finally won a majority government May 3, 2011.

Following the election, the Conservative's approach to child care remained the same;

> Finley … defended the government's decision to hand out monthly cheques instead of creating a federally-run system. She insisted that the issue provides choice for parents and that national daycare would remove that choice. ("Child care advocates")

LA LUTTE CONTINUES[7]

Minority or majority, the Harper Conservatives are the first government in modern Canada with a stated position of opposition to regulated child care.[8] Following the elimination of the Liberal's first steps in 2006, the Conservative's child care agenda has changed but little. In addition, research and organizational funds have been cut or eliminated so that even the groups who have long kept child care on the public agenda have been weakened and diminished as part of the attack on the fabric of Canada's civil society. Thus, child care is at risk as never before, together with many other advances for women.

At the time of the 2006 federal election, women from across Canada who had long advocated for a universal national child care program formed Code Blue for Child Care, a loose national coalition with goals dedicated to ensuring that the vision of a national child care program remains of front and centre. Code Blue has continued to advocate for its goals of high quality universal early childhood education and care through and beyond the 2011 election (Code Blue for Child Care). The woman-lead child care activism of the twenty-first century exemplified by Code Blue is multi-faceted, encompassing organizing, lobbying, research, public education, policy development and direct action and involves a wide range of sectors and players in all regions on Canada.

There is no doubt that the 2006 cancellation of the nascent national child care program by the minority Conservative government set child care back five years. Now, with a majority government with a reluctant (at best) attitude to child care in place for a four year fixed term, careful strategic thinking by the child care advocacy movement about resources, challenges and opportunities is more important than ever.

The child care movement is now finding energy in some new places, such as the labour movement. Driven by a unanimously-supported resolution at a national Canadian Labour Congress convention in 2011, collaboration among the national unions and child care advocates has developed a multi-union child care campaign to carry into the 2015 federal election. With a message to Rethink Child Care, the campaign is striving to tap the usual advocates but ordinary parents and grandparents, as well as to attract a force of new young feminists to ensure that child care is on the next election agenda ("Rethink child care").

Today, most Canadian families have changed. Most young children have a working mother; the historical male breadwinner family is increasingly rare and no longer universally desired. Women in Canada today are still struggling to balance work, family and personal lives without the support of a child care system but today it is a new generation of Canadian who are finding that they are in the same position vis-à-vis child care as were their mothers.. At the same time, most Canadians have come to understand the developmental or educational value of good quality child care programs. In addition, we often hear that good child care makes good economic sense, and the research supports this.

But most of all, child care makes sense because it is the right thing to do—a human right, a child's right and a key women's right. This means that if Canada is to be a twenty-first century country that does the right thing, we need a new approach to child care based on the best available twenty-first century evidence rather than on nineteenth century approaches that do not work.

Martha Friendly is the Director of the Childcare Resource and Research Unit and is based in Toronto. She is a policy researcher and an active part of the child care movement.

[1] Tasha Kheiriddin is the Ontario Director of the Canadian Taxpayers Federation and a frequent commentator from the right.
[2] On the occasion of shutting down regional Status of Women Canada offices.
[3] It should be noted that—although the Quebec government made very significant advances in ELCC in the late 1990s and first part of the 2000s, and provides much greater accessibility to publicly supported programs for all children who can find a space—when Quebec is compared to countries in Europe, it is apparent that there is still a long way to go. Space shortages, problems with quality and staff wages, surcharges, and cutbacks by subsequent Quebec governments are well documented both in the media and in the data. See Friendly 2006b for comparison of Quebec with the rest of Canada and Quebec with OECD countries vis-à-vis ELCC programs.
[4] Child care activists continued to advocate for stronger national policy, especially with regard to funding to for-profit child care.
[5] The agreements also committed to collaborative work on early learning and child care data, research and a national quality framework.
[6] Eventually all provinces but Quebec signed a bilateral agreement-in-principle with the federal government although several balked for some time. With Quebec, the agreement-in-principle stage was skipped and the federal government and

Quebec went right to a final five-year funding agreement. For an analysis of the intergovernmental child care agreements and their demise, see Friendly and White.

[7]The sources for the information on Code Blue in this section are www. buildchildcare.ca and the website of the Child Care Advocacy Association of Canada: <http://www.child careadvocacy.ca/action/codeBlue/index.html>.

[8]Usually, federal governments in the 1980s and 1990s stated commitment to child care although they didn't deliver or, at least, were silent on the issue (as was for example the Chretien federal election platform in 1997).

REFERENCES

"An agency well pruned." Editorial. *The Globe and Mail* 1 December 2006: A26.

Beach, J., J. Bertrand, B. Forer, D. Michal and J. Tougas. *Working for Change: Canada's Child Care Workforce. Labour Market Update Study.* Ottawa: Child care Human Resources Sector Council, 2004.

Child Care Advocacy Association of Canada. "Seven years and $15b gone: Nothing to show for the Universal Child Care Benefit." Information relation. February 6, 2013. Web.

"Child care advocates confront minister in Barrhaven park." *Metroland Media Ottawa* August 10, 2011. Web.

Code Blue for Child Care. Retrieved December 2, 2006. Web.

Conservative Party. A "New $1,200 Choice in Child Care Allowance for Pre-school Kids." December 6, 2006. Retrieved December 2, 2006. Web.

Cooke, K., J. London, R. Edwards, and R. Rose-Lizée. *Report of the Task Force on Child Care.* Ottawa: Status of Women Canada, 1986.

CTV News. "The Honourable Diane Finley. Federal Minister Responsible for Child Care." February 24, 2006.

Environics Research Group. *Canadians Attitudes Towards National Child Care Policy.* Toronto: Author, 2006.

Friendly, M. *Early Learning and Child Care: How Does Canada Measure Up? International Comparisons Using Data from Starting Strong II (OECD).* Toronto: Child Care Resource and Research Unit, University of Toronto, 2006a. Web.

Friendly, M. "Looking Beyond Our Borders: Early Learning and Child Care in Quebec, Canada and in the OECD." Powerpoint for a presentation at Politiques familiales et bien-être des enfants. Conseil de développement de la recherche sur la famille du Québec. Uniersité du Québec à Trois-Rivières, 2006b.

Friendly, M., J. Beach and C. Ferns. "Final Draft Report on Early Childhood Education and Care in Canada 2010." Prepared for Human Resources and Skills Development Canada, Fall, 2011.

Friendly, M. and L. White. "'No-lateralism': Paradoxes in Early Childhood Education and Care Policy in the Canadian Federation." *Canadian Federalism: Performance, Effectiveness and Legitimacy.* 3rd edition. Eds. H. Bakvis and G. Skogsted. Toronto: Oxford University Press, 2012.

Gauthier, A. H., T. M. Smeeding and F. Furstenberg, Jr. "Are Parents Investing Less Time in Children? Trends in Selected Industrialized Countries. Population and development Review 30 (4) (2004): 647-661.

Goelman, H., L. D. Doherty, A. LaGrange and J. Tougas. *You Bet I Care! Caring and Learning Environments: Quality in Child Care Centres across Canada.* Centre for Families, Work and Well-Being, University of Guelph, 2000.

Kheiriddin, T. "Colour the Liberal ghetto pink." *The Globe and Mail* December 1, 2006: A 27.

Lawton, V. "Ottawa, provinces sign day-care deal; 50,000 new spots over five years $900M program 'essential first step'." *Toronto Star* 14 March 2003: A1.

McDonald, M. "Steven Harper and the theo-cons. The rising clout of Canada's religious right." *The Walrus* October 2006. Retrieved December 2, 2006. Web.

"Minister Finley defends child care remarks." *Toronto Star* February 4, 2011: A-3.

Organization for Economic Co-operation and Development (OECD). *Starting Strong II. Early Childhood Education and Care.* Paris: Author, 2006.

Organization for Economic Co-operation and Development (OECD). *Thematic Review of Early Childhood Education and Care. Canada Country Note.* Paris: Author, 2004.

Prentice, S. *Changing Child Care: Five Decades of Child Care Advocacy and Policy in Canada.* Halifax: Fernwood Publishing, 2001.

Prentice, S. "Theorizing Political Difference in Toronto's Postwar Child Care Movement." Occasional Paper # 8. Child Care Resource and Research Unit. Toronto: University of Toronto, 1996.

Rebick, J. *Ten Thousand Roses: The Making of a Feminist Revolution.* Toronto: Penguin Books, 2005. "

"Rethink child care. There is a better way." Web. Accessed March 25, 2013.

Royal Commission on Equality in Employment. Ottawa: Minister of Supply and Services Canada, 1984.

Royal Commission on the Status of Women in Canada. *The Status of Women in Canada.* Ottawa: Minister of Supply and Services Canada, 1970.

Statistics Canada. *Women in Canada: Work Chapter Updates.* Ottawa: Author, 2003.

"The child-care challenge: Parents deserve a real choice." Editorial. *Toronto Star* February 6, 2011: A-14.

United Nations Educational, Scientific and Cultural Organization (UNESCO). *Strong Foundations: Early Childhood Care and Education. Education for All Monitoring Report.* New York: Author, 2006.

LIANNE MCTAVISH

Virtual Activism and the
Pro-Choice Movement in Canada

T HE ABORTION RIGHTS COALITION OF CANADA/Coalition pour le Droit
à l'Avortement au Canada (ARCC-CDAC) is a bilingual group formed in
October 2005. Feminist leaders and clinic directors from across Canada
decided to create a new pro-choice organization that would be overtly political in
nature. ARCC-CDAC is now actively devoted to expanding and defending women's
access to abortion, as well as to preventing reductions in reproductive health
services or rights. This article discusses the challenges faced by the founding
members of ARCC-CDAC as they strove to establish a national movement
with limited financial resources. It investigates how the group functions as a
"virtual organization" (www.arcc-cdac.ca) without a stable location, mailbox, or
phone number, as well as the political and historical implications of this virtual
existence. As a relatively new form of feminist organization, virtuality has many
benefits. This essay will also consider, however, the drawbacks of virtual forms
of communication and political activism, offering a frank assessment of the
effectiveness of ARCC-CDAC to date.

The creation of another national pro-choice group might seem surprising,
given the longstanding existence of the Canadian Abortion Rights Action League
(CARAL), formed in 1974. Yet the mandate of CARAL was met in 1988, when the
Supreme Court struck down Canada's unconstitutional abortion law. Though
CARAL continued to lobby for access to abortion, by 2005 members of the group
were working to close down the organization, believing it should be replaced
by one with goals more germane to the current situation in Canada. Therefore,
CARAL formed Canadians for Choice (CFC), a non-profit organization that
operates by raising public awareness and promoting education. As a group with
charitable status, however, CFC is not permitted to undertake political activity
such as lobbying. ARCC-CDAC thus compliments CFC. Unhindered by charitable
status, the new coalition directly participates in political activism in ways that
both continue and move beyond CARAL's original objectives.

There is much political work left to do. Abortion is difficult to access in
many parts of Canada, and this situation is of primary concern to ARCC-CDAC.
According to the Supreme Court's decision in 1988, Canadian women have a

right to obtain abortions without discriminatory barriers.[1] Nevertheless, almost 25 years later, women living in rural and northern areas continue to travel long distances for abortions. In Prince Edward Island women face especially dire conditions. There are no abortions performed in the province, and women often drive to Halifax's Victoria General Hospital or to Fredericton, paying for procedures done there at the Morgentaler Clinic. The situation is, however, scarcely better in New Brunswick. There women are routinely denied hospital abortions, and every year more than 600 have to pay out-of-pocket for this health service at the Morgentaler Clinic.[2] The government of New Brunswick refuses to pay for the abortions performed in clinics, though such funding is required under the *Canada Health Act* (ARCC-CDAC 2005a). The illegal user fees that numerous women must pay for their abortions are a form of gender discrimination because only women can get pregnant.

ARCC-CDAC is currently supporting Dr. Morgentaler's lawsuit, launched in 2003, meant to force the government of New Brunswick to fund abortions performed in clinics as well as hospitals update below? In 2001, the federal government began insisting that New Brunswick fully fund abortion services, but has been slow to take official steps toward remedying the situation (ARCC-CDAC 2005b). In April 2005, then-Federal Health Minister Ujjal Dosanjh began a dispute avoidance resolution process with the government of New Brunswick, but it has lost momentum. With the election of a Conservative majority government, it seems clear that women's right to fully funded abortion will not be supported at the federal level. At least 61.5 percent of the Conservative caucus is publicly anti-choice. ARCC-CDAC nevertheless has reason to believe that New Brunswick will ultimately be required to fund clinic abortions, for in August of 2006 a court judgment ordered the government of Quebec—which had been funding only part of the abortions performed in that province—to repay 13 million dollars to the approximately 45,000 women who had paid fees for their abortions in women's health centres and private clinics between 1999 and 2005 (Carroll and Dougherty). All the same, the New Brunswick government has managed to slow proceedings by challenging Dr. Morgentaler's standing, arguing that the abortion issue exclusively affects women. In January 2009 a judge ruled in Dr. Morgentaler's favour, allowing him to proceed with the lawsuit, but the province then appealed; in May of the same year, three appeal judges confirmed the initial finding (Canadian Press). As of 2011, the lawsuit continues to move forward, albeit at a snail's pace.

Even this brief discussion shows that Canadian women have very different experiences when seeking abortions.might suggest otherwise Recognition of this diversity prompted the founders of ARCC-CDAC to create a national coalition, made up of activists from across the country. They wanted a range of voices to be represented, instead of a centralized group—located in central or western Canada—trying to speak for all women. Joyce Arthur, a member of British Columbia's Pro-Choice Action Network, was an early organizer of ARCC-CDAC. She contacted clinic workers and community activists from across

Canada, inviting them to participate in the new organization. Eventually, representatives from such groups as the Ontario Coalition for Abortion Clinics, Le Collectif pour le Libre Choix, Planned Parenthood Alberta, Fédération du Québec pour le planning des naissances, Catholics for a Free Choice, and Pro-Choice New Brunswick, as well as many abortion clinics across Canada, joined ARCC-CDAC.

The coalition then had to determine the best method of organizing, which was not obvious given the range and geographical dispersal of its members. Choosing a name proved challenging, since referring to Canada risked alienating separatist Quebecers and implying a false unity. The term was retained in order to signify the nationwide participation of its membership, and so that federal as well as provincial reproductive health policies could be addressed. More crucial decisions involved how to create a broad organization with a national presence that existed in solidarity without becoming too centralized and concentrating authority into the hands of a few instead of collectively. During an initial teleconference, members decided that the group should exist virtually, with participants communicating by means of e-mail and a listserv. Decisions would be made by a Steering Committee consisting of representatives from each region in Canada, with input from other members. Information about ARCC-CDAC's mandate, vision and goals would be disseminated on an extensive web site. Now this web site additionally features recent press releases and position papers—brief written statements on topics such as why abortion is a medically required service, the abortion provider shortage, and emergency contraception. These papers are written by individual members, and then circulated electronically to the entire group for final editing. ARCC-CDAC's outreach and activist tools comprise three different listservs for members, one for volunteers who work on ARCC-CDAC projects, a forum for grass-roots pro-choice supporters, a regular newsletter, available both electronically and in print, that features news stories related to reproductive rights in Canada.

In practical and financial terms, this virtual existence has been successful. The group does not pay for office space, regular mail outs, telephones, or many of the other overhead costs traditionally borne by political organizations. Though without a centralized phone number, ARCC-CDAC provides the media with cell phone numbers for its spokespeople. The exchange of information and communication between members is immediate and regular. The website and listservs are available 24 hours a day, offering a wide range of political and practical information. During the last election campaign, ARCC-CDAC's web site included daily election updates, a list of anti-choice Members of Parliament, a history of Anti-Choice Private Member Bills and Motions, and a press release suggesting "What Could Happen to Reproductive Rights Under Harper?" This data received national attention, and was cited in the press, giving ARCC-CDAC further exposure (Timson). Though much information on the web site is aimed at the media and government officials, position papers such as "How to Get an Abortion in Canada," "All About Your Abortion (From Appointment to

Recovery)" and "Why Do Women Have Abortions?" strive to address a broader audience.

The virtual existence of ARCC-CDAC may nonetheless have implications extending beyond the matter-of-fact issues of expense and the efficient exchange of information. Virtual pro-choice activism is a relatively recent phenomenon, different from the consciousness raising groups and protest marches that have characterized the history of abortion activism in Canada. For example in 1970, the Abortion Caravan traveled over 3,000 miles from Vancouver to Ottawa to demand legal abortion. Nearly 500 women from across Canada joined the protest along the way, and on Mother's Day weekend the group demonstrated in Ottawa. Some 35 of the women chained themselves to the parliamentary gallery in the House of Commons, closing Parliament for the first time in Canadian history (Rebick 35-46). The Abortion Caravan helped politicize and activate women around the country. Can the ARCC-CDAC web site ever have a similar effect?

This comparison might be misplaced, for times are different and so are strategies, with greater emphasis now placed on changing or implementing government health policies. It may also imply that such "on the streets" pro-choice activism is no longer happening, which is clearly not the case. Many pro-choice people, including some members of ARCC-CDAC, help to organize community health clinics. Others participate in local pro-choice events, or volunteer at abortion clinics, as patient escorts. ARCC-CDAC certainly promotes such activity, and will continue to do so in the future. Nevertheless, as a virtual organization, ARCC-CDAC also participates in what is now commonly called "cyberfeminism," a contested term with various theoretical strands (Galloway). It is important to consider ARCC-CDAC within the contextof cyberfeminism in order to explore the impact of pro-choice virtual activism. This approach should both enable a fuller evaluation of ARCC-CDAC, and contribute to the ongoing assessment of cyberfeminism itself.

Since the 1990s a "utopian" branch of cyberfeminism has embraced technology, notably the Internet, arguing that it is a radically democratic medium that presents a plethora of voices able to undermine gender inequality. One author undertook a case study of web page use in a non-governmental organization in Colombia, concluding that "Networks—such as women's, environmental, ethnic and other social movements networks—are the location of new political actors and the source of promising cultural practices and possibilities" (Escobar 32).[4] In another formulation of the utopian position, Sadie Plant contends that computer technology is fundamentally female in both its nonlinear form, and its historical production by women such as nineteenth-century "computer programmer" Ada Lovelace (Plant). Her claims have some bearing on contemporary feminist activism online, reminding us that the use of communications technology is not entirely novel. Nineteenth-century abolitionists in Canada and the United States had, for example, "virtual" links with sympathetic European groups through their frequent exchange of letters.[5] Earlier forms of pro-choice activism functioned similarly, using fax trees, newsletters, and telephone hotlines to communicate. In a sense, ARCC-CDAC's virtual existence simply continues this tradition, while drawing on the utopian principle that virtuality can include diverse women from across Canada, bringing them together to fight the discrimination caused by women's unequal access to abortion.

Other cyberfeminists criticize this positive view. They claim the Internet is firmly embedded in sexist and racist frameworks, often promotes the exploitation of women, and on balance furthers the interests of capitalism rather than democracy (Gur-Ze'ev). Such arguments are relevant to contemporary abortion politics online. Entering the term "pro-choice" in an Internet search engine reveals a range of sites, including one called "ProChoice.com," which is actually an anti-choice site providing false information about abortion. In an effort to make women fear abortion, it links the procedure with various maladies, even breast cancer. All recognized health authorities, including the Canadian Cancer Society and the World Health Organization, have concluded that no link exists between abortion and an increased risk of breast cancer (ARCC-CDAC 2005c). This anti-choice web site is like the deceptive "pregnancy counselling centres" set up across the North America. Often using feminist-sounding names such as "Women's Care Centre," the centres are designed to reach women before they access an abortion provider, and bombard them with anti-abortion propaganda.[6] Clearly, the longstanding strategies of the anti-abortion movement have simply been moved online. Yet the success of these strategies may increase online, because the Internet is widely considered a democratic resource providing information to all who seek it. At the same time, anti-abortion groups often have more money than pro-choice groups, allowing their messages to dominate cyberspace.

The ARCC-CDAC web site intervenes in this situation, contributing to a pro-choice online presence. Various position papers on its web site are designed to counter anti-choice misinformation and harassment. One short essay discusses the medical facts about breast cancer, while another explains that so-called "partial-birth abortion" is a term invented by anti-abortionists trying to make all abortions illegal (see Mason 84-85). This kind of rebuttal is important, even though it is not new, as the ARCC-CDAC web site moves a standard pro-choice strategy online. For several decades, pro-choice groups have had to dispute the misinformation produced at an alarming rate by well-funded anti-abortion groups. Though necessary, this defensive activity detracts from the more proactive work pro-choice groups could be doing. In many ways, abortion politics-as-usual are now taking place in cyberspace as well as in the wider world.

ARCC-CDAC's virtual existence nevertheless fosters a new kind of pro-choice community, one that remains connected in defiance of time differences and geographical expanses. The more utopian approach to cyberfeminism studies how virtual feminist communities, created in gaming environments or interactive sites such as www.gurl.com, reconstitute identities (see, for example, Turkle). For them, cyberspace enables the proliferation of female selves, while the relationship between women and machines both empowers women and unsettles patriarchal binary distinctions. Yet critics claim that virtuality erases specificity, especially any concrete sense of place. According to philosopher Paul Virilio, the speed of virtual communication "no longer depends on the interval between places or things and so on the world's very extension, but on the interface of an instantaneous transmission of remote appearances" (Virilio 33). This denial of the interval between places and things privileges the *now* to the detriment of the *here*. When communications technologies paradoxically enable being everywhere at the same time but nowhere at all, they mark the loss of the site, city, and nation in a way that is at odds with democracy.

Virilio's claims are unsettling because the virtual existence of ARCC-CDAC is meant to insist on the specificity of place, particularly women's differing experiences of abortion based on their location within Canada. Are such goals undermined when a teleconference takes place "everywhere and nowhere," or when the ARCC-CDAC web site remains unanchored to a specific geographical location? These points are worth considering. It is true that many members of ARCC-CDAC have never met face to face. Some cyberfeminist critics contend, however, that it is possible to use these technologies while insisting on the rootedness of place, noting that virtual communities must include face-to-face meetings as well as other kinds of activism (Escobar 46). Active members of ARCC-CDAC have indeed met in person and will continue to do so. The existence of ARCC-CDAC has not reduced the continuing opportunities for abortion activists from around the country to meet. As well, the coalition plans to use Internet teleconferencing to host its Annual General Meetings, which will allow far more members across Canada to participate than would a traditional meeting in one geographical location. In this way, the virtual coalition undeniably enables a wider range of dialogue, bringing forward the voices of women in PEI, for example, which are otherwise far from the ear of the federal government and thus easily ignored. Arguably, virtual existence has its own kind of presence, one able to overcome the effects of absence within the context of abortion politics.

Virilio's assertions raise, however, an important possibility: perhaps virtuality will render invisible another important location in the abortion debate, namely the specificity of women's bodies. The pro-choice movement has always drawn attention to the bodies of individual women, and of pregnant women in particular. The voices of insistently present women contributed, for example, to the powerful effect of the pro-choice demonstrations in Ottawa in 1970. This strategy has been necessary because anti-choice rhetoric works to deny female subjectivity and bodily experience. Anti-abortionists portray the fetus in a fictional manner, as an individual entity able to exist separately from the maternal body.[7] The erasure of women is glaring in anti-choice imagery, especially on the Internet. Virtuality may support anti-choice politics if it allows for concrete places and bodies to be overlooked. This possibility has already been recognized by the pro-choice community, and addressed on web sites that feature the stories of real women who have had abortions, such as www.imnotsorry.net. This emphasis is not part of the ARCC-CDAC web site, and its members may need to devise additional strategies to counteract the disappearance of female embodiment both on and offline.

All the same, ARCC-CDAC members feel it has accomplished much. As a virtual entity with no funding, it has brought women together from across the country to articulate positions in relation to various reproductive issues, and it has been active in federal elections. Many of the challenges raised in this brief account of cyberfeminism can be addressed in the future, though ongoing attacks on fundamental reproductive rights in Canada mean that ARCC-CDAC members remain primarily focused on lobbying against these attacks and rebutting the cultural myths surrounding abortion. Members of the coalition can consider meeting face to face more formally, reaching out to include even more women, and devising strategies which insist on the specificity of individual female experiences. Clearly, pro-choice groups such as ARCC-CDAC complement more traditional pro-choice grassroots activism and must continue to insist that individual women make decisions about abortion based on their particular circumstances. And they must convey this message using multiple forms of communication and activism, including the Internet.

Lianne McTavish is a member of ARCC-CDAC, and former volunteer at the Morgentaler Clinic in Fredericton. A Professor in the Department of Art and Design at the University of Alberta since 2007, McTavish has published two books, Childbirth and the Display of Authority in Early Modern France (Ashgate, 2005), and Defining the Modern Museum (University of Toronto, 2012). She recently embarked on a new phase of feminist research by entering a bodybuilding competition, an experience analyzed in her blog: feministfiguregirl.com.

[1]For a transcript of this decision see: <www.lexum.umontreal.ca/csc-scc/en/pub/1988/vol1/html/1988scr1_0030.html>.

[2]This information was provided by Judy Burwell, Director of the Morgentaler Clinic in Fredericton from 1999-2005.

[3]For examples of press coverage during the 2006 election see: "Tories Would Curb Access to Abortion, Activists Warn"; For the 2011 election, see Timson.

[4]In Canada, Womenspace is a non-profit organization that promotes women's participation in information technologies, believing that "inclusive access, peer networking and creative uses of communication technologies are powerful vehicles for social equality."

[5]Alice Taylor's doctoral dissertation considers, among other things, the trans-Atlantic links between abolitionist women.

[6]The evidence against these deceptive pregnancy centres is overwhelming, but see, for example, the documentary produced by *W-Five*, and aired on 5 November 2000, which broadcast the story of a young woman's unpleasant and misleading experience with the Calgary Pregnancy Care Centre.

[7]There are many feminist critiques of contemporary fetal imagery, but see, for example, Petchesky; Stabile; Duden 99-106; Squier; Hartouni.

REFERENCES

Abortion Rights Coalition of Canada/Coalition pour le Droit à l'Avortement au Canada (ARCC-CDAC). "Abortion Clinics Must Be Fully Funded under *Canada Health Act*." Position Paper 2. 2005a. Web.

Abortion Rights Coalition of Canada/Coalition pour le Droit à l'Avortement au Canada (ARCC-CDAC). "Clinic Funding—Overview of Political Situation." Position Paper 3, 2005b. Online: www.arcc-cdac.ca.

Abortion Rights Coalition of Canada/Coalition pour le Droit à l'Avortement au Canada (ARCC-CDAC). "Abortion and Breast Cancer: An Evidence Based Perspective." Position Paper 70, 2005c. Web.

Binks, Georgie. "Stephen Harper may be the best thing to happen to the women's movement." *CBC News Viewpoint* 24 January 2006. Web.

Canadian Press. "N. B. Court of Appeal Paves Way for Morgentaler's Lawsuit." CBC News 21 May 2009. Accessed 25 September 2011. Web.

Carroll, Ann and Kevin Dougherty. "Province to refund abortions." *Montreal Gazette* 19 August 2006. Accessed 17 December 2006.

Duden, Barbara. *Disembodying Women: Perspectives on Pregnancy and the Unborn*. Trans. Lee Hoinacki. Cambridge, MA: Harvard University Press, 1993.

Escobar, Arturo. "Gender, Place and Networks: A Political Ecology of Cyberculture." *women@internet: Creating New Cultures in Cyberspace*. Ed. Wendy Harcourt. London: Zed Books, 1999. 32-49.

"Listing of Anti-Choice MPs." Abortion Rights Coalition of Canada/Coalition pour le Droit à l'Avortement au Canada (ARCC-CDAC). Web.

Galloway, Alex. "A Report on Cyberfeminism: Sadie Plant Relative to VNS Matrix." Switch/Electronic Gender: Art and the Interstice. Accessed 28 March 2006. Web.

Gur-Ze'ev, Ilan. "Cyberfeminism and Education in the Era of the Exile of Spirit." Accessed 28 March 2006. Web.

Hartouni, Valerie. "Fetal Exposures: Abortion Politics and the Optics of Allusion." *Camera Obscura* 29 (May 1992): 130-149.

Mason, Carol. *Killing for Life: The Apocalyptic Narrative of Pro-Life Politics*. Ithaca: Cornell University Press, 2002.

Rosalind Pollack Petchesky, "Foetal Images: The Power of Visual Culture in the Politics of Reproduction." *Reproductive Technologies: Gender, Motherhood and Medicine*. Ed. Michelle Stanworth. Minneapolis: University of Minnesota Press, 1987. 57-80.

Page, Shelley. "Anti-choice, pro-election: In the 98 ridings held by the Conservatives when this election was called, 70 MPs were against a woman's right to choose." *Ottawa Citizen* 21 January 2006: I2.

Plant, Sadie. *Zeros and Ones: Digital Women and the New Technoculture*. New York: Doubleday, 1997.

Rebick, Judy. "The Women are Coming: The Abortion Caravan." *Ten Thousand Roses: The Making of a Feminist Revolution*. Toronto: Penguin, 2005. 35-46.

Squier, Susan. "Fetal Subjects and Maternal Objects: Reproductive Technology and the New Fetal/Maternal Relation." *Journal of Medicine and Philosophy* 21 (October 1996): 515-35.

Stabile, Carol A. "The Traffic in Fetuses." *Fetal Subjects, Feminist Positions*. Eds. Lynn M. Morgan and Meredith W. Michaels. Philadelphia: University of Pennsylvania Press, 1999. 133-58.

Taylor, Alice. *Trading in Abolitionism: Women, Consumption, Material Culture at the Boston Anti-Slavery Fair, 1834-1863*. Ph.D. Diss., University of Western Ontario, 2006.

Timson, Judith. "Why Should Women Believe what Stephen Harper says about Abortion?" *The Globe and Mail* 28 April 2011. Accessed 25 September 2011. Web.

"Tories Would Curb Access to Abortion, Activists Warn." *The Globe and Mail* 21 January 2006: A12.

Turkle, Sherry. *Life on the Screen: Identity in the Age of the Internet*. New York: Touchstone, 1995.

Virilio, Paul. *Open Sky*. Trans. Julie Rose, London: Verso, 1997.

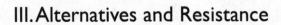

III. Alternatives and Resistance

WANDA NANIBUSH

Idle No More

Strong Hearts of Indigenous Women's Leadership

O N JANUARY 26, 2012, I found myself marching down a busy Toronto street beside grandmother Pauline Shirt and a number of Aboriginal women in front of hundreds of marchers. As a water carrier, I was holding a part of Lake Ontario in my hands. This water walk and ceremony was called together to bring attention to the Idle No More movement and the fight against the changes to the *Navigational Waters Protections Act* under Bill C-45 that legalized resource developments precedence over environmental protection. We were not protesting—we were speaking the spirit of the water. We were attempting to heal her from the pollution choking her life force, which in turn chokes our own.

The actions under the Idle No More banner have largely been peaceful and ceremonial in nature, thus markedly different from any other massive international Indigenous-led movement in history. It is a movement led largely by grassroots Indigenous women. The movement exhibits a post Cartesian Indigenous ethos where the mind, body, spirit and emotions are engaged together. Like the drum at the centre of the round dances is the heart of the mother earth, the women maintain the heart at the centre of the movement. It is a rare feeling to go to a political action and want to hug every stranger around you, to feel vulnerability at the centre of life and a desire to protect it.

Indigenous women's leadership has always been at the grassroots level having historically been shut out of *Indian Act*-based leadership until 1952. Many have forged their leadership skills in ceremonial spaces where pre contact cultural values around the roles of women have allowed us significant influence and power. The teachings gathered at the skirts of our grandmothers have also required a different set of principles for working cross culturally. While a return to and education about the Nation-to-Nation relationship that exists between Canada and the many Indigenous nations on whose soil this country was birthed has been the centre of the movement, it has also required understanding how we are to work together now and in the future. When the relationship is not defined from thought alone but also includes the spirit and the heart the work takes on a different character. The treaties (Nation to Nation agreements) and wampum belts that hold their history, speak of our relationships being based on peace and friendship with the values of trust, integrity, honesty, and truth as the basis for interaction. This is not a written contract to be analyzed and assessed but a contract of spirit and heart to be lived together.

Women who have worked at the ground level healing their communities from historical trauma, who deal with large socio-economic disparities and have counteracted cultural discontinuity—all brought on by colonialism and racism— bring a considerable knowledge base to the movement. Cross-cultural conflicts that are quite common in Canada come to fore in an Indigenous led movement like Idle No More. Canadians have been denied access to an education, which leads to deep mistrust and misunderstanding between Aboriginal and Non-Aboriginal participants in a struggle to protect the earth and water. Unity has been stressed and yet unity in difference is the goal. For this movement to work we must remain unified. This means no behind the back talk against each other. It means putting aside petty jealousies, envy, dislikes and old grudges. It means not having an ego. Indigenous concepts of the human that are non-ego based become important. It means true humility that listens before speaking, and that understands before judging, it means letting go of negativity and holding the fragility and dignity of fellow humans close.

It does not mean that we will all agree but the way we disagree is the main question. If I disagree I choose to disagree openly in front of the person, without anger or passive aggression as a form of peace offering towards understanding. I choose to ask questions and seek understanding, to deliberate before forming opinion. I choose to care for strangers. I choose to set aside my own desires for the larger picture. I choose to step forward and share my knowledge and skills for others. I choose to take the heat. I choose peaceful disobedience. I choose to obey ancient laws of respect. These tenets, if you will, are women's teachings that they bring to the movement and affect how it operates. The earth, for us, is considered a mother, mothering and creation is fore grounded for our identity. This does not mean that women cannot choose men's roles or have sexual relations with women. It does mean that there are specific knowledges within the acts of creation for both earth and women that are essential to the sustenance of our world and humanity. Creation is also an act of futural imagining which is what is at the heart of women's work. The creativity of the actions and the focus on our children's children's etc. future is part of what is expected of a woman living in a good way. Humanity is the weakest link in all of creation because it relies on all of creation to exist that is why they must ultimately protect it. The focus on male leadership under colonial rule has not quieted the voices of Indigenous women leaders. There is a strength derived from the attempted silencing in their closeness to the community, ceremony, children and creativity.

Wanda Nanibush is an Anishinabe-kwe writer, image maker, curator and cultural worker from Beausoleil First Nation. She has a Masters degree in Visual Studies from the University of Toronto. Currently she is a curator in residence at the Justina M. Barnicke gallery and an organizer for Idle No More Toronto.

SUNILA ABEYSEKARA

Racism, Ethnicity and Peace

THE WORLD CONFERENCE Against Racism, Racial Discrimination, Xenophobia and Related Intolerance (WCAR), held in Durban, South Africa in August/September 2001, provided an opportunity for new social movements grappling with a range of issues involving identity, identity-based politics, diversity, and difference to propose radical and critical redefinitions of racism and related intolerance within the global context of the twenty-first century.

Among the most critical of the discussions that took place around the process of preparing for the WCAR was a review and analysis of the definition of race-based discrimination as set out in the International Convention on the Elimination of All Forms of Racial Discrimination (ICERD)—"any distinction, exclusion, restriction or preference based on race, colour, descent, national or ethnic origin." Tribal and Indigenous people, Roma and Sinti people, and *Dalits*[1] were among the communities that used the space and environment created by the WCAR process to put on the main agenda a discussion about discrimination against members of these groups as a part of intolerance related to racism and racial discrimination.

The women's human rights lobby for the WCAR process focused on the need to address the specific impact of racism, racial discrimination, xenophobia, and related intolerance on women. As a prelude to this, their lobby supported the ICERD Committee to expound a General Recommendation (No. 25) on Gender-Related Dimensions of Racial Discrimination which clearly states: "Racial discrimination does not always affect women and men equally or in the same way." This opened up a space for a wide-ranging discussion on the interlocking forms of discrimination experienced by women and by other marginalized communities and led to the articulation of the concept of inter-sectionality of oppression and discrimination (see Crenshaw; Abeysekera).

In feminist circles, the discussion about intersectionality has its roots in the struggles against racism and xenophobia, against classism and Euro-centrism within women's movements across the world. In the 1960s and 1970s, pioneering black feminists and feminists of colour in the U.S. and Canada, such as Angela

505

Davis and bell hooks, raised the cross-cutting nature of class, sex and race in their feminist and political work and writings. Socialist feminists theorized on the links between racism, sexism and class privilege in their work on women and domestic labour (see Benston; "The Political Economy of Housework"). In more recent years, as feminists have reshaped the discussions on difference and diversity to include broader issues of democracy, representation and citizenship, issues of identity and identity-based politics have taken on new meanings.

In times of social, political or economic crisis, identity and belonging, or not belonging to a particular community or group, becomes a critical factor in determining one's access to power and resources. Competition over access to scarce resources and exclusion from power structures, and/or discrimination and suppression on the basis of perceived or real difference is what often leads to the emergence of tensions between different communities and social groups. It is in such situations, as identity assumes a divisive role, that women and their role in the community become critical in terms of the collective identity of the community.

My own line of inquiry is into the issue of identity as it provides the basis for social and political conflict and the construction of the female within that discourse on identity. In this article, I will especially focus on ethnicity since it has been the factor that has led to barbaric and horrible manifestations of conflict in several parts of the world over the past decades, in Rwanda, in the former Yugoslavia, in Indonesia and in Sri Lanka, to name a few of the more obvious cases.

In recent years, as competition for resources and power has grown, we have seen the emergence of social formations and political organizations that primarily define themselves on the basis of an ethnic identity. They re-create the community, they re-write its history, they re-invent traditions and customs in order to draw the community together, to reaffirm that their community is different from others and to provide symbolic and imaginary meaning to the unity that is called for to establish some degree of control over resources and power in the name of the community.

Ethnic difference is not so much based on physical appearance, since there may be several different ethnic groups within one racial category, but rather on dissimilarities of cultural and social practice. This is why people of diverse ethnic origins living within one nation state or region often adopt and highlight specific ethnic markers such as a particular form of dress or adornment, language use or food habits in order to project their identity to an outsider and observer and to affirm their membership of a certain community to others within that community.

As any social group begins to base its sense of belonging, community, and identity on factors of ethnicity and ethnic origin, a special role is ascribed to women in the construction and maintenance of this identity. Within the community, women are perceived as the biological and social reproducers of the community. Especially in situations in which a particular ethnic group is in the minority, the focus on biological reproduction as critical to the survival of the group places great pressure on women and men to marry and bear children, as many as possible. In their role as social reproducer, women bear the responsibility of preserving and passing on the traditions and culture of the community to the next generation. Because of their reproductive capacity, women become symbolic of the community, and of its honour. This in turn enables the community, especially male elders, to prescribe appropriate behaviour and practices for women. We have seen that this often means returning to traditional forms of dress and behaviour, even in communities that had abandoned these forms in previous years. The adoption of the *hijab* (head cover) among young Muslim women can be presented as an example. A process of affirmation of ethnic identity can also mean a resurrection of stereotypes of women from traditional folklore and myths; most often these women are identified by virtues of self-sacrifice and dignity in the face of adversity. Sita from the Ramayana story[2] is one such figure. These figures begin to re-appear in both traditional and modern guise in songs, stories, and television serials and become role models for women.

In addition, in such situations, women are told that since the pursuit of the community's rights and dignity is the most critical issue at that moment, they should refrain from raising issues that would divide the community from within. Thus, issues such as domestic violence, incest, and denial of equal rights to women in traditional law are perceived as divisive. Women who raise these issues are labeled as traitors or agents of alien interests. The fact that women are perceived as the bearers of the community's honour restricts their mobility and choice of partner. It also makes them vulnerable to all forms of violence and abuse at the hands of the other community. This is why the rape and sexual violation of women has been a strategy of war through the ages.

As the strengthening of ethnic identities perceived and proclaimed to be different from one another proceeds within a society, one soon sees a polarization of the society take place. As different sides emerge and the conflicts become more complex, some conflicts become violent. From civil strife to separatist war, conflict then results in the destruction of life and the devastation of all communities involved in the conflict. The conflict leads to militarization of the entire society and the conflict is battled out in a number of arenas, military, social, educational, ideological and cultural, to name a few.

One of the most chilling manifestations of ethnic conflict that we have seen emerge in recent times is that of ethnic cleansing in which the brutal and physical annihilation of an entire community is carried out by armed men as well as civilian groups working in collaboration and in consonance with each other. While it is women who are always the most brutalized and victimized in such circumstances, one cannot forget that women are also cast in the role of perpetrators of violence against women of othered communities.

Women civilians and women members of armed forces on all sides of ethnic divide have been known to engage in acts of violence and abuse against members of the enemy community. The example of the women cadres of the Liberation

Tigers of Tamil Eelam (LTTE) in Sri Lanka, and especially of their suicide-squad membership has led to inquiry as to the ideological and political basis for their extremism. More recently, similar work has been done on the women cadre of the Maoist militants in Nepal. The interaction between traditional notions of womanhood and femininity and the transformations of these notions in the context of conflict have evoked great academic interest. While some inquiries have been directed at the changing roles of women in the context of conflict-related displacement, widowhood, assumption of head of household status and imposed independence, others have looked at the impact of the process of transformation of women's role from mother and wife to armed militant.[3]

Women who belong to communities for whom ethnicity is the defining factor in self-identification find themselves torn between different loyalties—to their community and to the community of women. They cannot raise issues that are significant for women or that seem to call for equality within the community since this is often perceived as being contrary to the interests of the community. They cannot also easily maintain links with women outside the community because these women may more often than not belong to the other community and are, therefore, perceived as hostile. This places restraints on their ability to take collective action as women and places them at times in opposition to other women. In such a moment, unless there is critical understanding of the complexities of the situation, the divisions that are created can destroy a collectivity that has been nurtured over years of activism.

There are several extremely significant women's groups across the world that have maintained links across ethnic divides at moments of conflict and crisis and that have emerged as strong voices for peace and for an end to conflict not only in their own communities but in the world. Among these are the Women in Black initiatives in Israel/Palestine and in the former Yugoslavia. In South Asia, the North-East Network that brings together women from different ethnic and tribal communities in conflict with one another in the north-eastern region of India and networks such as Mothers and Daughters of Lanka, the Sri Lanka Women's NGO Forum and the Women's Alliance for Peace that work for peace and against the war with Sinhala. Tamil and Muslim women have demonstrated that strategic thinking and action among women can challenge existing divides and bear positive and constructive results.

Some critical issues that have emerged for us as feminist activists from examining these experiences have been:

- the need to respect women's needs to affirm their identity as a member of a community;
- the acceptance that criticism of a community that feels under siege best comes from within that community itself, with support from the outside when requested;
- the need to continue engaging in a dialogue about denial of equality to women in tradition, custom and religious practices with women

from communities in which such denial takes place most blatantly, but framed within the understanding that *all* societies contain elements that deny equality to women;

•the need to develop a feminist understanding of violence against women as a continuum of patriarchal domination, and to see the links between militarization at the state level and spousal abuse at the level of the family;

•the need to engage in a dialogue not only about discrimination but about privilege, on the understanding that women from majority/hegemonic communities need to address their own complicity in the conflict;

•the need to promote non-violent forms of conflict resolution at every level of society.

The challenge of working with and across ethnic diversity for peace, and for reconciliation, is a long and hard task. At times it seems as if there are more factors that divide us and promote hostility among us than there are factors that unite us and which provide the basis for collective action. Yet, it is clear that we can move forward in situations of conflict based on ethnic divisions only by working with differences and diversities, not denying them. The old slogan of "Unity in Diversity" now seems to smack of assimilation. We should rather affirm "Diversity for Unity" in the understanding that our differences enrich rather than diminish our activism and collective spirit. When communities are at war with one another, this is sometimes a difficult goal to pin our hopes on. Yet, in the end, I think feminism has taught us to understand the concept of identity as a constantly shifting and multi-faceted phenomenon. Therefore we can, in the abstract, imagine ways and means of coming through such conflicts, hanging on to our integrity as women while at the same time not denying ourselves the joy of belonging to our community. It should not be an either/or scenario. How to transform this abstract idea into reality, how to maintain friendships and express affection for one another while our communities are at war with one another, how to link our understanding of what it means to be women on either side of the ethnic divide: these are the key issues on which we must focus as we move towards developing strategies and actions for sustainable and just peace in all our societies.

This article was originally written in preparation for a discussion on feminist leadership and diversity at the World Conference Against Racism held in Durban in August/September 2001.

Sunila Abeysekera is a feminist and human rights defender from Sri Lanka. She has been a part of global advocacy for women's human rights since the 1990s and in 1998 was awarded the UN Human Rights Prize for the Asia Pacific region on the occasion of the fiftieth anniversary of the Universal Declaration of Human Rights.

She works as a human rights campaigner globally, as well as on issues of peace and human rights in Sri Lanka and is a member of the Women Human Rights Defenders International Coalition and Board Chair of the Urgent Action Fund for Women's Human Rights.

[1]*Dalits* is the term used by members of so-called low and scheduled caste communities in India to identify themselves.
[2]Sita is the epitome of wifely devotion and chastity and is presented to all women as the "ideal" Indian woman.
[3]See the work of Neloufer de Mel, Kumudini Samuel, Malathy de Alwis, Radhika Coomaraswamy on Sri Lanka, Shobha Gautam and Rita Manchanda on Nepal.

REFERENCES

Abeysekera, Sunila. "Intersectionality." *APWLD: Papers on Intersectionality.* Chiang Mai, Thailand: Asia Pacific Forum on Women, Law and Development, 2002.

Benston, Margaret. "The Political Economoy of Women's Liberation. *Monthly Review* (September 1969).

Crenshaw, Kimberle. "Intersectionality of Gender and Racism." Paper submitted to the Expert Group meeting on the World Conference Against Racism (WCAR) convened by the United Nations Division on the Advancement of Women, Zagreb, 2000.

Davis, Angela. *Race, Class and Sex.* Women's Press, 1981.

hooks, bell. *Feminist Theory: From Margin to Center.* Boston: South End Press, 1984.

"The Political Economy of Housework." *Bulletin of Social Economics* (Spring 1974).

LEE LAKEMAN, ANGELA MILES AND LINDA CHRISTIANSEN-RUFFMAN

Feminist Statement
on Guaranteed Living Income

VERY ISSUE OF *Canadian Woman Studies/les cahiers de la femme* involves gathering women from various locations to meet and read together and discuss the potential contents. Always that is a useful educational opportunity for those on the editorial board, for students, for the profession of women's studies, for activists and for the women's movement as a whole.

But in these times of great and increasing pressure on women and their activism, more is necessary. Editorial board members, potential authors, and readers are all feeling under attack. Women's places in the academy, centres, projects and wings of the movement as well as women's livelihood, dignity and autonomy are financially threatened in new ways. To write and to think creatively with political ingenuity and wisdom is difficult but essential in these circumstances.

The editorial board for the 2004 *CWS/cf* issue on "Benefitting Women? Women's Labour Rights" Vol. 23, nos. 3,4 responded to the challenge. Some of us were able to meet in person to discuss articles. Others contributed long distance using new technology. We recalled reliable women, encouraged discouraged women, suggested new names and new ideas from our various contacts to seek out points of view that might be helpful to the whole. We sought the work of academics, of women workers, and recipients of social programs and benefit programs. As usual, we sought the writing of activists as well as researchers and connected both.

For this issue, we also tried new strategies and drew on specifically feminist relations to knowledge, in line with activist research and theorizing. Two members of the *Canadian Woman's Studies* Executive Board and two members of the Guest Editorial Board for this issue were able to meet in Pictou, Nova Scotia with feminists from across the country for two days of intense dialogue around the themes of this issue. The mix of significant numbers of national groups with a substantial regional grass roots presence proved inspired.[1]

As a movement we are in need of much more contact with each other. We need a fuller discussion amongst ourselves that can renew our understanding of our shared feminist agenda's for action. We need to restate the relevance of each of our demands to each other's campaigns. It is in that coming together of our demands and actions that our hope emerges and is sustained. We had that opportunity at a meeting in Pictou and we rediscovered there that: feminism is alive and fighting in Canada and demands her share of a better world.

For our initial discussion we divided into two groups. Both used the time-honoured feminist process of starting from women's experiences. In one group participants shared information about the many economic security campaigns they had been involved in and reflected on how the varied issues are connnected and might be advanced from a feminist point of view. The other group, sharing information about women's lives including our increasing economic insecurity, imagined what changes would be needed to ensure the security and autonomy of all women. Both groups were asked to prioritize the implications for the poorest women, Indigenous women and immigrant women, and to include attention to international contexts. Information about proposals for an annual general income was provided in the participants' package of materials. The consensus that emerged in later dialogue informed by the themes of both groups was captured in the "Pictou Statement." The Pictou Statement has not been officially endorsed by individual participants or their respective groups. However, we are pleased to present this important contribution to feminist thinking on these issues here. We expect this statement will resound in the diverse member groups of the World March of Women, in labour and anti-poverty struggles, and in diverse grassroots women's groups across the country struggling on a daily and urgent basis with these issues. It will surely sugar the yeasty uprising of political activity among women refusing poverty and rewardless toil for all of us.

Lee Lakeman, World March of Women, CASAC
Linda Christiansen-Ruffman, CRIAW-Nova Scotia, FemJEPP
Angela Miles, Toronto Women for a Just and Healthy Planet

[1]Participants at the meeting held in Pictou, Nova Scotia, Sept. 18-20, 2004, included: Louise Aucoin, Coalition for Pay Equity; Linda Christiansen-Ruffman, Fishnet, FemJEPP, Feminist Allicance for International Action (FAFIA); Brenda Cranney, President, *CWS/cf*; Karen Dempsey (Vice President, Economics), National Council of Women; Michelle Genges Harris, Women's Network PEI; Sue Genges, Canadian Labour Congress (CLC); Lucille Harper, Antigonish Women's Centre, FemJEPP; Lee Lakeman, Canadian Association of Sexual Assault Centres (CASAC); Barbara Legault, Federation des Femmes du Québec (FFQ); Bernadette MacDonald, Pictou Women's Resource Centre; Angela Miles, Toronto Women for a Just and Healthy Planet; Doreen Paris, Nova Scotia Advisory Council; Katharine Reed, Canadian Centre for Policy Alternatives (CCPA); Angela Regnier, Canadian Federation of Students; Luciana Ricciutelli, Editor-in-chief, *CWS/cf*; Michelle Ridgeway, Women's Network PEI; Jane Robinson, Canadian Research Institute for the Advancement of Women (CRIAW); Jenny Robinson, YWCA; Gwen Wood, National Anti-Poverty Organization (NAPO).

FEMINIST STATEMENT ON GUARANTEED LIVING INCOME

PICTOU, NOVA SCOTIA, SEPTEMBER 18-20, 2004

For millennia women's work, along with the free gifts of nature, has provided most of the true wealth of our communities. Women's work has been central to individual and collective survival. In all our diverse communities women can be seen to work on the principle that everybody is entitled to economic and physical security and autonomy and a fair share of the common wealth.

Women in every community, context and racial group are still denied our rightful political power over the economics governing these communities and our world. To paraphrase "*A Women's Creed*," for thousands of years men have had power without responsibility while women have responsibility without power. This situation must change.

Feminists insist that all activities of government and business in our nation(s) and our diverse communities should be assessed in the light of the prime value of sustaining life and social priorities of universal entitlement, human security, autonomy and common wealth. Social priorities of universal entitlement, human security, autonomy and common wealth must become central in social life and in public policy.

W e refuse to accept market measures of wealth. They make invisible the important caring work in every society. They ignore the well-being of people and the planet, deny the value of women's work, and define the collective wealth of our social programs and public institutions as "costs" which cannot be borne. They undermine social connections and capacities (social currency).

We reject policies that sacrifice collective wealth and individual security in the interests of profit for transnational corporations.

Women in Canada expect full and generous provision for all people's basic needs from the common wealth. Social and collective provision for sustaining life must be generous and secure in Canada and must be delivered through national mechanisms appropriately influenced and controlled by the women of our many specific communities.

We expect all people's full and dignified participation in society including full individual and social sharing of the work and responsibility of sustaining life that has so far been gendered. Men must share equally in this work within and beyond monetary measures.

We expect our rightful share of the wealth we have created. Women's work must be recognized and valued both within and beyond monetary measures. We expect sustained and expanding collective provision for people's needs.

Women demand an indexed guaranteed living income for all individual resiidents set at a level to enable comfortable living. in society including full individual and social sharing of the work and responsibility of sustaining life that has so far been gendered. Men must share equally in this work within and beyond monetary measures.

We expect our rightful share of the wealth we have created. Women's work must be recognized and valued both within and beyond monetary measures. We expect sustained and expanding collective provision for people's needs.

Women demand an indexed guaranteed living income for all individual residents set at a level to enable comfortable living.

PATRICIA E. PERKINS

Social Diversity, Globalization, and Sustainability in Community-Based Economies

BIOREGIONAL AND "ECOLOGICAL ECONOMICS" theory describes the growth of local economic linkages as vital to move post-industrial economies in the direction of sustainability.[1] This involves expanding local stewardship over environmental and economic resources, so that progressively more production for local needs can be done within the community. Far from existing solely in the realm of theory, this is a pattern which is becoming more familiar in many parts of North America and Europe (see, for e.g., Rajan; Forsey; Dobson; Nozick; Mazmanian and Kraft; Hannum; Shuman; Beatley, Norberg-Hodge, Schor).[2]

The blossoming initiatives to create local, community economies can be understood in light of the long history of environmental challenges faced by people living in the industrialized North, and the economic blows of trade liberalization/globalization and recession. Many communities in North America and Europe have been organizing around environmental concerns for decades. Recession or trade-related layoffs in the early 1990s, and again since 2008, have given many people both time and incentives to exercise long-dormant skills for generating incomes and exchanging goods and services. Environmental awareness, community organizing, and "alternative" employment creation (e.g. in environmental remediation and energy conservation activities) form a natural and dynamic synergy which draws upon feminist theoretical insights and relies upon women's skills.

Stronger community-based economies not only help people to survive the vicissitudes of world market fluctuations, they hold the seed of more fundamental economic transformation.

> As individuals and households become more self-reliant and empowered, they lay the groundwork for new community responses to larger social and economic problems. When plant closings, layoffs, loss of local stores, or other large-scale economic hardships afflict their communities, such empowered, creative individuals may be more able to develop new solutions to these problems. And the new community

515

ties they have been forming through their shared activities serve as a base for building new economic structures and enterprises that more fully meet their community's needs. (Brandt 153)

Self-sufficient communities need the global economy less. In such communities, it is possible to live a healthy, fulfilling, productive life without consuming many goods and services which come from far away. But this requires knowing one's neighbours: their skills, needs, abilities, and trustworthiness. This makes possible the sorts of exchanges which are efficient and beneficial for everyone concerned— be they skills exchanges, community-supported agriculture, Local Enterprise Trading Systems, credit unions or informal credit circles, urban gardens, child-care and other cooperatives, environmental housing improvement programs or any other enterprises where local resources are transformed into goods and services which local people need (Norberg-Hodge). In many communities in both North and South, it is women who do the bulk of the networking, the conflict mediation, the organizing, and the fund-raising for such community endeavours.

Working toward self-sufficiency involves fostering the development, preservation, and appreciation of the skills needed to live our lives with more quality and less material consumption. To the extent that women are the guardians of these skills, and the teachers of young people, their role in skills transmission is central for any community's future self-sufficiency.

As Margo Adair and Sharon Howell state:

If we are to secure the future, we must reconstruct our communities. To do so, women's ways of talking, listening, and being together must come to define all public and political life. The qualities embodied in our relationships over the kitchen table are the very qualities needed for our talk of strategies and actions... For the world to survive, *everyone* must act like a woman. Let us reweave our communities, reclaim the wholeness of life, and empower ourselves to heal the future. (41)

Many of the things women all over the world are already thinking, writing, and doing in the face of globalization and global recession reflect the essence of Janine Brodie's statement that a feminist analysis

must begin with the premise that (global) restructuring represents a struggle over the appropriate boundaries of the public and the private, the constitution of gendered subjects within these spheres and ultimately, the objects of feminist political struggle. (Brodie 19)

Since local communities are, in a sense, intermediate between the "public" and the "private," they represent a terrain in which many women are comfortable acting politically. At the same time, it is exactly the fact that local communities are somewhat removed from national or international "public" life that can make them strong (and potentially subversive) bulwarks against centralized control, refuges of diversity, and incubators for creative human interaction.

CHARACTERISTICS OF COMMUNITY ECONOMIES

As Community Economic Development (CED) practitioners have demonstrated for decades, strong interactive multiplier effects can be created in communities by generating jobs and needed local services, and keeping money circulating within the local area.[3] "Green CED," as currently practiced, involves the extension of CED ideas to include financing of local economic initiatives via energy and other conservation measures, and environmental remediation as an important job creation focus (Jones, Carter). The particulars of how this works, and the potential for CED in a given community, are of course closely related to the specific situation.

Toronto, for example, is home to a vast and growing network of locally-based initiatives aimed at creating jobs by addressing environmental problems, and increasing local control of basic economic necessities: food, shelter, transportation, money.

When Central American refugees form an agricultural cooperative, lease land outside Toronto, and provide weekly food baskets of organic vegetables to urban consumers in a "community shared agriculture" project; or when the City of Toronto provides seed loans for energy-efficient retrofits of private housing and office towers which create construction jobs and save both energy and money; or when Afghan-born women begin a catering service in a church kitchen; all these initiatives contribute to the development of a more ecological, less wasteful, more locally-centred social economy.

There are countless more examples in Toronto of small-scale organizing and local economic initiatives involving people of all ethnicities and backgrounds:

•The GreenXChange Project creates energy-retrofit jobs, training programs, and pilot projects to include residents of Toronto's marginalized Jane-Finch neighbourhood in the growing green-collar economy.
•Yes In My Backyard links homeowners who have unused yard space with other city residents who are eager to garden, for increased local food production and social interaction.
•The Toronto Islands Residential Community Trust, negotiated by local residents, shows how complex land ownership and stewardship issues can be resolved using unconventional institutional approaches.
•The Access Community Capital Fund, linked with the Canadian Community Investment Network co-operative, helps promising local entrepreneurs gain access to new sources of financing for business start-ups.

•Not Far From the Tree mobilizes volunteers to pick fruit from Toronto trees which would otherwise go to waste. The harvest is split among the pickers, tree-owners, and local food banks and community kitchens.

•"Green Community" initiatives across Toronto have forged wide-ranging partnerships to create jobs by upgrading the energy efficiency and environmental quality of neighbourhood life. These include Autoshare, Toronto's first car-sharing program, the first wind turbine for distributed energy production, started by TREC Renewable Energy Co-operative, and the Solarshare Co-operative.

Several factors particular to Toronto have contributed to the development of a local economy. As the largest city in Canada, Toronto benefits from ethnic and cultural diversity and a wide range of community traditions; it also has relatively well-developed environmental and community organizations, and well-defined downtown urban neighbourhoods; pressing urban problems put attention to local environmental and job creation issues near the top of the public agenda; changing governments and downloading of social services to the municipal level have forced the city to develop ways of addressing local needs; downtown neighbourhoods, and at times the city as a whole, have generated progressive political leadership.

The fact that similar examples of burgeoning local economies can be found all over North America and Europe, however, indicates that in many different contexts the trend persists. This raises a number of interesting research questions, especially concerning the relationship between globalization and the growth of local economies.

GLOBALIZATION AND COMMUNITY ECONOMIES

The "restructuring" which is part of globalization inevitably leads to layoffs in some places, and laid-off workers often cannot move to where the jobs are, or be retrained for them. They may either have the wrong skills or be in the wrong places for the global economy to make use of them. They also, however, are likely to have very important knowledge of the places where they live—and community connections—which allow them to substitute local economic activity for whatever they formerly did. Such a substitution:

•provides personal satisfaction and contact with others;
•can provide basic goods and services which people need (food, clothing, shelter, personal services such as childcare and home repairs);
•makes money less necessary at a time when money is probably less available;
•facilitates the development, "remembering," and transmission of skills which are necessary for personal and community self-sufficiency (such as gardening, food preparation, crafts, construction and repair, music, etc.);

•encourages thrift and efficiency of resource use, and intrapersonal specialization.

All of these are things that people intuitively are attracted to and see as pleasant, worthwhile, and "good." De-linking from the global economy allows people to relax, depend on and learn from each other in a way that is impossible when time is precious and scarce because "time is money." When you are laid off, you can spend a week teaching your granddaughter how to rebuild a junked bicycle—*as long as* you've got a home to live in, health care, and food on the table.

At this stage we must ask a somewhat tricky question: Is this ridiculously naïve? Are local economies at best hopelessly anachronistic and at worst a futile dead end? This is a criticism of local economic thinking which I have heard from a number of progressive colleagues. I would like to offer a few thoughts on the theoretical importance of developing a local-economy focus along the lines sketched above.

First, any local-economy activist knows that global trends are driving the emergence of local economies. All of the grassroots initiatives described above involve awareness of and interaction with global-economy issues: fossil fuel depletion, climate change, food security, population and capital shifts. This does not mean, however, that local activists feel disempowered by globalization — quite the opposite! Their work is essentially a process of growing things in the cracks of globalization's splitting facade. The resulting micro-environments create space and support for a vast diversity of human-scale economic alternatives to dependence on the global economy. Simply because these are so diverse and far-flung, we should not have the false impression that they are weak and uncoordinated. Together, as I have attempted to outline above, they make up a picture of defiance and "refusal to be homogenized" that is a source of tremendous hope.

The "degrowth" movement, which aims to build social sources of value to replace material throughput as the driver of economic well-being, shares this perspective (Foster, Martinez Alier, Thomas).

Exactly because of their diversity and variety, local economies fly in the face of the simplifying forces of globalization. What local-economy theory is about is a new sort of economic development that honors ecological realities and finds efficiencies in small-scale, shared knowledge at the community level. By recognizing and refusing to accept the externalization of costs spun off by the juggernaut of broad-brush globalization, people in local places worldwide are in effect seeking to minimize those costs. From an ecological and "sustainable development" viewpoint as well as a social-economy viewpoint, this process is theoretically important.

Important conditions which make this vision of global-local restructuring feasible (and they are perhaps more realistic in Canada and some European countries than in other places) are a guaranteed basic income, such as that provided by an adequate welfare system or a Basic Income program, and healthcare or health insurance for all. In other words, while local economies can certainly contribute, people's basic needs must be met. Other factors which can facilitate the growth of a local economy include the following:

•Flexibility in the way basic social services are provided, which allows people to switch to locally-sourced and communally or barter-provided food, health care, and housing if they wish, using the money saved for other things. This implies welfare payments of a "guaranteed annual income" kind, rather than food stamps, government housing, etc.

•Dramatic economic upheavals or shocks. Large-scale economic change happening suddenly in a local area can be more conducive to development of local economic activity than protracted, smaller shifts. This is because in the former situation, people are less likely to feel personally responsible for being laid off; many people are in the same situation at once. When big changes hit a community, a unified response seems easier, and radically new institutions and lifestyles are more acceptable.

•Good examples. If pilot projects or small-scale local economic endeavours pre-exist a globalization shock, this can help people to see them as a viable solution to new problems. There may be an openness to community approaches within a short time following economic upheaval which dissipates over time as people "adjust" on their own, so a strong energy for creation of community-based economic institutions may be lost in the initial learning-by-doing phase. Pre-existing trials and and projects formerly seen as "fringe" can reduce this. Individual adjustment and alienation are dangerous because of the high costs in depression, family violence, alcoholism and other health effects. This has many gender implications.

•Strong communities. People who know each other well, have intergenerational connections, and participate in strong local institutions like churches, parents' groups, clubs, and sports leagues, can expand and develop their interpersonal ties into new areas. There is no substitute for this sort of community self-knowledge, which builds social resilience.

•Shared history. The longer most people have lived in the area, the easier it is for a local economy to develop. People need to know each other as individuals, including each others' non-work related skills, strengths, and needs They need to know how the community works—its institutions and history. And they need to know the local geographical area well: What grows readily in backyard gardens? Where can you get sand, or walnut planks, or locally-grown apples?

To the extent that globalization depends on accelerating consumption of nonrenewable resources, it is destined to be short-lived. Trade in goods which are produced and transported long distances using fossil fuels cannot continue at current rates. Transport prices will rise, the goods' final prices will rise, and locally-produced substitutes will become competitive. Anything made from metal, or which is otherwise energy-intensive in its production processes, will see a similar trend, as will goods which generate toxic or hazardous wastes as waste disposal costs rise (O'Connor). Production/consumption/disposal loops are already becoming shorter, and local economic linkages more important. The use of renewable energy sources is much easier in small-scale, dispersed settings. Decentralization is congruent with ecological economic development.

In the remainder of this article, I wish to focus particularly on the issue of social diversity as it affects the growth of locally-based economies.

DIVERSITY IN COMMUNITY ECONOMIES

From a bioregional and ecological perspective, cultural and biological diversity is a natural response to climatic and geographical differences across the earth's surface; cultural and biological diversity have evolved together (Coleman; Rajan; Bormann and Kellert). Ecologists detail the role of diversity in increasing an ecosystem's stability and chances of survival in the face of climatic or other shocks (see, for eg., "It's Natives vs. Newcomers, Down Under in Worm World; Bormann and Kellert). Diverse human cultures have played an important and largely unrecognized role worldwide in protecting plant and animal diversity, especially for species which are used as food (Rajan).

Humility *vis-a-vis* nature is linked to respect for other human cultures and diversity; cultural and social diversity allows for, accompanies, fosters and makes possible the growth of other ecological values (Coleman). "Green politics" is characterized by acceptance and embracing of functional differentiation, pluralism, decentralization and complexity; it is designed to unite diverse viewpoints in a cooperative participatory democracy leading to a deepening of community (Pepper; Coleman). "If diversity is good for an ecosystem, it's good for a social movement as well!" (Forman qtd. in Forsey).

New models of wealth involve wide variation in meeting ecological realities, a "new elegance" in respecting subsidiarity, anti-uniformity, and a "credo of diversity" (von Weizsacker 207-211). Diversity must be deliberately fostered to permit adaptation to future surprises (Norgaard; Yap). While most CED and ecological economics literature speaks favourably of social diversity as a goal, mention can also be found of the difficulties this can pose in practice for achieving consensus in decision-making processes. For one thing, differences can make "community" hard to achieve (Forsey; Gujit and Shah). A non-hierarchical process, "honouring what everyone can bring to the group," takes time and care, and conflict mediation skills may be necessary (Sandhill; Andruss and Wright). Moreover, decentralized communities may have the potential to become misogynistic, homophobic, racist, anti-Semitic, and otherwise repressive (Wallace). Social change may seem easier to accomplish in a group of like-minded people (Cousineau; Johnson and Tait).

Nonetheless, acceptance and welcoming of diversity in communities is a sign of their health; the skills required to mediate and develop community amidst diversity are extremely valuable for community stability (Coleman; Adair and Howell; Johnston). Often it is women, working together on food preparation, childcare, and/or income generation activities, who recognize commonalities across cultural divides, build respect and friendship, and create the social ties which become foundational for local economic stability in diverse communities.

It is a common theme in virtually all writing on CED, "Green CED," and ecological economics that social diversity, mirroring and enhancing biological diversity, is desirable, beneficial, "natural," and to be cultivated.

CONCLUSION

Marcia Nozick states,

> Feminine principles are forming the foundation for an alternative vision of society which is influencing how we work, organize and make decisions—smaller, more personal structures and processes, co-operative work situations, consensus decision making and reliance on community supports and the informal economy. They are values which support the building of sustainable communities. (38)

As community economies grow in response to economic globalization, climate change, and global ecological pressures, their characteristics and implications are becoming clearer. The examples cited above from Toronto, along with many others from elsewhere, demonstrate the importance of social diversity as a positive contributor to the stability and potential of local economic development.

Patricia E. (Ellie) Perkins is a professor at York University, where she teaches in the Faculty of Environmental Studies.

[1]See, for example, Merchant; Rifkin; Sale; Daly and Cobb, Jr; Hines; and the discussion in Perkins, "Exploring Sustainable Trade: Definitions and Indicators."
[2]Communities in the global South, of course, have struggled for centuries to maintain social and economic autonomy in the face of colonialism and neo-colonialism. The focus in this article is on the global North, although many parallels exist between South and North with regard to the role of diversity in community economies.
[3]An overview of this literature is contained in Boothroyd and Davis; see also Nozick; Roseland.

REFERENCES

Adair, Margo and Sharon Howell. "Women Weave Community." *Circles of*

Strength: Community Alternatives to Alienation. Ed. Helen Forsey. Gabriola Island, BC: New Society Publishers, 1993. 35-42.

Andruss, Van and E. Wright. "A People of Place." *Circles of Strength: Community Alternatives to Alienation.* Ed. Helen Forsey. Gabriola Island, BC: New Society Publishers, 1993. 105-110.

Beatley, Timothy. *Green Urbanism: Learning from European Cities.* Washington, DC: Island Press, 2000.

Boothroyd, P. and C. Davis. "The Meaning of Community Economic Development." University of British Columbia Planning Papers, Discussion Paper 25, School of Community and Regional Planning, University of British Columbia, Vancouver, BC, 1991.

Bormann, F. Herbert and Stephen R. Kellert. Eds. *Ecology, Economics, Ethics: The Broken Circle.* New Haven and London: Yale University Press, 1991.

Brandt, Barbara. *Whole Life Economics: Revaluing Daily Life.* Gabriola Island, BC: New Society Publishers, 1995.

Brodie, Janine. "Shifting the Boundaries: Gender and the Politics of Restructuring." *The Strategic Silence: Gender and Economic Policy.* Ed. Isabella Bakker. London: Zed Press, 1994. 19.

Carter, Majora. http://www.majoracartergroup.com/

Coleman, Daniel A. *Ecopolitics: Building a Green Society.* New Brunswick, NJ: Rutgers University Press, 1994.

Cousineau, Paige. "Of Mice and Elephants: The Individual, Community and Society." *Circles of Strength: Community Alternatives to Alienation.* Ed. Helen Forsey. Gabriola Island, BC: New Society Publishers, 1993. 67-72.

Daly, Herman and John Cobb Jr. *For the Common Good.* New York: Beacon Press, 1989.

Dobson, Ross. *Bringing the Economy Home From the Market.* Montreal: Black Rose Books, 1993.

Forsey, Helen, ed. *Circles of Strength: Community Alternatives to Alienation.* Gabriola Island, BC: New Society Publishers, 1993.

"It's Natives vs. Newcomers, Down Under in the Worm World." *The New York Times* March 28, 1995: B13.

Foster, John Bellamy. "Capitalism and Degrowth: An Impossibility Theorem." *Monthly Review* 62 (8) (January 2011). Web.

Gujit, Irene and Meera Kaul Shah. Eds. *The Myth of Community: Gender Issues in Participatory Development.* London: Intermediate Technology Publications, 1998.

Hannum, Hildegarde. Ed. *People, Land, and Community.* New Haven: Yale University Press, 1999.

Hines, Colin. *Localization: A Global Manifesto.* London: Earthscan, 2000.

Johnson, Sonia and Jean Tait, "A Passion for Women's World." *Circles of Strength: Community Alternatives to Alienation.* Ed. Helen Forsey. Gabriola Island, BC: New Society Publishers, 1993. 87-92.

Johnston, Barbara Rose, ed. *Who Pays the Price? The Sociocultural Context of*

Environmental Crisis. Washington, DC: Island Press, 1994.

Jones, Van. *The Green Collar Economy.* New York: HarperOne, 2008.

Martinez Alier, Joan. "Socially Sustainable Economic De-Growth." *Development and Change* 40 (6) (November 2009): 1099-1199.

Mazmanian, Daniel A. and Michael E. Kraft, eds. *Toward Sustainable Communities: Transition and Transformations in Environmental Policy.* Cambridge, MA:MIT Press, 1999.

Merchant, Carolyn. *Radical Ecology.* New York: Routledge, 1992.

Norberg-Hodge, Helena. "Building the Case Against Globalization and For Community-Based Economics." *International Society for Ecological Economics Newsletter* 5 (2) (April 1994): 3-4.

Norberg-Hodge, Helena. *Shifting Direction: From Global Dependence to Local Interdependence.* Berkeley: International Society for Ecology and Culture, 2000.

Nozick, Marcia. *No Place Like Home.* Ottawa: Canadian Council on Social Development, 1992.

O'Connor, Martin. ed. *Is Capitalism Sustainable?* New York: Guilford Press, 1994.

Pepper, David. *Eco-Socialiam: From Deep Ecology to Social Justice.* London: Routledge, 1993.

Perkins, Patricia E. "Exploring Sustainable Trade: Definitions and Indicators." *Global Political Ecology.* Eds. Bell, David V. J., Roger Keil, Leesa Fawcett and Peter Penz. London: Routledge, 1998. 207-242.

Rajan, Vidal. *Rebuilding Communities: Experiences and Experiments in Europe.* Totnes, Devon: Resurgence Books, 1993.

Rifkin, Jeremy. *Biosphere Politics.* New York: HarperCollins, 1991.

Roseland, Mark. *Eco-City Dimensions: Healthy Cities, Healthy Planet.* Gabriola Island, BC: New Society Publishers, 1997..

Sandhill, Laird. "Community as Crucible," *Circles of Strength: Community Alternatives to Alienation.* Ed. Helen Forsey. Gabriola Island, BC: New Society Publishers, 1993. 75-79.

Schor, Juliet. *Plenitude: The New Economics of True Wealth.* New York: Penguin, 2010.

Shuman, Michael H. *Going Local: Creating Self-Reliant Communities in a Global Age.* New York: The Free Press, 1998.

Thomas, Richard. "The Proximity Solution: Community Enterprise, Social Resilience and Slower Consumption." Paper presented at European Society for Ecological Economics conference, Istanbul, July 2011. Web. Accessed March 27, 2013.

von Weizsacker, Ernst Ulrich. *Earth Politics.* London: Zed Books, 1994.

Wallace, Ira. "The More We Do, The More We Know We Haven't Done," *Circles of Strength: Community Alternatives to Alienation.* Ed. Helen Forsey. Gabriola Island, BC: New Society Publishers, 1993. 51-55.

Yap, Nonita T. *Sustainable Community Development: An Introductory Guide.* Toronto: Ontario Environmental Network, 1989.

MARTHA MCMAHON

Alternatives to Globalization

Women Small-Scale Farmers and Local Food Systems

WHEN WE THINK ABOUT FARMING, many of us think about green fields and fresh produce. It is disturbing to learn that the institutionalization of new globalized agri-food systems through economic liberalization, World Trade Organization (WTO) agreements and Intellectual Property Rights Regimes (IPR) means that many developments in agriculture and food production have less to do with growing food or feeding people and more to do with financial speculation in agri-food and agri-fuel commodities (Clapp, Goldenberg, Paterson), power and the restructuring of capitalism (McMichael, Patal). And when they think of a farmer, most Canadians probably see a man (wearing a feed cap) driving a tractor across a Prairie landscape. In contrast, in the Global South, Marilee Karl points out, women make up the majority of farmers, producing between 60 percent and 80 percent of the food people eat and are central to local food security. It should not be surprising to learn, therefore, that despite the image of North American farmers as male, women farmers and women members of community supported agriculture (CSA) projects are central in building new local, ecological, alternative food systems. Nor should it surprise us to learn that internationally, those most hurt by globalized new food systems are women and children, especially rural women and small farmers (Karl; McMichael and Schneider; Patal). The significance of gender in understanding globalizing agri-food systems, however, is more complicated than the question of whether those most affected are men or women (Desmarais; McMahon 2001).

BACK FROM THE SHEEP BARN

I come in from the sheep barn. The sheep are due to lamb within a few days. Making tea and preparing the list of organic seed potatoes for spring planting, I listen to CBC. "Now we can get on with feeding a hungry planet," a spokesperson for the salmon farm industry here in BC announces as she welcomes the BC Liberal government's lifting of the moratorium on salmon farming. "Feeding the planet," I mentally note, catching how food provisioning is represented as a global and competitive project.

525

I hear her voice as both culturally masculine and feminine, rationally efficient yet caring. She (and the industry she speaks for) will "feed the world."

The local women small-scale farmers I have been interviewing here and in Ireland self-consciously represent themselves as feeding their communities. Are they simply small minded?

THINKING OF FOOD AS RELATIONSHIP AND RESISTING COMMODIFICATION

Talking with women organic and small-scale farmers on Vancouver Island and in the South West of Ireland has led me to attend deeply to their ideas about farming as being about feeding community and building relationships. On the one hand, focusing on the local and selling at farmers markets and through CSA projects looks like a sensible economic response to agri-business for small-scale farmers. It is ironic that small farmers near urban centres can use the (farmers') market to evade the corporate dominated "free-market." Direct sales of local organic produce can return up to 80 cents of each food dollar to the farmer. Conventional farmers often get less than five cents of each food dollar spent in a supermarket. Culturally, "doing community" is women's work, and women are over-represented among very small farmers. It is not surprising that they often focus on local markets.

Cone Abbott and Myhre point out, however, that the kind of locally oriented farming typical of the women farmers I talked to in British Columbia and Ireland is more radical than it seems. It represents a form of cultural resistance as well as economic resistance. It disrupts the disembeddedness and fragmentations of modernity (Giddens) and late capitalism. Food, especially ecologically-grown food, produced for and sold through local farmers markets and CSA projects has the potential for re-embedding people in time and place by linking them to particular farmers whom they know, and through them to specific pieces of land, the ecology of place and the seasons. It is a form of resistance to the commodification of life and farming under capitalism. Commodification, as Bove points out, destroys the "culture" in agriculture as well as the environment.

If we look at farming through an ecological feminist lens, resisting the commodification of farming and food requires that we think about food as the embodiment of relationships rather than simply as something we eat. A potato is not just a potato, it carries in it, and into us when we eat it, a host of social relationships such as those with the people who grow, harvest, or trade the potato and also with Nature, not in the abstract but with particular non-human others, things, and individual places. When we partake in food, we consume relationships. In refusing food, for example, Counihan explains, anorexic young women are refusing patriarchal relationships. Food embodies the relationships that organize and produce it, be they relations of inequality, or as in the movie *Like Water for Chocolate*, love.

Mauss's and Sahlin's anthropological work on non-capitalist societies shows how food exchanges build and strengthen social relationships and reduce social distance. Food in capitalist societies, on the other hand, Coulihan explains, is a commodity whose exchange creates distance and differentiation. Drawing on Sahlin's concept of "negative reciprocity," she emphasizes that people are separated and placed in antagonistic positions towards each other through capitalist food exchanges. Food becomes a vehicle of power (Coulihan).

When talking of globalization, it is important to distinguish corporate-driven globalization from above from globalization from below (Carroll), such as the loose webs of alliances and affinity groups connected in struggles for social justice and environment. The point is not to propose a new universalizing model that sees all trade as bad, or only local food as good, or that creates some exclusionary notion of community, but to understand food as the embodiment of relationships. Food can build life-sustaining and justice-enhancing relationships, as well as unjust ones. There are, for example, global networks of support for local food systems that express commitment to distant others, and a variety of models of fair trade relationships. There is also a global movement of peasants, landless rural people, women and small farmers and fishers call La Via Campesina that is working to promote food sovereignty built on social justice and respect for the natural world (Desmarais; Holt Gimenez and Shattuck).

"FEEDING THE WORLD": A UNIVERSALIZING AND MASCULINIST PROJECT THAT LEAVES PEOPLE HUNGRY?

The Food and Agriculture Organization (FAO) has estimated that the 2007/08 price spike in the globalized food system increased the number of undernourished people from about 850 million in 2007 to about 1023 million in 2009. Famine stalks up to 12 million people in the Horn of Africa. Yet there is more food produced every year than the world's population could consume. People are hungry, it seems, because they lack access. They do not have money to buy food or access to land on which to grow it, or an effective right to it. (UNSpecial Rapporteur on the Right to Food, Moore Lappe, Collins and Rosset). An unexpected natural event, whether crop disease (such as the Irish potato blight) or an extended drought can push people who have been already made vulnerable to hunger because of injustice, inequality or war from hunger into the horror of famine. That is, the dominant food system makes people vulnerable to chronic malnourishment, hunger and famine (Keneally; Patal; Fraser and Rimas).1 Feminist scholars like Vandana Shiva and others (Barndt; Bennholdt-Thomsen, and Mies), make it clear that this modern globalized hunger-making agriculture is a classed, raced, and gendered project. Many governmental and international organizations, policy makers and transnational corporations, in contrast, typically represent modern agriculture as a universal and moral project of "feeding the world."

In this latter representation, the inequitable gendered, raced, or classed nature of globalized food production and trade in agricultural products is largely invisible. Furthermore, we are told, local small-scale farming is far too inefficient, and cannot produce enough food for a growing world population. Concentration, specialization, biotechnology and reaping the advantages of comparative advantage and economies of scale through international trade, we are assured, is far more efficient.

A globalized agri-food system is thus constructed as a market imperative that becomes a moral imperative in a world of hungry people: "We must feed the world." "Losing" small farmers and family farms is the price to be paid, we are reminded, for ending world hunger and feeding the world. Like concerns about bioethics, concern about vanishing small farms is falsely dismissed as romantic and nostalgic, a luxury the Third World cannot afford. In practice, however, globalized agriculture does not help poor countries develop and escape poverty. A 2000 UN report on the world's 48 poorest countries reveals that as they opened their economies to international trade, poverty actually deepened (UNCTAD). Indeed, in the period when Kenyan food exports almost doubled, domestic consumption of fruit per person actually declined (FAO Food Balance Sheet Database). The 2010 UN report submitted by the Special Rapporteur on the Right to Food, Oliver de Schutter confirms that the global food system is continuing to fail the most vulnerable.

Janine Brodie explains that the discourse about global economic restructuring is invariably cased in gender-neutral terms, but it is usually women, both in first and third world countries, that are carrying the burden of economic restructuring. What is not said is that small-scale farmers are often women farmers, and that in the globalizing gaze of international trade regimes their food production counts for less, or is not counted at all (Waring) because it is produced for family, community, or a local market rather than for the export trade. On the one hand, small-scale women farmers, urban farmers, and other peasant farmers help feed their families and communities while global food regimes which claim to be able to feed the world leave millions hungry.

But like so much of women's work, much of women's agriculture is rendered invisible or devalued. On the other hand, an industrialized, globalized food system, liberalized international trade in agricultural products, and the benefits of biotechnology are offered as the efficient and moral alternative to peasant and subsistence farming in which women play such a central role. However, the work Miguel Altieri, Peter Rosset and Lori Ann Thrupp suggests that it is probably only small-scale, localized agroecology that can end hunger in the developing world.

More and more, agriculture is framed as a masculinist (and white) moral project of "feeding the world"—a moral project that is ideologically in the service of international trade. What is also not said is that corporate concentration of agriculture has increased with globalized agri-food systems which control nearly all aspects of American agriculture and much of the world's (Mittal and Kawaii). For example, by 2005 for livestock overall in the U.S., the top four agricultural companies within each sector are responsible for 83.5 percent of beef packing, 64 percent of pork packing, 49 percent of pork production and 51 percent of turkey production (Hendrickson and Heffernan, 2005) while Cargill and Continental control almost two-thirds of the grain trade in the world. Agri-food giants promote a model of agriculture that is driving third world peasants off the land (Mittal and Kawaii). Canadian, like U.S . farmers, are enlisted (perhaps I should say, conscripted) in the service of this project and annually warned that they must produce more or perish (Boyens; Qualman).

Many western governments speak two mutually incompatible discourses on food and farming. They say they are committed to sustainable food and farming systems, but they are also committed to globalization. The dis-local-izations of their economic policies undermine their environmental commitments.

The distance food is transported by road has increased over 50 percent in the last 20 years and food systems are now a major contributor to global climate change as well as other forms of environmental degradation (Jones). Especially disturbing are animal welfare issues. Live animals are transported greater and greater distances. Between 1989 and 1999 alone there was a 90 percent increase in road freight of food and agricultural products between the UK and Europe the food system accounts for over 40 percent of all UK road freight. Many countries seem to simply be "swapping" food. The UK for example exports and also imports millions of litres of milk per year. Buying organic is not necessarily the ecological alternative. One shopping basket of 26 imported organic products in the UK could have travelled 241,000 kms and released as much CO_2 into the atmosphere as an average four-bedroom household does in cooking meals for eight months (Sustain). However, food miles themselves are poor indicators of sustainability. Of more consequence is the transformation of the social and ecological relationships associated with globalizing food. As the issues of social inequality and environmental degradation associated with globalized agri-food systems become more visible, local food systems look more attractive. Several local and city councils in Canada and the UK, for example, have set up food policy councils or launched Local Food Links projects. Local food systems are being seen as ways of regenerating rural and inner city economies, strengthening community, improving community health, addressing food insecurity, protecting ecological biodiversity and ground water quality, and so on.

GENDERING AGRICULTURE AND DISRUPTING CONVENTIONAL IDENTITIES

This article draws on women organic farmers' experience and ideas. But it is an article about the gendered natures of agriculture and food systems rather than primarily an article about women farmers. Rather than use essentialized notions of women or women farmers, I want to argue that we can understand food systems as gendered. And these gendering lines, I suggest, can cross cut biologically and socially sexed bodies to disrupt the exclusions of class and economic power. I am using gender in a non-essentialist sense here to refer to social process that organizes meaning and produces a variety of exclusions and inclusions and functions to distribute power and privilege. Marshall, drawing on Patricia Williams, points out that the analytic category of gender is useful for some purposes, but needs to be fractured for other, and, I argue, ambiguously reconfigured for others.

On the one hand, empirically, small-scale farmers and urban farmers are very often women, especially in the third world, but also among organic farmers here locally in BC. On the other hand, small farmers, whether male or female, are culturally and politically "feminized" in discourse and economic regimes that construct them as powerless, unproductive, dependent, locally embedded, and parochial (reminiscent of depictions of women's bond of family), inefficient, and non-rational in their commitments to the local and traditional and in their failure to modernize or participate in agri-business (McMahon 2001). It is important, as Marshall points out, not to take gender as synonymous with women. As Other to the universal (masculine, white, classed) economic agent of the International Monetary Fund (IMF) and World Bank discourses, the economic man of neo-liberal economics (McMahon 1997), small farmers, male and female, are feminized. They are Other to economic man. Just as sex ideologically naturalizes gender, so the "natural law" of the market and economic efficiency naturalizes the gendering of small farmers as female-like. Not tough enough for the competitive real world.

Although feminism often sees gender as a way of distributing power and benefits according to marked bodies, we can extend the idea of marked embodiment to bodies embedded in local space, such as peasant bodies, Indigenous and tribal people's bodies, and associated embedding ties to land and place as a form of "marking"—an attributed gendered identity that is not a self-identity. Small-scale male farmers do not, after all, think of themselves as women, though they may experience economic restructuring in similar ways to many women.

The gendered discourses and representations of farmers and globalizing agri-food systems may be ideologically constructed, but the consequences are material. Gendered identities are linked in systematic ways to institutionalized forms of power. The women farmers' experiences I draw upon in writing this article are used to disrupt hegemonic stories about food, farming, and "feeding the world," rather than to represent women farmers or "women's ways" of farming. For this moment and this purpose, small-scale women farmers are the Other that exposes the oppressive face of the Master Narratives told about globalizing agriculture, food, hunger, and the environment.

Martha McMahon is an associate professor of Sociology at the University of Victoria and also a part-time farmer. <mcmahon@uvic.ca>.

[1]Martin Khor of the Third World World Network, speaking on behalf of the NGO Major Group to the UN General assembly at the opening of the

Multistakeholder Dialogue session at the 2nd preparatory commission (PrepCom 11) for the Johannesburg Summit Rio+10 later that year. Khor is stressing to his audience that the deterioration on both environment and development fronts over the previous ten years can be largely blamed on the "ascent of globalization," as policy, practice, and law.

REFERENCES:

Altieri, M., Rosset, P., and L. Thrupp._*The Potential of Agroecology to Combat Hunger in the Developing World.* Policy Brief, Institute for Food and Development Policy. Oakland California. Oct. 1998

Barndt, D. Ed. *Women Working the NAFTA Food Chain.* Toronto: Second Story Press, 1999.

Barrientos, S., A. Bee, A. Matear and I. Vogel. *Women in Agribusiness: Working Miracles in the Chilean Fruit Export Sector.* New York: St. Martin's Press, 1999.

Bove, Jose. *The World is Not For Sale: Farmers Against Junk Food.* London: Verso, 2001.

Boyens, I. *Another Season's Promise: Hope and Despair in Canada's Farm Country.* Toronto: Penguin Canada, 2001.

Brodie, J. "Shifting the Boundaries: Gender and the Politics of Restructuring." *Strategic Silence: Gender and Economic Policy.* Ed. E Bakker. London: Zed Books, 1994. 46-60.

Bennholdt-Thomsen, V. and M. Mies *The Subsistence Perspective: Beyond the Globalized Economy.* London: Zed Books, 1999.

Carroll, W. "Undoing the End of History: Canada-Centred Reflections on the Challenges of Globalization." *Socialist Studies Bulletin* 63-64 (Jan-June 2001): 5-31.

Clapp, Jennifer. "Food Price Vulnerability in the Global South: Considering the Global Economic Context." *Third World Quarterly* 30 (6) (2009): 1183-1196.

Cone, C. Abbott, and A. Myhre. "Community-Supported Agriculture: A Sustainable Alternative to Industrial Agriculture?" *Human Organization* 59 (2) (2000): 187-197

Counihan, C. *An Anthropology of Food and Body: Gender, Meaning, and Power.* New York: Routledge, 1999.

Desmarais, Annette. *La Via Campesina: Globalization and the Power of Peasants.* Halifax, NS: Fernwood, 2007.

Development Alternatives with Women for New Era (DAWN). "Biotech Weapons Worse than Nuclear Arsenal." Pakistan, Jan 28, 2002. Web.

Fraser, Evan and Andrew Rimas . *Empires of Food: Feast, Famine and the Rise and Fall of Civilizations.* New York: Free Press, 2010.

Food and Agriculture Organization (FAO). *Price Volatility and Food Security.* Accessed September 6, 2011. Web.

Giddens, A. *Modernity and Self-Identity: Self and Society in the Late Modern Age.* Stanford, CA: Stanford University Press, 1991.

Goldenberg, Suzanne. "U.S. Corn-belt Farmers: The Country Has Turned on U.S." *The Guardian* August 15, 2011. Web.

Hendrickson, J., and W. Heffernan. "Concentration of Agricultural Markets." *Domina Law* (2005). Web.

Holt Gimenez, Eric and Annie Shattuck. "Food Crises, Food Regimes and Food Movements." *Journal of Peasant Studies* 38 (1) (2010): 109-144.

Karl, Marilee. "Inseparable: The Crucial Role of Women in Food Security Revisited." Isis International, *Women in Action Series*, 2009. Accessed August 10, 2011. Web.

Keneally, Thomas. *Three Famines*. Australia: Random House, 2010.

Khor, M. "Introductory Statement on Behalf of NGO Major Group." Accessed January 2002. Web.

Marshall, B. *Reconfiguring Gender*. Toronto: Broadview Press, 2000.

Mauss, M. *The Gift*. New York: Norton, 1967.

McMahon, M. "Ecofeminism and Ecoagriculture." *Women and Environments International* 52/53 (Fall 2001): 36-37.

McMahon, M. "From the Ground Up: Ecofeminism and Ecological Economics." *Ecological Economics* 20 (1997): 163-173.

McMahon, Martha. "Standard Fare or Fairer Standards: Feminist Reflections on Agri-food Governance." *Agriculture and Human Values* 28 (2011): 401-412.

McMichael, Phillip. "A Food Regime Analysis of the Food Crisis." *Agriculture and Human Values* 26 (4) (2009): 281-295.

McMichael, Phillip and Mindi Schneider. "Food Security Politics and the Millennium Development Goals." *Third World Quarterly* 32 (1) (2011): 119-139.

Mittal, A. and M. Kawaai "Freedom to Trade?" *Institute for Food and Development Policy Backgrounder* 7 (4) (Fall 2001). Accessed December 2001. Web.

Moore Lappé, F., C. Collins and P. Rosset. *World Hunger: Twelve Myths*. New York: Grove Press, Food First, 1998.

Patal, Raj. *Stuffed and Starved: Markets, Power and the Hidden Battle for the World's Food System*. Toronto, Ontario: Harper Collins, 2007.

Paterson, Chris. "The Value of Food: More than Just Supply and Demand." *The agAdvance* (July 2011): 34-37. Accessed Sept 13, 2011. Web.

Qualman, D. "The Farm Crisis and Corporate Power." Ottawa: The Canadian Centre for Policy Alternatives, 2001.

Sahlins, M. *Stone Age Economics*. Hawthorne, NY: Aldine, 1972.

Shiva, Vandana. *Biopiracy: The Plunder of Nature and Knowledge*. Toronto: Between The Lines Press, 1997.

United Nations. "Report submitted by the Special Rapporteur on the Right to Food, Oliver de Schutter, Human Rights Council, General Assembly." December 20, 2010.

UN Commission on Trade and Development (UNCTAD). *Least Developed Countries Report 2000*. New York and Geneva: Author, 2000.

Waring, M. *If Women Counted: A New Feminist Economics*. New York: Harper Collins, 1988.

LESLEY MARPLE AND VICTORIA LATCHMORE

LGBTQ Activism

Small Town Social Change

RURAL LESBIAN, gay, bisexual, transgender and queer (LGBTQ) communities have the potential to find themselves in a state of dual isolation. There is first the difference experienced from heteronormative culture and society, and secondly the isolation from urban LGBTQ culture and political movements. Rural spaces do not always offer LGBTQ exclusive events, programs or communities and in exploring other examples of Rural LGBTQ programs, we were unable to find many similar models in Canada. This article will provide a brief description and analysis of the LGBTQ activism and programming that took place in Antigonish, Nova Scotia over a period of three years. Our aim is to document some of the quieter, smaller LGBTQ histories and evolutions, those events that may not capture headlines, but which are ongoing and transformative in the lives of LGBTQ individuals in our region.

Antigonish is unique when compared to other local rural regions. This is due to factors including the presence of a university in this town of 5,000, the town of Antigonish operating as a service centre for Antigonish County (population 19,500) (Statistics Canada), and Antigonish's designation as a Regional Health Centre. The student population at St. Francis Xavier University (StFX) is 4,000 students and each September, the population of Antigonish experiences a significant swell as students return and university classes resume. The presence of StFX University and the Regional Hospital means that there is significant migration into the Antigonish region when compared to other rural areas in North Eastern Nova Scotia. Despite this movement, the dominant local religious influence remains Catholic, with 80 percent of the population of the County identifying itself as such (Aslan). The local Catholic community remains traditional in its approach and has significant influence over local politics and education. Antigonish is often identified by members of local social justice organizations as a town of contradictions; for example despite the traditional nature of the region, there is a strong and vibrant feminist women's community. These contradictions result in interesting challenges and collaborative efforts for social change work.

Beginning in June 2004, Antigonish became the host site of the Lesbian, Gay, Bisexual, Transgender Community Safety Initiative funded in part by the National Crime Prevention Strategy. This was a locally initiated, rural community development project whose goal was to open a dialogue and continue the work of social change around acceptance and celebration of our local LGBTQ communities. The project developed out of student activism, and evolved into a community initiative that worked in conjunction with the local RCMP detachment, the Antigonish Women's Resource Centre, the regional school board, diverse service providers, students, and community members.

This project adapted from existing models of Positive Space and Ally training programs where participants attend a training session and display a symbol of their support for LGBTQ communities. Adaptations were made in order to ensure that the work was appropriate to a rural region. While the work of this project included male participants, volunteers, and advisory committee members, the focus of this article is to acknowledge and explore the impact of the LGBTQ project for women living in Antigonish and other surrounding rural regions.

Organized LGBTQ activism in Antigonish exists formally in two spheres: the Antigonish Women's Resource Centre (AWRC) and StFX University. Over the past ten years, the AWRC has organized awareness workshops, hosted a lesbian film festival, distributed information regarding lesbian communities through such forums as their newsletter, and provided ongoing support for women throughout the community. At StFX University, the Alliance for Sexual Diversity at X (ASD@X), formed in the late 1990s as an education and awareness raising organization, was the first public or "out" LGBTQ organization on campus. The LGBT Community Safety Initiative in its inception provided these two local communities, a feminist, service-based women's centre and a university, an opportunity to draw on each other's strengths and resources in order to support social change work on campus and throughout the region.

Much of the history of this project began at StFX with the student-run ASD@X group. ASD@X's mandate focuses on activism and the group organized a variety of events on campus and in the community at large. The work of this group was often missed or overlooked, with promotion made particularly challenging due to a persistent removal or destruction of most LGBTQ activity advertising and promotional materials on campus and in town. It was not until sexual health workshops were organized in February of 2003 by ASD@X that the group became better known in Antigonish. The intent of these workshops was to ensure that safe, accurate, and LGBTQ inclusive sexual health information be made available in the community. In response to the announcement of these workshops, representatives of the university-funded Chaplaincy department at StFX went to the president of the university to request that this student group not be permitted to use the Students' Union Building. The subject of the workshops was included in a homily delivered to hundreds of StFX students at the weekly university mass. Immediately following the service, a group of students left the church and destroyed the promotional banners and posters advertising the workshops on display in the Students' Union Building. The workshops took place nevertheless and were extremely well attended, although the second workshop attracted a group of students who formed a rosary circle outside of the event in protest. The resulting resistance led to both increased politicization of the LGBTQ and ally communities as well as an increased experience of oppression and victimization due to greater visibility of LGBTQ communities.

Following the incidents around the sexual health workshop female StFX students found themselves experiencing increased intimidation on campus. There were instances of harassment of women students by males while operating information tables in the Students' Union Building, students were criticized and ridiculed by males in their classes, and negative commentary regarding the LGBTQ communities were published in the campus newspaper. A lack of effective means through which to confront the issues inspired a desire to organize in a way which would better allow LGBTQ communities to address their own experiences of oppression, without a need to rely on existing forums which were homophobic, insensitive to the safety concerns of LGBTQ women, unaware of trans-politics, and intimidating to access.

Thus, in 2003, ASD@X held a focus group with discussion around experiences of LGBTQ students on campus. Stories of the negative experiences of LGBTQ students came out in this work along with an outline for what students needed in terms of support on campus. A proposal was prepared for StFX administration recommending that an LGBTQ Student Advisor be hired as exists for other student groups on campus. This proposal was accepted, but the university indicated that they were unable to invest money in this initiative. Efforts were then made to find outside funding sources.

The Community Mobilization Program (CMP) of Crime Prevention was identified as an excellent fit for the type of project funding required to implement the Lesbian, Gay, Bisexual, Transgender Community Safety Initiative. Although Crime Prevention was initially hesitant to fund a project addressing transphobia and homophobia as risks to community safety, funding was eventually secured. Crime Prevention affiliation offered the project levels of legitimacy in our conservative rural region which had not before been experienced by LGBTQ groups. The choice to operate out of the Antigonish Women's Resource Centre as a project of the Antigonish Women's Association situated the initiative in a feminist organization with over 20 years of history of local social change activism, a history that also provided the project with immediate connections within the community.

The initial stages of the project were aimed at grounding this work within the community. Historically, only a handful of non-LGBTQ allies would attend LGBTQ events. But the project found itself beginning this work in the midst of an interesting political climate. Same-sex marriage legislation was a key topic in the current federal election, the media was full of debates on these issues, and there was a broader public consciousness of LGBTQ issues than had existed previously. This public media attention gave a type of permission or incentive to local organizations to engage in LGBTQ work.

In a small rural community, challenge of the project included a conscious effort to ensure that the feminist and queer politics of the work were not sacrificed and to associate the project with well-known and respected community members. The advantage of a smaller community is the impact that can be had if this networking is successful. A Steering Committee made up of a small group of feminist women who had experience working both within the Antigonish community and with LGBTQ populations was established. The Steering Committee directed the development of a Community Advisory Committee that included representatives from health, justice, education, and community activists and gave the project access to large professional groups such as the Regional Health Authority, the regional School Board and StFX administration and faculty.

The Advisory Committee was an exciting balance between longt-ime community activists with political influence in the local community, as well as new and innovative university employees who brought their energy to challenge the local status quo. This group was made up almost exclusively of women who committed extensive energy and time to promotion of this work. The Community Advisory Committee was run on a collective model where meetings were facilitated to encourage members to contribute their ideas, skills, suggestions, and individual expertise to the work. At the first Advisory meeting members were provided with resource packages in order to introduce a topic to a population where many people had had little opportunity previously to discuss LGBT populations, promote collective ownership of the work, and to share resources as a tool in explaining and legitimizing the project to those who were skeptical of its validity. This group integrated the concepts and goals of the project into their respective workplaces that resulted in increased registrations and bookings for anti-oppression workshops.

A key success of the LGBT Community Safety Initiative was its local development, and presence in the community. The project was able to make adjustments to suit the local culture and climate. An example of this is the choice not to use the term "queer" in the project title. In the local region, "queer" is still a colloquial word, with many negative connotations. It was decided that in order to avoid offending both LGBTQ and non-LGBTQ individuals, this word would not be used in the project title. We saw this point as a key to the success of delivering LGBTQ training in a region without a history of activity in this area.

The first public event of the project was the launch of the Positive Space training program at StFX. This launch received supportive media attention from town and student newspapers. The StFX student newspaper, *The Xaverian,* reported the perspective of one professor,

"This seems like the culmination of various struggles," expressed Nancy Forestell of the Women's Studies and History Department.

"It has been frustrating at times to see wonderful people and students leave this school because there wasn't a safe space. This initiative gives me hope." (Dove 1)

Local media coverage in the Antigonish newspaper, *The Casket*, was seen as a tool for normalizing LGBTQ issues in the public mind. This Catholic publication provided a factual account of the project and resulted in an unprecedented lack of backlash ("Positive space program launched"). The importance of first having received media coverage, and second receiving no negative feedback was monumental for the town of Antigonish. We know that this was not only beneficial to the project, but also to the sense of belonging of LGBTQ community members and felt it indicated a significant shift in regards to the willingness of Antigonish to embrace change.

The first Positive Space training workshops of the project were held at StFX in the fall of 2004. These workshops were as participant driven as possible with the facilitator's role being to guide the conversation, or to provide information when necessary. Once the workshops began, the project had an ever increasing support base of allies. The use of a standard symbol, the sticker, and button, which could only be attained through participation in a workshop was an excellent means through which to promote this work and to inspire others to do the training. Many of the workshop participants wore their buttons, put up their stickers, and took responsibility for a piece of the education work in the community. The buttons and stickers were especially effective in our small community because they were displayed, and seen, by a large percentage of our community, a task that would have been much more challenging in a larger urban environment.

Because of the location of the work at the Antigonish Women's Resource Centre and a local history where women have been the primary leaders for social change in the community, the project was heavily influenced by women and feminist approaches to anti-oppression work. It was truly the women in our community who overwhelmingly responded to this work, and who brought it forward. Women in the community who were not LGBTQ identified, acted as key contributors to this work through both professional and personal connections. In looking at the influences of the work, the project's scope could be segmented into three groups: youth, LGBTQ identified women and non-LGBTQ women.

The youth who were actively engaged and who organized through the project were all women. Through the supports provided by the project, as well as the Antigonish Women's Resource Centre, these youth were able to overcome significant blocks and resistance in the local high school's administration in order to finally receive approval to operate a Gay Straight Alliance at their school. The youth also had an opportunity to participate in an event entitled *Reworking the Periphery* organized between StFX and the LGBT Community Safety Initiative. This weekend event included lectures, a drag show, and a one-day workshop. Youth we spoke to said it was the "greatest thing that ever happened in Antigonish." This initiative had a profound impact not only on youths' perceptions of themselves, but as was noted by one youth, it challenged her to realize "that things like this could happen in a rural place." One young organizer said she felt more "empowered and able to change stuff." The leadership development role that the project played with youth is a key piece of the LGBT Safety Initiative.

As a result of the overwhelmingly positive response to this work, the LGBTQ population in Antigonish received an unexpected boost in support. Antigonish's reaction to LGBTQ populations had previously only been evidenced in homophobic articles in the religion section and letters to the editor in *The Casket.* The levels of acceptance and support that existed in the community were unknown to us prior to this initiative but were clearly evident when a fundraiser for the LGBT Community Safety Initiative was attended by 200 community members.

This initiative was instrumental in giving voice to LGBTQ individuals and non-LGBTQ allies. The sessions were run with mixed groups, so that many LGBTQ individuals were given a supportive environment in which to analyze and discuss their challenges of living in a rural region. Non-LGBTQ individuals benefited from an opportunity to better hear and understand these experiences and to explore ways in which to confront issues of oppression and prejudice. There was a great deal of surprise amongst members of v communities, who had not anticipated a positive response to these workshops, let alone the overwhelming embracing of this work that was evident both during and after the project. As a result of the initiative, LGBTQ women described an improved sense of safety and belonging.

Through the many public Positive Space training sessions, many women had the opportunity to participate in this work and to discuss oppression and the operation of power in our community. This analysis was not kept exclusively to issues of gender identity and sexual orientation, but offered an occasion to discuss other forms of power and oppression experienced or observed by workshop participants. Exciting developments came out of these workshops. Many of the participants went on to organize training sessions within their places of employment, and to begin to challenge homophobia as they witnessed it in their lives. Three allies from one of the workshops decided to organize a positive space T-shirt campaign. These StFX students sold over 250 shirts in the Antigonish community, with participants all wearing the shirts on February 15, 2005 to coincide with Pink Triangle Day on February 14 as a sign of support for LGBT positive spaces.

What is most difficult to document is the shift in attitudes and perceptions, as well as the new sense of space and support that the LGBTQ community in the Antigonish region has experienced. This shift provided an opportunity for LGBTQ individuals to identify themselves publicly within safe social spaces, as well as the chance for non-LGBTQ allies to participate actively as visible supporters of this community. It has been inspiring for so many in the community to experience the way in which this project was embraced in a community that has often suffered a reputation of being closed-minded and unwelcoming. This project speaks to the possibility for rural communities to challenge and to grow despite external and internal perceptions of what is possible for these spaces. The rural sphere can be radical and the possibilities for rural engagement can even surprise those of us who call these communities home.

Lesley Marple developed and coordinated the LGBT Community Safety Initiative in Antigonish through the Antigonish Women's Association. She is currently working in health care in rural British Columbia.

Victoria Latchmore is a graduate of St. Francis Xavier University and worked as a summer research assistant for the Antigonish Women's Resource Center. She had ongoing involvement with the project as a volunteer facilitator and currently teaches high school in Ontario.

REFERENCES

Aslan, Luca. "Interview with Dr. Lucian Turcescu" *Radio Voice of America (Washington, DC)*. 23 Feb 2000. Accessed 25 August 2005. Web.

Dove, Amy. "Hate is not a family value" *The Xaverian* 27 October. 2004: 1.

"Positive space program launched." *The Casket* 27 October. 2004: 11.

Statistics Canada. *Census of Nova Scotia.* 2001. Accessed 26 August 2005.Web.

ANITA OLSEN HARPER

Is Canada Peaceful and Safe for Aboriginal Women?

ABORIGINAL WOMEN in Canada are the victims of very serious human rights violations. One blatant example is the legislative gap in both federal and provincial law in protecting a spouse's right to equal division of matrimonial real property on-reserve. All other Canadians are protected by provincial laws regarding this matter, but the same laws are not applicable on-reserve because only the federal government has jurisdiction over "lands reserved for Indians" and this includes real property on-reserve. There has never been a law enacted by the Canadian Parliament to address how real property, including matrimonial homes, will be divided when a marriage or common-law relationship breaks down. Aboriginal women and their children who reside on-reserve directly bear the brunt of this serious legislative gap. Further, because almost all reserves in Canada suffer from a severe lack of adequate housing, women who cannot remain in the family home are forced to go elsewhere with their children. This is only one example of the special ways in which the rights of on-reserve women remain unprotected.

These facts remain in spite of the fact that Canada is ranked very highly in the United Nations' Human Development Index (HDI). This index is based on a Quality of Life survey which examines the health, education and wealth of a country's citizens by measuring life expectancy, educational achievement, secondary and tertiary enrolment and standard of living.[1]

These findings would make one think that almost all Canadians citizens do quite well, and perhaps this is the case. For the Aboriginal people who have been living ab initio on these lands, this is simply not true. The disparity in health, educational attainment, accumulation of wealth, life expectancy and standard of living is a noticeably wide gap in comparison with the life experiences of most Canadians. Aboriginal women, in particular, suffer from inequality of status compared to both Aboriginal men and, especially, their non-Aboriginal counterparts.

In this and other respects, and mostly because Canada as a nation does not make it a priority to address issues such as these, it cannot "look in the mirror" and see a truly civilized and liberated nation.

Aboriginal women in Canada are subject to high rates of violence in all forms. In particular, racialized violence targeting Aboriginal women is especially disturbing because these experiences are passed on intergenerationally to children and youth in other violence-related forms such as through involvement in street gangs and other "street" misbehaviours. In far too many instances, extreme racialized violence against Aboriginal women leads to their disappearances and even murder. The life destroyed in these circumstances is not only the victim's, but those whom she has left behind: grandmothers, parents, sisters, aunts, children, other relatives and friends. Could the long-standing general lack of awareness within Canada about the extreme violence against Aboriginal women mean that the public simply does not want to know? Does the public think that these "uncomfortable" issues will perhaps just somehow "go away?"

REPRESENTATION OF ABORIGINAL PEOPLE IN CANADIAN HISTORY

The way Aboriginal people have been represented in Canadian history plays an important part in how Aboriginal people, including Aboriginal women, are perceived in today's Canadian society. In these times of rapid technological and other change, any statements about the importance of history seem almost naïve; modern western societies appear to self-define according to their future plans, not from their past or history. Nonetheless, such perceptions do not take away from the validity of understanding the past in order to understand the present. Only by thoroughly comprehending the paths that have been leading to the present can appropriate and timely steps be taken to solve long-term problems, such as those faced by Aboriginal women in Canada. Incidentally, Aboriginal tradition places a high importance on expending time and effort in teaching youngsters their family and tribal history because they believe that youth with a solid understanding of the past is a youth that values its own individual and collective identity.

There are many examples that demonstrate the reality that historical representation and its subsequent presentation is not necessarily trustworthy. In Canada, most recordings of the European-Aboriginal relationships have been preserved, presented and accepted according to the values, perceptions and general life philosophies of the prevailing Euro-Canadian society. Even within the relatively short span of that society, historiography points out an interesting phenomenon: narrations over time are recorded, shaped and fixed according to prevailing Eurocentric societal attitudes (Blaut 10). Paralleling any change in the view of the present is a change in the view of the past.

Historical presentations then, have many serious limitations. One of their functions is as a tool for propaganda to encourage thought and motivation into predetermined outcomes. The "battleground for the public mind" has always had many different fronts to serve certain specific purposes. For example, within their own societies at the time of contact, the roles of Aboriginal women were vastly different from those of European women. The latter held a status that was shared with minors and wards of the Crown; they were perceived as property—in their early lives, their father's property, and later when they married, the property of their husbands. Aboriginal women, on the other hand, headed family line,[2] exerted a great deal of power such as the authority to choose and oust their nation's chiefs, and were a vital part of consensus decision-making. Nevertheless, Canadian history presents these Aboriginal traditions in a negative light; the *Indian Act* of 1876 removed Aboriginal women's political powers by creating an elected chief and council system which stipulated that only men could be elected as chiefs and councilors.

Canadian history shows that stereotypical images were serving a purpose for those who endorsed them. The primary overall opinion of the first Europeans was cautiously optimistic for they relied on the First Peoples for all their basic livelihood needs. They condescendingly acknowledged that these "primitive" peoples needed civilizing, but were fully confident that this could be accomplished through educational processes that they themselves would predicate. Times began to change. The true imperialist ambitions of the colonialist powers began to emerge, and the fairly balanced early relationship began to crumble to give way to the birth of the interpretation of Aboriginal people as wretched and barbaric, even demonic. Many history and children's books of the nineteenth century were based on this imagery (Francis 159-164).

Settlement in Canada's "wild west" increased, but not by invitation of the First Nations themselves, who due to decimation from foreign diseases, increasingly found themselves on the fringes of their own territories. These times saw rampant theories of Native racial inferiority for these provided a rationale to the Europeans for indiscriminately taking lands that were not rightfully theirs (Hawkins 62). Newcomers willingly listened to academics who predicted the disappearance of the entire Indigenous peoples as God's way of using nature to weed out an inferior group in favour of a superior one (Le Conte 359-361). In the meantime, the First Peoples were being further marginalized into the undesired hinterlands and their suffering, if it was known at all, was treated with indifference by both the Canadian government and general public who were too busy and apathetic to involve themselves in any meaningful way.

RACISM AND ABORIGINAL WOMEN'S VULNERABILITY TO VIOLENCE

People treated with inequality by government are fair game for societal discrimination, and racism if they belong to a different ethnic group. Aboriginal people, meeting these conditions, are both discriminated against and suffer the consequences of racism. Further, because of the patriarchy of Canadian society, Aboriginal women are subject to even more inequality than Aboriginal men. There are many different arenas in "everyday Canadian life" in which Aboriginal women do not fare well at all.

Looking at Canada's Aboriginal women from an economic perspective, we see that, in one province (Manitoba), 42.7 percent off-reserve live in poverty (Donner, Busch and Fontaine). The corresponding figure for non-Aboriginal women is half that number. Aboriginal women's average annual income was $13,300; Aboriginal men's was $18,200 whereas that of non-Aboriginal women was $19,350 (NAPO 2). This synopsis is a prime example of Aboriginal women's inequality in relation to both Aboriginal men and non-Aboriginal women in the area of earning power for meeting basic livelihood needs.

Canada's child welfare system continues to be disastrous for Aboriginal families. Provincial government policies target Aboriginal children for transition into various agencies and adoption into non-Native families. While these practices are now being lobbied against by Native women's and other groups, policy changes are painstakingly slow. A significant but undesirable result is that, very often, the traditions and practices of most of these children, as grown adults, are not recognizable as Aboriginal and their connections to birth families tends to be weak at best. In 2004, a large proportion—30,000 out of a total of 76,000 children in care—is Aboriginal; this is an astonishing 39.5 percent (Blackstock and Trocme 1). More disturbingly, this large number of children has all but lost its true identity; searching out family roots and ties is problematic and traumatic for most.

In the area of education, there is a particularly large gap between the rates of non- and Aboriginal women with university degrees: in 2001, seven percent of Aboriginal women over 25 years of age had a university degree, compared with 17 percent for non-Aboriginal women within the same age group (Statistics Canada). While two-thirds of Aboriginal graduates are women, equal access to employment opportunities is still lagging; this is because gendered racism obstructs Aboriginal women's access to a fair share of the labour market (Jacobs). In the same year, 40 percent of Aboriginal women over the age of 25 had not graduated from high school compared with 29 percent among non-Aboriginal women (Statistics Canada 196).

Federal, provincial and territorial justice systems are other areas that discriminate against Aboriginal women on the basis of their race, gender and class. The systemic racism of all police forces albeit some "better" than others, and not applicable to every single member, is one way of explaining this. For example, most police officers need a fair and open attitude towards those working in the sex trade and must learn to treat street people as human beings—with dignity and respect. Another area that needs serious revision is the Court system. Court personnel often fail to either recognize or acknowledge the unique forms of injury that Aboriginal women suffer when they report being sexually assaulted or raped or any number of violations. Many Aboriginal women and girls are ostracized by their families or reserves when they go through with criminal charges; often, they themselves are blamed for their situations. This is especially harmful when so many live in the northern, more isolated areas of the country; a general lack of counseling and support services in many reserve communities does little to help and encourage these women.

The *Stolen Sisters* report by Amnesty International (Canada) made the following statements about the way in which police treat or relate to Aboriginal people:

•Most disturbingly, the inquiry concluded that police had long been aware of white men sexually preying on Indigenous women and girls in The Pas but "did not feel that the practice necessitated any particular vigilance." (1)

•The Inquiry explained that many police have come to view Indigenous people not as a community deserving protection, but a community from which the rest of society must be protected. (30)

•Many Indigenous families told Amnesty International that police did little when they reported a sister or daughter missing and seemed to be waiting for the woman to be found. (32)

•...few police forces have specific protocols on actions to be taken when Indigenous women and girls are reported missing. (33)

Amnesty International's report concluded that Canadian authorities and most police forces do not protect Aboriginal women from violent attacks (including murder) but, instead, tend to disregard these violations when they occur and are reported.

These long-standing realities, faced by all Aboriginal women in Canada, remain mostly unaddressed and given a low priority for change by governments. The status quo continues to place Aboriginal women at a much greater risk of social and economic marginalization, laying fertile ground for higher risks of victimization from all types of crimes—but most likely physical and sexual crime at the forefront. So far, no level of government has implemented the necessary legislative action and policy direction to decrease the risks that would help protect Aboriginal women from being targets of violence and other related criminal activity.

ABORIGINAL WOMEN'S RESISTANCE

In the meantime, not awaiting government policy and legislative change to address what became known as "racialized, sexualized" violence[3] against Aboriginal women, many began working with unrelenting perseverance in lobbying and involved advocacy efforts. This was taking place at both the grassroots and organizational levels in the Native community; one of those was the Native Women's Association of Canada (NWAC) and its Board of Directors who were Provincial/Territorial Member Associations (PTMAs). Many others were Aboriginal families and women themselves; they were helped by individual non-Aboriginal women and women's groups. Some of these were Amnesty International (Canada), KAIROS Canadian Ecumenical Justice Initiatives; the Canadian Association of Elizabeth Frye Societies, the Feminist Alliance for International Action (FAFIA), and the United, Anglican and other churches.

The year 2002 saw national momentum building up. Those involved pooled their efforts to raise awareness of the racially-motivated attacks on Aboriginal women. A"National Coalition for our Stolen Sisters" was established and adopted February 14 (Valentines Day) as "a day of love and hope and memory for our Stolen Sisters." This was the beginning of powerful Aboriginal women's voices being heard at the national level in an area that so long was a source of trauma for them.

The Coalition, spearheaded by NWAC, was simultaneously working to cultivate federal government allies; these were Indian and Northern Affairs Canada, the Department of Justice, Canadian International Development Agency, Public Safety and Emergency Preparedness Canada (part of which is the Royal Canadian Mounted Police), Foreign Affairs Canada and Status of Women Canada (SWC). Only one department made a formal agreement with NWAC. In November 2005, Status of Women Canada committed five-year[4] funding for Sisters in Spirit and this moved the campaign into a full research, education, national-awareness and policy initiative. The terms of the funding agreement provided NWAC with the fiscal and human resources to work in collaboration with other non- and Aboriginal women's organizations and with various federal government departments to improve the human rights of Aboriginal women in Canada, and to target the racialized and/or sexualized violence directed at this particular group.

From the 1980s through to the 2000s, concern for the safety of Aboriginal women was steadily increasing and posters of missing women were becoming a common sight anywhere Aboriginal people congregated—in community halls, stores and band offices, for example. Websites began to appear, listing the names of missing women, many being Aboriginal. Families of those missing and/or found murdered were starting to voice the pain, isolation, and trauma they were experiencing, and talked about the lack of support from police and other authorities when they tried to report on status of their loved ones.

In the early 1990s, sex trade workers in Vancouver's downtown east-side were noticing that, for at least the past decade, many of their peers were simply vanishing, never heard from again. For those friends and family members trying to get help from police, interactions were generally not fruitful. For example, in April 1999, there was a move to get police to offer a reward for information leading to information on the missing women, but instead the City of Vancouver[5] suggested offering $5,000 to any of the missing women to come forward. This offer reveals that authorities did not believe that the women were indeed missing, but had perhaps simply gone off somewhere. Then, the media became knowledgeable, and curious and involved. Journalists began to ask the same questions that family members had been asking for years. The eventual result was the formation of a joint Vancouver City Police/RCMP Taskforce; more than 70 women were listed as missing. An arrest was made in early 2002 and Robert Pickton was charged with 27 murders. It is believed that at least one-third of his victims were Aboriginal.

Statistically, Vancouver's Aboriginal population is about seven percent (Vancouver/Richmond Health Board 7). There is a high prevalence of prostitution in the city's downtown east-side where many Aboriginal women go missing. Aboriginal women are significantly overrepresented in Vancouver's sex trade and this "reflects not only their poverty but also their marginalized and devalued status as Canadians" (Farley, Lynne and Cotton 256). Victoria, the capital of British Columbia, reports a similar overrepresentation: 15 percent of women in escort prostitution are Aboriginal, although the Aboriginal population is only around two percent (Benoit and Millar 18).

Vancouver is not the only "hot spot" in the province. Another such area is now known as the "Highway of Tears" because of the large number of missing and/or murdered Aboriginal women along this nearly 500-mile stretch between Prince Rupert and Prince George. These murders started coming to light around 1994/1995 when three 15-year-old Aboriginal girls were found, in three separate instances, murdered in Prince George and Smithers. In March 2006, concerned community and family members held the "Highway of Tears Symposium" to address the urgent issue of the missing and murdered women along this highway. Nine families were officially listed as having members of their family go missing—including an entire family. Only one young woman was non-Aboriginal. The Symposium made four broad recommendations: [6]

•Emergency readiness must include an enhanced "amber alert" program which fast-tracks a public alert when someone goes missing, and preparation of an inventory of violent offenders for release into communities.
•Prevention programs must involve both families and communities as advocates for policy change in the area of regulations regarding missing persons; installing well-lit emergency telephones along this stretch of highway; creation of a hitch-hiker tracking system that would work somewhat like a block watch program; and, development of youth awareness programs such as "street smarts" and "stranger danger."
•Community development to address racism and oppression; identify "safe homes" along Highway 16; and, placing coordinators in Prince George and Terrace to move identified action plans.
•Counseling and support services that offer an Aboriginal focus on spirituality; advocates working with the RCMP in victim services.

CONCLUSION

Aboriginal women continue to work in many local and national initiatives to reduce the risks and increase the safety and security of all Aboriginal women in Canada, regardless of where they work or where they live; and to draw attention, recognition, and dignity to those Aboriginal women and girls who are still missing and those already found murdered. While their number is still unknown, most Aboriginal people, both men and women, would say that they know at least one person who simply disappeared from sight; some would know at least one who was murdered.

It is not hard to make the connection between being socially, economically and politically marginalized to being targets of hatred and violence. This is exactly the plight of Aboriginal people in Canada, particularly Aboriginal women. The effects of Canada's history are proving to be, without a doubt, disastrous for Aboriginal women. The ways this history is portrayed allows and perpetuates Aboriginal women continuing as targets of violence and death just because of their gender and race.

Clearly, Aboriginal women need their distinct voices heard in re-defining a better society in which they are included in positive and meaningful ways, ones that elevate their historic positions as significant decision-makers, choosers of chiefs, and land-owners. Indigenous truths, as a whole, need to be communicated everywhere in this country; worldviews and cosmologies must be known in educational institutions and political establishments, for example; no longer should room be made for the kind of cultural bigotry that sees Aboriginal women's thoughts and concerns as unsophisticated, undeveloped, or simply unapplicable in a contemporary highly-technological global society. Historically, the "Fathers of Confederation" deliberately excluded Aboriginal people, both men and women, from vital nation-building processes, and now there is a crucial need to restore the contributions of Indigenous people to an honourable and rightful place, and to recognize the enormous challenges they still face because of Canada's continuing discriminatory laws and practices.

The struggles of Aboriginal women striving to eliminate the objectification and dehumanizing activities that they have been subjected to since European contact, have a significant role to play in helping to change the attitudes, practices, policies and awareness of everyday Canadians. Though Canada still manages to maintain a relatively high global image—for this country's Aboriginal women, continuing to suffer from large scale inequalities, this has little meaning and no relevance.

Anita Olsen Harper convocated with her Ph.D. (Education) in 2011. She is Ojibwaa from the Lac Seul First Nation, Ontario, and lives in Ottawa with her husband, former MP, Elijah Harper.

[1]Real Gross Domestic Product per capita based on Purchasing Power Parts exchange rates (PPPs are the ratios of the prices in national currencies of the same goods or services in different countries).
[2]They were matrilineal and matriarchal, generally speaking.
[3]This is violence directed at a person because of their gender and race.
[4]The initiative ends in 2010.
[5]Vancouver, meanwhile, was being placed high on the annual Quality of Life survey. Other major Canadian cities were honoured for high levels of "personal safety and security" ("Vancouver 3rd in world in quality of life survey").
[6]The broad recommendations were fleshed out on the second day of the Symposium. The full report was released to the public on June 21, 2006.

REFERENCES

Amnesty International (Canada). *Stolen Sisters: A Human Rights Response to Discrimination and Violence Against Aboriginal Women in Canada.* Ottawa: Amnesty International (Canada), 2004.

Benoit, C. and A. Millar. "Dispelling Myths and Understanding Realities: Working Conditions, Health Status and Exiting Experiences of Sex Workers." 2001. Accessed May 13, 2006. Web.

Blackstock, Cindy and Nico Trocme. *Community-Based Child Welfare for Aboriginal Children: Supporting Resilience Through Structural Change.* First Nations Child and Family Caring Society and Centre of Excellence for Child Welfare, University of Toronto, October 9, 2004.

Blaut, I. M. *The Colonizer's Model of the World: Geographical Diffusionism and Eurocentric History.* New York: Guilford Press, 1993.

Donner, Lissa, Angela Busch and Nahanni Fontaine. "Women, Income and Health in Manitoba: An Overview and Ideas for Action." Women's Health Clinic website, 2002. Accessed on June 2, 2006. Web.

Farley, Melissa, Jacqueline Lynne and Ann J. Cotton. "Prostitution in Vancouver: Violence and the Colonization of First Nations Women." Transcultural Psychiatry 42 (2) (June 2005): 242 - 271.

Francis, Daniel. *The Imaginary Indian: The Image of the Indian in Canadian Culture.* Vancouver: Arsenal Pulp Press, 1995.

Hawkins, M. *Social Darwinism in European and American Thought.* Cambridge: Cambridge University Press, 1997.

"Highway of Tears" Symposium Broad Recommendations. Web.

Jacobs, Beverley. "Review of Beijing from an Indigenous Perspective; Secretariat Permanent Forum on Indigenous Issues." Paper presented at the Secretariat Permanent Forum on Indigenous Issues. New York. March 3, 2005.

Le Conte, J. "The Race Problem in the South." *Evolution Series No. 29: Man and the State.* New York: Appleton and Co, 1982.

National Anti-Poverty Organization (NAPO). T*he Face of Poverty in Canada: An Overview.* Updated January 2006. Web.

Statistics Canada. "Aboriginal Women in Canada." *Women in Canada 2005.* Catalogue No. 89-503-XIE. Ottawa: Statistics Canada, 2005.

"Vancouver 3rd in world in quality of life survey." CBC News 13 March 2005.

Vancouver/Richmond Health Board. *Healing Ways: Aboriginal Health and Service Review.* October 1999.

ANNETTE AURÉLIE DESMARAIS

Women Farm Leaders Speak Out About Resistance and Agrarian Activism

THIS ARTICLE is about Canadian farm activism, farmers' resistance, leadership and women's ways of working. It is the result of a collective interview with four women farm leaders of the National Farmers Union (NFU): Nettie Wiebe, Wendy Manson, Karen Pedersen and Martha Jane Robbins.[1] The NFU, formed in 1969, is the only federally-chartered, voluntary farm organization in Canada. It strives to build a sustainable food system that is based on the principles of social justice, gender equality and environmental sustainability. The NFU works on all types of issues related to rural communities from food production, distribution and consumption, to transportation of agricultural goods, free-trade agreements, corporatization of agriculture and food, rural day care, and rural health care. It is the only Canadian farm organization that has a structure designed specifically to also integrate the interests and needs of women and youth.

As leaders of the NFU, Nettie Wiebe, Wendy Manson, Karen Pedersen and Martha Jane Robbins have worked at the local, regional, national and international levels in efforts to effect progressive social change in the countryside and to build sustainable food systems based on the principles of gender equality and social justice. What follows is a glimpse into their perspectives, experiences and reflections.

Annette: *The targets of resistance often help shape the sites, forms and strategies of social movements. As farm leaders, what exactly is it that you are resisting?*

Wendy: I am surprised at how much of my resistance is about gender. Of course, we resist alongside many men. But a lot of the work that I have done, many of the positive things I've learned, many of the negative things I have experienced—a whole lot of it has to do with gender. The older I get, the more it seems like that to me.

Karen: Today "farm" seems to be like another "f" word—like feminism was. We are never "farm," instead we are "rural." It is the whole idea that: do you actually think people are going to pay you to do the dishes? It's that lack of recognition

549

combined with unpaid women's work that was carried onto not valuing cooking for the family. Now, producing for the family is no longer valued and it has all been moved into unpaid work. We won't even call it farming, we will just put it in the rural. We won't pay for it, and you're supposed to go and get a real job.

Nettie: This has a lot to do with the whole role of industrialization, the devaluing and discounting of the reproductive process of raw production of the farm, and reproductive work among women. As industrialization progressed that particular piece around food and farm got discounted, along with other kinds of reproductive work. And no matter how much we struggle to be somehow identified—either in the workforce or on the farm—with some other kind of production, it is still deeply true that the reproductive regenerative work is our work and it is discounted.

Wendy: I think that is why I sometimes feel so dissatisfied with the way men in our sector are handling resistance. In many ways they are so ill-equipped because under any other circumstances they have lived with the cultural view that power has worked out okay for them. Suddenly, they find themselves quite disabled. It is almost like underlying power has to be really obvious, as it now is in corporate concentration, before they get it. This is largely because there are so many other underlying power moments that they like.

Nettie: It is much harder for men, for example, to resist the viewpoint, the radical viewpoint around technology and industrialization than it is for women. It is much easier for us to see that the big tractor is actually not a step forward, and that the bigger half-ton isn't actually a symbol of progress, power, and prosperity.

It's interesting that when you talk about, and to, organic farmers, almost universally it is the women who were increasingly skeptical about the higher tech inputs and were pushing for organic production. I think that is also the case with genetically modified organisms too. It is a radical deep-seated resistance from women often before the men get there because the men are often not at the front end skeptical about the productive industrial process in the way women are.

I was very conscious of that when I was President of the NFU. You had to pick the issues that the male leadership around you understood and actually felt passionate about. Many of these were not the issues about which women actually felt most passionate, although they certainly understood that the trade portfolio, and the privatization and corporatization of resources were key.

But if we were just working within an all women resistance movement, we would also have talked a whole a lot more about the natural cycles, the damage to the ecological and regenerative power of the earth, communities and the cultural dynamic within communities, how one empowers communities and works on the ground with children of the community, what the value of this is, and why those are also farm movement issues. As an all women's resistance movement we would have worked much more assiduously on all of this. But because we work in the farm sector, if you are going to work with small-scale farmers and resistance, you are working with the family farm. You are working within a deeply patriarchal environment. So, you have to choose your issues and build resistance with that in mind.

When I think back to one of our most successful resistance campaigns, the BST campaign,[2] the way we convinced the Dairy Farmers of Canada (an all-male organization) to join the campaign was by persuading them that this was an economic issue. Yet the way in which the campaign was actually carried out in the malls, in the cities, and the movement was that women said, "BST in our milk and we are giving this to our children? Not on your life!" The women connected it to health, well-being, children, reproduction, growth, and a whole range of ecological, biological, and natural cycles.

Karen: This is the same with genetically engineered wheat. The women automatically look towards the precautionary principle.

Nettie: And women said "What? GMOs in our bread? We don't think so." And the men said: "It is going to trash our markets. Well, I guess we don't think so either. Pity, though, because it could have been really productive."

Martha Jane: One of our biggest hurdles is that we started with this industrial model. Internationally, there is a place to go back to where people look at production in a different way. For example, when the farmers' delegation from India was in Canada they talked about when women were the holders of the seeds and were the ones in the community who were in charge of reproduction. What they are trying to do now is reclaim that ground. We don't have that ground to reclaim because we started in a place that was already set up with a particular version of progress.

There is so much heart in the international work; this is how it connects to the local and why it is so important. Struggles there might be more immediate, there are more life and death situations. We censor ourselves a lot here. We care about community but we are very nervous about talking about it because it is not high tech. At the international level other people around the world are more willing to open themselves up. And once you do that, then it is easier to bring that back home.

Annette: *Together you represent over 50 years of agrarian activism. What have been your most difficult experiences and challenges as women farm leaders?*

Nettie: For a lot of women the hardest site of resistance is their own kitchens. I think there isn't a woman in the Farmers Union that hasn't had that struggle of finding, or knowing confidently enough, that you must go outside of your kitchen when there are all those undone dishes and when the demands within your own relationships in your own family are such that you are always trying to find a balance. In many cases women need to balance this while the scale is tipped with maybe not hostility, but resistance, from your partner around you leaving and devoting some energy to that other work. This is the hardest place, where you're balancing your leadership roles with your other intimate responsibilities and this is very specifically related to gender. I don't think that very often the home base is the first site of resistance for our male counterparts.

Karen: I work mostly with men and when I leave that farm work and have to justify my departure it is always the credibility issue: if I am going to take over the farm, am I going to be committed to it? Am I actually going to be serious about it?

Nettie: Which a male counterpart might or might not face. That might be a function of a young man on the farm who might face some skepticism about whether he is serious about farming. But everybody gets over that relatively quickly. Whereas for a woman, it will take a whole lot longer to assure everyone that you are indeed serious. This is also a key site, but there are others. In your community you really take a risk when you set yourself out there.

Wendy: There are a lot of power politics involved. In farm politics you have upwardly mobile people who want to be leaders and you have leaders of national farm organizations who clearly have a political agenda. This defines how the work of the movement is done because it takes place in that environment where people are brokering and working politically and so on. I am not in any way minimizing their commitment to improving the farm situation. In fact, they have a second wheel [their political aspirations] that helps to drive them sometimes. This is because, again, they have a better chance of achieving power inside the agricultural sector.

My goal isn't to be powerful. I just don't have that kind of second wheel. I just have a job I want to do, but in many ways I am marginalized. For example, I worked on transportation issues for a real long time. Then, when the Province of Saskatchewan organized a group of farm leaders to go to Vancouver to the port, well, it just never occured to them that they should ask me. And yet, they asked up-and-comers who were no more experienced than I was, and were equally radicalized by what was going on in transportation. It is as if I were just not seen. Because I wouldn't drive forward a political agenda that would have put me there, nobody thought to include me. Some of those men did not have a second wheel running or a political champion either, but then they didn't need one.

What I have found most difficult and challenging is that often I have to be more politically aggressive than I want to be just to have the opportunity to do the actual work I want to do. You have to work harder politically not to be marooned.

Annette: *What have been some of your most significant accomplishments?*

Wendy: When I know I helped make something happen—that I've helped to build capacity in such a way that people feel like they made it happen. I am quite often amazed that when we judge ourselves to be successful as women leaders, quite often it is as unsung heroes. The beauty in the way we do things is that it seems as though it just happened, that it happened without much work. That for me is one of the things that I value. It is like a little secret that you have, when you know that you did something and it made it all go well, and actually a lot of people thought they did it.

Martha Jane: For me it was participating in the protests of the WTO Ministerial meetings in Cancun and being part of La Vía Campesina process that really made a difference there.[3] Since I was the only NFU representative there I went feeling quite unsure of myself. You have to figure out your place and your space, where you might be useful, and where your voice is going to be heard the most.

That last protest march was such a huge accomplishment because it was so hard. Reaching consensus with so many people is insane! We were up the whole night before the final march negotiating terms with different groups, talking about who would play what role, and making sure that everyone was on side. In the end it was really collective and everyone felt that they had taken part. It was the first anti-globalization protest involving thousands of people where the strategies and tactics were collectively decided and there was no straying, nobody strayed, from those tactics. This had not happened at any of the other anti-globalization protests and it was the Vía Campesina that led the process.

Another thing that has been key for me is the generational dimension of the NFU. As a child you are in daycare [provided by the NFU] but you are also in the meeting. This makes you feel like you're part of the movement before you even start! And long before I was asked to run for Youth President, I remember spending lots of time at NFU conventions with the grandmothers of the movement.

Wendy: It also makes you feel less like you are flying solo and it makes you stronger. For example, I remember a time when there was tension in the organization about what direction the movement should take and who we were going to line up behind. One of the regional women who had years of experience in the organization was so clear-headed and she knew exactly what needed to be done. It was so much easier because she was there.

When I started as Women's Advisory, I constructed a project where we held meetings in four different places around the province. I went out and sat down with them and said: what are we going to do? In doing this I met and worked with women who had been with the organization for years. Can you imagine not having all of those women?

Nettie: When I was first elected NFU President, one of the sweetest moments for me was the time I went to Vegreville, Alberta, to speak at a big farm union meeting. After the meeting a group of older wonderful women from that area—whom I did not know personally but I had worked with their partners, the men in the organization—came and put their arms around me and said "Oh, we are so proud, now we are there too, now we are in." And that was for me just a really sweet moment to know that, yes, this is all of us.

Wendy: There is no doubt that that generation of women who are now in their 70s had worked so long and hard in the shadows; they had done so much uncelebrated work. And when the NFU was formed those women insisted that women have a place within the organization.[4] But it took that long and that much work before their contributions started coming through.

Karen: I'm from the third wave of feminism and we stupidly thought that we had arrived before we became feminists! Having grown up with this organization, what shocked me when I was going through the youth and women's filing cabinets was coming to the realization that when the organization was established in 1969 those youth and women's leadership positions were just token positions! And those women changed that, they forced those doors open.

Nettie: When the NFU was formed it was those women from the Saskatchewan Farmers Union and the Manitoba Farmers Union—and that goes way back to the United Grain Growers and the Violet MacNaughtons of this world— who had had those places and who were not ready to cede them in the new organization.[5] I do agree that when the NFU first had those places, they were a salve to the women of the Saskatchewan and Manitoba Farmers Unions, but they were not deemed to be real important positions at that time.

When I was the Women's President and was doing a speaking trip across Canada one woman who had been Women's President in the early 80s said to me: "That sure is different, they are letting a Women's President go out and speak on her own!" This certainly had not been her experience. The Women's President spoke as an auxiliary to the President. The real big farm meetings and the banquets—that was the President's work. This tells you just how token those positions were even in the early '80s!

That is why women's history is so important. That knowledge that there are others who have gone before you and who have worked in difficult circumstances. Not to romanticize the pioneering in any way but just to know that it has been done, that it can be done, circumstances change, but there we all are, sort of at the heart of what is strong and regenerative and progressive. Knowing that it goes on that it is not one single women's star that sort of rises and then drops. It is much earthier than that. It isn't about stars at all! It's about roots, shoots and seeds. And, it is regenerative.

Annette: *All of you have spent years developing progressive farm policy, building more vibrant rural communities and strengthening the farm movement in Canada and internationally. Yet, the farm crisis is getting worse and more farming families are being forced off the farms. What motivates you to continue to work for change?*

Martha Jane: I've now worked in two different movements: the farm movement and the student movement. The main difference with the farm movement is that it is tied to a sense of place, it is tied to communities, it's very tied to identity and also to livelihood. It is your life when you go home. The student movement is an issue—albeit a legitimate and politically critical issue. One of the hard parts about being motivated in the student movement is that I can go home at night and it's not who I am.

Wendy: That's exactly it, the farm movement is who you are and what you do. I can't see being a farm family or a farmer without being part of the social movement that speaks for farm people. I can't imagine what you would be doing out there if you weren't somehow part of the movement.

One of the reasons you keep going, is that you do have sort of magic moments when you suddenly feel a deep sense of satisfaction when you are sitting with someone from whom you've just learned something important. These are kind of private and sometimes painful things. For example, one woman taught me some things about being respectful of people's experiences and women's storytelling. It was like a gift from somebody. And those things are partly why you keep being involved because you wouldn't ever receive those gifts unless you hadn't already taken the risk by making yourself open and available.

Also, you continue because it deepens you. And then there are other times when it actually does the opposite, it unhooks you or frightens you. You do something, or you are suddenly in a place where you say to yourself, okay, I wouldn't be knowing how to do this! But then somebody has pushed you there and you wouldn't have done it on your own.

Karen: What keeps me working in the Farmers' Union is my belief in community and the fact that women and youth are involved. Commodity organizations don't really deal with community. The NFU is family that I grew up with and I can't imagine dropping family. Also, it is the mentoring. Who I am today is a product of mentoring. The women in this room are classic for throwing me into situations that I didn't want to experience and yet they put me there anyway all the while saying "you will do just fine." It is almost like you can't unhook yourself because there's constantly someone pushing you forward.

Martha Jane: A strong woman once told me that often it is women who don't necessarily want to be leaders, women who must be cajoled into running for leadership positions, often make the best leaders. They end up leaders because other people have gotten them there. That was certainly my case when others convinced me to run for Youth President.

Wendy: Yes, it is not that you are ever promised that you won't be uncomfortable, but you are mostly promised that you won't be alone.

Nettie: I think that is exactly it. It is not the promise that it's not going to be hard, it is going to be very difficult sometimes. It is not that you won't be criticized, or that you won't be very unhappy sometimes. It's the promise that you are not going to be alone. Because we are so relational we also understand something about movements and working together and that is, that actually, the things that really matter, that transform the places we live in and our communities, are never going to be solo acts. They are always going to be collective efforts. In some ways it is the power of that collective effort and being part of that which both keeps us so modest about what we can do as leaders but also strengthens us in doing what we need to do.

Annette Aurélie Desmarais is an Associate Professor in the International Studies Program at the University of Regina. Before obtaining a Ph.D. in Geography she farmed in Saskatchewan for 14 years. Annette is the author of La Vía Campesina: Globalization and the Power of Peasants *(2007). She also co-edited* Food Sovereignty: Reconnecting Food, Nature and Community *(2010) and* Food Sovereignty in Canada: Creating Just and Sustainable Food Systems *(2011).*

[1]Nettie Wiebe was elected NFU Women's Vice-President in 1988. She then served five consecutive years as the Women's President. In 1995, the NFU made history by electing its first woman, Nettie, as National President. She was re-elected in this position until 1998 when she decided not to run for re-election.

Wendy Manson has directed much of her efforts at the local and regional levels. She was re-elected NFU Women's Advisory Member for Saskatchewan from 1989-94. She then served as Chair of the NFU's Transportation Committee and member of the National Board of the NFU.

Karen Pedersen served as NFU Youth Advisory for Saskatchewan in 1994 and was elected National Youth President for the two consecutive years. Then, she was Women's Vice-President for one year and in 2002 was elected Women's President.

Martha Jane Robbins served as NFU Youth President for four years and has spent the last year as an NFU National Board member. In 2002, she was named as one of the *MacCleans Magazine's* 25 Leaders of Tomorrow.

All four interviewees provided the author with permission to conduct the collective interview, edit the transcript, and prepare it for publication.

[2]In the late 1990s the NFU along with many other Canadian organizations launched a campaign to block the registration of Recombinant Bovine Somatrotrophin (BST) or rBST in Canada. BST, developed by Monsanto, is a genetically engineered growth hormone that increases milk production in cows. Monsanto's nine-year struggle to introduce BST in Canada was controversial as newspaper headlines pointed to allegations of bribes, the disappearance of key research files and the "silencing" of key employees who wanted to go public on the issues involved. In January 1998 Health Canada declared a moratorium on the BST. William Leiss and Douglas Powell provide an interesting analysis of the rBST debate in Canada. An overview can also be accessed online at <http://www.tv.cbc.ca/newsinreview/mar99/milk>.

[3]La Vía Campesina is an international peasant and farm movement that embraces 148 organizations of peasants, small to medium-scale farmers, rural women, farm workers and Indigenous communities from Asia, the Americas, Europe and Africa. For an analysis of the formation, functioning and consolidation of La Vía Campesina see Edelman (2003) and Desmarais (2002, 2004, 2007 and 2008).

[4]The NFU is the only Canadian farm organization that has an affirmative action structure specifically designed to integrate the interests and needs of women and youth. To ensure greater participation and representation of women and youth the national leadership consists of six elected positions: National President and Vice-President, National Women's President and Vice-President, and National Youth President and Vice-President. In addition, each region of the NFU has a

Women's Advisory and a Youth Advisory position, and the district and local boards constitutionally guarantee positions for women and youth.

[5]Violet MacNaughton was involved in the women's suffrage movement in Saskatchewan. She was also a founding leader of the women's section of the Saskatchewan Grain Growers. As editor of the Women's Page of the Western Producer she provided farm women with an important forum for communication and debate. She is best known as a leader of agrarian feminism.

REFERENCES:

Desmarais, Annette Auríelie. *La Vía Campesina: Globalization and the Power of Peasants.* Halifax: Fernwood Publishing, 2007.

Desmarais, Annette Aurélie. *La Vía Campesina: Une réponse paysanne à la crise alimentaire.* Montréal: Écosociété, 2008.

Desmarais, Annette Aurélie. "The Vía Campesina: Peasant Women on the Frontiers of Food Sovereignty." *Canadian Woman Studies/les cahiers de la femme* 23 (1) (2004): 140-145.

Desmarais, Annette Aurélie. "The Vía Campesina: Consolidation of an International Peasant and Farm Movement." *Journal of Peasant Studies* 29 (2) (January 2002): 91-124.

Edelman, Mark. "Transnational Peasant and Farmer Movements and Networks." *Global Civil Society.* Eds. Mary Kaldor, Helmut Anheier and Marlies Glasius. Oxford: Oxford University Press, 2003: 185-220.

Leiss, William and Douglas Powell. *Mad Cows and Mother's Milk: The Perils of Poor Risk Communication.* Second Ed. Montreal: McGill-Queen's University Press, 2004.

WENDY MILNE

Women, Energy and Sustainability

Making Links, Taking Action

E NERGY, while a necessity for survival, presents many problems on the path to ecological sustainability, and equitable social and economic development. Dominant energy practices are non-renewable, large-scale, and highly technical requiring incalculable capital investment. Relations of power that control energy resources, distribution, and knowledge maintain inequities between nations and within nations, and marginalize the standpoint of women, the world's poor, and Indigenous populations. The lack of democratic control of energy use has obstructed critical analysis and fundamental change of current energy practices. Yet, change is precisely what is required as energy is at the forefront of local, regional, and global crises as diverse as deforestation, climate change, third world debt, and international conflict.

FROM RIO DE JANEIRO TO JOHANNESBURG TO RIO

There was some progress from Rio de Janeiro to Johannesburg to shift critical analysis of energy practices onto the international political agenda. Despite the role of energy in equitable sustainable development it was conspicuously absent from the formal deliberations at the 1992 United Nations Conference on Environment and Development (UNCED) in Rio de Janeiro. It was only after lobbying by civil society that energy was eventually placed within the context of climate change and included in the program areas of *Agenda 21* on protection of the atmosphere (Cecelski 1995). *Agenda 21* asserts that protection of the atmosphere requires the global promotion of an energy transition, energy efficiency, renewable energy sources and sustainable transportation systems.

In the years between Rio and Johannesburg the International Panel on Climate Change (IPCC) and other scientists concluded that human activities that produce greenhouse gases, like carbon dioxide, are altering the atmosphere and contributing to climate change (Raskin and Margolis; Skutch 2002). Three quarters of carbon dioxide comes from burning fossil fuel energy sources, and the rest is the result of land-use change like deforestation (Dankelman). Despite the science and the formation of international negotiation processes such as the Kyoto Protocol, politics and corporate alliances continue to deflect any substantive changes toward mitigating greenhouse gases through an energy transition.

Ten years after Rio at the World Summit on Sustainable Development (WSSD) in Johannesburg the inclusion of energy as one of five major negotiating themes signaled an opportunity for significant change. However, the negotiations failed to provide concrete actions on energy prompting the World Wildlife Fund, Oxfam, and Greenpeace to jointly declare that there was nothing for the poor, and nothing for the climate. Regrettably, the accomplishments of the WSSD were limited when it came to specific actions to alleviate poverty by delivering energy to the two billion people of the world with no access to energy services, and to start the renewable energy transition outlined in Agenda 21 that is required to protect the global climate.

Concurrent with this period of international negotiation and political inaction has been the development of diverse non-governmental and community organizations in the South and North working for a sustainable and equitable energy future. Initiatives by civil society to advance sustainable energy include renewable energy promotion, reforestation projects, research, political lobbying, policy development, community development, advocacy, education, and coalition building. Central to many alternative energy initiatives in the South, with no comparable network in the North, is the growing movement to make the link between gender and energy more visible (Cecelski 1995). Increasingly, strengthening women's participation in energy projects, policy development, research, and education is being recognized as a strategic entry point into improving women's lives and meeting the goals of sustainable development (UNDP 2000).

Twenty years later Rio + 20 was held in July 2012. According to NGOs like Women's Environment and Development Organization (WEDO) and World Wildlife Fund (WWF) the final document "The Future We Want" was a disappointment, lacking in any ambition to respond to the magnitude of current crises, including climate change and social inequities. Specific to gender, energy and climate change the results of Rio + 20 have been considered mixed. ENERGIA (Network for Gender and Sustainable Energy) concluded there were some encouraging outcomes including an acknowledgment of the connection between gender equality, social inclusion and access to sustainable energy services (ENERGIA 2012). While the Women's Major Group concluded that the link between gender and climate change was deleted in the final text, ignoring that women are most affected by the effects of climate disruption, as well as play an essential role in solutions (Bloomstrom 2012).

WOMEN AND ENERGY IN THE SOUTH

Energy is closely linked to the goals of sustainable development declared at Rio de Janeiro and Johannesburg. Eradicating poverty, expanding income-earning possibilities, increasing gender equity, improving education and health status, and protecting and regenerating the environment are all related to equitable access to energy (UNDP 1997). However, the majority of people in developing countries, particularly in rural areas, are lacking access to modern energy services. Many people continue to cook on traditional fuels like wood, charcoal, and dung, have limited or no available electricity for the household or workplace, and have minimal access to motorized transportation services (UNDP 2000).

Access to energy is limited further by gender and poverty. Women and girls suffer the most from the lack of appropriate and accessible energy sources and services (UNDP 2000). Men and women have different roles regarding energy within households and communities, different access to and control over energy resources, different incomes to buy energy, and different primary use of energy (Makan). Women and girl's primary responsibility for the basic survival of the household means they exert substantial amounts of time and physical energy in gathering fuels, preparing food, cooking on open fires, and washing and cleaning without any access to modern energy fuels or technology (Karlsson and Oparocha).

The intensive labour involved in energy-related activities for the household, not to mention the health and safety risks, seriously compromises the time for women to be involved in income-generating employment, continuing education, or community participation (UNDP 2000). Access to energy is also an essential resource for energy-intensive small enterprises and home industries like food-processing, beverage production, kiln operations, charcoal making and fuel distribution. Yet, past efforts to improve energy access and efficiency have tended to focus on large-scale producers ignoring women's productive activities (Cecelski 1995).

Recognizing gender in the energy sector has roots back to the 1970s. Early projects designed to respond to women's role in household energy use, and in the agriculture, small-enterprise, and forestry sectors had mixed results, however, as they tended to focus on the technical aspects of energy ignoring the social dimensions of energy practices (Skutch 1998). During the last decade the realization that energy, environment and development are clearly linked has made women's issues in the energy sector more visible and viable (Cecelski 1995). Along with this realization has emerged a substantial gender and energy network aimed at strengthening women's participation in energy research, policy development, project planning, and education. This network has broadened the conceptual thinking and empirical knowledge on the women and energy link by exploring a wide range of issues including studies on wood-fuel depletion, time spent on fuel acquisition, basic energy security, energy poverty, assessing women's opportunities as energy entrepreneurs, determining how to increase women's participation in the energy sector, and engendering national and international energy policy development (Cecelski 1995, 2000; Karlsson and Oparoacha; Makan; UNDP 2000).

Women have a pivotal role to play in a transition toward sustainable energy practices in the household, as they are the main users of energy, they influence family purchases, and are educators of children (Wakhungu and Cecelski). The assumption that women are not interested in learning about and maintaining technological energy systems has also been challenged through studies that confirm women are taking an active role in sustainable and renewable energy activities as consumers, mangers, micro-entrepreneurs, extension workers, leaders, networkers and lobbyists, and even as promoters and innovators of renewable energy technologies (Cecelski 2000).

The growing knowledge of the relevance of gender and energy and the lack of an international institution with an objective to promote a gender sensitive perspective on energy led to the 1995 formation of the gender and sustainable energy network ENERGIA. ENERGIA's mission is to engender energy and empower women through the promotion of information exchange, research, advocacy, and political action aimed at strengthening the role of women in sustainable energy development. At present ENERGIA has 1,500 members in Africa, Asia, Latin America, Europe and North America.

The ENERGIA network has worked skillfully to promote its mission. At the WSSD, ENERGIA was able to ensure that gender and energy issues were a component of the discussions. ENERGIA developed a background paper on gender and energy (ENERGIA 2001) and then created strategic alliances with other organizations to successfully lobby the Women's Caucus and the Climate Change Caucus to ensure that a gender and energy perspective appeared in their statements (Karlsson and Oaproacha). Ultimately the weakness in the political commitment to adequately address the linkages between energy, gender, and poverty in the WSSD Plan of Implementation (PoI) does not negate the success of ENERGIA in raising awareness of the issue and providing rationale for gender sensitive energy planning and policies for sustainable development (de Melo Branco and Roehr).

From Rio to Johannesburg there has been valid evidence that energy policies aimed at sustainability will remain flawed until gender is taking seriously. However, in the lives of everyday women in the South there has been minimal translation of these significant findings into change in the dominant political and economic policy approaches to energy.

WOMEN AND ENERGY IN THE NORTH

Energy presents a much different profile in the North. Energy is accessible everyday, taken for granted, and ultimately rendered unseen. It is consumed at an alarming rate with little knowledge of the consequences. Canadians, for example, are for the most part unaware that they consume more energy per capita than in any other country, and more energy as a nation than all African nations combined (Suzuki Foundation).

Accordingly, and in sharp contrast to the South, recognition of the link between energy and gender is virtually invisible in the North. Energy is considered gender-neutral; women and men are seen as equal in their use of and attitudes about energy (Clancy and Roehr). The tendency to believe that women's role in energy use ends once modern forms of energy became readily available (Wakhungu and Cecelski) is reflected in current approaches to energy policies, programs, research, and education.

Along with the many differences concerning energy in the North and the South there are crucial similarities. Sustainability in the North, like in the South, requires social, economic, and environmental justice, and sustainable energy use demands equitable access and influence in energy decision-making. As well, the limited research on women and energy in the North indicates there are gendered differences in relation to energy consumption, energy sector involvement, and decision-making capacity over energy issues. Women in the North have also demonstrated the potential to be substantial contributors in the energy sector, and to energy efficiency, conservation and in energy transition.

Household energy use reflects the gendered dimensions of society. While a significant number of women in the North are in the paid labour force the growing distinction between wealth and the feminization of poverty means that more women than men, especially in northern climates like Canada, live in fuel poverty (defined as spending more than 20 percent of their household income on fuel) (ENERGIA 2001). Many single women, senior women and women-led families spend at least 20 percent of their income on heating and electricity, especially since poverty is linked to less energy-efficient housing and reliance on older inefficient appliances (Clancy and Roehr).

There is a growing network of women working in the energy sector but the ability to shape energy decisions continues as a male domain (Clancy and Roehr). Statistics Canada data on the energy sector in Canada indicates that women make for 24.2 percent of employees in the petroleum sector, with 60 percent of these women working in support, sales and service, and one quarter of the professional positions in the sector being held by women (Dowse, Horton, Lele and Sherk). The report *Women and the Oil and Gas Sector in Canada* (Dowse et al.) concludes that the number of women working in the energy field has increased in the last decade, particularly after the sector has attempted to address a number of equity issues. Gender-related equity initiatives that have been implemented in the energy sector include: subsidized childcare, the introduction of training opportunities for non-traditional occupations, anti-harassment training, and diversity sensitive hiring policies. Despite an increase in women working in the energy sector studies in Canada and Europe suggest that female employees are reluctant to address gender aspects of energy due to the male-dominated organizational culture and established process and rules (Dowse et al.).

Women have been successful in building the capacity to work outside the established power structures to affect change toward sustainable energy. Studies confirm that women are more supportive than men of renewable energy and conservation, and demonstrate less support for highly technical and potentially environmentally damaging energy sources like nuclear power (ENERGIA 2001). A study on the gender differences in support for soft energy (renewable) and hard energy (oil, gas and nuclear) concludes that hard energy sources are more opposed by women than men, and that reliance on oil that leads to war is more opposed by women than men (Longstreath). These kinds of gender differences are reflected in the leading roles that women and women's organizations have taken in the nuclear disarmament movement (Wittner) and in the anti-nuclear energy movement (Clancy and Roehr).

Currently, the direct link between climate change and energy use is increasing the potential for women in the North to once again become actively engaged in energy issues and take a role in shaping a gender sensitive movement toward sustainability.

CLIMATE CHANGE AND WOMEN

Climate change from fossil fuel energy use presents a serious and imminent threat to the sustainability of the planet. The International Panel on Climate Change (IPCC) concludes that regional climate changes like temperature increases are already affecting many physical and biological systems and increasing floods and droughts in some areas. The effects of climate change are threatening livelihoods and human security around the globe. The IPCC further concludes that the impacts of climate change will be experienced differently by region, age, class, income, occupations and gender, and that those with limited resources are not only the most vulnerable to the effects of climate change, but have the least capacity to respond and recover from the changes (IPCC).

Climate change like energy is not gender neutral. Fatma Denton (2000) observes that the topic of gender and climate change is such a burgeoning area of study that the findings are often more theoretical than empirical. However, it is being argued that women, particularly in the South, will be especially vulnerable to the effects of climate change (Denton 2002; Dankleman). Building on existing research in gender and energy, environment and sustainable development a number of factors have been identified that make women particularly vulnerable to climate change. The possible health effects of climate change and caring for the ill will fall within women's areas of responsibility, as will expected nutritional problems, food and water shortages (Villagrasa). The affects of climate change on agriculture, fishing, and the tourism sectors also have the potential to affect women more than men (Denton 2000). As well, there is some indication that women are more vulnerable to disasters related to climate change (Dankleman; Skutch 2002).

Women are also vulnerable to the changes that will be required to curb fossil fuel energy use, particularly in the household (Wamukonya and Skutch). While women around the world have a primary role in the use and conservation of household energy the responsibility of mitigating greenhouse gases has not been considered within a gendered framework. In Canada, for example, the climate change plan asks that citizens reduce their greenhouse gas emissions by one tonne by taking actions at home, at work, and on the road (Government of Canada). While the plan states it intends to develop an approach that is fair and equitable across regions and sectors it does not currently consider other dimensions of inequity like gender and poverty.

A strategy to ensure meaningful consideration of gender in climate change issues is being formulated through the gender and energy networks. At the outset, responses for equitable climate change requires increasing women's participation in climate change negotiations, and building the capacity of women's organizations to work on the issues of climate change and energy (Villagrasa).

The two principal treaties related to climate change, the UN Framework Convention for Climate Change (UNFCCC) and the Kyoto Protocol, are lacking references to women, gender, and poverty, and only generally refer to social and economic sustainable development (Skutch 2002). Gender sensitive responses to climate change require more women on the various commissions within the climate change development process, and gender needs to be included in future policy formulations and activities (Denton 2002; Villagrassa). Women need to be active participants in policy-making on mitigation strategies, vulnerability studies, and in projects for adaptation, technology transfer, and capacity building (Wamukonya and Skutch). Skutch (2002) adds that explicitly including gender considerations in all climate change negotiations and strategies will increase the efficiency of the negotiation process and keep gender equity issues on the international agenda.

Women have already demonstrated the positive role they can play in climate protection by influencing the outcome of previous negotiations and preparatory meetings (Danklemen; Villagrasa). Delia Villagrasa reports that during the Kyoto negotiations the small number of female delegates representing the government sector differentiated themselves from their male colleagues by actively building alliances with other delegates, particularly from developing countries, to push for the adoption of the protocol despite powerful opposition. Also women representing the NGO sector were able to make significant contributions by working together, despite differences, to ensure that the debates came to a successful outcome and that there was a flow of accurate information from the meetings to the public (Villagrasa).

Ensuring that more women are involved in the complex negotiation process for climate change and are able to be directly involved in the development and delivery of sustainable energy technology requires capacity building through education and training, and access to funding mechanisms (Dankelman). According to Skutch (2002) the international community has formally recognized capacity building as necessary for implementing climate change plans, but there remain major gender-based inequities in capacity building plans.

Women's groups require mentoring on the complex and detailed nature of climate change negotiations. Women's groups in the South require support from NGOs now active on climate change to secure plans for climate protection that are compatible with the goals of sustainable development and improved livelihoods (Villagrasa). Women's groups in the North need to develop the capacity to respond to climate change as they have had limited involvement in the issue. However, Villagrasa argues that, "if mobilized, they could put tremendous pressure on wealthier countries to provide the policies and measures needed for climate protection, such as stronger development of renewable energy technologies" (43).

Women in the North can take this opportunity to learn with women around the world how to shape actions for a transition toward sustainability that will address excessive energy use in the North while enabling women in the South to escape poverty and equitably share in energy resources and alternatives.

CONCLUSION

A sustainable energy future is about placing energy in the context of the broader transition to social and environmental sustainability. It is about changing the way energy is currently controlled by power interests. It is about all citizens, including women, having an opportunity to influence the direction of energy supply, use and alternatives. Ulrike Roehr argues that,

> the solution is not to take part in destructive power structures.... At the local level, both Southern and Northern, women can work toward decentralized production from renewable sources. At the international level, women should work together to change the structures and instruments, and to develop new ones that are environmentally and climate friendly, and at the same time ensure that these are just, both socially and in terms of gender. (16)

From Rio de Janeiro through to Johannesburg to Rio 2012, women have been working toward alternatives to current energy practices. But much more needs to be done. There needs to be more research in the South and North on the linkages across gender, energy, and sustainability. Women must continue to build global networks that are essential for research, advocacy, and action on energy and climate change that effect women around the world. Only then will there be a chance for equitable sustainable development supported by gender and climate justice.

Wendy Milne has a Ph.D. in Rural Studies. She is a researcher/consultant and part-time educator on gender, renewable energy, environmental justice, energy literacy, and sustainable rural communities.

REFERENCES

Bloomstrom, Eleanor. "Women's Major Group on Rio+20: Taking Stock and

Moving Forward." 2012. Web.

Cecelski, Elizabeth. "From Rio to Beijing: Engendering the Energy Debate." *Energy Policy* 23 (6) (1995). 561-575.

Cecelski, Elizabeth. *The Role of Women in Sustainable Energy Development.* Golden, Colorado: National Renewable Energy Laboratory, 2000.

Clancy, Joy and Ulrike Roehr. "Gender and Energy: Is there a Northern Perspective?" *Energy for Sustainable Development* 7 (3) (2003): 44-49.

Dankelman, Irene. "Climate Change: Learning from Gender Analysis and Women's Experiences of Organizing for Sustainable Development." *Gender and Development* 10 (2) (2002): 21-29.

de Melo Branco, Adélia and Ulrike Roehr. "The WSSD and its Results Regarding Gender and Energy." *ENERGIA News* 5 (4) (December 2002): 1-2.

Denton, Fatma. "Gendered Impacts of Climate Change: A Human Security Dimension." *ENERGIA News* 3 (3) (2000): 13-14.

Denton, Fatma. "Climate Change Vulnerability, Impacts, and Adaptation: Why Does Gender Matter?" *Gender and Development* 10 (2) (2002): 10-20.

Dowse, Susan, Kimberly Horton, Dorothy Lele and Susan Sherk. *Women in Canada's Oil and Gas Sector.* Report for CIDA Oil and Gas Sector Program Pakistan, 1999.

ENERGIA. "Gender Perspectives on Energy for the CSD-9: Draft Position Paper." ENERGIA, International Network on Gender and Sustainable Energy, 2001. Web.

ENERGIA. "Energia's Engagement and Results at Rio 20+." 2012. Web.

Government of Canada. "Climate Change: Achieving our Commitments Together: Climate Change Plan for Canada." 2002.

International Panel on Climate Change (IPCC). "Summary for Policy Makers: Impacts, Adaptation, and Vulnerability. Report of Working Group IPCC." 2001. Web.

Karlsson, Gail and Sheila Oparoacha. 'The Road to Johnnesburg and Beyond: Networking for Gender and Energy.' *Energy for Sustainable Development* 7 (3) (2003): 62-67.

Longstreth, Molly. "Support for Soft and Hard Path American Energy Policies: Does Gender Play a Role?" *Women's Studies International Forum* 1(2) (1989): 213-226.

Makan, Amita. "Power for Women and Men: Towards a Gendered Approach to Domestic Energy Policy and Planning in South Africa." *Third World Planning Review* 17 (2) (1995): 183-198.

Raskin, P. D. and R. M. Margolis. "Global Energy, Sustainability and the Conventional Development Paradigm." *Energy Sources* 20 (1998): 263-283.

Rio Declaration on Environment and Development and Agenda 21: Programme of Action for Sustainable Development, 1992. New York: United Nations, 1994.

Roehr, Ulrike. "Gender and Energy in the North: Background Paper for Expert Workshop Gender Perspectives for Earth Summit 2002: Energy Transport Information Decision-Making." Berlin, Germany. Federal Ministry for the

Environment, Nature Protection and Nuclear Safety and the Heinrich Boell Foundation, 2002.

Skutch, Margaret. "The Gender Issue in Energy Project Planning: Welfare, Empowerment or Efficiency?" *Energy Policy* 26 (12) (1998): 945-955.

Skutch, Margaret. "Protocols, Treaties and Action: The Climate Change Process Viewed Through Gender Spectacles." *Gender and Development* 10 (3) (2002): 30-39.

Suzuki Foundation. *Climate of Change, Canadian Solutions: Practical and Affordable Steps to Fight Climate Change.* Vancouver: Suzuki Foundation and Pembina Institute. 1998.

United Nations (UN). *Rio Declaraction on Environment and Development and Agenda 21: Programme of Action for Sustainable Development.* 1992. New York: United, 1994.

United Nations Development Program (UNDP). *Energy After Rio: Prospects and Challenges.* New York: UNDP, 1997.

United Nation Development Program (UNDP). *Gender and Energy: How is Gender Relevant for Sustainable Energy Policies?* New York: UNDP, Sustainable Energy and Environment Division, 2000.

Villagrasa, Delia. "Kyoto Protocol Negotiations: Reflections on the Role of Women." *Gender and Development* 10 (2) (2002): 40-44.

Wakhungu, Judi and Elizabeth Cecelski. *A Crisis in Power: Missing Links: Gender Equity in Science and Technology for Development.* International Development Research Centre, Intermediate Technology Publications, and United Nations Development Fund for Women, 1995.

Wamukonya, Njeri and Margaret Skutch. "Is There a Gender Angle to Climate Change Negotiations." Energy and Environment 13 (2002): 115-124.

Wittner, Lawrence S. "Gender Roles in Nuclear Disarmament Activism, 1954-1965." *Gender and History* 12 (1) (2000): 197-222.

STARHAWK

Why We Need Women's Actions and Feminist Voices for Peace

W OMEN ARE DEEPLY IMPACTED by war, racism and poverty—the three evils named by Martin Luther King. But when we stand for peace as women, it is not to make a case for our special victimhood, but to represent a different vision of strength. Women-initiated and women-led actions have a special energy and power. That power comes not from excluding men—most of these actions welcome men as participants—but because of the joy and visionary potential that arise when we come together as women to defend the values of life and caring that we hold dear.

To defend those values, we need not just women's voices against the war, but specifically feminist voices. For feminism allows us to analyze patriarchy, the constellation of values, ideas and beliefs that reinforces male control over women.

No set of qualities is innately or exclusively "female" or "male." Men can be compassionate, loving and kind, as women can be tough, brave, or callous. But patriarchy assigns the qualities associated with aggression and competition to men, and relegates to women the devalued roles of nurturing and service. Patriarchy values the hard over the soft, the tough over the tender; punishment, vengeance and vindictiveness over compassion, negotiation, and reconciliation. The "hard" qualities are identified with power, success and masculinity, and exalted. The "soft" qualities are identified with weakness, powerlessness, and femininity, and denigrated.

Under patriarchy, men are shamed and considered weak if they exhibit qualities associated with women. Politicians win elections by being tough—tough on terror, tough on crime, tough on drugs, tough on welfare mothers. Calls for cooperation, negotiation, compassion or recognition of our mutual interdependence are equated with womanly weakness. In the name of "toughness," the power holders deprive the poor of the means of life, the troubled and the ill of treatment and care, the ordinary citizen of our privacy and civil rights. Force, punishment, and violence are patriarchy's answer to conflicts and social problems.

Patriarchy finds its ultimate expression in war. War is the field in which the tough can prove their toughness and the winners triumph over the losers.

Soldiers can be coerced into dying or killing when their fear of being called womanlike or cowardly overrides their reluctance to face or deal death. War removes every argument for tenderness and dissolves all strictures on violence. War is the justification for the clampdown that lets the rulers impose control on every aspect of life.

Wise feminists do not claim that women are innately kinder, gentler, more compassionate than men per se. If we did, the Margaret Thatchers and Condoleeza Rices of the world would soon prove us wrong. We do claim that patriarchy encourages and rewards behaviour that is brutal and stupid. We need raucous, incautious feminist voices to puncture the pomposity, the arrogance, the hypocrisy of the warmongers, to point out that gorilla chest-beating does not constitute diplomacy, that having the world's largest collection of phallic projectile weapons does not constitute moral authority, that invasion and penetration are not acts of liberation.

And we need to remind the world that modern warfare never spares the civilian population. Rape is always a weapon of war, and women's bodies are used as prizes for the conquerors. Women and children and men, too, who have no say in the policies of their rulers face death, maiming, wounding, and the loss of their homes, livelihoods, and loved ones in a war.

Patriarchy is the brother of racism, which sets one group of people above another, dehumanizing and devaluing the "other," who is seen as deserving of punishment, fair game for violence and annihilation.

We need feminist voices for peace because the issues of women's freedom and autonomy are being used cynically to justify anti-Arab racism and military takeovers of Arab countries.

The U.S. and its allies, who now pose as the liberators of women in the Muslim world, are the same powers which gave the Taliban, Saddam Hussein, and Al Qaeda their start-up funds, supported them and put them in power, with no consideration for their impact on women. The "liberators" of Afghan women ignored the grassroots women's organizations such as the Revolutionary Association of the Women of Afghanistan (RAWA) installed a new government almost equally as oppressive as the Taliban, and excluded the heraic women who have risked their lives to educate their daughters and maintain some sense of freedom under oppressive rule.

We protest the hypocrisy that trumpets the oppression of women in Arab societies while the oppression of women in the West is never raised as an issue. Nor are the racism, economic oppression and endemic violence of Western culture acknowledged when the West is hailed as the flag bearer of freedom. Women cannot walk safely through the streets of the West, nor can we be assured of the means of life for our children, of health care in our illnesses, of care and support in our old age. The ongoing daily violence against women and children worldwide, the violence of battering, sexual assault, poverty, and lack of opportunity, the global traffic in women's bodies is ignored. And the vast global inequalities that benefit the West are also not acknowledged. Nor is the history, that Western exploitation of the East and South generated the wealth that allowed our greater "development" and "enlightenment."

Oppression of women is real, in Muslim societies and non-Muslim societies, around the globe. But women cannot be liberated by the tanks and bombs of those who are continuing centuries-old policies of exploitation, commandeering resources for themselves, and fomenting prejudice against the culture and heritage which are also deep parts of a woman's being.

We need a feminist voice for peace to say that those who truly care about life and freedom will work to support, not conquer, those women in every culture who are struggling for liberation and social justice.

The war against Iraq is not about safety, security, or liberation. The war's real aims include gaining control of Iraq's rich oil reserves and establishing U.S. hegemony over the Middle East. Racism is the ideology of empire, the set of beliefs that tell us we deserve to rule because we are superior to some other group.

Racism and patriarchy are the recruitment tools for the legions of enforcers: the soldiers, police, judges, bureaucrats and officials who protect institutions of power. Patriarchy, racism, homophobia, discrimination against Arabs and Muslims, anti-Semitism, ageism and all forms of prejudice keep our eyes trained downward, looking at those we see as beneath us, instead of looking upward and seeing clearly how we are being manipulated.

We need strong feminist voices to cry out that there is no hierarchy of human value, that every child must be cherished, that we claim common ground with women, children, and men around the world.

Oil is the lifeblood, and the military is the ultimate enforcer of economic policies which disenfranchise the poor and undercut the livelihoods of working people around the globe, consolidating wealth and power in fewer and fewer hands, devouring the family farm, the vibrant neighborhood, the old-growth forest and the last remaining wilderness, eroding the soil, poisoning the atmosphere, disrupting the earth's climate and threatening every life support system of the planet. The global corporate capitalist system also exalts toughness and ruthless competition, and exhibits utter disdain for caring, compassion, and nurturing values. Women staff the *maquiladoras* and the sweatshops that produce the cheap goods of the global economy. The vast majority of the world's poor are women and children. A feminist voice for peace must identify and address the root causes of war. "Peace" cannot be separated from justice, including economic justice. And real security can only come when we weave a new global web of mutual aid and support.

We need women's actions to make these larger connections, to assert that compassion is not weakness and brutality is not strength, to dramatize our support for nurturing and life-affirming values. And ultimately, we need women and men both to join our voices and roar like a mother tiger in defense of our interconnectedness with all of life, the true ground of peace.

Starhawk, committed global justice activist and organizer, is the author or coauthor of twelve books, including The Spiral Dance, The Fifth Sacred Thing, *and* The Earth Path. *Her latest is* The Empowerment Manual: A Guide for Collaborative Groups. *She is a veteran of progressive movements, from anti-war to anti-nukes, is a highly influential voice in the revival of earth-based spirituality and Goddess religion, and has brought many innovative techniques of spirituality and magic to her political work. Her website is* <www.starhawk.org>.

JENNY FOSTER

Tear Gas in Utero

Quebec City

NEOLIBERAL ECONOMIC POLICIES are often promoted as means of advancing democracy worldwide. However, the negotiation of these policies and their short- and long-term outcomes raise serious concerns about democratic processes and freedoms in general. The multitude of summits hosting political leaders (often joined by business representatives) are persistently confronted by demonstrators, who in turn are persistently confronted by repressive and dangerous crowd control attitudes and techniques in the name of security.

I was pissed off before the Free Trade Area of the Americas summit even began. Before the agenda was officially secret, before the fence went up around the conference site in Quebec City, and before I knew I was pregnant. I was disgusted at the arrogance of leaders who could put so much on the line—risking environmental degradation, erosion of labour standards, and increased polarization of living standards—with so little accountability for their actions. Once the conference began, the only means of communicating these concerns was on the streets outside the baracades, amid water cannons, rubber bullets, and dense clouds of tear gas. The decision to protest with six friends was a no-brainer: the stakes were so high, the process so flawed. What we did not know was that the thousands and thousands of tear gas canisters launched randomly at demonstrators would cause unknown harm to those at particular risk in the crowds, including my unborn daughter.

We expected oppressive security measures at the Quebec Summit including arrests and lots of tear gas. We expected a twisted form of democracy. We expected that we would have to protect each other amidst the street-level struggles. But we were going as pacifists and observers. We were not planning to attack the six-kilometre long perimeter sheltering conference delegates from civil society. Aside from a couple of rough nights sleep and potential run-ins with security, what did we have to lose? There were only two women in our group; we agreed to keep an especially close eye on each other and make sure that we didn't get separated. Resisting neo-liberalism was worth it.

For two days we gasped, coughed and wiped away tears as we exercised our constitutional right to demonstrate. On the third day conference organizers did not even need to spray tear gas at demonstrators. Its burning residue hung thick in the air and covered buildings, sidewalks, trees, statues, lampposts, and all other surfaces. We returned to Toronto worn out, but with strengthened resolve about the critical need to resist globalization and protect civil liberties.

When my doctor delivered the shock three weeks later that I was already five weeks pregnant, one of the first things I grappled with was the possibility that my child had been exposed to tear gas. I remembered all of the warnings circulating in Quebec City about pregnancy and tear gas. Distributed by diverse organizations, they all cautioned anyone who was pregnant, might be pregnant, or was planning to become pregnant soon to stay well clear of the noxious clouds. I had been exposed at least 12 times. To make matters worse, I soon discovered that the tear gas was mixed with methyl chloride for ease of dispersal. Methyl chloride is a known carcinogen with human toxicity to the liver, kidneys, and central nervous system. I decided not to panic. I resolved to find out as much as I could and make informed decisions about proceeding with the pregnancy.

But where to start? Astonishingly, there is no published research whatsoever related to the effects of tear gas on human pregnancy. Meanwhile, a 1989 review published in the *Journal of the American Medical Association* raised serious medical concerns about the use of tear gas as a harassing agent for dispersal of demonstrators and subdual of criminals. The authors conclude that:

> The possibility of long-term health consequences such as tumour formulation, reproductive effects, and pulmonary disease is especially disturbing in view of the multiple exposures sustained by demonstrators and non-demonstrators alike in some areas of civilian unrest. (Hu, Fine, Epstein, Kelsey, Reynolds and Walker 662)

The report emphasizes the urgent need for epidemiological and laboratory research. Rarely does a refereed medical journal publish articles advancing concerns about human rights and civil liberties. However, this report makes clear links between medical uncertainty surrounding tear gas exposure and human rights. A sample of statements to this effect include the following:

> … the evidence already assembled regarding the pattern of use of tear gas, as well as its toxicology, raises the question of whether its further use can be condoned under any conditions. (663)

> At a time when the world has recently seen the recurrence of the use of mustard gas … it is also worthy to note that in 1969, at the United Nations General Assembly, 80 countries voted to ban the use of any chemical in war, including tear gas, under the Geneva Protocol. (663)

It is the hallmark of repressive regimes to equate the voicing of dissent with disorder and to deny opponents the freedom of assembly and speech, rights guaranteed universally among signatories to the Universal Declaration of Human Rights. (663)

Implementation of the *Access to information Act* reveals that the RCMP alone launched 3009 canisters of tear gas during the FTAA summit (Picard, 2001). This is a staggering figure, but represents only a portion of the tear gas dispersed. Corresponding figures for the other two security forces commissioned for the summit, the Sûreté du Québec and the Police Municipal de Quebec, are indeterminate but presumably equally high. Although data concerning the demographics of demonstrators at Quebec City have not been collected, it is fair to assume that at least half of these were women, scores of whom must also have been pregnant.

I probed my doctor for any further information whatsoever relating to tear gas and pregnancy. She came up with nothing and referred me to Motherisk, an organization run out of The Hospital for Sick Children in Toronto devoted to public education, counselling, and research pertaining to fetal risks associated with drug, chemical, infection, disease, and radiation exposure during pregnancy. Consultation with Motherisk turned up nothing either. The report I later received from Motherisk briefly concluded that "there is limited data published on effects of chlorobenzylidonemalanonitrate, a component of tear gas" (Ratnapalan).

At eight weeks, I still did not know what I was going to do about the pregnancy. I was already feeling strong maternal instincts, protecting the young fetus with a careful diet, regular exercise, and lots of sleep. But what hazards had it been exposed to in Quebec City? Nobody could answer this question, and I had serious misgivings about basic health and prenatal development. The day before my birthday I started bleeding heavily with painful abdominal cramps. After an internal exam, my doctor diagnosed a miscarriage, one of the purported effects of tear gas exposure (stillbirth and genotoxicity are others). I was sad and angry. Strangely though, after only two days the bleeding stopped and I still felt pregnant. Blood tests confirmed that I was still pregnant, that I had probably lost a twin. A week later, I considered terminating the pregnancy. I felt that this fetus had already been exposed to undue stress, and my own anxiety level about the whole matter was very high. But after seeing an ultrasound image of the shrimp-like baby I just could not follow through with an abortion. I dearly wanted to hold it in my hands and tell it I loved it and would do whatever I could to protect it. Although the baby had been tear gassed and its living environment was traumatized with a miscarriage, this young sprout passed the five basic criteria defining appropriate prenatal development: it had a heartbeat, a spinal column, a yolk sac, intestines, and a brain.

Although Health Canada provides national leadership to develop health policy and enforces health regulations, it has expressed no interest in the issue of massive use of tear gas on the public. As far as I can tell, Health Canada maintains responsibility for at least three federal acts (the Food and Drugs Act, the Hazardous Materials Information Review Act, and the Hazardous Products Act) which should have caused the ministry to at least question the indiscriminant use of tear gas in Quebec City (and at other demonstrations). Yet, Health Canada raised no concerns before, during, or after the Quebec Summit.

My baby was born in early January 2002. All of the tests conducted so far tell me that she has developed in a healthy manner. But there are significant limitations to what can be tested both pre- and postnatally. Weighing a healthy 9 pounds 5 ounces at birth, my daughter has grown like a weed over the past six months. She squirms and wiggles practically non-stop, and has a twinkling two-toothed smile that captures even the most dour faces we meet. Despite vigourous growth and endearing charm, concern about the effects of tear gas linger. Specifically, the article published in the *Journal of the American Medical Association* reports that tear gas is potentially genotoxic (622).

As is the experience of most child-bearing women I know, I have encountered some negative socio-cultural response to pregnancy and pending motherhood. For example, a couple of people responded poorly to the news of my pregnancy, questioning the wisdom of bringing a baby into the world. But most were extremely supportive. I have learned to recognize the numerous ways in which pregnant women and mothers are often desexualized and infantilised. It is also true that many people feel they can comfortably overstep boundaries of decorum and baseline respect by trying to tell pregnant women and mothers exactly what they should and should not do. I encounter these irritations regularly, combined with the physical effects of hosting a gestating human being, gining birth, sleep deprivation and general exhaustion. Yet these pale in comparison to the stress and anxiety of an unstable pregnancy provoked by tear gas and the shortage of information relating to associated health risks.

There is no proof that tear gas is safe for public consumption. If anything, the scant research that has been conducted in this area indicates that there are grounds to assume it is unsafe, especially for people at particular risk. An outstanding example is risk to prenatal development. I went to Quebec City as a citizen exercising my democratic right to protest. I was Jane Public, one of over 50,000 people who felt strongly enough about globalization to stand up and be counted. There is no reasonable way that I or the vast majority could be perceived as a security threat. Yet, we were gassed repeatedly. For many people, the Quebec Summit was an intensely politicizing event. It certainly confirmed my own commitment to resisting the negative effects of globalization and fighting to protect civil liberties. But the urgent need for thorough testing of the human toxicity of tear gas prior to any further dissemination of the compounds must be underscored. This must become part of the policy agenda surrounding Canadian civil liberties, health, and safety.

Jenny Foster is an Associate Professor in the Faculty of Environmental Studies at York University. She is the Coordinator of the Urban Ecologies Certificate and is a Registered Professional Planner.

REFERENCES

Hu, Howard., Jonathan Fine, Paul Epstein, Karl Kelsey, Preston Reynolds and Bailus Walker. "Tear Gas: Harassing Agent or Toxic Weapon?" *Journal of the American Medical Association* 262 (5) (1989): 660-663.

Picard, J. Christian. (Departmental Privacy and Access to Information Coordinator, RCMP). Personal communication, 4 July 2001.

Ratnapalan, Savitri. (Specialty Fellow in Clinical Pharmacology, The Hospital for Sick Children). Personal communication, 14 September 2001.

JUDY REBICK

Occupy and Feminism

WHEN I FIRST WROTE and spoke about the movements that had influenced Occupy, the civil rights, anti-globalization, and labour movement influences were clear to me. But even though I had spent most of my activist life in the women's movement, I did not see the influence of feminism. On the contrary, it seemed that Occupy had forgotten the lessons of four decades of feminism and anti-racism in their singular focus on economic inequality. Women seemed to be leaders in Occupy Wall Street but in Occupy Nova Scotia and Occupy Vancouver, men seemed quite dominant. When I visited Occupy Vancouver, a couple of women there asked me to give a talk and then a workshop on anti-oppression policy. They were having a hard time convincing the General Assembly (GA) that they needed safer spaces for women even though there had already been some serious sexual harassment. In Occupy Toronto while women were clearly in the leadership, I kept hearing about problems on the site and the refusal of the GA to deal with it.

The only mention of feminism as an influence in my book, *Occupy This!*, published in March 2012, was in the section on democracy.

In the 1960s, feminism, and the New Age movement challenged authoritarianism in many institutions. However, the political Left never managed to change its authoritarian and patriarchal mode of functioning. The Left believed that to be effective and take on a centralized and authoritarian power, they, too, had to concentrate power. For the social democratic Left, the pressure of the media to conform to highly managed political interventions and, eventually, to highly managed political conventions, was deadly to internal party democracy.

But the problem goes beyond patriarchal modes of functioning to our very notions of power. We have always seen power as being located in the state and in the corporations. The way to change the world was to get state power and make changes to state and economic structures. Then, the women's movement, anti-racist groups, and the environmental movement introduced the idea that we must also change our personal behaviour if we want to change the world. These movements, and other similar ones, broadened the idea of politics into the realm of the personal relationships between people and the relationship between humans and the environment. Power was understood as something each of us exercises in our lives as part of a dominant group, including our human dominance over nature and its creatures. These ideas about power were influential in organizations and in community, but somehow didn't alter our ideas of how political change could be achieved. Today we are seeing the beginnings of that kind of change in the notions of transformative power. It is these ideas that make "Occupy" such a brilliant slogan.

British feminist Hilary Wainright who has been analyzing the need for more democracy and inclusion on the left for decades, points out in her saucy magazine *Red Pepper*:

These new understandings of knowledge point towards an emphasis on the horizontal sharing and exchange of knowledge and collaborative attempts to build connected alternatives and shared memories. They stress the gaining of knowledge as a process of discovery and therefore see political action … as itself a source of knowledge, revealing unpredicted problems or opportunities implying debate driven not so much by the struggle for positions of power as by a search for truth about the complexity of social change.

This is precisely what the General Assemblies and Working Group structures of Occupy are looking for.

While the book was at the publisher, I got a twitter message from Stephanie Rogers, a young woman involved with WOW (Women Occupying Wall St.). "I'd like to interview you for an article I am doing for *Ms.* on the influence of feminism on Occupy Wall Street. My friends say I should talk to you." I agreed to an interview but on the phone I said I wasn't really sure that feminism had any influence on Occupy. Her questions made me realize that I was quite wrong about that. She was most interested in consciousness raising groups. Here is how she put it in her article published in *Ms.*:

And one of the things I love most about the Occupy Wall Street movement is that it borrows so much of its activism, specifically pertaining to how the protesters interact with one another, from the feminist consciousness-raising model of the 1960s and '70s. Like consciousness-raising, Occupy Wall Street started with small groups of oppressed people who spoke to one another about their personal struggles, and in doing so, learned they weren't alone or insane or weak or lazy, the way Those In Charge suggested. That discovery gave them the strength to channel the individual anger and suffering they experienced into a larger collective call to action.

If the personal has ever been political in this country, take a look at the concerns driving the Occupy Wall Street movement: home foreclosures, college loan debts, health problems representing the leading cause of personal bankruptcy, lay-offs and skyrocketing unemployment rates, rapidly diminishing pensions, unaffordable education, unaffordable and inaccessible childcare....

Other examples of consciousness-raising at Occupy Wall Street include discussion groups reminiscent of those started by '70s' feminists. There's the Divine Feminine, a group in which female-bodied or female-identified women talk about the oppressions they experience; Ambiguous UpSparkles, started by Eve Ensler, where people come together and share their personal stories of oppression using the people's mic; and similar groups, like POCcupy (People of Color), a group for people of color to talk about oppression; WOW (Women Occupying Wall Street) and Safer Spaces, two groups that focus on the presence and safety of women in the movement.

So other than some variations on the feminist understanding of knowledge coming from our life experience and a variation on the flat structures and consensus practiced in the women's movement, how has feminism been part of Occupy?

The most obvious sign is the way in which women are organizing in Occupy. Occupy Wall Street has had feminist organizing from fairly early on with WOW, and Occupy Patriarchy, but it took until May 17, 2012 to have the first feminist general assembly. I had talked with quite a few of the young women playing leadership roles in Occupy Toronto but feminism never really came up. So I interviewed two women who were involved in writing about or organizing around women and Occupy. Both told the same story but had quite a different approach.

Megan Kinch is an activist who was involved in organizing around the G-20 a couple of years ago and in CUPE at York University. Magdelena Diaz is a 55-year-old Latina feminist who has been an activist since she was 15. Both describe the first GAs as dominated by young white males. Megan tried to intervene to suggest that the GA should vote on whether or not to have a 100 percent consensus rule. She said, "I love consensus, but 100 percent consensus can't work in an open group." She was trying to use some of the lessons from the Tyranny of Structurelessness and her union meetings. In a blog at the time she wrote,

I said that the decision on using consensus or not has to be made by the group, not by the facilitators, and that we should vote and/or come to consensus on it. I started with a 50 percent voting proposal, but I accepted as a friendly amendment a motion for 80 percent to pass. There was no consensus. My call for a vote/consensus on how to make decisions was shouted down, and I was called out for being "oppressive" because I was yelling, even though I was on the speakers list and every person who'd spoken had yelled as we hadn't started using "the people's mic."

Magdelana saw similar problems in the GA. Her solution was to join a women's caucus so that women could figure out how to have a stronger voice to deal with some sexist language that was emerging and to create a safe space for women to sleep. It just so happened, she told me, that all the women who became part of this group were Latina.

Another women's group was also set up but they weren't feminist. According to Magdelana, they were critical of feminism thinking it was anti-male. Megan said they were more into a spiritual approach to feminine energy, for example thinking women are closer to nature, than into speaking up for women's participation or safety. Megan told me,

> *Feminist work at Occupy was not feminist political work but really just making space for women to be political. To speak or even to be physically present in the park. Most of the work we did as women was to make space.*
>
> *Women were playing a strong leadership role but not so much as women. My biggest regret is that we didn't organize an Occupy Feminism group earlier. I was never in a feminist group before because I didn't feel I had to in the unions or on the left. But it became clear that women were having special problems in the park.*

The reason for the danger and marginalization women faced didn't seem much like the sexism my generation faced in the '60s and '70s based on male power and denying the ability of women to lead. On the other hand, the language and grammar of equality that has been developed over the last decades in our movements to deal with racism and sexism were unknown to a large number of Occupy participants, including many women. Madelaine explained it this way:

> *There was definitely resistance and fear. People at Occupy were strangers to each other. Trust needed to be built and relationships needed to develop. Much of the resistance encountered came from preconceived ideas on feminism and the fears of an anti-men movement sprouting in the middle of Occupy.*
>
> *Also, many of the white males seen as the leaders within occupy self-identified themselves as having no prejudice, as being inclusive and sensitive to diversity, and as being free from racism. They were not aware of the subtle ways in which they manifested gender bias, racism and exclusion.*

Part of the problem was a kind of radical inclusion where the wonderful instinct of Occupy to include everyone, especially those who have been discarded by society like homeless people and people with serious mental illness, was taken too far to the idea that no-one could be excluded.

"People were so idealistic they didn't want to create any rules," says Megan. "They were so utopian. It made it very difficult to create a safe space." We didn't want to use the police in most cases but we don't really have a way to deal with truly destructive individuals ourselves."

Magdelena added, "We were all learning to negotiate a collective space, learning to work together and trying to build trust, while dealing with a lot of complex personal history. We were making it up as we moved along. It was a big learning experience for all of us."

Both Megan and Magdelena agree that the marshalls played an important role in ensuring safety and for changing the atmosphere at Occupy so that individuals who were violent, abusive or disruptive could be removed from the park.

Magdelena, who calls herself a peace maker, says she really saw people change over the course of Occupy.

> *Of course, some people never change. But the male leaders, who I had problems with at the beginning really changed. Now they are much more sensitive to the needs of women in participating in the group. I do believe that learning took place and that today many of us are much better off because of occupy. We continue to learn together with much lesser friction and a greater sense of solidarity.*

Magdelena is still part of a feminist group of Occupy but now they include some men who identify as feminists as well. Megan says if she had it to do again, she would have organized a feminist group from day one.

Judy Rebick is a well known feminist and writer. Her latest book is Occupy This! *is a Penguin ebook (2012).*

REFERENCES

Rebick, Judy. *Occupy This!* Toronto: Penguin Canada, 2012.
Rogers, Stephanie. *Ms Magazine* December 13, 2011.
Wainright, Hilary. *Red Pepper* February 2008.

MEGAN BOLER

Occupy Patriarchy

Will Feminism's Fourth Wave Be a Swell or a Ripple?

O N MAY DAY 2012, women around the world streamed into the streets by thousands ("Women Protest"). Seen and unseen, women have been on the front lines throughout the Arab Spring, the uprisings in Russia, in Spain and London, and within the Occupy Wall Street (OWS) movement. Marching mile after mile through city streets, creating and carrying her creative demands on placards and signs in marches and protests, writing hundreds of emails and blogs, carefully strategizing, facilitating countless meetings and discussions—while cooking, cleaning, taking care of children—women have claimed a large and potentially defining role in demanding that those in the Occupy movement "check their privilege."[1]

TURNING TIDE

The 1970s women's liberation movement evolved in part because of the sexism inherent in free speech, antiwar and civil rights social movements in which men assumed leadership as visionaries and strategists and too often assigned women to menial labour making copies and serving coffee. Over the past decades, "feminist"
has become a highly-contested term. During the second wave of feminism, tensions ran high about whether and how, for example, women of colour were named, included, described and represented underneath the banner "feminism;" Alice Walker coined the term "womanist"; bell hooks uses "white male capitalist patriarchy," while Patricia Hill Collins develops what she entitles "black feminist thought." By the end of the 1980s, systematic conservative and liberal backlash had managed a public relations spin painting our society as "post-feminist."

But the tide seems to have turned. Feminism's re-emergence has been spotted on the horizon by numerous long-term feminist organizers. Kathy Miriam, a professor and feminist organizer who lives in Brooklyn, recognizes this as a, "fluid, dynamic moment" (cited in *The F Word*) in which anything is possible. As Miriam wrote in a blog post during the autumn of OWS:

Can feminist solidarity reap the whirlwind and reinvent itself within new forms of social association too? ...[T]he dynamism released by Occupy Wall Street [OWS] involves women—lots and lots of young women—who, like their male counter-parts are caught up in the momentum of movement-creating. This means that women are agitating, aroused anew as political actors on the stage of history. If there is any situation then, in which feminist ideas might stick and take root, this is it.

Will Occupy Wall Street be open to re-orientation through the lens of feminist action and vision? Will feminism re-invent itself as a *movement* within the new political situation and its forcefield of political possibilities?

During the early weeks of Occupy Wall Street, feminist manifestos were cropping up online. A single-entry Wordpress blog (with no information as to its author(s) and only one solitary entry dated October 15, 2010 said:

> As feminists we call for clarification of the fact that neoliberal capitalism is also patriarchal to the core. The poorest of the world's poor are women who also do two thirds of the world's work and own 1 percent of the means of production. Women are the other 99 percent—the vast majority of whom "hold up half the sky" mostly on their under or unpaid backs. ("Feminism Now!")

The same week in October saw the publication of "Radical Feminism Enters the 21st Century," an insightful analysis by Vliet Tiptree. Now, one finds dozens of women caucuses affiliated with Occupy groups across North America: Occupy Patriarchy; Women Occupy, Women Occupying Wall Street and Global Women's Strike to name a few.

WOMEN'S INTERVENTIONS IN OCCUPY

Making space for women and women of color requires courage and energy. Occupy participant Manissa Maharawal, "a South Asian woman, has been one of Occupy Wall Street's most eloquent and passionate defenders," according to a March article in Counterpunch (Vohra and Flaherty). Her well-wrought and impassioned story, "So Real It Hurts" hit headlines on October 4, 2011, and has been widely read and commented upon; it is a warning, and a beacon of hope.

Curious to check out OWS, Maharawal began attending meetings despite her fears of encountering the usual white-male-dominated left. And though young white folks constitute the majority of the crowds and much of the horizontal helm, she found enough powerful energy, promise and people of color to inspire her to join. Through general assembly (GA) meetings and other events, Maharawal became connected and invested in the community and movement.

At a GA in early October, participants were approving, "a document called the 'Declaration of the Occupation,' and she felt language in the document erased oppression faced by people of color," reported *Counterpunch* (Vohra and Flaherty). "She did not want to have to block the proposal and face the angry stares of hundreds of people. However, says Maharawal, it's something she had to do." The article offers more of her perspective:

> What struck me then was that if I want Occupy to be something that's around for a long time in my life … it needs from the very beginning to be a movement that's taking these things on," she explained. "And that is thinking about not just corporate greed and financial institutions, but is thinking about how these things are connected to racism, to patriarchy, to oppression generally. (Vohra and Flaherty)

Ultimately, Maharawal and others who agreed with her succeeded in changing the language of the declaration.

Maharawal's bold defense of inclusivity as a foundation of Occupy required courage, as well as investment of significant energy to "raise consciousness," in the words popularized by earlier feminists, to educate those ignorant about structural social inequalities. As she wrote in *Racialicious*:

> There in that circle, on that street-corner we did a crash course on racism, white privilege, structural racism, oppression. We did a course on history and the declaration of independence and colonialism and slavery. It was hard. It was real. It hurt. But people listened. We had to fight for it. I'm going to say that again: we had to fight for it. But it felt worth it.
>
> Let me tell you what it feels like to stand in front of a white man and explain privilege to him. It hurts. It makes you tired. Sometimes it makes you want to cry. Sometimes it is exhilarating. Every single time it is hard. Every single time I get angry that I have to do this, that this is my job, that this shouldn't be my job. Every single time I am proud of myself that I've been able to say these things because I used to not be able to and because some days I just don't want to.

Her willing commitment to the long-haul sense of this movement and to process being as important as goals inspired activists and readers around the world. As Maharawal aptly described to *Counterpunch*: "[T]his movement is about creating a real alternative to our current system, and, for her, that means fighting these systemic issues. 'Why are we going to create a system that just re-creates all these oppressions? That recreates racism, that recreates oppression, that recreates gender hierarchy? Why would I want to be a part of that?'" (Vohra and Flaherty).

Why "create a system that just re-creates all these oppressions" is indeed the million-dollar question. Many are committed to changing the very roots of society, in order to overhaul the existing corporate oligarchy and political system that defines Western democracies. Reformist measures—interventions in policy, legislation, partisan politics—are seen by many young activists as useless bandaids. Further, the movement aims for its own processes to match and embody the ideals and visions of a just society, hence its commitment to consensus and to a leaderless "horizontal" organizational structure.

MAKING SPACE FOR MARGINALIZED MEMBERS OF OCCUPY

Our interviews with women activists reveal that issues related to gender or sexism have not been articulated as part of the fundamental visions or aims of Occupy. Furthermore, issues of gender oppression have required persistent reminders and calling out as problems, during the course of General Assemblies, working groups, and within the internal dynamics of the movements. The common vocabularies used to address gender issues tend to avoid "feminism" and instead include other concepts such as critiques of "rape culture," calls to "occupy" or "smash" patriarchy, the need to create "safe spaces" (especially within/during the camps), and "check your privilege."

Why, some may ask, is an analysis of gender needed? If we're fighting for the 99 percent, that covers women, doesn't it? "The concept of patriarchy," explains Kathy Miriam, "goes farther than capitalism in explaining why it is that capitalism depends for its sustainability on the extraction of surplus value from women's unpaid work—women's unpaid and unvalued work is equal to 50 percent of the world's GDP and yet women only control one percent of the means of production."

Dynamics around white male dominance, misogyny, sexism, and racism have been addressed in Occupy through the creation of "safe spaces", debates within the General Assemblies about adopting "progressive stack" (for which a facilitator takes down names of people to ensure that those traditionally silenced or marginalized in public spaces have an opportunity to speak), and challenging the imperialist connotations and histories of "occupy," suggesting instead alternative terms such as "decolonize..

One of the first visible instances of women's distinctive needs and rights within Occupy was the call for what is often referred to in activist and advocacy circles, as well as elsewhere, as "safe spaces." Safe spaces were created to counter women's vulnerability in Occupy's public spaces and camps. During the encampments, women experienced sexual harassment and even rape. (Concerns with violence against women extend now to police brutality and a new level of aggression toward women's bodies. In one incident, a police officer reportedly broke a woman's wrist while arresting her at a protest in New York City after she confronted an officer about grabbing her breast as police moved protesters out of Zuccotti Park [Graeber].)

Another frequent clarion call is a style of dialogue and consensus-building known as "step up, step back." Marginalized members are encouraged to step up in a conversation and dominant members (whose dominance may originate in social status or simply by virtue of personalities that take up enormous space) are asked to step back. Some Occupy groups have adopted what is called a "progressive stack." Take Occupy Montreal's example:

> We urge that the Assembly recognize the concept of stepping back: that dominant voices and identities recognize privilege and power in the room and in themselves, and 'step back' from monopolizing a conversation in the interest of hearing a diversity of voices and experiences on the topic. We are not here to reproduce the same monopolization of voice and power as the "1%," we are here to diversify spaces for radical inclusion, and to name centuries of privilege and exploitation of particular demographics of the population, including but not limited to: women, people of colour, members of the LGBTQ populations, non-status individuals, differently-abled persons, the very young and the very old ... all these voices are regularly marginalised in our societies. In devising alternate modes of being and redistribution of power in the world, it is our duty and responsibility to listen and learn from prioritising these voices that are traditionally and systemically silenced in our dominant culture. Let us be accountable to our own declarations of values—let us put these principles into practice in order to devise alternate ways of being in the world. (Occupy Patriarchy)

Efforts at greater inclusion—challenging the "Occupy" term and calling for its replacement with "decolonize" and urging the adoption of progressive stack at GAs—have been met with support, as well as strong backlash. In such conflicts, one sees clearly how race and gender intersect, and how persistent the problem of white male dominance can be on the left. Unable to see the need to address systemic or structural racism and sexism, and instead operating as if we live already in a world where the playing field is level, some Occupy members accuse those trying to ensure equity of "playing the race card" (Jacobson) and of "wasting another hour" (Stevedigiboytv) on issues of gender and racial equality.

The exclusion of women and people of color in public panels about Occupy is defended by some as a necessary for unity. "At a recent panel discussion on the Occupy movement, a left-leaning professor from New York University speculated that identity politics—the prioritizing of issues of race and gender in movements for justice—could be a plot funded by the CIA to undermine activism," Counterpunch reported (Vohra and Flaherty). In our research, we are asking about interviewee's experiences with police and whether they have observed members who seem to be "infiltrators" or "counter intelligence" agitators. Indeed, there is concern and suspicion that some "participants" may in fact be "plants" to create conflict and disruption within group discussions and process both on- and offline.

The need for consciousness-raising becomes apparent through all manner of conflicts. In October, Steven Greenstreet posted a controversial video and a tumblr site of photos titled, "Hot Chicks of Occupy." Subsequently retitled "Inspiring Women of Occupy Wall Street," the comments and stormy reaction to critiques of Greenstreet's video reflect the reality that the ranks of Occupy include many who have not yet thought through the deep violence of power or the violence of images within male-dominated culture.

OVERCOMING HISTORIES: HOPE FOR A FOURTH WAVE

What are the similarities and differences between the conditions for the second wave of feminism and today? Resonant with United Sluts of America's "Take Back Your Vagina from invasive Conservative Politicians!" campaign, the 1970s second wave of feminism was also rooted in fighting violence against women and for women's reproductive rights.

Occupy is built on principles and processes familiar to those of second-wave of feminism—a leaderless movement built on horizontal decisionmaking. Consciousness-raising is being used today, as Maharawal's story and many others reveal, showing similarities across generations of feminist organizing.

Is there hope that decades of learning about the intersections of race, class and gender will support coalition-building across differences? In comments on a recent *Ms. Magazine* article discussing what Occupy owes to the legacy of feminist consciousness-raising, these challenges are made clear:

> White women feminist groups like code pink are getting press and yet everywhere i look its women of color/ transnational women who are leading the POC committees of occupy/decolonize sites. 4 Indigenous women led the resolution proposal at a recent general assembly to try to change the name to decolonize in Oakland. Stop white-washing our feminism. (Rogers)

Another commenter responds:

> On November 25th, AF3IRM led a coalition of organizations in a women's assembly at Foley Square, followed by a march to Zuccotti Park, to denounce Wall Street as violence against women. About 200 women participated, many of color, many transnational....
>
> AF3IRM chapters have been conducting teach-ins, marches, speakouts at Occupy sites in Oakland, Los Angeles, Riverside, San Diego and other places.
>
> As these events have been led by transnational women of color, they have not received as much attention from either the media or the feminist world, it seems.

Will difference be recognized for its richness, as a fund from which to draw, as Audre Lorde wrote in the 1980s?

> Difference must be not merely tolerated, but seen as a fund of necessary polarities between which our creativity can spark like a dialectic....Only within that interdependency of different strengths, acknowledged and equal, can the power to seek new ways of being in the world generate, as well as the courage and sustenance to act where there are no charters.

Although the struggle is never finished, it is not always thankless—nor without victories, as Maharawal's comments to *Counterpunch* attest:

> Nearly two months later, one of the white male activists who had expressed his frustration with her came up to her to thank her for her intervention. "I'm really glad you did that, I learned a lot right then," he told her.
> "Making these connections is difficult, it's been like constant work in this movement," says Maharawal. But, she adds "this stuff doesn't feel like minutia, it feels fundamental to me."

The essay was originally published just prior prior to the 1st Feminist General Assembly in New York. Over the summer of 2012, there were four FemGAs held in NYC, as well as a large Feminist General Assembly at the July National Gathering of Occupy in Philadelphia. (Though the Fem GAs were well attended by NYC participants, few of those we interviewed in the Occupy sites on West Coast were aware of these gatherings.) With respect to the turning tide of feminism, it is significant to note that in the North American context, in spring 2012 U.S. right wing conservatives added fuel to the fire with the right's so-called "war on women." Rush Limbaugh's misogynist vitriol regarding health care coverage for contraception sparked a populist feminist movement including renowned "Slutwalk" protests, and two popular Facebook sites launched in March 2012 "Rock the Slut Vote" and "One Million Vaginas"—humorous but serious and organized and ongoing protest of right wing attacks on women.

Our ongoing interviews with young women activists reveal that women are breaking the barriers of exclusions that kept many out of the "Media Tents" at the different Occupy camps. Women have taught themselves and each other the technological and media skills to ustream and livestream events, and have adopted roles as the active and dedicated "admins" for the Facebook pages for different Occupy sites (FB pages remain the central organizing hub for Occupy communities around the country).

What might a fourth wave of feminism look like; what unique forms may it take; how can it create new banners for solidarity and coalition within the globally- and locally-shared ongoing oppression of women? Who feels included under this banner; who are the allies inside and outside of OWS who are committed to a fourth wave of feminism? Can a fourth wave of feminism move beyond identity politics and work towards coalition? Will other non-hierarchically led groups recognize and support the importance of women's reasons for assembling?

As the Occupy movement and the other social movements of this global discontent reveal, economic justice requires challenging patriarchy as much as it requires challenging capitalism.

Today, a growing number of male allies express hope that indeed, women will take on the leadership. As Sea, a professor participating in Occupy Cafe, urges in a series of reflections on women's knowledge and values: "How bad could it be if Occupy adopted a strong womanist stance? Men need to get out of the way. Men need to beg women to take over." And one thing is clear from our research into the women organizing these hybrid online/offline twenty-first century social movements: a call for conscious awakening appears to be a global zeitgeist, quietly but humbly envisioned, practiced, and led by countless brave and tireless women around the world.

An earlier version of this article orginally appeared online at Truth-Out.Org, May 18, 2012. ©Truthout.org. <http://truth-out.org/news/item/9188-occupy-women-will-fourth-wave-feminism-be-a-wave-or-a-ripple>. Reprinted with permission.

Megan M. Boler is a professor at the Ontario Institute of Studies in Education/ University of Toronto. Her books include Feeling Power: Emotions and Education *(1999),* Democratic Dialogue in Education: Troubling Speech, Disturbing Silences *(2004) and* Digital Media and Democracy: Tactic in Hard Times *(2008); and* DIY Citizenship: Critical Making and Social Media *(eds. M. Ratto and M Boler, forthcoming 2014).*

[1]This essay is based on a three-year project entitled "Social Media in the Hands of Young Citizens," funded by the Canadian Social Sciences and Humanities Research Council; see www. meganboler.net.

REFERENCES

"Declaration of the Occupation of New York City." New York General Assembly. September 29, 2011. Web.

Stevedigiboytv. "Vancouver Occupy Pro facilitator raises race/gender card against majority." YouTube. October 20, 2011. Web.

"Feminism Now!" FEMINISMNOWOWS. October 2011. Web.

Graeber, David. "New Police Strategy in New York – Sexual Assault Against Peaceful Protestors." Truth-Out.org May 4, 2012. Web.

Greenstreet, Steven. "Inspiring Women of Wall Street." YouTube. October 29, 2011. Web.

"Hot Chicks of Occupy Wall Street: The Sexy Side of Protesting Corruption." Tumblr.com. Web.

Jacobson, William. "A Saturday Night Card Game (Dominant progressive white males in the #OccupyWallStreet mist)." Legal Insurrection. October 8, 2011. Web.

Kanfo, Saki. "Philadelphia Convention Plans Lead to a Rift in Occupy Movement."*Huffington Post.com*. February 23, 2012. Web.

Lorde, Audre. "The Master's Tools Will Never Dismantle the Master's House." *Sister Outsider: Essays and Speeches*. Freedom, CA: The Crossing Press, 1984.

Maharawal, Manissa McCleave. "So Real It Hurts: Notes on Occupy Wall Street." *Racialicious* October 3, 2011. Web.

McKeown, Maeve. "Rape and the Occupy Movement." New Left Project. n.d. Web.

Miriam, Kathy. "Manifest(o)ing Feminism: Occupy Patriarchy!"November 4, 2011. Blog.

Occupy Patriarchy. "Confronting Misogyny at Occupy Montreal." February 10, 2012. Web.

Rogers, Stephanie. "What Occupy Wall Street Owes to Feminist Consciousness Raising." *Ms. Magazine* December 13, 2011. Web.

The F Word, Meghan Murphy. "Feminism and Occupy Wall Street." November 4, 2011. Podcast.

Tiptree, Vliet. "Radical Feminism Enters the 21st Century." Radfem Hub: A Radical Feminist Collective Blog. October 2011. Web.

Vohra, Sweta and Jordan Flaherty. "Race, Gender and Occupy." Counterpunch March 20, 2012. Web.

Walters, Patrick. "Occupy National Convention to Be Held in Philadelphia." *Huffington Post.com*. February 22, 2012. Web.

"What Occupy Wall Street Owes to Feminist Consciousness-Raising." *Ms. Magazine* December 13, 2011. Web.

"Women Protest Worldwide Mayday 2012." Cryptome Protest Series. 1 May 2012. Web.

Index